TRAVELS IN ALASKA

JOHN MUIR

GIBBS SMITH

TO ENRICH AND INSPIRE HUMANKIND

26 25 24 23 22   9 8 7 6 5

Cover © 2016 Gibbs Smith

First Gibbs Smith Edition published in 2016

Originally published by Houghton Mifflin in 1915

Published by
Gibbs Smith
P.O. Box 667
Layton, Utah 84041

1.800.835.4993 orders
www.gibbs-smith.com

Cover art by Seth Lucas
Printed and bound in China

Gibbs Smith books are printed on either recycled, 100% post-consumer waste, FSC-certified papers or on paper produced from sustainable PEFC-certified forest/controlled wood source. Learn more at www. pefc.org.

Library of Congress Cataloging-in-Publication Data
Names: Muir, John, 1838–1914.
Title: Travels in Alaska / John Muir.
    Originally published: Boston : Houghton Mifflin, 1915.
Identifiers: LCCN 2015051084 | ISBN 9781423644743
Subjects: LCSH: Alaska—Description and travel. | Muir, John,
    1838–1914—Travel—Alaska. | Natural history—Alaska.
Classification: LCC F908 .M95 2016 | DDC 917.9804—dc23
LC record available at http://lccn.loc.gov/2015051084

CONTENTS

PART ONE

THE TRIP OF 1879

1

PUGET SOUND AND BRITISH COLUMBIA

After eleven years of study and exploration in the Sierra Nevada of California and the mountain ranges of the Great Basin, studying in particular their glaciers, forests, and wild life, above all their ancient glaciers and the influence they exerted in sculpturing the rocks over which they passed with tremendous pressure, making new landscapes, scenery, and beauty which so mysteriously influence every human being, and to some extent all life, I was anxious to gain some knowledge of the regions to the northward, about Puget Sound and Alaska. With this grand object in view I left San Francisco in May, 1879, on the steamer Dakota, without any definite plan, as with the exception of a few of the Oregon peaks and their forests all the wild north was new to me.

To the mountaineer a sea voyage is a grand, inspiring, restful change. For forests and plains with their flowers and fruits we have new scenery, new life of every sort; water hills and dales in eternal visible motion for rock waves, types of permanence.

It was curious to note how suddenly the eager countenances of the passengers were darkened as soon as the good ship passed through the Golden Gate and began to heave on the waves of the open ocean. The crowded deck was speedily deserted on account of seasickness. It seemed strange that nearly every one afflicted should be more or less ashamed.

Next morning a strong wind was blowing, and the sea was gray and white, with long breaking waves, across which the Dakota was racing half-buried in spray. Very few of the passengers were on deck to enjoy the wild scenery. Every wave seemed to be making enthusiastic, eager haste to the shore, with long, irised tresses streaming from its tops, some of its outer fringes borne away in scud to refresh the wind, all the rolling, pitching, flying water exulting in the beauty of rainbow light. Gulls and albatrosses, strong, glad life in the midst of the stormy beauty, skimmed the waves against the wind, seemingly without effort, oftentimes flying nearly a mile without a single wing-beat, gracefully swaying from side to side and tracing the curves of the briny water hills with the finest precision, now and then just grazing the highest.

And yonder, glistening amid the irised spray, is still more striking revelation of warm life in the so-called howling waste—a half-dozen whales, their broad backs like glaciated bosses of granite heaving aloft in near view, spouting lustily, drawing a long breath, and plunging down home in colossal health and comfort. A merry school of porpoises, a square mile of them, suddenly appear, tossing themselves into the air in abounding strength and hilarity, adding foam to the waves and making all the wilderness wilder. One cannot but feel sympathy with and be proud of these brave neighbors, fellow citizens in the commonwealth of the world, making a living like the rest of us. Our good ship also seemed like a thing of life, its great iron heart beating on through calm and storm, a truly noble spectacle. But think of the hearts of these whales, beating warm against the sea, day and night, through dark and light, on and on for centuries; how the red blood must rush and gurgle in and out, bucketfuls, barrelfuls at a beat!

The cloud colors of one of the four sunsets enjoyed on the voyage were remarkably pure and rich in tone. There was a well-defined range of cumuli a few degrees above the horizon, and a massive, dark-gray rain cloud above it, from which depended long, bent fringes overlapping the lower cumuli and partially veiling them; and from time to time sunbeams poured through narrow openings and painted the exposed bosses and fringes in ripe yellow tones, which, with the reflections on the water, made magnificent pictures. The scenery of the ocean, however sublime in vast expanse, seems far less beautiful to us dry-shod animals than that of the land seen only in comparatively small patches; but when we contemplate the whole globe as one great dewdrop, striped and dotted with continents and islands, flying through space with other stars all singing and shining together as one, the whole universe appears as an infinite storm of beauty.

The California coast hills and cliffs look bare and uninviting as seen from the ship, the magnificent forests keeping well back out of sight beyond the reach of the sea winds; those of Oregon and Washington are in some places clad with conifers nearly down to the shore; even the little detached islets, so marked a feature to the northward, are mostly tree-crowned. Up through the Straits of Juan de Fuca the forests, sheltered from the ocean gales and favored with abundant rains, flourish in marvelous luxuriance on the glacier-sculptured mountains of the Olympic Range.

We arrived in Esquimalt Harbor, three miles from Victoria, on the evening of the fourth day, and drove to the town through a magnificent forest of Douglas spruce—with an undergrowth in open spots of oak, madrone, hazel, dogwood, alder, spiraea, willow, and wild rose—and around many an upswelling *moutonné* rock, freshly glaciated and furred with yellow mosses and lichens.

Victoria, the capital of British Columbia, was in 1879 a small old-fashioned English town on the south end of Vancouver Island. It was said to contain about six thousand inhabitants. The government buildings and some of the business blocks were noticeable, but the attention of the traveler was more worthily attracted to the neat cottage homes found here, embowered in the freshest and floweriest climbing roses and honeysuckles conceivable. Californians may well be proud of their home roses loading sunny verandas, climbing to the tops of the roofs and falling over the gables in white and red cascades. But here, with so much bland fog and dew and gentle laving rain, a still finer development of some of the commonest garden plants is reached. English honeysuckle seems to have found here a most congenial home. Still more beautiful were the wild roses, blooming in wonderful luxuriance along the woodland paths, with corollas two and three inches wide. This rose and three species of spiraea fairly filled the air with fragrance after showers; and how brightly then did the red dogwood berries shine amid the green leaves beneath trees two hundred and fifty feet high.

Strange to say, all of this exuberant forest and flower vegetation was growing upon fresh moraine material scarcely at all moved or in any way modified by post-glacial agents. In the town gardens and orchards, peaches and apples fell upon glacier-polished rocks, and the streets were graded in moraine gravel; and I observed scratched and grooved rock bosses as unweathered and telling as those of the High Sierra of California eight thousand feet or more above sea level. The Victoria Harbor is plainly glacial in origin, eroded from the solid; and the rock islets that rise here and there in it are unchanged to any appreciable extent by all the waves that have broken over them since first they came to light toward the close of the glacial period. The shores also of the harbor are strikingly grooved and scratched and in every way as glacial in all their characteristics as those of newborn glacial lakes. That the domain of the sea is being slowly extended over the land by incessant wave-action is well known; but in this freshly glaciated region the shores have been so short a time exposed to wave-action that they are scarcely at all wasted. The extension of the sea affected by its own action in post-glacial times is probably less than the millionth part of that affected by glacial action during the last glacier period. The direction of the flow of the ice sheet to which all the main features of this wonderful region are due was in general southward.

From this quiet little English town I made many short excursions—up the coast to Nanaimo, to Burrard Inlet, now the terminus of the Canadian Pacific Railroad, to Puget Sound, up Fraser River to New Westminster and Yale at the head of navigation, charmed everywhere with the wild, newborn scenery. The most interesting of these and the most difficult to leave was the Puget Sound region, famous the world over for the wonderful forests of gigantic trees about its shores. It is an arm and many-fingered hand of the sea, reaching southward from the Straits of Juan de Fuca about a hundred miles into the heart of one of the noblest coniferous forests on the face of the globe. All its scenery is wonderful—broad riverlike reaches sweeping in beautiful curves around bays and capes and jutting promontories, opening here and there into smooth, blue, lakelike expanses dotted with islands and feathered with tall, spiry evergreens, their beauty doubled on the bright mirror-water.

Sailing from Victoria, the Olympic Mountains are seen right ahead, rising in bold relief against the sky, with jagged crests and peaks from six to eight thousand feet high—small residual glaciers and ragged snowfields beneath them in wide amphitheatres opening down through the forest-filled valleys. These valleys mark the courses of the Olympic glaciers at the period of their greatest extension, when they poured their tribute into that portion of the great northern ice sheet that overswept Vancouver Island and filled the strait between it and the mainland.

On the way up to Olympia, then a hopeful little town situated at the end of one of the longest fingers of the Sound, one is often reminded of Lake Tahoe, the scenery of the widest expanses is so lakelike in the clearness and stillness of the water and the luxuriance of the surrounding forests. Doubling cape after cape, passing uncounted islands, new combinations break on the view in endless variety, sufficient to satisfy the lover of wild beauty through a whole life. When the clouds come down, blotting out everything, one feels as if at sea; again lifting a little, some islet may be seen standing alone with the tops of its trees dipping out of sight in gray misty fringes; then the ranks of spruce and cedar bounding the water's edge come to view; and when at length the whole sky is clear the colossal cone of Mt. Rainier may be seen in spotless white, looking down over the dark woods from a distance of fifty or sixty miles, but so high and massive and so sharply outlined, it seems to be just back of a strip of woods only a few miles wide.

Mt. Rainier, or Tahoma (the Indian name), is the noblest of the volcanic cones extending from Lassen Butte and Mt. Shasta along the Cascade Range to Mt. Baker. One of the most telling views of it hereabouts is obtained near Tacoma. From a bluff back of the town it was revealed in all its glory, laden with glaciers and snow down to the forested foothills around its finely curved base. Up to this time (1879) it had been ascended but once. From observations made on the summit with a single aneroid barometer, it was estimated to be about 14,500 feet high. Mt. Baker, to the northward, is about 10,700 feet high, a noble mountain. So also are Mt. Adams, Mt. St. Helens, and Mt. Hood. The latter, overlooking the town of Portland, is perhaps the best known. Rainier, about the same height as Shasta, surpasses them all in massive icy grandeur—the most majestic solitary mountain I had ever yet beheld. How eagerly I gazed and longed to climb it and study its history only the mountaineer may know, but I was compelled to turn away and bide my time.

The species forming the bulk of the woods here is the Douglas spruce (*Pseudotsuga douglasii*), one of the greatest of the western giants. A specimen that I measured near Olympia was about three hundred feet in height and twelve feet in diameter four feet above

7

the ground. It is a widely distributed tree, extending northward through British Columbia, southward through Oregon and California, and eastward to the Rocky Mountains. The timber is used for shipbuilding, spars, piles, and the framework of houses, bridges, etc. In the California lumber markets it is known as "Oregon pine." In Utah, where it is common on the Wasatch Mountains, it is called "red pine." In California, on the western slope of the Sierra Nevada, it forms, in company with the yellow pine, sugar pine, and incense cedar, a pretty well-defined belt at a height of from three to six thousand feet above the sea; but it is only in Oregon and Washington, especially in this Puget Sound region, that it reaches its very grandest development—tall, straight, and strong, growing down close to tidewater.

All the towns of the Sound had a hopeful, thrifty aspect. Port Townsend, picturesquely located on a grassy bluff, was the port of clearance for vessels sailing to foreign parts. Seattle was famed for its coal mines, and claimed to be the coming town of the North Pacific Coast. So also did its rival, Tacoma, which had been selected as the terminus of the much-talked-of Northern Pacific Railway. Several coal veins of astonishing thickness were discovered the winter before on the Carbon River, to the east of Tacoma, one of them said to be no less than twenty-one feet, another twenty feet, another fourteen, with many smaller ones, the aggregate thickness of all the veins being upwards of a hundred feet. Large deposits of magnetic iron ore and brown hematite, together with limestone, had been discovered in advantageous proximity to the coal, making a bright outlook for the Sound region in general in connection with its railroad hopes, its unrivaled timber resources, and its far-reaching geographical relations.

After spending a few weeks in the Puget Sound region with a friend from San Francisco, we engaged passage on the little mail steamer California, at Portland, Oregon, for Alaska. The sail down the broad lower reaches of the Columbia and across its foamy bar, around Cape Flattery, and up the Juan de Fuca Strait, was delightful; and after calling again at Victoria and Port Townsend we got fairly off for icy Alaska.

2

ALEXANDER ARCHIPELAGO AND THE HOME I FOUND IN ALASKA

To the lover of pure wildness Alaska is one of the most wonderful countries in the world. No excursion that I know of may be made into any other American wilderness where so marvelous an abundance of noble, newborn scenery is so charmingly brought to view as on the trip through the Alexander Archipelago to Fort Wrangell and Sitka. Gazing from the deck of the steamer, one is borne smoothly over calm blue waters, through the midst of countless forest-clad islands. The ordinary discomforts of a sea voyage are not felt, for nearly all the whole long way is on inland waters that are about as waveless as rivers and lakes. So numerous are the islands that they seem to have been sown broadcast; long tapering vistas between the largest of them open in every direction.

Day after day in the fine weather we enjoyed, we seemed to float in true fairyland, each succeeding view seeming more and more beautiful, the one we chanced to have before us the most surprisingly beautiful of all. Never before this had I been embosomed in scenery so hopelessly beyond description. To sketch picturesque bits, definitely bounded, is comparatively easy—a lake in the woods, a glacier meadow, or a cascade in its dell; or even a grand master view of mountains beheld from some commanding outlook after climbing from height to height above the forests. These may be attempted, and more or less telling pictures made of them; but in these coast landscapes there is such indefinite, on-leading expansiveness, such a multitude of features without apparent redundance, their lines graduating delicately into one another in endless succession, while the whole is so fine, so tender, so ethereal, that all pen work seems hopelessly unavailing. Tracing shining ways through fjord and sound, past forests and waterfalls, islands and mountains and far azure headlands, it seems as if surely we must at length reach the very paradise of the poets, the abode of the blessed.

Some idea of the wealth of this scenery may be gained from the fact that the coastline of Alaska is about twenty-six thousand miles long, more than twice as long as all the rest of the United States. The islands of the Alexander Archipelago, with the straits, channels, canals, sounds, passages, and fjords, form an intricate web of land and water embroidery sixty or seventy miles wide, fringing the lofty icy chain of coast mountains from Puget Sound to Cook Inlet; and, with infinite variety, the general pattern is harmonious throughout its whole extent of nearly a thousand miles. Here you glide into a narrow channel hemmed in by mountain walls, forested down to the water's edge, where there is no distant view, and your attention is concentrated on the objects close about you—the crowded spires of the spruces and hemlocks rising higher and higher on the steep green slopes; stripes of paler green where winter avalanches have cleared away the trees, allowing grasses and willows to spring up; zigzags of cascades appearing and disappearing among the bushes and trees; short, steep glens with brawling streams hidden beneath alder and dogwood, seen only where they emerge on the brown algae of the shore; and retreating hollows, with lingering snowbanks marking the fountains of ancient glaciers. The steamer is often so near the shore that you may distinctly see the cones clustered on the tops of the trees, and the ferns and bushes at their feet. .

But new scenes are brought to view with magical rapidity. Rounding some bossy cape, the eye is called away into far-reaching vistas, bounded on either hand by headlands in charming array, one dipping gracefully beyond another and growing fainter and more ethereal in the distance. The tranquil channel stretching riverlike between, may be stirred here and there by the silvery plashing of upspringing salmon, or by flocks of white gulls floating like water lilies among the sun spangles; while mellow, tempered sunshine is streaming over all, blending sky, land, and water in pale, misty blue. Then, while you are dreamily gazing into the depths of this leafy ocean lane, the little steamer, seeming hardly larger than a duck, turning into some passage not visible until the moment of entering it, glides into a wide expanse—a sound filled with islands, sprinkled and clustered in forms and compositions such as nature alone can invent; some of them so small the trees growing on them seem like single handfuls culled from the neighboring woods and set in the water to keep them fresh, while here and there at wide intervals you may notice bare rocks just above the water, mere dots punctuating grand, outswelling sentences of islands.

The variety we find, both as to the contours and the collocation of the islands, is due chiefly to differences in the structure and composition of their rocks, and the unequal glacial denudation different portions of the coast were subjected to. This influence must have been especially heavy toward the end of the glacial period, when the main ice sheet began to break up into separate glaciers. Moreover, the mountains of the larger islands nourished local glaciers, some of them of considerable size, which sculptured their summits and sides, forming in some cases wide cirques with canyons or valleys leading down from them into the channels and sounds. These causes have produced much of the bewildering variety of which nature is so fond, but nonetheless will the studious observer see the underlying harmony—the general trend of the islands in the direction of the flow of the main ice-mantle from the mountains of the Coast Range, more or less varied by subordinate foothill ridges and mountains. Furthermore, all the islands, great and small, as well as the headlands and promontories of the mainland, are seen to have a rounded, overrubbed appearance produced by the oversweeping ice flood during the period of greatest glacial abundance.

The canals, channels, straits, passages, sounds, etc., are subordinate to the same glacial conditions in their forms, trends, and extent as those which determined the forms, trends, and distribution of the land-masses, their basins being the parts of the pre-glacial margin of the continent, eroded to varying depths below sea level, and into which, of course, the ocean waters flowed as the ice was melted out of them. Had the general glacial denudation been much less, these ocean ways over which we are sailing would have

been valleys and canyons and lakes; and the islands
rounded hills and ridges, landscapes with undulating
features like those found above sea level wherever
the rocks and glacial conditions are similar. In general, the island-bound channels are like rivers, not
only in separate reaches as seen from the deck of a
vessel, but continuously so for hundreds of miles in
the case of the longest of them. The tide currents, the
fresh driftwood, the inflowing streams, and the luxuriant foliage of the out-leaning trees on the shores make
this resemblance all the more complete. The largest
islands look like part of the mainland in any view to be
had of them from the ship, but far the greater number
are small, and appreciable as islands, scores of them
being less than a mile long. These the eye easily takes
in and revels in their beauty with ever fresh delight.
In their relations to each other the individual members of a group have evidently been derived from the
same general rock mass, yet they never seem broken
or abridged in any way as to their contour lines, however abruptly they may dip their sides. Viewed one
by one, they seem detached beauties, like extracts
from a poem, while, from the completeness of their
lines and the way that their trees are arranged, each
seems a finished stanza in itself. Contemplating the
arrangement of the trees on these small islands, a
distinct impression is produced of their having been
sorted and harmonized as to size like a well-balanced
bouquet. On some of the smaller tufted islets a group
of tapering spruces is planted in the middle, and two
smaller groups that evidently correspond with each
other are planted on the ends at about equal distances
from the central group; or the whole appears as one
group with marked fringing trees that match each

other spreading around the sides, like flowers leaning outward against the rim of a vase. These harmonious tree relations are so constant that they evidently are the result of design, as much so as the arrangement of the feathers of birds or the scales of fishes.

Thus perfectly beautiful are these blessed evergreen islands, and their beauty is the beauty of youth, for though the freshness of their verdure must be ascribed to the bland moisture with which they are bathed from warm ocean currents, the very existence of the islands, their features, finish, and peculiar distribution, are all immediately referable to ice-action during the great glacial winter just now drawing to a close.

We arrived at Wrangell July 14, and after a short stop of a few hours went on to Sitka and returned on the 20th to Wrangell, the most inhospitable place at first sight I had ever seen. The little steamer that had been my home in the wonderful trip through the archipelago, after taking the mail, departed on her return to Portland, and as I watched her gliding out of sight in the dismal blurring rain, I felt strangely lonesome. The friend that had accompanied me thus far now left for his home in San Francisco, with two other interesting travelers who had made the trip for health and scenery, while my fellow passengers, the missionaries, went direct to the Presbyterian home in the old fort. There was nothing like a tavern or lodging house in the village, nor could I find any place in the stumpy, rocky, boggy ground about it that looked dry enough to camp on until I could find a way into the wilderness to begin my studies. Every place within a mile or two of the town seemed strangely shelterless and inhospitable, for all the trees had long ago been felled for building-timber and firewood. At the worst, I thought,

I could build a bark hut on a hill back of the village, where something like a forest loomed dimly through the draggled clouds.

I had already seen some of the high glacier-bearing mountains in distant views from the steamer, and was anxious to reach them. A few whites of the village, with whom I entered into conversation, warned me that the Indians were a bad lot, not to be trusted, that the woods were well-nigh impenetrable, and that I could go nowhere without a canoe. On the other hand, these natural difficulties made the grand wild country all the more attractive, and I determined to get into the heart of it somehow or other with a bag of hardtack, trusting to my usual good luck. My present difficulty was in finding a first base camp. My only hope was on the hill. When I was strolling past the old fort I happened to meet one of the missionaries, who kindly asked me where I was going to take up my quarters.

"I don't know," I replied. "I have not been able to find quarters of any sort. The top of that little hill over there seems the only possible place."

He then explained that every room in the mission house was full, but he thought I might obtain leave to spread my blanket in a carpenter shop belonging to the mission. Thanking him, I ran down to the sloppy wharf for my little bundle of baggage, laid it on the shop floor, and felt glad and snug among the dry, sweet-smelling shavings.

The carpenter was at work on a new Presbyterian mission building, and when he came in I explained that Dr. Jackson had suggested that I might be allowed to sleep on the floor, and after I assured him that I would not touch his tools or be in his way, he good-naturedly gave me the freedom of the shop and also of his small private side room where I would find a washbasin.

I was here only one night, however, for Mr. Vanderbilt, a merchant, who with his family occupied the best house in the fort, hearing that one of the late arrivals, whose business none seemed to know, was compelled to sleep in the carpenter shop, paid me a good-Samaritan visit and after a few explanatory words on my glacier and forest studies, with fine hospitality offered me a room and a place at his table. Here I found a real home, with freedom to go on all sorts of excursions as opportunity offered. Annie Vanderbilt, a little doctor of divinity two years old, ruled the household with love sermons and kept it warm.

Mr. Vanderbilt introduced me to prospectors and traders and some of the most influential of the Indians. I visited the mission school and the home for Indian girls kept by Mrs. MacFarland, and made short excursions to the nearby forests and streams, and studied the rate of growth of the different species of trees and their age, counting the annual rings on stumps in the large clearings made by the military when the fort was occupied, causing wondering speculation among the Wrangell folk, as was reported by Mr. Vanderbilt.

"What can the fellow be up to?" they inquired. "He seems to spend most of his time among stumps and weeds. I saw him the other day on his knees, looking at a stump as if he expected to find gold in it. He seems to have no serious object whatever."

One night when a heavy rainstorm was blowing I unwittingly caused a lot of wondering excitement among the whites as well as the superstitious Indians. Being anxious to see how the Alaska trees behave in storms and hear the songs they sing, I stole quietly

17

away through the gray drenching blast to the hill back of the town, without being observed. Night was falling when I set out and it was pitch dark when I reached the top. The glad, rejoicing storm in glorious voice was singing through the woods, noble compensation for mere body discomfort. But I wanted a fire, a big one, to see as well as hear how the storm and trees were behaving. After long, patient groping I found a little dry punk in a hollow trunk and carefully stored it beside my matchbox and an inch or two of candle in an inside pocket that the rain had not yet reached; then, wiping some dead twigs and whittling them into thin shavings, stored them with the punk. I then made a little conical bark hut about a foot high, and, carefully leaning over it and sheltering it as much as possible from the driving rain, I wiped and stored a lot of dead twigs, lighted the candle, and set it in the hut, carefully added pinches of punk and shavings, and at length got a little blaze, by the light of which I gradually added larger shavings, then twigs all set on end astride the inner flame, making the little hut higher and wider. Soon I had light enough to enable me to select the best dead branches and large sections of bark, which were set on end, gradually increasing the height and corresponding light of the hut fire. A considerable area was thus well lighted, from which I gathered abundance of wood, and kept adding to the fire until it had a strong, hot heart and sent up a pillar of flame thirty or forty feet high, illuminating a wide circle in spite of the rain, and casting a red glare into the flying clouds. Of all the thousands of campfires I have elsewhere built none was just like this one, rejoicing in triumphant strength and beauty in the heart of the rain-laden gale. It was wonderful—the illumined rain and clouds mingled together and the trees glowing against the jet background, the colors of the mossy, lichened trunks with sparkling streams pouring down the furrows of the bark, and the gray-bearded old patriarchs bowing low and chanting in passionate worship!

My fire was in all its glory about midnight, and, having made a bark shed to shelter me from the rain and partially dry my clothing, I had nothing to do but look and listen and join the trees in their hymns and prayers.

Neither the great white heart of the fire nor the quivering enthusiastic flames shooting aloft like auroral lances could be seen from the village on account of the trees in front of it and its being back a little way over the brow of the hill; but the light in the clouds made a great show, a portentous sign in the stormy heavens unlike anything ever before seen or heard of in Wrangell. Some wakeful Indians, happening to see it about midnight, in great alarm aroused the Collector of Customs and begged him to go to the missionaries and get them to pray away the frightful omen, and inquired anxiously whether white men had ever seen anything like that sky-fire, which instead of being quenched by the rain was burning brighter and brighter. The Collector said he had heard of such strange fires, and this one he thought might perhaps be what the white man called a "volcano, or an *ignis fatuus.*" When Mr. Young was called from his bed to pray, he, too, confoundedly astonished and at a loss for any sort of explanation, confessed that he had never seen anything like it in the sky or anywhere else in such cold wet weather, but that it was probably some sort of spontaneous combustion "that the white man called St. Elmo's fire, or Will-of-the-Wisp." These explanations, though not convincingly clear, perhaps served to veil their own astonishment and in some measure to diminish the superstitious fears of the natives; but from what I heard, the few whites who happened to see the strange light wondered about as wildly as the Indians.

I have enjoyed thousands of campfires in all sorts of weather and places, warm-hearted, short-flamed, friendly little beauties glowing in the dark on open spots in high Sierra gardens, daisies and lilies circled about them, gazing like enchanted children; and large fires in silver fir forests, with spires of flame towering like the trees about them, and sending up multitudes of starry sparks to enrich the sky; and still greater fires on the mountains in winter, changing camp climate to summer, and making the frosty snow look like beds of white flowers, and oftentimes mingling their swarms of swift-flying sparks with falling snow crystals when the clouds were in bloom. But this Wrangell campfire, my first in Alaska, I shall always remember for its triumphant storm-defying grandeur, and the wondrous beauty of the psalm-singing, lichen-painted trees which it brought to light.

3

WRANGELL ISLAND AND ALASKA SUMMERS

Wrangell Island is about fourteen miles long, separated from the mainland by a narrow channel or fjord, and trending in the direction of the flow of the ancient ice sheet. Like all its neighbors, it is densely forested down to the water's edge with trees that never seem to have suffered from thirst or fire or the axe of the lumberman in all their long century lives. Beneath soft, shady clouds, with abundance of rain, they flourish in wonderful strength and beauty to a good old age, while the many warm days, half cloudy, half clear, and the little groups of pure sun-days enable them to ripen their cones and send myriads of seeds flying every autumn to insure the permanence of the forests and feed the multitude of animals.

The Wrangell village was a rough place. No mining hamlet in the placer gulches of California, nor any backwoods village I ever saw, approached it in picturesque, devil-may-care *abandon*. It was a lawless draggle of wooden huts and houses, built in crooked lines, wrangling around the boggy shore of the island for a mile or so in the general form of the letter S, without the slightest subordination to the points of the compass or to building laws of any kind. Stumps and logs, like precious monuments, adorned its two streets, each stump and log, on account of the moist climate, moss-grown and tufted with grass and bushes, but muddy on the sides below the limit of the bog line. The ground in general was an oozy, mossy bog on a foundation of jagged rocks, full of concealed pitholes. These picturesque rock, bog, and stump obstructions, however, were not so very much in the way, for there were no wagons or carriages there. There was not a horse on the island. The domestic animals were represented by chickens, a lonely cow, a few sheep, and hogs of a breed well calculated to deepen and complicate the mud of the streets.

Most of the permanent residents of Wrangell were engaged in trade. Some little trade was carried on in fish and furs, but most of the quickening business of the place was derived from the Cassiar gold mines, some two hundred and fifty or three hundred miles inland, by way of the Stickeen River and Dease Lake. Two stern-wheel steamers plied on the river between Wrangell and Telegraph Creek at the head of navigation, a hundred and fifty miles from Wrangell, carrying freight and passengers and connecting with pack trains for the mines. These placer mines, on tributaries of the Mackenzie River, were discovered in the year 1874. About eighteen hundred miners and prospectors were said to have passed through Wrangell that season of 1879, about half of them being Chinamen. Nearly a third of this whole number set out from here in the month of February, traveling on the Stickeen River, which usually remains safely frozen until toward the end of April. The main body of the miners, however, went up on the steamers in May and

June. On account of the severe winters they were all compelled to leave the mines the end of September. Perhaps about two thirds of them passed the winter in Portland and Victoria and the towns of Puget Sound. The rest remained here in Wrangell, dozing away the long winter as best they could.

Indians, mostly of the Stickeen tribe, occupied the two ends of the town, the whites, of whom there were about forty or fifty, the middle portion; but there was no determinate line of demarcation, the dwellings of the Indians being mostly as large and solidly built of logs and planks as those of the whites. Some of them were adorned with tall totem poles.

The fort was a quadrangular stockade with a dozen block and frame buildings located upon rising ground just back of the business part of the town. It was built by our Government shortly after the purchase of Alaska, and was abandoned in 1872, reoccupied by the military in 1875, and finally abandoned and sold to private parties in 1877. In the fort and about it there were a few good, clean homes, which shone all the more brightly in their somber surroundings. The ground occupied by the fort, by being carefully leveled and drained, was dry, though formerly a portion of the general swamp, showing how easily the whole town could have been improved. But in spite of disorder and squalor, shaded with clouds, washed and wiped by rain and sea winds, it was triumphantly salubrious through all the seasons. And though the houses seemed to rest uneasily among the miry rocks and stumps, squirming at all angles as if they had been tossed and twisted by earthquake shocks, and showing but little more relation to one another than may be observed among moraine boulders, Wrangell was a tranquil place. I never heard a noisy brawl in the streets, or a clap of thunder, and the waves seldom spoke much above a whisper along the beach. In summer the rain comes straight down, steamy and tepid. The clouds are usually united, filling the sky, not racing along in threatening ranks suggesting energy of an overbearing destructive kind, but forming a bland, mild, laving bath. The cloudless days are calm, pearl-gray, and brooding in tone, inclining to rest and peace; the islands seem to drowse and float on the glassy water, and in the woods scarce a leaf stirs.

The very brightest of Wrangell days are not what Californians would call bright. The tempered sunshine sifting through the moist atmosphere makes no dazzling glare, and the town, like the landscape, rests beneath a hazy, hushing, Indian-summerish spell. On the longest days the sun rises about three o'clock, but it is daybreak at midnight. The cocks crowed when they woke, without reference to the dawn, for it is never quite dark; there were only a few full-grown roosters in Wrangell, half a dozen or so, to awaken the town and give it a civilized character. After sunrise a few languid smoke columns might be seen, telling the first stir of the people. Soon an Indian or two might be noticed here and there at the doors of their barn-like cabins, and a merchant getting ready for trade; but scarcely a sound was heard, only a dull, muffled stir gradually deepening. There were only two white babies in the town, so far as I saw, and as for Indian babies, they woke and ate and made no crying sound. Later you might hear the croaking of ravens, and the strokes of an axe on firewood. About eight or nine o'clock the town was awake. Indians, mostly women and children, began to gather on the front platforms of the half-dozen stores, sitting carelessly on their blankets, every other face hideously blackened, a naked circle around the eyes, and perhaps a spot on the cheekbone and the nose where the smut has been rubbed off. Some of the little children were also blackened, and none were over-clad, their light and airy costume consisting of a calico shirt reaching only to the waist. Boys eight or ten years old sometimes had an additional garment—a pair of castaway miner's overalls wide enough and ragged enough for extravagant ventilation. The larger girls and young women were arrayed in showy calico, and wore jaunty straw hats, gorgeously ribboned, and glowed among the blackened and blanketed old crones like scarlet tanagers in a flock of blackbirds. The women, seated on the steps and platform of the traders' shops, could hardly be called loafers, for they had berries to sell, basketfuls of huckleberries, large yellow salmonberries, and bog raspberries that looked wondrous fresh and clean amid the surrounding squalor. After patiently waiting for purchasers until hungry, they ate what they could not sell, and went away to gather more.

Yonder you see a canoe gliding out from the shore, containing perhaps a man, a woman, and a child or two, all paddling together in natural, easy rhythm. They are going to catch a fish, no difficult matter, and when this is done their day's work is done. Another party puts out to capture bits of driftwood, for it is easier to procure fuel in this way than to drag it down from the outskirts of the woods through rocks and bushes. As the day advances, a fleet of canoes may be seen along the shore, all fashioned alike, high and long beak-like prows and sterns, with lines as fine as those of the breast of a duck. What the mustang is to the Mexican *vaquero*, the canoe is to these coast

Indians. They skim along the shores to fish and hunt and trade, or merely to visit their neighbors, for they are sociable, and have family pride remarkably well developed, meeting often to inquire after each other's health, attend potlatches and dances, and gossip concerning coming marriages, births, deaths, etc. Others seem to sail for the pure pleasure of the thing, their canoes decorated with handfuls of the tall purple epilobium.

Yonder goes a whole family, grandparents and all, making a direct course for some favorite stream and campground. They are going to gather berries, as the baskets tell. Never before in all my travels, north or south, had I found so lavish an abundance of berries as here. The woods and meadows are full of them, both on the lowlands and mountains—huckleberries of many species, salmonberries, blackberries, raspberries, with serviceberries on dry open places, and cranberries in the bogs, sufficient for every bird, beast, and human being in the territory and thousands of tons to spare. The huckleberries are especially abundant. A species that grows well up on the mountains is the best and largest, a half-inch and more in diameter and delicious in flavor. These grow on bushes three or four inches to a foot high. The berries of the commonest species are smaller and grow almost everywhere on the low grounds on bushes from three to six or seven feet high. This is the species on which the Indians depend most for food, gathering them in large quantities, beating them into a paste, pressing the paste into cakes about an inch thick, and drying them over a slow fire to enrich their winter stores. Salmonberries and serviceberries are preserved in the same way.

A little excursion to one of the best huckleberry

fields adjacent to Wrangell, under the direction of the
Collector of Customs, to which I was invited, I greatly
enjoyed. There were nine Indians in the party, mostly
women and children going to gather huckleberries.
As soon as we had arrived at the chosen campground
on the bank of a trout stream, all ran into the bushes
and began eating berries before anything in the way
of campmaking was done, laughing and chattering in
natural animal enjoyment. The Collector went up the
stream to examine a meadow at its head with reference to the quantity of hay it might yield for his cow,
fishing by the way. All the Indians except the two
eldest boys who joined the Collector, remained among
the berries.

The fishermen had rather poor luck, owing, they
said, to the sunny brightness of the day, a complaint
seldom heard in this climate. They got good exercise, however, jumping from boulder to boulder in
the brawling stream, running along slippery logs and
through the bushes that fringe the bank, casting here
and there into swirling pools at the foot of cascades,
imitating the tempting little skips and whirls of flies
so well known to fishing parsons, but perhaps still better known to Indian boys. At the lake basin the Collector, after he had surveyed his hay meadow, went
around it to the inlet of the lake with his brown pair of
attendants to try their luck, while I botanized in the
delightful flora which called to mind the cool sphagnum and carex bogs of Wisconsin and Canada. Here I
found many of my old favorites the heathworts—kalmia, pyrola, chiogenes, huckleberry, cranberry, etc.
On the margin of the meadow, darling linnaea was in
its glory; purple panicled grasses in full flower reached
over my head, and some of the carices and ferns were

almost as tall. Here, too, on the edge of the woods I found the wild apple tree, the first I had seen in Alaska. The Indians gather the fruit, small and sour as it is, to flavor their fat salmon. I never saw a richer bog and meadow growth anywhere. The principal forest trees are hemlock, spruce, and Nootka cypress, with a few pines (*P. contorta*) on the margin of the meadow, some of them nearly a hundred feet high, draped with gray usnea, the bark also gray with scale lichens.

We met all the berry pickers at the lake, excepting only a small girl and the camp keeper. In their bright colors they made a lively picture among the quivering bushes, keeping up a low pleasant chanting as if the day and the place and the berries were according to their own hearts. The children carried small baskets, holding two or three quarts; the women two large ones swung over their shoulders. In the afternoon, when the baskets were full, all started back to the campground, where the canoe was left. We parted at the lake, I choosing to follow quietly the stream through the woods. I was the first to arrive at camp. The rest of the party came in shortly afterwards, singing and humming like heavy-laden bees. It was interesting to note how kindly they held out handfuls of the best berries to the little girl, who welcomed them all in succession with smiles and merry words that I did not understand. But there was no mistaking the kindliness and serene good nature.

While I was at Wrangell the chiefs and head men of the Stickeen tribe got up a grand dinner and entertainment in honor of their distinguished visitors, three doctors of divinity and their wives, fellow passengers on the steamer with me, whose object was to organize the Presbyterian church. To both the dinner and dances I was invited, was adopted by the Stickeen tribe, and given an Indian name (Ancoutahan) said to mean adopted chief. I was inclined to regard this honor as being unlikely to have any practical value, but I was assured by Mr. Vanderbilt, Mr. Young, and others that it would be a great safeguard while I was on my travels among the different tribes of the archipelago. For travelers without an Indian name might be killed and robbed without the offender being called to account as long as the crime was kept secret from the whites; but, being adopted by the Stickeens, no one belonging to the other tribes would dare attack me, knowing that the Stickeens would hold them responsible.

The dinner tables were tastefully decorated with flowers, and the food and general arrangements were in good taste, but there was no trace of Indian dishes. It was mostly imported canned stuff served Boston fashion. After the dinner we assembled in Chief Shakes's large blockhouse and were entertained with lively examples of their dances and amusements, carried on with great spirit, making a very novel barbarous durbar. The dances seemed to me wonderfully like those of the American Indians in general, a monotonous stamping accompanied by hand-clapping, head-jerking, and explosive grunts kept in time to grim drum beats. The chief dancer and leader scattered great quantities of downy feathers like a snowstorm as blessings on everybody, while all chanted, "Hee-ee-ah-ah, hee-ee-ah-ah," jumping up and down until all were bathed in perspiration.

After the dancing excellent imitations were given of the gait, gestures, and behavior of several animals under different circumstances—walking, hunting, capturing, and devouring their prey, etc. While all were quietly seated, waiting to see what next was going to happen, the door of the big house was suddenly thrown open and in bounced a bear, so true to life in form and gestures we were all startled, though it was only a bearskin nicely fitted on a man who was intimately acquainted with the animals and knew how to imitate them. The bear shuffled down into the middle of the floor and made the motion of jumping into a stream and catching a wooden salmon that was ready for him, carrying it out on to the bank, throwing his head around to listen and see if any one was coming, then tearing it to pieces, jerking his head from side to side, looking and listening in fear of hunters' rifles. Besides the bear dance, there were porpoise and deer dances with one of the party imitating the animals by stuffed specimens with an Indian inside, and the movements were so accurately imitated that they seemed the real thing.

These animal plays were followed by serious speeches, interpreted by an Indian woman: "Dear Brothers and Sisters, this is the way we used to dance. We liked it long ago when we were blind, we always danced this way, but now we are not blind. The Good Lord has taken pity upon us and sent his son, Jesus Christ, to tell us what to do. We have danced today only to show you how blind we were to like to dance in this foolish way. We will not dance anymore."

Another speech was interpreted as follows: "'Dear Brothers and Sisters,' the chief says, 'this is the way we used to dance and play. We do not wish to do so any more. We will give away all the dance dresses you have seen us wearing, though we value them very highly.' He says he feels much honored to have so many white brothers and sisters at our dinner and plays."

Several short explanatory remarks were made all

through the exercises by Chief Shakes, presiding with grave dignity. The last of his speeches concluded thus: "Dear Brothers and Sisters, we have been long, long in the dark. You have led us into strong guiding light and taught us the right way to live and the right way to die. I thank you for myself and all my people, and I give you my heart."

At the close of the amusements there was a potlatch when robes made of the skins of deer, wild sheep, marmots, and sables were distributed, and many of the fantastic headdresses that had been worn by Shamans. One of these fell to my share.

The floor of the house was strewn with fresh hemlock boughs, bunches of showy wild flowers adorned the walls, and the hearth was filled with huckleberry branches and epilobium. Altogether it was a wonderful show.

I have found southeastern Alaska a good, healthy country to live in. The climate of the islands and shores of the mainland is remarkably bland and temperate and free from extremes of either heat or cold throughout the year. It is rainy, however—so much so that haymaking will hardly ever be extensively engaged in here, whatever the future may show in the way of the development of mines, forests, and fisheries. This rainy weather, however, is of good quality, the best of the kind I ever experienced, mild in temperature, mostly gentle in its fall, filling the fountains of the rivers and keeping the whole land fresh and fruitful, while anything more delightful than the shining weather in the midst of the rain, the great round sundays of July and August, may hardly be found anywhere, north or south. An Alaska summer day is a day without night. In the Far North, at Point Barrow, the

sun does not set for weeks, and even here in southeastern Alaska it is only a few degrees below the horizon at its lowest point, and the topmost colors of the
sunset blend with those of the sunrise, leaving no gap
of darkness between. Midnight is only a low noon, the
middle point of the gloaming. The thin clouds that
are almost always present are then colored yellow
and red, making a striking advertisement of the sun's
progress beneath the horizon. The day opens slowly.
The low arc of light steals around to the northeastward with gradual increase of height and span and
intensity of tone; and when at length the sun appears,
it is without much of that stirring, impressive pomp,
of flashing, awakening, triumphant energy, suggestive of the Bible imagery, a bridegroom coming out of
his chamber and rejoicing like a strong man to run
a race. The red clouds with yellow edges dissolve in
hazy dimness; the islands, with grayish-white ruffs
of mist about them, cast ill-defined shadows on the
glistening waters, and the whole down-bending firmament becomes pearl-gray. For three or four hours
after sunrise there is nothing especially impressive in
the landscape. The sun, though seemingly unclouded,
may almost be looked in the face, and the islands and
mountains, with their wealth of woods and snow and
varied beauty of architecture, seem comparatively
sleepy and uncommunicative.

As the day advances toward high noon, the sun-
flood streaming through the damp atmosphere lights
the water levels and the sky to glowing silver. Brightly
play the ripples about the bushy edges of the islands
and on the plume-shaped streaks between them, ruffled by gentle passing wind currents. The warm air
throbs and makes itself felt as a life-giving, energizing

ocean, embracing all the landscape, quickening the imagination, and bringing to mind the life and motion about us—the tides, the rivers, the flood of light streaming through the satiny sky; the marvelous abundance of fishes feeding in the lower ocean; the misty flocks of insects in the air; wild sheep and goats on a thousand grassy ridges; beaver and mink far back on many a rushing stream; Indians floating and basking along the shores; leaves and crystals drinking the sunbeams; and glaciers on the mountains, making valleys and basins for new rivers and lakes and fertile beds of soil.

Through the afternoon, all the way down to the sunset, the day grows in beauty. The light seems to thicken and become yet more generously fruitful without losing its soft mellow brightness. Everything seems to settle into conscious repose. The winds breathe gently or are wholly at rest. The few clouds visible are downy and luminous and combed out fine on the edges. Gulls here and there, winnowing the air on easy wing, are brought into striking relief; and every stroke of the paddles of Indian hunters in their canoes is told by a quick, glancing flash. Bird choirs in the grove are scarce heard as they sweeten the brooding stillness; and the sky, land, and water meet and blend in one inseparable scene of enchantment. Then comes the sunset with its purple and gold, not a narrow arch on the horizon, but oftentimes filling all the sky. The level cloud-bars usually present are fired on the edges, and the spaces of clear sky between them are greenish-yellow or pale amber, while the orderly flocks of small overlapping clouds, often seen higher up, are mostly touched with crimson like the out-leaning sprays of maple groves in the beginning of an Eastern Indian Summer. Soft, mellow purple flushes the sky to the zenith and fills the air, fairly steeping and transfiguring the islands and making all the water look like wine. After the sun goes down, the glowing gold vanishes, but because it descends on a curve nearly in the same plane with the horizon, the glowing portion of the display lasts much longer than in more southern latitudes, while the upper colors with gradually lessening intensity of tone sweep around to the north, gradually increase to the eastward, and unite with those of the morning.

The most extravagantly colored of all the sunsets I have yet seen in Alaska was one I enjoyed on the voyage from Portland to Wrangell, when we were in the midst of one of the most thickly islanded parts of the Alexander Archipelago. The day had been showery, but late in the afternoon the clouds melted away from the west, all save a few that settled down in narrow level bars near the horizon. The evening was calm and the sunset colors came on gradually, increasing in extent and richness of tone by slow degrees as if requiring more time than usual to ripen. At a height of about thirty degrees there was a heavy cloud bank, deeply reddened on its lower edge and the projecting parts of its face. Below this were three horizontal belts of purple edged with gold, while a vividly defined, spreading fan of flame streamed upward across the purple bars and faded in a feather edge of dull red. But beautiful and impressive as was this painting on the sky, the most novel and exciting effect was in the body of the atmosphere itself, which, laden with moisture, became one mass of color—a fine translucent purple haze in which the islands with softened outlines seemed to float, while a dense red ring lay around the base of each of them as a fitting border. The peaks, too, in the distance, and the snowfields and glaciers and fleecy rolls of mist that lay in the hollows, were flushed with a deep, rosy alpenglow of ineffable loveliness. Everything near and far, even the ship, was comprehended in the glorious picture and the general color effect. The mission divines we had aboard seemed then to be truly divine as they gazed transfigured in the celestial glory. So also seemed our bluff, storm-fighting old captain, and his tarry sailors and all.

About one third of the summer days I spent in the Wrangell region were cloudy with very little or no rain, one-third decidedly rainy, and one-third clear. According to a record kept here of a hundred and forty-seven days beginning May 17 of that year, there were sixty-five on which rain fell, forty-three cloudy with no rain, and thirty-nine clear. In June rain fell on eighteen days, in July eight days, in August fifteen days, in September twenty days. But on some of these days there was only a few minutes' rain, light showers scarce enough to count, while as a general thing the rain fell so gently and the temperature was so mild, very few of them could be called stormy or dismal; even the bleakest, most bedraggled of them all usually had a flush of late or early color to cheer them, or some white illumination about the noon hours. I never before saw so much rain fall with so little noise. None of the summer winds make roaring storms, and thunder is seldom heard. I heard none at all. This wet, misty weather seems perfectly healthful. There is no mildew in the houses, as far as I have seen, or any tendency toward moldiness in nooks hidden from the sun; and neither among the people nor the plants do we find anything flabby or dropsical.

In September clear days were rare, more than three

fourths of them were either decidedly cloudy or rainy, and the rains of this month were, with one wild exception, only moderately heavy, and the clouds between showers drooped and crawled in a ragged, unsettled way without betraying hints of violence such as one often sees in the gestures of mountain storm clouds.

July was the brightest month of the summer, with fourteen days of sunshine, six of them in uninterrupted succession, with a temperature at 7 A.M. of about 60 degrees, at 12 M., 70 degrees. The average 7 A.M. temperature for June was 54.3 degrees; the average 7 A.M. temperature for July was 55.3 degrees; at 12 M. the average temperature was 61.45 degrees; the average 7 A.M. temperature for August was 54.12 degrees; 12 M., 61.48 degrees; the average 7 A.M. temperature for September was 52.14 degrees; and 12 M., 56.12 degrees.

The highest temperature observed here during the summer was seventy-six degrees. The most remarkable characteristic of this summer weather, even the brightest of it, is the velvet softness of the atmosphere. On the mountains of California, throughout the greater part of the year, the presence of an atmosphere is hardly recognized, and the thin, white, bodiless light of the morning comes to the peaks and glaciers as a pure spiritual essence, the most impressive of all the terrestrial manifestations of God. The clearest of Alaskan air is always appreciably substantial, so much so that it would seem as if one might test its quality by rubbing it between the thumb and finger. I never before saw summer days so white and so full of subdued luster.

The winter storms, up to the end of December when I left Wrangell, were mostly rain at a temperature of thirty-five or forty degrees, with strong winds which sometimes roughly lash the shores and carry scud far into the woods. The long nights are then gloomy enough and the value of snug homes with crackling yellow cedar fires may be finely appreciated. Snow falls frequently, but never to any great depth or to lie long. It is said that only once since the settlement of Fort Wrangell has the ground been covered to a depth of four feet. The mercury seldom falls more than five or six degrees below the freezing point, unless the wind blows steadily from the mainland. Back from the coast, however, beyond the mountains, the winter months are very cold. On the Stickeen River at Glenora, less than a thousand feet above the level of the sea, a temperature of from thirty to forty degrees below zero is not uncommon.

4

THE STICKEEN RIVER

The most interesting of the short excursions we made from Fort Wrangell was the one up the Stickeen River to the head of steam navigation. From Mt. St. Elias the coast range extends in a broad, lofty chain beyond the southern boundary of the territory, gashed by stupendous canyons, each of which carries a lively river, though most of them are comparatively short, as their highest sources lie in the icy solitudes of the range within forty or fifty miles of the coast. A few, however, of these foaming, roaring streams— the Alsek, Chilcat, Chilcoot, Taku, Stickeen, and perhaps others—head beyond the range with some of the southwest branches of the Mackenzie and Yukon.

The largest side branches of the main trunk canyons of all these mountain streams are still occupied by glaciers which descend in showy ranks, their messy, bulging snouts lying back a little distance in the shadows of the walls, or pushing forward among the cottonwoods that line the banks of the rivers, or even stretching all the way across the main canyons, compelling the rivers to find a channel beneath them.

The Stickeen was, perhaps, the best known of the rivers that cross the Coast Range, because it was the best way to the Mackenzie River Cassiar gold mines. It is about three hundred and fifty miles long, and is navigable for small steamers a hundred and fifty miles to Glenora, and sometimes to Telegraph Creek, fifteen miles farther. It first pursues a westerly course through grassy plains darkened here and there with groves of spruce and pine; then, curving southward and receiving numerous tributaries from the north, it enters the Coast Range, and sweeps across it through a magnificent canyon three thousand to five thousand feet deep, and more than a hundred miles long. The majestic cliffs and mountains forming the canyon walls display endless variety of form and sculpture, and are wonderfully adorned and enlivened with glaciers and waterfalls, while throughout almost its whole extent the floor is a flowery landscape garden, like Yosemite. The most striking features are the glaciers, hanging over the cliffs, descending the side canyons and pushing forward to the river, greatly enhancing the wild beauty of all the others.

Gliding along the swift-flowing river, the views change with bewildering rapidity. Wonderful, too, are the changes dependent on the seasons and the weather. In spring, when the snow is melting fast, you enjoy the countless rejoicing waterfalls; the gentle breathing of warm winds; the colors of the young leaves and flowers when the bees are busy and wafts of fragrance are drifting hither and thither from miles of wild roses, clover, and honeysuckle; the swaths of birch and willow on the lower slopes following the melting of the winter avalanche snowbanks; the bossy cumuli swelling in white and purple piles above the highest peaks; gray rain clouds wreathing the outstanding brows and battlements of the walls; and the breaking forth of the sun after the rain; the shining of the leaves and streams and crystal architecture of the glaciers; the rising of fresh fragrance; the song of the happy birds; and the serene color-grandeur of the morning and evening sky. In summer you find the groves and gardens in full dress; glaciers melting rapidly under sunshine and rain; waterfalls in all their glory; the river rejoicing in its strength; young birds trying their wings; bears enjoying salmon and berries; all the life of the canyon brimming full like the streams. In autumn comes rest, as if the year's work were done. The rich hazy sunshine streaming over the cliffs calls forth the last of the gentians and goldenrods; the groves and thickets and meadows bloom again as their leaves change to red and yellow petals; the rocks also, and the glaciers, seem to bloom like the plants in the mellow golden light. And so goes the song, change succeeding change in sublime harmony through all the wonderful seasons and weather.

My first trip up the river was made in the spring with the missionary party soon after our arrival at Wrangell. We left Wrangell in the afternoon and anchored for the night above the river delta, and started up the river early next morning when the heights above the "Big Stickeen" Glacier and the smooth domes and copings and arches of solid snow along the tops of the canyon walls were glowing in the early beams. We arrived before noon at the old trading post called "Buck's" in front of the Stickeen Glacier, and remained long enough to allow the few passengers who wished a nearer view to cross the river to the terminal moraine. The sunbeams streaming through the ice pinnacles along its terminal wall produced a wonderful glory of color, and the broad, sparkling crystal prairie and the distant snowy fountains were wonderfully attractive and made me pray for opportunity to explore them.

Of the many glaciers, a hundred or more, that adorn the walls of the great Stickeen River Canyon, this is the largest. It draws its sources from snowy mountains within fifteen or twenty miles of the coast, pours through a comparatively narrow canyon about two miles in width in a magnificent cascade, and expands in a broad fan five or six miles in width, separated from the Stickeen River by its broad terminal moraine, fringed with spruces and willows. Around the beautifully drawn curve of the moraine the Stickeen River flows, having evidently been shoved by the glacier out of its direct course. On the opposite side of the canyon another somewhat smaller glacier, which now terminates four or five miles from the river, was once united front to front with the greater glacier, though at first both were tributaries of the main Stickeen Glacier which once filled the whole grand canyon. After the main trunk canyon was melted out, its side branches, drawing their sources from a height of three or four to five or six thousand feet, were cut off, and of course became separate glaciers, occupying cirques and branch canyons along the tops and sides of the walls. The Indians have a tradition that the river used to run through a tunnel under the united fronts of the two large tributary glaciers mentioned above, which entered the main canyon from either side; and that on one occasion an Indian, anxious to get rid of his wife, had her sent adrift in a canoe down through the ice tunnel, expecting that she would trouble him no more. But to his surprise she floated through under the ice in safety. All the evidence connected with the present appearance of these two glaciers indicates that they were united and formed a dam across the river after the smaller tributaries had been melted off and had receded to a greater or lesser height above the valley floor.

The big Stickeen Glacier is hardly out of sight ere you come upon another that pours a majestic crystal flood through the evergreens, while almost every hollow and tributary canyon contains a smaller one, the size, of course, varying with the extent of the area drained. Some are like mere snowbanks; others, with the blue ice apparent, depend in massive bulging curves and swells, and graduate into the riverlike forms that maze through the lower forested regions and are so striking and beautiful that they are admired even by the passing miners with gold dust in their eyes.

Thirty-five miles above the Big Stickeen Glacier is the "Dirt Glacier," the second in size. Its outlet is a fine stream, abounding in trout. On the opposite side of the river there is a group of five glaciers, one of them descending to within a hundred feet of the river.

Near Glenora, on the northeastern flank of the main Coast Range, just below a narrow gorge called "The Canyon," terraces first make their appearance, where great quantities of moraine material have been swept through the flood-choked gorge and of course outspread and deposited on the first open levels below. Here, too, occurs a marked change in climate and consequently in forests and general appearance of the face of the country. On account of destructive fires the woods are younger and are composed of smaller trees about a foot to eighteen inches in diameter and seventy-five feet high, mostly two-leaved pines which hold their seeds for several years after they are ripe. The woods here are without a trace of those deep accumulations of mosses, leaves, and decaying trunks which make so damp and unclearable a mass in the coast forests. Whole mountainsides are covered with gray moss and lichens where the forest has been utterly destroyed. The riverbank cottonwoods are also smaller, and the birch and contorta pines mingle freely with the coast hemlock and spruce. The birch is common on the lower slopes and is very effective, its round, leafy, pale-green head contrasting with the dark, narrow spires of the conifers and giving a striking character to the forest. The "tamarac pine" or black pine, as the variety of *P. contorta* is called here, is yellowish-green, in marked contrast with the dark lichen-draped spruce which grows above the pine at a height of about two thousand feet, in groves and belts where it has escaped fire and snow avalanches. There is another handsome spruce hereabouts, *Picea alba*, very slender and graceful in habit, drooping at the top like a mountain hemlock. I saw fine specimens a hundred and twenty-five feet high on deep bottom land a few miles below Glenora. The tops of some of them were almost covered with dense clusters of yellow and brown cones.

We reached the old Hudson's Bay trading post at Glenora about one o'clock, and the captain informed me that he would stop here until the next morning, when he would make an early start for Wrangell.

At a distance of about seven or eight miles to the northeastward of the landing, there is an outstanding group of mountains crowning a spur from the main chain of the Coast Range, whose highest point rises about eight thousand feet above the level of the sea; and as Glenora is only a thousand feet above the sea, the height to be overcome in climbing this peak is about seven thousand feet. Though the time was short I determined to climb it, because of the advantageous position it occupied for general views of the peaks and glaciers of the east side of the great range.

Although it was now twenty minutes past three and the days were getting short, I thought that by rapid climbing I could reach the summit before sunset, in time to get a general view and a few pencil sketches, and make my way back to the steamer in the night. Mr. Young, one of the missionaries, asked permission to accompany me, saying that he was a good walker and climber and would not delay me or cause any trouble. I strongly advised him not to go, explaining that it involved a walk, coming and going, of fourteen or sixteen miles, and a climb through brush and boulders of seven thousand feet, a fair day's work for a seasoned mountaineer to be done in less than half a day and part of a night. But he insisted that he was a strong walker, could do a mountaineer's day's work in half a day, and would not hinder me in any way.

"Well, I have warned you," I said, "and will not assume responsibility for any trouble that may arise."

He proved to be a stout walker, and we made rapid progress across a brushy timbered flat and up the mountain slopes, open in some places, and in others thatched with dwarf firs, resting a minute here and there to refresh ourselves with huckleberries, which grew in abundance in open spots. About half an hour before sunset, when we were near a cluster of crumbling pinnacles that formed the summit, I had ceased to feel anxiety about the mountaineering strength and skill of my companion, and pushed rapidly on. In passing around the shoulder of the highest pinnacle, where the rock was rapidly disintegrating and the danger of slipping was great, I shouted in a warning voice, "Be very careful here, this is dangerous."

Mr. Young was perhaps a dozen or two yards behind me, but out of sight. I afterwards reproached myself for not stopping and lending him a steadying hand, and showing him the slight footsteps I had made by kicking out little blocks of the crumbling surface, instead of simply warning him to be careful. Only a few seconds after giving this warning, I was startled by a scream for help, and hurrying back, found the missionary face downward, his arms outstretched, clutching little crumbling knobs on the brink of a gully that plunges down a thousand feet or more to a small residual glacier. I managed to get below him, touched one of his feet, and tried to encourage him by saying, "I am below you. You are in no danger. You can't slip past me and I will soon get you out of this."

He then told me that both of his arms were dislocated. It was almost impossible to find available footholds on the treacherous rock, and I was at my wits' end to know how to get him rolled or dragged to a place where I could get about him, find out how much he was hurt, and a way back down the mountain. After narrowly scanning the cliff and making footholds, I managed to roll and lift him a few yards to a place where the slope was less steep, and there I attempted to set his arms. I found, however, that this was impossible in such a place. I therefore tied his arms to his sides with my suspenders and necktie, to prevent as much as possible inflammation from movement. I then left him, telling him to lie still, that I would be back in a few minutes, and that he was now safe from slipping. I hastily examined the ground and saw no way of getting him down except by the steep glacier gully. After scrambling to an outstanding point that commands a view of it from top to bottom, to make sure that it was not interrupted by sheer precipices, I concluded that with great care and the digging of slight footholds he could be slid down to the glacier, where I could lay him on his back and perhaps be able to set his arms. Accordingly, I cheered him up, telling him I had found a way, but that it would require lots of time and patience. Digging a footstep in the sand or crumbling rock five or six feet beneath him, I reached up, took hold of him by one of his feet, and gently slid him down on his back, placed his heels in the step, then descended another five or six feet, dug heel notches, and slid him down to them. Thus the whole distance was made by a succession of narrow steps at very short intervals, and the glacier was reached perhaps about midnight. Here I took off one of my boots, tied a handkerchief around his wrist for a good hold, placed my heel in his armpit, and succeeded in getting one of his arms into place, but my utmost strength was insufficient to reduce the dislocation of the other. I therefore bound it closely to his side, and asked him if in his exhausted and trembling condition he was still able to walk.

"Yes," he bravely replied.

So, with a steadying arm around him and many stops for rest, I marched him slowly down in the starlight on the comparatively smooth, unassured surface of the little glacier to the terminal moraine, a distance of perhaps a mile, crossed the moraine, bathed his head at one of the outlet streams, and after many rests reached a dry place and made a brush fire. I then went ahead looking for an open way through the bushes to where larger wood could be had, made a good lasting fire of resiny silver-fir roots, and a leafy bed beside it. I now told him I would run down the mountain, hasten back with help from the boat, and carry him down in comfort. But he would not hear of my leaving him.

"No, no," he said, "I can walk down. Don't leave me."

I reminded him of the roughness of the way, his nerve-shaken condition, and assured him I would not be gone long. But he insisted on trying, saying on no account whatever must I leave him. I therefore concluded to try to get him to the ship by short walks from one fire and resting place to another. While he was resting I went ahead, looking for the best way through the brush and rocks, then returning, got him on his feet and made him lean on my shoulder while I steadied him to prevent his falling. This slow, staggering struggle from fire to fire lasted until long after sunrise. When at last we reached the ship and stood at the foot of the narrow single plank without side rails that reached from the bank to the deck at a considerable angle, I briefly explained to Mr. Young's companions, who stood looking down at us, that he had been hurt in an accident, and requested one of them to assist me in getting him aboard. But strange to say, instead of coming down to help, they made haste to reproach him for having gone on a "wild goose chase" with Muir.

"These foolish adventures are well enough for Mr. Muir," they said, "but you, Mr. Young, have a work to do; you have a family; you have a church, and you have no right to risk your life on treacherous peaks and precipices."

The captain, Nat Lane, son of Senator Joseph Lane, had been swearing in angry impatience for being compelled to make so late a start and thus encounter a dangerous wind in a narrow gorge, and was threatening to put the missionaries ashore to seek their lost companion, while he went on down the river about his business. But when he heard my call for help, he hastened forward, and elbowed the divines away from the end of the gangplank, shouting in angry irreverence, "Oh, blank! This is no time for preaching! Don't you see the man is hurt?"

He ran down to our help, and while I steadied my trembling companion from behind, the captain kindly led him up the plank into the saloon, and made him drink a large glass of brandy. Then, with a man holding down his shoulders, we succeeded in getting the bone into its socket, notwithstanding the inflammation and contraction of the muscles and ligaments. Mr. Young was then put to bed, and he slept all the way back to Wrangell.

In his mission lectures in the East, Mr. Young oftentimes told this story. I made no record of it in my notebook and never intended to write a word about it; but after a miserable, sensational caricature of the story had appeared in a respectable magazine, I thought it but fair to my brave companion that it should be told just as it happened.

5

A CRUISE IN THE CASSIAR

Shortly after our return to Wrangell the missionaries planned a grand mission excursion up the coast of the mainland to the Chilcat country, which I gladly joined, together with Mr. Vanderbilt, his wife, and a friend from Oregon. The river steamer Cassiar was chartered, and we had her all to ourselves, ship and officers at our command to sail and stop where and when we would, and of course everybody felt important and hopeful. The main object of the missionaries was to ascertain the spiritual wants of the warlike Chilcat tribe, with a view to the establishment of a church and school in their principal village; the merchant and his party were bent on business and scenery; while my mind was on the mountains, glaciers, and forests.

This was toward the end of July, in the very brightest and best of Alaska summer weather, when the icy mountains towering in the pearly sky were displayed in all their glory, and the islands at their feet seemed to float and drowse on the shining mirror waters.

After we had passed through the Wrangell Narrows, the mountains of the mainland came in full view, gloriously arrayed in snow and ice, some of the largest and most riverlike of the glaciers flowing through wide, high-walled valleys like Yosemite, their sources far back and concealed, others in plain sight, from their highest fountains to the level of the sea.

Cares of every kind were quickly forgotten, and though the Cassiar engines soon began to wheeze and sigh with doleful solemnity, suggesting coming trouble, we were too happy to mind them. Every face glowed with natural love of wild beauty. The islands were seen in long perspective, their forests dark green in the foreground, with varying tones of blue growing more and more tender in the distance; bays full of hazy shadows, graduating into open, silvery fields of light, and lofty headlands with fine arching insteps dipping their feet in the shining water. But every eye was turned to the mountains. Forgotten now were the Chilcats and missions while the word of God was being read in these majestic hieroglyphics blazoned along the sky. The earnest, childish wonderment with which this glorious page of Nature's Bible was contemplated was delightful to see. All evinced eager desire to learn.

"Is that a glacier," they asked, "down in that canyon? And is it all solid ice?"

"Yes."

"How deep is it?"

"Perhaps five hundred or a thousand feet."

"You say it flows. How can hard ice flow?"

"It flows like water, though invisibly slow."

"And where does it come from?"

"From snow that is heaped up every winter on the mountains."

"And how, then, is the snow changed into ice?"

"It is welded by the pressure of its own weight."

"Are these white masses we see in the hollows glaciers also?"

"Yes."

"Are those bluish draggled masses hanging down from beneath the snowfields what you call the snouts of the glaciers?"

"Yes."

"What made the hollows they are in?"

"The glaciers themselves, just as traveling animals make their own tracks."

"How long have they been there?"

"Numberless centuries," etc. I answered as best I could, keeping up a running commentary on the subject in general, while busily engaged in sketching and noting my own observations, preaching glacial gospel in a rambling way, while the Cassiar, slowly wheezing and creeping along the shore, shifted our position so that the icy canyons were opened to view and closed again in regular succession, like the leaves of a book.

About the middle of the afternoon we were directly opposite a noble group of glaciers some ten in number, flowing from a chain of craterlike snow fountains, guarded around their summits and well down their sides by jagged peaks and cols and curving mural ridges. From each of the larger clusters of fountains, a wide, sheer-walled canyon opens down to the sea. Three of the trunk glaciers descend to within a few feet of the sea level. The largest of the three, probably about fifteen miles long, terminates in a magnificent valley like Yosemite, in an imposing wall of ice about two miles long, and from three to five hundred feet high, forming a barrier across the valley from wall to wall. It was to this glacier that the ships of the Alaska Ice Company resorted for the ice they carried to San Francisco and the Sandwich Islands, and, I believe, also to China and Japan. To load, they had only to sail up the fjord within a short distance of the front and drop anchor in the terminal moraine.

Another glacier, a few miles to the south of this one, receives two large tributaries about equal in size, and then flows down a forested valley to within a hundred feet or so of sea level. The third of this low-descending group is four or five miles farther south, and, though less imposing than either of the two sketched above, is still a truly noble object, even as imperfectly seen from the channel, and would of itself be well worth a visit to Alaska to any lowlander so unfortunate as never to have seen a glacier.

The boilers of our little steamer were not made for seawater, but it was hoped that fresh water would be found at available points along our course where streams leap down the cliffs. In this particular we failed, however, and were compelled to use salt water an hour or two before reaching Cape Fanshawe, the supply of fifty tons of fresh water brought from Wrangell having then given out. To make matters worse, the captain and engineer were not in accord concerning the working of the engines. The captain repeatedly called for more steam, which the engineer refused to furnish, cautiously keeping the pressure low because the salt water foamed in the boilers and some of it passed over into the cylinders, causing heavy thumping at the end of each piston stroke, and threatening to knock out the cylinder heads. At seven o'clock in the evening we had made only about seventy miles, which caused dissatisfaction, especially among the divines, who thereupon called a meeting in the cabin to consider what had better be done. In the discussions that followed, much indignation and economy were brought to light. We had chartered the boat for sixty dollars per day, and the round trip was to have been made in four or five days. But at the present rate of speed it was found that the cost of the trip for each passenger would be five or ten dollars above the first estimate. Therefore, the majority ruled that we must return next day to Wrangell, the extra dollars outweighing the mountains and missions as if they had suddenly become dust in the balance.

Soon after the close of this economical meeting, we came to anchor in a beautiful bay, and as the long northern day had still hours of good light to offer, I gladly embraced the opportunity to go ashore to see the rocks and plants. One of the Indians, employed as a deckhand on the steamer, landed me at the mouth of a stream. The tide was low, exposing a luxuriant growth of algae, which sent up a fine, fresh sea smell. The shingle was composed of slate, quartz, and granite, named in the order of abundance. The first land plant met was a tall grass, nine feet high, forming a meadowlike margin in front of the forest. Pushing my way well back into the forest, I found it composed almost entirely of spruce and two hemlocks (*Picea sitchensis, Tsuga heterophylla* and *T. mertensiana*) with a few specimens of yellow cypress. The ferns were developed in remarkable beauty and size—aspidiums, one of which is about six feet high, a woodsia, lomaria, and several species of polypodium. The underbrush is chiefly alder, rubus, ledum, three species of vaccinium, and *Echinopanax horrida*, the whole about from six to eight feet high, and in some places closely intertangled and hard to penetrate. On the opener spots beneath the trees the ground is covered to a depth of two or three feet with mosses of indescribable freshness and beauty, a few dwarf conifers often planted on their rich furred bosses, together with pyrola, coptis, and Solomon's seal. The tallest of the trees are about a hundred and fifty feet high, with a diameter of about four or five feet, their branches mingling together and making a perfect shade. As the twilight began to fall, I sat down on the mossy instep of a spruce. Not a bush or tree was moving; every leaf seemed hushed in brooding repose. One bird, a thrush, embroidered the silence with cheery notes, making the solitude familiar and sweet, while the solemn monotone of the stream sifting through the woods seemed like the very voice of God, humanized, terrestrialized, and entering one's heart as to a home prepared for it. Go where we will, all the world over, we seem to have been there before.

The stream was bridged at short intervals with picturesque, moss-embossed logs, and the trees on its banks, leaning over from side to side, made high embowering arches. The log bridge I crossed was, I think, the most beautiful of the kind I ever saw. The massive log is plushed to a depth of six inches or more with mosses of three or four species, their different tones of yellow shading finely into each other, while their delicate fronded branches and foliage lie in exquisite order, inclining outward and down the sides in rich, furred, clasping sheets overlapping and felted together until the required thickness is attained. The pedicels and spore cases give a purplish tinge, and the whole bridge is enriched with ferns and a row of small seedling trees and currant bushes with colored leaves, every one of which seems to have been culled from the woods for this special use, so perfectly do they harmonize in size, shape, and color with the mossy cover, the width of the span, and the luxuriant, brushy abutments.

Sauntering back to the beach, I found four or five Indian deckhands getting water, with whom I returned aboard the steamer, thanking the Lord for so noble an addition to my life as was this one big mountain, forest, and glacial day.

Next morning most of the company seemed uncomfortably conscience-stricken, and ready to do anything in the way of compensation for our broken excursion that would not cost too much. It was not found difficult, therefore, to convince the captain and disappointed passengers that instead of creeping back to Wrangell direct we should make an expiatory branch excursion to the largest of the three low-descending glaciers we had passed. The Indian pilot, well acquainted with this part of the coast, declared himself willing to guide us. The water in these fjord channels is generally deep and safe, and though at wide intervals rocks rise abruptly here and there, lacking only a few feet in height to enable them to take rank as islands, the flat-bottomed Cassiar drew but little more water than a duck, so that even the most timid raised no objection on this score. The cylinder heads of our engines were the main source of anxiety; provided they could be kept on all might yet be well. But in this matter there was evidently some distrust, the engineer having imprudently informed some of the passengers that in consequence of using salt water in his frothing boilers the cylinder heads might fly off at any moment. To the glacier, however, it was at length decided we should venture.

Arriving opposite the mouth of its fjord, we steered straight inland between beautiful wooded shores, and the grand glacier came in sight in its granite valley, glowing in the early sunshine and extending a noble invitation to come and see. After we passed between the two mountain rocks that guard the gate of the fjord, the view that was unfolded fixed every eye in wondering admiration. No words can convey anything like an adequate conception of its sublime grandeur—the noble simplicity and fineness of the sculpture of the walls; their magnificent proportions; their cascades, gardens, and forest adornments; the placid fjord between them; the great white and blue ice wall, and the snow-laden mountains beyond. Still more impotent are words in telling the peculiar awe one experiences in entering these mansions of the icy North, notwithstanding it is only the natural effect of appreciable manifestations of the presence of God.

Standing in the gateway of this glorious temple, and regarding it only as a picture, its outlines may be easily traced, the water foreground of a pale-green color, a smooth mirror sheet sweeping back five or six miles like one of the lower reaches of a great river, bounded at the head by a beveled barrier wall of bluish-white ice four or five hundred feet high. A few snowy mountaintops appear beyond it, and on either hand rise a series of majestic, pale-gray granite rocks from three to four thousand feet high, some of them thinly forested and striped with bushes and flowery grass on narrow shelves, especially about half way up, others severely sheer and bare and built together into walls like those of Yosemite, extending far beyond the ice barrier, one immense brow appearing beyond another with their bases buried in the glacier. This is a Yosemite Valley in process of formation, the modeling and sculpture of the walls nearly completed and well planted, but no groves as yet or gardens or meadows on the raw and unfinished bottom. It is as if the explorer, in entering the Merced Yosemite, should find the walls nearly in their present condition, trees and flowers in the warm nooks and along the sunny portions of the moraine-covered brows, but the bottom of the valley still covered with water and beds of gravel and mud, and the grand glacier that formed it slowly receding but still filling the upper half of the valley.

Sailing directly up to the edge of the low, outspread, water-washed terminal moraine, scarce noticeable in a general view, we seemed to be separated from the glacier only by a bed of gravel a hundred yards or so in width; but on so grand a scale are all the main features of the valley, we afterwards found the distance to be a mile or more.

The captain ordered the Indian deckhands to get out the canoe, take as many of us ashore as wished to go, and accompany us to the glacier in case we should need their help. Only three of the company, in the first place, availed themselves of this rare opportunity of meeting a glacier in the flesh—Mr. Young, one of the doctors, and myself. Paddling to the nearest and driest-looking part of the moraine flat, we stepped ashore, but gladly wallowed back into the canoe; for the gray mineral mud, a paste made of fine-ground mountain meal kept unstable by the tides, at once began to take us in, swallowing us feet foremost with becoming glacial deliberation. Our next attempt, made nearer the middle of the valley, was successful, and we soon found ourselves on firm gravelly ground, and made haste to the huge ice wall, which seemed to recede as we advanced. The only difficulty we met was a network of icy streams, at the largest of which we halted, not willing to get wet in fording. The Indian attendant promptly carried us over on his back. When my turn came I told him I would ford, but he bowed his shoulders in so ludicrously persuasive a manner I thought I would try the queer mount, the only one of the kind I had enjoyed since boyhood days in playing leapfrog. Away staggered my perpendicular mule over the boulders into the brawling torrent, and in spite of top-heavy predictions to the contrary, crossed without a fall. After being ferried in this way over several more of these glacial streams, we at length reached the foot of the glacier wall. The doctor simply played tag on it, touched it gently as if it were a dangerous wild beast, and hurried back to the boat, taking the portage Indian with him for safety, little knowing what he was missing. Mr. Young and I traced the glorious crystal wall, admiring its wonderful architecture, the play of light in the rifts and caverns, and the structure of the ice as displayed in the less fractured sections, finding fresh beauty everywhere and facts for study. We then tried to climb it, and by dint of patient zigzagging and doubling among the crevasses, and cutting steps here and there, we made our way up over the brow and back a mile or two to a height of about seven hundred feet. The whole front of the glacier is gashed and sculptured into a maze of shallow caves and crevasses, and a bewildering variety of novel architectural forms, clusters of glittering lance-tipped spires, gables, and obelisks, bold outstanding bastions and plain mural cliffs, adorned along the top with fretted cornice and battlement, while every gorge and crevasse, groove and hollow, was filled with light, shimmering and throbbing in pale-blue tones of ineffable tenderness and beauty. The day was warm, and back on the broad melting bosom of the glacier beyond the crevassed front, many streams were rejoicing, gurgling, ringing, singing, in frictionless channels worn down through the white disintegrated ice of the surface into the quick and living blue, in which they flowed with a grace of motion and flashing of light to be found only on the crystal hillocks and ravines of a glacier.

Along the sides of the glacier we saw the mighty flood grinding against the granite walls with tremendous pressure, rounding outswelling bosses, and deepening the retreating hollows into the forms they are destined to have when, in the fullness of appointed time, the huge ice tool shall be withdrawn by the sun. Every feature glowed with intention, reflecting the plans of God. Back a few miles from the front, the glacier is now probably but little more than a thousand feet deep; but when we examine the records on the walls, the rounded, grooved, striated, and polished features so surely glacial, we learn that in the earlier days of the ice age they were all overswept, and that this glacier has flowed at a height of from three to four thousand feet above its present level, when it was at least a mile deep.

Standing here, with facts so fresh and telling and held up so vividly before us, every seeing observer, not to say geologist, must readily apprehend the earth-sculpturing, landscape-making action of flowing ice. And here, too, one learns that the world, though made, is yet being made; that this is still the morning of creation; that mountains long conceived are now being born, channels traced for coming rivers, basins hollowed for lakes; that moraine soil is being ground and outspread for coming plants—coarse boulders and gravel for forests, finer soil for grasses and flowers— while the finest part of the grist, seen hastening out to sea in the draining streams, is being stored away in darkness and builded particle on particle, cementing and crystallizing, to make the mountains and valleys and plains of other predestined landscapes, to be followed by still others in endless rhythm and beauty.

Gladly would we have camped out on this grand old landscape mill to study its ways and works; but we had no bread and the captain was keeping the Cassiar whistle screaming for our return. Therefore, in mean haste, we threaded our way back through the crevasses and down the blue cliffs, snatched a few flowers from a warm spot on the edge of the ice, plashed across the moraine streams, and were paddled aboard, rejoicing in the possession of so blessed a day, and feeling that in very foundational truth we had been in one of God's own temples and had seen Him and heard Him working and preaching like a man.

Steaming solemnly out of the fjord and down the coast, the islands and mountains were again passed in review; the clouds that so often hide the mountaintops even in good weather were now floating high above them, and the transparent shadows they cast were scarce perceptible on the white glacier fountains. So abundant and novel are the objects of interest in a pure wilderness that unless you are pursuing special studies it matters little where you go, or how often to the same place. Wherever you chance to be always seems at the moment of all places the best; and you feel that there can be no happiness in this world or in any other for those who may not be happy here. The bright hours were spent in making notes and sketches and getting more of the wonderful region into memory. In particular a second view of the mountains made me raise my first estimate of their height. Some of them must be seven or eight thousand feet at the least. Also the glaciers seemed larger and more numerous. I counted nearly a hundred, large and small, between a point ten or fifteen miles to the north of Cape Fanshawe and the mouth of the Stickeen River. We made no more landings, however, until we had passed through the Wrangell Narrows and dropped anchor for the night in a small sequestered bay. This was about sunset, and I eagerly seized the opportunity to go ashore in the canoe and see what I could learn. It is here only a step from the marine algae to terrestrial vegetation of almost tropical luxuriance. Parting the alders and huckleberry bushes and the crooked stems of the prickly panax, I made my way into the woods, and lingered in the twilight doing nothing in particular, only measuring a few of the trees, listening to learn what birds and animals might be about, and gazing along the dusky aisles.

In the meantime another excursion was being invented, one of small size and price. We might have reached Fort Wrangell this evening instead of anchoring here; but the owners of the Cassiar would then receive only ten dollars fare from each person, while they had incurred considerable expense in fitting up the boat for this special trip, and had treated us well. No, under the circumstances, it would never do to return to Wrangell so meanly soon.

It was decided, therefore, that the Cassiar Company should have the benefit of another day's hire, in visiting the old deserted Stickeen village fourteen miles to the south of Wrangell.

"We shall have a good time," one of the most influential of the party said to me in a semi-apologetic tone, as if dimly recognizing my disappointment in not going on to Chilcat. "We shall probably find stone axes and other curiosities. Chief Kadachan is going to guide us, and the other Indians aboard will dig for us, and there are interesting old buildings and totem poles to be seen."

It seemed strange, however, that so important a mission to the most influential of the Alaskan tribes should end in a deserted village. But divinity abounded nevertheless; the day was divine and there was plenty of natural religion in the newborn landscapes that were being baptized in sunshine, and sermons in the glacial boulders on the beach where we landed.

The site of the old village is on an outswelling strip of ground about two hundred yards long and fifty wide, sloping gently to the water with a strip of gravel and tall grass in front, dark woods back of it, and charming views over the water among the islands—a delightful place. The tide was low when we arrived, and I noticed that the exposed boulders on the beach—granite erratics that had been dropped by the melting ice toward the close of the glacial period—were piled in parallel rows at right angles to the shoreline, out of the way of the canoes that had belonged to the village.

Most of the party sauntered along the shore; for the ruins were overgrown with tall nettles, elder bushes, and prickly rubus vines through which it was difficult to force a way. In company with the most eager of the relic-seekers and two Indians, I pushed back among the dilapidated dwellings. They were deserted some sixty or seventy years before, and some of them were at least a hundred years old. So said our guide, Kadachan, and his word was corroborated by the venerable aspect of the ruins. Though the damp climate is destructive, many of the house timbers were still in a good state of preservation, particularly those hewn from the yellow cypress, or cedar as it is called here.

The magnitude of the ruins and the excellence of the workmanship manifest in them was astonishing as belonging to Indians. For example, the first dwelling we visited was about forty feet square, with walls built of planks two feet wide and six inches thick. The ridgepole of yellow cypress was two feet in diameter, forty feet long, and as round and true as if it had been turned in a lathe; and, though lying in the damp weeds, it was still perfectly sound. The nibble marks of the stone adze were still visible, though crusted over with scale lichens in most places. The pillars that had supported the ridgepole were still standing in some of the ruins. They were all, as far as I observed, carved into life-size figures of men, women, and children, fishes, birds, and various other animals, such as the beaver, wolf, or bear. Each of the wall planks had evidently been hewn out of a whole log, and must have required sturdy deliberation as well as skill. Their geometrical truthfulness was admirable. With the same tools not one in a thousand of our skilled mechanics could do as good work. Compared with it the bravest work of civilized backwoodsmen is feeble and bungling. The completeness of form, finish, and proportion of these timbers suggested skill of a wild and positive kind, like that which guides the woodpecker in drilling round holes, and the bee in making its cells.

The carved totem-pole monuments are the most striking of the objects displayed here. The simplest of them consisted of a smooth, round post fifteen or twenty feet high and about eighteen inches in diameter, with the figure of some animal on top—a bear, porpoise, eagle, or raven, about life-size or larger. These were the totems of the families that occupied the houses in front of which they stood. Others supported the figure of a man or woman, life-size or larger, usually in a sitting posture, said to resemble the dead whose ashes were contained in a closed cavity in the pole. The largest were thirty or forty feet high, carved from top to bottom into human and animal totem figures, one above another, with their limbs grotesquely doubled and folded. Some of the most imposing were said to commemorate some event of an historical character. But a telling display of family pride seemed to have been the prevailing motive. All the figures were more or less rude, and some were broadly grotesque, but there was never any feebleness or obscurity in the expression. On the contrary, every feature showed grave force and decision; while the childish audacity displayed in the designs, combined with manly strength in their execution, was truly wonderful.

The colored lichens and mosses gave them a venerable air, while the larger vegetation often found on such as were most decayed produced a picturesque effect. Here, for example, is a bear five or six feet long, reposing on top of his lichen-clad pillar, with paws comfortably folded, a tuft of grass growing in each ear and rubus bushes along his back. And yonder is an old chief poised on a taller pillar, apparently gazing out over the landscape in contemplative mood, a tuft of bushes leaning back with a jaunty air from the top of his weather-beaten hat, and downy mosses about his massive lips. But no rudeness or grotesqueness that may appear, however combined with the decorations that nature has added, may possibly provoke mirth. The whole work is serious in aspect and brave and true in execution.

Similar monuments are made by other Thlinkit tribes. The erection of a totem pole is made a grand affair, and is often talked of for a year or two beforehand. A feast, to which many are invited, is held, and the joyous occasion is spent in eating, dancing, and the distribution of gifts. Some of the larger specimens cost a thousand dollars or more. From one to two hundred blankets, worth three dollars apiece, are paid to the genius who carves them, while the presents and feast usually cost twice as much, so that only the wealthy families can afford them. I talked with an old Indian who pointed out one of the carvings he had made in the Wrangell village, for which he told me he had received forty blankets, a gun, a canoe, and other articles, all together worth about $170. Mr. Swan, who has contributed much information concerning the British Columbian and Alaskan tribes, describes a totem pole that cost $2,500. They are always planted firmly in the ground and stand fast, showing the sturdy erectness of their builders.

While I was busy with my pencil, I heard chopping going on at the north end of the village, followed by a heavy thud, as if a tree had fallen. It appeared that after digging about the old hearth in the first dwelling visited without finding anything of consequence, the archaeological doctor called the steamer deckhands to one of the most interesting of the totems and directed them to cut it down, saw off the principal figure—a woman measuring three feet three inches across the shoulders—and convey it aboard the steamer, with a view to taking it on East to enrich some museum or other. This sacrilege came near causing trouble and would have cost us dear had the totem not chanced to belong to the Kadachan family, the representative of which is a member of the newly organized Wrangell Presbyterian Church. Kadachan looked very seriously into the face of the reverend doctor and pushed home the pertinent question: "How would you like to have an Indian go to a graveyard and break down and carry away a monument belonging to your family?"

However, the religious relations of the parties and a few trifling presents embedded in apologies served to hush and mend the matter.

Some time in the afternoon the steam whistle called us together to finish our memorable trip. There was no trace of decay in the sky; a glorious sunset gilded the water and cleared away the shadows of our meditations among the ruins. We landed at the Wrangell wharf at dusk, pushed our way through a group of inquisitive Indians, across the two crooked streets, and up to our homes in the fort. We had been away only three days, but they were so full of novel scenes and impressions the time seemed indefinitely long, and our broken Chilcat excursion, far from being a failure as it seemed to some, was one of the most memorable of my life.

6

THE CASSIAR TRAIL

I made a second trip up the Stickeen in August and from the head of navigation pushed inland for general views over dry grassy hills and plains on the Cassiar trail.

Soon after leaving Telegraph Creek I met a merry trader who encouragingly assured me that I was going into the most wonderful region in the world, that "the scenery up the river was full of the very wildest freaks of nature, surpassing all other sceneries either natural or artificial, on paper or in nature. And give yourself no bothering care about provisions, for wild food grows in prodigious abundance everywhere. A man was lost four days up there, but he feasted on vegetables and berries and got back to camp in good condition. A mess of wild parsnips and pepper, for example, will actually do you good. And here's my advice—go slow and take the pleasures and sceneries as you go."

At the confluence of the first North Fork of the Stickeen I found a band of Toltan or Stick Indians catching their winter supply of salmon in willow traps, set where the fish are struggling in swift rapids on their way to the spawning grounds. A large supply had already been secured, and of course the Indians were well fed and merry. They were camping in large booths made of poles set on end in the ground, with many binding cross-pieces on which tons of salmon were being dried. The heads were strung on separate poles and the roes packed in willow baskets, all being well smoked from fires in the middle of the floor. The largest of the booths near the bank of the river was about forty feet square. Beds made of spruce and pine boughs were spread all around the walls, on which some of the Indians lay asleep; some were braiding ropes, others sitting and lounging, gossiping and courting, while a little baby was swinging in a hammock. All seemed to be lighthearted and jolly, with work enough and wit enough to maintain health and comfort. In the winter they are said to dwell in substantial huts in the woods, where game, especially caribou, is abundant. They are pale copper-colored, have small feet and hands, are not at all negroish in lips or cheeks like some of the coast tribes, nor so thickset, short-necked, or heavy-featured in general.

One of the most striking of the geological features of this region are immense gravel deposits displayed in sections on the walls of the river gorges. About two miles above the North Fork confluence there is a bluff of basalt three hundred and fifty feet high, and above this a bed of gravel four hundred feet thick, while beneath the basalt there is another bed at least fifty feet thick.

From "Ward's," seventeen miles beyond Telegraph, and about fourteen hundred feet above sea level, the trail ascends a gravel ridge to a pine and fir–covered plateau twenty-one hundred feet above the sea. Thence for three miles the trail leads through a forest of short, closely planted trees to the second North Fork

of the Stickeen, where a still greater deposit of stratified gravel is displayed, a section at least six hundred
feet thick resting on a red jaspery formation.

Nine hundred feet above the river there is a
slightly dimpled plateau diversified with aspen and
willow groves and mossy meadows. At "Wilson's," one
and a half miles from the river, the ground is carpeted
with dwarf manzanita and the blessed *Linnaea borealis*, and forested with small pines, spruces, and aspens,
the tallest fifty to sixty feet high.

From Wilson's to "Caribou," fourteen miles, no
water was visible, though the nearly level, mossy
ground is swampy-looking. At "Caribou Camp," two
miles from the river, I saw two fine dogs, a Newfoundland and a spaniel. Their owner told me that he paid
only twenty dollars for the team and was offered one
hundred dollars for one of them a short time afterwards. The Newfoundland, he said, caught salmon on
the ripples, and could be sent back for miles to fetch
horses. The fine jet-black curly spaniel helped to carry
the dishes from the table to the kitchen, went for
water when ordered, took the pail and set it down at
the stream-side, but could not be taught to dip it full.
But their principal work was hauling camp supplies
on sleds up the river in winter. These two were said to
be able to haul a load of a thousand pounds when the
ice was in fairly good condition. They were fed on dried
fish and oatmeal boiled together.

The timber hereabouts is mostly willow or poplar
on the low ground, with here and there pine, birch, and
spruce about fifty feet high. None seen much exceeded
a foot in diameter. Thousand-acre patches have been
destroyed by fire. Some of the green trees had been
burned off at the root, the raised roots, packed in dry

moss, being readily attacked from beneath. A range of mountains about five thousand to six thousand feet high trending nearly north and south for sixty miles is forested to the summit. Only a few cliff faces and one of the highest points patched with snow are treeless. No part of this range as far as I could see is deeply sculptured, though the general denudation of the country must have been enormous as the gravel beds show.

At the top of a smooth, flowery pass about four thousand feet above the sea, beautiful Dease Lake comes suddenly in sight, shining like a broad tranquil river between densely forested hills and mountains. It is about twenty-seven miles long, one to two miles wide, and its waters, tributary to the Mackenzie, flow into the Arctic Ocean by a very long, roundabout, romantic way, the exploration of which in 1789 from Great Slave Lake to the Arctic Ocean must have been a glorious task for the heroic Scotchman, Alexander Mackenzie, whose name it bears.

Dease Creek, a fine rushing stream about forty miles long and forty or fifty feet wide, enters the lake from the west, drawing its sources from grassy mountain ridges. Thibert Creek, about the same size, and McDames and Defot Creeks, with their many branches, head together in the same general range of mountains or on moor-like tablelands on the divide between the Mackenzie and Yukon and Stickeen. All these Mackenzie streams had proved rich in gold. The wing-dams, flumes, and sluice boxes on the lower five or ten miles of their courses showed wonderful industry, and the quantity of glacial and perhaps pre-glacial gravel displayed was enormous. Some of the beds were not unlike those of the so-called Dead Rivers of California. Several ancient drift-filled channels on Thibert

Creek, blue at bedrock, were exposed and had been worked. A considerable portion of the gold, though mostly coarse, had no doubt come from considerable distances, as boulders included in some of the deposits show. The deepest beds, though known to be rich, had not yet been worked to any great depth on account of expense. Diggings that yield less than five dollars a day to the man were considered worthless. Only three of the claims on Defot Creek, eighteen miles from the mouth of Thibert Creek, were then said to pay. One of the nuggets from this creek weighed forty pounds.

While wandering about the banks of these gold-besprinkled streams, looking at the plants and mines and miners, I was so fortunate as to meet an interesting French Canadian, an old *coureur de bois*, who after a few minutes' conversation invited me to accompany him to his gold mine on the head of Defot Creek, near the summit of a smooth, grassy mountain ridge which he assured me commanded extensive views of the region at the heads of Stickeen, Taku, Yukon, and Mackenzie tributaries. Though heavy-laden with flour and bacon, he strode lightly along the rough trails as if his load was only a natural balanced part of his body. Our way at first lay along Thibert Creek, now on gravel benches, now on bedrock, now close down on the bouldery edge of the stream. Above the mines the stream is clear and flows with a rapid current. Its banks are embossed with moss and grass and sedge well mixed with flowers—daisies, larkspurs, solidagos, parnassia, potentilla, strawberry, etc. Small strips of meadow occur here and there, and belts of slender arrowy fir and spruce with moss-clad roots grow close to the water's edge. The creek is about forty-five miles long, and the richest of its gold-bearing beds so far discovered were on the lower four miles of the creek; the higher four-or-five-dollars-a-day diggings were considered very poor on account of the high price of provisions and shortness of the season. After crossing many smaller streams with their strips of trees and meadows, bogs and bright wild gardens, we arrived at the Le Claire cabin about the middle of the afternoon. Before entering it he threw down his burden and made haste to show me his favorite flower, a blue forget-me-not, a specimen of which he found within a few rods of the cabin, and proudly handed it to me with the finest respect, and telling its many charms and lifelong associations, showed in every endearing look and touch and gesture that the tender little plant of the mountain wilderness was truly his best-loved darling.

After luncheon we set out for the highest point on the dividing ridge about a mile above the cabin, and sauntered and gazed until sundown, admiring the vast expanse of open rolling prairie-like highlands dotted with groves and lakes, the fountainheads of countless cool, glad streams.

Le Claire's simple, childlike love of nature, preserved undimmed through a hard wilderness life, was delightful to see. The grand landscapes with their lakes and streams, plants and animals, all were dear to him. In particular he was fond of the birds that nested near his cabin, watched the young, and in stormy weather helped their parents to feed and shelter them. Some species were so confiding they learned to perch on his shoulders and take crumbs from his hand.

A little before sunset snow began to fly, driven by a cold wind, and by the time we reached the cabin, though we had not far to go, everything looked wintry. At half past nine we ate supper, while a good fire crackled cheerily in the ingle and a wintry wind blew hard. The little log cabin was only ten feet long, eight wide, and just high enough under the roof peak to allow one to stand upright. The bedstead was not wide enough for two, so Le Claire spread the blankets on the floor, and we gladly lay down after our long, happy walk, our heads under the bedstead, our feet against the opposite wall, and though comfortably tired, it was long ere we fell asleep, for Le Claire, finding me a good listener, told many stories of his adventurous life with Indians, bears and wolves, snow and hunger, and of his many camps in the Canadian woods, hidden like the nests and dens of wild animals; stories that have a singular interest to everybody, for they awaken inherited memories of the lang, lang syne when we were all wild. He had nine children, he told me, the youngest eight years of age, and several of his daughters were married. His home was in Victoria.

Next morning was cloudy and windy, snowy and cold, dreary December weather in August, and I gladly ran out to see what I might learn. A gray ragged-edged cloud capped the top of the divide, its snowy fringes drawn out by the wind. The flowers, though most of them were buried or partly so, were to some extent recognizable, the bluebells bent over, shining like eyes through the snow, and the gentians, too, with their corollas twisted shut; cassiope I could recognize under any disguise; and two species of dwarf willow with their seeds already ripe, one with comparatively small leaves, were growing in mere cracks and crevices of rock ledges where the dry snow could not lie. Snowbirds and ptarmigan were flying briskly in the cold wind, and on the edge of a grove I saw a spruce from which a bear had stripped large sections of bark for food.

About nine o'clock the clouds lifted and I enjoyed another wide view from the summit of the ridge of the vast grassy fountain region with smooth rolling features. A few patches of forest broke the monotony of color, and the many lakes, one of them about five miles long, were glowing like windows. Only the highest ridges were whitened with snow, while rifts in the clouds showed beautiful bits of yellow-green sky. The limit of tree growth is about five thousand feet.

Throughout all this region from Glenora to Cassiar the grasses grow luxuriantly in openings in the woods and on dry hillsides where the trees seem to have been destroyed by fire, and over all the broad prairies above the timberline. A kind of bunchgrass in particular is often four or five feet high, and close enough to be mowed for hay. I never anywhere saw finer or more bountiful wild pasture. Here the caribou feed and grow fat, braving the intense winter cold, often forty to sixty degrees below zero. Winter and summer seem to be the only seasons here. What may fairly be called summer lasts only two or three months, winter nine or ten, for of pure well-defined spring or autumn there is scarcely a trace. Were it not for the long severe winters, this would be a capital stock country, equaling Texas and the prairies of the old West. From my outlook on the Defot ridge I saw thousands of square miles of this prairie-like region drained by tributaries of the Stickeen, Taku, Yukon, and Mackenzie Rivers.

Le Claire told me that the caribou, or reindeer, were very abundant on this high ground. A flock of fifty or more was seen a short time before at the head of Defot Creek—fine, hardy, able animals like their near relatives the reindeer of the Arctic tundras. The Indians hereabouts, he said, hunted them with dogs, mostly in the fall and winter. On my return trip I met several bands of these Indians on the march, going north to hunt. Some of the men and women were carrying puppies on top of their heavy loads of dried salmon, while the grown dogs had saddlebags filled with odds and ends strapped on their backs. Small puppies, unable to carry more than five or six pounds, were thus made useful. I overtook another band going south, heavy-laden with furs and skins to trade. An old woman, with short dress and leggings, was carrying a big load of furs and skins, on top of which was perched a little girl about three years old.

A brown, speckled marmot, one of Le Claire's friends, was getting ready for winter. The entrance to his burrow was a little to one side of the cabin door. A well-worn trail led to it through the grass and another to that of his companion, fifty feet away. He was a most amusing pet, always on hand at meal times for breadcrumbs and bits of bacon rind, came when called, answering in a shrill whistle, moving like a squirrel with quick, nervous impulses, jerking his short flat tail. His fur clothing was neat and clean, fairly shining in the wintry light. The snowy weather that morning must have called winter to mind; for as soon as he got his breakfast, he ran to a tuft of dry grass, chewed it into fuzzy mouthfuls, and carried it to his nest, coming and going with admirable industry, forecast, and confidence. None watching him as we did could fail to sympathize with him; and I fancy that in practical weather wisdom no government forecaster with all his advantages surpasses this little Alaska rodent, every hair and nerve a weather instrument.

I greatly enjoyed this little inland side trip—the wide views; the miners along the branches of the great river, busy as moles and beavers; young men dreaming and hoping to strike it rich and rush home to marry their girls faithfully waiting; others hoping to clear off weary farm mortgages, and brighten the lives of the anxious home folk; but most, I suppose, just struggling blindly for gold enough to make them indefinitely rich to spend their lives in aimless affluence, honor, and ease. I enjoyed getting acquainted with the trees, especially the beautiful spruce and silver fir; the flower gardens and great grassy caribou pastures; the cheery, able marmot mountaineer; and above all the friendship and kindness of Mr. Le Claire, whom I shall never forget. Bidding goodbye, I sauntered back to the head of navigation on the Stickeen, happy and rich without a particle of obscuring gold dust care.

7

GLENORA PEAK

On the trail to the steamboat landing at the foot of Dease Lake, I met a Douglas squirrel, nearly as red and rusty in color as his Eastern relative the chickaree. Except in color, he differs but little from the California Douglas squirrel. In voice, language, gestures, temperament, he is the same fiery, indomitable little king of the woods. Another darker and probably younger specimen met near the Caribou House, barked, chirruped, and showed off in fine style on a tree within a few feet of us.

"What does the little rascal mean?" said my companion, a man I had fallen in with on the trail. "What is he making such a fuss about? I cannot frighten him."

"Never mind," I replied; "just wait until I whistle 'Old Hundred' and you will see him fly in disgust." And so he did, just as his California brethren do. Strange that no squirrel or spermophile I yet have found ever seemed to have anything like enough of Scotch religion to enjoy this grand old tune.

The taverns along the Cassiar gold trail were the worst I had ever seen, rough shacks with dirt floors, dirt roofs, and rough meals. The meals are all alike—a potato, a slice of something like bacon, some gray stuff called bread, and a cup of muddy, semi-liquid coffee like that which the California miners call "slickers" or "slumgullion." The bread was terrible and sinful. How the Lord's good wheat could be made into stuff so mysteriously bad is past finding out. The very de'il, it would seem, in wicked anger and ingenuity, had been the baker.

On our walk from Dease Lake to Telegraph Creek we had one of these rough luncheons at three o'clock in the afternoon of the first day, then walked on five miles to Ward's, where we were solemnly assured that we could not have a single bite of either supper or breakfast, but as a great favor we might sleep on his best gray bunk. We replied that, as we had lunched at the lake, supper would not be greatly missed, and as for breakfast we would start early and walk eight miles to the next roadhouse. We set out at half past four, glad to escape into the fresh air, and reached the breakfast place at eight o'clock. The landlord was still abed, and when at length he came to the door, he scowled savagely at us as if our request for breakfast was preposterous and criminal beyond anything ever heard of in all goldful Alaska. A good many in those days were returning from the mines dead broke, and he probably regarded us as belonging to that disreputable class. Anyhow, we got nothing and had to tramp on.

As we approached the next house, three miles ahead, we saw the tavern keeper keenly surveying us, and, as we afterwards learned, taking me for a certain judge whom for some cause he wished to avoid, he hurriedly locked his door and fled. Half a mile farther on we discovered him in a thicket a little way off the trail, explained our wants, marched him back to his house, and at length obtained a little sour bread, sour milk, and old salmon, our only lonely meal between the Lake and Telegraph Creek.

We arrived at Telegraph Creek, the end of my two-hundred-mile walk, about noon. After luncheon I went on down the river to Glenora in a fine canoe owned and manned by Kitty, a stout, intelligent-looking Indian woman, who charged her passengers a dollar for the fifteen-mile trip. Her crew was four Indian paddlers. In the rapids she also plied the paddle, with stout, telling strokes, and a keen-eyed old man, probably her husband, sat high in the stern and steered. All seemed exhilarated as we shot down through the narrow gorge on the rushing, roaring, throttled river, paddling all the more vigorously the faster the speed of the stream, to hold good steering way. The canoe danced lightly amid gray surges and spray as if alive and enthusiastically enjoying the adventure. Some of the passengers were pretty thoroughly drenched. In unskillful hands the frail dugout would surely have been wrecked or upset. Most of the season goods for the Cassiar gold camps were carried from Glenora to Telegraph Creek in canoes, the steamers not being able to overcome the rapids except during high water. Even then they had usually to line two of the rapids—that is, take a line ashore, make it fast to a tree on the bank, and pull up on the capstan. The freight canoes carried about three or four tons, for which fifteen dollars per ton was charged. Slow progress was made by poling along the bank out of the swiftest part of the current. In the rapids a tow line was taken ashore, only one of the crew remaining aboard to steer. The trip took a day unless a favoring wind was blowing, which often happened.

Next morning I set out from Glenora to climb Glenora Peak for the general view of the great Coast

Range that I failed to obtain on my first ascent on account of the accident that befell Mr. Young when we were within a minute or two of the top. It is hard to fail in reaching a mountaintop that one starts for, let the cause be what it may. This time I had no companion to care for, but the sky was threatening. I was assured by the local weather-prophets that the day would be rainy or snowy because the peaks in sight were muffled in clouds that seemed to be getting ready for work. I determined to go ahead, however, for storms of any kind are well worthwhile, and if driven back I could wait and try again.

With crackers in my pocket and a light rubber coat that a kind Hebrew passenger on the steamer Gertrude loaned me, I was ready for anything that might offer, my hopes for the grand view rising and falling as the clouds rose and fell. Anxiously I watched them as they trailed their draggled skirts across the glaciers and fountain peaks as if thoughtfully looking for the places where they could do the most good. From Glenora there is first a terrace two hundred feet above the river covered mostly with bushes, yellow apocynum on the open spaces, together with carpets of dwarf manzanita, bunch-grass, and a few of the compositae, galiums, etc. Then comes a flat stretch a mile wide, extending to the foothills, covered with birch, spruce, fir, and poplar, now mostly killed by fire and the ground strewn with charred trunks. From this black forest the mountain rises in rather steep slopes covered with a luxuriant growth of bushes, grass, flowers, and a few trees, chiefly spruce and fir, the firs gradually dwarfing into a beautiful chaparral, the most beautiful, I think, I have ever seen, the flat fan-shaped plumes thickly foliaged and imbricated by snow pressure, forming a smooth, handsome thatch which bears cones and thrives as if this repressed condition were its very best. It extends up to an elevation of about fifty-five hundred feet. Only a few trees more than a foot in diameter and more than fifty feet high are found higher than four thousand feet above the sea. A few poplars and willows occur on moist places, gradually dwarfing like the conifers. Alder is the most generally distributed of the chaparral bushes, growing nearly everywhere; its crinkled stems an inch or two thick form a troublesome tangle to the mountaineer. The blue geranium, with leaves red and showy at this time of the year, is perhaps the most telling of the flowering plants. It grows up to five thousand feet or more. Larkspurs are common, with epilobium, senecio, erigeron, and a few solidagos. The harebell appears at about four thousand feet and extends to the summit, dwarfing in stature but maintaining the size of its handsome bells until they seem to be lying loose and detached on the ground as if like snow flowers they had fallen from the sky; and, though frail and delicate-looking, none of its companions is more enduring or rings out the praises of beauty-loving Nature in tones more appreciable to mortals, not forgetting even Cassiope, who also is here, and her companion, Bryanthus, the loveliest and most widely distributed of the alpine shrubs. Then come crowberry, and two species of huckleberry, one of them from about six inches to a foot high with delicious berries, the other a most lavishly prolific and contented-looking dwarf, few of the bushes being more than two inches high, counting to the topmost leaf, yet each bearing from ten to twenty or more large berries. Perhaps more than half the bulk of the whole plant is fruit, the largest and finest-flavored of all the huckleberries or blueberries I ever tasted, spreading fine feasts for the grouse and ptarmigan and many others of Nature's mountain people. I noticed three species of dwarf willows, one with narrow leaves, growing at the very summit of the mountain in cracks of the rocks, as well as on patches of soil, another with large, smooth leaves now turning yellow. The third species grows between the others as to elevation; its leaves, then orange-colored, are strikingly pitted and reticulated. Another alpine shrub, a species of sericocarpus, covered with handsome heads of feathery achenia, beautiful dwarf echeverias with flocks of purple flowers pricked into their bright grass-green, cushion-like bosses of mosslike foliage, and a fine forget-me-not reach to the summit. I may also mention a large mertensia, a fine anemone, a veratrum, six feet high, a large blue daisy, growing up to three to four thousand feet, and at the summit a dwarf species, with dusky, hairy involucres, and a few ferns, aspidium, gymnogramma, and small rock cheilanthes, leaving scarce a foot of ground bare, though the mountain looks bald and brown in the distance like those of the desert ranges of the Great Basin in Utah and Nevada.

Charmed with these plant people, I had almost forgotten to watch the sky until I reached the top of the highest peak, when one of the greatest and most impressively sublime of all the mountain views I have ever enjoyed came full in sight—more than three hundred miles of closely packed peaks of the great Coast Range, sculptured in the boldest manner imaginable, their naked tops and dividing ridges dark in color, their sides and the canyons, gorges, and valleys between them loaded with glaciers and snow. From this standpoint I counted upwards of two hundred glaciers, while dark-centered luminous clouds with fringed edges hovered and crawled over them, now slowly descending, casting transparent shadows on the ice and snow, now rising high above them, lingering like loving angels guarding the crystal gifts they had bestowed. Although the range as seen from this Glenora mountaintop seems regular in its trend, as if the main axis were simple and continuous, it is, on the contrary, far from simple. In front of the highest ranks of peaks are others of the same form with their own glaciers, and lower peaks before these, and yet lower ones with their ridges and canyons, valleys and foothills. Alps rise beyond alps as far as the eye can reach, and clusters of higher peaks here and there closely crowded together; clusters, too, of needles and pinnacles innumerable like trees in groves. Everywhere the peaks seem comparatively slender and closely packed, as if Nature had here been trying to see how many noble well-dressed mountains could be crowded into one grand range.

The black rocks, too steep for snow to lie upon, were brought into sharp relief by white clouds and snow and glaciers, and these again were outlined and made tellingly plain by the rocks. The glaciers so grandly displayed are of every form, some crawling through gorge and valley like monster glittering serpents; others like broad cataracts pouring over cliffs into shadowy gulfs; others, with their main trunks winding through narrow canyons, display long, white fingerlike tributaries descending from the summits of pinnacled ridges. Others lie back in fountain cirques walled in all around save at the lower edge over which they pour in blue cascades. Snow, too, lay in folds and patches of every form on blunt, rounded ridges in curves, arrowy lines, dashes, and narrow ornamental flutings among the summit peaks and in broad radiating wings on smooth slopes. And on many a bulging headland and lower ridge there lay heavy, over-curling copings and smooth, white domes where wind-driven snow was pressed and wreathed and packed into every form and in every possible place and condition. I never before had seen so richly sculptured a range or so many awe-inspiring inaccessible mountains crowded together. If a line were drawn east and west from the peak on which I stood, and extended both ways to the horizon, cutting the whole round landscape in two equal parts, then all of the south half would be bounded by these icy peaks, which would seem to curve around half the horizon and about twenty degrees more, though extending in a general straight, or but moderately curved, line. The deepest and thickest and highest of all this wilderness of peaks lie to the southwest. They are probably from about nine to twelve thousand feet high, springing to this elevation from near the sea level. The peak on which these observations were made is somewhere about seven thousand feet high, and from here I estimated the height of the range. The highest peak of all, or that seemed so to me, lies to the westward at an estimated distance of about one hundred and fifty or two hundred miles. Only its solid white summit was visible. Possibly it may be the topmost peak of St. Elias. Now look northward around the other half of the horizon, and instead of countless peaks crowding into the sky, you see a low brown region, heaving and swelling in gentle curves, apparently scarcely more waved than a rolling prairie. The so-called canyons of several forks of the upper Stick-een are visible, but even where best seen in the fore-ground and middle ground of the picture, they are like mere sunken gorges, making scarce perceptible marks on the landscape, while the tops of the high-est mountain-swells show only small patches of snow and no glaciers.

Glenora Peak, on which I stood, is the highest point of a spur that puts out from the main range in a northerly direction. It seems to have been a rounded, broad-backed ridge which has been sculptured into its present irregular form by short residual glaciers, some of which, a mile or two long, are still at work.

As I lingered, gazing on the vast show, luminous shadowy clouds seemed to increase in glory of color and motion, now fondling the highest peaks with infinite tenderness of touch, now hovering above them like eagles over their nests.

When night was drawing near, I ran down the flowery slopes exhilarated, thanking God for the gift of this great day. The setting sun fired the clouds. All the world seemed newborn. Every thing, even the commonest, was seen in new light and was looked at with new interest as if never seen before. The plant people seemed glad, as if rejoicing with me, the little ones as well as the trees, while every feature of the peak and its traveled boulders seemed to know what I had been about and the depth of my joy, as if they could read faces.

8

EXPLORATION OF THE STICKEEN GLACIERS

Next day I planned an excursion to the so-called Dirt Glacier, the most interesting to Indians and steamer men of all the Stickeen glaciers from its mysterious floods. I left the steamer Gertrude for the glacier delta an hour or two before sunset. The captain kindly loaned me his canoe and two of his Indian deckhands, who seemed much puzzled to know what the rare service required of them might mean, and on leaving bade a merry adieu to their companions. We camped on the west side of the river opposite the front of the glacier, in a spacious valley surrounded by snowy mountains. Thirteen small glaciers were in sight and four waterfalls. It was a fine, serene evening, and the highest peaks were wearing turbans of flossy, gossamer cloudstuff. I had my supper before leaving the steamer, so I had only to make a campfire, spread my blanket, and lie down. The Indians had their own bedding and lay beside their own fire.

The Dirt Glacier is noted among the river men as being subject to violent flood outbursts once or twice a year, usually in the late summer. The delta of this glacier stream is three or four miles wide where it fronts the river, and the many rough channels with which it is guttered and the uprooted trees and huge boulders that roughen its surface manifest the power of the floods that swept them to their places; but under ordinary conditions the glacier discharges its drainage water into the river through only four or five of the delta channels.

Our camp was made on the south or lower side of the delta, below all the draining streams, so that I would not have to ford any of them on my way to the glacier. The Indians chose a sandpit to sleep in; I chose a level spot back of a drift log. I had but little to say to my companions as they could speak no English, nor I much Thlinkit or Chinook. In a few minutes after landing they retired to their pit and were soon asleep and asnore. I lingered by the fire until after ten o'clock, for the night sky was clear, and the great white mountains in the starlight seemed nearer than by day and to be looking down like guardians of the valley, while the waterfalls, and the torrents escaping from beneath the big glacier, roared in a broad, low monotone, sounding as if close at hand, though, as it proved next day, the nearest was three miles away. After wrapping myself in my blankets, I still gazed into the marvelous sky and made out to sleep only about two hours. Then, without waking the noisy sleepers, I arose, ate a piece of bread, and set out in my shirtsleeves, determined to make the most of the time at my disposal. The captain was to pick us up about noon at a woodpile about a mile from here; but if in the meantime the steamer should run aground and he should need his canoe, a three-whistle signal would be given.

Following a dry channel for about a mile, I came suddenly upon the main outlet of the glacier, which in the imperfect light seemed as large as the river, about one hundred and fifty feet wide, and perhaps three or four feet deep. A little farther up it was only about fifty feet wide and rushing on with impetuous roaring force in its rocky channel, sweeping forward sand, gravel, cobblestones, and boulders, the bump and rumble sounds of the largest of these rolling stones being readily heard in the midst of the roaring. It was too swift and rough to ford, and no bridge tree could be found, for the great floods had cleared everything out of their way. I was therefore compelled to keep on up the right bank, however difficult the way. Where a strip of bare boulders lined the margin, the walking was easy, but where the current swept close along the ragged edge of the forest, progress was difficult and slow on account of snow-crinkled and interlaced thickets of alder and willow, reinforced with fallen trees and thorny devil's-club (*Echinopanax horridum*), making a jungle all but impenetrable. The mile of this extravagantly difficult growth through which I struggled, inch by inch, will not soon be forgotten. At length arriving within a few hundred yards of the glacier, full of panax barbs, I found that both the glacier and its unfordable stream were pressing hard against a shelving cliff, dangerously steep, leaving no margin, and compelling me to scramble along its face before I could get on to the glacier. But by sunrise all these cliff, jungle, and torrent troubles were overcome and I gladly found myself free on the magnificent ice river.

The curving, out-bulging front of the glacier is about two miles wide, two hundred feet high, and its surface for a mile or so above the front is strewn with moraine detritus, giving it a strangely dirty, dusky look, hence its name, the "Dirt Glacier," this detritus-laden portion being all that is seen in passing up the river. A mile or two beyond the moraine-covered part I was surprised to find alpine plants growing on the ice, fresh and green, some of them in full flower. These curious glacier gardens, the first I had seen, were evidently planted by snow avalanches from the high walls. They were well watered, of course, by the melting surface of the ice and fairly well nourished by humus still attached to the roots, and in some places formed beds of considerable thickness. Seedling trees and bushes also were growing among the flowers. Admiring these novel floating gardens, I struck out for the middle of the pure white glacier, where the ice seemed smoother, and then held straight on for about eight miles, where I reluctantly turned back to meet the steamer, greatly regretting that I had not brought a week's supply of hardtack to allow me to explore the glacier to its head, and then trust to some passing canoe to take me down to Buck Station, from which I could explore the Big Stickeen Glacier.

Altogether, I saw about fifteen or sixteen miles of the main trunk. The grade is almost regular, and the walls on either hand are about from two to three thousand feet high, sculptured like those of Yosemite Valley. I found no difficulty of an extraordinary kind. Many a crevasse had to be crossed, but most of them were narrow and easily jumped, while the few wide ones that lay in my way were crossed on sliver bridges or avoided by passing around them. The structure of the glacier was strikingly revealed on its melting surface. It is made up of thin vertical or inclined sheets or slabs set on edge and welded together. They represent, I think, the successive snowfalls from heavy storms on the tributaries. One of the tributaries on the right side, about three miles above the front, has been entirely melted off from the trunk and has receded two or three miles, forming an independent glacier. Across the mouth of this abandoned part of its channel the main glacier flows, forming a dam which gives rise to a lake. On the head of the detached tributary there are some five or six small residual glaciers, the drainage of which, with that of the snowy mountain slopes above them, discharges into the lake, whose outlet is through a channel or channels beneath the damming glacier. Now these subchannels are occasionally blocked and the water rises until it flows alongside of the glacier, but as the dam is a moving one, a grand outburst is sometimes made, which, draining the large lake, produces a flood of amazing power, sweeping down immense quantities of moraine material and raising the river all the way down to its mouth, so that several trips may occasionally be made by the steamers after the season of low water has laid them up for the year. The occurrence of these floods are, of course, well known to the Indians and steamboat men, though they know nothing of their cause. They simply remark, "The Dirt Glacier has broken out again."

I greatly enjoyed my walk up this majestic ice river, charmed by the pale-blue, ineffably fine light in the crevasses, moulins, and wells, and the innumerable azure pools in basins of azure ice, and the network of surface streams, large and small, gliding, swirling with wonderful grace of motion in their frictionless channels, calling forth devout admiration at almost every step and filling the mind with a sense of Nature's endless beauty and power. Looking ahead from the middle of the glacier, you see the broad white flood, though apparently rigid as iron, sweeping in graceful curves between its high mountain-like walls, small glaciers hanging in the hollows on either side, and snow in every form above them, and the great down-plunging granite buttresses and headlands of the walls marvelous in bold massive sculpture; forests in side canyons to within fifty feet of the glacier; avalanche pathways overgrown with alder and willow; innumerable cascades keeping up a solemn harmony of water sounds blending with those of the glacier moulins and rills; and as far as the eye can reach, tributary glaciers at short intervals silently descending from their high, white fountains to swell the grand central ice river.

In the angle formed by the main glacier and the lake that gives rise to the river floods, there is a massive granite dome sparsely feathered with trees, and just beyond this yosemitic rock is a mountain, perhaps ten thousand feet high, laden with ice and snow which seemed pure pearly white in the morning light. Last evening as seen from camp it was adorned with a cloud streamer, and both the streamer and the peak were flushed in the alpenglow. A mile or two above this mountain, on the opposite side of the glacier, there is a rock like the Yosemite Sentinel; and in general all the wall rocks as far as I saw them are more or less yosemitic in form and color and streaked with cascades.

But wonderful as this noble ice river is in size and depth and in power displayed, far more wonderful was the vastly greater glacier three or four thousand feet, or perhaps a mile, in depth, whose size and general history is inscribed on the sides of the walls and over the tops of the rocks in characters which have not yet been greatly dimmed by the weather. Comparing its present size with that when it was in its prime, is like comparing a small rivulet to the same stream when it is a roaring torrent.

The return trip to the camp past the shelving cliff
and through the weary devil's-club jungle was made
in a few hours. The Indians had gone off picking berries, but were on the watch for me and hailed me as I
approached. The captain had called for me, and, after
waiting three hours, departed for Wrangell without
leaving any food, to make sure, I suppose, of a quick
return of his Indians and canoe. This was no serious
matter, however, for the swift current swept us down
to Buck Station, some thirty-five miles distant, by
eight o'clock. Here I remained to study the "Big Stickeen Glacier," but the Indians set out for Wrangell
soon after supper, though I invited them to stay till
morning.

The weather that morning, August 27, was dark
and rainy, and I tried to persuade myself that I ought
to rest a day before setting out on new ice work. But
just across the river the "Big Glacier" was staring me
in the face, pouring its majestic flood through a broad
mountain gateway and expanding in the spacious
river valley to a width of four or five miles, while dim
in the gray distance loomed its high mountain fountains. So grand an invitation displayed in characters
so telling was of course irresistible, and body-care and
weather-care vanished.

Mr. Choquette, the keeper of the station, ferried me
across the river, and I spent the day in getting general views and planning the work that had been long
in mind. I first traced the broad, complicated terminal
moraine to its southern extremity, climbed up the west
side along the lateral moraine three or four miles, making my way now on the glacier, now on the moraine-covered bank, and now compelled to climb up through the
timber and brush in order to pass some rocky headland,

until I reached a point commanding a good general view of the lower end of the glacier. Heavy, blotting rain then began to fall, and I retraced my steps, oftentimes stopping to admire the blue ice caves into which glad, rejoicing streams from the mountainside were hurrying as if going home, while the glacier seemed to open wide its crystal gateways to welcome them.

The following morning blotting rain was still falling, but time and work were too precious to mind it. Kind Mr. Choquette put me across the river in a canoe, with a lot of biscuits his Indian wife had baked for me and some dried salmon, a little sugar and tea, a blanket, and a piece of light sheeting for shelter from rain during the night, all rolled into one bundle.

"When shall I expect you back?" inquired Choquette, when I bade him good-bye.

"Oh, any time," I replied. "I shall see as much as possible of the glacier, and I know not how long it will hold me."

"Well, but when will I come to look for you, if anything happens? Where are you going to try to go? Years ago Russian officers from Sitka went up the glacier from here and none ever returned. It's a mighty dangerous glacier, all full of damn deep holes and cracks. You've no idea what ticklish deceiving traps are scattered over it."

"Yes, I have," I said. "I have seen glaciers before, though none so big as this one. Do not look for me until I make my appearance on the riverbank. Never mind me. I am used to caring for myself." And so, shouldering my bundle, I trudged off through the moraine boulders and thickets.

My general plan was to trace the terminal moraine to its extreme north end, pitch my little tent, leave the blanket and most of the hardtack, and from this main camp go and come as hunger required or allowed.

After examining a cross section of the broad moraine, roughened by concentric masses, marking interruptions in the recession of the glacier of perhaps several centuries, in which the successive moraines were formed and shoved together in closer or wider order, I traced the moraine to its northeastern extremity and ascended the glacier for several miles along the left margin, then crossed it at the grand cataract and down the right side to the river, and along the moraine to the point of beginning.

On the older portions of this moraine I discovered several kettles in process of formation and was pleased to find that they conformed in the most striking way with the theory I had already been led to make from observations on the old kettles which form so curious a feature of the drift covering Wisconsin and Minnesota and some of the larger moraines of the residual glaciers in the California Sierra. I found a pit eight or ten feet deep with raw shifting sides countersunk abruptly in the rough moraine material, and at the bottom, on sliding down by the aid of a lithe spruce tree that was being undermined, I discovered, after digging down a foot or two, that the bottom was resting on a block of solid blue ice which had been buried in the moraine perhaps a century or more, judging by the age of the tree that had grown above it. Probably more than another century will be required to complete the formation of this kettle by the slow melting of the buried ice-block. The moraine material of course was falling in as the ice melted, and the sides maintained an angle as steep as the material would lie. All sorts of theories have been advanced for the formation of these kettles, so abundant in the drift over a great part of the United States, and I was glad to be able to set the question at rest, at least as far as I was concerned.

The glacier and the mountains about it are on so grand a scale and so generally inaccessible in the ordinary sense, it seemed to matter but little what course I pursued. Everything was full of interest, even the weather, though about as unfavorable as possible for wide views, and scrambling through the moraine jungle brush kept one as wet as if all the way was beneath a cascade.

I pushed on, with many a rest and halt to admire the bold and marvelously sculptured ice front, looking all the grander and more striking in the gray mist with all the rest of the glacier shut out, until I came to a lake about two hundred yards wide and two miles long with scores of small bergs floating in it, some aground, close inshore against the moraine, the light playing on their angles and shimmering in their blue caves in ravishing tones. This proved to be the largest of the series of narrow lakelets that lie in shallow troughs between the moraine and the glacier, a miniature Arctic Ocean, its ice cliffs played upon by whispering, rippling waveless and its small berg floes drifting in its currents or with the wind, or stranded here and there along its rocky moraine shore.

Hundreds of small rills and good-sized streams were falling into the lake from the glacier, singing in low tones, some of them pouring in sheer falls over blue cliffs from narrow ice valleys, some spouting from pipelike channels in the solid front of the glacier, others gurgling out of arched openings at the base. All these water streams were riding on the parent ice stream, their voices joined in one grand anthem telling the wonders of their near and far-off fountains. The lake itself is resting in a basin of ice, and the forested moraine, though seemingly cut off from the glacier and probably more than a century old, is in great part resting on buried ice left behind as the glacier receded, and melting slowly on account of the protection afforded by the moraine detritus, which keeps shifting and falling on the inner face long after it is overgrown with lichens, mosses, grasses, bushes, and even good-sized trees; these changes going on with marvelous deliberation until in fullness of time the whole moraine settles down upon its bedrock foundation.

The outlet of the lake is a large stream, almost a river in size, one of the main draining streams of the glacier. I attempted to ford it where it begins to break in rapids in passing over the moraine, but found it too deep and rough on the bottom. I then tried to ford at its head, where it is wider and glides smoothly out of the lake, bracing myself against the current with a pole, but found it too deep, and when the icy water reached my shoulders I cautiously struggled back to the moraine. I next followed it down through the rocky jungle to a place where in breaking across the moraine dam it was only about thirty-five feet wide. Here I found a spruce tree which I felled for a bridge; it reached across, about ten feet of the top holding in the bank brush. But the force of the torrent, acting on the submerged branches and the slender end of the trunk, bent it like a bow and made it very unsteady, and after testing it by going out about a third of the way over, it seemed likely to be carried away when bent deeper into the current by my weight. Fortunately, I discovered another larger tree well situated a little farther down, which I felled, and though a few feet in the middle was submerged, it seemed perfectly safe.

As it was now getting late, I started back to the lakeside where I had left my bundle, and in trying to hold a direct course found the interlaced jungle still more difficult than it was along the bank of the torrent. For over an hour I had to creep and struggle close to the rocky ground like a fly in a spiderweb without being able to obtain a single glimpse of any guiding feature of the landscape. Finding a little willow taller than the surrounding alders, I climbed it, caught sight of the glacier front, took a compass bearing, and sunk again into the dripping, blinding maze of brush, and at length emerged on the lakeshore seven hours after leaving it, all this time as wet as though I had been swimming, thus completing a trying day's work. But everything was deliciously fresh, and I found new and old plant friends, and lessons on Nature's Alaska moraine landscape gardening that made everything bright and light.

It was now near dark, and I made haste to make up my flimsy little tent. The ground was desperately rocky. I made out, however, to level down a strip large enough to lie on, and by means of slim alder stems bent over it and tied together soon had a home. While thus busily engaged I was startled by a thundering roar across the lake. Running to the top of the moraine, I discovered that the tremendous noise was only the outcry of a newborn berg about fifty or sixty feet in diameter, rocking and wallowing in the waves it had raised as if enjoying its freedom after its long grinding work as part of the glacier. After this fine last lesson I managed to make a small fire out of wet twigs, got a cup of tea, stripped off my dripping clothing, wrapped myself in a blanket and lay brooding on the gains of the day and plans for the morrow, glad, rich, and almost comfortable.

It was raining hard when I awoke, but I made up my mind to disregard the weather, put on my dripping clothing, glad to know it was fresh and clean; ate biscuits and a piece of dried salmon without attempting to make a tea fire; filled a bag with hardtack, slung it over my shoulder, and with my indispensable ice axe plunged once more into the dripping jungle. I found my bridge holding bravely in place against the swollen torrent, crossed it and beat my way around pools and logs and through two hours of tangle back to the moraine on the north side of the outlet—a wet, weary battle but not without enjoyment. The smell of the washed ground and vegetation made every breath a pleasure, and I found *Calypso borealis*, the first I had seen on this side of the continent, one of my darlings, worth any amount of hardship; and I saw one of my Douglas squirrels on the margin of a grassy pool. The drip of the rain on the various leaves was pleasant to hear. More especially marked were the flat low-toned bumps and splashes of large drops from the trees on the broad horizontal leaves of *Echinopanax horridum*, like the drumming of thundershower drops on veratrum and palm leaves, while the mosses were indescribably beautiful, so fresh, so bright, so cheerily green, and all so low and calm and silent, however heavy and wild the wind and the rain blowing and pouring above them. Surely never a particle of dust has touched leaf or crown of all these blessed mosses; and how bright were the red rims of the cladonia cups beside them, and the fruit of the dwarf cornel! And the wet berries, Nature's precious jewelry, how beautiful they were!—huckleberries with pale bloom and a crystal drop on each; red and yellow salmonberries, with clusters of smaller drops; and the glittering, berrylike raindrops adorning the interlacing arches of bent grasses and sedges around the edges of the pools, every drop a mirror with all the landscape in it. A' that and a' that and twice as muckle's a' that in this glorious Alaska day, recalling, however different, George Herbert's "Sweet day, so cool, so calm, so bright."

In the gardens and forests of this wonderful moraine one might spend a whole joyful life.

When I at last reached the end of the great moraine and the front of the mountain that forms the north side of the glacier basin, I tried to make my way along its side, but, finding the climbing tedious and difficult, took to the glacier and fared well, though a good deal of step cutting was required on its ragged, crevassed margin. When night was drawing nigh, I scanned the steep mountainside in search of an accessible bench, however narrow, where a bed and a fire might be gathered for a camp. About dark great was my delight to find a little shelf with a few small mountain hemlocks growing in cleavage joints. Projecting knobs below it enabled me to build a platform for a fireplace and a bed, and by industrious creeping from one fissure to another, cutting bushes and small trees and sliding them down to within reach of my rock shelf, I made out to collect wood enough to last through the night. In an hour or two I had a cheery fire, and spent the night in turning from side to side, steaming and drying after being wet two days and a night. Fortunately this night it did not rain, but it was very cold.

Pushing on next day, I climbed to the top of the glacier by ice steps and along its side to the grand cataract two miles wide where the whole majestic flood of the glacier pours like a mighty surging river down a steep declivity in its channel. After gazing a long time on the glorious show, I discovered a place beneath the edge of the cataract where it flows over a hard, resisting granite rib, into which I crawled and enjoyed the novel and instructive view of a glacier pouring over my head, showing not only its grinding, polishing action, but how it breaks off large angular boulder masses—a most telling lesson in earth sculpture, confirming many I had already learned in the glacier basins of the High Sierra of California. I then crossed to the south side, noting the forms of the huge blocks into which the glacier was broken in passing over the brow of the cataract, and how they were welded.

The weather was now clear, opening views according to my own heart far into the high snowy fountains. I saw what seemed the farthest mountains, perhaps thirty miles from the front, everywhere winterbound, but thick forested, however steep, for a distance of at least fifteen miles from the front, the trees, hemlock and spruce, clinging to the rock by rootholds among cleavage joints. The greatest discovery was in methods of denudation displayed beneath the glacier.

After a few more days of exhilarating study I returned to the riverbank opposite Choquette's landing. Promptly at sight of the signal I made, the kind Frenchman came across for me in his canoe. At his house I enjoyed a rest while writing out notes; then examined the smaller glacier fronting the one I had been exploring, until a passing canoe bound for Fort Wrangell took me aboard.

9

A CANOE VOYAGE TO NORTHWARD

I arrived at Wrangell in a canoe with a party of Cassiar miners in October while the icy regions to the northward still burned in my mind. I had met several prospectors who had been as far as Chilcat at the head of Lynn Canal, who told wonderful stories about the great glaciers they had seen there. All the high mountains up there, they said, seemed to be made of ice, and if glaciers "are what you are after, that's the place for you," and to get there "all you have to do is to hire a good canoe and Indians who know the way."

But it now seemed too late to set out on so long a voyage. The days were growing short and winter was drawing nigh when all the land would be buried in snow. On the other hand, though this wilderness was new to me, I was familiar with storms and enjoyed them. The main channels extending along the coast remain open all winter, and, their shores being well forested, I knew that it would be easy to keep warm in camp, while abundance of food could be carried. I determined, therefore, to go ahead as far north as possible, to see and learn what I could, especially with reference to future work. When I made known my plans to Mr. Young, he offered to go with me, and, being acquainted with the Indians, procured a good canoe and crew, and with a large stock of provisions and blankets, we left Wrangell October 14, eager to welcome weather of every sort, as long as food lasted.

I was anxious to make an early start, but it was half past two in the afternoon before I could get my Indians together—Toyatte, a grand old Stickeen nobleman, who was made captain, not only because he owned the canoe, but for his skill in woodcraft and sea-manship; Kadachan, the son of a Chilcat chief; John, a Stickeen, who acted as interpreter; and Sitka Char-ley. Mr. Young, my companion, was an adventurous evangelist, and it was the opportunities the trip might afford to meet the Indians of the different tribes on our route with reference to future missionary work, that induced him to join us.

When at last all were aboard and we were about to cast loose from the wharf, Kadachan's mother, a woman of great natural dignity and force of character, came down the steps alongside the canoe oppressed with anxious fears for the safety of her son. Standing silent for a few moments, she held the missionary with her dark, bodeful eyes, and with great solemnity of speech and gesture accused him of using undue influence in gaining her son's consent to go on a dangerous voyage among unfriendly tribes; and like an ancient sibyl fore-told a long train of bad luck from storms and enemies, and finished by saying, "If my son comes not back, on you will be his blood, and you shall pay. I say it."

Mr. Young tried in vain to calm her fears, promis-ing Heaven's care as well as his own for her precious son, assuring her that he would faithfully share every danger that he encountered, and if need be die in his defense.

"We shall see whether or not you die," she said, and turned away.

Toyatte also encountered domestic difficulties. When he stepped into the canoe I noticed a cloud of anxiety on his grand old face, as if his doom now drawing near was already beginning to overshadow him. When he took leave of his wife, she refused to shake hands with him, wept bitterly, and said that his enemies, the Chilcat chiefs, would be sure to kill him in case he reached their village. But it was not on this trip that the old hero was to meet his fate, and when we were fairly free in the wilderness and a gentle breeze pressed us joyfully over the shining waters these gloomy forebodings vanished.

We first pursued a westerly course, through Sumner Strait, between Kupreanof and Prince of Wales Islands, then, turning northward, sailed up the Kiku Strait through the midst of innumerable picturesque islets, across Prince Frederick's Sound, up Chatham Strait, thence northwestward through Icy Strait and around the then uncharted Glacier Bay. Thence returning through Icy Strait, we sailed up the beautiful Lynn Canal to the Davidson Glacier and the lower village of the Chilcat tribe and returned to Wrangell along the coast of the mainland, visiting the icy Sum Dum Bay and the Wrangell Glacier on our route. Thus we made a journey more than eight hundred miles long, and though hardships and perhaps dangers were encountered, the great wonderland made compensation beyond our most extravagant hopes. Neither rain nor snow stopped us, but when the wind was too wild, Kadachan and the old captain stayed on guard in the camp and John and Charley went into the woods deer-hunting, while I examined the adjacent rocks and woods. Most of our campgrounds were in sheltered nooks where good firewood was abundant, and where the precious canoe could be safely drawn up beyond reach of the waves. After supper we sat long around the fire, listening to the Indian's stories about the wild animals, their hunting adventures, wars, traditions, religion, and customs. Every Indian party we met we interviewed, and visited every village we came to.

Our first camp was made at a place called the Island of the Standing Stone, on the shore of a shallow bay. The weather was fine. The mountains of the mainland were unclouded, excepting one, which had a horizontal ruff of dull slate color, but its icy summit covered with fresh snow towered above the cloud, flushed like its neighbors in the alpenglow. All the large islands in sight were densely forested, while many small rock islets in front of our camp were treeless or nearly so. Some of them were distinctly glaciated even below the tideline, the effects of wave washing and general weathering being scarce appreciable as yet. Some of the larger islets had a few trees, others only grass. One looked in the distance like a two-masted ship flying before the wind under press of sail.

Next morning the mountains were arrayed in fresh snow that had fallen during the night down to within a hundred feet of the sea level. We made a grand fire, and after an early breakfast pushed merrily on all day along beautiful forested shores embroidered with autumn-colored bushes. I noticed some pitchy trees that had been deeply hacked for kindling wood and torches, precious conveniences to belated voyagers on stormy nights. Before sundown we camped in a beautiful nook of Deer Bay, shut in from every wind by gray-bearded trees and fringed with rose bushes,

rubus, potentilla, asters, etc. Some of the lichen tresses
depending from the branches were six feet in length.

A dozen rods or so from our camp we discovered a
family of Kake Indians snugly sheltered in a portable
bark hut, a stout middle-aged man with his wife, son,
and daughter, and his son's wife. After our tent was
set and fire made, the head of the family paid us a visit
and presented us with a fine salmon, a pair of mallard
ducks, and a mess of potatoes. We paid a return visit
with gifts of rice and tobacco, etc. Mr. Young spoke
briefly on mission affairs and inquired whether their
tribe would be likely to welcome a teacher or missionary. But they seemed unwilling to offer an opinion on
so important a subject. The following words from the
head of the family was the only reply:

"We have not much to say to you fellows. We
always do to Boston men as we have done to you, give
a little of whatever we have, treat everybody well and
never quarrel. This is all we have to say."

Our Kake neighbors set out for Fort Wrangell
next morning, and we pushed gladly on toward Chilcat. We passed an island that had lost all its trees
in a storm, but a hopeful crop of young ones was
springing up to take their places. I found no trace
of fire in these woods. The ground was covered
with leaves, branches, and fallen trunks perhaps a
dozen generations deep, slowly decaying, forming a
grand mossy mass of ruins, kept fresh and beautiful. All that is repulsive about death was here hidden
beneath abounding life. Some rocks along the shore
were completely covered with crimson-leafed huckleberry bushes; one species still in fruit might well be
called the winter huckleberry. In a short walk I found
vetches eight feet high leaning on raspberry bushes,

and tall ferns and *Smilacina unifolia* with leaves six inches wide growing on yellow-green moss, producing a beautiful effect.

Our Indians seemed to be enjoying a quick and merry reaction from the doleful domestic dumps in which the voyage was begun. Old and young behaved this afternoon like a lot of truant boys on a lark. When we came to a pond fenced off from the main channel by a moraine dam, John went ashore to seek a shot at ducks. Creeping up behind the dam, he killed a mallard fifty or sixty feet from the shore and attempted to wave it within reach by throwing stones back of it. Charley and Kadachan went to his help, enjoying the sport, especially enjoying their own blunders in throwing in front of it and thus driving the duck farther out. To expedite the business John then tried to throw a rope across it, but failed after repeated trials, and so did each in turn, all laughing merrily at their awkward bungling. Next they tied a stone to the end of the rope to carry it further and with better aim, but the result was no better. Then majestic old Toyatte tried his hand at the game. He tied the rope to one of the canoe poles, and taking aim threw it, harpoon fashion, beyond the duck, and the general merriment was redoubled when the pole got loose and floated out to the middle of the pond. At length John stripped, swam to the duck, threw it ashore, and brought in the pole in his teeth, his companions meanwhile making merry at his expense by splashing the water in front of him and making the dead duck go through the motions of fighting and biting him in the face as he landed.

The morning after this delightful day was dark and threatening. A high wind was rushing down the strait dead against us, and just as we were about ready to start, determined to fight our way by creeping close inshore, pelting rain began to fly. We concluded therefore to wait for better weather. The hunters went out for deer and I to see the forests. The rain brought out the fragrance of the drenched trees, and the wind made wild melody in their tops, while every brown bole was embroidered by a network of rain rills. Perhaps the most delightful part of my ramble was along a stream that flowed through a leafy arch beneath overleaping trees which met at the top. The water was almost black in the deep pools and fine clear amber in the shallows. It was the pure, rich wine of the woods with a pleasant taste, bringing spicy spruce groves and widespread bog and beaver meadows to mind. On this amber stream I discovered an interesting fall. It is only a few feet high, but remarkably fine in the curve of its brow and blending shades of color, while the mossy, bushy pool into which it plunges is inky black, but wonderfully brightened by foam bells larger than common that drift in clusters on the smooth water around the rim, each of them carrying a picture of the overlooking trees leaning together at the tips like the teeth of moss capsules before they rise.

I found most of the trees here fairly loaded with mosses. Some broadly palmated branches had beds of yellow moss so wide and deep that when wet they must weigh a hundred pounds or even more. Upon these mossbeds ferns and grasses and even good-sized seedling trees grow, making beautiful hanging gardens in which the curious spectacle is presented of old trees holding hundreds of their own children in their arms, nourished by rain and dew and the decaying leaves showered down to them by their parents. The branches upon which these beds of mossy soil rest become flat and irregular like weathered roots or the antlers of deer, and at length die; and when the whole tree has thus been killed it seems to be standing on its head with roots in the air. A striking example of this sort stood near the camp and I called the missionary's attention to it.

"Come, Mr. Young," I shouted. "Here's something wonderful, the most wonderful tree you ever saw; it is standing on its head."

"How in the world," said he in astonishment, "could that tree have been plucked up by the roots, carried high in the air, and dropped down head foremost into the ground. It must have been the work of a tornado."

Toward evening the hunters brought in a deer. They had seen four others, and at the campfire talk said that deer abounded on all the islands of considerable size and along the shores of the mainland. But few were to be found in the interior on account of wolves that ran them down where they could not readily take refuge in the water. The Indians, they said, hunted them on the islands with trained dogs which went into the woods and drove them out, while the hunters lay in wait in canoes at the points where they were likely to take to the water. Beaver and black bear also abounded on this large island. I saw but few birds there, only ravens, jays, and wrens. Ducks, gulls, bald eagles, and jays are the commonest birds hereabouts. A flock of swans flew past, sounding their startling humanlike cry which seemed yet more striking in this lonely wilderness. The Indians said that geese, swans, cranes, etc., making their long journeys in regular order thus called aloud to encourage each other and enable them to keep stroke and time like men in rowing or marching (a sort of "Row, brothers, row," or "Hip, hip" of marching soldiers).

October 18 was about half sunshine, half rain and wet snow, but we paddled on through the midst of the innumerable islands in more than half comfort, enjoying the changing effects of the weather on the dripping wilderness. Strolling a little way back into the woods when we went ashore for luncheon, I found fine specimens of cedar, and here and there a birch, and small thickets of wild apple. A hemlock, felled by Indians for breadbark, was only twenty inches thick at the butt, a hundred and twenty feet long, and about five hundred and forty years old at the time it was felled. The first hundred of its rings measured only four inches, showing that for a century it had grown in the shade of taller trees and at the age of one hundred years was yet only a sapling in size. On the mossy trunk of an old prostrate spruce about a hundred feet in length, thousands of seedlings were growing. I counted seven hundred on a length of eight feet, so favorable is this climate for the development of tree seeds and so fully do these trees obey the command to multiply and replenish the earth. No wonder these islands are densely clothed with trees. They grow on solid rocks and logs as well as on fertile soil. The surface is first covered with a plush of mosses in which the seeds germinate; then the interlacing roots form a sod, fallen leaves soon cover their feet, and the young trees, closely crowded together, support each other, and the soil becomes deeper and richer from year to year.

I greatly enjoyed the Indian's campfire talk this evening on their ancient customs, how they were taught by their parents ere the whites came among them, their religion, ideas connected with the next world, the stars, plants, the behavior and language of animals under different circumstances, manner of

getting a living, etc. When our talk was interrupted
by the howling of a wolf on the opposite side of the
strait, Kadachan puzzled the minister with the question, "Have wolves souls?" The Indians believe that
they have, giving as foundation for their belief that
they are wise creatures who know how to catch seals
and salmon by swimming slyly upon them with their
heads hidden in a mouthful of grass, hunt deer in
company, and always bring forth their young at the
same and most favorable time of the year. I inquired
how it was that with enemies so wise and powerful
the deer were not all killed. Kadachan replied that
wolves knew better than to kill them all and thus cut
off their most important food supply. He said they
were numerous on all the large islands, more so than
on the mainland, that Indian hunters were afraid of
them and never ventured far into the woods alone,
for these large gray and black wolves attacked man
whether they were hungry or not. When attacked, the
Indian hunter, he said, climbed a tree or stood with
his back against a tree or rock as a wolf never attacks
face to face. Wolves, and not bears, Indians regard as
masters of the woods, for they sometimes attack and
kill bears, but the wolverine they never attack, "for,"
said John, "wolves and wolverines are companions in
sin and equally wicked and cunning."

On one of the small islands we found a stockade,
sixty by thirty-five feet, built, our Indians said, by the
Kake tribe during one of their many warlike quarrels.
Toyatte and Kadachan said these forts were common
throughout the canoe waters, showing that in this
foodful, kindly wilderness, as in all the world beside,
man may be man's worst enemy.

We discovered small bits of cultivation here and

there, patches of potatoes and turnips, planted mostly on the cleared sites of deserted villages. In spring the most industrious families sailed to their little farms of perhaps a quarter of an acre or less, and ten or fifteen miles from their villages. After preparing the ground, and planting it, they visited it again in summer to pull the weeds and speculate on the size of the crop they were likely to have to eat with their fat salmon. The Kakes were then busy digging their potatoes, which they complained were this year injured by early frosts.

We arrived at Klugh-Quan, one of the Kupreanof Kake villages, just as a funeral party was breaking up. The body had been burned and gifts were being distributed—bits of calico, handkerchiefs, blankets, etc., according to the rank and wealth of the deceased. The death ceremonies of chiefs and head men, Mr. Young told me, are very weird and imposing, with wild feasting, dancing, and singing. At this little place there are some eight totem poles of bold and intricate design, well executed, but smaller than those of the Stickeens. As elsewhere throughout the archipelago, the bear, raven, eagle, salmon, and porpoise are the chief figures. Some of the poles have square cavities, mortised into the back, which are said to contain the ashes of members of the family. These recesses are closed by a plug. I noticed one that was caulked with a rag where the joint was imperfect.

Strolling about the village, looking at the tangled vegetation, sketching the totems, etc., I found a lot of human bones scattered on the surface of the ground or partly covered. In answer to my inquiries, one of our crew said they probably belonged to Sitka Indians, slain in war. These Kakes are shrewd, industrious, and rather good-looking people. It was at their largest village that an American schooner was seized and all the crew except one man murdered. A gunboat sent to punish them burned the village. I saw the anchor of the ill-fated vessel lying near the shore.

Though all the Thlinkit tribes believe in witchcraft, they are less superstitious in some respects than many of the lower classes of whites. Chief Yana Taowk seemed to take pleasure in kicking the Sitka bones that lay in his way, and neither old nor young showed the slightest trace of superstitious fear of the dead at any time.

It was at the northmost of the Kupreanof Kake villages that Mr. Young held his first missionary meeting, singing hymns, praying, and preaching, and trying to learn the number of the inhabitants and their readiness to receive instruction. Neither here nor in any of the other villages of the different tribes that we visited was there anything like a distinct refusal to receive schoolteachers or ministers. On the contrary, with but one or two exceptions, all with apparent good faith declared their willingness to receive them, and many seemed heartily delighted at the prospect of gaining light on subjects so important and so dark to them. All had heard ere this of the wonderful work of the Reverend Mr. Duncan at Metlakatla, and even those chiefs who were not at all inclined to anything like piety were yet anxious to procure schools and churches that their people should not miss the temporal advantages of knowledge, which with their natural shrewdness they were not slow to recognize. "We are all children," they said, "groping in the dark. Give us this light and we will do as you bid us."

The chief of the first Kupreanof Kake village we came to was a venerable-looking man, perhaps seventy years old, with massive head and strongly marked features, a bold Roman nose, deep, tranquil eyes, shaggy eyebrows, a strong face set in a halo of long gray hair. He seemed delighted at the prospect of receiving a teacher for his people. "This is just what I want," he said. "I am ready to bid him welcome."

"This," said Yana Taowk, chief of the larger north village, "is a good word you bring us. We will be glad to come out of our darkness into your light. You Boston men must be favorites of the Great Father. You know all about God, and ships and guns and the growing of things to eat. We will sit quiet and listen to the words of any teacher you send us."

While Mr. Young was preaching, some of the congregation smoked, talked to each other, and answered the shouts of their companions outside, greatly to the disgust of Toyatte and Kadachan, who regarded the Kakes as mannerless barbarians. A little girl, frightened at the strange exercises, began to cry and was turned out of doors. She cried in a strange, low, wild tone, quite unlike the screech crying of the children of civilization.

The following morning we crossed Prince Frederick Sound to the west coast of Admiralty Island. Our frail shell of a canoe was tossed like a bubble on the swells coming in from the ocean. Still, I suppose, the danger was not so great as it seemed. In a good canoe, skillfully handled, you may safely sail from Victoria to Chilcat, a thousand-mile voyage frequently made by Indians in their trading operations before the coming of the whites. Our Indians, however, dreaded this crossing so late in the season. They spoke of it repeatedly before we reached it as the one great danger of our voyage.

John said to me just as we left the shore, "You and Mr. Young will be scared to death on this broad water."

"Never mind us, John," we merrily replied, "perhaps some of you brave Indian sailors may be the first to show fear."

Toyatte said he had not slept well a single night thinking of it, and after we rounded Cape Gardner and entered the comparatively smooth Chatham Strait, they all rejoiced, laughing and chatting like frolicsome children.

We arrived at the first of the Hootsenoo villages on Admiralty Island shortly after noon and were welcomed by everybody. Men, women, and children made haste to the beach to meet us, the children staring as if they had never before seen a Boston man. The chief, a remarkably good-looking and intelligent fellow, stepped forward, shook hands with us Boston fashion, and invited us to his house. Some of the curious children crowded in after us and stood around the fire staring like half-frightened wild animals. Two old women drove them out of the house, making hideous gestures, but taking good care not to hurt them. The merry throng poured through the round door, laughing and enjoying the harsh gestures and threats of the women as all a joke, indicating mild parental government in general. Indeed, in all my travels I never saw a child, old or young, receive a blow or even a harsh word. When our cook began to prepare luncheon our host said through his interpreter that he was sorry we could not eat Indian food, as he was anxious to entertain us. We thanked him, of course, and expressed our sense of his kindness. His brother, in the meantime, brought a dozen turnips, which he peeled and sliced and served in a clean dish. These we ate raw as dessert, reminding me of turnip-field feasts when I was a boy in Scotland. Then a box was brought from some corner and opened. It seemed to be full of tallow or butter. A sharp stick was thrust into it, and a lump of something five or six inches long, three or four wide, and an inch thick was dug up, which proved to be a section of the back fat of a deer, preserved in fish oil and seasoned with boiled spruce and other spicy roots. After stripping off the lard-like oil, it was cut into small pieces and passed round. It seemed white and wholesome, but I was unable to taste it even for manner's sake. This disgust, however, was not noticed, as the rest of the company did full justice to the precious tallow and smacked their lips over it as a great delicacy. A lot of potatoes about the size of walnuts, boiled and peeled and added to a potful of salmon, made a savory stew that all seemed to relish. An old, cross-looking, wrinkled crone presided at the steaming chowder-pot, and as she peeled the potatoes with her fingers she, at short intervals, quickly thrust one of the best into the mouth of a little wild-eyed girl that crouched beside her, a spark of natural love which charmed her withered face and made all the big gloomy house shine. In honor of our visit, our host put on a genuine white shirt. His wife also dressed in her best and put a pair of dainty trousers on her two-year-old boy, who seemed to be the pet and favorite of the large family and indeed of the whole village. Toward evening messengers were sent through the village to call everybody to a meeting. Mr. Young delivered the usual missionary sermon and I also was called on to say something. Then the chief arose and made an eloquent reply, thanking us for our good words and for the hopes we had inspired of obtaining a teacher for their children. In particular, he said, he wanted to hear all we could tell him about God.

This village was an offshoot of a larger one, ten miles to the north, called Killisnoo. Under the prevailing patriarchal form of government each tribe is divided into comparatively few families; and because of quarrels, the chief of this branch moved his people to this little bay, where the beach offered a good landing for canoes. A stream which enters it yields abundance of salmon, while in the adjacent woods and mountains berries, deer, and wild goats abound.

"Here," he said, "we enjoy peace and plenty; all we lack is a church and a school, particularly a school for the children." His dwelling so much with benevolent aspect on the children of the tribe showed, I think, that he truly loved them and had a right intelligent insight concerning their welfare. We spent the night under his roof, the first we had ever spent with Indians, and I never felt more at home. The loving kindness bestowed on the little ones made the house glow.

Next morning, with the hearty good wishes of our Hootsenoo friends, and encouraged by the gentle weather, we sailed gladly up the coast, hoping soon to see the Chilcat glaciers in their glory. The rock hereabouts is mostly a beautiful blue marble, waveworn into a multitude of small coves and ledges. Fine sections were thus revealed along the shore, which with their colors, brightened with showers and late-blooming leaves and flowers, beguiled the weariness of the way. The shingle in front of these marble cliffs is also mostly marble, well polished and rounded and mixed with a small percentage of glacier-borne slate and granite erratics.

We arrived at the upper village about half past one o'clock. Here we saw Hootsenoo Indians in a very different light from that which illumined the lower village. While we were yet half a mile or more away, we heard sounds I had never before heard—a storm of strange howls, yells, and screams rising from a base of gasping, bellowing grunts and groans. Had I been alone, I should have fled as from a pack of fiends, but our Indians quietly recognized this awful sound, if such stuff could be called sound, simply as the "whiskey howl" and pushed quietly on. As we approached the landing, the demoniac howling so greatly increased I tried to dissuade Mr. Young from attempting to say a single word in the village, and as for preaching one might as well try to preach in Tophet. The whole village was afire with bad whiskey. This was the first time in my life that I learned the meaning of the phrase "a howling drunk." Even our Indians hesitated to venture ashore, notwithstanding whiskey storms were far from novel to them. Mr. Young, however, hoped that in this Indian Sodom at least one man might be found so righteous as to be in his right mind and able to give trustworthy information. Therefore I was at length prevailed on to yield consent to land. Our canoe was drawn up on the beach and one of the crew left to guard it. Cautiously we strolled up the hill to the main row of houses, now a chain of alcoholic volcanoes. The largest house, just opposite the landing, was about forty feet square, built of immense planks, each hewn from a whole log, and, as usual, the only opening was a mere hole about two and a half feet in diameter, closed by a massive hinged plug like the breach of a cannon. At the dark door-hole a few black faces appeared and were suddenly withdrawn. Not a single person was to be seen on the street. At length a couple of old, crouching men, hideously blackened, ventured out and stared at us, then, calling to their companions, other black and burning heads appeared, and we began to fear that like the Alloway Kirk witches the whole legion was about to sally forth. But, instead, those outside suddenly crawled and tumbled in again. We were thus allowed to take a general view of the place and return to our canoe unmolested. But ere we could get away, three old women came swaggering and grinning down to the beach, and Toyatte was discovered by a man with whom he had once had a business misunderstanding, who, burning for revenge, was now jumping and howling and threatening as only a drunken Indian may, while our heroic old captain, in severe icy majesty, stood erect and motionless, uttering never a word. Kadachan, on the contrary, was well nigh smothered with the drunken caresses of one of his father's *tillicums* (friends), who insisted on his going back with him into the house. But reversing the words of St. Paul in his account of his shipwreck, it came to pass that we all at length got safe to sea and by hard rowing managed to reach a fine harbor before dark, fifteen sweet, serene miles from the howlers.

Our camp this evening was made at the head of a narrow bay bordered by spruce and hemlock woods. We made our beds beneath a grand old Sitka spruce five feet in diameter, whose broad, winglike branches were outspread immediately above our heads. The night picture as I stood back to see it in the firelight was this one great tree, relieved against the gloom of the woods back of it, the light on the low branches revealing the shining needles, the brown, sturdy trunk grasping an outswelling mossy bank, and a fringe of illuminated bushes within a few feet of the tree with the firelight on the tips of the sprays.

Next morning, soon after we left our harbor, we were caught in a violent gust of wind and dragged over the seething water in a passionate hurry, though our sail was close-reefed, flying past the gray headlands in most exhilarating style, until fear of being capsized made us drop our sail and run into the first little nook we came to for shelter. Captain Toyatte remarked that in this kind of wind no Indian would dream of traveling, but since Mr. Young and I were with him he was willing to go on, because he was sure that the Lord loved us and would not allow us to perish.

We were now within a day or two of Chilcat. We had only to hold a direct course up the beautiful Lynn Canal to reach the large Davidson and other glaciers at its head in the canyons of the Chilcat and Chilcoot Rivers. But rumors of trouble among the Indians there now reached us. We found a party taking shelter from the stormy wind in a little cove, who confirmed the bad news that the Chilcats were drinking and fighting, that Kadachan's father had been shot, and that it would be far from safe to venture among them until blood money had been paid and the quarrels settled. I decided, therefore, in the meantime, to turn westward and go in search of the wonderful "ice mountains" that Sitka Charley had been telling us about. Charley, the youngest of my crew, noticing my interest in glaciers, said that when he was a boy he had gone with his father to hunt seals in a large bay full of ice, and that though it was long since he had been there, he thought he could find his way to it. Accordingly, we pushed eagerly on across Chatham Strait to the north end of Icy Strait, toward the new and promising ice field.

On the south side of Icy Strait we ran into a picturesque bay to visit the main village of the Hoona tribe. Rounding a point on the north shore of the bay, the charmingly located village came in sight, with a group of the inhabitants gazing at us as we approached. They evidently recognized us as strangers or visitors from the shape and style of our canoe, and perhaps even determining that white men were aboard, for these Indians have wonderful eyes. While we were yet half a mile off, we saw a flag unfurled on a tall mast in front of the chief's house. Toyatte hoisted his United States flag in reply, and thus arrayed we made for the landing. Here we were met and received by the chief, Kashoto, who stood close to the water's edge, barefooted and bareheaded, but wearing so fine a robe and standing so grave, erect, and serene, his dignity was complete. No white man could have maintained sound dignity under circumstances so disadvantageous. After the usual formal salutations, the chief, still standing as erect and motionless as a tree, said that he was not much acquainted with our people and feared that his house was too mean for visitors so distinguished as we were. We hastened of course to assure him that we were not proud of heart, and would be glad to have the honor of his hospitality and friendship. With a smile of relief he then led us into his large fort house to the seat of honor prepared for us. After we had been allowed to rest unnoticed and unquestioned for fifteen minutes or so, in accordance with good Indian manners in case we should be weary or embarrassed, our cook began to prepare luncheon;

and the chief expressed great concern at his not being able to entertain us in Boston fashion.

Luncheon over, Mr. Young as usual requested him to call his people to a meeting. Most of them were away at outlying camps gathering winter stores. Some ten or twelve men, however, about the same number of women, and a crowd of wondering boys and girls were gathered in, to whom Mr. Young preached the usual gospel sermon. Toyatte prayed in Thlinkit, and the other members of the crew joined in the hymn singing. At the close of the mission exercises the chief arose and said that he would now like to hear what the other white chief had to say. I directed John to reply that I was not a missionary, that I came only to pay a friendly visit and see the forests and mountains of their beautiful country. To this he replied, as others had done in the same circumstances, that he would like to hear me on the subject of their country and themselves; so I had to get on my feet and make some sort of a speech, dwelling principally on the brotherhood of all races of people, assuring them that God loved them and that some of their white brethren were beginning to know them and become interested in their welfare; that I seemed this evening to be among old friends with whom I had long been acquainted, though I had never been here before; that I would always remember them and the kind reception they had given us; advised them to heed the instructions of sincere self-denying mission men who wished only to do them good and desired nothing but their friendship and welfare in return. I told them that in some far-off countries, instead of receiving the missionaries with glad and thankful hearts, the Indians killed and ate them; but I hoped, and indeed felt sure, that his people would find a better use for missionaries than putting them, like salmon, in pots for food. They seemed greatly interested, looking into each other's faces with emphatic nods and a-ahs and smiles.

The chief then slowly arose and, after standing silent a minute or two, told us how glad he was to see us; that he felt as if his heart had enjoyed a good meal; that we were the first to come humbly to his little out-of-the-way village to tell his people about God; that they were all like children groping in darkness, but eager for light; that they would gladly welcome a missionary and teacher and use them well; that he could easily believe that whites and Indians were the children of one Father just as I had told them in my speech; that they differed little and resembled each other a great deal, calling attention to the similarity of hands, eyes, legs, etc., making telling gestures in the most natural style of eloquence and dignified composure. "Oftentimes," he said, "when I was on the high mountains in the fall, hunting wild sheep for meat, and for wool to make blankets, I have been caught in snowstorms and held in camp until there was nothing to eat, but when I reached my home and got warm, and had a good meal, then my body felt good. For a long time my heart has been hungry and cold, but to-night your words have warmed my heart, and given it a good meal, and now my heart feels good."

The most striking characteristic of these people is their serene dignity in circumstances that to us would be novel and embarrassing. Even the little children behave with natural dignity, come to the white men when called, and restrain their wonder at the strange prayers, hymn singing, etc. This evening an old woman fell asleep in the meeting and began to snore; and though both old and young were shaken with suppressed mirth, they evidently took great pains to conceal it. It seems wonderful to me that these so-called savages can make one feel at home in their families. In good breeding, intelligence, and skill in accomplishing whatever they try to do with tools they seem to me to rank above most of our uneducated white laborers. I have never yet seen a child ill-used, even to the extent of an angry word. Scolding, so common a curse in civilization, is not known here at all. On the contrary the young are fondly indulged without being spoiled. Crying is very rarely heard.

In the house of this Hoona chief, a pet marmot (Parry's) was a great favorite with old and young. It was therefore delightfully confiding and playful and human. Cats were petted, and the confidence with which these cautious, thoughtful animals met strangers showed that they were kindly treated.

There were some ten or a dozen houses, all told, in the village. The count made by the chief for Mr. Young showed some seven hundred and twenty-five persons in the tribe.

10

THE DISCOVERY OF GLACIER BAY

From here, on October 24, we set sail for Guide Charley's ice mountains. The handle of our heaviest axe was cracked, and as Charley declared that there was no firewood to be had in the big ice mountain bay, we would have to load the canoe with a store for cooking at an island out in the Strait a few miles from the village. We were therefore anxious to buy or trade for a good sound axe in exchange for our broken one. Good axes are rare in rocky Alaska. Soon or late an unlucky stroke on a stone concealed in moss spoils the edge. Finally one in almost perfect condition was offered by a young Hoona for our broken-handled one and a half-dollar to boot; but when the broken axe and money were given he promptly demanded an additional twenty-five cents' worth of tobacco. The tobacco was given him, then he required a half-dollar's worth more of tobacco, which was also given; but when he still demanded something more, Charley's patience gave way and we sailed in the same condition as to axes as when we arrived. This was the only contemptible commercial affair we encountered among these Alaskan Indians.

We reached the wooded island about one o'clock,

made coffee, took on a store of wood, and set sail direct for the icy country, finding it very hard indeed to believe the woodless part of Charley's description of the Icy Bay, so heavily and uniformly are all the shores forested wherever we had been. In this view we were joined by John, Kadachan, and Toyatte, none of them on all their lifelong canoe travels having ever seen a woodless country.

We held a northwesterly course until long after dark, when we reached a small inlet that sets in near the mouth of Glacier Bay, on the west side. Here we made a cold camp on a desolate snow-covered beach in stormy sleet and darkness. At daybreak I looked eagerly in every direction to learn what kind of place we were in; but gloomy rain clouds covered the mountains, and I could see nothing that would give me a clue, while Vancouver's chart, hitherto a faithful guide, here failed us altogether. Nevertheless, we made haste to be off; and fortunately, for just as we were leaving the shore, a faint smoke was seen across the inlet, toward which Charley, who now seemed lost, gladly steered. Our sudden appearance so early that gray morning had evidently alarmed our neighbors, for as soon as we were within hailing distance an Indian with his face blackened fired a shot over our heads, and in a blunt, bellowing voice roared, "Who are you?"

Our interpreter shouted, "Friends and the Fort Wrangell missionary."

Then men, women, and children swarmed out of the hut, and awaited our approach on the beach. One of the hunters having brought his gun with him, Kadachan sternly rebuked him, asking with superb indignation whether he was not ashamed to meet a

missionary with a gun in his hands. Friendly relations, however, were speedily established, and as a
cold rain was falling, they invited us to enter their
hut. It seemed very small and was jammed full of
oily boxes and bundles; nevertheless, twenty-one persons managed to find shelter in it about a smoky fire.
Our hosts proved to be Hoona seal hunters laying in
their winter stores of meat and skins. The packed hut
was passably well ventilated, but its heavy, meaty
smells were not the same to our noses as those we
were accustomed to in the sprucy nooks of the evergreen woods. The circle of black eyes peering at us
through a fog of reek and smoke made a novel picture.
We were glad, however, to get within reach of information, and of course asked many questions concerning the ice mountains and the strange bay, to most
of which our inquisitive Hoona friends replied with
counter-questions as to our object in coming to such a
place, especially so late in the year. They had heard of
Mr. Young and his work at Fort Wrangell, but could
not understand what a missionary could be doing in
such a place as this. Was he going to preach to the
seals and gulls, they asked, or to the ice mountains?
And could they take his word? Then John explained
that only the friend of the missionary was seeking
ice mountains, that Mr. Young had already preached
many good words in the villages we had visited, their
own among the others, that our hearts were good and
every Indian was our friend. Then we gave them a
little rice, sugar, tea, and tobacco, after which they
began to gain confidence and to speak freely. They
told us that the big bay was called by them Sit-a-
da-kay, or Ice Bay; that there were many large ice
mountains in it, but no gold mines; and that the ice

mountain they knew best was at the head of the bay, where most of the seals were found.

Notwithstanding the rain, I was anxious to push on and grope our way beneath the clouds as best we could, in case worse weather should come; but Charley was ill at ease, and wanted one of the seal hunters to go with us, for the place was much changed. I promised to pay well for a guide, and in order to lighten the canoe proposed to leave most of our heavy stores in the hut until our return. After a long consultation one of them consented to go. His wife got ready his blanket and a piece of cedar matting for his bed, and some provisions—mostly dried salmon, and seal sausage made of strips of lean meat plaited around a core of fat. She followed us to the beach, and just as we were pushing off said with a pretty smile, "It is my husband that you are taking away. See that you bring him back."

We got under way about 10 A.M. The wind was in our favor, but a cold rain pelted us, and we could see but little of the dreary, treeless wilderness which we had now fairly entered. The bitter blast, however, gave us good speed; our bedraggled canoe rose and fell on the waves as solemnly as a big ship. Our course was northwestward, up the southwest side of the bay, near the shore of what seemed to be the mainland, smooth marble islands being on our right. About noon we discovered the first of the great glaciers, the one I afterward named for James Geikie, the noted Scotch geologist. Its lofty blue cliffs, looming through the draggled skirts of the clouds, gave a tremendous impression of savage power, while the roar of the newborn icebergs thickened and emphasized the general roar of the storm. An hour and a half beyond the Geikie Glacier we ran into a slight harbor where the shore is low, dragged the canoe beyond the reach of drifting icebergs, and, much against my desire to push ahead, encamped, the guide insisting that the big ice mountain at the head of the bay could not be reached before dark, that the landing there was dangerous even in daylight, and that this was the only safe harbor on the way to it. While camp was being made, I strolled along the shore to examine the rocks and the fossil timber that abounds here. All the rocks are freshly glaciated, even below the sea level, nor have the waves as yet worn off the surface polish, much less the heavy scratches and grooves and lines of glacial contour.

The next day being Sunday, the minister wished to stay in camp; and so, on account of the weather, did the Indians. I therefore set out on an excursion, and spent the day alone on the mountain slopes above the camp, and northward, to see what I might learn. Pushing on through rain and mud and sludgy snow, crossing many brown, boulder-choked torrents, wading, jumping, and wallowing in snow up to my shoulders was mountaineering of the most trying kind. After crouching cramped and benumbed in the canoe, poulticed in wet or damp clothing night and day, my limbs had been asleep. This day they were awakened and in the hour of trial proved that they had not lost the cunning learned on many a mountain peak of the High Sierra. I reached a height of fifteen hundred feet, on the ridge that bounds the second of the great glaciers. All the landscape was smothered in clouds and I began to fear that as far as wide views were concerned I had climbed in vain. But at length the clouds lifted a little, and beneath their gray fringes I saw the berg-filled expanse of the bay, and the feet of the mountains that stand about it, and the imposing fronts of five huge glaciers, the nearest being immediately beneath me. This was my first general view of Glacier Bay, a solitude of ice and snow and newborn rocks, dim, dreary, mysterious. I held the ground I had so dearly won for an hour or two, sheltering myself from the blast as best I could, while with benumbed fingers I sketched what I could see of the landscape, and wrote a few lines in my notebook. Then, breasting the snow again, crossing the shifting avalanche slopes and torrents, I reached camp about dark, wet and weary and glad.

While I was getting some coffee and hardtack, Mr. Young told me that the Indians were discouraged, and had been talking about turning back, fearing that I would be lost, the canoe broken, or in some other mysterious way the expedition would come to grief if I persisted in going farther. They had been asking him what possible motive I could have in climbing mountains when storms were blowing; and when he replied that I was only seeking knowledge, Toyatte said, "Muir must be a witch to seek knowledge in such a place as this and in such miserable weather."

After supper, crouching about a dull fire of fossil wood, they became still more doleful, and talked in tones that accorded well with the wind and waters and growling torrents about us, telling sad old stories of crushed canoes, drowned Indians, and hunters frozen in snowstorms. Even brave old Toyatte, dreading the treeless, forlorn appearance of the region, said that his heart was not strong, and that he feared his canoe, on the safety of which our lives depended, might be entering a skookum-house (jail) of ice, from which there might be no escape; while the Hoona guide said bluntly that if I was so fond of danger, and meant to go close up to the noses of the ice mountains, he would not consent to go any farther; for we should all be lost, as many of his tribe had been, by the sudden rising of bergs from the bottom. They seemed to be losing heart with every howl of the wind, and, fearing that they might fail me now that I was in the midst of so grand a congregation of glaciers, I made haste to reassure them, telling them that for ten years I had wandered alone among mountains and storms, and good luck always followed me; that with me, therefore, they need fear nothing. The storm would soon cease and the sun would shine to show us the way we should go, for God cares for us and guides us as long as we are trustful and brave, therefore all childish fear must be put away. This little speech did good. Kadachan, with some show of enthusiasm, said he liked to travel with good-luck people; and dignified old Toyatte declared that now his heart was strong again, and he would venture on with me as far as I liked for my "wawa" was "delait" (my talk was very good). The old warrior even became a little sentimental, and said that even if the canoe was broken he would not greatly care, because on the way to the other world he would have good companions.

Next morning it was still raining and snowing, but the south wind swept us bravely forward and swept the bergs from our course. In about an hour we reached the second of the big glaciers, which I afterwards named for Hugh Miller. We rowed up its fjord and landed to make a slight examination of its grand frontal wall. The berg-producing portion we found to be about a mile and a half wide, and broken into an imposing array of jagged spires and pyramids, and flat-topped towers and battlements, of many shades of blue, from pale, shimmering, limpid tones in the crevasses and hollows, to the most startling, chilling, almost shrieking vitriol blue on the plain mural spaces from which bergs had just been discharged. Back from the front for a few miles the glacier rises in a series of wide steps, as if this portion of the glacier had sunk in successive sections as it reached deep water, and the sea had found its way beneath it. Beyond this it extends indefinitely in a gently rising prairie-like expanse, and branches along the slopes and canyons of the Fairweather Range.

From here a run of two hours brought us to the head of the bay, and to the mouth of the northwest fjord, at the head of which lie the Hoona sealing-grounds, and the great glacier now called the Pacific, and another called the Hoona. The fjord is about five miles long, and two miles wide at the mouth. Here our Hoona guide had a store of dry wood, which we took aboard. Then, setting sail, we were driven wildly up the fjord, as if the storm-wind were saying, "Go, then, if you will, into my icy chamber; but you shall stay in until I am ready to let you out." All this time sleety rain was falling on the bay, and snow on the mountains; but soon after we landed the sky began to open. The camp was made on a rocky bench near the front of the Pacific Glacier, and the canoe was carried beyond the reach of the bergs and berg-waves. The bergs were now crowded in a dense pack against the discharging front, as if the storm-wind had determined to make the glacier take back her crystal offspring and keep them at home.

While camp affairs were being attended to, I set out to climb a mountain for comprehensive views; and before I had reached a height of a thousand feet the rain ceased, and the clouds began to rise from the lower altitudes, slowly lifting their white skirts, and lingering in majestic, wing-shaped masses about the mountains that rise out of the broad, icy sea, the highest of all the white mountains, and the greatest of all the glaciers I had yet seen. Climbing higher for a still broader outlook, I made notes and sketched, improving the precious time while sunshine streamed through the luminous fringes of the clouds and fell on the green waters of the fjord, the glittering bergs, the crystal bluffs of the vast glacier, the intensely white, far-spreading fields of ice, and the ineffably chaste and spiritual heights of the Fairweather Range, which were now hidden, now partly revealed, the whole making a picture of icy wildness unspeakably pure and sublime.

Looking southward, a broad ice sheet was seen extending in a gently undulating plain from the Pacific Fjord in the foreground to the horizon, dotted and ridged here and there with mountains which were as white as the snow-covered ice in which they were half, or more than half, submerged. Several of the great glaciers of the bay flow from this one grand fountain. It is an instructive example of a general glacier covering the hills and dales of a country that is not yet ready to be brought to the light of day—not only covering but creating a landscape with the features it is destined to have when, in the fullness of time, the fashioning ice sheet shall be lifted by the sun, and the land become warm and fruitful. The view to the westward is bounded and almost filled by the glorious Fairweather Mountains, the highest among them springing aloft in sublime beauty to a height of nearly sixteen thousand feet, while from base to summit every peak and spire and dividing ridge of all the mighty host was spotless white, as if painted. It would seem that snow could never be made to lie on the steepest slopes and precipices unless plastered on when wet, and then frozen. But this snow could not have been wet. It must have been fixed by being driven and set in small particles like the storm-dust of drifts, which, when in this condition, is fixed not only on sheer cliffs, but in massive, overcurling cornices. Along the base of this majestic range sweeps the Pacific Glacier, fed by innumerable cascading tributaries, and discharging into the head of its fjord by two mouths only partly separated by the brow of an island rock about one thousand feet high, each nearly a mile wide.

Dancing down the mountain to camp, my mind glowing like the sunbeaten glaciers, I found the Indians seated around a good fire, entirely happy now that the farthest point of the journey was safely reached and the long, dark storm was cleared away. How hopefully, peacefully bright that night were the stars in the frosty sky, and how impressive was the thunder of the icebergs, rolling, swelling, reverberating through the solemn stillness! I was too happy to sleep.

About daylight next morning we crossed the fjord and landed on the south side of the rock that divides the wall of the great glacier. The whiskered faces of seals dotted the open spaces between the bergs, and I could not prevent John and Charley and Kadachan from shooting at them. Fortunately, few, if any, were hurt. Leaving the Indians in charge of the canoe, I managed to climb to the top of the wall by a good deal of step cutting between the ice and dividing rock, and gained a good general view of the glacier. At one favorable place I descended about fifty feet below the side of the glacier, where its denuding, fashioning action was clearly shown. Pushing back from here, I found the surface crevassed and sunken in steps, like the Hugh Miller Glacier, as if it were being undermined by the action of tidewaters. For a distance of fifteen or twenty miles the riverlike ice flood is nearly level, and when it recedes, the ocean water will follow it, and thus form a long extension of the fjord, with features essentially the same as those now extending into the continent farther south, where many great glaciers once poured into the sea, though scarce a vestige of them now exists. Thus the domain of the sea has been, and is being, extended in these ice-sculptured lands, and the scenery of their shores enriched. The brow of the dividing rock is about a thousand feet high, and is hard beset by the glacier. A short time ago it was at least two thousand feet below the surface of the over-sweeping ice; and under present climatic conditions it will soon take its place as a glacier-polished island in the middle of the fjord, like a thousand others in the magnificent archipelago. Emerging from its icy sepulchre, it gives a most telling illustration of the birth of a marked feature of a landscape. In this instance it is not the mountain, but the glacier, that is in labor, and the mountain itself is being brought forth.

The Hoona Glacier enters the fjord on the south side, a short distance below the Pacific, displaying a broad and far-reaching expanse, over which many lofty peaks are seen; but the front wall, thrust into the fjord, is not nearly so interesting as that of the Pacific, and I did not observe any bergs discharged from it.

In the evening, after witnessing the unveiling of the majestic peaks and glaciers and their baptism in the down-pouring sunbeams, it seemed inconceivable that nature could have anything finer to show us. Nevertheless, compared with what was to come the next morning, all that was as nothing. The calm dawn gave no promise of anything uncommon. Its most impressive features were the frosty clearness of the sky and a deep, brooding stillness made all the more striking by the thunder of the newborn bergs. The sunrise we did not see at all, for we were beneath the shadows of the fjord cliffs; but in the midst of our studies, while the Indians were getting ready to sail, we were startled by the sudden appearance of a red light burning with a strange unearthly splendor on the topmost peak of the Fairweather Mountains. Instead of vanishing as suddenly as it had appeared, it spread and spread until the whole range down to the level of the glaciers was filled with the celestial fire. In color it was at first a vivid crimson, with a thick, furred appearance, as fine as the alpenglow, yet indescribably rich and deep—not in the least like a garment or mere external flush or bloom through which one might expect to see the rocks or snow, but every mountain apparently was glowing from the heart like molten metal fresh from a furnace. Beneath the frosty shadows of the fjord we stood hushed and awestricken, gazing at the holy vision; and had we seen the heavens opened and God made manifest, our attention could not have been more tremendously strained. When the highest peak began to burn, it did not seem to be steeped in sunshine, however glorious, but rather as if it had been thrust into the body of the sun itself. Then the supernal fire slowly descended, with a sharp line of demarcation separating it from the cold, shaded region beneath; peak after peak, with their spires and ridges and cascading glaciers, caught the heavenly glow, until all the mighty host stood transfigured, hushed, and thoughtful, as if awaiting the coming of the Lord. The white, rayless light of morning, seen when I was alone amid the peaks of the California Sierra, had always seemed to me the most telling of all the terrestrial manifestations of God. But here the mountains themselves were made divine, and declared His glory in terms still more impressive. How long we gazed I never knew. The glorious vision passed away in a gradual, fading change through a thousand tones of color to pale yellow and white, and then the work of the ice world went on again in everyday beauty. The green waters of the fjord were filled with sun spangles; the fleet of icebergs set forth on their voyages with the upspringing breeze; and on the innumerable mirrors and prisms of these bergs, and on those of the shattered crystal walls of the glaciers, common white light and rainbow light began to burn, while the mountains shone in their frosty jewelry, and loomed again in the thin azure in serene terrestrial majesty. We turned and sailed away, joining the outgoing bergs, while "Gloria in excelsis" still seemed to be sounding over all the white landscape, and our burning hearts were ready for any fate, feeling that, whatever the future might have in store, the treasures we had gained this glorious morning would enrich our lives forever.

When we arrived at the mouth of the fjord, and rounded the massive granite headland that stands guard at the entrance on the north side, another large glacier, now named the Reid, was discovered at the head of one of the northern branches of the bay. Pushing ahead into this new fjord, we found that it was not only packed with bergs, but that the spaces between the bergs were crusted with new ice, compelling us to turn back while we were yet several miles from the discharging frontal wall. But though we were not then allowed to set foot on this magnificent glacier, we obtained a fine view of it, and I made the Indians cease rowing while I sketched its principal features. Thence, after steering northeastward a few miles, we discovered still another large glacier, now named the Carroll. But the fjord into which this glacier flows was, like the last, utterly inaccessible on account of ice, and we had to be content with a general view and sketch of it, gained as we rowed slowly past at a distance of three or four miles. The mountains back of it and on each side of its inlet are sculptured in a singularly rich and striking style of architecture, in which subordinate peaks and gables appear in wonderful profusion, and an imposing conical mountain with a wide, smooth base stands out in the main current of the glacier, a mile or two back from the discharging ice wall.

We now turned southward down the eastern shore of the bay, and in an hour or two discovered a glacier of the second class, at the head of a comparatively short fjord that winter had not yet closed. Here we landed, and climbed across a mile or so of rough boulder beds, and back upon the wildly broken, receding front of the glacier, which, though it descends to the level of the sea, no longer sends off bergs. Many large masses, detached from the wasting front by irregular melting, were partly buried beneath mud, sand, gravel, and boulders of the terminal moraine. Thus protected, these fossil icebergs remain unmelted for many years, some of them for a century or more, as shown by the age of trees growing above them, though there are no trees here as yet. At length melting, a pit with sloping sides is formed by the falling in of the overlying moraine material into the space at first occupied by the buried ice. In this way are formed the curious depressions in drift-covered regions called kettles or sinks. On these decaying glaciers we may also find many interesting lessons on the formation of boulders and boulder beds, which in all glaciated countries exert a marked influence on scenery, health, and fruitfulness.

Three or four miles farther down the bay, we came to another fjord, up which we sailed in quest of more glaciers, discovering one in each of the two branches into which the fjord divides. Neither of these glaciers quite reaches tidewater. Notwithstanding the apparent fruitfulness of their fountains, they are in the first stage of decadence, the waste from melting and evaporation being greater now than the supply of new ice from their snowy fountains. We reached the one in the north branch, climbed over its wrinkled brow, and gained a good view of the trunk and some of the tributaries, and also of the sublime gray cliffs of its channel.

Then we sailed up the south branch of the inlet, but failed to reach the glacier there, on account of a thin sheet of new ice. With the tent poles we broke a lane for the canoe for a little distance; but it was slow work, and we soon saw that we could not reach the glacier before dark. Nevertheless, we gained a fair view of it as it came sweeping down through its gigantic gateway of massive Yosemite rocks three or four thousand feet high. Here we lingered until sundown, gazing and sketching; then turned back, and encamped on a bed of cobblestones between the forks of the fjord.

We gathered a lot of fossil wood and after supper made a big fire, and as we sat around it the brightness of the sky brought on a long talk with the Indians about the stars; and their eager, childlike attention was refreshing to see as compared with the deathlike apathy of weary town dwellers, in whom natural curiosity has been quenched in toil and care and poor shallow comfort.

After sleeping a few hours, I stole quietly out of the camp, and climbed the mountain that stands between the two glaciers. The ground was frozen, making the climbing difficult in the steepest places; but the views over the icy bay, sparkling beneath the stars, were enchanting. It seemed then a sad thing that any part of so precious a night had been lost in sleep. The starlight was so full that I distinctly saw not only the berg-filled bay, but most of the lower portions of the glaciers, lying pale and spirit-like amid the mountains. The nearest glacier in particular was so distinct that it seemed to be glowing with light that came from within itself. Not even in dark nights have I ever found any difficulty in seeing large glaciers; but on this mountaintop, amid so much ice, in the heart of so clear and frosty a night, everything was more or less luminous, and I seemed to be poised in a vast hollow between two skies of almost equal brightness. This exhilarating scramble made me glad and strong and I rejoiced that my studies called me before the glorious night succeeding so glorious a morning had been spent!

I got back to camp in time for an early breakfast, and by daylight we had everything packed and were again under way. The fjord was frozen nearly to its mouth, and though the ice was so thin it gave us but little trouble in breaking a way for the canoe, yet it showed us that the season for exploration in these waters was well-nigh over. We were in danger of being imprisoned in a jam of icebergs, for the water spaces between them freeze rapidly, binding the floes into one mass. Across such floes it would be almost impossible to drag a canoe, however industriously we might ply the axe, as our Hoona guide took great pains to warn us. I would have kept straight down the bay from here, but the guide had to be taken home, and the provisions we left at the bark hut had to be got on board. We therefore crossed over to our Sunday storm-camp, cautiously boring a way through the bergs. We found the shore lavishly adorned with a fresh arrival of assorted bergs that had been left stranded at high tide. They were arranged in a curving row, looking intensely clear and pure on the gray sand, and, with the sunbeams pouring through them, suggested the jewel-paved streets of the New Jerusalem.

On our way down the coast, after examining the front of the beautiful Geikie Glacier, we obtained our first broad view of the great glacier afterwards named the Muir, the last of all the grand company to be seen, the stormy weather having hidden it when we first entered the bay. It was now perfectly clear, and the spacious, prairie-like glacier, with its many tributaries extending far back into the snowy recesses of its fountains, made a magnificent display of its wealth, and I was strongly tempted to go and explore it at all hazards. But winter had come, and the freezing of its fjords was an insurmountable obstacle. I had, therefore, to be content for the present with sketching and studying its main features at a distance.

When we arrived at the Hoona hunting camp, men, women, and children came swarming out to welcome us. In the neighborhood of this camp I carefully noted the lines of demarkation between the forested and deforested regions. Several mountains here are only in part deforested, and the lines separating the bare and the forested portions are well defined. The soil, as well as the trees, had slid off the steep slopes, leaving the edge of the woods raw looking and rugged.

At the mouth of the bay a series of moraine islands show that the trunk glacier that occupied the bay halted here for some time and deposited this island material as a terminal moraine; that more of the bay was not filled in shows that, after lingering here, it receded comparatively fast. All the level portions of trunks of glaciers occupying ocean fjords, instead of melting back gradually in times of general shrinking and recession, as inland glaciers with sloping chan-nels do, melt almost uniformly over all the surface until they become thin enough to float. Then, of course, with each rise and fall of the tide, the seawater, with a temperature usually considerably above the freez-ing point, rushes in and out beneath them, causing rapid waste of the nether surface, while the upper is being wasted by the weather, until at length the fjord portions of these great glaciers become comparatively thin and weak and are broken up and vanish almost simultaneously.

Glacier Bay is undoubtedly young as yet. Vancou-ver's chart, made only a century ago, shows no trace of it, though found admirably faithful in general. It seems probable, therefore, that even then the entire bay was occupied by a glacier of which all those described above, great though they are, were only trib-utaries. Nearly as great a change has taken place in Sum Dum Bay since Vancouver's visit, the main trunk glacier there having receded from eighteen to twenty five miles from the line marked on his chart. Char-ley, who was here when a boy, said that the place had so changed that he hardly recognized it, so many new islands had been born in the meantime and so much ice had vanished. As we have seen, this Icy Bay is being still farther extended by the recession of the glaciers. That this whole system of fjords and channels was added to the domain of the sea by glacial action is to my mind certain.

We reached the island from which we had obtained our store of fuel about half past six and camped here for the night, having spent only five days in Sitadaka, sailing round it, visiting and sketching all the six glaciers excepting the largest, though I landed only on three of them—the Geikie, Hugh Miller, and Grand Pacific—the freezing of the fjords in front of the others rendering them inaccessible at this late season.

11

THE COUNTRY OF THE CHILCATS

On October 30 we visited a camp of Hoonas at the mouth of a salmon chuck. We had seen some of them before, and they received us kindly. Here we learned that peace reigned in Chilcat. The reports that we had previously heard were, as usual in such cases, wildly exaggerated. The little camp hut of these Indians was crowded with the food supplies they had gathered—chiefly salmon, dried and tied in bunches of convenient size for handling and transporting to their villages, bags of salmon roe, boxes of fish oil, a lot of mountain-goat mutton, and a few porcupines. They presented us with some dried salmon and potatoes, for which we gave them tobacco and rice. About 3 P.M. we reached their village, and in the best house, that of a chief, we found the family busily engaged in making whiskey. The still and mash were speedily removed and hidden away with apparent shame as soon as we came in sight. When we entered and passed the regular greetings, the usual apologies as to being unable to furnish Boston food for us and inquiries whether we could eat Indian food were gravely made. Toward six or seven o'clock Mr. Young explained the object of his visit and held a short service. The chief replied with grave deliberation, saying that he would be heartily glad to have a teacher sent to his poor ignorant people, upon whom he now hoped the light of a better day was beginning to break. Hereafter he would gladly do whatever the white teachers told him to do and would have no will of his own. This under the whiskey circumstances seemed too good to be quite true. He thanked us over and over again for coming so far to see him, and complained that Port Simpson Indians, sent out on a missionary tour by Mr. Crosby, after making a good-luck board for him and nailing it over his door, now wanted to take it away. Mr. Young promised to make him a new one, should this threat be executed, and remarked that since he had offered to do his bidding he hoped he would make no more whiskey. To this the chief replied with fresh complaints concerning the threatened loss of his precious board, saying that he thought the Port Simpson Indians were very mean in seeking to take it away, but that now he would tell them to take it as soon as they liked for he was going to get a better one at Wrangell. But no effort of the missionary could bring him to notice or discuss the whiskey business. The luck board nailed over the door was about two feet long and had the following inscription: "The Lord will bless those who do his will. When you rise in the morning, and when you retire at night, give him thanks. Heccla Hockla Popla."

This chief promised to pray like a white man every morning, and to bury the dead as the whites do. "I often wondered," he said, "where the dead went to. Now I am glad to know;" and at last acknowledged the whiskey, saying he was sorry to have been caught making the bad stuff. The behavior of all, even the little ones circled around the fire, was very good. There was no laughter when the strange singing commenced. They only gazed like curious, intelligent animals. A little daughter of the chief with the glow of the firelight on her eyes made an interesting picture, head held aslant. Another in the group, with upturned eyes, seeming to half understand the strange words about God, might have passed for one of Raphael's angels.

The chief's house was about forty feet square, of the ordinary fort kind, but better built and cleaner than usual. The side-room doors were neatly paneled, though all the lumber had been nibbled into shape with a small narrow Indian adze. We had our tent pitched on a grassy spot near the beach, being afraid of wee beasties; which greatly offended Kadachan and old Toyatte, who said, "If this is the way you are to do up at Chilcat, we will be ashamed of you." We promised them to eat Indian food and in every way behave like good Chilcats.

We set out direct for Chilcat in the morning against a brisk headwind. By keeping close inshore and working hard, we made about ten miles by two or three o'clock, when, the tide having turned against us, we could make scarce any headway, and therefore landed in a sheltered cove a few miles up the west side of Lynn Canal. Here I discovered a fine growth of yellow cedar, but none of the trees were very large, the tallest only seventy-five to one hundred feet high. The flat, drooping, plumelike branchlets hang edgewise, giving the trees a thin, open, airy look. Nearly every tree that I saw in a long walk was more or less marked by the knives and axes of the Indians, who use the bark for matting, for covering house roofs, and making temporary portable huts. For this last purpose, sections five or six feet long and two or three wide are pressed flat and secured from warping or splitting by binding them with thin strips of wood at the end. These they carry about with them in their canoes, and in a few minutes they can be put together against slim poles and made into a rainproof hut. Every paddle that I have seen along the coast is made of the light, tough, handsome yellow wood of this tree. It is a tree of moderately rapid growth and usually chooses ground that is rather boggy and mossy. Whether its network of roots makes the bog or not, I am unable as yet to say.

Three glaciers on the opposite side of the canal were in sight, descending nearly to sea level, and many smaller ones that melt a little below timberline. While I was sketching these, a canoe hove in sight, coming on at a flying rate of speed before the wind. The owners, eager for news, paid us a visit. They proved to be Hoonas, a man, his wife, and four children, on their way home from Chilcat. The man was sitting in the stern steering and holding a sleeping child in his arms. Another lay asleep at his feet. He told us that Sitka Jack had gone up to the main Chilcat village the day before he left, intending to hold a grand feast and potlatch, and that whiskey up there was flowing like water. The news was rather depressing to Mr. Young and myself, for we feared the effect of the poison on Toyatte's old enemies. At 8.30 P.M. we set out again on the turn of the tide, though the crew did not relish this night work. Naturally enough, they liked to stay in camp when wind and tide were against us, but didn't care to make up lost time after dark however wooingly wind and tide might flow and blow. Kadachan, John, and Charley rowed, and Toyatte steered and paddled, assisted now and then by me. The wind moderated and almost died away, so that we made about fifteen miles in six hours, when the tide turned and snow began to fall. We ran into a bay nearly opposite Berner's Bay, where three or four families of Chilcats were camped who shouted when they heard us landing and demanded our names. Our men ran to the huts for news before making camp. The Indians proved to be hunters, who said there were plenty of wild sheep on the mountains back a few miles from the head of the bay. This interview was held at three o'clock in the morning, a rather early hour. But Indians never resent any such disturbance provided there is anything worthwhile to be said or done. By four o'clock we had our tents set, a fire made and some coffee, while the snow was falling fast. Toyatte was out of humor with this night business. He wanted to land an hour or two before we did, and then, when the snow began to fall and we all wanted to find a camping ground as soon as possible, he steered out into the middle of the canal, saying grimly that the tide was good. He turned, however, at our orders, but read us a lecture at the first opportunity, telling us to start early if we were in a hurry, but not to travel in the night like thieves.

After a few hours' sleep, we set off again, with the wind still against us and the sea rough. We were all tired after making only about twelve miles, and camped in a rocky nook where we found a family of Hoonas in their bark hut beside their canoe. They presented us with potatoes and salmon and a big bucketful of berries, salmon roe, and grease of some sort, probably fish oil, which the crew consumed with wonderful relish.

A fine breeze was blowing next morning from the south, which would take us to Chilcat in a few hours, but unluckily the day was Sunday and the good wind was refused. Sunday, it seemed to me, could be kept as well by sitting in the canoe and letting the Lord's wind waft us quietly on our way. The day was rainy and the clouds hung low. The trees here are remarkably well developed, tall and straight. I observed three or four hemlocks which had been struck by lightning—the first I noticed in Alaska. Some of the species on windy outjutting rocks become very picturesque, almost as much so as old oaks, the foliage becoming dense and the branchlets tufted in heavy plume-shaped horizontal masses.

Monday was a fine clear day, but the wind was dead ahead, making hard, dull work with paddles and oars. We passed a long stretch of beautiful marble cliffs enlivened with small merry waterfalls, and toward noon came in sight of the front of the famous Chilcat or Davidson Glacier, a broad white flood reaching out two or three miles into the canal with wonderful effect. I wanted to camp beside it but the head wind tired us out before we got within six or eight miles of it. We camped on the west side of a small rocky island in a narrow cove. When I was looking among the rocks and bushes for a smooth spot for a bed, I found a human skeleton. My Indians seemed not in the least shocked or surprised, explaining that it was only the remains of a Chilcat slave. Indians never bury or burn the bodies of slaves, but just cast them away anywhere. Kind Nature was covering the poor bones with moss and leaves, and I helped in the pitiful work.

The wind was fair and joyful in the morning, and away we glided to the famous glacier. In an hour or so we were directly in front of it and beheld it in all its crystal glory descending from its white mountain fountains and spreading out in an immense fan three or four miles wide against its tree-fringed terminal moraine. But, large as it is, it long ago ceased to discharge bergs.

The Chilcats are the most influential of all the Thlinkit tribes. Whenever on our journey I spoke of the interesting characteristics of other tribes we had visited, my crew would invariably say, "Oh, yes, these are pretty good Indians, but wait till you have seen the Chilcats." We were now only five or six miles distant from their lower village, and my crew requested time to prepare themselves to meet their great rivals. Going ashore on the moraine with their boxes that had not been opened since we left Fort Wrangell, they sat on boulders and cut each other's hair, carefully washed and perfumed themselves and made a complete change in their clothing, even to white shirts, new boots, new hats, and bright neckties. Meanwhile, I scrambled across the broad, brushy, forested moraine, and on my return scarcely recognized my crew in their dress suits. Mr. Young also made some changes in his clothing, while I, having nothing dressy in my bag, adorned my cap with an eagle's feather I found on the moraine, and thus arrayed we set forth to meet the noble Thlinkits.

We were discovered while we were several miles from the village, and as we entered the mouth of the river we were hailed by a messenger from the chief, sent to find out who we were and the objects of our extraordinary visit.

"Who are you?" he shouted in a heavy, far-reaching voice. "What are your names? What do you want? What have you come for?"

On receiving replies, he shouted the information

to another messenger, who was posted on the river-bank at a distance of a quarter of a mile or so, and he to another and another in succession, and by this living telephone the news was delivered to the chief as he sat by his fireside. A salute was then fired to welcome us, and a swarm of musket bullets, flying scarce high enough for comfort, pinged over our heads. As soon as we reached the landing at the village, a dignified young man stepped forward and thus addressed us—

"My chief sent me to meet you, and to ask if you would do him the honor to lodge in his house during your stay in our village?"

We replied, of course, that we would consider it a great honor to be entertained by so distinguished a chief.

The messenger then ordered a number of slaves, who stood behind him, to draw our canoe out of the water, carry our provisions and bedding into the chief's house, and then carry the canoe back from the river where it would be beyond the reach of floating ice. While we waited, a lot of boys and girls were playing on a meadow near the landing—running races, shooting arrows, and wading in the icy river without showing any knowledge of our presence beyond quick stolen glances. After all was made secure, he conducted us to the house, where we found seats of honor prepared for us.

The old chief sat barefooted by the fireside, clad in a calico shirt and blanket, looking down, and though we shook hands as we passed him he did not look up. After we were seated, he still gazed into the fire without taking the slightest notice of us for about ten or fifteen minutes. The various members of the chief's family, also—men, women, and children—went about

their usual employment and play as if entirely unconscious that strangers were in the house, it being considered impolite to look at visitors or speak to them
before time had been allowed them to collect their
thoughts and prepare any message they might have
to deliver.

At length, after the politeness period had passed,
the chief slowly raised his head and glanced at his visitors, looked down again, and at last said, through our
interpreter—

"I am troubled. It is customary when strangers
visit us to offer them food in case they might be hungry, and I was about to do so, when I remembered that
the food of you honorable white chiefs is so much better than mine that I am ashamed to offer it."

We, of course, replied that we would consider it a
great honor to enjoy the hospitality of so distinguished
a chief as he was.

Hearing this, he looked up, saying, "I feel relieved;"
or, in John the interpreter's words, "He feels good now,
he says he feels good."

He then ordered one of his family to see that the
visitors were fed. The young man who was to act as
steward took up his position in a corner of the house
commanding a view of all that was going on, and
ordered the slaves to make haste to prepare a good
meal; one to bring a lot of the best potatoes from the
cellar and wash them well; another to go out and pick
a basketful of fresh berries; another to broil a salmon;
while others made a suitable fire, pouring oil on the
wet wood to make it blaze. Speedily the feast was prepared and passed around. The first course was potatoes, the second fish oil and salmon, next berries and
rose hips; then the steward shouted the important

news, in a loud voice like a herald addressing an army, "That's all!" and left his post.

Then followed all sorts of questions from the old chief. He wanted to know what Professor Davidson had been trying to do a year or two ago on a mountaintop back of the village, with many strange things looking at the sun when it grew dark in the daytime; and we had to try to explain eclipses. He asked us if we could tell him what made the water rise and fall twice a day, and we tried to explain that the sun and moon attracted the sea by showing how a magnet attracted iron.

Mr. Young, as usual, explained the object of his visit and requested that the people might be called together in the evening to hear his message. Accordingly all were told to wash, put on their best clothing, and come at a certain hour. There was an audience of about two hundred and fifty, to whom Mr. Young preached. Toyatte led in prayer, while Kadachan and John joined in the singing of several hymns. At the conclusion of the religious exercises the chief made a short address of thanks, and finished with a request for the message of the other chief. I again tried in vain to avoid a speech by telling the interpreter to explain that I was only traveling to see the country, the glaciers, and mountains and forests, etc., but these subjects, strange to say, seemed to be about as interesting as the gospel, and I had to deliver a sort of lecture on the fine foodful country God had given them and the brotherhood of man, along the same general lines I had followed at other villages. Some five similar meetings were held here, two of them in the daytime, and we began to feel quite at home in the big blockhouse with our hospitable and warlike friends.

At the last meeting an old white-haired shaman of

grave and venerable aspect, with a high wrinkled fore-head, big, strong Roman nose and light-colored skin, slowly and with great dignity arose and spoke for the first time.

"I am an old man," he said, "but I am glad to listen to those strange things you tell, and they may well be true, for what is more wonderful than the flight of birds in the air? I remember the first white man I ever saw. Since that long, long-ago time I have seen many, but never until now have I ever truly known and felt a white man's heart. All the white men I have heretofore met wanted to get something from us. They wanted furs and they wished to pay for them as small a price as possible. They all seemed to be seeking their own good—not our good. I might say that through all my long life I have never until now heard a white man speak. It has always seemed to me while trying to speak to traders and those seeking gold mines that it was like speaking to a person across a broad stream that was running fast over stones and making so loud a noise that scarce a single word could be heard. But now, for the first time, the Indian and the white man are on the same side of the river, eye to eye, heart to heart. I have always loved my people. I have taught them and ministered to them as well as I could. Here-after, I will keep silent and listen to the good words of the missionaries, who know God and the places we go to when we die so much better than I do."

At the close of the exercises, after the last ser-mon had been preached and the last speech of the Indian chief and headmen had been made, a number of the sub-chiefs were talking informally together. Mr. Young, anxious to know what impression he had made on the tribe with reference to mission work, requested

John to listen and tell him what was being said.

"They are talking about Mr. Muir's speech," he reported. "They say he knows how to talk and beats the preacher far." Toyatte also, with a teasing smile, said: "Mr. Young, mika tillicum hi yu tola wawa" (your friend leads you far in speaking).

Later, when the sending of a missionary and teacher was being considered, the chief said they wanted me, and, as an inducement, promised that if I would come to them they would always do as I directed, follow my councils, give me as many wives as I liked, build a church and school, and pick all the stones out of the paths and make them smooth for my feet.

They were about to set out on an expedition to the Hootsenoos to collect blankets as indemnity or blood money for the death of a Chilcat woman from drinking whiskey furnished by one of the Hootsenoo tribe. In case of their refusal to pay, there would be fighting, and one of the chiefs begged that we would pray them good luck, so that no one would be killed. This he asked as a favor, after begging that we would grant permission to go on this expedition, promising that they would avoid bloodshed if possible. He spoke in a very natural and easy tone and manner always serene and so much of a polished diplomat that all polish was hidden. The younger chief stood while speaking, the elder sat on the floor. None of the congregation had a word to say, though they gave approving nods and shrugs.

The house was packed at every meeting, two a day. Some climbed on the roof to listen around the smoke opening. I tried in vain to avoid speechmaking, but, as usual, I had to say something at every meeting. I made five speeches here, all of which seemed to be gladly heard, particularly what I said on the different kinds of white men and their motives, and their own kindness and good manners in making strangers feel at home in their houses.

The chief had a slave, a young and good-looking girl, who waited on him, cooked his food, lighted his pipe for him, etc. Her servitude seemed by no means galling. In the morning, just before we left on the return trip, interpreter John overheard him telling her that after the teacher came from Wrangell, he was going to dress her well and send her to school and use her in every way as if she were his own daughter. Slaves are still owned by the richest of the Thlinkits. Formerly, many of them were sacrificed on great occasions, such as the opening of a new house or the erection of a totem pole. Kadachan ordered John to take a pair of white blankets out of his trunk and wrap them about the chief's shoulders, as he sat by the fire. This gift was presented without ceremony or saying a single word. The chief scarcely noticed the blankets, only taking a corner in his hand, as if testing the quality of the wool. Toyatte had been an inveterate enemy and fighter of the Chilcats, but now, having joined the church, he wished to forget the past and bury all the hard feuds and be universally friendly and peaceful. It was evident, however, that he mistrusted the proud and warlike Chilcats and doubted the acceptance of his friendly advances, and as we approached their village became more and more thoughtful.

"My wife said that my old enemies would be sure to kill me. Well, never mind. I am an old man and may as well die as not." He was troubled with palpitation, and oftentimes, while he suffered, he put his hand over his heart and said, "I hope the Chilcats will shoot me here."

Before venturing up the river to the principal village, located some ten miles up the river, we sent Sitka Charley and one of the young Chilcats as messengers to announce our arrival and inquire whether we would be welcome to visit them, informing the chief that both Kadachan and Toyatte were Mr. Young's friends and mine, that we were "all one meat" and any harm done them would also be done to us.

While our messengers were away, I climbed a pure white, dome-crowned mountain about fifty-five hundred feet high and gained noble telling views to the northward of the main Chilcat glaciers and the multitude of mighty peaks from which they draw their sources. At a height of three thousand feet I found a mountain hemlock, considerably dwarfed, in company with Sitka spruce and the common hemlock, the tallest about twenty feet high, sixteen inches in diameter. A few stragglers grew considerably higher, say at about four thousand feet. Birch and two-leaf pine were common.

The messengers returned next day, bringing back word that we would all be heartily welcomed excepting Toyatte; that the guns were loaded and ready to be fired to welcome us, but that Toyatte, having insulted a Chilcat chief not long ago in Wrangell, must not come. They also informed us in their message that they were very busy merrymaking with other visitors, Sitka Jack and his friends, but that if we could get up to the village through the running ice on the river, they would all be glad to see us; they had been drinking and Kadachan's father, one of the principal chiefs, said plainly that he had just waked up out of a ten days' sleep. We were anxious to make this visit, but, taking the difficulties and untoward circumstances into account, the danger of being frozen in at so late a time, while Kadachan would not be able to walk back on account of a shot in his foot, the danger also from whiskey, the awakening of old feuds on account of Toyatte's presence, etc., we reluctantly concluded to start back on the home journey at once. This was on Friday and a fair wind was blowing, but our crew, who loved dearly to rest and eat in these big hospitable houses, all said that Monday would be *hyas klosh* for the starting day. I insisted, however, on starting Saturday morning, and succeeded in getting away from our friends at ten o'clock. Just as we were leaving, the chief who had entertained us so handsomely requested a written document to show that he had not killed us, so in case we were lost on the way home he could not be held accountable in any way for our death.

12

THE RETURN TO FORT WRANGELL

The day of our start for Wrangell was bright and the Hoon, the north wind, strong. We passed around the east side of the larger island which lies near the south extremity of the point of land between the Chilcat and the Chilcoot channels and thence held a direct course down the east shore of the canal. At sunset we encamped in a small bay at the head of a beautiful harbor three or four miles south of Berner's Bay, and the next day, being Sunday, we remained in camp as usual, though the wind was fair and it is not a sin to go home. The Indians spent most of the day in washing, mending, eating, and singing hymns with Mr. Young, who also gave them a Bible lesson, while I wrote notes and sketched. Charley made a sweathouse and all the crew got good baths. This is one of the most delightful little bays we have thus far enjoyed, girdled with tall trees whose branches almost meet, and with views of pure-white mountains across the broad, riverlike canal.

Seeing smoke back in the dense woods, we went ashore to seek it and discovered a Hootsenoo whiskey-factory in full blast. The Indians said that an old man, a friend of theirs, was about to die and they were making whiskey for his funeral.

Our Indians were already out of oily flesh, which they regard as a necessity and consume in enormous quantities. The bacon was nearly gone and they eagerly inquired for flesh at every camp we passed. Here we found skinned carcasses of porcupines and a heap of wild mutton lying on the confused hut floor. Our cook boiled the porcupines in a big pot with a lot of potatoes we obtained at the same hut, and although the potatoes were protected by their skins, the awfully wild penetrating porcupine flavor found a way through the skins and flavored them to the very heart. Bread and beans and dried fruit we had in abundance, and none of these rank aboriginal dainties ever came nigh any meal of mine. The Indians eat the hips of wild roses entire like berries, and I was laughed at for eating only the outside of this fruit and rejecting the seeds.

When we were approaching the village of the Auk tribe, venerable Toyatte seemed to be unusually pensive, as if weighed down by some melancholy thought. This was so unusual that I waited attentively to find out the cause of his trouble.

When at last he broke silence it was to say, "Mr. Young, Mr. Young,"—he usually repeated the name—"I hope you will not stop at the Auk village."

"Why, Toyatte?" asked Mr. Young.

"Because they are a bad lot, and preaching to them can do no good."

"Toyatte," said Mr. Young, "have you forgotten what Christ said to his disciples when he charged them to go forth and preach the gospel to everybody; and that we should love our enemies and do good to those who use us badly?"

"Well," replied Toyatte, "if you preach to them, you

must not call on me to pray, because I cannot pray for Auks."

"But the Bible says we should pray for all men, however bad they may be."

"Oh, yes, I know that, Mr. Young; I know it very well. But Auks are not men, good or bad—they are dogs."

It was now nearly dark and quite so ere we found a harbor, not far from the fine Auk Glacier which descends into the narrow channel that separates Douglas Island from the mainland. Two of the Auks followed us to our camp after eight o'clock and inquired into our object in visiting them, that they might carry the news to their chief. One of the chief's houses is opposite our camp a mile or two distant, and we concluded to call on him next morning.

I wanted to examine the Auk Glacier in the morning, but tried to be satisfied with a general view and sketch as we sailed around its wide fan-shaped front. It is one of the most beautiful of all the coast glaciers that are in the first stage of decadence. We called on the Auk chief at daylight, when he was yet in bed, but he arose good-naturedly, put on a calico shirt, drew a blanket around his legs, and comfortably seated himself beside a small fire that gave light enough to show his features and those of his children and the three women that one by one came out of the shadows. All listened attentively to Mr. Young's message of goodwill. The chief was a serious, sharp-featured, dark-complexioned man, sensible-looking and with good manners. He was very sorry, he said, that his people had been drinking in his absence and had used us so ill; he would like to hear us talk and would call his people together if we would return to the village. This offer we had to decline. We gave him good words and tobacco and bade him good-bye.

The scenery all through the channel is magnificent, something like Yosemite Valley in its lofty avalanche-swept wall cliffs, especially on the mainland side, which are so steep few trees can find footing. The lower island side walls are mostly forested. The trees are heavily draped with lichens, giving the woods a remarkably gray, ancient look. I noticed a good many two-leafed pines in boggy spots. The water was smooth, and the reflections of the lofty walls striped with cascades were charmingly distinct.

It was not easy to keep my crew full of wild flesh. We called at an Indian summer camp on the mainland about noon, where there were three very squalid huts crowded and jammed full of flesh of many colors and smells, among which we discovered a lot of bright fresh trout, lovely creatures about fifteen inches long, their sides adorned with vivid red spots. We purchased five of them and a couple of salmon for a box of gun caps and a little tobacco. About the middle of the afternoon we passed through a fleet of icebergs, their number increasing as we neared the mouth of the Taku Fjord, where we camped, hoping to explore the fjord and see the glaciers where the bergs, the first we had seen since leaving Icy Bay, are derived.

We left camp at six o'clock, nearly an hour before daybreak. My Indians were glad to find the fjord barred by a violent wind, against which we failed to make any headway; and as it was too late in the season to wait for better weather, I reluctantly gave up this promising work for another year, and directed the crew to go straight ahead down the coast. We sailed across the mouth of the happy inlet at fine speed, keeping a man at the bow to look out for the smallest of the bergs, not easily seen in the dim light, and another bailing the canoe as the tops of some of the white caps broke over us. About two o'clock we passed a large bay or fjord, out of which a violent wind was blowing, though the main Stephens Passage was calm. About dusk, when we were all tired and anxious to get into camp, we reached the mouth of Sum Dum Bay, but nothing like a safe landing could we find. Our experienced captain was indignant, as well he might be, because we did not see fit to stop early in the afternoon at a good campground he had chosen. He seemed determined to give us enough of night sailing as a punishment to last us for the rest of the voyage. Accordingly, though the night was dark and rainy and the bay full of icebergs, he pushed grimly on, saying that we must try to reach an Indian village on the other side of the bay or an old Indian fort on an island in the middle of it. We made slow, weary, anxious progress while Toyatte, who was well acquainted with every feature of this part of the coast and could find his way in the dark, only laughed at our misery. After a mile or two of this dismal night work we struck across toward the island, now invisible, and came near being wrecked on a rock which showed a smooth round back over which the waves were breaking. In the hurried Indian shouts that followed and while we were close against the rock, Mr. Young shouted, as he leaned over against me, "It's a whale, a whale!" evidently fearing its tail, several specimens of these animals, which were probably still on his mind, having been seen in the forenoon. While we were passing along the east shore of the island, we saw a light on the opposite shore, a joyful sight, which Toyatte took for a fire in the Indian village, and steered for it. John stood in the bow, as guide through the bergs. Suddenly, we ran aground on a sand bar. Clearing this, and running back half a mile or so, we again stood for the light, which now shone brightly. I thought it strange that Indians should have so large a fire. A broad white mass dimly visible back of the fire Mr. Young took for the glow of the fire on the clouds. This proved to be the front of a glacier. After we had effected a landing and stumbled up toward the fire over a ledge of slippery, algae-covered rocks, and through the ordinary tangle of shore grass, we were astonished to find white men instead of Indians, the first we had seen for a month. They proved to be a party of seven gold-seekers from Fort Wrangell. It was now about eight o'clock and they were in bed, but a jolly Irishman got up to make coffee for us and find out who we were, where we had come from, where going, and the objects of our travels. We unrolled our chart and asked for information as to the extent and features of the bay. But our benevolent friend took great pains to pull wool over our eyes, and made haste to say that if "ice and sceneries" were what we were looking for, this was a very poor, dull place. There were "big rocks, gulches, and sceneries" of a far better quality down the coast on the way to Wrangell. He and his party were prospecting, he said, but thus far they had found only a few colors and they proposed going over to Admiralty Island in the morning to try their luck.

In the morning, however, when the prospectors were to have gone over to the island, we noticed a smoke half a mile back on a large stream, the outlet of the glacier we had seen the night before, and an Indian told us that the white men were building a big log house up there. It appeared that they had found a promising placer mine in the moraine and feared we might find it and spread the news. Daylight revealed a magnificent fjord that brought Glacier Bay to mind. Miles of bergs lay stranded on the shores, and the waters of the branch fjords, not on Vancouver's chart, were crowded with them as far as the eye could reach. After breakfast we set out to explore an arm of the bay that trends southeastward, and managed to force a way through the bergs about ten miles. Farther we could not go. The pack was so close no open water was in sight, and, convinced at last that this part of my work would have to be left for another year, we struggled across to the west side of the fjord and camped.

I climbed a mountain next morning, hoping to gain a view of the great fruitful glaciers at the head of the fjord or, at least, of their snowy fountains. But in this also I failed; for at a distance of about sixteen miles from the mouth of the fjord a change to the northward in its general trend cut off all its upper course from sight.

Returning to camp baffled and weary, I ordered all hands to pack up and get out of the ice as soon as possible. And how gladly was that order obeyed! Toyatte's grand countenance glowed like a sun-filled glacier, as he joyfully and teasingly remarked that "the big Sum Dum ice mountain had hidden his face from me and refused to let me pay him a visit." All the crew worked hard boring a way down the west side of the fjord, and early in the afternoon we reached comparatively open water near the mouth of the bay. Resting a few minutes among the drifting bergs, taking last lingering looks at the wonderful place I might never see again, and feeling sad over my weary failure to explore it, I was cheered by a friend I little expected to meet here. Suddenly, I heard the familiar whir of an ousel's wings, and, looking up, saw my little comforter coming straight from the shore. In a second or two he was with me, and flew three times around my head with a happy salute, as if saying, "Cheer up, old friend, you see I am here and all's well." He then flew back to the shore, alighted on the topmost jag of a stranded iceberg, and began to nod and bow as though he were on one of his favorite rocks in the middle of a sunny California mountain cataract.

Mr. Young regretted not meeting the Indians here, but mission work also had to be left until next season. Our happy crew hoisted sail to a fair wind, shouted "Good-bye, Sum Dum!" and soon after dark reached a harbor a few miles north of Hobart Point.

We made an early start the next day, a fine, calm morning, glided smoothly down the coast, admiring the magnificent mountains arrayed in their winter robes, and early in the afternoon reached a lovely harbor on an island five or six miles north of Cape Fanshawe. Toyatte predicted a heavy winter storm, though only a mild rain was falling as yet. Everybody was tired and hungry, and as the voyage was nearing the end, I consented to stop here. While the shelter tents were being set up and our blankets stowed under cover, John went out to hunt and killed a deer within two hundred yards of the camp. When we were at the campfire in Sum Dum Bay, one of the prospectors, replying to Mr. Young's complaint that they were oftentimes out of meat, asked Toyatte why he and his men did not shoot plenty of ducks for the minister. "Because the duck's friend would not let us," said Toyatte; "when we want to shoot, Mr. Muir always shakes the canoe."

Just as we were passing the south headland of Port Houghton Bay, we heard a shout, and a few minutes later saw four Indians in a canoe paddling rapidly after us. In about an hour they overtook us. They were an Indian, his son, and two women with a load of fish oil and dried salmon to sell and trade at Fort Wrangell. They camped within a dozen yards of us; with their sheets of cedar bark and poles they speedily made a hut, spread spruce boughs in it for a carpet, unloaded the canoe, and stored their goods under cover. Toward evening the old man came smiling with a gift for Toyatte—a large fresh salmon, which was promptly boiled and eaten by our captain and crew as if it were only a light refreshment like a biscuit between meals. A few minutes after the big salmon had vanished, our generous neighbor came to Toyatte with a second gift of dried salmon, which after being toasted a few minutes tranquilly followed the fresh one as though it were a mere mouthful. Then, from the same generous hands, came a third gift—a large milkpanful of huckleberries and grease boiled together—and, strange to say, this wonderful mess went smoothly down to rest on the broad and deep salmon foundation. Thus refreshed, and appetite sharpened, my sturdy crew made haste to begin on the buck, beans, bread, etc., and, boiling and roasting, managed to get comfortably full on but little more than half of it by sundown, making a good deal of sport of my pity for the deer and refusing to eat any of it and nicknaming me the ice *ancou* and the deer and duck's *tillicum*.

Sunday was a wild, driving, windy day with but little rain but big promise of more. I took a walk back in the woods. The timber here is very fine, about as large as any I have seen in Alaska, much better than farther north. The Sitka spruce and the common hemlock, one hundred and fifty and two hundred feet high, are slender and handsome. The Sitka spruce makes good firewood even when green, the hemlock very poor. Back a little way from the sea, there was a good deal of yellow cedar, the best I had yet seen. The largest specimen that I saw and measured on the trip was five feet three inches in diameter and about one hundred and forty feet high. In the evening Mr. Young gave the Indians a lesson, calling in our Indian neighbors. He told them the story of Christ coming to save the world. The Indians wanted to know why the Jews had killed him. The lesson was listened to with very marked attention. Toyatte's generous friend caught a devilfish about three feet in diameter to add to his stores of food. It would be very good, he said, when boiled in berry and colicon-oil soup. Each arm of this savage animal with its double row of button-like suction discs closed upon any object brought within reach with a grip nothing could escape. The Indians tell me that devilfish live mostly on crabs, mussels, and clams, the shells of which they easily crunch with their strong, parrotlike beaks. That was a wild, stormy, rainy night. How the rain soaked us in our tents!

"Just feel that," said the minister in the night, as he took my hand and plunged it into a pool about three inches deep in which he was lying.

"Never mind," I said, "it is only water. Everything is wet now. It will soon be morning and we will dry at the fire."

Our Indian neighbors were, if possible, still wetter. Their hut had been blown down several times during the night. Our tent leaked badly, and we were lying in a mossy bog, but around the big campfire we were soon warm and half dry. We had expected to reach Wrangell by this time. Toyatte said the storm might last several days longer. We were out of tea and coffee, much to Mr. Young's distress. On my return from a walk I brought in a good big bunch of glandular ledum and boiled it in the teapot. The result of this experiment was a bright, clear amber-colored, rank-smelling liquor which I did not taste, but my suffering companion drank the whole potful and praised it. The rain was so heavy we decided not to attempt to leave camp until the storm somewhat abated, as we were assured by Toyatte that we would not be able to round Cape Fanshawe, a sheer, outjutting headland, the nose as he called it, past which the wind sweeps with great violence in these southeastern storms. With what grateful enthusiasm the trees welcomed the life-giving rain! Strong, towering spruces, hemlocks, and cedars tossed their arms, bowing, waving, in every leap, quivering and rejoicing together in the gray, roaring storm. John and Charley put on their gun coats and went hunting for another deer, but returned later in the afternoon with clean hands, having fortunately failed to shed any more blood. The wind still held in the south, and Toyatte, grimly trying to comfort us, told us that we might be held here a week or more, which we should not have minded much, for we had abundance of provisions. Mr. Young and I shifted our tent and tried to dry blankets. The wind moderated considerably, and at 7 A.M. we started but met a rough sea and so stiff a wind we barely succeeded in rounding the cape by all hands pulling their best. Thence we struggled down the coast, creeping close to the shore and taking advantage of the shelter of protecting rocks, making slow, hard-won progress until about the middle of the afternoon, when the sky opened and the blessed sun shone out over the beautiful waters and forests with

rich amber light; and the high, glacier-laden mountains, adorned with fresh snow, slowly came to view
in all their grandeur, the bluish-gray clouds crawling
and lingering and dissolving until every vestige of
them vanished. The sunlight made the upper snow-
fields pale, creamy yellow, like that seen on the Chilcat mountains the first day of our return trip. Shortly
after the sky cleared, the wind abated and changed
around to the north, so that we ventured to hoist our
sail, and then the weary Indians had rest. It was interesting to note how speedily the heavy swell that had
been rolling for the last two or three days was subdued
by the comparatively light breeze from the opposite
direction. In a few minutes the sound was smooth and
no trace of the storm was left, save the fresh snow and
the discoloration of the water. All the water of the
sound as far as I noticed was pale coffee color like that
of the streams in boggy woods. How much of this color
was due to the inflow of the flooded streams many
times increased in size and number by the rain, and
how much to the beating of the waves along the shore
stirring up vegetable matter in shallow bays, I cannot
determine. The effect, however, was very marked.

About four o'clock we saw smoke on the shore and
ran in for news. We found a company of Taku Indians, who were on their way to Fort Wrangell, some
six men and about the same number of women. The
men were sitting in a bark hut, handsomely reinforced
and embowered with fresh spruce boughs. The women
were out at the side of a stream, washing their many
bits of calico. A little girl, six or seven years old, was
sitting on the gravelly beach, building a playhouse of
white quartz pebbles, scarcely caring to stop her work
to gaze at us. Toyatte found a friend among the men,

and wished to encamp beside them for the night, assuring us that this was the only safe harbor to be found within a good many miles. But we resolved to push on a little farther and make use of the smooth weather after being stormbound so long, much to Toyatte and his companion's disgust. We rowed about a couple of miles and ran into a cozy cove where wood and water were close at hand. How beautiful and homelike it was! Plushy moss for mattresses decked with red corner berries, noble spruce standing guard about us and spreading kindly protecting arms. A few ferns, aspidiums, polypodiums, with dewberry vines, coptis, pyrola, leafless huckleberry bushes, and ledum grow beneath the trees. We retired at eight o'clock, and just then Toyatte, who had been attentively studying the sky, presaged rain and another southeaster for the morrow.

The sky was a little cloudy next morning, but the air was still and the water smooth. We all hoped that Toyatte, the old weather prophet, had misread the sky signs. But before reaching Point Vanderpeut the rain began to fall and the dreaded southeast wind to blow, which soon increased to a stiff breeze, next thing to a gale, that lashed the sound into ragged white caps. Cape Vanderpeut is part of the terminal of an ancient glacier that once extended six or eight miles out from the base of the mountains. Three large glaciers that once were tributaries still descend nearly to the sea level, though their fronts are back in narrow fjords, eight or ten miles from the sound. A similar point juts out into the sound five or six miles to the south, while the missing portion is submerged and forms a shoal.

All the cape is forested save a narrow strip about a mile long, composed of large boulders against which the waves beat with loud roaring. A bar of foam a mile or so farther out showed where the waves were breaking on a submerged part of the moraine, and I supposed that we would be compelled to pass around it in deep water, but Toyatte, usually so cautious, determined to cross it, and after giving particular directions, with an encouraging shout every oar and paddle was strained to shoot through a narrow gap. Just at the most critical point a big wave heaved us aloft and dropped us between two huge rounded boulders, where, had the canoe been a foot or two closer to either of them, it must have been smashed. Though I had offered no objection to our experienced pilot's plan, it looked dangerous, and I took the precaution to untie my shoes so they could be quickly shaken off for swimming. But after crossing the bar we were not yet out of danger, for we had to struggle hard to keep from being driven ashore while the waves were beating us broadside on. At length we discovered a little inlet, into which we gladly escaped. A pure-white iceberg, weathered to the form of a cross, stood amid drifts of kelp and the black rocks of the wave-beaten shore in sign of safety and welcome. A good fire soon warmed and dried us into common comfort. Our narrow escape was the burden of conversation as we sat around the fire. Captain Toyatte told us of two similar adventures while he was a strong young man. In both of them his canoe was smashed and he swam ashore out of the surge with a gun in his teeth. He says that if we had struck the rocks he and Mr. Young would have been drowned, all the rest of us probably would have been saved. Then, turning to me, he asked me if I could have made a fire in such a case without matches, and found a way to Wrangell without canoe or food.

We started about daybreak from our blessed white cross harbor, and, after rounding a bluff cape opposite the mouth of Wrangell Narrows, a fleet of icebergs came in sight, and of course I was eager to trace them to their source. Toyatte naturally enough was greatly excited about the safety of his canoe and begged that we should not venture to force a way through the bergs, risking the loss of the canoe and our lives now that we were so near the end of our long voyage.

"Oh, never fear, Toyatte," I replied. "You know we are always lucky—the weather is good. I only want to see the Thunder Glacier for a few minutes, and should the bergs be packed dangerously close, I promise to turn back and wait until next summer."

Thus assured, he pushed rapidly on until we entered the fjord, where we had to go cautiously slow. The bergs were close packed almost throughout the whole extent of the fjord, but we managed to reach a point about two miles from the head—commanding a good view of the down-plunging lower end of the glacier and blue, jagged ice wall. This was one of the most imposing of the first-class glaciers I had as yet seen, and with its magnificent fjord formed a fine triumphant close for our season's ice work. I made a few notes and sketches and turned back in time to escape from the thickest packs of bergs before dark. Then Kadachan was stationed in the bow to guide through the open portion of the mouth of the fjord and across Soutchoi Strait. It was not until several hours after dark that we were finally free from ice. We occasionally encountered stranded packs on the delta, which in the starlight seemed to extend indefinitely in every direction. Our danger lay in breaking the canoe on small bergs hard to see and in getting too near the larger ones that might split or roll over.

"Oh, when will we escape from this ice?" moaned much-enduring old Toyatte.

We ran aground in several places in crossing the Stickeen delta, but finally succeeded in groping our way over muddy shallows before the tide fell, and encamped on the boggy shore of a small island, where we discovered a spot dry enough to sleep on, after tumbling about in a tangle of bushes and mossy logs.

We left our last camp November 21 at daybreak. The weather was calm and bright. Wrangell Island came into view beneath a lovely rosy sky, all the forest down to the water's edge silvery gray with a dusting of snow. John and Charley seemed to be seriously distressed to find themselves at the end of their journey while a portion of the stock of provisions remained uneaten. "What is to be done about it?" they asked, more than half in earnest. The fine, strong, and specious deliberation of Indians was well illustrated on this eventful trip. It was fresh every morning. They all behaved well, however, exerted themselves under tedious hardships without flinching for days or weeks at a time; never seemed in the least nonplussed; were prompt to act in every exigency; good as servants, fellow travelers, and even friends.

We landed on an island in sight of Wrangell and built a big smoky signal fire for friends in town, then set sail, unfurled our flag, and about noon completed our long journey of seven or eight hundred miles. As we approached the town, a large canoeful of friendly Indians came flying out to meet us, cheering and handshaking in lusty Boston fashion. The friends of Mr. Young had intended to come out in a body to welcome him back, but had not had time to complete their arrangements before we landed. Mr. Young was eager for news. I told him there could be no news of importance about a town. We only had real news, drawn from the wilderness. The mail steamer had left Wrangell eight days before, and Mr. Vanderbilt and family had sailed on her to Portland. I had to wait a month for the next steamer, and though I would have liked to go again to Nature, the mountains were locked for the winter and canoe excursions no longer safe.

So I shut myself up in a good garret alone to wait and work. I was invited to live with Mr. Young but concluded to prepare my own food and enjoy quiet work. How grandly long the nights were and short the days! At noon the sun seemed to be about an hour high, the clouds colored like sunset. The weather was rather stormy. North winds prevailed for a week at a time, sending down the temperature to near zero and chilling the vapor of the bay into white reek, presenting a curious appearance as it streamed forward on the wind, like combed wool. At Sitka the minimum was eight degrees plus; at Wrangell, near the storm-throat of the Stickeen, zero. This is said to be the coldest weather ever experienced in southeastern Alaska.

13

ALASKA INDIANS

Looking back on my Alaska travels, I have always been glad that good luck gave me Mr. Young as a companion, for he brought me into confiding contact with the Thlinkit tribes, so that I learned their customs, what manner of men they were, how they lived and loved, fought and played, their morals, religion, hopes and fears, and superstitions, how they resembled and differed in their characteristics from our own and other races. It was easy to see that they differed greatly from the typical American Indian of the interior of this continent. They were doubtless derived from the Mongol stock. Their down-slanting oval eyes, wide cheekbones, and rather thick, outstanding upper lips at once suggest their connection with the Chinese or Japanese. I have not seen a single specimen that looks in the least like the best of the Sioux, or indeed of any of the tribes to the east of the Rocky Mountains. They also differ from other North American Indians in being willing to work, when free from the contamination of bad whites. They manage to feed themselves well, build good substantial houses, bravely fight their enemies, love their wives and children and friends, and cherish a quick sense of honor. The best of them prefer death to dishonor, and sympathize with their neighbors in their misfortunes and sorrows. Thus when a family loses a child by death, neighbors visit them to cheer and console. They gather around the fire and smoke, talk kindly and naturally, telling the sorrowing parents not to grieve too much, reminding them of the better lot of their child in another world and of the troubles and trials the little ones escape by dying young, all this in a perfectly natural, straightforward way, wholly unlike the vacant, silent, hesitating behavior of most civilized friends, who oftentimes in such cases seem nonplussed, awkward, and afraid to speak, however sympathetic.

The Thlinkits are fond and indulgent parents. In all my travels I never heard a cross, fault-finding word, or anything like scolding inflicted on an Indian child, or ever witnessed a single case of spanking, so common in civilized communities. They consider the want of a son to bear their name and keep it alive the saddest and most deplorable ill fortune imaginable.

The Thlinkit tribes give a hearty welcome to Christian missionaries. In particular they are quick to accept the doctrine of the atonement, because they themselves practice it, although to many of the civilized whites it is a stumbling block and rock of offense. As an example of their own doctrine of atonement they told Mr. Young and me one evening that twenty or thirty years ago there was a bitter war between their own and the Sitka tribe, great fighters, and pretty evenly matched. After fighting all summer in a desultory, squabbling way, fighting now under cover, now in the open, watching for every chance for a shot, none of the women dared venture to the salmon streams or berry fields to procure their winter stock of food. At this crisis one of the Stickeen chiefs came out of his blockhouse fort into an open space midway between their fortified camps, and shouted that he wished to speak to the leader of the Sitkas.

When the Sitka chief appeared he said:

"My people are hungry. They dare not go to the salmon streams or berry fields for winter supplies, and if this war goes on much longer most of my people will die of hunger. We have fought long enough; let us make peace. You brave Sitka warriors go home, and we will go home, and we will all set out to dry salmon and berries before it is too late."

The Sitka chief replied:

"You may well say let us stop fighting, when you have had the best of it. You have killed ten more of my tribe than we have killed of yours. Give us ten Stickeen men to balance our blood account; then, and not till then, will we make peace and go home."

"Very well," replied the Stickeen chief, "you know my rank. You know that I am worth ten common men and more. Take me and make peace."

This noble offer was promptly accepted; the Stickeen chief stepped forward and was shot down in sight of the fighting bands. Peace was thus established, and all made haste to their homes and ordinary work. That chief literally gave himself a sacrifice for his people. He died that they might live. Therefore, when missionaries preached the doctrine of atonement, explaining that when all mankind had gone astray, had broken God's laws and deserved to die, God's son came forward, and, like the Stickeen chief, offered himself as a sacrifice to heal the cause of God's wrath and set all the people of the world free, the doctrine was readily accepted.

"Yes, your words are good," they said. "The Son of God, the Chief of chiefs, the Maker of all the world, must be worth more than all mankind put together;

therefore, when His blood was shed, the salvation of the world was made sure."

A telling illustration of the ready acceptance of this doctrine was displayed by Shakes, head chief of the Stickeens at Fort Wrangell. A few years before my first visit to the Territory, when the first missionary arrived, he requested Shakes to call his people together to hear the good word he had brought them. Shakes accordingly sent out messengers throughout the village, telling his people to wash their faces, put on their best clothing, and come to his blockhouse to hear what their visitor had to say. When all were assembled, the missionary preached a Christian sermon on the fall of man and the atonement whereby Christ, the Son of God, the Chief of chiefs, had redeemed all mankind, provided that this redemption was voluntarily accepted with repentance of their sins and the keeping of his commandments.

When the missionary had finished his sermon, Chief Shakes slowly arose, and, after thanking the missionary for coming so far to bring them good tidings and taking so much unselfish interest in the welfare of his tribe, he advised his people to accept the new religion, for he felt satisfied that because the white man knew so much more than the Indian, the white man's religion was likely to be better than theirs.

"The white man," said he, "makes great ships. We, like children, can only make canoes. He makes his big ships go with the wind, and he also makes them go with fire. We chop down trees with stone axes; the Boston man with iron axes, which are far better. In everything the ways of the white man seem to be better than ours. Compared with the white man we are only blind children, knowing not how best to live either here or in the country we go to after we die. So I wish you to learn this new religion and teach it to your children, that you may all go when you die into that good heaven country of the white man and be happy. But I am too old to learn a new religion, and besides, many of my people who have died were bad and foolish people, and if this word the missionary has brought us is true, and I think it is, many of my people must be in that bad country the missionary calls 'Hell,' and I must go there also, for a Stickeen chief never deserts his people in time of trouble. To that bad country, therefore, I will go, and try to cheer my people and help them as best I can to endure their misery."

Toyatte was a famous orator. I was present at the meeting at Fort Wrangell at which he was examined and admitted as a member of the Presbyterian Church. When called upon to answer the questions as to his ideas of God, and the principal doctrines of Christianity, he slowly arose in the crowded audience, while the missionary said, "Toyatte, you do not need to rise. You can answer the questions seated."

To this he paid no attention, but stood several minutes without speaking a word, never for a moment thinking of sitting down like a tired woman while making the most important of all the speeches of his life. He then explained in detail what his mother had taught him as to the character of God, the great Maker of the world; also what the shamans had taught him; the thoughts that often came to his mind when he was alone on hunting expeditions, and what he first thought of the religion which the missionaries had brought them. In all his gestures, and in the language in which he expressed himself, there was a noble simplicity and earnestness and majestic bearing which made the sermons and behavior of the three distinguished divinity doctors present seem commonplace in comparison.

Soon after our return to Fort Wrangell this grand
old man was killed in a quarrel in which he had taken
no other part than that of peacemaker. A number of
the Taku tribe came to Fort Wrangell, camped near the
Stickeen village, and made merry, manufacturing and
drinking *hootchenoo*, a vile liquor distilled from a mash
made of flour, dried apples, sugar, and molasses, and
drunk hot from the still. The manufacture of *hootchenoo*
being illegal, and several of Toyatte's tribe having been
appointed deputy constables to prevent it, they went
to the Taku camp and destroyed as much of the liquor
as they could find. The Takus resisted, and during the
quarrel one of the Stickeens struck a Taku in the face—
an unpardonable offense. The next day messengers from
the Taku camp gave notice to the Stickeens that they
must make atonement for that blow, or fight with guns.
Mr. Young, of course, was eager to stop the quarrel and
so was Toyatte. They advised the Stickeen who had
struck the Taku to return to their camp and submit to
an equal blow in the face from the Taku. He did so; went
to the camp, said he was ready to make atonement, and
invited the person whom he had struck to strike him.
This the Taku did with so much force that the balance of
justice was again disturbed. The attention of the Takus
was called to the fact that this atoning blow was far
harder than the one to be atoned for, and immediately a
sort of general free fistfight began, and the quarrel was
thus increased in bitterness rather than diminished.

Next day the Takus sent word to the Stickeens to get
their guns ready, for tomorrow they would come up and
fight them, thus boldly declaring war. The Stickeens
in great excitement assembled and loaded their guns
for the coming strife. Mr. Young ran hither and thither
amongst the men of his congregation, forbidding them

to fight, reminding them that Christ told them when they were struck to offer the other cheek instead of giving a blow in return, doing everything in his power to still the storm, but all in vain. Toyatte stood outside one of the big blockhouses with his men about him, awaiting the onset of the Takus. Mr. Young tried hard to get him away to a place of safety, reminding him that he belonged to his church and no longer had any right to fight. Toyatte calmly replied:

"Mr. Young, Mr. Young, I am not going to fight. You see I have no gun in my hand; but I cannot go inside of the fort to a place of safety like women and children while my young men are exposed to the bullets of their enemies. I must stay with them and share their dangers, but I will not fight. But you, Mr. Young, you must go away; you are a minister and you are an important man. It would not do for you to be exposed to bullets. Go to your home in the fort; pretty soon 'hi yu poogh'" (much shooting).

At the first fire Toyatte fell, shot through the breast. Thus died for his people the noblest old Roman of them all.

On this first Alaska excursion I saw Toyatte under all circumstances—in rain and snow, landing at night in dark storms, making fires, building shelters, exposed to all kinds of discomfort—but never under any circumstances did I ever see him do anything, or make a single gesture, that was not dignified, or hear him say a word that might not be uttered anywhere. He often deplored the fact that he had no son to take his name at his death, and expressed himself as very grateful when I told him that his name would not be forgotten—that I had named one of the Stickeen glaciers for him.

PART TWO

THE TRIP OF 1880

14

SUM DUM BAY

I arrived early on the morning of the eighth of August on the steamer California to continue my explorations of the fjords to the northward, which were closed by winter the previous November. The noise of our cannon and whistle was barely sufficient to awaken the sleepy town. The morning shout of one good rooster was the only evidence of life and health in all the place. Everything seemed kindly and familiar—the glassy water; evergreen islands; the Indians with their canoes and baskets and blankets and berries; the jet ravens, prying and flying about the streets and spruce trees; and the bland, hushed atmosphere brooding tenderly over all.

How delightful it is, and how it makes one's pulses bound to get back into this reviving northland wilderness! How truly wild it is, and how joyously one's heart responds to the welcome it gives, its waters and mountains shining and glowing like enthusiastic human faces! Gliding along the shores of its network of channels, we may travel thousands of miles without seeing any mark of man, save at long intervals some little Indian village or the faint smoke of a campfire. Even these are confined to the shore. Back a few yards from the beach the forests are as trackless as the sky, while the mountains, wrapped in their snow and ice and clouds, seem never before to have been even looked at.

For those who really care to get into hearty contact with the coast region, travel by canoe is by far the better way. The larger canoes carry from one to three tons, rise lightly over any waves likely to be met on the inland channels, go well under sail, and are easily paddled alongshore in calm weather or against moderate winds, while snug harbors where they may ride at anchor or be pulled up on a smooth beach are to be found almost everywhere. With plenty of provisions packed in boxes, and blankets and warm clothing in rubber or canvas bags, you may be truly independent, and enter into partnership with Nature; to be carried with the winds and currents, accept the noble invitations offered all along your way to enter the mountain fjords, the homes of the waterfalls and glaciers, and encamp almost every night beneath hospitable trees.

I left Fort Wrangell the 16th of August, accompanied by Mr. Young, in a canoe about twenty-five feet long and five wide, carrying two small square sails and manned by two Stickeen Indians—Captain Tyeen and Hunter Joe—and a half-breed named Smart Billy. The day was calm, and bright, fleecy, clouds hung about the lowest of the mountain brows, while far above the clouds the peaks were seen stretching grandly away to the northward with their ice and snow shining in as calm a light as that which was falling on the glassy waters. Our Indians welcomed the work that lay before them, dipping their oars in exact time with hearty goodwill as we glided past island after island across the delta of the Stickeen into Soutchoi Channel.

By noon we came in sight of a fleet of icebergs from

Hutli Bay. The Indian name of this icy fjord is Hutli, or Thunder Bay, from the sound made by the bergs in falling and rising from the front of the inflowing glacier.

As we floated happily on over the shining waters, the beautiful islands, in ever-changing pictures, were an unfailing source of enjoyment; but chiefly our attention was turned upon the mountains. Bold granite headlands with their feet in the channel, or some broad-shouldered peak of surpassing grandeur, would fix the eye, or some one of the larger glaciers, with far-reaching tributaries clasping entire groups of peaks and its great crystal river pouring down through the forest between gray ridges and domes. In these grand picture lessons the day was spent, and we spread our blankets beneath a Menzies spruce on moss two feet deep.

Next morning we sailed around an outcurving bank of boulders and sand ten miles long, the terminal moraine of a grand old glacier on which last November we met a perilous adventure. It is located just opposite three large converging glaciers which formerly united to form the vanished trunk of the glacier to which the submerged moraine belonged. A few centuries ago it must have been the grandest feature of this part of the coast, and, so well preserved are the monuments of its greatness, the noble old ice river may be seen again in imagination about as vividly as if present in the flesh, with snow clouds crawling about its fountains, sunshine sparkling on its broad flood, and its ten-mile ice wall planted in the deep waters of the channel and sending off its bergs with loud resounding thunder.

About noon we rounded Cape Fanshawe, scudding swiftly before a fine breeze, to the delight of our Indians, who had now only to steer and chat. Here we overtook two Hoona Indians and their families on their way home from Fort Wrangell. They had exchanged five sea otter furs, worth about a hundred dollars apiece, and a considerable number of fur seal, land otter, marten, beaver, and other furs and skins, some $800 worth, for a new canoe valued at $80, some flour, tobacco, blankets, and a few barrels of molasses for the manufacture of whiskey. The blankets were not to wear, but to keep as money, for the almighty dollar of these tribes is a Hudson's Bay blanket. The wind died away soon after we met, and as the two canoes glided slowly side by side, the Hoonas made minute inquiries as to who we were and what we were doing so far north. Mr. Young's object in meeting the Indians as a missionary they could in part understand, but mine in searching for rocks and glaciers seemed past comprehension, and they asked our Indians whether gold mines might not be the main object. They remembered, however, that I had visited their Glacier Bay ice mountains a year ago, and seemed to think there might be, after all, some mysterious interest about them of which they were ignorant. Toward the middle of the afternoon they engaged our crew in a race. We pushed a little way ahead for a time, but, though possessing a considerable advantage, as it would seem, in our long oars, they at length overtook us and kept up until after dark, when we camped together in the rain on the bank of a salmon stream among dripping grass and bushes some twenty-five miles beyond Cape Fanshawe.

These cold northern waters are at times about as brilliantly phosphorescent as those of the warm South, and so they were this evening in the rain and darkness, with the temperature of the water at forty-nine degrees, the air fifty-one. Every stroke of the oar made a vivid surge of white light, and the canoes left shining tracks.

As we neared the mouth of the well-known salmon stream where we intended making our camp, we noticed jets and flashes of silvery light caused by the startled movement of the salmon that were on their way to their spawning grounds. These became more and more numerous and exciting, and our Indians shouted joyfully, "Hi yu salmon! Hi yu muck-a-muck!" while the water about the canoe and beneath the canoe was churned by thousands of fins into silver fire. After landing two of our men to commence camp work, Mr. Young and I went up the stream with Tyeen to the foot of a rapid, to see him catch a few salmon for supper. The stream was so filled with them there seemed to be more fish than water in it, and we appeared to be sailing in boiling, seething silver light marvelously relieved in the jet darkness. In the midst of the general auroral glow and the specially vivid flashes made by the frightened fish darting ahead and to right and left of the canoe, our attention was suddenly fixed by a long, steady, comet-like blaze that seemed to be made by some frightful monster that was pursuing us. But when the portentous object reached the canoe, it proved to be only our little dog, Stickeen.

After getting the canoe into a side eddy at the foot of the rapids, Tyeen caught half a dozen salmon in a few minutes by means of a large hook fastened to the end of a pole. They were so abundant that he simply groped for them in a random way, or aimed at them by the light they themselves furnished. That food to last a month or two may thus be procured in less than an hour is a striking illustration of the fruitfulness of these Alaskan waters.

Our Hoona neighbors were asleep in the morning at sunrise, lying in a row, wet and limp like dead salmon. A little boy about six years old, with no other covering than a remnant of a shirt, was lying peacefully on his back, like Tam o' Shanter, despising wind and rain and fire. He is up now, looking happy and fresh, with no clothes to dry and no need of washing while this weather lasts. The two babies are firmly strapped on boards, leaving only their heads and hands free. Their mothers are nursing them, holding the boards on end, while they sit on the ground with their breasts level with the little prisoners' mouths.

This morning we found out how beautiful a nook we had got into. Besides the charming picturesqueness of its lines, the colors about it, brightened by the rain, made a fine study. Viewed from the shore, there was first a margin of dark-brown algae, then a bar of yellowish-brown, next a dark bar on the rugged rocks marking the highest tides, then a bar of granite boulders with grasses in the seams, and above this a thick, bossy, overleaning fringe of bushes colored red and yellow and green. A wall of spruces and hemlocks draped and tufted with gray and yellow lichens and mosses embowered the campground and overarched the little river, while the campfire smoke, like a stranded cloud, lay motionless in their branches. Down on the beach ducks and sandpipers in flocks of hundreds were getting their breakfasts, bald eagles were seen perched on dead spars along the edge of the woods, heavy-looking and overfed, gazing stupidly like gorged vultures, and porpoises were blowing and plunging outside.

As for the salmon, as seen this morning urging their way up the swift current—tens of thousands of them, side by side, with their backs out of the water in shallow places now that the tide was low—nothing that I could write might possibly give anything like a fair conception of the extravagance of their numbers. There was more salmon apparently, bulk for bulk, than water in the stream. The struggling multitudes, crowding one against another, could not get out of our way when we waded into the midst of them. One of our men amused himself by seizing them above the tail and swinging them over his head. Thousands could thus be taken by hand at low tide, while they were making their way over the shallows among the stones.

Whatever may be said of other resources of the Territory, it is hardly possible to exaggerate the importance of the fisheries. Not to mention cod, herring, halibut, etc., there are probably not less than a thousand salmon streams in southeastern Alaska as large or larger than this one (about forty feet wide) crowded with salmon several times a year. The first run commenced that year in July, while the king salmon, one of the five species recognized by the Indians, was in the Chilcat River about the middle of the November before.

From this wonderful salmon camp we sailed joyfully up the coast to explore icy Sum Dum Bay, beginning my studies where I left off the previous November. We started about six o'clock, and pulled merrily on through fog and rain, the beautiful wooded shore on our right, passing bergs here and there, the largest of which, though not over two hundred feet long, seemed many times larger as they loomed gray and indistinct through the fog. For the first five hours the sailing was open and easy, nor was there anything very exciting to be seen or heard, save now and then the thunder of a falling berg rolling and echoing from cliff to cliff, and the sustained roar of cataracts.

About eleven o'clock we reached a point where the fjord was packed with ice all the way across, and we ran ashore to fit a block of wood on the cutwater of our canoe to prevent its being battered or broken. While Captain Tyeen, who had had considerable experience among berg ice, was at work on the canoe, Hunter Joe and Smart Billy prepared a warm lunch.

The sheltered hollow where we landed seems to be a favorite camping ground for the Sum Dum seal hunters. The pole-frames of tents, tied with cedar bark, stood on level spots strewn with seal bones, bits of salmon, and spruce bark.

We found the work of pushing through the ice rather tiresome. An opening of twenty or thirty yards would be found here and there, then a close pack that had to be opened by pushing the smaller bergs aside with poles. I enjoyed the labor, however, for the fine lessons I got, and in an hour or two we found zigzag lanes of water, through which we paddled with but little interruption, and had leisure to study the wonderful variety of forms the bergs presented as we glided past them. The largest we saw did not greatly exceed two hundred feet in length, or twenty-five or thirty feet in height above the water. Such bergs would draw from one hundred and fifty to two hundred feet of water. All those that have floated long undisturbed have a projecting base at the waterline, caused by the more rapid melting of the immersed portion. When a portion of the berg breaks off, another base line is formed, and the old one, sharply cut, may be seen rising at all angles, giving it a marked character. Many of the oldest bergs are beautifully ridged by the melting out of narrow furrows strictly parallel throughout the mass, revealing the bedded structure of the ice, acquired perhaps centuries ago, on the mountain snow fountains. A berg suddenly going to pieces is a grand sight, especially when the water is calm and no motion is visible save perchance the slow drift of the tide current. The prolonged roar of its fall comes with startling effect, and heavy swells are raised that haste away in every direction to tell what has taken place, and tens of thousands of its neighbors rock and swash in sympathy, repeating the news over and over again. We were too near several large ones that fell apart as we passed them, and our canoe had narrow escapes. The seal hunters, Tyeen says, are frequently lost in these sudden berg accidents.

In the afternoon, while we were admiring the scenery, which, as we approached the head of the fjord, became more and more sublime, one of our Indians called attention to a flock of wild goats on a mountain overhead, and soon afterwards we saw two other flocks, at a height of about fifteen hundred feet, relieved against the mountains as white spots. They are abundant here and throughout the Alaskan Alps in general, feeding on the grassy slopes above the timberline. Their long, yellowish hair is shed at this time of year and they were snowy white. None of nature's cattle are better fed or better protected from the cold. Tyeen told us that before the introduction of guns they used to hunt them with spears, chasing them with their wolf-dogs, and thus bringing them to bay among the rocks, where they were easily approached and killed.

The upper half of the fjord is about from a mile to a mile and a half wide, and shut in by sublime Yosemite cliffs, nobly sculptured, and adorned with waterfalls and fringes of trees, bushes, and patches of flowers; but amid so crowded a display of novel beauty it was not easy to concentrate the attention long enough on any portion of it without giving more days and years than our lives could afford. I was determined to see at least the grand fountain of all this ice. As we passed headland after headland, hoping as each was rounded we should obtain a view of it, it still remained hidden.

"Ice mountain hi yu kumtux hide,"—glaciers know how to hide extremely well—said Tyeen, as he rested for a moment after rounding a huge granite shoulder of the wall whence we expected to gain a view of the extreme head of the fjord. The bergs, however, were less closely packed and we made good progress, and at half past eight o'clock, fourteen and a half hours after setting out, the great glacier came in sight at the head of a branch of the fjord that comes in from the northeast.

The discharging front of this fertile, fast-flowing glacier is about three quarters of a mile wide, and probably eight or nine hundred feet deep, about one hundred and fifty feet of its depth rising above the water as a grand blue barrier wall. It is much wider a few miles farther back, the front being jammed between sheer granite walls from thirty-five hundred to four thousand feet high. It shows grandly from where it broke on our sight, sweeping boldly forward and downward in its majestic channel, swaying from side to side in graceful fluent lines around stern, unflinching rocks. While I stood in the canoe making a sketch of it, several bergs came off with tremendous dashing and thunder, raising a cloud of ice dust and spray to a height of a hundred feet or more.

"The ice mountain is well disposed toward you," said Tyeen. "He is firing his big guns to welcome you."

After completing my sketch and entering a few notes, I directed the crew to pull around a lofty burnished rock on the west side of the channel, where, as I knew from the trend of the canyon, a large glacier once came in; and what was my delight to discover that the glacier was still there and still pouring its ice into a branch of the fjord. Even the Indians shared my joy and shouted with me. I expected only one first-class glacier here, and found two. They are only about two miles apart. How glorious a mansion that precious pair dwell in! After sunset we made haste to seek a campground. I would fain have shared these upper chambers with the two glaciers, but there was no landing place in sight, and we had to make our way back a few miles in the twilight to the mouth of a side canyon where we had seen timber on the way up. There seemed to be a good landing as we approached the shore, but, coming nearer, we found that the granite fell directly into deep water without leading any level margin, though the slope a short distance back was not very steep.

After narrowly scanning the various seams and steps that roughened the granite, we concluded to attempt a landing rather than grope our way farther down the fjord through the ice. And what a time we had climbing on hands and knees up the slippery glacier-polished rocks to a shelf some two hundred feet above the water and dragging provisions and blankets after us! But it proved to be a glorious place, the very best campground of all the trip—a perfect garden, ripe berries nodding from a fringe of bushes around its edges charmingly displayed in the light of our big fire. Close alongside there was a lofty mountain capped with ice, and from the blue edge of that ice cap there were sixteen silvery cascades in a row, falling about four thousand feet, each one of the sixteen large enough to be heard at least two miles.

How beautiful was the firelight on the nearest larkspurs and geraniums and daisies of our garden! How hearty the wave greeting on the rocks below brought to us from the two glaciers! And how glorious a song the sixteen cascades sang!

The cascade songs made us sleep all the sounder, and we were so happy as to find in the morning that the berg-waves had spared our canoe. We set off in high spirits down the fjord and across to the right side to explore a remarkably deep and narrow branch of the main fjord that I had noted on the way up, and that, from the magnitude of the glacial characters on the two colossal rocks that guard the entrance, promised a rich reward for our pains.

After we had sailed about three miles up this side fjord, we came to what seemed to be its head, for trees and rocks swept in a curve around from one side to the other without showing any opening, although the walls of the canyon were seen extending back indefinitely, one majestic brow beyond the other.

When we were tracing this curve, however, in a leisurely way, in search of a good landing, we were startled by Captain Tyeen shouting, "Skookum chuck! Skookum chuck!" (strong water, strong water), and found our canoe was being swept sideways by a powerful current, the roar of which we had mistaken for a waterfall. We barely escaped being carried over a rocky bar on the boiling flood, which, as we afterwards learned, would have been only a happy shove on our way. After we had made a landing a little distance back from the brow of the bar, we climbed the highest rock near the shore to seek a view of the channel beyond the inflowing tide rapids, to find out whether or no we could safely venture in. Up over rolling, mossy, bushy, burnished rock waves we scrambled for an hour or two, which resulted in a fair view of the deep-blue waters of the fjord stretching on and on along the feet of the most majestic Yosemite rocks we had yet seen. This determined our plan of shooting the rapids and exploring it to its farthest recesses. This novel interruption of the channel is a bar of exceedingly hard resisting granite, over which the great glacier that once occupied it swept, without degrading it to the general level, and over which tidewaters now rush in and out with the violence of a mountain torrent.

Returning to the canoe, we pushed off, and in a few moments were racing over the bar with lightning speed through hurrahing waves and eddies and sheets of foam, our little shell of a boat tossing lightly as a bubble. Then, rowing across a belt of back-flowing water, we found ourselves on a smooth mirror reach between granite walls of the very wildest and most exciting description, surpassing in some ways those of the far-famed Yosemite Valley.

As we drifted silent and awe-stricken beneath the shadows of the mighty cliffs, which, in their tremendous height and abruptness, seemed to overhang at the top, the Indians gazing intently, as if they, too, were impressed with the strange, awe-inspiring grandeur that shut them in, one of them at length broke the silence by saying, "This must be a good place for woodchucks; I hear them calling."

When I asked them, further on, how they thought this gorge was made, they gave up the question, but offered an opinion as to the formation of rain and soil. The rain, they said, was produced by the rapid whirling of the earth by a stout mythical being called Yek. The water of the ocean was thus thrown up, to descend again in showers, just as it is thrown off a wet grindstone. They did not, however, understand why the ocean water should be salt, while the rain from it is fresh. The soil, they said, for the plants to grow on is formed by the washing of the rain on the rocks and gradually accumulating. The grinding action of ice in this connection they had not recognized.

Gliding on and on, the scenery seemed at every turn to become more lavishly fruitful in forms as well as more sublime in dimensions—snowy falls booming in splendid dress; colossal domes and battle meets and sculptured arches of a fine neutral-gray tint, their bases raved by the blue fjord water; green ferny dells; bits of flower-bloom on ledges; fringes of willow and birch; and glaciers above all. But when we approached the base of a majestic rock like the Yosemite Half Dome at the head of the fjord, where two short branches put out, and came in sight of another glacier of the first order sending off bergs, our joy was complete. I had a most glorious view of it, sweeping in grand majesty from high mountain fountains, swaying around one mighty bastion after another, until it fell into the fjord in shattered overleaning fragments. When we had feasted awhile on this unhoped-for treasure, I directed the Indians to pull to the head of the left fork of the fjord, where we found a large cascade with a volume of water great enough to be called a river, doubtless the outlet of a receding glacier not in sight from the fjord.

This is in form and origin a typical Yosemite valley, though as yet its floor is covered with ice and water—ice above and beneath, a noble mansion in which to spend a winter and a summer! It is about ten miles long, and from three quarters of a mile to one mile wide. It contains ten large falls and cascades, the finest one on the left side near the head. After coming in an admirable rush over a granite brow where it is first seen at a height of nine hundred or a thousand feet, it leaps a sheer precipice of about two hundred and fifty feet, then divides and reaches the tidewater in broken rapids over boulders. Another about a thousand feet high drops at once on to the margin of the glacier two miles back from the front. Several of the others are upwards of three thousand feet high, descending through narrow gorges as richly feathered with ferns as any channel that water ever flowed in, though tremendously abrupt and deep. A grander array of rocks and waterfalls I have never yet beheld in Alaska.

The amount of timber on the walls is about the same as that on the Yosemite walls, but owing to greater moisture, there is more small vegetation—bushes, ferns, mosses, grasses, etc.; though by far the greater portion of the area of the wall surface is bare and shining with the polish it received when occupied by the glacier that formed the fjord. The deep-green patches seen on the mountains back of the walls at the limits of vegetation are grass, where the wild goats, or chamois rather, roam and feed. The still greener and more luxuriant patches farther down in gullies and on slopes where the declivity is not excessive, are made up mostly of willows, birch, and huckleberry bushes, with a varying amount of prickly ribes and rubus and echinopanax. This growth, when approached, especially on the lower slopes near the level of the sea at the jaws of the great side canyons, is found to be the most impenetrable and tedious and toilsome combination of fighting bushes that the weary explorer ever fell into, incomparably more punishing than the buckthorn and manzanita tangles of the Sierra.

The cliff gardens of this hidden Yosemite are exceedingly rich in color. On almost every rift and bench, however small, as well as on the wider table-rocks where a little soil has lodged, we found gay multitudes of flowers, far more brilliantly colored than would be looked for in so cool and beclouded a region— larkspurs, geraniums, painted cups, bluebells, gentians, saxifrages, epilobiums, violets, parnassia, veratrum, spiranthes and other orchids, fritillaria, smilax, asters, daisies, bryanthus, cassiope, linnaea, and a great variety of flowering ribes and rubus and heathworts. Many of the above, though with soft stems and leaves, are yet as brightly painted as those of the warm sunlands of the south. The heathworts in particular are very abundant and beautiful, both in flower and fruit, making delicate green carpets for the rocks, flushed with pink bells, or dotted with red and blue berries. The tallest of the grasses have ribbon leaves well tempered and arched, and with no lack of bristly spikes and nodding purple panicles. The alpine grasses of the Sierra, making close carpets on the glacier meadows, I have not yet seen in Alaska.

The ferns are less numerous in species than in California, but about equal in the number of fronds. I have seen three aspidiums, two woodsias, a lomaria, polypodium, cheilanthes, and several species of pteris.

In this eastern arm of Sum Dum Bay and its Yosemite branch, I counted from my canoe, on my way up and down, thirty small glaciers back of the walls, and we saw three of the first order; also thirty-seven cascades and falls, counting only those large enough to make themselves heard several miles. The whole bay, with its rocks and woods and ice, reverberates with their roar. How many glaciers may be disclosed in the other great arm that I have not seen as yet, I cannot say, but, judging from the bergs it sends down, I guess not less than a hundred pour their turbid streams into the fjord, making about as many joyful, bouncing cataracts.

About noon we began to retrace our way back into the main fjord, and arrived at the gold mine camp after dark, rich and weary.

On the morning of August 21, I set out with my three Indians to explore the right arm of this noble bay, Mr. Young having decided, on account of mission work, to remain at the gold mine. So here is another fine lot of Sum Dum ice—thirty-five or forty square miles of bergs, one great glacier of the first class descending into the fjord at the head, the fountain whence all these bergs were derived, and thirty-one smaller glaciers that do not reach tidewater; also nine cascades and falls, large size, and two rows of Yosemite rocks from three to four thousand feet high, each row about eighteen or twenty miles long, burnished and sculptured in the most telling glacier style, and well trimmed with spruce groves and flower gardens; a' that and more of a kind that cannot here be catalogued.

For the first five or six miles there is nothing excepting the icebergs that is very striking in the scenery as compared with that of the smooth unencumbered outside channels, where all is so evenly beautiful. The mountain wall on the right as you go up is more precipitous than usual, and a series of small glaciers is seen along the top of it, extending their blue-crevassed fronts over the rims of pure-white snow fountains, and from the end of each front a hearty stream coming in a succession of falls and rapids over the terminal moraines, through patches of dwarf willows, and then through the spruce woods into the bay, singing and dancing all the way down. On the opposite side of the bay from here there is a small side bay about three miles deep, with a showy group of glacier-bearing mountains back of it. Everywhere else the view is bounded by comparatively low mountains densely forested to the very top.

After sailing about six miles from the mine, the experienced mountaineer could see some evidence of an opening from this wide lower portion, and on reaching it, it proved to be the continuation of the main west arm, contracted between stupendous walls of gray granite, and crowded with bergs from shore to shore, which seem to bar the way against everything but wings. Headland after headland, in most imposing array, was seen plunging sheer and bare from dizzy heights, and planting its feet in the ice-encumbered water without leaving a spot on which one could land from a boat, while no part of the great glacier that pours all these miles of ice into the fjord was visible. Pushing our way slowly through the packed bergs, and passing headland after headland, looking eagerly forward, the glacier and its fountain mountains were still beyond sight, cut off by other projecting headland capes, toward which I urged my way, enjoying the extraordinary grandeur of the wild unfinished Yosemite. Domes swell against the sky in fine lines as lofty and as perfect in form as those of the California valley, and rock-fronts stand forward, as sheer and as nobly sculptured. No ice work that I have ever seen surpasses this, either in the magnitude of the features or effectiveness of composition.

On some of the narrow benches and tables of the walls rows of spruce trees and two-leaved pines were growing, and patches of considerable size were found on the spreading bases of those mountains that stand back inside the canyons, where the continuity of the walls is broken. Some of these side canyons are cut down to the level of the water and reach far back, opening views into groups of glacier fountains that give rise to many a noble stream; while all along the tops of the walls on both sides small glaciers are seen, still busily engaged in the work of completing their sculpture. I counted twenty-five from the canoe. Probably the drainage of fifty or more pours into this fjord. The average elevation at which they melt is about eighteen hundred feet above sea level, and all of them are residual branches of the grand trunk that filled the fjord and overflowed its walls when there was only one Sum Dum glacier.

The afternoon was wearing away as we pushed on and on through the drifting bergs without our having obtained a single glimpse of the great glacier. A Sum Dum seal hunter, whom we met groping his way deftly through the ice in a very small, unsplitable cottonwood canoe, told us that the ice mountain was yet fifteen miles away. This was toward the middle of the afternoon, and I gave up sketching and making notes and worked hard with the Indians to reach it before dark. About seven o'clock we approached what seemed to be the extreme head of the fjord, and still no great glacier in sight—only a small one, three or four miles long, melting a thousand feet above the sea.

Presently, a narrow side opening appeared between tremendous cliffs sheer to a height of four thousand feet or more, trending nearly at right angles to the general trend of the fjord, and apparently terminated by a cliff, scarcely less abrupt or high, at a distance of a mile or two. Up this bend we toiled against wind and tide, creeping closely along the wall on the right side, which, as we looked upward, seemed to be leaning over, while the waves beating against the bergs and rocks made a discouraging kind of music. At length, toward nine o'clock, just before the gray darkness of evening fell, a long, triumphant shout told that the glacier, so deeply and desperately hidden, was at last hunted back to its benmost bore. A short distance around a second bend in the canyon, I reached a point where I obtained a good view of it as it pours its deep, broad flood into the fjord in a majestic course from between the noble mountains, its tributaries, each of which would be regarded elsewhere as a grand glacier, converging from right and left from a fountain set far in the silent fastnesses of the mountains.

"There is your lost friend," said the Indians laughing; "he says, 'Sagh-a-ya'" (how do you do)? And while berg after berg was being born with thundering uproar, Tyeen said, "Your friend has klosh tumtum (good heart). Hear! Like the other big-hearted one he is firing his guns in your honor."

I stayed only long enough to make an outline sketch, and then urged the Indians to hasten back some six miles to the mouth of a side canyon I had noted on the way up as a place where we might camp in case we should not find a better. After dark we had to move with great caution through the ice. One of the Indians was stationed in the bow with a pole to push aside the smaller fragments and look out for the most promising openings, through which he guided us, shouting, "Friday! Tucktay!" (shoreward, seaward) about ten times a minute. We reached this landing place after ten o'clock, guided in the darkness by the roar of a glacier torrent. The ground was all boulders and it was hard to find a place among them, however small, to lie on. The Indians anchored the canoe well out from the shore and passed the night in it to guard against berg-waves and drifting waves, after assisting me to set my tent in some sort of way among the stones well back beyond the reach of the tide. I asked them as they were returning to the canoe if they were not going to eat something. They answered promptly:

"We will sleep now, if your ice friend will let us. We will eat tomorrow, but we can find some bread for you if you want it."

"No," I said, "go to rest. I, too, will sleep now and eat tomorrow." Nothing was attempted in the way of light or fire. Camping that night was simply lying down. The boulders seemed to make a fair bed after finding the best place to take their pressure.

During the night I was awakened by the beating of the spent ends of berg-waves against the side of my tent, though I had fancied myself well beyond their reach. These special waves are not raised by wind or tide, but by the fall of large bergs from the snout of the glacier, or sometimes by the overturning or breaking of large bergs that may have long floated in perfect poise. The highest berg-waves oftentimes travel half a dozen miles or farther before they are much spent, producing a singularly impressive uproar in the far recesses of the mountains on calm dark nights when all beside is still. Far and near they tell the news that a berg is born, repeating their story again and again, compelling attention and reminding us of earthquake waves that roll on for thousands of miles, taking their story from continent to continent.

When the Indians came ashore in the morning and saw the condition of my tent they laughed heartily and said, "Your friend [meaning the big glacier] sent you a good word last night, and his servant knocked at your tent and said, 'Sagh-a-ya, are you sleeping well?'"

I had fasted too long to be in very good order for hard work, but while the Indians were cooking, I made out to push my way up the canyon before breakfast to seek the glacier that once came into the fjord, knowing from the size and muddiness of the stream that drains it that it must be quite large and not far off. I came in sight of it after a hard scramble of two hours through thorny chaparral and across steep avalanche taluses of rocks and snow. The front reaches across the canyon from wall to wall, covered with rocky detritus, and looked dark and forbidding in the shadow cast by the cliffs, while from a low, cavelike hollow its draining stream breaks forth, a river in size, with a reverberating roar that stirs all the canyon. Beyond, in a cloudless blaze of sunshine, I saw many tributaries, pure and white as new-fallen snow, drawing their sources from clusters of peaks and sweeping down waving slopes to unite their crystal currents with the trunk glacier in the central canyon. This fine glacier reaches to within two hundred and fifty feet of the level of the sea, and would even yet reach the fjord and send off bergs but for the waste it suffers in flowing slowly through the trunk canyon, the declivity of which is very slight.

Returning, I reached camp and breakfast at ten o'clock; then had everything packed into the canoe, and set off leisurely across the fjord to the mouth of another wide and low canyon, whose lofty outer cliffs, facing the fjord, are telling glacial advertisements. Gladly I should have explored it all, traced its streams of water and streams of ice, and entered its highest chambers, the homes and fountains of the snow. But I had to wait. I only stopped an hour or two, and climbed to the top of a rock through the common underbrush, whence I had a good general view. The front of the main glacier is not far distant from the fjord, and sends off small bergs into a lake. The walls of its tributary canyons are remarkably jagged and high, cut in a red variegated rock, probably slate. On the way back to the canoe I gathered ripe salmonberries an inch and a half in diameter, ripe huckleberries, too, in great abundance, and several interesting plants I had not before met in the territory.

About noon, when the tide was in our favor, we set out on the return trip to the gold mine camp. The sun shone free and warm. No wind stirred. The water spaces between the bergs were as smooth as glass, reflecting the unclouded sky, and doubling the ravishing beauty of the bergs as the sunlight streamed through their innumerable angles in rainbow colors.

Soon a light breeze sprang up, and dancing lily spangles on the water mingled their glory of light with that burning on the angles of the ice.

On days like this, true sun-days, some of the bergs show a purplish tinge, though most are white from the disintegrating of their weathered surfaces. Now and then a newborn one is met that is pure blue crystal throughout, freshly broken from the fountain or recently exposed to the air by turning over. But in all of them, old and new, there are azure caves and rifts of ineffable beauty, in which the purest tones of light pulse and shimmer, lovely and untainted as anything on earth or in the sky.

As we were passing the Indian village I presented a little tobacco to the headmen as an expression of regard, while they gave us a few smoked salmon, after putting many questions concerning my exploration of their bay and bluntly declaring their disbelief in the ice business.

About nine o'clock we arrived at the gold camp, where we found Mr. Young ready to go on with us the next morning, and thus ended two of the brightest and best of all my Alaska days.

15

FROM TAKU RIVER TO TAYLOR BAY

I never saw Alaska looking better than it did when we bade farewell to Sum Dum on August 22 and pushed on northward up the coast toward Taku. The morning was clear, calm, bright—not a cloud in all the purple sky, nor wind, however gentle, to shake the slender spires of the spruces or dew-laden grass around the shores. Over the mountains and over the broad white bosoms of the glaciers the sunbeams poured, rosy as ever fell on fields of ripening wheat, drenching the forests and kindling the glassy waters and icebergs into a perfect blaze of colored light. Every living thing seemed joyful, and nature's work was going on in glowing enthusiasm, not less appreciable in the deep repose that brooded over every feature of the landscape, suggesting the coming fruitfulness of the icy land and showing the advance that has already been made from glacial winter to summer. The care-laden commercial lives we lead close our eyes to the operations of God as a workman, though openly carried on that all who will look may see. The scarred rocks here and the moraines make a vivid showing of the old winter-time of the glacial period, and mark the bounds of the *mer-de-glace* that once filled the bay and covered the surrounding mountains. Already that sea of ice is replaced by water, in which multitudes of fishes are fed, while the hundred glaciers lingering about the bay and the streams that pour from them are busy night and day bringing in sand and mud and stones, at the rate of tons every minute, to fill it up. Then, as the seasons grow warmer, there will be fields here for the plough.

Our Indians, exhilarated by the sunshine, were garrulous as the gulls and plovers, and pulled heartily at their oars, evidently glad to get out of the ice with a whole boat.

"Now for Taku," they said, as we glided over the shining water. "Good-bye, Ice Mountains; good-bye, Sum Dum." Soon a light breeze came, and they unfurled the sail and laid away their oars and began, as usual in such free times, to put their goods in order, unpacking and sunning provisions, guns, ropes, clothing, etc. Joe has an old flintlock musket suggestive of Hudson's Bay times, which he wished to discharge and reload. So, stepping in front of the sail, he fired at a gull that was flying past before I could prevent him, and it fell slowly with outspread wings alongside the canoe, with blood dripping from its bill. I asked him why he had killed the bird, and followed the question by a severe reprimand for his stupid cruelty, to which he could offer no other excuse than that he had learned from the whites to be careless about taking life. Captain Tyeen denounced the deed as likely to bring bad luck.

Before the whites came most of the Thlinkits held, with Agassiz, that animals have souls, and that it was wrong and unlucky to even speak disrespectfully of the fishes or any of the animals that supplied them with food. A case illustrating their superstitious beliefs in this connection occurred at Fort Wrangell while I was there the year before. One of the sub-chiefs of the Stickeens had a little son five or six years old, to whom he was very much attached, always taking him with him in his short canoe trips, and leading him by the hand while going about town. Last summer the boy was taken sick, and gradually grew weak and thin, whereupon his father became alarmed, and feared, as is usual in such obscure cases, that the boy had been bewitched. He first applied in his trouble to Dr. Carliss, one of the missionaries, who gave medicine, without effecting the immediate cure that the fond father demanded. He was, to some extent, a believer in the powers of missionaries, both as to material and spiritual affairs, but in so serious an exigency it was natural that he should go back to the faith of his fathers. Accordingly, he sent for one of the shamans, or medicine men, of his tribe, and submitted the case to him, who, after going through the customary incantations, declared that he had discovered the cause of the difficulty.

"Your boy," he said, "has lost his soul, and this is the way it happened. He was playing among the stones down on the beach when he saw a crawfish in the water, and made fun of it, pointing his finger at it and saying, 'Oh, you crooked legs! Oh, you crooked legs! You can't walk straight; you go sidewise,' which made the crab so angry that he reached out his long nippers, seized the lad's soul, pulled it out of him and made off with it into deep water. And," continued the medicine man, "unless his stolen soul is restored to him and put back in its place he will die. Your boy is really dead already; it is only his lonely, empty body that is living now, and though it may continue to live in this way for a year or two, the boy will never be of any account, not strong, nor wise, nor brave."

The father then inquired whether anything could be done about it; was the soul still in possession of the crab, and if so, could it be recovered and reinstalled in his forlorn son? Yes, the doctor rather thought it might be charmed back and reunited, but the job would be a difficult one, and would probably cost about fifteen blankets.

After we were fairly out of the bay into Stephens Passage, the wind died away, and the Indians had to take to their oars again, which ended our talk. On we sped over the silvery level, close alongshore. The dark forests extending far and near, planted like a field of wheat, might seem monotonous in general views, but the appreciative observer, looking closely, will find no lack of interesting variety, however far he may go. The steep slopes on which they grow allow almost every individual tree, with its peculiarities of form and color, to be seen like an audience on seats rising above one another—the blue-green, sharply tapered spires of the Menzies spruce, the warm yellow-green Mertens spruce with their fingerlike tops all pointing in the same direction, or drooping gracefully like leaves of grass, and the airy, feathery, brownish-green Alaska cedar. The outer fringe of bushes along the shore and hanging over the brows of the cliffs, the white mountains above, the shining water beneath, the changing sky over all, form pictures of divine beauty in which no healthy eye may ever grow weary.

Toward evening at the head of a picturesque bay we came to a village belonging to the Taku tribe. We found it silent and deserted. Not a single shaman or policeman had been left to keep it. These people are so happily rich as to have but little of a perishable kind to keep, nothing worth fretting about. They were away catching salmon, our Indians said. All the Indian villages hereabout are thus abandoned at regular periods every year, just as a tent is left for a day, while they repair to fishing, berrying, and hunting stations, occupying each in succession for a week or two at a time, coming and going from the main, substantially built villages. Then, after their summer's work is done, the winter supply of salmon dried and packed, fish oil and seal oil stored in boxes, berries and spruce bark pressed into cakes, their trading trips completed, and the year's stock of quarrels with the neighboring tribe patched up in some way, they devote themselves to feasting, dancing, and hootchenoo drinking. The Takus, once a powerful and warlike tribe, were at this time, like most of the neighboring tribes, whiskied nearly out of existence. They had a larger village on the Taku River, but, according to the census taken that year by the missionaries, they numbered only 269 in all—109 men, 79 women, and 81 children, figures that show the vanishing condition of the tribe at a glance.

Our Indians wanted to camp for the night in one of the deserted houses, but I urged them on into the clean wilderness until dark, when we landed on a rocky beach fringed with devil's clubs, greatly to the disgust of our crew. We had to make the best of it, however, as it was too dark to seek farther. After supper was accomplished among the boulders, they retired to the canoe, which they anchored a little way out, beyond low tide, while Mr. Young and I at the expense of a good deal of scrambling and panax stinging, discovered a spot on which we managed to sleep.

The next morning, about two hours after leaving our thorny camp, we rounded a great mountain rock nearly a mile in height and entered the Taku fjord. It is about eighteen miles long and from three to five miles wide, and extends directly back into the heart of the mountains, draining hundreds of glaciers and streams. The ancient glacier that formed it was far too deep and broad and too little concentrated to erode one of those narrow canyons, usually so impressive in sculpture and architecture, but it is all the more interesting on this account when the grandeur of the ice work accomplished is recognized. This fjord, more than any other I have examined, explains the formation of the wonderful system of channels extending along the coast from Puget Sound to about latitude 59 degrees, for it is a marked portion of the system—a branch of Stephens Passage. Its trends and general sculpture are as distinctly glacial as those of the narrowest fjord, while the largest tributaries of the great glacier that occupied it are still in existence. I counted some forty-five altogether, big and little, in sight from the canoe in sailing up the middle of the fjord. Three of them, drawing their sources from magnificent groups of snowy mountains, came down to the level of the sea and formed a glorious spectacle. The middle one of the three belongs to the first class, pouring its majestic flood, shattered and crevassed, directly into the fjord, and crowding about twenty-five square miles of it with bergs. The next below it also sends off bergs occasionally, though a narrow strip of glacial detritus separates it from the tidewater. That forenoon a large mass fell from it, damming its draining stream, which at length broke the dam, and the resulting flood swept forward thousands of small bergs across the mudflat into the fjord. In a short time all was quiet again; the floodwaters receded, leaving only a large blue scar on the front of the glacier and stranded bergs on the moraine flat to tell the tale.

These two glaciers are about equal in size—two miles wide—and their fronts are only about a mile and a half apart. While I sat sketching them from a point among the drifting icebergs where I could see far back into the heart of their distant fountains, two Taku seal hunters, father and son, came gliding toward us in an extremely small canoe. Coming alongside with a goodnatured "Sagh-a-ya," they inquired who we were, our objects, etc., and gave us information about the river, their village, and two other large glaciers that descend nearly to the sea level a few miles up the river canyon. Crouching in their little shell of a boat among the great bergs, with paddle and barbed spear, they formed a picture as arctic and remote from anything to be found in civilization as ever was sketched for us by the explorers of the Far North.

Making our way through the crowded bergs to the extreme head of the fjord, we entered the mouth of the river, but were soon compelled to turn back on account of the strength of the current. The Taku River is a large stream, nearly a mile wide at the mouth, and, like the Stickeen, Chilcat, and Chilcoot, draws its sources from far inland, crossing the mountain chain from the interior through a majestic canyon, and draining a multitude of glaciers on its way.

The Taku Indians, like the Chilcats, with a keen appreciation of the advantages of their position for trade, hold possession of the river and compel the

Indians of the interior to accept their services as middlemen, instead of allowing them to trade directly with the whites.

When we were baffled in our attempt to ascend the river, the day was nearly done, and we began to seek a campground. After sailing two or three miles along the left side of the fjord, we were so fortunate as to find a small nook described by the two Indians, where firewood was abundant, and where we could drag our canoe up the bank beyond reach of the bergwaves. Here we were safe, with a fine outlook across the fjord to the great glaciers and near enough to see the birth of the icebergs and the wonderful commotion they make, and hear their wild, roaring rejoicing. The sunset sky seemed to have been painted for this one mountain mansion, fitting it like a ceiling. After the fjord was in shadow the level sunbeams continued to pour through the miles of bergs with ravishing beauty, reflecting and refracting the purple light like cut crystal. Then all save the tips of the highest became dead white. These, too, were speedily quenched, the glowing points vanishing like stars sinking beneath the horizon. And after the shadows had crept higher, submerging the glaciers and the ridges between them, the divine alpenglow still lingered on their highest fountain peaks as they stood transfigured in glorious array. Now the last of the twilight purple has vanished, the stars begin to shine, and all trace of the day is gone. Looking across the fjord the water seems perfectly black, and the two great glaciers are seen stretching dim and ghostly into the shadowy mountains now darkly massed against the starry sky.

Next morning it was raining hard, everything looked dismal, and on the way down the fjord a growling head wind battered the rain in our faces, but we held doggedly on and by 10 A.M. got out of the fjord into Stephens Passage. A breeze sprung up in our favor that swept us bravely on across the passage and around the end of Admiralty Island by dark. We camped in a boggy hollow on a bluff among scraggy, usnea-bearded spruces. The rain, bitterly cold and driven by a stormy wind, thrashed us well while we floundered in the stumpy bog trying to make a fire and supper.

When daylight came we found our campground a very savage place. How we reached it and established ourselves in the thick darkness it would be difficult to tell. We crept along the shore a few miles against strong head winds, then hoisted sail and steered straight across Lynn Canal to the mainland, which we followed without great difficulty, the wind having moderated toward evening. Near the entrance to Icy Strait we met a Hoona who had seen us last year and who seemed glad to see us. He gave us two salmon, and we made him happy with tobacco and then pushed on and camped near Sitka Jack's deserted village.

Though the wind was still ahead next morning, we made about twenty miles before sundown and camped on the west end of Farewell Island. We bumped against a hidden rock and sprung a small leak that was easily stopped with resin. The salmonberries were ripe. While climbing a bluff for a view of our course, I discovered moneses, one of my favorites, and saw many well-traveled deer trails, though the island is cut off from the mainland and other islands by at least five or six miles of icy, berg-encumbered water.

We got under way early next day—a gray, cloudy morning with rain and wind. Fair and head winds were about evenly balanced throughout the day. Tides run fast here, like great rivers. We rowed and paddled around Point Wimbledon against both wind and tide, creeping close to the feet of the huge, bold rocks of the north wall of Cross Sound, which here were very steep and awe-inspiring as the heavy swells from the open sea coming in past Cape Spencer dashed white against them, tossing our frail canoe up and down lightly as a feather. The point reached by vegetation shows that the surf dashes up to a height of about seventy-five or a hundred feet. We were awe-stricken and began to fear that we might be upset should the ocean waves rise still higher. But little Stickeen seemed to enjoy the storm, and gazed at the foam-wreathed cliffs like a dreamy, comfortable tourist admiring a sunset. We reached the mouth of Taylor Bay about two or three o'clock in the afternoon, when we had a view of the open ocean before we entered the bay. Many large bergs from Glacier Bay were seen drifting out to sea past Cape Spencer. We reached the head of the fjord now called Taylor Bay at five o'clock and camped near an immense glacier with a front about three miles wide stretching across from wall to wall. No icebergs are discharged from it, as it is separated from the water of the fjord at high tide by a low, smooth mass of outspread, overswept moraine material, netted with torrents and small shallow rills from the glacier front, with here and there a lakelet, and patches of yellow mosses and garden spots bright with epilobium, saxifrage, grass tufts, sedges, and creeping willows on the higher ground. But only the mosses were sufficiently abundant to make conspicuous masses of color to relieve the dull slaty gray of the glacial mud and gravel. The front of the glacier, like all those which do not discharge icebergs, is rounded like a brow, smooth-looking in general views, but cleft and furrowed, nevertheless, with chasms and grooves in which the light glows and shimmers in glorious beauty. The granite walls of the fjord, though very high, are not deeply sculptured. Only a few deep side canyons with trees, bushes, grassy and flowery spots interrupt their massive simplicity, leaving but few of the cliffs absolutely sheer and bare like those of Yosemite, Sum Dum, or Taku. One of the side canyons is on the left side of the fjord, the other on the right, the tributaries of the former leading over by a narrow tide channel to the bay next to the eastward, and by a short portage over into a lake into which pours a branch glacier from the great glacier. Still another branch from the main glacier turns to the right. Counting all three of these separate fronts, the width of this great Taylor Bay Glacier must be about seven or eight miles.

While camp was being made, Hunter Joe climbed the eastern wall in search of wild mutton, but found none. He fell in with a brown bear, however, and got a shot at it, but nothing more. Mr. Young and I crossed the moraine slope, splashing through pools and streams up to the ice wall, and made the interesting discovery that the glacier had been advancing of late years, ploughing up and shoving forward moraine soil that had been deposited long ago, and overwhelming and grinding and carrying away the forests on the sides and front of the glacier. Though not now sending off icebergs, the front is probably far below sea level at the bottom, thrust forward beneath its wave-washed moraine.

Along the base of the mountain wall we found abundance of salmonberries, the largest measuring an inch and a half in diameter. Strawberries, too, are found hereabouts. Some which visiting Indians brought us were as fine in size and color and flavor as any I ever saw anywhere. After wandering and wondering an hour or two, admiring the magnificent rock and crystal scenery about us, we returned to camp at sundown, planning a grand excursion for the morrow.

I set off early the morning of August 30 before any one else in camp had stirred, not waiting for breakfast, but only eating a piece of bread. I had intended getting a cup of coffee, but a wild storm was blowing and calling, and I could not wait. Running out against the rain-laden gale and turning to catch my breath, I saw that the minister's little dog had left his bed in the tent and was coming boring through the storm, evidently determined to follow me. I told him to go back, that such a day as this had nothing for him.

"Go back," I shouted, "and get your breakfast." But he simply stood with his head down, and when I began to urge my way again, looking around, I saw he was still following me. So I at last told him to come on if he must and gave him a piece of the bread I had in my pocket.

Instead of falling, the rain, mixed with misty shreds of clouds, was flying in level sheets, and the wind was roaring as I had never heard wind roar before. Over the icy levels and over the woods, on the mountains, over the jagged rocks and spires and chasms of the glacier it boomed and moaned and roared, filling the fjord in even, gray, structureless gloom, inspiring and awful. I first struggled up in the face of the blast to the east end of the ice wall, where a patch of forest had been carried away by the glacier when it was advancing. I noticed a few stumps well out on the moraine flat, showing that its present bare, raw condition was not the condition of fifty or a hundred years ago. In front of this part of the glacier there is a small moraine lake about half a mile in length, around the margin of which are a considerable number of trees standing knee-deep, and of course dead. This also is a result of the recent advance of the ice.

Pushing up through the ragged edge of the woods on the left margin of the glacier, the storm seemed to increase in violence, so that it was difficult to draw breath in facing it; therefore I took shelter back of a tree to enjoy it and wait, hoping that it would at last somewhat abate. Here the glacier, descending over an abrupt rock, falls forward in grand cascades, while a stream swollen by the rain was now a tor-rent—wind, rain, ice torrent, and water torrent in one grand symphony.

At length the storm seemed to abate somewhat, and I took off my heavy rubber boots, with which I had waded the glacial streams on the flat, and laid them with my overcoat on a log, where I might find them on my way back, knowing I would be drenched anyhow, and firmly tied my mountain shoes, tightened my belt, shouldered my ice axe, and, thus free and ready for rough work, pushed on, regardless as possible of mere rain. Making my way up a steep granite slope, its pro-jecting polished bosses encumbered here and there by boulders and the ground and bruised ruins of the rag-ged edge of the forest that had been uprooted by the glacier during its recent advance, I traced the side of the glacier for two or three miles, finding everywhere evidence of its having encroached on the woods, which here run back along its edge for fifteen or twenty miles. Under the projecting edge of this vast ice river I could see down beneath it to a depth of fifty feet or so in some places, where logs and branches were being crushed to pulp, some of it almost fine enough for paper, though most of it stringy and coarse.

After thus tracing the margin of the glacier for three or four miles, I chopped steps and climbed to the top, and as far as the eye could reach, the nearly level glacier stretched indefinitely away in the gray cloudy sky, a prairie of ice. The wind was now almost moderate, though rain continued to fall, which I did not mind, but a tendency to mist in the drooping draggled clouds made me hesitate about attempting to cross to the opposite shore. Although the distance was only six or seven miles, no traces at this time could be seen of the mountains on the other side, and in case the sky should grow darker, as it seemed inclined to do, I feared that when I got out of sight of land and perhaps into a maze of crevasses I might find difficulty in winning a way back.

Lingering a while and sauntering about in sight of the shore, I found this eastern side of the glacier remarkably free from large crevasses. Nearly all I met were so narrow I could step across them almost anywhere, while the few wide ones were easily avoided by going up or down along their sides to where they narrowed. The dismal cloud ceiling showed rifts here and there, and, thus encouraged, I struck out for the west shore, aiming to strike it five or six miles above the front wall, cautiously taking compass bearings at short intervals to enable me to find my way back should the weather darken again with mist or rain or snow. The structure lines of the glacier itself were, however, my main guide. All went well. I came to a deeply furrowed section about two miles in width where I had to zigzag in long, tedious tacks and make narrow doublings, tracing the edges of wide longitudinal furrows and chasms until I could find a bridge connecting their sides, oftentimes making the direct distance ten times over. The walking was good of its kind, however, and by dint of patient doubling and axe work on dangerous places, I gained the opposite shore in about three hours, the width of the glacier at this point being about seven miles. Occasionally, while making my way, the clouds lifted a little, revealing a few bald, rough mountains sunk to the throat in the broad, icy sea which encompassed them on all sides, sweeping on forever and forever as we count time, wearing them away, giving them the shape they are destined to take when in the fullness of time they shall be parts of new landscapes.

Ere I lost sight of the east-side mountains, those on the west came in sight, so that holding my course was easy, and, though making haste, I halted for a moment to gaze down into the beautiful pure blue crevasses and to drink at the lovely blue wells, the most beautiful of all Nature's water basins, or at the rills and streams outspread over the ice-land prairie, never ceasing to admire their lovely color and music as they glided and swirled in their blue crystal channels and potholes, and the rumbling of the moulins, or mills, where streams poured into blue-walled pits of unknown depth, some of them as regularly circular as if bored with augers. Interesting, too, were the cascades over blue cliffs, where streams fell into crevasses or slid almost noiselessly down slopes so smooth and frictionless their motion was concealed. The round or oval wells, however, from one to ten feet wide, and from one to twenty or thirty feet deep, were perhaps the most beautiful of all, the water so pure as to be almost invisible. My widest views did not probably exceed fifteen miles, the rain and mist making distances seem greater.

On reaching the farther shore and tracing it a few miles to northward, I found a large portion of the glacier-current sweeping out westward in a bold and beautiful curve around the shoulder of a mountain as if going direct to the open sea. Leaving the main trunk, it breaks into a magnificent uproar of pinnacles and spires and upheaving, splashing wave-shaped masses, a crystal cataract incomparably greater and wilder than a score of Niagaras.

Tracing its channel three or four miles, I found that it fell into a lake, which it fills with bergs. The front of this branch of the glacier is about three miles wide. I first took the lake to be the head of an arm of the sea, but, going down to its shore and tasting it, I found it fresh, and by my aneroid perhaps less than a hundred feet above sea level. It is probably separated from the sea only by a moraine dam. I had not time to go around its shores, as it was now near five o'clock and I was about fifteen miles from camp, and I had to make haste to recross the glacier before dark, which would come on about eight o'clock. I therefore made haste up to the main glacier, and, shaping my course by compass and the structure lines of the ice, set off from the land out on to the grand crystal prairie again. All was so silent and so concentered, owing to the low dragging mist, the beauty close about me was all the more keenly felt, though tinged with a dim sense of danger, as if coming events were casting shadows. I was soon out of sight of land, and the evening dusk that on cloudy days precedes the real night gloom came stealing on and only ice was in sight, and the only sounds, save the low rumbling of the mills and the rattle of falling stones at long intervals, were the low, terribly earnest moanings of the wind or distant waterfalls coming through the thickening gloom. After two hours of hard work I came to a maze of crevasses of appalling depth and width which could not be passed apparently either up or down. I traced them with firm nerve developed by the danger, making wide jumps, poising cautiously on dizzy edges after cutting footholds, taking wide crevasses at a grand leap at once frightful and inspiring. Many a mile was thus traveled, mostly up and down the glacier, making but little real headway, running much of the time as the danger of having to pass the night on the ice became more and more imminent. This I could do, though with the weather and my rain-soaked condition it would be trying at best. In treading the mazes of this crevassed section I had frequently to cross bridges that were only knife-edges for twenty or thirty feet, cutting off the sharp tops and leaving them flat so that little Stickeen could follow me. These I had to straddle, cutting off the top as I progressed and hitching gradually ahead like a boy riding a rail fence. All this time the little dog followed me bravely, never hesitating on the brink of any crevasse that I had jumped, but now that it was becoming dark and the crevasses became more troublesome, he followed close at my heels instead of scampering far and wide, where the ice was at all smooth, as he had in the forenoon. No land was now in sight. The mist fell lower and darker and snow began to fly. I could not see far enough up and down the glacier to judge how best to work out of the bewildering labyrinth, and how hard I tried while there was yet hope of reaching camp that night! A hope which was fast growing dim like the sky. After dark, on such ground, to keep from freezing, I could only jump up and down until morning on a piece of flat ice between the crevasses, dance to the boding music of the winds and waters, and as I was already tired and hungry I would be in bad condition for such ice work. Many times I was put to my mettle, but with a firm-braced nerve, all the more unflinching as the dangers thickened, I worked out of that terrible ice-web, and with blood fairly up Stickeen and I ran over common danger without fatigue. Our very hardest trial was in getting across the very last of the sliver bridges. After examining the first of the two widest crevasses, I followed its edge half a mile or so up and down and discovered that its narrowest spot was about eight feet wide, which was the limit of what I was able to jump. Moreover, the side I was on—that is, the west side—was about a foot higher than the other, and I feared that in case I should be stopped by a still wider impassable crevasse ahead that I would hardly be able to take back that jump from its lower side. The ice beyond, however, as far as I could see it, looked temptingly smooth. Therefore, after carefully making a socket for my foot on the rounded brink, I jumped, but found that I had nothing to spare and more than ever dreaded having to retrace my way. Little Stickeen jumped this, however, without apparently taking a second look at it, and we ran ahead joyfully over smooth, level ice, hoping we were now leaving all danger behind us. But hardly had we gone a hundred or two yards when to our dismay we found ourselves on the very widest of all the longitudinal crevasses we had yet encountered. It was about forty feet wide. I ran anxiously up the side of it to northward, eagerly hoping that I could get around its head, but my worst fears were realized when at a distance of about a mile or less it ran into the crevasse that I had just jumped. I then ran down the edge for a mile or more below the point where I had first met it, and found that its lower end also united with the crevasse I had jumped, showing dismally that we were on an island two or three hundred yards wide and about two miles long and the only way of escape from this island was by turning back and jumping again that crevasse which I dreaded, or venturing ahead across the giant crevasse by the very worst of the sliver bridges I had ever seen. It was so badly weathered and melted down that it formed a knife-edge, and extended across from side to side in a low, drooping curve like that made by a loose rope attached at each end at the same height. But the worst difficulty was that the ends of the down-curving sliver were attached to the sides at a depth of about eight or ten feet below the surface of the glacier. Getting down to the end of the bridge, and then after crossing it getting up the other side, seemed hardly possible. However, I decided to dare the dangers of the fearful sliver rather than to attempt to retrace my steps. Accordingly I dug a low groove in the rounded edge for my knees to rest in and, leaning over, began to cut a narrow foothold on the steep, smooth side. When I was doing this, Stickeen came up behind me, pushed his head over my shoulder, looked into the crevasses and along the narrow knife-edge, then turned and looked in my face, muttering and whining as if trying to say, "Surely you are not going down there." I said, "Yes, Stickeen, this is the only way." He then began to cry and ran wildly along the rim of the crevasse, searching for a better way, then, returning baffled, of course, he came behind me and lay down and cried louder and louder.

After getting down one step I cautiously stooped and cut another and another in succession until I reached the point where the sliver was attached to the wall. There, cautiously balancing, I chipped down the upcurved end of the bridge until I had formed a small level platform about a foot wide, then, bending forward, got astride of the end of the sliver, steadied myself with my knees, then cut off the top of the sliver, hitching myself forward an inch or two at a time, leaving it about four inches wide for Stickeen. Arrived at the farther end of the sliver, which was about seventy-five feet long, I chipped another little platform on its upcurved end, cautiously rose to my feet, and with infinite pains cut narrow notch steps and fingerholds in the wall and finally got safely across. All this dreadful time poor little Stickeen was crying as if his heart was broken, and when I called to him in as reassuring a voice as I could muster, he only cried the louder, as if trying to say that he never, never could get down there—the only time that the brave little fellow appeared to know what danger was. After going away as if I was leaving him, he still howled and cried without venturing to try to follow me. Returning to the edge of the crevasse, I told him that I must go, that he could come if he only tried, and finally in despair he hushed his cries, slid his little feet slowly down into my footsteps out on the big sliver, walked slowly and cautiously along the sliver as if holding his breath, while the snow was falling and the wind was moaning and threatening to blow him off. When he arrived at the foot of the slope below me, I was kneeling on the brink ready to assist him in case he should be unable to reach the top. He looked up along the row of notched steps I had made, as if fixing them in his mind, then with a nervous spring he whizzed up and passed me out on to the level ice, and ran and cried and barked and rolled about fairly hysterical in the sudden revulsion from the depth of despair to triumphant joy. I tried to catch him and pet him and tell him how good and brave he was, but he would not be caught. He ran round and round, swirling like autumn leaves in an eddy, lay down and rolled head over heels. I told him we still had far to go and that we must now stop all nonsense and get off the ice before dark. I knew by the ice lines that every step was now taking me nearer the shore and soon it came in sight. The headland four or five miles back from the front, covered with spruce trees, loomed faintly but surely through the mist and light fall of snow not more than two miles away. The ice now proved good all the way across, and we reached the lateral moraine just at dusk, then with trembling limbs, now that the danger was over, we staggered and stumbled down the bouldery edge of the glacier and got over the dangerous rocks by the cascades while yet a faint light lingered. We were safe, and then, too, came limp weariness such as no ordinary work ever produces, however hard it may be. Wearily we stumbled down through the woods, over logs and brush and roots, devil's clubs pricking us at every faint blundering tumble. At last we got out on the smooth mud slope with only a mile of slow but sure dragging of weary limbs to camp. The Indians had been firing guns to guide me and had a fine supper and fire ready, though fearing they would be compelled to seek us in the morning, a care not often applied to me. Stickeen and I were too tired to eat much, and, strange to say, too tired to sleep. Both of us, springing up in the night again and again, fancied we were still on that dreadful ice bridge in the shadow of death.

Nevertheless, we arose next morning in newness of life. Never before had rocks and ice and trees seemed so beautiful and wonderful, even the cold, biting rainstorm that was blowing seemed full of loving-kindness, wonderful compensation for all that we had endured, and we sailed down the bay through the gray, driving rain rejoicing.

16

GLACIER BAY

While Stickeen and I were away, a Hoona, one of the head men of the tribe, paid Mr. Young a visit, and presented him with porpoise meat and berries and much interesting information. He naturally expected a return visit, and when we called at his house, a mile or two down the fjord, he said his wives were out in the rain gathering fresh berries to complete a feast prepared for us. We remained, however, only a few minutes, for I was not aware of this arrangement or of Mr. Young's promise until after leaving the house. Anxiety to get around Cape Wimbledon was the cause of my haste, fearing the storm might increase. On account of this ignorance, no apologies were offered him, and the upshot was that the good Hoona became very angry. We succeeded, however, in the evening of the same day, in explaining our haste, and by sincere apologies and presents made peace.

After a hard struggle we got around stormy Wimbledon and into the next fjord to the northward (Klunastucksana—Dundas Bay). A cold, drenching rain was falling, darkening but not altogether hiding its extraordinary beauty, made up of lovely reaches and side fjords, feathery headlands and islands, beautiful

every one and charmingly collocated. But how it rained,
and how cold it was, and how weary we were pulling
most of the time against the wind! The branches of this
bay are so deep and so numerous that, with the rain
and low clouds concealing the mountain landmarks,
we could hardly make out the main trends. While groping and gazing among the islands through the misty
rain and clouds, we discovered wisps of smoke at the
foot of a sheltering rock in front of a mountain, where
a choir of cascades were chanting their rain songs.
Gladly we made for this camp, which proved to belong
to a rare old Hoona sub-chief, so tall and wide and dignified in demeanor he looked grand even in the sloppy
weather, and every inch a chief in spite of his bare
legs and the old shirt and draggled, ragged blanket in
which he was dressed. He was given to much handshaking, gripping hard, holding on and looking you
gravely in the face while most emphatically speaking
in Thlinkit, not a word of which we understood until
interpreter John came to our help. He turned from
one to the other of us, declaring, as John interpreted,
that our presence did him good like food and fire, that
he would welcome white men, especially teachers,
and that he and all his people compared to ourselves
were only children. When Mr. Young informed him
that a missionary was about to be sent to his people,
he said he would call them all together four times and
explain that a teacher and preacher were coming and
that they therefore must put away all foolishness and
prepare their hearts to receive them and their words.
He then introduced his three children, one a naked
lad five or six years old who, as he fondly assured
us, would soon be a chief, and later to his wife, an
intelligent-looking woman of whom he seemed proud.

When we arrived she was out at the foot of the cascade mountain gathering salmonberries. She came in dripping and loaded. A few of the fine berries saved for the children she presented, proudly and fondly beginning with the youngest, whose only clothing was a nose ring and a string of beads. She was lightly appareled in a cotton gown and bit of blanket, thoroughly bedraggled, but after unloading her berries she retired with a dry calico gown around the corner of a rock and soon returned fresh as a daisy and with becoming dignity took her place by the fireside. Soon two other berry-laden women came in, seemingly enjoying the rain like the bushes and trees. They put on little clothing so that they may be the more easily dried, and as for the children, a thin shirt of sheeting is the most they encumber themselves with, and get wet and half dry without seeming to notice it while we shiver with two or three dry coats. They seem to prefer being naked. The men also wear but little in wet weather. When they go out for all day they put on a single blanket, but in choring around camp, getting firewood, cooking, or looking after their precious canvas, they seldom wear anything, braving wind and rain in utter nakedness to avoid the bother of drying clothes. It is a rare sight to see the children bringing in big chunks of firewood on their shoulders, balancing in crossing boulders with firmly set bowlegs and bulging back muscles.

We gave Ka-hood-oo-shough, the old chief, some tobacco and rice and coffee, and pitched our tent near his hut among tall grass. Soon after our arrival the Taylor Bay sub-chief came in from the opposite direction from ours, telling us that he came through a cut-off passage not on our chart. As stated above, we took pains to conciliate him and soothe his hurt feelings. Our words and gifts, he said, had warmed his sore heart and made him glad and comfortable.

The view down the bay among the islands was, I thought, the finest of this kind of scenery that I had yet observed.

The weather continued cold and rainy. Nevertheless Mr. Young and I and our crew, together with one of the Hoonas, an old man who acted as guide, left camp to explore one of the upper arms of the bay, where we were told there was a large glacier. We managed to push the canoe several miles up the stream that drains the glacier to a point where the swift current was divided among rocks and the banks were overhung with alders and willows. I left the canoe and pushed up the right bank past a magnificent waterfall some twelve hundred feet high, and over the shoulder of a mountain, until I secured a good view of the lower part of the glacier. It is probably a lobe of the Taylor Bay or Brady Glacier.

On our return to camp, thoroughly drenched and cold, the old chief came to visit us, apparently as wet and cold as ourselves.

"I have been thinking of you all day," he said, "and pitying you, knowing how miserable you were, and as soon as I saw your canoe coming back I was ashamed to think that I had been sitting warm and dry at my fire while you were out in the storm; therefore I made haste to strip off my dry clothing and put on these wet rags to share your misery and show how much I love you."

I had another long talk with Ka-hood-oo-shough the next day.

"I am not able," he said, "to tell you how much good

your words have done me. Your words are good, and they are strong words. Some of my people are foolish, and when they make their salmon traps they do not take care to tie the poles firmly together, and when the big rain-floods come the traps break and are washed away because the people who made them are foolish people. But your words are strong words and when storms come to try them they will stand the storms."

There was much handshaking as we took our leave and assurances of eternal friendship. The grand old man stood on the shore watching us and waving farewell until we were out of sight.

We now steered for the Muir Glacier and arrived at the front on the east side the evening of the third, and camped on the end of the moraine, where there was a small stream. Captain Tyeen was inclined to keep at a safe distance from the tremendous threatening cliffs of the discharging wall. After a good deal of urging he ventured within half a mile of them, on the east side of the fjord, where with Mr. Young I went ashore to seek a campground on the moraine, leaving the Indians in the canoe. In a few minutes after we landed a huge berg sprung aloft with awful commotion, and the frightened Indians incontinently fled down the fjord, plying their paddles with admirable energy in the tossing waves until a safe harbor was reached around the south end of the moraine. I found a good place for a camp in a slight hollow where a few spruce stumps afforded firewood. But all efforts to get Tyeen out of his harbor failed. "Nobody knew," he said, "how far the angry ice mountain could throw waves to break his canoe." Therefore I had my bedding and some provisions carried to my stump camp, where I could watch the bergs as they were discharged and get night views of the brow of the glacier and its sheer jagged face all the way across from side to side of the channel. One night the water was luminous and the surge from discharging icebergs churned the water into silver fire, a glorious sight in the darkness. I also went back up the east side of the glacier five or six miles and ascended a mountain between its first two eastern tributaries, which, though covered with grass near the top, was exceedingly steep and difficult. A bulging ridge near the top I discovered was formed of ice, a remnant of the glacier when it stood at this elevation which had been preserved by moraine material and later by a thatch of dwarf bushes and grass.

Next morning at daybreak I pushed eagerly back over the comparatively smooth eastern margin of the glacier to see as much as possible of the upper fountain region. About five miles back from the front I climbed a mountain twenty-five hundred feet high, from the flowery summit of which, the day being clear, the vast glacier and its principal branches were displayed in one magnificent view. Instead of a stream of ice winding down a mountain-walled valley like the largest of the Swiss glaciers, the Muir looks like a broad undulating prairie streaked with medial moraines and gashed with crevasses, surrounded by numberless mountains from which flow its many tributary glaciers. There are seven main tributaries from ten to twenty miles long and from two to six miles wide where they enter the trunk, each of them fed by many secondary tributaries; so that the whole number of branches, great and small, pouring from the mountain fountains perhaps number upward of two hundred, not counting the smallest. The area drained by this one grand glacier can hardly be less than seven or eight hundred miles, and probably contains as much ice as all the eleven hundred Swiss glaciers combined. Its length from the frontal wall back to the head of its farthest fountain seemed to be about forty or fifty miles, and the width just below the confluence of the main tributaries about twenty-five miles. Though apparently motionless as the mountains, it flows on forever, the speed varying in every part with the seasons, but mostly with the depth of the current, and the declivity, smoothness and directness of the different portions of the basin. The flow of the central cascading portion near the front, as determined by Professor Reid, is at the rate of from two and a half to five inches an hour, or from five to ten feet a day. A strip of the main trunk about a mile in width, extending along the eastern margin about fourteen miles to a lake filled with bergs, has so little motion and is so little interrupted by crevasses, a hundred horsemen might ride abreast over it without encountering very much difficulty.

But far the greater portion of the vast expanse looking smooth in the distance is torn and crumpled into a bewildering network of hummocky ridges and blades, separated by yawning gulfs and crevasses, so that the explorer, crossing it from shore to shore, must always have a hard time. In hollow spots here and there in the heart of the icy wilderness are small lakelets fed by swift-glancing streams that flow without friction in blue shining channels, making delightful melody, singing and ringing in silvery tones of peculiar sweetness, radiant crystals like flowers ineffably fine growing in dazzling beauty along their banks. Few, however, will be likely to enjoy them. Fortunately to most travelers the thundering ice wall, while comfortably accessible, is also the most strikingly interesting portion of the glacier.

The mountains about the great glacier were also seen from this standpoint in exceedingly grand and telling views, ranged and grouped in glorious array. Along the valleys of the main tributaries to the northwestward I saw far into their shadowy depths, one noble peak in its snowy robes appearing beyond another in fine perspective. One of the most remarkable of them, fashioned like a superb crown with delicately fluted sides, stands in the middle of the second main tributary, counting from left to right. To the westward the magnificent Fairweather Range is displayed in all its glory, lifting its peaks and glaciers into the blue sky. Mt. Fairweather, though not the highest, is the noblest and most majestic in port and architecture of all the sky-dwelling company. La Perouse, at the south end of the range, is also a magnificent mountain, symmetrically peaked and sculptured, and wears its robes of snow and glaciers in noble style. Lituya, as seen from here, is an immense tower, severely plain and massive. It makes a fine and terrible and lonely impression. Crillon, though the loftiest of all (being nearly sixteen thousand feet high), presents no well-marked features. Its ponderous glaciers have ground it away into long, curling ridges until, from this point of view, it resembles a huge twisted shell. The lower summits about the Muir Glacier, like this one, the first that I climbed, are richly adorned and enlivened with flowers, though they make but a faint show in general views. Lines and dashes of bright green appear on the lower slopes as one approaches them from the glacier, and a fainter green tinge may be noticed on the subordinate summits at a height of two thousand or three thousand feet. The lower are mostly alder bushes and the topmost a lavish profusion of flowering plants, chiefly cassiope, vaccinium, pyrola, erigeron, gentiana, campanula, anemone, larkspur, and columbine, with a few grasses and ferns. Of these cassiope is at once the commonest and the most beautiful and influential. In some places its delicate stems make mattresses more than a foot thick over several acres, while the bloom is so abundant that a single handful plucked at random contains hundreds of its pale pink bells. The very thought of this Alaska garden is a joyful exhilaration. Though the storm-beaten ground it is growing on is nearly half a mile high, the glacier centuries ago flowed over it as a river flows over a boulder; but out of all the cold darkness and glacial crushing and grinding comes this warm, abounding beauty and life to teach us that what we in our faithless ignorance and fear call destruction is creation finer and finer.

When night was approaching I scrambled down out of my blessed garden to the glacier, and returned to my lonely camp, and, getting some coffee and bread, again went up the moraine to the east end of the great ice wall. It is about three miles long, but the length of the jagged, berg-producing portion that stretches across the fjord from side to side like a huge green-and-blue barrier is only about two miles and rises above the water to a height of from two hundred and fifty to three hundred feet. Soundings made by Captain Carroll show that seven hundred and twenty feet of the wall is below the surface, and a third unmeasured portion is buried beneath the moraine detritus deposited at the foot of it. Therefore, were the water and rocky detritus cleared away, a sheer precipice of ice would be presented nearly two miles long and more than a thousand feet high. Seen from a distance, as you come up the fjord, it seems comparatively regular in form, but it is far otherwise; bold, jagged capes jut forward into the fjord, alternating with deep reentering angles and craggy hollows with plain bastions, while the top is roughened with innumerable spires and pyramids and sharp hacked blades leaning and toppling or cutting straight into the sky.

The number of bergs given off varies somewhat with the weather and the tides, the average being about one every five or six minutes, counting only those that roar loud enough to make themselves heard at a distance of two or three miles. The very largest, however, may under favorable conditions be heard ten miles or even farther. When a large mass sinks from the upper fissured portion of the wall, there is first a keen, prolonged, thundering roar, which slowly subsides into a low muttering growl, followed by numerous smaller grating clashing sounds from the agitated bergs that dance in the waves about the newcomer as if in welcome; and these again are followed by the swash and roar of the waves that are raised and hurled up the beach against the moraines. But the largest and most beautiful of the bergs, instead of thus falling from the upper weathered portion of the wall, rise from the submerged portion with a still grander commotion, springing with tremendous voice and gestures nearly to the top of the wall, tons of water streaming like hair down their sides, plunging and rising again and again before they finally settle in perfect poise, free at last, after having formed part of the slow-crawling glacier for centuries. And as we contemplate their history, as they sail calmly away down the fjord to the sea, how wonderful it seems that ice formed from pressed snow on the far-off mountains two or three hundred years ago should still be pure and lovely in color after all its travel and toil in the rough mountain quarries, grinding and fashioning the features of predestined landscapes.

When sunshine is sifting through the midst of the multitude of icebergs that fill the fjord and through the jets of radiant spray ever rising from the tremendous dashing and splashing of the falling and upspringing bergs, the effect is indescribably glorious. Glorious, too, are the shows they make in the night when the moon and stars are shining. The berg-thunder seems far louder than by day, and the projecting buttresses seem higher as they stand forward in the pale light, relieved by gloomy hollows, while the newborn bergs are dimly seen, crowned with faint lunar rainbows in the up-dashing spray. But it is in the darkest nights when storms are blowing and the waves are phosphorescent that the most impressive displays are made. Then the long range of ice-bluffs is plainly seen stretching through the gloom in weird, unearthly splendor, luminous wave foam dashing against every bluff and drifting berg; and ever and anon amid all this wild auroral splendor some huge newborn berg dashes the living water into yet brighter foam, and the streaming torrents pouring from its sides are worn as robes of light, while they roar in awful accord with the winds and waves, deep calling unto deep, glacier to glacier, from fjord to fjord over all the wonderful bay.

After spending a few days here, we struck across to the main Hoona village on the south side of Icy Strait, thence by a long cutoff with one short portage to Chatham Strait, and thence down through Peril Strait, sailing all night, hoping to catch the mail steamer at Sitka. We arrived at the head of the strait about daybreak. The tide was falling, and rushing down with the swift current as if descending a majestic cataract was a memorable experience. We reached Sitka the same night, and there I paid and discharged my crew, making allowance for a couple of days or so for the journey back home to Fort Wrangell, while I boarded the steamer for Portland and thus ended my explorations for this season.

PART THREE

THE TRIP OF 1890

17

IN CAMP AT GLACIER BAY

I left San Francisco for Glacier Bay on the steamer City of Pueblo, June 14, 1890, at 10 A.M., this being my third trip to southeastern Alaska and fourth to Alaska, including northern and western Alaska as far as Unalaska and Pt. Barrow and the northeastern coast of Siberia. The bar at the Golden Gate was smooth, the weather cool and pleasant. The redwoods in sheltered coves approach the shore closely, their dwarfed and shorn tops appearing here and there in ravines along the coast up to Oregon. The windswept hills, beaten with scud, are of course bare of trees. Along the Oregon and Washington coast the trees get nearer the sea, for spruce and contorted pine endure the briny winds better than the redwoods. We took the inside passage between the shore and Race Rocks, a long range of islets on which many a good ship has been wrecked. The breakers from the deep Pacific, driven by the gale, made a glorious display of foam on the bald islet rocks, sending spray over the tops of some of them a hundred feet high or more in sublime, curving, jagged-edged and flame-shaped sheets. The gestures of these upspringing, purple-tinged waves as they dashed and broke were sublime and serene, combining displays of graceful beauty of motion and form with tremendous power—a truly glorious show. I noticed several small villages on the green slopes between the timbered mountains and the shore. Long Beach made quite a display of new houses along the beach, north of the mouth of the Columbia.

I had pleasant company on the Pueblo and sat at the chief engineer's table, who was a good and merry talker. An old San Francisco lawyer, rather stiff and dignified, knew my father-in-law, Dr. Strentzel. Three ladies, opposed to the pitching of the ship, were absent from table the greater part of the way. My best talker was an old Scandinavian sea captain, who was having a new bark built at Port Blakely—an interesting old salt, every sentence of his conversation flavored with sea brine, bluff and hearty as a sea wave, keen-eyed, courageous, self-reliant, and so stubbornly skeptical he refused to believe even in glaciers.

"After you see your bark," I said, "and find everything being done to your mind, you had better go on to Alaska and see the glaciers."

"Oh, I haf seen many glaciers already."

"But are you sure that you know what a glacier is?" I asked.

"Vell, a glacier is a big mountain all covered up vith ice."

"Then a river," said I, "must be a big mountain all covered with water."

I explained what a glacier was and succeeded in exciting his interest. I told him he must reform, for a man who neither believed in God nor glaciers must be very bad, indeed the worst of all unbelievers.

At Port Townsend I met Mr. Loomis, who had agreed to go with me as far as the Muir Glacier. We sailed from here on the steamer Queen. We touched again at Victoria, and I took a short walk into the adjacent woods and gardens and found the flowery vegetation in its glory, especially the large wild rose for which the region is famous, and the spiraea and English honeysuckle of the gardens.

June 18. We sailed from Victoria on the Queen at 10.30 A.M. The weather all the way to Fort Wrangell was cloudy and rainy, but the scenery is delightful even in the dullest weather. The marvelous wealth of forests, islands, and waterfalls, the cloud-wreathed heights, the many avalanche slopes and slips, the pearl-gray tones of the sky, the browns of the woods, their purple flower edges and mist fringes, the endless combinations of water and land and ever-shifting clouds—none of these greatly interest the tourists. I noticed one of the small whales that frequent these channels and mentioned the fact, then called attention to a charming group of islands, but they turned their eyes from the islands, saying, "Yes, yes, they are very fine, but where did you see the whale?"

The timber is larger and apparently better every way as you go north from Victoria, that is on the islands, perhaps on account of fires from less rain to the southward. All the islands have been overswept by the ice sheet and are but little changed as yet, save a few of the highest summits which have been sculptured by local residual glaciers. All have approximately the form of greatest strength with reference to the overflow of an ice sheet, excepting those mentioned above, which have been more or less eroded by local residual glaciers. Every channel also has the form of greatest strength with reference to ice-action. Islands, as we have seen, are still being born in Glacier Bay and elsewhere to the northward.

I found many pleasant people aboard, but strangely ignorant on the subject of earth sculpture and land-scape-making. Professor Niles, of the Boston Institute of Technology, is aboard; also Mr. Russell and Mr. Kerr of the Geological Survey, who are now on their way to Mt. St. Elias, hoping to reach the summit; and a granddaughter of Peter Burnett, the first governor of California.

We arrived at Wrangell in the rain at 10.30 P.M. There was a grand rush on shore to buy curiosities and see totem poles. The shops were jammed and mobbed, high prices paid for shabby stuff manufactured expressly for tourist trade. Silver bracelets hammered out of dollars and half dollars by Indian smiths are the most popular articles, then baskets, yellow cedar toy canoes, paddles, etc. Most people who travel look only at what they are directed to look at. Great is the power of the guidebook-maker, however ignorant. I inquired for my old friends Tyeen and Shakes, who were both absent.

June 20. We left Wrangell early this morning and passed through the Wrangell Narrows at high tide. I noticed a few bergs near Cape Fanshawe from Wrangell Glacier. The water ten miles from Wrangell is colored with particles derived mostly from the Stickeen River glaciers and Le Conte Glacier. All the waters of the channels north of Wrangell are green or yellowish from glacier erosion. We had a good view of the glaciers all the way to Juneau, but not of their high, cloud-veiled fountains. The stranded bergs on the moraine bar at the mouth of Sum Dum Bay looked just as they did when I first saw them ten years ago.

Before reaching Juneau, the Queen proceeded up

the Taku Inlet that the passengers might see the fine glacier at its head, and ventured to within half a mile of the berg-discharging front, which is about three quarters of a mile wide. Bergs fell but seldom, perhaps one in half an hour. The glacier makes a rapid descent near the front. The inlet, therefore, will not be much extended beyond its present limit by the recession of the glacier. The grand rocks on either side of its channel show ice-action in telling style. The Norris Glacier, about two miles below the Taku is a good example of a glacier in the first stage of decadence. The Taku River enters the head of the inlet a little to the east of the glaciers, coming from beyond the main coast range. All the tourists are delighted at seeing a grand glacier in the flesh. The scenery is very fine here and in the channel at Juneau. On Douglas Island there is a large mill of two hundred and forty stamps, all run by one small waterwheel, which, however, is acted on by water at enormous pressure. The forests around the mill are being rapidly nibbled away. Wind is here said to be very violent at times, blowing away people and houses and sweeping scud far up the mountainside. Winter snow is seldom more than a foot or two deep.

June 21. We arrived at Douglas Island at five in the afternoon and went sightseeing through the mill. Six hundred tons of low-grade quartz are crushed per day. Juneau, on the mainland opposite the Douglas Island mills, is quite a village, well supplied with stores, churches, etc. A dance house in which Indians are supposed to show native dances of all sorts is perhaps the best patronized of all the places of amusement. A Mr. Brooks, who prints a paper here, gave us some information on Mt. St. Elias, Mt. Wrangell, and the Cook Inlet and Prince William Sound region. He told Russell that he would never reach the summit of St. Elias, that it was inaccessible. He saw no glaciers that discharged bergs into the sea at Cook Inlet, but many in Prince William Sound.

June 22. Leaving Juneau at noon, we had a good view of the Auk Glacier at the mouth of the channel between Douglas Island and the mainland, and of Eagle Glacier a few miles north of the Auk on the east side of Lynn Canal. Then the Davidson Glacier came in sight, finely curved, striped with medial moraines, and girdled in front by its magnificent tree-fringed terminal moraine; and besides these many others of every size and pattern on the mountains bounding Lynn Canal, most of them comparatively small, completing their sculpture. The mountains on either hand and at the head of the canal are strikingly beautiful at any time of the year. The sky today is mostly clear, with just clouds enough hovering about the mountains to show them to best advantage as they stretch onward in sustained grandeur like two separate and distinct ranges, each mountain with its glaciers and clouds and fine sculpture glowing bright in smooth, graded light. Only a few of them exceed five thousand feet in height; but as one naturally associates great height with ice-and-snow-laden mountains and with glacial sculpture so pronounced, they seem much higher. There are now two canneries at the head of Lynn Canal. The Indians furnish some of the salmon at ten cents each. Everybody sits up to see the midnight sky. At this time of the year there is no night here, though the sun drops a degree or two below the horizon. One may read at twelve o'clock San Francisco time.

June 23. Early this morning we arrived in Glacier Bay. We passed through crowds of bergs at the mouth of the bay, though, owing to wind and tide, there were but few at the front of Muir Glacier. A fine, bright day, the last of a group of a week or two, as shown by the dryness of the sand along the shore and on the moraine—rare weather hereabouts. Most of the passengers went ashore and climbed the moraine on the east side to get a view of the glacier from a point a little higher than the top of the front wall. A few ventured on a mile or two farther. The day was delightful, and our one hundred and eighty passengers were happy, gazing at the beautiful blue of the bergs and the shattered pinnacled crystal wall, awed by the thunder and commotion of the falling and rising ice bergs, which ever and anon sent spray flying several hundred feet into the air and raised swells that set all the fleet of bergs in motion and roared up the beach, telling the story of the birth of every iceberg far and near. The number discharged varies much, influenced in part no doubt by the tides and weather and seasons, sometimes one every five minutes for half a day at a time on the average, though intervals of twenty or thirty minutes may occur without any considerable fall, then three or four immense discharges will take place in as many minutes. The sound they make is like heavy thunder, with a prolonged roar after deep thudding sounds—a perpetual thunderstorm easily heard three or four miles away. The roar in our tent and the shaking of the ground one or two miles distant from points of discharge seems startlingly near.

I had to look after camp supplies and left the ship late this morning, going with a crowd to the glacier; then, taking advantage of the fine weather, I pushed off alone into the silent icy prairie to the east, to Nunatak Island, about five hundred feet above the ice. I discovered a small lake on the larger of the two islands, and many battered and ground fragments of fossil wood, large and small. They seem to have come from trees that grew on the island perhaps centuries ago. I mean to use this island as a station in setting out stakes to measure the glacial flow. The top of Mt. Fairweather is in sight at a distance of perhaps thirty miles, the ice all smooth on the eastern border, wildly broken in the central portion. I reached the ship at 2.30 P.M. I had intended getting back at noon and sending letters and bidding friends goodbye, but could not resist this glacier saunter. The ship moved off as soon as I was seen on the moraine bluff, and Loomis and I waved our hats in farewell to the many wavings of handkerchiefs of acquaintances we had made on the trip.

Our goods—blankets, provisions, tent, etc.—lay in a rocky moraine hollow within a mile of the great terminal wall of the glacier, and the discharge of the rising and falling icebergs kept up an almost continuous thundering and echoing, while a few gulls flew about on easy wing or stood like specks of foam on the shore. These were our neighbors.

After my twelve-mile walk, I ate a cracker and planned the camp. I found that one of my boxes had been left on the steamer, but still we have more than enough of everything. We obtained two cords of dry wood at Juneau which Captain Carroll kindly had his men carry up the moraine to our campground. We piled the wood as a windbreak, then laid a floor of lumber brought from Seattle for a square tent, nine feet by nine. We set the tent, stored our provisions in it, and made our beds. This work was done by 11.30 P.M., good daylight lasting to this time. We slept well in our roomy cotton house, dreaming of California home nests in the wilderness of ice.

June 25. A rainy day. For a few hours I kept count of the number of bergs discharged, then sauntered along the beach to the end of the crystal wall. A portion of the way is dangerous, the moraine bluff being capped by an overlying lobe of the glacier, which as it melts sends down boulders and fragments of ice, while the strip of sandy shore at high tide is only a few rods wide, leaving but little room to escape from the falling moraine material and the berg-waves. The view of the ice cliffs, pinnacles, spires and ridges was very telling, a magnificent picture of nature's power and industry and love of beauty. About a hundred or a hundred and fifty feet from the shore a large stream issues from an arched, tunnellike channel in the wall of the glacier, the blue of the ice hall being of an exquisite tone, contrasting with the strange sooty, smoky, brown-colored stream. The front wall of the Muir Glacier is about two and a half or three miles wide. Only the central portion about two miles wide discharges icebergs. The two wings advanced over the washed and stratified moraine deposits have little or no motion, melting and receding as fast, or perhaps faster, than it advances. They have been advanced at least a mile over the old re-formed moraines, as is shown by the overlying, angular, recent moraine deposits, now being laid down, which are continuous with the medial moraines of the glacier.

In the old stratified moraine banks, trunks and branches of trees showing but little sign of decay occur at a height of about a hundred feet above tidewater.

I have not yet compared this fossil wood with that of the opposite shore deposits. That the glacier was once withdrawn considerably back of its present limit seems plain. Immense torrents of water had filled in the inlet with stratified moraine material, and for centuries favorable climatic conditions allowed forests to grow upon it. At length the glacier advanced, probably three or four miles, uprooting and burying the trees which had grown undisturbed for centuries. Then came a great thaw, which produced the flood that deposited the uprooted trees. Also the trees which grew around the shores above reach of floods were shed off, perhaps by the thawing of the soil that was resting on the buried margin of the glacier, left on its retreat and protected by a covering of moraine-material from melting as fast as the exposed surface of the glacier. What appear to be remnants of the margin of the glacier when it stood at a much higher level still exist on the left side and probably all along its banks on both sides just below its present terminus.

June 26. We fixed a mark on the left wing to measure the motion if any. It rained all day, but I had a grand tramp over mud, ice, and rock to the east wall of the inlet. Brown metamorphic slate, close-grained in places, dips away from the inlet, presenting edges to ice-action, which has given rise to a singularly beautiful and striking surface, polished and grooved and fluted.

All the next day it rained. The mountains were smothered in dull-colored mist and fog, the great glacier looming through the gloomy gray fog fringes with wonderful effect. The thunder of bergs booms and rumbles through the foggy atmosphere. It is bad weather for exploring but delightful nevertheless, making all the strange, mysterious region yet stranger and more mysterious.

June 28. A light rain. We were visited by two parties of Indians. A man from each canoe came ashore, leaving the women in the canoe to guard against the berg-waves. I tried my Chinook and made out to say that I wanted to hire two of them in a few days to go a little way back on the glacier and around the bay. They are seal hunters and promised to come again with "Charley," who "hi yu kumtux wawa Boston"— knew well how to speak English.

I saw three huge bergs born. Spray rose about two hundred feet. Lovely reflections showed of the pale-blue tones of the ice wall and mountains in the calm water. Mirages are common, making the stranded bergs along the shore look like the sheer frontal wall of the glacier from which they were discharged.

I am watching the ice wall, berg life and behavior, etc. Yesterday and today a solitary small flycatcher was feeding about camp. A sandpiper on the shore, loons, ducks, gulls, and crows, a few of each, and a bald eagle are all the birds I have noticed thus far. The glacier is thundering gloriously.

June 30. Clearing clouds and sunshine. In less than a minute I saw three large bergs born. First there is usually a preliminary thundering of comparatively small masses as the large mass begins to fall, then the grand crash and boom and reverberating roaring. Oftentimes three or four heavy main throbbing thuds and booming explosions are heard as the main mass falls in several pieces, and also secondary thuds and thunderings as the mass or masses plunge and rise again and again ere they come to rest. Seldom, if ever, do the towers, battlements, and pinnacles into which the front of the glacier is broken fall forward headlong from their bases like falling trees at the water level or above or below it. They mostly sink vertically or nearly so, as if undermined by the melting action of the water of the inlet, occasionally maintaining their upright position after sinking far below the level of the water, and rising again a hundred feet or more into the air with water streaming like hair down their sides from their crowns, then launch forward and fall flat with yet another thundering report, raising spray in magnificent, flame-like, radiating jets and sheets, occasionally to the very top of the front wall. Illumined by the sun, the spray and angular crystal masses are indescribably beautiful. Some of the discharges pour in fragments from clefts in the wall like waterfalls, white and mealy-looking, even dusty with minute swirling ice particles, followed by a rushing succession of thunder-tones combining into a huge, blunt, solemn roar. Most of these crumbling discharges are from the excessively shattered central part of the ice wall; the solid deep-blue masses from the ends of the wall forming the large bergs rise from the bottom of the glacier.

Many lesser reports are heard at a distance of a mile or more from the fall of pinnacles into crevasses or from the opening of new crevasses. The berg discharges are very irregular, from three to twenty-two an hour. On one rising tide, six hours, there were sixty bergs discharged, large enough to thunder and be heard at distances of from three quarters to one and a half miles; and on one succeeding falling tide, six hours, sixty-nine were discharged.

July 1. We were awakened at four o'clock this morning by the whistle of the steamer George W. Elder. I went out on the moraine and waved my hand in salute and was answered by a toot from the whistle. Soon a party came ashore and asked if I was Professor Muir. The leader, Professor Harry Fielding Reid of Cleveland, Ohio, introduced himself and his companion, Mr. Cushing, also of Cleveland, and six or eight young students who had come well provided with instruments to study the glacier. They landed seven or eight tons of freight and pitched camp beside ours. I am delighted to have companions so congenial—we have now a village.

As I set out to climb the second mountain, three thousand feet high, on the east side of the glacier, I met many tourists returning from a walk on the smooth east margin of the glacier, and had to answer many questions. I had a hard climb, but wonderful views were developed and I sketched the glacier from this high point and most of its upper fountains.

Many fine alpine plants grew here, an anemone on the summit, two species of cassiope in shaggy mats, three or four dwarf willows, large blue hairy lupines eighteen inches high, parnassia, phlox, solidago, dandelion, white-flowered bryanthus, daisy, pedicularis, epilobium, etc., with grasses, sedges, mosses, and lichens, forming a delightful deep spongy sod. Woodchucks stood erect and piped dolefully for an hour "Chee-chee!" with jaws absurdly stretched to emit so thin a note—rusty-looking, seedy fellows, also a smaller striped species which stood erect and cheeped and whistled like a Douglas squirrel. I saw three or four species of birds. A finch flew from her nest at my

feet; and I almost stepped on a family of young ptarmigan ere they scattered, little bunches of downy brown
silk, small but able to run well. They scattered along a
snowbank, over boulders, through willows, grass, and
flowers, while the mother, very lame, tumbled and
sprawled at my feet. I stood still until the little ones
began to peep; the mother answered "Too-too-too" and
showed admirable judgment and devotion. She was in
brown plumage with white on the wing primaries. She
had fine grounds on which to lead and feed her young.

Not a cloud in the sky today; a faint film to the
north vanished by noon, leaving all the sky full of soft,
hazy light. The magnificent mountains around the
widespread tributaries of the glacier; the great, gently undulating, prairie-like expanse of the main trunk,
bluish on the east, pure white on the west and north;
its trains of moraines in magnificent curving lines and
many colors—black, gray, red, and brown; the stormy,
cataract-like, crevassed sections; the hundred fountains; the lofty, pure white Fairweather Range; the
thunder of the plunging bergs; the fleet of bergs sailing tranquilly in the inlet—formed a glowing picture
of nature's beauty and power.

July 2. I crossed the inlet with Mr. Reid and Mr.
Adams today. The stratified drift on the west side all
the way from top to base contains fossil wood. On the
east side, as far as I have seen it, the wood occurs only
in one stratum at a height of about a hundred and
twenty feet in sand and clay. Some in a bank of the
west side are rooted in clay soil. I noticed a large grove
of stumps in a washed-out channel near the glacier
front but had no time to examine closely. Evidently
a flood carrying great quantities of sand and gravel

had overwhelmed and broken off these trees, leaving high stumps. The deposit, about a hundred feet or more above them, had been recently washed out by one of the draining streams of the glacier, exposing a part of the old forest floor certainly two or three centuries old.

I climbed along the right bank of the lowest of the tributaries and set a signal flag on a ridge fourteen hundred feet high. This tributary is about one and a fourth or one and a half miles wide and has four secondary tributaries. It reaches tidewater but gives off no bergs. Later I climbed the large Nunatak Island, seven thousand feet high, near the west margin of the glacier. It is composed of crumbling granite draggled with washed boulders, but has some enduring bosses which on sides and top are polished and scored rigidly, showing that it had been heavily overswept by the glacier when it was thousands of feet deeper than now, like a submerged boulder in a river channel. This island is very irregular in form, owing to the variations in the structure joints of the granite. It has several small lakelets and has been loaded with glacial drift, but by the melting of the ice about its flanks is shedding it off, together with some of its own crumbling surface. I descended a deep rock gully on the north side, the rawest, dirtiest, dustiest, most dangerous that I have seen hereabouts. There is also a large quantity of fossil wood scattered on this island, especially on the north side, that on the south side having been cleared off and carried away by the first tributary glacier, which, being lower and melting earlier, has allowed the soil of the moraine material to fall, together with its forest, and be carried off. That on the north side is now being carried off or buried. The last of the main ice foundation is melting and the moraine material re-formed over and over again, and the fallen tree trunks, decayed or half decayed or in a fair state of preservation, are also unburied and buried again or carried off to the terminal or lateral moraine.

I found three small seedling Sitka spruces, feeble beginnings of a new forest. The circumference of the island is about seven miles. I arrived at camp about midnight, tired and cold. Sailing across the inlet in a cranky rotten boat through the midst of icebergs was dangerous, and I was glad to get ashore.

July 4. I climbed the east wall to the summit, about thirty-one hundred feet or so, by the northernmost ravine next to the yellow ridge, finding about a mile of snow in the upper portion of the ravine and patches on the summit. A few of the patches probably lie all the year, the ground beneath them is so plantless. On the edge of some of the snowbanks I noticed cassiope. The thin, green, mosslike patches seen from camp are composed of a rich, shaggy growth of cassiope, white-flowered bryanthus, dwarf vaccinium with bright pink flowers, saxifrages, anemones, bluebells, gentians, small erigeron, pedicularis, dwarf willow and a few species of grasses. Of these, *Cassiope tetragona* is far the most influential and beautiful. Here it forms mats a foot thick and an acre or more in area, the sections being measured by the size and drainage of the soil patches. I saw a few plants anchored in the less crumbling parts of the steep-faced bosses and steps—parnassia, potentilla, hedysarum, lutkea, etc. The lower, rough-looking patches half way up the mountain are mostly alder bushes ten or fifteen feet high. I had a fine view of the top of the mountain-mass which forms the boundary wall of the upper portion of the inlet on the west side, and of several glaciers, tributary to the first of the eastern tributaries of the main Muir Glacier. Five or six of these tributaries were seen, most of them now melted off from the trunk and independent. The highest peak to the eastward has an elevation of about five thousand feet or a little less. I also had glorious views of the Fairweather Range, La Perouse, Crillon, Lituya, and Fairweather. Mt. Fairweather is the most beautiful of all the giants that stand guard about Glacier Bay. When the sun is shining on it from the east or south its magnificent glaciers and colors are brought out in most telling display. In the late afternoon its features become less distinct. The atmosphere seems pale and hazy, though around to the north and northeastward of Fairweather innumerable white peaks are displayed, the highest fountainheads of the Muir Glacier crowded together in bewildering array, most exciting and inviting to the mountaineer. Altogether I have had a delightful day, a truly glorious celebration of the fourth.

July 6. I sailed three or four miles down the east coast of the inlet with the Reid party's cook, who is supposed to be an experienced camper and prospector, and landed at a stratified moraine bank. It was here that I camped in 1880, a point at that time less than half a mile from the front of the glacier, now one and a half miles. I found my Indian's old camp made just ten years ago, and Professor Wright's of five years ago. Their alder-bough beds and fireplace were still marked and but little decayed. I found thirty-three species of plants in flower, not counting willows—a showy garden on the shore only a few feet above high tide, watered by a fine stream. Lutkea, hedysarum, parnassia, epilobium, bluebell, solidago, habenaria, strawberry with fruit half grown, arctostaphylos, mertensia, erigeron, willows, tall grasses and alder are the principal species. There are many butterflies in this garden. Gulls are breeding near here. I saw young in the water today.

On my way back to camp I discovered a group of monumental stumps in a washed-out valley of the moraine and went ashore to observe them. They are in the dry course of a flood channel about eighty feet above mean tide and four or five hundred yards back from the shore, where they have been pounded and battered by boulders rolling against them and over them, making them look like gigantic shaving brushes. The largest is about three feet in diameter and probably three hundred years old. I mean to return and examine them at leisure. A smaller stump, still firmly rooted, is standing astride of an old crumbling trunk, showing that at least two generations of trees flourished here undisturbed by the advance or retreat of the glacier or by its draining stream floods. They are Sitka spruces and the wood is mostly in a good state of preservation. How these trees were broken off without being uprooted is dark to me at present. Perhaps most of their companions were uprooted and carried away.

July 7. Another fine day; scarce a cloud in the sky. The icebergs in the bay are miraged in the distance to look like the frontal wall of a great glacier. I am writing letters in anticipation of the next steamer, the Queen.

She arrived about 2.30 P.M. with two hundred and

thirty tourists. What a show they made with their ribbons and kodaks! All seemed happy and enthusiastic, though it was curious to see how promptly all of them ceased gazing when the dinner bell rang, and how many turned from the great thundering crystal world of ice to look curiously at the Indians that came alongside to sell trinkets, and how our little camp and kitchen arrangements excited so many to loiter and waste their precious time prying into our poor hut.

July 8. A fine clear day. I went up the glacier to observe stakes and found that a marked point near the middle of the current had flowed about a hundred feet in eight days. On the medial moraine one mile from the front there was no measureable displacement. I found a raven devouring a tomcod that was alive on a shallow at the mouth of the creek. It had probably been wounded by a seal or eagle.

July 10. I have been getting acquainted with the main features of the glacier and its fountain mountains with reference to an exploration of its main tributaries and the upper part of its prairie-like trunk, a trip I have long had in mind. I have been building a sled and must now get fully ready to start without reference to the weather. Yesterday evening I saw a large blue berg just as it was detached sliding down from the front. Two of Professor Reid's party rowed out to it as it sailed past the camp, estimating it to be two hundred and forty feet in length and one hundred feet high.

18

MY SLED-TRIP ON THE MUIR GLACIER

I started off the morning of July 11 on my memorable sled-trip to obtain general views of the main upper part of the Muir Glacier and its seven principal tributaries, feeling sure that I would learn something and at the same time get rid of a severe bronchial cough that followed an attack of the grippe and had troubled me for three months. I intended to camp on the glacier every night, and did so, and my throat grew better every day until it was well, for no lowland microbe could stand such a trip. My sled was about three feet long and made as light as possible. A sack of hardtack, a little tea and sugar, and a sleeping bag were firmly lashed on it so that nothing could drop off however much it might be jarred and dangled in crossing crevasses.

Two Indians carried the baggage over the rocky moraine to the clear glacier at the side of one of the eastern Nunatak Islands. Mr. Loomis accompanied me to this first camp and assisted in dragging the empty sled over the moraine. We arrived at the middle Nunatak Island about nine o'clock. Here I sent back my Indian carriers, and Mr. Loomis assisted me the first day in hauling the loaded sled to my second camp at the foot of Hemlock Mountain, returning the next morning.

July 13. I skirted the mountain to eastward a few miles and was delighted to discover a group of trees high up on its ragged rocky side, the first trees I had seen on the shores of Glacier Bay or on those of any of its glaciers. I left my sled on the ice and climbed the mountain to see what I might learn. I found that all the trees were mountain hemlock (*Tsuga mertensiana*), and were evidently the remnant of an old well-established forest, standing on the only ground that was stable, all the rest of the forest below it having been sloughed off with the soil from the disintegrating slate bedrock. The lowest of the trees stood at an elevation of about two thousand feet above the sea, the highest at about three thousand feet or a little higher. Nothing could be more striking than the contrast between the raw, crumbling, deforested portions of the mountain, looking like a quarry that was being worked, and the forested part with its rich, shaggy beds of cassiope and bryanthus in full bloom, and its sumptuous cushions of flower-enameled mosses. These garden patches are full of gay colors of gentian, erigeron, anemone, larkspur, and columbine, and are enlivened with happy birds and bees and marmots. Climbing to an elevation of twenty-five hundred feet, which is about fifteen hundred feet above the level of the glacier at this point, I saw and heard a few marmots, and three ptarmigans that were as tame as barnyard fowls. The sod is sloughing off on the edges, keeping it ragged. The trees are storm-bent from the southeast. A few are standing at an elevation of nearly three thousand feet; at twenty-five hundred feet, pyrola, veratrum, vaccinium, fine grasses, sedges, willows, mountain ash, buttercups, and acres of the most luxuriant cassiope are in bloom.

A lake encumbered with icebergs lies at the end of Divide Glacier. A spacious, level-floored valley beyond it, eight or ten miles long, with forested mountains on its west side, perhaps discharges to the southeastward into Lynn Canal. The divide of the glacier is about opposite the third of the eastern tributaries. Another berg-dotted lake into which the drainage of the Braided Glacier flows lies a few miles to the westward and is one and a half miles long. Berg Lake is next to the remarkable Girdled Glacier to the southeastward.

When the ice-period was in its prime, much of the Muir Glacier that now flows northward into Howling Valley flowed southward into Glacier Bay as a tributary of the Muir. All the rock contours show this, and so do the medial moraines. Berg Lake is crowded with bergs because they have no outlet and melt slowly. I heard none discharged. I had a hard time crossing the Divide Glacier, on which I camped. Half a mile back from the lake I gleaned a little fossil wood and made a fire on moraine boulders for tea. I slept fairly well on the sled. I heard the roar of four cascades on a shaggy green mountain on the west side of Howling Valley and saw three wild goats fifteen hundred feet up in the steep grassy pastures.

July 14. I rose at four o'clock this cloudy and dismal morning and looked for my goats, but saw only one. I thought there must be wolves where there were goats, and in a few minutes heard their low, dismal, far-reaching howling. One of them sounded very near and came nearer until it seemed to be less than a quarter of a mile away on the edge of the glacier. They had evidently seen me, and one or more had come down to observe me, but I was unable to catch sight of any of them. About half an hour later, while I was eating breakfast, they began howling again, so near I began to fear they had a mind to attack me, and I made haste to the shelter of a big square boulder, where, though I had no gun, I might be able to defend myself from a front attack with my alpenstock. After waiting half an hour or so to see what these wild dogs meant to do, I ventured to proceed on my journey to the foot of Snow Dome, where I camped for the night.

There are six tributaries on the northwest side of Divide arm, counting to the Gray Glacier, next after Granite Canyon Glacier going northwest. Next is Dirt Glacier, which is dead. I saw bergs on the edge of the main glacier a mile back from here which seem to have been left by the draining of a pool in a sunken hollow. A circling rim of driftwood, back twenty rods on the glacier, marks the edge of the lakelet shore where the bergs lie scattered and stranded. It is now half past ten o'clock and getting dusk as I sit by my little fossil-wood fire writing these notes. A strange bird is calling and complaining. A stream is rushing into a glacier well on the edge of which I am camped, back a few yards from the base of the mountain for fear of falling stones. A few small ones are rattling down the steep slope. I must go to bed.

July 15. I climbed the dome to plan a way, scan the glacier, and take bearings, etc., in case of storms. The main divide is about fifteen hundred feet; the second divide, about fifteen hundred also, is about one and one half miles southeastward. The flow of water on the glacier noticeably diminished last night though there was no frost. It is now already increasing. Stones begin to roll into the crevasses and into new positions, sliding against each other, half turning over or falling on moraine ridges. Mud pellets with small pebbles slip and roll slowly from ice hummocks again and again. How often and by how many ways are boulders finished and finally brought to anything like permanent form and place in beds for farms and fields, forests and gardens. Into crevasses and out again, into moraines, shifted and reinforced and reformed by avalanches, melting from pedestals, etc. Rain, frost, and dew help in the work; they are swept in rills, caught and ground in pot hole mills. Moraines of washed pebbles, like those on glacier margins, are formed by snow avalanches deposited in crevasses, then weathered out and projected on the ice as shallow raised moraines. There is one such at this camp.

A ptarmigan is on a rock twenty yards distant, as if on show. It has red over the eye, a white line, not conspicuous, over the red, belly white, white markings over the upper parts on ground of brown and black wings, mostly white as seen when flying, but the coverts the same as the rest of the body. Only about three inches of the folded primaries show white. The breast seems to have golden iridescent colors, white under the wings. It allowed me to approach within twenty feet. It walked down a sixty degree slope of the rock, took flight with a few whirring wing-beats, then sailed with wings perfectly motionless four hundred yards down a gentle grade, and vanished over the brow of a cliff. Ten days ago Loomis told me that he found a nest with nine eggs. On the way down to my sled I saw four more ptarmigans. They utter harsh notes when alarmed. "Crack, chuck, crack," with the *r* rolled and prolonged. I also saw fresh and old goat tracks and some bones that suggest wolves.

There is a pass through the mountains at the head of the third glacier. Fine mountains stand at the head on each side. The one on the northeast side is the higher and finer every way. It has three glaciers, tributary to the third. The third glacier has altogether ten tributaries, five on each side. The mountain on the left side of White Glacier is about six thousand feet high. The moraines of Girdled Glacier seem scarce to run anywhere. Only a little material is carried to Berg Lake. Most of it seems to be at rest as a terminal on the main glacier field, which here has little motion. The curves of these last as seen from this mountain-top are very beautiful.

It has been a glorious day, all pure sunshine. An hour or more before sunset, the distant mountains, a vast host, seemed more softly ethereal than ever, pale blue, ineffably fine, all angles and harshness melted off in the soft evening light. Even the snow and the grinding, cascading glaciers became divinely tender and fine in this celestial amethystine light. I got back to camp at 7.15, not tired. After my hardtack supper I could have climbed the mountain again and got back before sunrise, but dragging the sled tires me. I have been out on the glacier examining a moraine-like mass about a third of a mile from camp. It is perhaps a mile long, a hundred yards wide, and is thickly strewn with wood. I think that it has been brought down the mountain by a heavy snow avalanche, loaded on the ice, then carried away from the shore in the direction of the flow of the glacier. This explains detached moraine-masses. This one seems to have been derived from a big roomy cirque or amphitheatre on the northwest side of this Snow Dome Mountain.

To shorten the return journey I was tempted to glissade down what appeared to be a snow-filled ravine, which was very steep. All went well until

I reached a bluish spot which proved to be ice, on which I lost control of myself and rolled into a gravel talus at the foot without a scratch. Just as I got up and was getting myself orientated, I heard a loud fierce scream, uttered in an exulting, diabolical tone of voice which startled me, as if an enemy, having seen me fall, was glorying in my death. Then suddenly two ravens came swooping from the sky and alighted on the jag of a rock within a few feet of me, evidently hoping that I had been maimed and that they were going to have a feast. But as they stared at me, studying my condition, impatiently waiting for bone-picking time, I saw what they were up to and shouted, "Not yet, not yet!"

July 16. At 7 A.M. I left camp to cross the main glacier. Six ravens came to the camp as soon as I left. What wonderful eyes they must have! Nothing that moves in all this icy wilderness escapes the eyes of these brave birds. This is one of the loveliest mornings I ever saw in Alaska; not a cloud or faintest hint of one in all the wide sky. There is a yellowish haze in the east, white in the west, mild and mellow as a Wisconsin Indian Summer, but finer, more ethereal, God's holy light making all divine.

In an hour or so I came to the confluence of the first of the seven grand tributaries of the main Muir Glacier and had a glorious view of it as it comes sweeping down in wild cascades from its magnificent, pure-white, mountain-girt basin to join the main crystal sea, its many fountain peaks, clustered and crowded, all pouring forth their tribute to swell its grand current. I crossed its front a little below its confluence, where its shattered current, about two or three miles wide, is reunited, and many rills and good-sized brooks glide gurgling and ringing in pure blue channels, giving delightful animation to the icy solitude.

Most of the ice surface crossed today has been very uneven, and hauling the sled and finding a way over hummocks has been fatiguing. At times I had to lift the sled bodily and to cross many narrow, nerve-trying, ice-sliver bridges, balancing astride of them, and cautiously shoving the sled ahead of me with tremendous chasms on either side. I had made perhaps not more than six or eight miles in a straight line by six o'clock this evening when I reached ice so hummocky and tedious I concluded to camp and not try to take the sled any farther. I intend to leave it here in the middle of the basin and carry my sleeping bag and provisions the rest of the way across to the west side. I am cozy and comfortable here resting in the midst of glorious icy scenery, though very tired. I made out to get a cup of tea by means of a few shavings and splinters whittled from the bottom board of my sled, and made a fire in a little can, a small campfire, the smallest I ever made or saw, yet it answered well enough as far as tea was concerned. I crept into my sack before eight o'clock as the wind was cold and my feet wet. One of my shoes is about worn out. I may have to put on a wooden sole. This day has been cloudless throughout, with lovely sunshine, a purple evening and morning. The circumference of mountains beheld from the midst of this world of ice is marvelous, the vast plain reposing in such soft tender light, the fountain mountains so clearly cut, holding themselves aloft with their loads of ice in supreme strength and beauty of architecture. I found a skull and most of the other bones of a goat on the glacier about two miles from the nearest land. It had probably been chased out of its mountain home by wolves and devoured here. I carried its horns with me. I saw many considerable depressions in the glacial surface, also a pitlike hole, irregular, not like the ordinary wells along the slope of the many small dirt-clad hillocks, faced to the south. Now the sun is down and the sky is saffron yellow, blending and fading into purple around to the south and north. It is a curious experience to be lying in bed writing these notes, hummock waves rising in every direction, their edges marking a multitude of crevasses and pits, while all around the horizon rise peaks innumerable of most intricate style of architecture. Solemnly growling and grinding moulins contrast with the sweet low-voiced whispering and warbling of a network of rills, singing like water ouzels, glinting, gliding with indescribable softness and sweetness of voice. They are all around, one within a few feet of my hard sled bed.

July 17. Another glorious cloudless day is dawning in yellow and purple and soon the sun over the eastern peak will blot out the blue peak shadows and make all the vast white ice prairie sparkle. I slept well last night in the middle of the icy sea. The wind was cold but my sleeping bag enabled me to lie neither warm nor intolerably cold. My three-months cough is gone. Strange that with such work and exposure one should know nothing of sore throats and of what are called colds. My heavy, thick-soled shoes, resoled just before starting on the trip six days ago, are about worn out and my feet have been wet every night. But no harm comes of it, nothing but good. I succeeded in getting a warm breakfast in bed. I reached over the edge of my sled, got hold of a small cedar stick that I had been carrying, whittled a lot of thin shavings from it, stored them on my breast, then set fire to a piece of paper in a shallow tin can, added a pinch of shavings, held the cup of water that always stood at my bedside over the tiny blaze with one hand, and fed the fire by adding little pinches of shavings until the water boiled, then pulling my bread sack within reach, made a good warm breakfast, cooked and eaten in bed. Thus refreshed, I surveyed the wilderness of crevassed, hummocky ice and concluded to try to drag my little sled a mile or two farther, then, finding encouragement, persevered, getting it across innumerable crevasses and streams and around several lakes and over and through the midst of hummocks, and at length reached the western shore between five and six o'clock this evening, extremely fatigued. This I consider a hard job well done, crossing so wildly broken a glacier, fifteen miles of it from Snow Dome Mountain, in two days with a sled weighing altogether not less than a hundred pounds. I found innumerable crevasses, some of them brimful of water. I crossed in most places just where the ice was close pressed and welded after descending cascades and was being shoved over an upward slope, thus closing the crevasses at the bottom, leaving only the upper sun-melted beveled portion open for water to collect in.

Vast must be the drainage from this great basin. The waste in sunshine must be enormous, while in dark weather rains and winds also melt the ice and add to the volume produced by the rain itself. The winds also, though in temperature they may be only a degree or two above freezing point, dissolve the ice as fast, or perhaps faster, than clear sunshine. Much of the water caught in tight crevasses doubtless freezes during the winter and gives rise to many of the irregular veins seen in the structure of the glacier. Saturated snow also freezes at times and is incorporated with the ice, as only from the lower part of the glacier is the snow melted during the summer. I have noticed many traces of this action. One of the most beautiful things to be seen on the glacier is the myriads of minute and intensely brilliant radiant lights burning in rows on the banks of streams and pools and lakelets from the tips of crystals melting in the sun, making them look as if bordered with diamonds. These gems are rayed like stars and twinkle; no diamond radiates keener or more brilliant light. It was perfectly glorious to think of this divine light burning over all this vast crystal sea in such ineffably fine effulgence, and over how many other of icy Alaska's glaciers where nobody sees it. To produce these effects I fancy the ice must be melting rapidly, as it was being melted today. The ice in these pools does not melt with anything like an even surface, but in long branches and leaves, making fairy forests of points, while minute bubbles of air are constantly being set free. I am camped tonight on what I call Quarry Mountain from its raw, loose, plantless condition, seven or eight miles above the front of the glacier. I found enough fossil wood for tea. Glorious is the view to the eastward from this camp. The sun has set, a few clouds appear, and a torrent rushing down a gully and under the edge of the glacier is making a solemn roaring. No tinkling, whistling rills this night. Ever and anon I hear a falling boulder. I have had a glorious and instructive day, but am excessively weary and to bed I go.

July 18. I felt tired this morning and meant to rest today. But after breakfast at 8 A.M. I felt I must be up and doing, climbing, sketching new views up the great tributaries from the top of Quarry Mountain. Weariness vanished and I could have climbed, I think, five thousand feet. Anything seems easy after sled-dragging over hummocks and crevasses, and the constant nerve strain in jumping crevasses so as not to slip in making the spring. Quarry Mountain is the barest I have seen, a raw quarry with infinite abundance of loose decaying granite all on the go. Its slopes are excessively steep. A few patches of epilobium make gay purple spots of color. Its seeds fly everywhere seeking homes. Quarry Mountain is cut across into a series of parallel ridges by oversweeping ice. It is still overswept in three places by glacial flows a half to three quarters of a mile wide, finely arched at the top of the divides. I have been sketching, though my eyes are much inflamed and I can scarce see. All the lines I make appear double. I fear I shall not be able to make the few more sketches I want tomorrow, but must try. The day has been gloriously sunful, the glacier pale yellow toward five o'clock. The hazy air, white with a yellow tinge, gives an Indian-summerish effect. Now the blue evening shadows are creeping out over the icy plain, some ten miles long, with sunny yellow belts between them. Boulders fall now and again with dull, blunt booming, and the gravel pebbles rattle.

July 19. Nearly blind. The light is intolerable and I fear I may be long unfitted for work. I have been lying on my back all day with a snow poultice bound over my eyes. Every object I try to look at seems double; even the distant mountain ranges are doubled, the upper an exact copy of the lower, though somewhat faint. This is the first time in Alaska that I have had too much sunshine. About four o'clock this afternoon, when I was waiting for the evening shadows to enable me to get nearer the main camp, where I could be more easily found in case my eyes should become still more inflamed and I should be unable to travel, thin clouds cast a grateful shade over all the glowing landscape. I gladly took advantage of these kindly clouds to make an effort to cross the few miles of the glacier that lay between me and the shore of the inlet. I made a pair of goggles but am afraid to wear them. Fortunately the ice here is but little broken, therefore I pulled my cap well down and set off about five o'clock. I got on pretty well and camped on the glacier in sight of the main camp, which from here in a straight line is only five or six miles away. I went ashore on Granite Island and gleaned a little fossil wood with which I made tea on the ice.

July 20. I kept wet bandages on my eyes last night as long as I could, and feel better this morning, but all the mountains still seem to have double summits, giving a curiously unreal aspect to the landscape. I packed everything on the sled and moved three miles farther down the glacier, where I want to make measurements. Twice today I was visited on the ice by a hummingbird, attracted by the red lining of the bearskin sleeping bag.

I have gained some light on the formation of gravel beds along the inlet. The material is mostly sifted and sorted by successive railings and washings along the margins of the glacier tributaries, where the supply is abundant beyond anything I ever saw elsewhere.

The lowering of the surface of a glacier when its walls are not too steep leaves a part of the margin dead and buried and protected from the wasting sunshine beneath the lateral moraines. Thus a marginal valley is formed, clear ice on one side, or nearly so, buried ice on the other. As melting goes on, the marginal trough, or valley, grows deeper and wider, since both sides are being melted, the land side slower. The dead, protected ice in melting first sheds off the large boulders, as they are not able to lie on slopes where smaller ones can. Then the next larger ones are rolled off, and pebbles and sand in succession. Meanwhile this material is subjected to torrent action, as if it were cast into a trough. When floods come it is carried forward and stratified, according to the force of the current, sand, mud, or larger material. This exposes fresh surfaces of ice and melting goes on again, until enough material has been undermined to form a veil in front; then follows another washing and carrying-away and depositing where the current is allowed to spread. In melting, protected margin terraces are oftentimes formed. Perhaps these terraces mark successive heights of the glacial surface. From terrace to terrace the grist of stone is rolled and sifted. Some, meeting only feeble streams, have only the fine particles carried away and deposited in smooth beds; others, coarser, from swifter streams, overspread the fine beds, while many of the large boulders no doubt roll back upon the glacier to go on their travels again.

It has been cloudy mostly today, though sunny in the afternoon, and my eyes are getting better. The steamer Queen is expected in a day or two, so I must try to get down to the inlet tomorrow and make signal to have some of the Reid party ferry me over.

I must hear from home, write letters, get rest and more to eat.

Near the front of the glacier the ice was perfectly free, apparently, of anything like a crevasse, and in walking almost carelessly down it I stopped opposite the large granite Nunatak Island, thinking that I would there be partly sheltered from the wind. I had not gone a dozen steps toward the island when I suddenly dropped into a concealed water-filled crevasse, which on the surface showed not the slightest sign of its existence. This crevasse like many others was being used as the channel of a stream, and at some narrow point the small cubical masses of ice into which the glacier surface disintegrates were jammed and extended back farther and farther till they completely covered and concealed the water. Into this I suddenly plunged, after crossing thousands of really dangerous crevasses, but never before had I encountered a danger so completely concealed. Down I plunged over head and ears, but of course bobbed up again, and after a hard struggle succeeded in dragging myself out over the farther side. Then I pulled my sled over close to Nunatak cliff, made haste to strip off my clothing, threw it in a sloppy heap and crept into my sleeping bag to shiver away the night as best I could.

July 21. Dressing this rainy morning was a miserable job, but might have been worse. After wringing my sloppy underclothing, getting it on was far from pleasant. My eyes are better and I feel no bad effect from my icy bath. The last trace of my three months' cough is gone. No lowland grippe microbe could survive such experiences.

I have had a fine telling day examining the ruins

of the old forest of Sitka spruce that no great time ago grew in a shallow mud-filled basin near the southwest corner of the glacier. The trees were protected by a spur of the mountain that puts out here, and when the glacier advanced they were simply flooded with fine sand and overborne. Stumps by the hundred, three to fifteen feet high, rooted in a stream of fine blue mud on cobbles, still have their bark on. A stratum of decomposed bark, leaves, cones, and old trunks is still in place. Some of the stumps are on rocky ridges of gravelly soil about one hundred and twenty-five feet above the sea. The valley has been washed out by the stream now occupying it, one of the glacier's draining streams a mile long or more and an eighth of a mile wide.

I got supper early and was just going to bed, when I was startled by seeing a man coming across the moraine, Professor Reid, who had seen me from the main camp and who came with Mr. Loomis and the cook in their boat to ferry me over. I had not intended making signals for them until tomorrow but was glad to go. I had been seen also by Mr. Case and one of his companions, who were on the western mountainside above the fossil forest, shooting ptarmigans. I had a good rest and sleep and leisure to find out how rich I was in new facts and pictures and how tired and hungry I was.

19

AURORAS

A few days later I set out with Professor Reid's party to visit some of the other large glaciers that flow into the bay, to observe what changes have taken place in them since October, 1879, when I first visited and sketched them. We found the upper half of the bay closely choked with bergs, through which it was exceedingly difficult to force a way. After slowly struggling a few miles up the east side, we dragged the whale boat and canoe over rough rocks into a fine garden and comfortably camped for the night.

The next day was spent in cautiously picking a way across to the west side of the bay; and as the strangely scanty stock of provisions was already about done, and the ice jam to the northward seemed impenetrable, the party decided to return to the main camp by a comparatively open, roundabout way to the southward, while with the canoe and a handful of food scraps I pushed on northward. After a hard, anxious struggle, I reached the mouth of the Hugh Miller fjord about sundown, and tried to find a camp spot on its steep, boulder-bound shore. But no landing place where it seemed possible to drag the canoe above high-tide mark was discovered after examining a mile or more of this dreary, forbidding barrier, and as night was closing down, I decided to try to grope my way across the mouth of the fjord in the starlight to an open sandy spot on which I had camped in October, 1879, a distance of about three or four miles.

With the utmost caution I picked my way through the sparkling bergs, and after an hour or two of this nerve-trying work, when I was perhaps less than half-way across and dreading the loss of the frail canoe which would include the loss of myself, I came to a pack of very large bergs which loomed threateningly, offering no visible thoroughfare. Paddling and pushing to right and left, I at last discovered a sheer-walled opening about four feet wide and perhaps two hundred feet long, formed apparently by the splitting of a huge iceberg. I hesitated to enter this passage, fearing that the slightest change in the tide current might close it, but ventured nevertheless, judging that the dangers ahead might not be greater than those I had already passed. When I had got about a third of the way in, I suddenly discovered that the smooth-walled ice lane was growing narrower, and with desperate haste backed out. Just as the bow of the canoe cleared the sheer walls they came together with a growling crunch. Terror-stricken, I turned back, and in an anxious hour or two gladly reached the rock-bound shore that had at first repelled me, determined to stay on guard all night in the canoe or find some place where with the strength that comes in a fight for life I could drag it up the boulder wall beyond ice danger. This at last was happily done about midnight, and with no thought of sleep I went to bed rejoicing.

My bed was two boulders, and as I lay wedged and bent on their up-bulging sides, beguiling the hard, cold

time in gazing into the starry sky and across the sparkling bay, magnificent upright bars of light in bright
prismatic colors suddenly appeared, marching swiftly
in close succession along the northern horizon from
west to east as if in diligent haste, an auroral display
very different from any I had ever before beheld. Once
long ago in Wisconsin I saw the heavens draped in rich
purple auroral clouds fringed and folded in most magnificent forms; but in this glory of light, so pure, so
bright, so enthusiastic in motion, there was nothing in
the least cloud-like. The short color bars, apparently
about two degrees in height, though blending, seemed
to be as well defined as those of the solar spectrum.

How long these glad, eager soldiers of light held on
their way I cannot tell; for sense of time was charmed
out of mind and the blessed night circled away in measureless rejoicing enthusiasm.

In the early morning after so inspiring a night I
launched my canoe feeling able for anything, crossed
the mouth of the Hugh Miller fjord, and forced a way
three or four miles along the shore of the bay, hoping
to reach the Grand Pacific Glacier in front of Mt. Fairweather. But the farther I went, the ice pack, instead
of showing inviting little open streaks here and there,
became so much harder jammed that on some parts of
the shore the bergs, drifting south with the tide, were
shoving one another out of the water beyond high-tide
line. Farther progress to northward was thus rigidly
stopped, and now I had to fight for a way back to my
cabin, hoping that by good tide luck I might reach it
before dark. But at sundown I was less than halfway
home, and though very hungry was glad to land on a
little rock island with a smooth beach for the canoe
and a thicket of alder bushes for fire and bed and a

little sleep. But shortly after sundown, while these arrangements were being made, lo and behold another aurora enriching the heavens! And though it proved to be one of the ordinary almost colorless kind, thrusting long, quivering lances toward the zenith from a dark cloud-like base, after last night's wonderful display one's expectations might well be extravagant and I lay wide awake watching.

On the third night I reached my cabin and food. Professor Reid and his party came in to talk over the results of our excursions, and just as the last one of the visitors opened the door after bidding good night, he shouted, "Muir, come look here. Here's something fine."

I ran out in auroral excitement, and sure enough here was another aurora, as novel and wonderful as the marching rainbow-colored columns—a glowing silver bow spanning the Muir Inlet in a magnificent arch right under the zenith, or a little to the south of it, the ends resting on the top of the mountain walls. And though colorless and steadfast, its intense, solid, white splendor, noble proportions, and fineness of finish excited boundless admiration. In form and proportion it was like a rainbow, a bridge of one span five miles wide; and so brilliant, so fine and solid and homogeneous in every part, I fancy that if all the stars were raked together into one windrow, fused and welded and run through some celestial rolling mill, all would be required to make this one glowing white colossal bridge.

After my last visitor went to bed, I lay down on the moraine in front of the cabin and gazed and watched. Hour after hour the wonderful arch stood perfectly motionless, sharply defined and substantial-looking as if it were a permanent addition to the furniture of the sky. At length while it yet spanned the inlet in serene, unchanging splendor, a band of fluffy, pale-gray, quivering ringlets came suddenly all in a row over the eastern mountaintop, glided in nervous haste up and down the under side of the bow and over the western mountain wall. They were about one and a half times the apparent diameter of the bow in length, maintained a vertical posture all the way across, and slipped swiftly along as if they were suspended like a curtain on rings. Had these lively auroral fairies marched across the fjord on the top of the bow instead of shuffling along the under side of it, one might have fancied they were a happy band of spirit people on a journey making use of the splendid bow for a bridge. There must have been hundreds of miles of them; for the time required for each to cross from one end of the bridge to the other seemed only a minute or less, while nearly an hour elapsed from their first appearance until the last of the rushing throng vanished behind the western mountain, leaving the bridge as bright and solid and steadfast as before they arrived. But later, half an hour or so, it began to fade. Fissures or cracks crossed it diagonally through which a few stars were seen, and gradually it became thin and nebulous until it looked like the Milky Way, and at last vanished, leaving no visible monument of any sort to mark its place.

I now returned to my cabin, replenished the fire, warmed myself, and prepared to go to bed, though too aurorally rich and happy to go to sleep. But just as I was about to retire, I thought I had better take another look at the sky, to make sure that the glorious show was over; and, contrary to all reasonable expectations, I found that the pale foundation for another bow was being laid right overhead like the first. Then losing all thought of sleep, I ran back to my cabin, carried out blankets and lay down on the moraine to keep watch until daybreak, that none of the sky wonders of the glorious night within reach of my eyes might be lost.

I had seen the first bow when it stood complete in full splendor, and its gradual fading decay. Now I was to see the building of a new one from the beginning. Perhaps in less than half an hour the silvery material was gathered, condensed, and welded into a glowing, evenly proportioned arc like the first and in the same part of the sky. Then in due time over the eastern mountain wall came another throng of restless electric auroral fairies, the infinitely fine pale-gray garments of each lightly touching those of their neighbors as they swept swiftly along the under side of the bridge and down over the western mountain like the merry band that had gone the same way before them, all keeping quivery step and time to music too fine for mortal ears.

While the gay throng was gliding swiftly along, I watched the bridge for any change they might make upon it, but not the slightest could I detect. They left no visible track, and after all had passed the glowing arc stood firm and apparently immutable, but at last faded slowly away like its glorious predecessor.

Excepting only the vast purple aurora mentioned above, said to have been visible over nearly all the continent, these two silver bows in supreme, serene, supernal beauty surpassed everything auroral I ever beheld.

GLOSSARY OF WORDS
IN THE CHINOOK JARGON

Boston: English
Chuck: Water, stream
Deliat: Very, or very good
Friday: Shoreward
Hi yu: A great quantity of, plenty of
Hootchenoo: A native liquor
Hyas: Big, very
Klosh: Good
Kumtux: Know, understand
Mika: You, your (singular)
Muck-a-muck: Food
Poogh: Shoot, shooting
Sagh-a-ya: How do you do?
Skookum: Strong
Skookum-house: Jail
Tillicum: Friend
Tola: Lead (verb)
Tucktay: Seaward
Tumtum: Mind, heart
Wawa: Talk (noun or verb)

Also Available

Continue your journey with adventure writers
and literary naturalists, from Gibbs Smith:

Wild Animals I Have Known
By Ernest Thompson Seton
Hardcover, $16.99
ISBN: 978-1-4236-5488-9

Nature and Other Essays
By Ralph Waldo Emerson
Hardcover, $16.99
ISBN: 978-1-4236-5269-4

Canoeing in the Wilderness
By Henry David Thoreau
Hardcover, $14.99
ISBN: 978-1-4236-4914-4

Walden: Life in the Woods
By Henry David Thoreau
Hardcover, $16.99
ISBN: 978-1-4236-4679-2

Natural History Essays
By Henry David Thoreau
Hardcover, $16.99
ISBN: 978-1-4236-2228-4

Leaves of Grass
By Walt Whitman
Hardcover, $16.99
ISBN: 978-1-4236-4774-4

Call of the Wild
By Jack London
Hardcover, $14.99
ISBN: 978-1-4236-4677-8

Roughing It
By Mark Twain
Hardcover, $16.99
ISBN: 978-1-4236-4772-0

The Grand Canyon Expedition
By John Wesley Powell
Hardcover, $16.99
ISBN: 978-1-4236-5166-6

GIBBS SMITH
TO ENRICH AND INSPIRE HUMANKIND

our NATIONAL PARKS

JOHN MUIR

our NATIONAL PARKS

GIBBS SMITH

TO ENRICH AND INSPIRE HUMANKIND

Published by
Gibbs Smith
P.O. Box 667
Layton, Utah 84041

1.800.835.4993 orders
www.gibbs-smith.com

Cover art by Seth Lucas
Printed and bound in China

Gibbs Smith books are printed on either recycled, 100% post-consumer waste, FSC-certified papers or on paper produced from sustainable PEFC-certified forest/controlled wood source. Learn more at www. pefc.org.

Names: Muir, John, 1838–1914, author.
Title: Our national parks / John Muir.
Identifiers: LCCN 2018000357 | ISBN 9781423650393 (hardcover)
Subjects: LCSH: National parks and reserves—United States. |
   Yellowstone National Park. | Yosemite National Park (Calif.) |
   Sequoia National Park (Calif.) | Kings Canyon National Park (Calif.)
Classification: LCC E160 .M957 2018 | DDC 973—dc23
LC record available at https://lccn.loc.gov/2018000357

26 25 24 23 22   13 12 11 10 9

CONTENTS

I

THE WILD PARKS AND FOREST RESERVATIONS OF THE WEST

"Keep not standing fix'd and rooted,
Briskly venture, briskly roam;
Head and hand, where'er thou foot it,
And stout heart are still at home.
In each land the sun does visit
We are gay, whate'er betide:
To give room for wandering is it
That the world was made so wide."

The tendency nowadays to wander in wildernesses is delightful to see. Thousands of tired, nerve-shaken, over-civilized people are beginning to find out that going to the mountains is going home; that wildness is a necessity; and that mountain parks and reservations are useful not only as fountains of timber and irrigating rivers, but as fountains of life. Awakening from the stupefying effects of the vice of over-industry and the deadly apathy of luxury, they are trying as best they can to mix and enrich their own little ongoings with those of Nature, and to get rid of rust and disease. Briskly venturing and roaming, some are washing off sins and cobweb cares of the devil's spinning in all-day storms on mountains; sauntering in rosiny pinewoods or in gentian meadows, brushing through chaparral, bending down and parting sweet, flowery sprays; tracing rivers to their sources, getting in touch with the nerves of Mother Earth; jumping from rock to rock, feeling the life of them, learning the songs

1

of them, panting in whole-souled exercise, and rejoicing in deep, long-drawn breaths of pure wildness. This is fine and natural and full of promise. So also is the growing interest in the care and preservation of forests and wild places in general, and in the half wild parks and gardens of towns. Even the scenery habit in its most artificial forms, mixed with spectacles, silliness, and kodaks; its devotees arrayed more gorgeously than scarlet tanagers, frightening the wild game with red umbrellas,—even this is encouraging, and may well be regarded as a hopeful sign of the times.

All the Western mountains are still rich in wildness, and by means of good roads are being brought nearer civilization every year. To the sane and free it will hardly seem necessary to cross the continent in search of wild beauty, however easy the way, for they find it in abundance wherever they chance to be. Like Thoreau they see forests in orchards and patches of huckleberry brush, and oceans in ponds and drops of dew. Few in these hot, dim, strenuous times are quite sane or free; choked with care like clocks full of dust, laboriously doing so much good and making so much money,—or so little,—they are no longer good for themselves.

When, like a merchant taking a list of his goods, we take stock of our wildness, we are glad to see how much of even the most destructible kind is still unspoiled. Looking at our continent as scenery when it was all wild, lying between beautiful seas, the starry sky above it, the starry rocks beneath it, to compare its sides, the East and the West, would be like comparing the sides of a rainbow. But it is no longer equally beautiful. The rainbows of to-day are, I suppose, as bright as those that first spanned the sky; and some of our landscapes are growing more beautiful from year to year, notwithstanding the clearing, trampling work of civilization. New plants and animals are enriching woods and gardens, and many landscapes wholly new, with divine sculpture and architecture, are just now coming to the light of day as the mantling folds of creative glaciers are being withdrawn, and life in a thousand cheerful, beautiful forms is pushing into them, and new-born rivers are beginning to sing and shine in them. The old rivers, too, are growing longer, like healthy trees, gaining new branches and lakes as the residual glaciers at their highest sources on the mountains recede, while the rootlike branches in the flat deltas are at same time spreading farther and wider into the seas and making new lands.

Under the control of the vast mysterious forces of the interior of the earth all the continents and islands are slowly rising or sinking. Most of the mountains are diminishing in size under the wearing action of the weather, though a few are increasing in height and girth, especially the volcanic ones, as fresh floods of molten rocks are piled on their summits and spread in successive layers, like the wood-rings of trees, on their sides. New mountains, also, are being created from time to time as islands in lakes and seas, or as subordinate cones on the slopes of old ones, thus in some measure balancing the waste of old beauty with new. Man, too, is making many far-reaching changes. This most influential half animal, half angel is rapidly multiplying and spreading, covering the seas and lakes with ships, the land with huts, hotels, cathedrals, and clustered city shops and homes, so that soon, it would seem, we may have to go farther than Nansen to find a good sound solitude. None of Nature's landscapes are ugly so long as they are wild; and much, we can say comfortingly, must always be in great part wild, particularly the sea and the sky, the floods of light from the stars, and the warm, unspoilable heart of the earth, infinitely beautiful, though only dimly visible to the eye of imagination. The geysers, too, spouting from the hot underworld; the steady, long-lasting glaciers on the mountains, obedient only to the sun; Yosemite domes and the tremendous grandeur of rocky cañons and mountains in general,—these must always be wild, for man can change them and mar them hardly more than can the butterflies that hover above them. But the continent's outer beauty is fast passing away, especially the plant part of it, the most destructible and most universally charming of all.

Only thirty years ago, the great Central Valley of California, five hundred miles long and fifty miles wide, was one bed of golden and purple flowers. Now it is ploughed and pastured out of existence, gone forever,—scarce a memory of it left in fence corners and along the bluffs of the streams. The gardens of the Sierra, also, and the noble forests in both the reserved and unreserved portions are sadly hacked and trampled, notwithstanding, the ruggedness of the topography,—all excepting those of the parks guarded by a few soldiers. In the noblest forests of the world, the ground, once divinely beautiful, is desolate and repulsive, like a face ravaged by disease. This is true also of many other Pacific Coast and Rocky Mountain valleys and forests. The same fate, sooner or later, is awaiting them all, unless awakening public opinion comes forward to stop it. Even the great deserts in Arizona, Nevada, Utah, and New Mexico, which offer so little to attract settlers, and which a few years ago pioneers were afraid of, as places of desolation and death, are now taken as pastures at the rate of one or two square miles per cow, and of course their plant treasures are passing away,—the delicate abronias, phloxes, gilias, etc. Only a few of the bitter, thorny, unbitable shrubs are left, and the sturdy cactuses that defend themselves with bayonets and spears.

Most of the wild plant wealth of the East also has vanished,—gone into dusty history. Only vestiges of its glorious prairie and woodland wealth remain to bless humanity in boggy, rocky, unploughable places. Fortunately, some of these are purely wild, and go far to keep Nature's love visible. White water-lilies, with rootstocks deep and safe in mud, still send up every summer a Milky Way of starry, fragrant flowers around a thousand lakes, and many a tuft of wild grass waves its panicles on mossy rocks, beyond reach of trampling feet, in company with saxifrages, bluebells, and ferns. Even in the midst of farmers fields, precious sphagnum bogs, too soft for the feet of cattle, are preserved with their charming plants unchanged,—chiogenes, Andromeda, Kalmia, Linnæa, Arethusa, etc. Calypso borealis still hides in the arbor vitæ swamps of Canada, and away to the southward there are a few unspoiled swamps, big ones, where miasma, snakes, and alligators, like guardian angels, defend their treasures and keep them as pure as paradise. And beside a that and a that, the East is blessed with good winters and blossoming clouds that shed white flowers over all the land, covering every scar and making the saddest landscape divine at least once a year.

The most extensive, least spoiled, and most unspoilable of the gardens of the continent are the vast tundras of Alaska. In summer they extend smooth, even, undulating, continuous beds of flowers and leaves from about lat. 62 to the shores of the Arctic Ocean; and in winter sheets of snow-flowers make all the country shine, one mass of white radiance like a star. Nor are these Arctic plant people the pitiful frost-pinched unfortunates they are guessed to be by those who have never seen them. Though lowly in stature, keeping near the frozen ground as if loving it, they are bright and cheery, and speak Nature's love as plainly as their big relatives of the South. Tenderly happed and tucked in beneath downy snow to sleep through the long, white winter, they make haste to bloom in the spring without trying to grow tall, though some rise high enough to ripple and wave in the wind, and display masses of color,—yellow, purple, and blue,—so rich that they look like beds of rainbows, and are visible miles and miles away.

As early as June one may find the showy Geum glaciale in flower, and the dwarf willows putting forth myriads of fuzzy catkins, to be followed quickly, especially on the dryer ground, by mertensia, eritrichium, polemonium, oxytropis, astragalus, lathyrus, lupinus, myosotis, dodecatheon, arnica, chrysanthemum, nardosmia, saussurea, senecio, erigeron, matrecaria, caltha, valeriana, stellaria, Tofieldia, polygonum, papaver, phlox, lychnis, cheiranthus, Linnæa, and a host of drabas, saxifrages, and heathworts, with bright stars and bells in glorious profusion, particularly Cassiope, Andromeda, ledum, pyrola, and vaccinium,—Cassiope the most abundant and beautiful of them all. Many grasses also grow here, and wave fine purple spikes and panicles over the other flowers,—poa, aira, calamagrostis, alopecurus, trisetum, elymus, festuca, glyceria, etc. Even ferns are found thus far north, carefully and comfortably unrolling their precious fronds,—aspidium, cystopteris, and woodsia, all growing on a sumptuous bed of mosses and lichens; not the scaly lichens seen on rails and trees and fallen logs to the southward, but massive, roundheaded, finely colored plants like corals, wonderfully beautiful, worth going round the world to see. I should like to mention all the plant friends I found in a summer's wanderings in this cool reserve, but I fear few would care to read their names, although everybody, I am sure, would love them could they see them blooming and rejoicing at home.

On my last visit to the region about Kotzebue sound, near the middle of September, 1881, the weather was so fine and mellow that it suggested the Indian summer of the Eastern States. The winds were hushed, the tundra glowed in creamy golden sunshine, and the colors of the ripe foliage of the heathworts, willows, and birch—red, purple, and yellow, in pure bright tones—were enriched with those of berries which were scattered everywhere, as if they had been showered from the clouds like hail. When I was back a mile or two from the shore, reveling in this color-glory, and thinking how fine it would be could I cut a square of the tundra sod of conventional picture size, frame it, and hang it among the paintings on my study walls at home, saying to myself, "Such a Nature painting taken at random from any part of the thousand-mile bog would make the other pictures look dim and coarse," I heard merry shouting, and, looking round, saw a band of Eskimos—men, women, and children, loose and hairy like wild animals—running towards me. I could not guess at first what they were seeking, for they seldom leave the shore; but soon they told me, as they threw themselves down, sprawling and laughing, on the mellow bog, and began to feast on the berries. A lively picture they made, and a pleasant one, as they frightened the whirring ptarmigans, and surprised their oily stomachs with the beautiful acid berries of many kinds, and filled sealskin bags with them to carry away for festive days in winter.

Nowhere else on my travels have I seen so much warm-blooded, rejoicing life as in this grand Arctic reservation, by so many regarded as desolate. Not only are there whales in abundance along the shores, and innumerable seals, walruses, and white bears, but on the tundras great herds of fat reindeer and wild sheep, foxes, hares, mice, piping marmots, and birds. Perhaps more birds are born here than in any other region of equal extent on the continent. Not only do strong-winged hawks, eagles, and water-fowl, to whom the length of the continent is merely a pleasant excursion, come up here every summer in great numbers, but also many short-winged warblers, thrushes, and finches, repairing hither to rear their young in safety, reinforce the plant bloom with their plumage, and sweeten the wilderness with song; flying all the way, some of them, from Florida, Mexico, and Central America. In coming north they are coming home, for they were born here, and they go south only to spend the winter months, as New Englanders go to Florida. Sweet-voiced troubadours, they sing in orange groves and vine-clad magnolia woods in winter, in thickets of dwarf birch and alder in summer, and sing and chatter more or less all the way back and forth, keeping the whole country glad. Oftentimes, in New England, just as the last snow-patches are melting and the sap in the maples begins to flow, the blessed wanderers may be heard about orchards and the edges of fields where they have stopped to glean a scanty meal, not tarrying long, knowing they have far to go. Tracing the footsteps of spring, they arrive in their tundra homes in June or July, and set out on their return journey in September, or as soon as their families are able to fly well.

This is Nature's own reservation, and every lover of wildness will rejoice with me that by kindly frost it is so well defended. The discovery lately made that it is sprinkled with gold may cause some alarm; for the strangely exciting stuff makes the timid bold enough for anything, and the lazy destructively industrious. Thousands at least half insane are now pushing their way into it, some by the southern passes over the mountains, perchance the first mountains they have ever seen,—sprawling, struggling, gasping for breath, as, laden with awkward, merciless burdens of provisions and tools, they climb over rough-angled boulders and cross thin miry bogs. Some are going by the mountains and rivers to the eastward through Canada, tracing the old romantic ways of the Hudson Bay traders; others by Bering Sea and the Yukon, sailing all the way, getting glimpses perhaps of the famous fur-seals, the ice-floes, and the innumerable islands and bars of the great Alaska river. In spite of frowning hardships and the frozen ground, the Klondike gold will increase the crusading crowds for years to come, but comparatively little harm will be done. Holes will be burned and dug into the hard ground here and there, and into the quartz-ribbed mountains and hills; ragged towns like beaver and muskrat villages will be built, and mills and locomotives will make rumbling, screeching, disenchanting noises; but the miner's pick will not be followed far by the plough, at least not until Nature is ready to unlock the frozen soil-beds with her slow-turning climate key. On the other hand, the roads of the pioneer miners will lead many a lover of wildness into the heart of the reserve, who without them would never see it.

In the meantime, the wildest health and pleasure grounds accessible and available to tourists seeking escape from care and dust and early death are the parks and reservations of the West. There are four national parks,[1]—the Yellowstone, Yosemite, General Grant, and Sequoia,—all within easy reach, and thirty forest reservations, a magnificent realm of woods, most of which, by railroads and trails and open ridges, is also fairly accessible, not only to the determined traveler rejoicing in difficulties, but to those (may their tribe increase) who, not tired, not sick, just naturally take wing every summer in search of wildness. The forty million acres of these reserves are in the main unspoiled as yet, though sadly wasted and threatened on their more open margins by the axe and fire of the lumberman and prospector, and by hoofed locusts, which, like the winged ones, devour every leaf within reach, while the shepherds and owners set fires with the intention of making a blade of grass grow in the place of every tree, but with the result of killing both the grass and the trees.

In the million acre Black Hills Reserve of South Dakota, the easternmost of the great forest reserves, made for the sake of the farmers and miners, there are delightful, reviving sauntering-grounds in open parks of yellow pine, planted well apart, allowing plenty of sunshine to warm the ground. This tree is one of the most variable and most widely distributed of American pines. It grows sturdily on all kinds of soil and rocks, and, protected by a mail of thick bark, defies frost and fire and disease alike, daring every danger in firm, calm beauty and strength. It occurs here mostly on the outer hills and slopes where no other tree can grow. The ground beneath it is yellow most of the summer with showy Wythia, arnica, applopappus, solidago, and other sun-loving plants, which, though they form no heavy entangling growth, yet give abundance of color and make all the woods a garden. Beyond the yellow pine woods there lies a world of rocks of wildest architecture, broken, splintery, and spiky, not very high, but the strangest in form and style of grouping imaginable. Countless towers and spires, pinnacles and slender domed columns, are crowded together, and feathered with sharp-pointed Engelmann spruces, making curiously mixed forests,—half trees, half rocks. Level gardens here and there in the midst of them offer charming surprises, and so do the many small lakes with lilies on their meadowy borders, and bluebells, anemones, daises, castilleias, comandras, etc., together forming landscapes delightfully novel, and made still wilder by many interesting animals,—elk, deer, beavers, wolves squirrels, and birds. Not very long ago this was the richest of all the red man's hunting-grounds hereabout. After the season's buffalo hunts were over,—as described by Parkman, who, with a picturesque cavalcade of Sioux savages, passed through these famous hills in 1846,—every winter deficiency was here made good, and hunger was unknown until, in spite of most determined, fighting, killing opposition, the white gold-hunters entered the fat game reserve and spoiled it. The Indians are dead now, and so are most of the hardly less striking free trappers of the early romantic Rocky Mountain times. Arrows, bullets, scalping-knives, need no longer be feared; and all the wilderness is peacefully open.

9

The Rocky Mountain reserves are the Teton, Yellowstone, Lewis and Clark, Bitter Root, Priest River and Flathead, comprehending more than twelve million acres of mostly unclaimed, rough, forest-covered mountains in which the great rivers of the country take their rise. The commonest tree in most of them is the brave, indomitable, and alto- gether admirable Pinus contorta, widely distributed in all kinds of climate and soil, growing cheerily in frosty Alaska, breathing the damp salt air of the sea as well as the dry bit- ing blasts of the Arctic interior, and making itself at home on the most dangerous flame-swept slopes and bridges of the Rocky Mountains in immeasurable abundance and variety of forms. Thousands of acres of this species are destroyed by running fires nearly every summer, but a new growth springs quickly from the ashes. It is generally small, and yields few sawlogs of commercial value, but is of incalcu- lable importance to the farmer and miner; supplying fenc- ing, mine timbers, and firewood, holding the porous soil on steep slopes, preventing landslips and avalanches, and giving kindly, nourishing shelter to animals and the widely outspread sources of the life-giving rivers. The other trees are mostly spruce, mountain pine, cedar, juniper, larch, and balsam fir; some of them, especially on the western slopes of the mountains, attaining grand size and furnishing abun- dance of fine timber.

Perhaps the least known of all this grand group of reserves is the Bitter Root, of more than four million acres. It is the wildest, shaggiest block of forest wildness in the Rocky Mountains, full of happy, healthy, storm-loving trees, full of streams that dance and sing in glorious array, and full of Nature's animals,—elk, deer, wild sheep, bears, cats, and innumerable smaller people.

In calm Indian summer, when the heavy winds are hushed, the vast forests covering hill and dale, rising and falling over the rough topography and vanishing in the dis- tance, seem lifeless. No moving thing is seen as we climb the peaks, and only the low, mellow murmur of falling water is heard, which seems to thicken the silence. Nevertheless, how many hearts with warm red blood in them are beating under cover of the woods, and how many teeth and eyes are shining! A multitude of animal people, intimately related to us, but of whose lives we know almost nothing, are as busy about their own affairs as we are about ours: beavers are building and mending dams and huts for winter, and storing them with food; bears are studying winter quarters as they stand thoughtful in open spaces, while the gentle breeze ruffles the long hair on their backs; elk and deer, assembling on the heights, are considering cold pastures where they will be farthest away from the wolves; squirrels and marmots are busily laying up provisions and lining their nests against coming frost and snow foreseen; and countless thousands of birds are forming parties and gathering their young about them for flight to the southlands; while butterflies and bees, apparently with no thought of hard times to come, are hovering above the late-blooming goldenrods, and, with countless other insect folk, are dancing and humming right merrily in the sunbeams and shaking all the air into music.

Wander here a whole summer, if you can. Thousands of God's wild blessings will search you and soak you as if you were sponge, and the big days will go by uncounted. If you are business-tangled, and so burdened with duty that only weeks can be got out of the heavy-laden year, then go to the Flathead Reserve; for it is easily and quickly reached by the Great Northern Railroad. Get off the track at Belton Station, and in a few minutes you will find yourself in the midst of what you are sure to say is the best care-killing scenery on the continent,—beautiful lakes derived straight from glaciers, lofty mountains steeped in lovely nemophila-blue skies and clad with forests and glaciers, mossy, ferny waterfalls in their hollows, nameless and numberless, and meadowy gardens abounding in the best of everything. When you are calm enough for discriminating observation, you will find the king of the larches, one of the best of the Western giants, beautiful, picturesque, and regal in port, easily the grandest of all the larches in the world. It grows to a height of one hundred and fifty to two hundred feet, with a diameter at the ground of five to eight feet, throwing out its branches into the light as no other tree does. To those who before have seen only the European larch or the Lyall species of the eastern Rocky Mountains, or the little tamarack or hackmatack of the Eastern States and Canada, this Western king must be a revelation.

Associated with this grand tree in the making of the Flathead forests is the large and beautiful mountain pine, or Western white pine (*Pinus monticola*), the invincible contorta or lodge-pole pine, and spruce and cedar. The forest floor is covered with the richest beds of Linnæa borealis I ever saw, thick fragrant carpets, enriched with shining mosses here and there, and with Clintonia, pyrola, moneses, and vaccinium, weaving hundred-mile beds of bloom that would have made blessed old Linnæus weep for joy.

Lake McDonald, full of brisk trout, is in the heart of this forest, and Avalanche Lake is ten miles above McDonald, at the feet of a group of glacier-laden mountains. Give a month at least to this precious reserve. The time will not be taken from the sum of your life. Instead of shortening, it will indefinitely lengthen it and make you truly immortal. Nevermore will time seem short or long, and cares will never again fall heavily on you, but gently and kindly as gifts from heaven.

The vast Pacific Coast reserves in Washington and Oregon—the Cascade, Washington, Mount Rainier, Olympic, Bull Run, and Ashland, named in order of size—include more than 12,500,000 acres of magnificent forests of beautiful and gigantic trees. They extend over the wild, unexplored Olympic Mountains and both flanks of the Cascade Range, the wet and the dry. On the east side of the Cascades the woods are sunny and open, and contain principally yellow pine, of moderate size, but of great value as a cover for the irrigating streams that flow into the dry interior, where agriculture on a grand scale is being carried on. Along the moist, balmy, foggy, west flank of the mountains, facing the sea, the woods reach their highest development, and, excepting the California redwoods, are the heaviest on the continent. They are made up mostly of the Douglas spruce (*Pseudotsuga taxifolia*), with the giant arbor vitæ, or cedar, and several species of fir and hemlock in varying abundance, forming a forest kingdom unlike any other, in which limb meets limb, touching and overlapping in bright, lively, triumphant exuberance, two hundred and fifty, three hundred, and even four hundred feet above the shady, mossy ground. Over all the other species the Douglas spruce reigns supreme. It is not only a large tree, the tallest in America next to the redwood, but a very beautiful one, with bright green drooping foliage, handsome pendent cones, and a shaft exquisitely straight and round and regular. Forming extensive forests by itself in many places, it lifts its spiry tops into the sky close together with as even a growth as a well-tilled field of grain. No ground has been better tilled for wheat than these Cascade Mountains for trees: They were ploughed by mighty glaciers, and harrowed and mellowed and outspread by the broad streams that flowed from the ice-ploughs as they were withdrawn at the close of the glacial period.

In proportion to its weight when dry, Douglas spruce timber is perhaps stronger than that of any other large conifer in the country, and being tough, durable, and elastic, it is admirably suited for ship-building, piles, and heavy timbers in general; but its hardness and liability to warp when it is cut into boards render it unfit for fine work. In the lumber markets of California it is called "Oregon pine." When lumbering is going on in the best Douglas woods, especially about Puget Sound, many of the long, slender boles are saved for spars; and so superior is their quality that they are called for in almost every shipyard in the world, and it is interesting to follow their fortunes. Felled and peeled and dragged to tide-water, they are raised again as yards and masts for ships, given iron roots and canvas foliage, decorated with flags, and sent to sea, where in glad motion they go cheerily over the ocean prairie in every latitude and longitude, singing and bowing responsive to the same winds that waved them when they were in the woods. After standing in one place for centuries they thus go round the world like tourists, meeting many a friend from the old home forest; some traveling like themselves, some standing head downward in muddy harbors, holding up the platforms of wharves, and others doing all kinds of hard timber work, showy or hidden.

This wonderful tree also grows far northward in British Columbia, and southward along the coast and middle regions of Oregon and California; flourishing with the redwood wherever it can find an opening, and with the sugar pine, yellow pine, and libocedrus in the Sierra. It extends into the San Gabriel, San Bernardino, and San Jacinto Mountains of southern California. It also grows well on the Wasatch Mountains, where it is called "red pine," and on many parts of the Rocky Mountains and short interior ranges of the Great Basin. But though thus widely distributed, only in Oregon, Washington, and some parts of British Columbia does it reach perfect development.

To one who looks from some high standpoint over its vast breadth, the forest on the west side of the Cascades seems all one dim, dark, monotonous field, broken only by the white volcanic cones along the summit of the range. Back in the untrodden wilderness a deep furred carpet of brown and yellow mosses covers the ground like a garment, pressing about the feet of the trees, and rising in rich bosses softly and kindly over every rock and mouldering trunk, leaving no spot uncared for; and dotting small prairies, and fringing the meadows and the banks of streams not seen in general views, we find, besides the great conifers, a considerable number of hard-wood trees,—oak, ash, maple, alder, wild apple, cherry, arbutus, Nuttall's flowering dogwood, and in some places chestnut. In a few favored spots the broad-leaved maple grows to a height of a hundred feet in forests by itself, sending out large limbs in magnificent interlacing arches covered with mosses and ferns, thus forming lofty sky-gardens, and rendering the underwoods delightfully cool. No finer forest ceiling is to be found than these maple arches, while the floor, ornamented with tall ferns and rubus vines, and cast into hillocks by the bulging, moss-covered roots of the trees, matches it well.

Passing from beneath the heavy shadows of the woods, almost anywhere one steps into lovely gardens of lilies, orchids, heathworts, and wild roses. Along the lower slopes, especially in Oregon, where the woods are less dense, there are miles of rhododendron, making glorious masses

14

of purple in the spring, while all about the streams and the lakes and the beaver meadows there is a rich tangle of hazel, plum, cherry, crab-apple, cornel, gaultheria, and rubus, with myriads of flowers and abundance of other more delicate bloomers, such as erythronium, Brodiæa, fritillaria, calochortus, Clintonia, and the lovely hider of the north, Calypso. Beside all these bloomers there are wonderful ferneries about the many misty waterfalls, some of the fronds ten feet high, others the most delicate of their tribe, the maidenhair fringing the rocks within reach of the lightest dust of the spray, while the shading trees on the cliffs above them, leaning over, look like eager listeners anxious to catch every tone of the restless waters. In the autumn berries of every color and flavor abound, enough for birds, bears, and everybody, particularly about the stream-sides and meadows where sunshine reaches the ground: huckleberries, red, blue, and black, some growing close to the ground others on bushes ten feet high; gaultheria berries, called "sal-al" by the Indians; salmon berries, an inch in diameter, growing in dense prickly tangles, the flowers, like wild roses, still more beautiful than the fruit; raspberries, gooseberries, currants, blackberries, and strawberries. The underbrush and meadow fringes are in great part made up of these berry bushes and vines; but in the depths of the woods there is not much underbrush of any kind,—only a thin growth of rubus, huckleberry, and vine-maple.

Notwithstanding the outcry against the reservations last winter in Washington, that uncounted farms, towns, and villages were included in them, and that all business was threatened or blocked, nearly all the mountains in which the reserves lie are still covered with virgin forests. Though lumbering has long been carried on with tremendous energy along their boundaries, and home-seekers have explored the woods for openings available for farms, however small, one may wander in the heart of the reserves for weeks without meeting a human being, Indian or white man, or any conspicuous trace of one. Indians used to ascend the main streams on their way to the mountains for wild goats, whose wool furnished them clothing. But with food in abundance on the coast there was little to draw them into the woods, and the monuments they have left there are scarcely more conspicuous than those of birds and squirrels; far less so than those of the beavers, which have dammed streams and made clearings that will endure for centuries. Nor is there much in these woods to attract cattle-keepers. Some of the first settlers made farms on the small bits of prairie and in the comparatively open Cowlitz and Chehalis valleys of Washington; but before the gold period most of the immigrants from the Eastern States settled in the fertile and open Willamette Valley of Oregon. Even now, when the search for tillable land is so keen, excepting the bottom-lands of the rivers around Puget Sound, there are few cleared spots in all western Washington. On every meadow or opening of any sort some one will be found keeping cattle, raising hops, or cultivating patches of grain, but these spots are few and far between. All the larger spaces were taken long ago; therefore most of the newcomers build their cabins where the beavers built theirs. They keep a few cows, laboriously widen their little meadow openings by hacking, girdling, and burning the rim of the close-pressing forest, and scratch and plant among the huge blackened logs and stamps, girdling and killing themselves in killing the trees.

Most of the farm lands of Washington and Oregon, excepting the valleys of the Willamette and Rogue rivers, lie on the east side of the mountains. The forests on the eastern slopes of the Cascades fail altogether ere the foot of the range is reached, stayed by drought as suddenly as on the west side they are stopped by the sea; showing strikingly how dependent are these forest giants on the generous rains and fogs so often complained of in the coast climate. The lower portions of the reserves are solemnly soaked and poulticed in rain and fog during the winter months, and there is a sad dearth of sunshine, but with a little knowledge of woodcraft any one may enjoy an excursion into these woods even in the rainy season. The big, gray days are exhilarating, and the colors of leaf and branch and mossy bole are then at their best. The mighty trees getting their food are seen to be wide-awake, every needle thrilling in the welcome nourishing storms, chanting and bowing low in glorious harmony, while every raindrop and snowflake is seen as a beneficent messenger from the sky. The snow that falls on the lower woods is mostly soft, coming through the trees in downy tufts, loading their branches, and bending them down against the trunks until they look like arrows, while a strange muffled silence prevails, making everything impressively solemn. But these lowland snowstorms and their effects quickly vanish. The snow melts in a day or two, sometimes in a few hours, the bent branches spring up again, and all the forest work is left to the fog and the rain. At the same time, dry snow is falling on the upper forests and mountain tops. Day after day, often for weeks, the big clouds give their flowers without ceasing, as if knowing how important is the work they have to do. The glinting, swirling swarms thicken the blast, and the trees and rocks are covered to a depth of ten to twenty feet. Then the mountaineer, snug in a grove with bread and fire, has nothing to do but gaze and listen and enjoy. Ever and anon the deep, low roar of the storm is broken by the booming of avalanches, as the snow slips from the overladen heights and crushes down the long white slopes to fill the fountain hollows. All the smaller streams are crushed and buried, and the young groves of spruce and fir near the edge of the timber-line are gently bowed to the ground and put to sleep, not again to see the light of day or stir branch or leaf until the spring.

These grand reservations should draw thousands of admiring visitors at least in summer, yet they are neglected as if of no account, and spoilers are allowed to ruin them as fast as they like.[2] A few peeled spars cut here were set up in London, Philadelphia, and Chicago, where they excited wondering attention; but the countless hosts of living trees rejoicing at home on the mountains are scarce considered at all. Most travelers here are content with what they can see from car windows or the verandas of hotels, and in going from place to place cling to their precious trains and stages like wrecked sailors to rafts. When an excursion into the woods is proposed, all sorts of dangers are imagined,— snakes, bears, Indians. Yet it is far safer to wander in God's woods than to travel on black highways or to stay at home. The snake danger is so slight it is hardly worth mentioning. Bears are a peaceable people, and mind their own business, instead of going about like the devil seeking whom they may devour. Poor fellows, they have been poisoned, trapped, and shot at until they have lost confidence in brother man, and it is not now easy to make their acquaintance. As to Indians, most of them are dead or civilized into useless innocence. No American wilderness that I know of is so dangerous as a city home "with all the modern improvements." One should go to the woods for safety, if for nothing else. Lewis and Clark, in their famous trip across the continent in 1804-1805, did not lose a single man by Indians or animals, though all the West was then wild. Captain Clark was bitten on the hand as he lay asleep. That was one bite among more than a hundred men while traveling nine thousand miles. Loggers are far more likely to be met than Indians or bears in the reserves or about their boundaries, brown weather-tanned men with faces furrowed like bark, tired-looking, moving slowly, swaying like the trees they chop. A little of everything in the woods is fastened to their clothing, rosiny and smeared with balsam, and rubbed into it, so that their scanty outer garments grow thicker with use and never wear out. Many a forest giant have these old woodmen felled, but, round-shouldered and stooping, they too are leaning over and tottering to their fall. Others, however, stand ready to take their places, stout young fellows, erect as saplings; and always the foes of trees outnumber their friends. Far up the white peaks one can hardly fail to meet the wild goat, or American chamois,—an admirable mountaineer, familiar with woods and glaciers as well as rocks,—and in leafy thickets deer will be found; while gliding about unseen there are many sleek furred animals enjoying their beautiful lives, and birds also, notwithstanding few are noticed in hasty walks. The ousel sweetens the glens and gorges where the streams flow fastest, and every grove has its singers, however silent it seems,—thrushes, linnets, warblers; humming-birds glint about the fringing bloom of the meadows and peaks, and the lakes are stirred into lively pictures by water-fowl.

The Mount Rainier Forest Reserve should be made a national park and guarded while yet its bloom is on;[3] for if in the making of the West Nature had what we call parks in mind,—places for rest, inspiration, and prayers,—this Rainier region must surely be one of them. In the centre of it there is a lonely mountain capped with ice; from the ice-cap glaciers radiate in every direction, and young rivers from the glaciers; while its flanks, sweeping down in beautiful curves, are clad with forests and gardens, and filled with birds and animals. Specimens of the best of Nature's treasures have been lovingly gathered here and arranged in simple symmetrical beauty within regular bounds.

Of all the fire-mountains which, like beacons, once blazed along the Pacific Coast, Mount Rainier is the noblest in form, has the most interesting forest cover, and, with perhaps the exception of Shasta, is the highest and most flowery. Its massive white dome rises out of its forests, like a world by itself, to a height of fourteen thousand to fifteen thousand feet. The forests reach to a height of a little over six thousand feet, and above the forests there is a zone of the loveliest flowers, fifty miles in circuit and nearly two miles wide, so closely planted and luxuriant that it seems as if Nature, glad to make an open space between woods so dense and ice so deep, were economizing the precious ground, and trying to see how many of her darlings she can get together in one mountain wreath,—daisies, anemones, geraniums, columbines, erythroniums, larkspurs, etc., among which we wade knee-deep and waist-deep, the bright corollas in myriads touching petal to petal. Picturesque detached groups of the spiry Abies lasiocarpa stand like islands along the lower margin of the garden zone, while on the upper margin there are extensive beds of bryanthus, Cassiope, Kalmia, and other heathworts, and higher still saxifrages and drabas, more and more lowly, reach up to the edge of the ice. Altogether this is the richest subalpine garden I ever found, a perfect floral elysium. The icy dome needs none of man's care, but unless the reserve is guarded the flower bloom will soon be killed, and nothing of the forests will be left but black stump monuments.

The Sierra of California is the most openly beautiful and useful of all the forest reserves, and the largest excepting the Cascade Reserve of Oregon and the Bitter Root of Montana and Idaho. It embraces over four million acres of the grandest scenery and grandest trees on the continent, and its forests are planted just where they do the most good, not only for beauty, but for farming in the great San Joaquin Valley beneath them. It extends southward from the Yosemite National Park to the end of the range, a distance of nearly two hundred miles. No other coniferous forest in the world contains so many species or so many large and beautiful trees,—Sequoia gigantea, king of conifers, "the noblest of a noble race," as Sir Joseph Hooker well says; the sugar pine, king of all the world's pines, living or extinct; the yellow pine, next in rank, which here reaches most perfect development, forming noble towers of verdure two hundred feet high; the mountain pine, which braves the coldest blasts far up the mountains on grim, rocky slopes; and five others, flourishing each in its place, making eight species of pine in one forest, which is still further enriched by the great Douglas spruce, libocedrus, two species of silver fir, large trees and exquisitely beautiful, the Paton hemlock, the most graceful of evergreens, the curious tumion, oaks of many species, maples, alders, poplars, and flowering dogwood, all fringed with flowery underbrush, manzanita, ceanothus, wild rose, cherry, chestnut, and rhododendron. Wandering at random through these friendly, approachable woods, one comes here and there to the loveliest lily gardens, some of the lilies ten feet high, and the smoothest gentian meadows, and Yosemite valleys known only to mountaineers. Once I spent a night by a camp-fire on Mount Shasta with Asa Gray and Sir Joseph Hooker, and, knowing that they were acquainted with all the great forests of the world, I asked whether they knew any coniferous forest that rivaled that of the Sierra. They unhesitatingly said: "No. In the beauty and grandeur of individual trees, and in number and variety of species, the Sierra forests surpass all others."

This Sierra Reserve, proclaimed by the President of the United States in September, 1893, is worth the most thoughtful care of the government for its own sake, without considering its value as the fountain of the rivers on which the fertility of the great San Joaquin Valley depends. Yet it gets no care at all. In the fog of tariff, silver, and annexation politics it is left wholly unguarded, though the management of the adjacent national parks by a few soldiers shows how well and how easily it can be preserved. In the meantime, lumbermen are allowed to spoil it at their will, and sheep in uncountable ravenous hordes to trample it and devour every green leaf within reach; while the shepherds, like destroying angels, set innumerable fires, which burn not only the undergrowth of seedlings on which the permanence of the forest depends, but countless thousands of the venerable giants. If every citizen could take one walk through this reserve, there would be no more trouble about its care; for only in darkness does vandalism flourish.[4] The reserves of southern California,—the San Gabriel, San Bernardino, San Jacinto, and Trabuco,—though not large, only about two million acres together, are perhaps the best appreciated. Their slopes are covered with a close, almost impenetrable growth of flowery bushes, beginning on the sides of the fertile coast valleys and the dry interior plains. Their higher ridges, however, and mountains are open, and fairly well forested with sugar pine, yellow pine, Douglas spruce, libocedrus, and white fir. As timber fountains they amount to little, but as bird and bee pastures, cover for the precious streams that irrigate the lowlands, and quickly available retreats from dust and heat and care, their value is incalculable. Good roads have been graded into them, by which in a few hours lowlanders can get well up into the sky and find refuge in hospitable camps and club-houses, where, while breathing reviving ozone, they may absorb the beauty about them, and look comfortably down on the busy towns and the most beautiful orange groves ever planted since gardening began.

The Grand Cañon Reserve of Arizona, of nearly two million acres, or the most interesting part of it, as well as the Rainier region, should be made into a national park, on account of their supreme grandeur and beauty. Setting out

from Flagstaff, a station on the Atchison, Topeka, and Santa
Fé Railroad, on the way to the cañon you pass through beautiful forests of yellow pine,—like those of the Black Hills,
but more extensive,—and curious dwarf forests of nut pine
and juniper, the spaces between the miniature trees planted
with many interesting species of eriogonum, yucca, and
cactus. After riding or walking seventy-five miles through
these pleasure-grounds, the San Francisco and other mountains, abounding in flowery parklike openings and smooth
shallow valleys with long vistas which in fineness of finish
and arrangement suggest the work of a consummate landscape artist, watching you all the way, you come to the most
tremendous cañon in the world. It is abruptly countersunk
in the forest plateau, so that you see nothing of it until you
are suddenly stopped on its brink, with its immeasurable
wealth of divinely colored and sculptured buildings before
you and beneath you. No matter how far you have wandered hitherto, or how many famous gorges and valleys you
have seen, this one, the Grand Cañon of the Colorado, will
seem as novel to you, as unearthly in the color and grandeur
and quantity of its architecture, as if you had found it after
death, on some other star; so incomparably lovely and grand
and supreme is it above all the other cañons in our fire-
moulded, earthquake-shaken, rain-washed, wave-washed,
river and glacier sculptured world. It is about six thousand
feet deep where you first see it, and from rim to rim ten to
fifteen miles wide. Instead of being dependent for interest
upon waterfalls, depth, wall sculpture, and beauty of park-
like floor, like most other great cañons, it has not waterfalls
in sight, and no appreciable floor spaces. The big river has
just room enough to flow and roar obscurely, here and there
groping its way as best it can, like a weary, murmuring,
overladen traveler trying to escape from the tremendous,
bewildering labyrinthic abyss, while its roar serves only to
deepen the silence. Instead of being filled with air, the vast
space between the walls is crowded with Nature's grandest
buildings,—a sublime city of them, painted in every color,
and adorned with richly fretted cornice and battlement
spire and tower in endless variety of style and architecture.

Every architectural invention of man has been anticipated, and far more, in this grandest of God's terrestrial cities.

[1] There are now five parks and thirty-eight reservations.

[2] The outlook over forest affairs is now encouraging. Popular interest, more practical than sentimental in whatever touches the welfare of the country's forests, is growing rapidly, and a hopeful beginning has been made by the Government in real protection for the reservations as well as for the parks. From July 1, 1900, there have been 9 superintendents, 39 supervisors, and from 330 to 445 rangers of reservations.

[3] This was done shortly after the above was written. "One of the most important measures taken during the past year in connection with forest reservations was the action of Congress in withdrawing from the Mount Rainier Forest Reserve a portion of the region immediately surrounding Mount Rainier and setting it apart as a national park." (Report of Commissioner of General Land Office, for the year ended June, 1899.) But the park as it now stands is far too small.]

[4] [See note 3.]

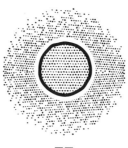

II

THE YELLOWSTONE NATIONAL PARK

Of the four national parks of the West, the Yellowstone is far the largest. It is a big, wholesome wilderness on the broad summit of the Rocky Mountains, favored with abundance of rain and snow,—a place of fountains where the greatest of the American rivers take their rise. The central portion is a densely forested and comparatively level volcanic plateau with an average elevation of about eight thousand feet above the sea, surrounded by an imposing host of mountains belonging to the subordinate Gallatin, Wind River, Teton, Absaroka, and snowy ranges. Unnumbered lakes shine in it, united by a famous band of streams that rush up out of hot lava beds, or fall from the frosty peaks in channels rocky and bare, mossy and bosky, to the main rivers, singing cheerily on through every difficulty, cunningly dividing and finding their way east and went to the two far-off seas.

Glacier meadows and beaver meadows are out-spread with charming effect along the banks of the streams, park-like expanses in the woods, and innumerable small gardens in rocky recesses of the mountains, some of them containing more petals than leaves, while the whole wilderness is enlivened with happy animals.

Beside the treasures common to most mountain regions that are wild and blessed with a kind climate, the park is full of exciting wonders. The wildest geysers in the world, in bright, triumphant bands, are dancing and singing in it amid thousands of boiling springs, beautiful and awful, their basins arrayed in gorgeous colors like gigantic flowers; and hot paint-pots, mud springs, mud volcanoes, mush and broth caldrons whose contents are of every color and consistency, plash and heave and roar in bewildering abundance. In the adjacent mountains, beneath the living trees the edges of petrified forests are exposed to view, like specimens on the shelves of a museum, standing on ledges tier above tier where they grew, solemnly silent in rigid crystalline beauty after swaying in the winds thousands of centuries ago, opening marvelous views back into the years and climates and life of the past. Here, too, are hills of sparkling crystals, hills of sulphur, hills of glass, hills of cinders and ashes, mountains of every style of architecture, icy or forested, mountains covered with honey-bloom sweet as Hymettus, mountains boiled soft like potatoes and colored like a sunset sky. A' that and a' that, and twice as muckle's a' that, Nature has on show in the Yellowstone Park. Therefore it is called Wonderland, and thousands of tourists and travelers stream into it every summer, and wander about in it enchanted.

Fortunately, almost as soon as it was discovered it was dedicated and set apart for the benefit of the people, a piece of legislation that shines benignly amid the common dust-and-ashes history of the public domain, for which the world must thank Professor Hayden above all others; for he led the first scientific exploring party into it, described it, and with admirable enthusiasm urged Congress to preserve it. As delineated in the year 1872, the park, contained about 3344 square miles. On March 30, 1891 it was to all intents and purposes enlarged by the Yellowstone National Park Timber Reserve, and in December, 1897, by the Teton Forest Reserve; thus nearly doubling its original area, and extending the southern boundary far enough to take in the sublime Teton range and the famous pasture-lands of the big Rocky Mountain game animals. The withdrawal of this large tract from the public domain did no harm to any one; for its height, 6000 to over 13,000 feet above the sea, and its thick mantle of volcanic rocks, prevent its ever being available for agriculture or mining, while on the other hand its geographical position, reviving climate, and wonderful scenery combine to make it a grand health, pleasure, and study resort,—a gathering-place for travelers from all the world.

The national parks are not only withdrawn from sale and entry like the forest reservations, but are efficiently managed and guarded by small troops of United States cavalry, directed by the Secretary of the Interior. Under this care the forests are flourishing, protected from both axe and fire; and so, of course, are the shaggy beds of underbrush and the herbaceous vegetation. The so-called curiosities, also, are preserved, and the furred and feathered tribes, many of which, in danger of extinction a short time ago, are now increasing in numbers,—a refreshing thing to see amid the blind, ruthless destruction that is going on in the adjacent regions. In pleasing contrast to the noisy, ever changing management, or mismanagement, of blundering, plundering, money-making vote-sellers who receive their places from boss politicians as purchased goods, the soldiers do their duty so quietly that the traveler is scarce aware of their presence.

This is the coolest and highest of the parks. Frosts occur every month of the year. Nevertheless, the tenderest tourist finds it warm enough in summer. The air is electric and full of ozone, healing, reviving, exhilarating, kept pure by frost and fire, while the scenery is wild enough to awaken the dead. It is a glorious place to grow in and rest in; camping on the shores of the lakes, in the warm openings of the woods golden with sunflowers, on the banks of the streams, by the snowy waterfalls, beside the exciting wonders or away from them in the scallops of the mountain walls sheltered from every wind, on smooth silky lawns enameled with gentians, up in the fountain hollows of the ancient glaciers between the peaks, where cool pools and brooks and gardens of precious plants charmingly embowered are never wanting, and good rough rocks with every variety of cliff and scaur are invitingly near for outlooks and exercise.

From these lovely dens you may make excursions whenever you like into the middle of the park, where the geysers and hot springs are reeking and spouting in their beautiful basins, displaying an exuberance of color and strange motion and energy admirably calculated to surprise and frighten, charm and shake up the least sensitive out of apathy into newness of life.

However orderly your excursions or aimless, again and again amid the calmest, stillest scenery you will be brought to a standstill hushed and awe-stricken before phenomena wholly new to you. Boiling springs and huge deep pools of purest green and azure water, thousands of them, are plashing and heaving in these high, cool mountains as if a fierce furnace fire were burning beneath each one of them; and a hundred geysers, white torrents of boiling water and steam, like inverted waterfalls, are ever and anon rushing up out of the hot, black underworld. Some of these ponderous geyser columns are as large as sequoias,—five to sixty feel in diameter, one hundred and fifty to three hundred feet high,—and are sustained at this great height with tremendous energy for a few minutes, or perhaps nearly an hour, standing rigid and erect, hissing, throbbing, booming, as if thunderstorms were raging beneath their roots, their sides roughened or fluted like the furrowed boles of trees, their tops dissolving in feathery branches, while the irised spray, like misty bloom is at times blown aside, revealing the massive shafts shining against a background of pine-covered hills. Some of them lean more or less, as if storm-bent, and instead of being round are flat or fan-shaped, issuing from irregular slits in silex pavements with radiate structure, the sunbeams sifting through them in ravishing splendor. Some are broad and round-headed like oaks; others are low and bunchy, branching near the ground like bushes; and a few are hollow in the centre like big daisies or water-lilies. No frost cools them, snow never covers them nor lodges in their branches; winter and summer they welcome alike; all of them, of whatever form or size, faithfully rising and sinking in fairy rhythmic dance night and day, in all sorts of weather, at varying periods of minutes, hours, or weeks, growing up rapidly, uncontrollable as fate, tossing their pearly branches in the wind, bursting into bloom and vanishing like the frailest flowers,—plants of which Nature raises hundreds or thousands of crops a year with no apparent exhaustion of the fiery soil.

The so-called geyser basins, in which this rare sort of vegetation is growing, are mostly open valleys on the central plateau that were eroded by glaciers after the greater volcanic fires had ceased to burn. Looking down over the forests as you approach them from the surrounding heights, you see a multitude of white columns, broad, reeking masses, and irregular jets and puffs of misty vapor ascending from the bottom of the valley, or entangled like smoke among the neighboring trees, suggesting the factories of some busy town or the camp-fires of an army. These mark the position of each mush-pot, paint-pot, hot spring, and geyser, or gusher, as the Icelandic words mean. And when you saunter into the midst of them over the bright sinter pavements, and see how pure and white and pearly gray they are in the shade of the mountains, and how radiant in the sunshine, you are fairly enchanted. So numerous they are and varied, Nature seems to have gathered them from all the world as specimens of her rarest fountains, to show in one place what she can do. Over four thousand hot springs have been counted in the park, and a hundred geysers; how many more there are nobody knows.

These valleys at the heads of the great rivers may be regarded as laboratories and kitchens, in which, amid a thousand retorts and pots, we may see Nature at work as chemist or cook, cunningly compounding an infinite variety of mineral messes; cooking whole mountains; boiling and steaming flinty rocks to smooth paste and mush,— yellow, brown, red, pink, lavender, gray, and creamy white,—making the most beautiful mud in the world; and distilling the most ethereal essences. Many of these pots and caldrons have been boiling thousands of years. Pots of sulphurous mush, stringy and lumpy, and pots of broth as black as ink, are tossed and stirred with constant care, and thin transparent essences, too pure and fine to be called water, are kept simmering gently in beautiful sinter cups and bowls that grow ever more beautiful the longer they are used. In some of the spring basins, the waters, though still warm, are perfectly calm, and shine blandly in a sod of overleaning grass and flowers, as if they were thoroughly cooked at last, and set aside to settle and cool. Others are wildly boiling over as if running to waste, thousands of tons of the precious liquids being thrown into the air to fall in scalding floods on the clean coral floor of the establishment, keeping onlookers at a distance. Instead of holding limpid pale green or azure water, other pots and craters are filled with scalding mud, which is tossed up from three or four feet to thirty feet, in sticky, rank-smelling masses, with gasping, belching, thudding sounds, plastering the branches of neighboring trees; every flask, retort, hot spring, and geyser has something special in it, no two being the same in temperature, color, or composition.

In these natural laboratories one needs stout faith to feel at ease. The ground sounds hollow underfoot, and the awful subterranean thunder shakes one's mind as the ground is shaken, especially at night in the pale moonlight, or when the sky is overcast with storm-clouds. In the solemn gloom, the geysers, dimly visible, look like monstrous dancing ghosts, and their wild songs and the earthquake thunder replying to the storms overhead seem doubly terrible, as if divine government were at an end. But the trembling hills keep their places. The sky clears, the rosy dawn is reassuring, and up comes the sun like a god, pouring his faithful beams across the mountains and forest, lighting each peak and tree and ghastly geyser alike, and shining into the eyes of the reeking springs, clothing them with rainbow light, and dissolving the seeming chaos of darkness into varied forms of harmony. The ordinary work of the world goes on. Gladly we see the flies dancing in the sun-beams, birds feeding their young, squirrels gathering nuts, and hear the blessed ouzel singing confidingly in the shallows of the river,—most faithful evangel, calming every fear, reducing everything to love.

The variously tinted sinter and travertine formations, outspread like pavements over large areas of the
geyser valleys, lining the spring basins and throats of the
craters, and forming beautiful coral-like rims and curbs
about them, always excite admiring attention; so also does
the play of the waters from which they are deposited. The
various minerals in them are rich in colors, and these are
greatly heightened by a smooth, silky growth of brilliantly
colored confervæ which lines many of the pools and channels and terraces. No bed of flower-bloom is more exquisite
than these myriads of minute plants, visible only in mass,
growing in the hot waters. Most of the spring borders are
low and daintily scalloped, crenelated, and beaded with
sinter pearls. Some of the geyser craters are massive and
picturesque, like ruined castles or old burned-out sequoia
stumps, and are adorned on a grand scale with outbulging,
cauliflower-like formations. From these as centres the silex
pavements slope gently away in thin, crusty, overlapping
layers, slightly interrupted in some places by low terraces.
Or, as in the case of the Mammoth Hot Springs, at the north
end of the park, where the building waters issue from the
side of a steep hill, the deposits form a succession of higher
and broader terraces of white travertine tinged with purple,
like the famous Pink Terrace at Rotomahana, New Zealand,
draped in front with clustering stalactites, each terrace
having a pool of indescribably beautiful water upon it in a
basin with a raised rim that glistens with confervæ—the
whole, when viewed at a distance of a mile or two, looking
like a broad, massive cascade pouring over shelving rocks in
snowy purpled foam.

The stones of this divine masonry, invisible particles of
lime or silex, mined in quarries no eye has seen, go to their
appointed places in gentle, tinkling, transparent currents
or through the dashing turmoil of floods, as surely guided as
the sap of plants streaming into bole and branch, leaf and
flower. And thus from century to century this beauty-work
has gone on and is going on.

Passing through many a mile of pine and spruce woods,
toward the centre of the park you come to the famous

Yellowstone Lake. It is about twenty miles long and fifteen wide, and lies at a height of nearly 8000 feet above the level of the sea, amid dense black forests and snowy mountains. Around its winding, wavering shores, closely forested and picturesquely varied with promontories and bays, the distance is more than 100 miles. It is not very deep, only from 200 to 300 feet, and contains less water than the celebrated Lake Tahoe of the California Sierra, which is nearly the same size, lies at a height of 6400 feet, and is over 1600 feet deep. But no other lake in North America of equal area lies so high as the Yellowstone, or gives birth to so noble a river. The terraces around its shores show that at the close of the glacial period its surface was about 160 feet higher than it is now, and its area nearly twice as great.

It is full of trout, and a vast multitude of birds—swans, pelicans, geese, ducks, cranes, herons, curlews, plovers, snipe—feed in it and upon its shores; and many forest animals come out of the woods, and wade a little way in shallow, sandy places to drink and look about them, and cool themselves in the free flowing breezes.

In calm weather it is a magnificent mirror for the woods and mountains and sky, now pattered with hail and rain, now roughened with sudden storms that send waves to fringe the shores and wash its border of gravel and sand. The Absaroka Mountains and the Wind River Plateau on the east and south pour their gathered waters into it, and the river issues from the north side in a broad, smooth, stately current, silently gliding with such serene majesty that one fancies it knows the vast journey of four thousand miles that lies before it, and the work it has to do. For the first twenty miles its course is in a level, sunny valley lightly fringed with trees, through which it flows in silvery reaches stirred into spangles here and there by ducks and leaping trout, making no sound save a low whispering among the pebbles and the dipping willows and sedges of its banks. Then suddenly, as if preparing for hard work; it rushes eagerly, impetuously forward rejoicing in its strength, breaks into foam-bloom, and goes thundering down into the Grand Cañon in two magnificent falls, one hundred and three hundred feet high.

The cañon is so tremendously wild and impressive that even these great falls cannot hold your attention. It is about twenty miles long and a thousand feet deep,—a weird, unearthly-looking gorge of jagged, fantastic architecture, and most brilliantly colored. Here the Washburn range, forming the northern rim of the Yellowstone basin, made up mostly of beds of rhyolite decomposed by the action of thermal waters, has been cut through and laid open to view by the river; and a famous section it has made. It is not the depth or the shape of the cañon nor the waterfall, nor the green and gray river chanting its brave song as it goes foaming on its way, that most impresses the observer, but the colors of the decomposed volcanic rocks. With few exceptions, the traveler in strange lands finds that, however much the scenery and vegetation in different countries may change, Mother Earth is ever familiar and the same. But here the very ground is changed, as if belonging to some other world. The walls of the cañon from top to bottom burn in a perfect glory of color, confounding and dazzling when the sun is shining,—white, yellow, green, blue, vermilion, and various other shades of red indefinitely blending. All the earth hereabouts seems to be paint. Millions of tons of it lie in sight, exposed to wind and weather as if of no account, yet marvelously fresh and bright, fast colors not to be washed out or bleached out by either sunshine or storms. The effect is so novel and awful, we imagine that even a river might be afraid to enter such a place. But the rich and gentle beauty of the vegetation is reassuring. The lovely Linnæa borealis hangs her twin bells over the brink of the cliffs, forests and gardens extend their treasures in smiling confidence on either side, nuts and berries ripen well whatever may be going on below; blind fears varnish, and the grand gorge seems a kindly, beautiful part of the general harmony, full of peace and joy and good will.

The park is easy of access. Locomotives drag you to its northern boundary at Cinnabar, and horses and guides do the rest. From Cinnabar you will be whirled in coaches along the foaming Gardiner River to Mammoth Hot Springs; thence through woods and meadows, gulches and ravines along branches of the Upper Gallatin, Madison, and Firehole rivers to the main geyser basins; thence over the Continental Divide and back again, up and down through dense pine, spruce, and fir woods to the magnificent Yellowstone Lake, along its northern shore to the outlet, down the river to the falls and Grand Cañon, and thence back through the woods to Mammoth Hot Springs and Cinnabar; stopping here and there at the so-called points of interest among the geysers, springs, paint-pots, mud volcanoes, etc., where you will be allowed a few minutes or hours to saunter over the sinter pavements, watch the play of a few of the geysers, and peer into some of the most beautiful and terrible of the craters and pools. These wonders you will enjoy, and also the views of the mountains, especially the Gallatin and Absaroka ranges, the long, willowy glacier and beaver meadows, the beds of violets, gentians, phloxes, asters, phacelias, goldenrods, eriogonums, and many other flowers, some species giving color to whole meadows and hillsides. And you will enjoy your short views of the great lake and river and cañon. No scalping Indians will you see. The Blackfeet and Bannocks that once roamed here are gone; so are the old beaver-catchers, the Coulters and Bridgers, with all their attractive buckskin and romance. There are several bands of buffaloes in the park, but you will not thus cheaply in tourist fashion see them nor many of the other large animals hidden in the wilderness. The song-birds, too, keep mostly out of sight of the rushing tourist, though off the roads thrushes, warblers, orioles, grosbeaks, etc., keep the air sweet and merry. Perhaps in passing rapids and falls you may catch glimpses of the water-ouzel, but in the whirling noise you will not hear his song. Fortunately, no road noise frightens the Douglas squirrel, and his merry play and gossip will amuse you all through the woods. Here and there a deer may be seen crossing the road, or a bear. Most likely, however, the only bears you will see are the half tame ones that go to the hotels every night for dinner-table scraps,— yeast-powder biscuit, Chicago canned stuff, mixed pickles, and beefsteaks that have proved too tough for the tourists.

Among the gains of a coach trip are the acquaintances made and the fresh views into human nature; for the wilderness is a shrewd touchstone, even thus lightly approached, and brings many a curious trait to view. Setting out, the driver cracks his whip, and the four horses go off at half gallop, half trot, in trained, showy style, until out of sight of the hotel. The coach is crowded, old and young side by side, blooming and fading, full of hope and fun and care. Some look at the scenery or the horses, and all ask questions, an odd mixed lot of them: "Where is the umbrella? What is the name of that blue flower over there? Are you sure the little bag is aboard? Is that hollow yonder a crater? How is your throat this morning? How high did you say the geysers spout? How does the elevation affect your head? Is that a geyser reeking over there in the rocks, or only a hot spring?" A long ascent is made, the solemn mountains come to view, small cares are quenched, and all become natural and silent, save perhaps some unfortunate expounder who has been reading guidebook geology, and rumbles forth foggy subsidences and upheavals until he is in danger of being heaved overboard. The driver will give you the names of the peaks and meadows and streams as you come to them, call attention to the glass road, tell how hard it was to build,—how the obsidian cliffs naturally pushed the surveyor's lines to the right, and the industrious beavers, by flooding the valley in front of the cliff, pushed them to the left.

Geysers, however, are the main objects, and as soon as they come in sight other wonders are forgotten. All gather around the crater of the one that is expected to play first. During the eruptions of the smaller geysers, such as the Beehive and Old Faithful, though a little frightened at first, all welcome the glorious show with enthusiasm, and shout, "Oh, how wonderful, beautiful, splendid. majestic!" Some venture near enough to stroke the column with a stick, as if it were a stone pillar or a tree, so firm and substantial and permanent it seems. While tourists wait around a large geyser, such as the Castle or the Giant, there is a chatter of small talk in anything but solemn mood; and during the intervals between the preliminary splashes and upheavals some adventurer occasionally looks down the throat of the crater, admiring the silex formations and wondering whether Hades is as beautiful. But when, with awful uproar as if avalanches were falling and storms thundering in the depths, the tremendous outburst begins, all run away to a safe distance, and look on, awe-stricken and silent, in devout, worshiping wonder.

The largest and one of the most wonderfully beautiful of the springs is the Prismatic, which the guide will be sure to show you. With a circumference of 300 yards, it is more like a lake than a spring. The water is pure deep blue in the centre, fading to green on the edges, and its basin and the slightly terraced pavement about it are astonishingly bright and varied in color. This one of the multitude of Yellowstone fountains is of itself object enough for a trip across the continent. No wonder that so many fine myths have originated in springs; that so many fountains were held sacred in the youth of the world, and had miraculous virtues ascribed to them. Even in these cold, doubting, questioning, scientific times many of the Yellowstone fountains seem able to work miracles. Near the Prismatic Spring is the great Excelsior Geyser, which is said to throw a column of boiling water 60 to 70 feet in diameter to a height of from 50 to 300 feet, at irregular periods. This is the greatest of all the geysers yet discovered anywhere. The Firehole River, which sweeps past it, is, at ordinary states, a stream about 100 yards wide and 3 feet deep; but when the geyser is in eruption, so great is the quantity of water discharged that the volume of the river is doubled, and it is rendered too hot and rapid to be forded.

Geysers are found in many other volcanic regions,—in Iceland, New Zealand, Japan, the Himalayas, the Eastern Archipelago, South America, the Azores, and elsewhere; but only in Iceland, New Zealand, and this Rocky Mountain park do they display their grandest forms, and of these three famous regions the Yellowstone is easily first, both in the number and in the size of its geysers. The greatest height of the column of the Great Geyser of Iceland actually measured was 212 feet, and of the Strokhr 162 feet.

In New Zealand, the Te Pueia at Lake Taupo, the Waikite at Rotorna, and two others are said to lift their waters occasionally to a height of 100 feet, while the celebrated Te Tarata at Rotomahana sometimes lifts a boiling column 20 feet in diameter to a height of 60 feet. But all these are far surpassed by the Excelsior. Few tourists, however, will see the Excelsior in action, or a thousand other interesting features of the park that lie beyond the wagon-roads and the hotels. The regular trips—from three to five days—are too short. Nothing can be done well at a speed of forty miles a day. The multitude of mixed, novel impressions rapidly piled on one another make only a dreamy, bewildering, swirling blur, most of which is unrememberable. Far more time should be taken. Walk away quietly in any direction and taste the freedom of the mountaineer. Camp out among the grass and gentians of glacier meadows, in craggy garden nooks full of Nature's darlings. Climb the mountains and get their good tidings. Nature's peace will flow into you as sunshine flows into trees. The winds will blow their own freshness into you, and the storms their energy, while cares will drop off like autumn leaves. As age comes on, one source of enjoyment after another is closed, but Nature's sources never fail. Like a generous host, she offers here brimming cups in endless variety, served in a grand hall, the sky its ceiling, the mountains its walls, decorated with glorious paintings and enlivened with bands of music ever playing. The petty discomforts that beset the awkward guest, the unskilled camper, are quickly forgotten, while all that is precious remains. Fears vanish as soon as one is fairly free in the wilderness.

Most of the dangers that haunt the unseasoned citizen are imaginary; the real ones are perhaps too few rather than too many for his good. The bears that always seem to spring up thick as trees, in fighting, devouring attitudes before the frightened tourist whenever a camping trip is proposed, are gentle now, finding they are no longer likely to be shot; and rattlesnakes, the other big irrational dread of over-civilized people, are scarce here, for most of the park lies above the snake-line. Poor creatures, loved only by their Maker, they are timid and bashful, as mountaineers know; and though perhaps not possessed of much of that charity that suffers long and is kind, seldom, either by mistake or by mishap, do harm to any one. Certainly they cause not the hundredth part of the pain and death that follow the footsteps of the admired Rocky Mountain trapper. Nevertheless, again and again, in season and out of season, the question comes up, "What are rattlesnakes good for?" As if nothing that does not obviously make for the benefit of man had any right to exist; as if our ways were God's ways. Long ago, an Indian to whom a French traveler put this old question replied that their tails were good for toothache, and their heads for fever. Anyhow, they are all, head and tail, good for themselves, and we need not begrudge them their share of life.

Fear nothing. No town park you have been accustomed to saunter in is so free from danger as the Yellowstone. It is a hard place to leave. Even its names in your guidebook are attractive, and should draw you far from wagon-roads,—all save the early ones, derived from the infernal regions: Hell Roaring River, Hell Broth Springs, The Devil's Caldron, etc. Indeed, the whole region was at first called Coulter's Hell, from the fiery brimstone stories told by trapper Coulter, who left the Lewis and Clark expedition and wandered through the park, in the year 1807, with a band of Bannock Indians. The later names, many of which we owe to Mr. Arnold Hague of the U. S. Geological Survey, are so telling and exhilarating that they set our pulses dancing and make us begin to enjoy the pleasures of excursions ere they are commenced. Three River Peak, Two Ocean Pass, Continental Divide, are capital geographical descriptions, suggesting thousands of miles of rejoicing streams and all that belongs to them. Big Horn Pass, Bison Peak, Big Game Ridge, bring brave mountain animals to mind. Birch Hills, Garnet Hills, Amethyst Mountain, Storm Peak, Electric Peak, Roaring Mountain, are bright, bracing names. Wapiti, Beaver, Tern, and Swan lakes, conjure up fine pictures, and so also do Osprey and Ouzel falls. Antelope Creek, Otter, Mink, and Grayling creeks, Geode, Jasper, Opal, Carnelian, and Chalcedony creeks, are lively and sparkling names that help the streams to shine; and Azalea, Stellaria, Arnica, Aster, and Phlox creeks, what pictures these bring up! Violet, Morning Mist, Hygeia, Beryl, Vermilion, and Indigo springs, and many beside, give us visions of fountains more beautifully arrayed than Solomon in all his purple and golden glory. All these and a host of others call you to camp. You may be a little cold some nights, on mountain tops above the timber-line, but you will see the stars, and by and by you can sleep enough in your town bed, or at least in your grave. Keep awake while you may in mountain mansions so rare.

If you are not very strong, try to climb Electric Peak when a big bossy, well-charged thunder-cloud is on it, to breathe the ozone set free, and get yourself kindly shaken and shocked. You are sure to be lost in wonder and praise, and every hair of your head will stand up and hum and sing like an enthusiastic congregation.

After this reviving experience, you should take a look into a few of the tertiary volumes of the grand geological library of the park, and see how God writes history. No technical knowledge is required; only a calm day and a calm mind. Perhaps nowhere else in the Rocky Mountains have the volcanic forces been so busy. More than ten thousand square miles hereabouts have been covered to a depth of at least five thousand feet with material spouted from chasms and craters during the tertiary period, forming broad sheets of basalt, andesite, rhyolite, etc., and marvelous masses of ashes, sand, cinders, and stones now consolidated into conglomerates, charged with the remains of plants and animals that lived in the calm, genial periods that separated the volcanic outbursts.

Perhaps the most interesting and telling of these rocks to the hasty tourist, are those that make up the mass of Amethyst Mountain. On its north side it presents a section two thousand feet high of roughly stratified beds of sand, ashes, and conglomerates coarse and fine, forming the untrimmed edges of a wonderful set of volumes lying on their sides,—books a million years old, well bound, miles in size, with full-page illustrations. On the ledges of this one section we see trunks and stumps of fifteen or twenty ancient forests ranged one above another, standing where they grew, or prostrate and broken like the pillars of ruined temples in desert sands,—a forest fifteen or twenty stories high, the roots of each spread above the tops of the next beneath it, telling wonderful tales of the bygone centuries, with their winters and summers, growth and death, fire, ice, and flood.

There were giants in those days. The largest of the standing opal and agate stumps and prostrate sections of the trunks are from two or three to fifty feet in height or length, and from five to ten feet in diameter; and so perfect is the petrifaction that the annual rings and ducts are clearer and more easily counted than those of living trees, centuries of burial having brightened the records instead of blurring them. They show that the winters of the tertiary period gave as decided a check to vegetable growth as do those of the present time. Some trees favorably located grew rapidly, increasing twenty inches in diameter in as many years, while others of the some species, on poorer soil or overshadowed, increased only two or three inches in the same time.

Among the roots and stumps on the old forest floors we find the remains of ferns and bushes, and the seeds and leaves of trees like those now growing on the southern Alleghanies,—such as magnolia, sassafras, laurel, linden, persimmon, ash, alder, dogwood. Studying the lowest of these forests, the soil it grew on and the deposits it is buried in, we see that it was rich in species, and flourished in a genial, sunny climate. When its stately trees were in their glory, volcanic fires broke forth from chasms and craters, like larger geysers, spouting ashes, cinders, stones and mud, which fell on the doomed forest like hail and snow; sifting, hurtling through the leaves and branches, choking the streams, covering the ground, crushing bushes and ferns, rapidly deepening, packing around the trees and breaking them, rising higher until the topmost boughs of the giants were buried, leaving not a leaf or twig in sight, so complete was the desolation. At last the volcanic storm

began to abate, the fiery soil settled; mud floods and boulder floods passed over it, enriching it, cooling it; rains fell
and mellow sunshine, and it became fertile and ready for
another crop. Birds, and the winds, and roaming animals
brought seeds from more fortunate woods, and a new forest
grew up on the top of the buried one. Centuries of genial
growing seasons passed. The seedling trees became giants,
and with strong outreaching branches spread a leafy canopy
over the gray land.

The sleeping subterranean fires again awake and shake
the mountains, and every leaf trembles. The old craters,
with perhaps new ones, are opened, and immense quantities of ashes, pumice, and cinders are again thrown into the
sky. The sun, shorn of his beams, glows like a dull red ball,
until hidden in sulphurous clouds. Volcanic snow, hail, and
floods fall on the new forest, burying it alive, like the one
beneath its roots. Then come another noisy band of mud
floods and boulder floods, mixing, settling, enriching the
new ground, more seeds, quickening sunshine and showers;
and a third noble magnolia forest is carefully raised on the
top of the second. And so on. Forest was planted above forest
and destroyed, as if Nature were ever repenting, undoing
the work she had so industriously done, and burying it.

Of course this destruction was creation, progress in
the march of beauty through death. How quickly these old
monuments excite and hold the imagination! We see the
old stone stumps budding and blossoming and waving in
the wind as magnificent trees, standing shoulder to shoulder, branches interlacing in grand varied round-headed
forests; see the sunshine of morning and evening gilding
their mossy trunks, and at high noon spangling on the thick
glossy leaves of the magnolia, filtering through translucent
canopies of linden and ash, and falling in mellow patches
on the ferny floor; see the shining after rain, breathe the
exhaling fragrance, and hear the winds and birds and the
murmur of brooks and insects. We watch them from season
to season; see the swelling buds when the sap begins to flow
in the spring, the opening leaves and blossoms, the ripening of summer fruits, the colors of autumn, and the maze

of leafless branches and sprays in winter; and we see the sudden oncome of the storms that overwhelmed them.

One calm morning at sunrise I saw the oaks and pines in Yosemite Valley shaken by an earthquake, their tops swishing back and forth, and every branch and needle shuddering as if in distress like the frightened screaming birds. One may imagine the trembling, rocking, tumultuous waving of those ancient Yellowstone woods, and the terror of their inhabitants when the first foreboding shocks were felt, the sky grew dark, and rock-laden floods began to roar. But though they were close pressed and buried, cut off from sun and wind, all their happy leaf-fluttering and waving done, other currents coursed through them, fondling and thrilling every fibre, and beautiful wood was replaced by beautiful stone. Now their rocky sepulchres are partly open, and show forth the natural beauty of death.

After the forest times and fire times had passed away, and the volcanic furnaces were banked and held in abeyance, another great change occurred. The glacial winter came on. The sky was again darkened, not with dust and ashes, but with snow which fell in glorious abundance, piling deeper, deeper, slipping from the overladen heights in booming avalanches, compacting into glaciers, that flowed over all the landscape, wiping off forests, grinding, sculpturing, fashioning the comparatively featureless lava beds into the beautiful rhythm of hill and dale and ranges of mountains we behold to-day; forming basins for lakes, channels for streams, few soils for forests, gardens, and meadows. While this ice-work was going on, the slumbering volcanic fires were boiling the subterranean waters, and with curious chemistry decomposing the rocks, making beauty in the darkness; these forces, seemingly antagonistic, working harmoniously together. How wild their meetings on the surface were we may imagine. When the glacier period began, geysers and hot springs were playing in grander volume, it may be, than those of to-day. The glaciers flowed over them while they spouted and thundered, carrying away their fine sinter and travertine structures, and shortening their mysterious channels.

The soils made in the down-grinding required to bring
the present features of the landscape into relief are possibly
no better than were some of the old volcanic soils that were
carried away, and which, as we have seen, nourished magnificent forests, but the glacial landscapes are incomparably
more beautiful than the old volcanic ones were. The glacial
winter has passed away, like the ancient summers and fire
periods, though in the chronology of the geologist all these
times are recent. Only small residual glaciers on the cool
northern slopes of the highest mountains are left of the vast
all-embracing ice-mantle, as solfataras and geysers are all
that are left of the ancient volcanoes.

Now the post-glacial agents are at work on the grand
old palimpsest of the park region, inscribing new characters;
but still in its main telling features it remains distinctly
glacial. The moraine soils are being leveled, sorted, refined,
re-formed, and covered with vegetation; the polished pavements and scoring and other superficial glacial inscriptions
on the crumbling lavas are being rapidly obliterated; gorges
are being cut in the decomposed rhyolites and loose conglomerates, and turrets and pinnacles seem to be springing
up like growing trees; while the geysers are depositing miles
of sinter and travertine. Nevertheless, the ice-work is scarce
blurred as yet. These later effects are only spots and wrinkles on the grand glacial countenance of the park.

Perhaps you have already said that you have seen
enough for a lifetime. But before you go away you should
spend at least one day and a night on a mountain top, for
a last general, calming, settling view. Mount Washburn is
a good one for the purpose, because it stands in the middle of the park, is unencumbered with other peaks, and
is so easy of access that the climb to its summit is only a
saunter. First your eye goes roving around the mountain
rim amid the hundreds of peaks; some with plain flowing
skirts, others abruptly precipitous and defended by sheer
battlemented escarpments; flat-topped or round; heaving
like sea-waves or spired and turreted like Gothic cathedrals; streaked with snow in the ravines, and darkened
with files of adventurous trees climbing the ridges. The

nearer peaks are perchance clad in sapphire blue, others far off in creamy white. In the broad glare of noon they seem to shrink and crouch to less than half their real stature, and grow dull and uncommunicative,—mere dead, draggled heaps of waste ashes and stone, giving no hint of the multitude of animals enjoying life in their fastnesses, or of the bright bloom-bordered streams and lakes. But when storms blow they awake and arise, wearing robes of cloud and mist in majestic speaking attitudes like gods. In the color glory of morning and evening they become still more impressive; steeped in the divine light of the alpenglow their earthiness disappears, and, blending with the heavens, they seem neither high nor low.

Over all the central plateau, which from here seems level, and over the foothills and lower slopes of the mountains, the forest extends like a black uniform bed of weeds, interrupted only by lakes and meadows and small burned spots called parks,—all of them, except the Yellowstone Lake, being mere dots and spangles in general views, made conspicuous by their color and brightness. About eighty-five per cent of the entire area of the park is covered with trees, mostly the indomitable lodge-pole pine (*Pinus contorta*, var. *Murrayana*), with a few patches and sprinklings of Douglas spruce, Engelmann spruce, silver fir (*Abies lasiocarpa*), Pinus flexilis, and a few alders, aspens, and birches. The Douglas spruce is found only on the lowest portions, the silver fir on the highest, and the Engelmann spruce on the dampest places, best defended from fire. Some fine specimens of the flexilis pine are growing on the margins of openings,—wide-branching, sturdy trees, as broad as high, with trunks five feet in diameter, leafy and shady, laden with purple cones and rose-colored flowers. The Engelmann spruce and sub-alpine silver fir are beautiful and notable trees—tall, spiry hardy, frost and snow defying, and widely distributed over the West, wherever there is a mountain to climb or a cold moraine slope to cover. But neither of these is a good fire-fighter. With rather thin bark, and scattering their seeds every year as soon as they are ripe, they are quickly driven out of fire-swept regions. When the glaciers

were melting, these hardy mountaineering trees were probably among the first to arrive on the new moraine soil beds;
but as the plateau became drier and fires began to run, they
were driven up the mountains, and into the wet spots and
islands where we now find them, leaving nearly all the park
to the lodge-pole pine, which, though as thin-skinned as
they and as easily killed by fire, takes pains to store up its
seeds in firmly closed cones, and holds them from three to
nine years, so that, let the fire come when it may, it is ready
to die and ready to live again in a new generation. For when
the killing fires have devoured the leaves and thin resinous bark, many of the cones, only scorched, open as soon as
the smoke clears away; the hoarded store of seeds is sown
broadcast on the cleared ground, and a new growth immediately springs up triumphant out of the ashes. Therefore,
this tree not only holds its ground, but extends its conquests
farther after every fire. Thus the evenness and closeness of
its growth are accounted for. In one part of the forest that
I examined, the growth was about as close as a cane-brake.
The trees were from four to eight inches in diameter, one
hundred feet high, and one hundred and seventy-five years
old. The lower limbs die young and drop off for want of light.
Life with these close-planted trees is a race for light, more
light, and so they push straight for the sky. Mowing off ten
feet from the top of the forest would make it look like a
crowded mass of telegraph-poles; for only the sunny tops are
leafy. A sapling ten years old, growing in the sunshine, has
as many leaves as a crowded tree one or two hundred years
old. As fires are multiplied and the mountains become drier,
this wonderful lodge-pole pine bids fair to obtain possession
of nearly all the forest ground in the West.

How still the woods seem from here, yet how lively a
stir the hidden animals are making; digging, gnawing, biting, eyes shining, at work and play, getting food, rearing
young, roving through the underbrush, climbing the rocks,
wading solitary marshes, tracing the banks of the lakes and
streams! Insect swarms are dancing in the sunbeams, burrowing in the ground, diving, swimming,—a cloud of witnesses telling Nature's joy. The plants are as busy as the

animals, every cell in a swirl of enjoyment, humming like a hive, singing the old new song of creation. A few columns and puffs of steam are seen rising above the treetops, some near, but most of them far off, indicating geysers and hot springs, gentle-looking and noiseless as downy clouds, softly hinting the reaction going on between the surface and the hot interior. From here you see them better than when you are standing beside them, frightened and confused, regarding them as lawless cataclysms. The shocks and out-bursts of earthquakes, volcanoes, geysers, storms, the pounding of waves, the uprush of sap in plants, each and all tell the orderly love-beats of Nature's heart.

Turning to the eastward, you have the Grand Cañon and reaches of the river in full view; and yonder to the southward lies the great lake, the largest and most important of all the high fountains of the Missouri-Mississippi, and the last to be discovered.

In the year 1541, when De Soto, with a romantic band of adventurers, was seeking gold and glory and the fountain of youth, he found the Mississippi a few hundred miles above its mouth, and made his grave beneath its floods. La Salle, in 1682, after discovering the Ohio, one of the largest and most beautiful branches of the Mississippi, traced the latter to the sea from the mouth of the Illinois, through adventures and privations not easily realized now. About the same time Joliet and Father Marquette reached the "Father of Waters" by way of the Wisconsin, but more than a century passed ere its highest sources in these mountains were seen. The advancing stream of civilization has ever followed its guidance toward the west, but none of the thousand tribes of Indians living on its banks could tell the explorer whence it came. From those romantic De Soto and La Salle days to these times of locomotives and tourists, how much has the great river seen and done! Great as it now is, and still growing longer through the ground of its delta and the basins of receding glaciers at its head, it was immensely broader toward the close of the glacial period, when the ice-mantle of the mountains was melting: then with its three hundred thousand miles of branches out-spread over the plains and valleys of the continent, laden with fertile mud, it made the biggest and most generous bed of soil in the world.

Think of this mighty stream springing in the first place in vapor from the sea, flying on the wind, alighting on the mountains in hail and snow and rain, lingering in many a fountain feeding the trees and grass; then gathering its scattered waters, gliding from its noble lake, and going back home to the sea, singing all the way! On it sweeps, through the gates of the mountains, across the vast prairies and plains, through many a wild, gloomy forest, cane-brake, and sunny savanna; from glaciers and snowbanks and pine woods to warm groves of magnolia and palm; geysers dancing at its head keeping time with the sea-waves at its mouth; roaring and gray in rapids, booming in broad, bossy falls, murmuring, gleaming in long, silvery reaches, swaying now hither, now thither, whirling, bending in huge doubling, eddying folds, serene, majestic, ungovernable, overflowing all its metes and bounds, frightening the dwellers upon its banks; building, wasting, uprooting, planting; engulfing old islands and making new ones, taking away fields and towns as if in sport, carrying canoes and ships of commerce in the midst of its spoils and drift, fertilizing the continent as one vast farm. Then, its work done, it gladly vanishes in its ocean home, welcomed by the waiting waves.

Thus naturally, standing here in the midst of its fountains, we trace the fortunes of the great river. And how much more comes to mind as we overlook this wonderful wilderness! Fountains of the Columbia and Colorado lie before us, interlaced with those of the Yellowstone and Missouri, and fine it would be to go with them to the Pacific; but the sun is already in the west, and soon our day will be done.

Yonder is Amethyst Mountain, and other mountains hardly less rich in old forests, which now seem to spring up again in their glory; and you see the storms that buried them,—the ashes and torrents laden with boulders and mud, the centuries of sunshine, and the dark, lurid nights. You see again the vast floods of lava, red-hot and white-hot, pouring out from gigantic geysers, usurping the basins of lakes and streams, absorbing or driving away their hissing, screaming waters, flowing around hills and ridges, submerging every subordinate feature. Then you see the snow and glaciers taking possession of the land, making new landscapes. How admirable it is that, after passing through so many vicissitudes of frost and fire and flood, the physiognomy and even the complexion of the landscape should still be so divinely fine!

Thus reviewing the eventful past, we see Nature working with enthusiasm like a man, blowing her volcanic forges like a blacksmith blowing his smithy fires, shoving glaciers over the landscapes like a carpenter shoving his planes, clearing, ploughing, harrowing, irrigating, planting, and sowing broadcast like a farmer and gardener, doing rough work and fine work, planting sequoias and pines, rosebushes and daisies; working in gems, filling every crack and hollow with them; distilling fine essences; painting plants and shells, clouds, mountains, all the earth and heavens, like an artist,—ever working toward beauty higher and higher. Where may the mind find more stimulating, quickening pasturage? A thousand Yellowstone wonders are calling, "Look up and down and round about you!" And a multitude of still, small voices may be heard directing you to look through all this transient, shifting show of things called "substantial" into the truly substantial, spiritual world whose forms flesh and wood, rock and water, air and sunshine, only veil and conceal, and to learn that here is heaven and the dwelling-place of the angels.

The sun is setting; long, violet shadows are growing out over the woods from the mountains along the western rim of the park; the Absaroka range is baptized in the divine light of the alpenglow, and its rocks and trees are transfigured. Next to the light of the dawn on high mountain tops, the alpenglow is the most impressive of all the terrestrial manifestations of God.

Now comes the gloaming. The alpenglow is fading into earthy, murky gloom, but do not let your town habits draw you away to the hotel. Stay on this good fire-mountain and spend the night among the stars. Watch their glorious bloom until the dawn, and get one more baptism of light. Then, with fresh heart, go down to your work, and whatever your fate, under whatever ignorance or knowledge you may afterward chance to suffer, you will remember these fine, wild views, and look back with joy to your wanderings in the blessed old Yellowstone Wonderland.

III

THE YOSEMITE NATIONAL PARK

Of all the mountain ranges I have climbed, I like the Sierra Nevada the best. Though extremely rugged, with its main features on the grandest scale in height and depth, it is nevertheless easy of access and hospitable; and its marvelous beauty, displayed in striking and alluring forms, wooes the admiring wanderer on and on, higher and higher, charmed and enchanted. Benevolent, solemn, fateful, pervaded with divine light, every landscape glows like a countenance hallowed in eternal repose; and every one of its living creatures, clad in flesh and leaves, and every crystal of its rocks, whether on the surface shining in the sun or buried miles deep in what we call darkness, is throbbing and pulsing with the heartbeats of God. All the world lies warm in one heart, yet the Sierra seems to get more light than other mountains. The weather is mostly sunshine embellished with magnificent storms, and nearly everything shines from base to summit,—the rocks, streams, lakes, glaciers, irised falls, and the forests of silver fir and silver pine. And how bright is the shining after summer showers and dewy nights, and after frosty nights in spring and autumn, when the morning sunbeams are pouring through the crystals on the bushes and grass, and in winter through the snow-laden trees!

The average cloudiness for the whole year is perhaps less than ten hundredths. Scarcely a day of all the summer is dark, though there is no lack of magnificent thundering cumuli. They rise in the warm midday hours, mostly over the middle region, in June and July, like new mountain ranges, higher Sierras, mightily augmenting the grandeur of the scenery while giving rain to the forests and gardens and bringing forth their fragrance. The wonderful weather and beauty inspire everybody to be up and doing. Every summer day is a workday to be confidently counted on, the short dashes of rain forming, not interruptions, but rests. The big blessed storm days of winter, when the whole range stands white, are not a whit less inspiring and kind. Well may the Sierra be called the Range of Light, not the Snowy Range; for only in winter is it white; while all the year it is bright.

Of this glorious range the Yosemite National Park is a central section, thirty-six miles in length and forty-eight miles in breadth. The famous Yosemite Valley lies in the heart of it, and it includes the head waters of the Tuolumne and Merced rivers, two of the most songful streams in the world; innumerable lakes and waterfalls and smooth silky lawns; the noblest forests, the loftiest granite domes, the deepest ice-sculptured canons, the brightest crystalline pavements, and snowy mountains soaring into the sky twelve and thirteen thousand feet, arrayed in open ranks and spiry pinnacled groups partially separated by tremendous cañons and amphitheatres; gardens on their sunny brows avalanches thundering down their long white slopes, cataracts roaring gray and foaming in the crooked rugged gorges. and glaciers in their shadowy recesses working in silence, slowly completing their sculpture; new-born lakes at their feet, blue and green, free or encumbered with drifting icebergs like miniature Arctic Oceans, shining, sparkling, calm as stars.

Nowhere will you see the majestic operations of nature more clearly revealed beside the frailest, most gentle and peaceful things. Nearly all the park is a profound solitude. Yet it is full of charming company, full of God's thoughts, a place of peace and safety amid the most exalted grandeur and eager enthusiastic action, a new song, a place of beginnings abounding in first lessons on life, mountain-building, eternal, invincible, unbreakable order; with sermons in stones, storms, trees, flowers, and animals brimful of humanity. During the last glacial period, just past, the former features of the range were rubbed off as a chalk sketch from a blackboard, and a new beginning was made. Hence the wonderful clearness and freshness of the rocky pages.

But to get all this into words is a hopeless task. The leanest sketch of each feature would need a whole chapter. Nor would any amount of space, however industriously scribbled, be of much avail. To defrauded town toilers,parks in magazine articles are like pictures of bread to the hungry. I can write only hints to incite good wanderers to come to the feast.

While this glorious park embraces big, generous samples of the very best of the Sierra treasure, it is, fortunately, at the same time, the most accessible portion. It lies opposite San Francisco, at a distance of about one hundred and forty miles. Railroads connected with all the continent reach into the foothills, and three good carriage roads, from Big Oak Flat, Coulterville, and Raymond, run into Yosemite Valley. Another, called the Tioga road, runs from Crocker's Station on the Yosemite Big Oak Flat road near the Tuolumne Big Tree Grove, right across the park to the summit of the range by way of Lake Tenaya, the Big Tuolumne Meadows, and Mount Dana. These roads, with many trails that radiate from Yosemite Valley, bring most of the park within reach of everybody, well or half well.

The three main natural divisions of the park, the lower, middle, and alpine regions, are fairly well defined in altitude, topographical features, and vegetation. The lower, with an average elevation of about five thousand feet, is the region of the great forests, made up of sugar pine, the largest and most beautiful of all the pines in the world; the silvery yellow pine, the next in rank; Douglas spruce, libocedrus, the white and red silver firs, and the Sequoia gigantea, or "big tree," the king of conifers, the noblest of a noble race. On warm slopes next the foothills there are a few Sabine nut pines; oaks make beautiful groves in the cañon valleys; and poplar, alder, maple, laurel, and Nuttall's flowering dogwood shade the banks of the streams. Many of the pines are more than two hundred feet high, but they are not crowded together. The sunbeams streaming through their feathery arches brighten the ground, and you walk beneath the radiant ceiling in devout subdued mood, as if you were in a grand cathedral with mellow light sifting through colored windows, while the flowery pillared aisles open enchanting vistas in every direction. Scarcely a peak or ridge in the whole region rises bare above the forests, though they are thinly planted in some places where the soil is shallow. From the cool breezy heights you look abroad over a boundless waving sea of evergreens, covering hill and ridge and smooth-flowing slope as far as the eye can reach, and filling every hollow and down-plunging ravine in glorious triumphant exuberance.

Perhaps the best general view of the pine forests of the park, and one of the best in the range, is obtained from the top of the Merced and Tuolumne divide near Hazel Green. On the long, smooth, finely folded slopes of the main ridge, at a height of five to six thousand feet above the sea, they reach most perfect development and are marshaled to view in magnificent towering ranks, their colossal spires and domes and broad palmlike crowns, deep in the kind sky, rising above one another,—a multitude of giants in perfect health and beauty,—sun-fed mountaineers rejoicing in their strength, chanting with the winds, in accord with the falling waters. The ground is mostly open and inviting to walkers. The fragrant chamæbatia is outspread in rich carpets miles in extent; the manzanita, in orchard-like groves, covered with pink bell-shaped flowers in the spring, grows in openings facing the sun, hazel and buckthorn in the dells; warm brows are purple with mint, yellow with sunflowers and violets; and tall lilies ring their bells around the borders of meadows and along the ferny, mossy banks of the streams. Never was mountain forest more lavishly furnished.

Hazel Green is a good place quietly to camp and study, to get acquainted with the trees and birds, to drink the reviving water and weather, and to watch the changing lights of the big charmed days. The rose light of the dawn, creeping higher among the stars, changes to daffodil yellow; then come the level enthusiastic sunbeams pouring across the feathery ridges, touching pine after pine, spruce and fir, libocedrus and lordly sequoia, searching every recess, until all are awakened and warmed. In the white noon they shine in silvery splendor, every needle and cell in bole and branch thrilling and tingling with ardent life; and the whole landscape glows with consciousness, like the face of a god. The hours go by uncounted. The evening flames with purple and gold. The breeze that has been blowing from the lowlands dies away, and far and near the mighty host of trees baptized in the purple flood stand hushed and thoughtful, awaiting the sun's blessing and farewell,—as impressive a ceremony as if it were never to rise again. When the daylight fades, the night breeze from the snowy summits begins to blow, and the trees, waving and rustling beneath the stars, breathe free again.

It is hard to leave such camps and woods; nevertheless, to the large majority of travelers the middle region of the park is still more interesting, for it has the most striking features of all the Sierra scenery,—the deepest sections of the famous cañons, of which the Yosemite Valley, Hetch-Hetchy Valley, and many smaller ones are wider portions, with level parklike floors and walls of immense height and grandeur of sculpture. This middle region holds also the greater number of the beautiful glacier lakes and glacier meadows, the great granite domes, and the most brilliant and most extensive of the glacier pavements. And though in large part it is severely rocky and bare, it is still rich in trees. The magnificent silver fir (*Abies magnifica*), which ranks with the giants, forms a continuous belt across the park above the pines at an elevation of from seven to nine thousand feet, and north and south of the park boundaries to the extremities of the range, only slightly interrupted by the main cañons. The two-leaved or tamarack pine makes another less regular belt along the upper margin of the region, while between these two belts, and mingling with them, in groves or scattered, are the mountain hemlock, the most graceful of evergreens; the noble mountain pine; the Jeffrey form of the yellow pine, with big cones and long needles; and the brown, burly, sturdy Western juniper. All these, except the juniper, which grows on bald rocks, have plenty of flowery brush about them, and gardens in open spaces.

Here, too, lies the broad, shining heavily sculptured region of primeval granite, which best tells the story of the glacial period on the Pacific side of the continent. No other mountain chain on the globe, as far as I know, is so rich as the Sierra in bold, striking, well-preserved glacial monuments, easily understood by anybody capable of patient observation. Every feature is more or less glacial, and this park portion of the range is the brightest and clearest of all. Not a peak, ridge, dome, cañon, lake basin, garden, forest, or stream but in some way explains the past existence and modes of action of flowing, grinding, sculpturing, soil-making, scenery-making ice. For, notwithstanding the post-glacial agents—air, rain, frost, rivers, earthquakes, avalanches—have been at work upon the greater part of the range for tens of thousands of stormy years, engraving their own characters over those of the ice, the latter are so heavily emphasized and enduring they still rise in sublime relief, clear and legible through every after inscription. The streams have traced only shallow wrinkles as yet, and avalanche, wind, rain, and melting snow have made blurs and scars, but the change effected on the face of the landscape is not greater than is made on the face of a mountaineer by a single year of weathering.

Of all the glacial phenomena presented here, the most striking and attractive to travelers are the polished pavements, because they are so beautiful, and their beauty is of so rare a kind,—unlike any part of the loose earthy lowlands where people dwell and earn their bread. They are simply flat or gently undulating areas of solid resisting granite, the unchanged surface over which the ancient glaciers flowed. They are found in the most perfect condition at an elevation of from eight to nine thousand feet above sea level. Some are miles in extent, only slightly blurred or scarred by spots that have at last yielded to the weather; while the best preserved portions are brilliantly polished, and reflect the sunbeams as calm water or glass, shining as if rubbed and burnished every day, notwithstanding they have been exposed to plashing, corroding rains, dew, frost, and melting sloppy snows for thousands of years.

The attention of hunters and prospectors, who see so much in their wild journeys, is seldom attracted by moraines, however regular and artificial-looking; or rocks, however boldly sculptured; or cañons, however deep and sheer-walled. But when they come to these pavements, they go down on their knees and rub their hands admiringly on the glistening surface, and try hard to account for its mysterious smoothness and brightness. They may have seen the winter avalanches come down the mountains, through the woods, sweeping away the trees and scouring the ground; but they conclude that this cannot be the work of avalanches, because the striæ show that the agent, whatever it was, flowed along and around and over the top of high ridges and domes, and also filled the deep cañons. Neither can they see how water could be the agent, for the strange polish is found thousands of feet above the reach of any conceivable flood. Only the winds seem capable of moving over the face of the country in the directions indicated by the lines and grooves.

The pavements are particularly fine around Lake Tenaya, and have suggested the Indian name Py-we-ack, the Lake of the Shining Rocks. Indians seldom trouble themselves with geological questions, but a Mono Indian once came to me and asked if I could tell him what made the rocks so smooth at Tenaya. Even dogs and horses, on their first journeys into this region, study geology to the extent of gazing wonderingly at the strange brightness of the ground, and pawing it and smelling it, as if afraid of falling or sinking.

In the production of this admirable hard finish, the glaciers in many places exerted a pressure of more than a hundred tons to the square foot, planing down granite, slate, and quartz alike, showing their structure, and making beautiful mosaics where large feldspar crystals form the greater part of the rock. On such pavements the sunshine is at times dazzling, as if the surface were of burnished silver.

Here, also, are the brightest of the Sierra landscapes in general. The regions lying at the same elevation to the north and south were perhaps subjected to as long and intense a glaciation; but because the rocks are less resisting, their polished surfaces have mostly given way to the weather, leaving here and there only small imperfect patches on the most enduring portions of cañon walls protected from the action of rain and snow, and on hard bosses kept comparatively dry by boulders. The short, steeply inclined canons of the east flank of the range are in some places brightly polished, but they are far less magnificent than those of the broad west flank.

One of the best general views of the middle region of the park is to be had from the top of a majestic dome which long ago I named the Glacier Monument. It is situated a few miles to the north of Cathedral Peak, and rises to a height of about fifteen hundred feet above its base and ten thousand above the sea. At first sight it seems sternly inaccessible, but a good climber will find that it may be scaled on the south side. Approaching it from this side you pass through a dense bryanthus-fringed grove of mountain hemlock, catching glimpses now and then of the colossal dome towering to an immense height above the dark evergreens; and when at last you have made your way across woods, wading through azalea and ledum thickets, you step abruptly out of the tree shadows and mossy leafy softness upon a bare porphyry pavement, and behold the dome unveiled in all its grandeur. Fancy a nicely proportioned monument, eight or ten feet high, hewn from one stone, standing in a pleasure ground; magnify it to a height of fifteen hundred feet, retaining its simplicity of form and fineness, and cover its surface with crystals; then you may gain an idea of the sublimity and beauty of this ice-burnished dome, one of many adorning this wonderful park.

In making the ascent, one finds that the curve of the base rapidly steepens, until one is in danger of slipping; but feldspar crystals, two or three inches long, that have been weathered into relief, afford slight footholds. The summit is in part burnished, like the sides and base, the striæ and scratches indicating that the mighty Tuolumne Glacier, two or three thousand feet deep, overwhelmed it while it stood firm like a boulder at the bottom of a river. The pressure it withstood must have been enormous. Had it been less solidly built, it would have been ground and crushed into moraine fragments, like the general mass of the mountain flank in which at first it lay imbedded; for it is only a hard residual knob or knot with a concentric structure of superior strength, brought into relief by the removal of the less resisting rock about it,—an illustration in stone of the survival of the strongest and most favorably situated.

Hardly less wonderful, when we contemplate the storms it has encountered since first it saw the light, is its present unwasted condition. The whole quantity of postglacial wear and tear it has suffered has not diminished its stature a single inch, as may be readily shown by measuring from the level of the unchanged polished portions of the surface. Indeed, the average postglacial denudation of the entire region, measured in the same way, is found to be less than two inches,—a mighty contrast to that of the ice; for the glacial denudation here has been not less than a mile; that is, in developing the present landscapes, an amount of rock a mile in average thickness has been silently carried away by flowing ice during the last glacial period.

A few erratic boulders nicely poised on the founded summit of the monument tell an interesting story. They came from a mountain on the crest of the range, about twelve miles to the eastward, floating like chips on the frozen sea, and were stranded here when the top of the monument emerged to the light of day, while the companions of these boulders, whose positions chanced to be over the slopes where they could not find rest, were carried farther on by the shallowing current.

The general view from the summit consists of a sublime assemblage of iceborn mountains and rocks and long wavering ridges, lakes and streams and meadows, moraines in wide-sweeping belts, and beds covered and dotted with

forests and groves,—hundreds of square miles of them composed in wild harmony. The snowy mountains on the axis of
the range, mostly sharp-peaked and crested, rise in a noble
array along the sky to the eastward and northward; the
gray-pillared Hoffman spur and the Yosemite domes and
a countless number of others to the westward; Cathedral
Peak with its many spires and companion peaks and domes
to the southward; and a smooth billowy multitude of rocks,
from fifty feet or less to a thousand feet high, which from
their peculiar form seem to be rolling on westward, fill
most of the middle ground. Immediately beneath you are
the Big Tuolumne Meadows, with an ample swath of dark
pine woods on either side, enlivened by the young river, that
is seen sparkling and shimmering as it sways from side to
side, tracing as best it can its broad glacial channel.

The ancient Tuolumne Glacier, lavishly flooded by
many a noble affluent from the snow-laden flanks of
Mounts Dana, Gibbs, Lyell, Maclure, and others nameless as yet, poured its majestic overflowing current, four
or five miles wide, directly against the high outstanding
mass of Mount Hoffman, which divided and deflected it
right and left, just as a river is divided against an island
that stands in the middle of its channel. Two distinct glaciers were thus formed, one of which flowed through the Big
Tuolumne Cañon and Hetch-Hetchy Valley, while the other
swept upward five hundred feet in a broad current across
the divide between the basins of the Tuolumne and Merced
into the Tenaya basin, and thence down through the Tenaya
Cañon and Yosemite Valley.

The maplike distinctness and freshness of this glacial landscape cannot fail to excite the attention of every
observer, no matter how little of its scientific significance
he may at first recognize. These bald, glossy, westward-
leaning rocks in the open middle ground, with their
rounded backs and shoulders toward the glacier fountains
of the summit mountains and their split angular fronts
looking in the opposite direction, every one of them displaying the form of greatest strength with reference to physical
structure and glacial action, show the tremendous force

with which through unnumbered centuries the ice flood swept over them, and also the direction of the flow; while the mountains, with their sharp summits and abraded sides, indicate the height to which the glacier rose; and the moraines, curving and swaying in beautiful lines, mark the boundaries of the main trunk and its tributaries as they existed toward the close of the glacial winter. None of the commercial highways of the sea or land, marked with buoys and lamps, fences and guideboards, is so unmistakably indicated as are these channels of the vanished Tuolumne glaciers.

The action of flowing ice, whether in the form of river-like glaciers or broad mantling folds, is but little understood as compared with that of other sculpturing agents. Rivers work openly where people dwell, and so do the rain, and the sea thundering on all the shores of the world; and the universal ocean of air, through unseen, speaks aloud in a thousand voices and explains its modes of working and its power. But glaciers, back in their cold solitudes, work apart from men, exerting their tremendous energies in silence and darkness. Coming in vapor from the sea, flying invisible on the wind, descending in snow, changing to ice, white, spiritlike, they brood outspread over the predestined landscapes, working on unwearied through unmeasured ages, until in the fullness of time the mountains and valleys are brought forth, channels furrowed for the rivers, basins made for meadows and lakes, and soil beds spread for the forests and fields that man and beast may be fed. Then vanishing like clouds, they melt into streams and go singing back home to the sea.

To an observer upon this adamantine old monument in the midst of such scenery, getting glimpses of the thoughts of God, the day seems endless, the sun stands still. Much faithless fuss is made over the passage in the Bible telling of the standing still of the sun for Joshua. Here you may learn that the miracle occurs for every devout mountaineer, for everybody doing anything worth doing, seeing anything worth seeing. One day is as a thousand years, a thousand years as one day, and while yet in the flesh you enjoy immortality.

From the monument you will find an easy way down through the woods and along the Big Tuolumne Meadows to Mount Dana, the summit of which commands a grand telling view of the alpine region. The scenery all the way is inspiring, and you saunter on without knowing that you are climbing. The spacious sunny meadows, through the midst of which the bright river glides, extend with but little interruption ten miles to the eastward, dark woods rising on either side to the limit of tree growth, and above the woods a picturesque line of gray peaks and spires dotted with snow banks; while, on the axis of the Sierra, Mount Dana and his noble compeers repose in massive sublimity, their vast size and simple flowing contours contrasting in the most striking manner with the clustering spires and thin-pinnacled crests crisply outlined on the horizon to the north and south of them.

Tracing the silky lawns, gradually ascending, gazing at the sublime scenery more and more openly unfolded, noting the avalanche gaps in the upper forests, lingering over beds of blue gentians and purple-flowered bryanthus and cassiope, and dwarf willows an inch high in close-felted gray carpets, brightened here and there with kalmia and soft creeping mats of vaccinium sprinkled with pink bells that seem to have been showered down from the sky like hail,— thus beguiled and enchanted, you reach the base of the mountain wholly unconscious of the miles you have walked. And so on to the summit. For all the way up the long red slate slopes, that in the distance seemed barren, you find little garden beds and tufts of dwarf phlox, ivesia, and blue arctic daisies that go straight to your heart, blessed fellow mountaineers kept safe and warm by a thousand miracles. You are now more than thirteen thousand feet above the sea, and to the north and south you behold a sublime wilderness of mountains in glorious array, their snowy summits towering together in crowded, bewildering abundance, shoulder to shoulder, peak beyond peak. To the east lies the Great Basin, barren-looking and silent, apparently a land of pure desolation, rich only in beautiful light. Mono Lake, fourteen miles long, is outspread below you at a depth of nearly seven thousand feet, its shores of volcanic ashes and sand, treeless and sunburned; a group of volcanic cones, with well-formed, unwasted craters rises to the south of the lake; while up from its eastern shore innumerable mountains with soft flowing outlines extend range beyond range, gray, and pale purple, and blue,—the farthest gradually fading on the flowing horizon. Westward you look down and over the countless moraines, glacier meadows, and grand sea of domes and rock waves of the upper Tuolumne basin, the Cathedral and Hoffman mountains with their wavering lines and zones of forest, the wonderful region to the north of the Tuolumne Cañon, and across the dark belt of silver firs to the pale mountains of the coast.

In the icy fountains of the Mount Lyell and Ritter groups of peaks, to the south of Dana, three of the most important of the Sierra rivers—the Tuolumne, Merced, and San Joaquin—take their rise, their highest tributaries being within a few miles of one another as they rush forth on their adventurous courses from beneath snow banks and glaciers.

Of the small shrinking glaciers of the Sierra, remnants of the majestic system that sculptured the range, I have seen sixty-five. About twenty-five of them are in the park, and eight are in sight from Mount Dana.

The glacier lakes are sprinkled over all the alpine and subalpine regions, gleaming like eyes beneath heavy rock brows, tree-fringed or bare, embosomed in the woods, or lying in open basins with green and purple meadows around them; but the greater number are in the cool shadowy hollows of the summit mountains not far from the glaciers, the highest lying at an elevation of from eleven to nearly twelve thousand feet above the sea. The whole number in the Sierra, not counting the smallest, can hardly be less than fifteen hundred, of which about two hundred and fifty are in the park. From one standpoint, on Red Mountain, I counted forty-two, most of them within a radius of ten miles. The glacier meadows, which are spread over the filled-up basins of vanished lakes and form one of the most charming features of the scenery, are still more numerous than the lakes.

An observer stationed here, in the glacial period, would have overlooked a wrinkled mantle of ice as continuous as that which now covers the continent of Greenland; and of all the vast landscape now shining in the sun, he would have seen only the tops of the summit peaks, rising darkly like storm-beaten islands, lifeless and hopeless, above rock-encumbered ice waves. If among the agents that nature has employed in making these mountains there be one that above all other deserves the name of Destroyer, it is the glacier. But we quickly learn that destruction is creation. During the dreary centuries through which the Sierra lay in darkness, crushed beneath the ice folds of the glacial winter, there was a steady invincible advance toward the warm life and beauty of to-day; and it is just where the glaciers crushed most destructively that the greatest amount of beauty is made manifest. But as these landscapes have succeeded the preglacial landscapes, so they in turn are giving place to others already planned and foreseen. The granite domes and pavements, apparently imperishable, we take as symbols of permanence, while these crumbling peaks, down whose frosty gullies avalanches are ever falling, are symbols of change and decay. Yet all alike, fast or slow, are surely vanishing away.

Nature is ever at work building and pulling down, creating and destroying, keeping everything whirling and flowing, allowing no rest but in rhythmical motion, chasing everything in endless song out of one beautiful form into another.

IV

THE FORESTS OF THE YOSEMITE PARK

The coniferous forests of the Yosemite Park, and of the Sierra in general, surpass all others of their kind in America or indeed in the world, not only in the size and beauty of the trees, but in the number of species assembled together, and the grandeur of the mountains they are growing on. Leaving the workaday lowlands, and wandering into the heart of the mountains, we find a new world, and stand beside the majestic pines and firs and sequoias silent and awe-stricken, as if in the presence of superior beings new arrived from some other star, so calm and bright and godlike they are.

Going to the woods is going home; for I suppose we came from the woods originally. But in some of nature's forests the adventurous traveler seems a feeble, unwelcome creature; wild beasts and the weather trying to kill him, the rank, tangled vegetation, armed with spears and stinging needles, barring his way and making life a hard struggle. Here everything is hospitable and kind, as if planned for your pleasure, ministering to every want of body and soul. Even the storms are friendly and seem to regard you as a brother, their beauty and tremendous fateful earnestness charming alike. But the weather is mostly sunshine, both winter and summer and the clear sunny brightness of the park is one of its most striking characteristics. Even the heaviest portions of the main forest belt, where the trees are tallest and stand closest, are not in the least gloomy. The sunshine falls in glory through the colossal spires and crowns, each a symbol of health and strength, the noble shafts faithfully upright like the pillars of temples, upholding a roof of infinite leafy interlacing arches and fretted skylights. The more open portions are like spacious parks, carpeted with small shrubs, or only with the fallen needles sprinkled here and there with flowers. In some places, where the ground is level or slopes gently, the trees are assembled in groves, and the flowers and underbrush in trim beds and thickets as in landscape gardens or the lovingly planted grounds of homes; or they are drawn up in orderly rows around meadows and lakes and along the brows of cañons. But in general the forests are distributed in wide belts in accordance with climate and the comparative strength of each kind in gaining and holding possession of the ground, while anything like monotonous uniformity is prevented by the grandly varied topography,and by the arrangement of the best soilbeds in intricate patterns like embroidery; for these soilbeds are the moraines of ancient glaciers more or less modified by weathering and stream action, and the trees trace them over the hills and ridges, and far up the sides of the mountains, rising with even growth on levels, and towering above one another on the long rich slopes prepared for them by the vanished glaciers.

Had the Sierra forests been cheaply accessible, the most valuable of them commercially would ere this have fallen a prey to the lumberman. Thus far the redwood of the Coast Mountains and the Douglas spruce of Oregon and Washington have been more available for lumber than the pine of the Sierra. It cost less to go a thousand miles up the coast for timber, where the trees came down to the shores of navigable rivers and bays, than fifty miles up the mountains. Nevertheless, the superior value of the sugar pine for many purposes has tempted capitalists to expend large sums on flumes and railroads to reach the best forests, though perhaps none of these enterprises has paid. Fortunately, the lately established system of parks and reservations has put a stop to any great extension of the business hereabouts in its most destructive forms. And as the Yosemite Park region has escaped the millmen, and the all-devouring hordes of hoofed locusts have been banished, it is still in the main a pure wilderness, unbroken by axe clearings except on the lower margin, where a few settlers have opened spots beside hay meadows for their cabins and gardens. But these are mere dots of cultivation, in no appreciable degree disturbing the grand solitude. Twenty or thirty years ago a good many trees were felled for their seeds; traces of this destructive method of seed-collecting are still visible along the trails; but these as well as the shingle-makers ruins are being rapidly overgrown, the gardens and beds of underbrush once devastated by sheep are blooming again in all their wild glory, and the park is a paradise that makes even the loss of Eden seem insignificant.

On the way to Yosemite Valley, you get some grand views over the forests of the Merced and Tuolumne basins and glimpses of some of the finest trees by the roadside without leaving your seat in the stage. But to learn how they live and behave in pure wildness, to see them in their varying aspects through the seasons and weather, rejoicing in the great storms, in the spiritual mountain light, putting forth their new leaves and flowers when all the streams are in flood and the birds are singing, and sending away their seeds in the thoughtful Indian summer when all the landscape is glowing in deep calm enthusiasm,—for this you must love them and live with them, as free from schemes and cares and time as the trees themselves.

And surely nobody will find anything hard in this. Even the blind must enjoy these woods, drinking their fragrance, listening to the music of the winds in their groves, and fingering their flowers and plumes and cones and richly furrowed boles. The kind of study required is as easy and natural as breathing. Without any great knowledge of botany or wood-craft, in a single season you may learn the name and something more of nearly every kind of tree in the park.

With few exceptions all the Sierra trees are growing in the park,—nine species of pine, two of silver fir, one each of Douglas spruce, libocedrus, hemlock, juniper, and sequoia,—sixteen conifers in all, and about the same number of round-headed trees, oaks, maples, poplars, laurel, alder, dogwood, tumion, etc.

The first of the conifers you meet in going up the range from the west is the digger nut-pine (*Pinus Sabiniana*), a remarkably open, airy, wide-branched tree, forty to sixty feet high, with long, sparse, grayish green foliage and large cones. At a height of fifteen to thirty feet from the ground the trunk usually divides into several main branches, which, after bearing away from one another, shoot straight up and form separate heads as if the axis of the tree had been broken, while the secondary branches divide again and again into rather slender sprays loosely tasseled, with leaves eight to twelve inches long. The yellow and purple flowers are about an inch long, the staminate in showy clusters. The big, rough, burly cones, five to eight or ten inches in length and five or six in diameter, are rich brown in color when ripe, and full of hard-shelled nuts that are greatly prized by Indians and squirrels. This strange-looking pine, enjoying hot sunshine like a palm, is sparsely distributed along the driest part of the Sierra among small oaks and chaparral, and with its gray mist of foliage, strong trunk and branches, and big cones seen in relief on the glowing sky, forms the most striking feature of the foothill vegetation.

Pinus attenuata is a small, slender, arrowy tree, with pale green leaves in threes, clustered flowers half an inch long, brownish yellow and crimson, and cones whorled in conspicuous clusters around the branches and also around the trunk. The cones never fall off or open until the tree dies. They are about four inches long, exceedingly strong and solid, and varnished with hard resin forming a waterproof and almost worm and squirrel proof package, in which the seeds are kept fresh and safe during the lifetime of the tree. Sometimes one of the trunk cones is overgrown and imbedded in the heart wood like a knot, but nearly all are pushed out and kept on the surface by the pressure of the successive layers of wood against the base.

This admirable little tree grows on brushy, sun-beaten slopes, which from their position and the inflammable character of the vegetation are most frequently fire-swept. These grounds it is able to hold against all comers, however big and strong, by saving its seeds until death, when all it has produced are scattered over the bare cleared ground, and a new generation quickly springs out of the ashes. Thus the curious fact that all the trees of extensive groves and belts are of the same age is accounted for, and their slender habit; for the lavish abundance of seed sown at the same time makes a crowded growth, and the seedlings with an even start rush up in a hurried race for light and life.

Only a few of the attenuata and Sabiniana pines are within the boundaries of the park, the former on the side of the Merced Cañon, the latter on the walls of Hetch-Hetchy Valley and in the cañon below it.

The nut-pine (*Pinus monophylla*) is a small, hardy, contended-looking tree, about fifteen or twenty feet high and a foot in diameter. In its youth the close radiating and aspiring branches form a handsome broad-based pyramid, but when fully grown it becomes round-topped, knotty, and irregular, throwing out crooked divergent limbs like an apple tree. The leaves are pale grayish green, about an inch and a half long, and instead of being divided into clusters they are single, round, sharp-pointed, and rigid like spikes, amid which in the spring the red flowers glow brightly. The cones are only about two inches in length and breadth, but nearly half of their bulk is made up of sweet nuts.

This fruitful little pine grows on the dry east side of the park, along the margin of the Mono sage plain, and is the commonest tree of the short mountain ranges of the Great Basins. Tens of thousands of acres are covered with it, forming bountiful orchards for the Red-man. Being so low and accessible, the cones are easily beaten off with poles, and the nuts procured by roasting until the scales open. To the tribes of the desert and sage plains these seeds are the staff of life. They are eaten either raw or parched, or in the form of mush or cakes after being pounded into meal. The time of nut harvest in the autumn is the Indian's merriest time of all the year. An industrious squirrelish family can gather fifty or sixty bushels in a single month before the snow comes, and then their bread for the winter is sure.

The white pine (*Pinus flexilis*) is widely distributed through the Rocky Mountains and the ranges of the Great Basin, where in many places it grows to a good size, and is an important timber tree where none better is to be found. In the park it is sparsely scattered along the eastern flank of the range from Mono Pass southward, above the nut-pine, at an elevation of from eight to ten thousand feet, dwarfing to a tangled bush near the timber-line, but under favorable conditions attaining a height of forty or fifty feet, with a diameter of three to five. The long branches show a tendency to sweep out in bold curves, like those of the mountain and sugar pines to which it is closely related. The needles are in clusters of five, closely packed on the ends of the branchlets. The cones are about five inches long,—the smaller ones nearly oval, the larger cylindrical. But the most interesting feature of the tree is its bloom, the vivid red pistillate flowers glowing among the leaves like coals of fire.

The dwarfed pine or white-barked pine (*Pinus albicaulis*) is sure to interest every observer on account of its curious low matted habit, and the great height on the snowy mountains at which it bravely grows. It forms the extreme edge of the timber-line on both flanks of the summit mountains—if so lowly a tree can be called timber—at an elevation of ten to twelve thousand feet above the level of the sea. Where it is first met on the lower limit of its range it may be thirty or forty feet high, but farther up the rocky wind-swept slopes, where the snow lies deep and heavy for six months of the year, it makes shaggy clumps and beds, crinkled and pressed flat, over which you can easily walk. Nevertheless in this crushed, down-pressed, felted condition it clings hardily to life, puts forth fresh leaves every spring on the ends of its tasseled branchlets, blooms bravely in the lashing blasts with abundance of gay red and purple flowers, matures its seeds in the short summers, and often outlives the favored giants of the sun lands far below. One of the trees that I examined was only about three feet high, with a stem six inches in diameter at the ground, and branches that spread out horizontally as if they had grown up against a ceiling; yet it was four hundred and twenty-six years old, and one of its supple branchlets, about an eighth of an inch in diameter inside the bark, was seventy-five years old, and so tough that I tied it into knots. At the age of this dwarf many of the sugar and yellow pines and sequoias are seven feet in diameter and over two hundred feet high.

In detached clumps never touched by fire the fallen needles of centuries of growth make fine elastic mattresses for the weary mountaineer, while the tasseled branchlets spread a roof over him, and the dead roots, half resin, usually found in abundance, make capital camp-fires, unquenchable in thickest storms of rain or snow. Seen from a distance the belts and patches darkening the mountain sides look like mosses on a roof, and bring to mind Dr. Johnson's remarks on the trees of Scotland. His guide, anxious for the honor of Mull, was still talking of its woods and pointing them out. "Sir," said Johnson, "I saw at Tobermory what they called a wood, which I unluckily took for heath. If you show me what I shall take for furze, it will be something."

The mountain pine (*Pinus monticola*) is far the largest of the Sierra tree mountaineers. Climbing nearly as high as the dwarf albicaulis, it is still a giant in size, bold and strong, standing erect on the storm-beaten peaks and ridges, tossing its cone-laden branches in the rough winds, living a thousand years, and reaching its greatest size—ninety to a hundred feet in height, six to eight in diameter—just where other trees, its companions, are dwarfed. But it is not able to endure burial in snow so long as the albicaulis and flexilis. Therefore, on the upper limit of its range it is found on slopes which, from their steepness or exposure, are least snowy. Its soft graceful beauty in youth, and its leaves, cones, and out-sweeping feathery branches constantly remind you of the sugar pine, to which it is closely allied. An admirable tree, growing nobler in form and size the colder and balder the mountains about it.

The giants of the main forest in the favored middle region are the sequoia, sugar pine, yellow pine, libocedrus, Douglas spruce, and the two silver firs. The park sequoias are restricted to two small groves, a few miles apart, on the Tuolumne and Merced divide, about seventeen miles from

Yosemite Valley. The Big Oak Flat road to the valley runs
through the Tuolumne Grove, the Coulterville through
the Merced. The more famous and better known Mariposa
Grove, belonging to the state, lies near the southwest corner
of the park, a few miles above Wawona.

The sugar pine (*Pinus Lambertiana*) is first met in the
park in open, sunny, flowery woods, at an elevation of about
thirty-five hundred feet above the sea, attains full development at a height between five and six thousand feet, and
vanishes at the level of eight thousand feet. In many places,
especially on the northern slopes of the main ridges between
the rivers, it forms the bulk of the forest, but mostly it is intimately associated with its noble companions, above which it
towers in glorious majesty on every hill, ridge, and plateau
from one extremity of the range to the other, a distance of
five hundred miles,—the largest, noblest, and most beautiful of all the seventy or eighty species of pine trees in the
world, and of all the conifers second only to King Sequoia.

A good many are from two hundred to two hundred and
twenty feet in height, with a diameter at four feet from the
ground of six to eight feet, and occasionally a grand patriarch, seven or eight hundred years old, is found that is ten
or even twelve feet in diameter and two hundred and forty
feet high, with a magnificent crown seventy feet wide. David
Douglas, who discovered "this most beautiful and immensely
grand tree" in the fall of 1826 in southern Oregon, says that
the largest of several that had been blown down, "at three
feet from the ground was fifty-seven feet nine inches in
circumference" (or fully eighteen feet in diameter); "at one
hundred and thirty-four feet, seventeen feet five inches;
extreme length, two hundred and forty-five feet." Probably
for fifty-seven we should read thirty-seven for the base measurement, which would make it correspond with the other
dimensions; for none of this species with anything like so
great a girth has since been seen. A girth of even thirty feet
is uncommon. A fallen specimen that I measured was nine
feet three inches in diameter inside the bark at four feet
from the ground, and six feet in diameter at a hundred feet
from the ground. A comparatively young tree, three hundred

and thirty years old, that had been cut down, measured seven feet across the stump. was three feet three inches in diameter at a height of one hundred and fifty feet, and two hundred and ten feet in length.

The trunk is a round, delicately tapered shaft with finely furrowed purplish-brown bark, usually free of limbs for a hundred feet or more. The top is furnished with long and comparatively slender branches, which sweep gracefully downward and outward, feathered with short tasseled branchlets, and divided only at the ends, forming a palm-like crown fifty to seventy-five feet wide, but without the monotonous uniformity of palm crowns or of the spires of most conifers. The old trees are as tellingly varied and picturesque as oaks. No two are alike, and we are tempted to stop and admire every one we come to, whether as it stands silent in the calm balsam-scented sunshine or waving in accord with enthusiastic storms. The leaves are about three or four inches long, in clusters of five, finely tempered, bright lively green, and radiant. The flowers are but little larger than those of the dwarf pine, and far less showy. The immense cylindrical cones, fifteen to twenty or even twenty-four inches long and three in diameter, hang singly or in clusters, like ornamental tassels, at the ends of the long branches, green, flushed with purple on the sunward side. Like those of almost all the pines they ripen in the autumn of the second season from the flower, and the seeds of all that have escaped the Indians, bears, and squirrels take wing and fly to their places. Then the cones become still more effective as ornaments, for by the spreading of the scales the diameter is nearly doubled, and the color changes to a rich brown. They remain on the tree the following winter and summer; therefore few fertile trees are ever found without them. Nor even after they fall is the beauty work of these grand cones done, for they make a fine show on the flowery, needle-strewn ground. The wood is pale yellow, fine in texture, and deliciously fragrant. The sugar, which gives name to the tree, exudes from the heart wood on wounds made by fire or the axe, and forms irregular crisp white candy-like masses. To the taste of most people it is as good as maple sugar, though it cannot be eaten in large quantities.

No traveler, whether a tree lover or not, will ever forget his first walk in a sugar-pine forest. The majestic crowns approaching one another make a glorious canopy, through the feathery arches of which the sunbeams pour, silvering the needles and gilding the stately columns and the ground into a scene of enchantment.

The yellow pine (*Pinus ponderosa*) is surpassed in size and nobleness of port only by its kingly companion. Full-grown trees in the main forest where it is associated with the sugar pine, are about one hundred and seventy-five feet high, with a diameter of five to six feet, though much larger specimens may easily be found. The largest I ever measured was little over eight feet in diameter four feet above the ground, and two hundred and twenty feet high. Where there is plenty of sunshine and other conditions are favorable, it is a massive symmetrical spire, formed of a strong straight shaft clad with innumerable branches, which are divided again and again into stout branchlets laden with bright shining needles and green or purple cones. Where the growth is at all close half or more of the trunk is branchless. The species attains its greatest size and most majestic form in open groves on the deep, well-drained soil of lake basins at an elevation of about four thousand feet. There nearly all the old trees are over two hundred feet high, and the heavy, leafy, much-divided branches sumptuously clothe the trunk almost to the ground. Such trees are easily climbed, and in going up the winding stairs of knotty limbs to the top you will gain a most telling and memorable idea of the height, the richness and intricacy of the branches, and the marvelous abundance and beauty of the long shining elastic foliage. In tranquil weather, you will see the firm outstanding needles in calm content, shimmering and throwing off keen minute rays of light like lances of ice; but when heavy winds are blowing, the strong towers bend and wave in the blast with eager wide-awake enthusiasm, and every tree in the grove glows and flashes in one mass of white sunfire.

Both the yellow and sugar pines grow rapidly on good soil where they are not crowded. At the age of a hundred years they are about two feet in diameter and a hundred or more high. They are then very handsome, though very unlike: the sugar pine, lithe, feathery, closely clad with ascending branches; the yellow, open, showing its axis from the ground to the top, its whorled branches but little divided as yet, spreading and turning up at the ends with magnificent tassels of long stout bright needles, the terminal shoot with its leaves being often three or four feet long and a foot and a half wide, the most hopeful looking and the handsomest tree-top in the woods. But instead of increasing, like its companion, in wildness and individuality of form with age, it becomes more evenly and compactly spiry. The bark is usually very thick, four to six inches at the ground, and arranged in large plates, some of them on the lower part of the trunk four or five feet long and twelve to eighteen inches wide, forming a strong defense against fire. The leaves are in threes, and from three inches to a foot long. The flowers appear in May: the staminate pink or brown, in conspicuous clusters two or three inches wide; the pistillate crimson, a fourth of an inch wide, and mostly hidden among the leaves on the tips of the branchlets. The cones vary from about three to ten inches in length, two to five in width, and grow in sessile outstanding clusters near the ends of the upturned branchlets.

Being able to endure fire and hunger and many climates this grand tree is widely distributed: eastward from the coast across the broad Rocky Mountain ranges to the Black Hills of Dakota, a distance of more than a thousand miles, and southward from British Columbia, near latitude 51, to Mexico, about fifteen hundred miles. South of the Columbia River it meets the sugar pine, and accompanies it all the way down along the Coast and Cascade mountains and the Sierra and southern ranges to the mountains of the peninsula of Lower California, where they find their southmost homes together. Pinus ponderosa is extremely variable, and much bother it gives botanists who try to catch and confine the unmanageable proteus in two or a dozen species,—Jeffreyi, deflexa, Apacheca latifolia, etc. But in all its wanderings, in every form, it manifests noble strength. Clad in thick bark like a warrior in mail, it extends its bright ranks over all the high ranges of the wild side of the continent: flourishes in the drenching fog and rain of the northern coast at the level of the sea, in the snow-laden blasts of the mountains, and the white glaring sunshine of the interior plateaus and plains, on the borders of mirage-haunted deserts, volcanoes, and lava beds, waving its bright plumes in hot winds undaunted, blooming every year for centuries, and tossing big ripe cones among the cinders and ashes of nature's hearths.

The Douglas spruce grows with the great pines, especially on the cool north sides of ridges and cañons, and is here nearly as large as the yellow pine, but less abundant. The wood is strong and tough, the bark thick and deeply furrowed, and on vigorous, quick-growing trees the stout, spreading branches are covered with innumerable slender, swaying sprays, handsomely clothed with short leaves. The flowers are about three fourths of an inch in length, red or greenish, not so showy as the pendulous bracted cones. But in June and July, when the young bright yellow leaves appear, the entire tree seems to be covered with bloom.

It is this grand tree that forms the famous forests of western Oregon, Washington, and the adjacent coast regions of British Columbia, where it attains its greatest size and is most abundant, making almost pure forests over thousands of square miles, dark and close and almost inaccessible, many of the trees towering with straight, imperceptibly tapered shafts to a height of three hundred feet, their heads together shutting out the light,—one of the largest, most widely distributed, and most important of all the Western giants.

The incense cedar (*Libocedrus decurrens*), when full grown, is a magnificent tree, one hundred and twenty to nearly two hundred feet high, five to eight and occasionally twelve feet in diameter, with cinnamon-colored bark and warm yellow-green foliage, and in general appearance like an arbor vitæ. It is distributed through the main forest from an elevation of three to six thousand feet, and in sheltered portions of cañons on the warm sides to seven thousand five hundred. In midwinter, when most trees are asleep, it puts forth its flowers. The pistillate are pale green and inconspicuous; but the staminate are yellow, about one fourth of an inch long, and are produced in myriads, tingeing all the branches with gold, and making the tree as it stands in the snow look like a gigantic goldenrod. Though scattered rather sparsely amongst its companions in the open woods, it is seldom out of sight, and its bright brown shafts and warm masses of plumy foliage make a striking feature of the landscape. While young and growing fast in an open situation no other tree of its size in the park forms so exactly tapered a pyramid. The branches, outspread in flat plumes and beautifully fronded, sweep gracefully downward and outward, except those near the top, which aspire; the lowest droop to the ground, overlapping one another, shedding off rain and snow, and making fine tents for storm-bound mountaineers and birds. In old age it becomes irregular and picturesque, mostly from accidents: running fires, heavy wet snow breaking the branches, lightning shattering the top, compelling it to try to make new summits out of side branches, etc. Still it frequently lives more than a thousand years, invincibly beautiful, and worthy its place beside the Douglas spruce and the great pines.

This unrivaled forest is still further enriched by two majestic silver firs, Abies magnifica and Abies concolor, bands of which come down from the main fir belt by cool shady ridges and glens. Abies magnifica is the noblest of its race, growing on moraines, at an elevation of seven thousand to eight thousand five hundred feet above the sea, to a height of two hundred or two hundred and fifty feet, and five to seven in diameter; and with these noble dimensions there is a richness and symmetry and perfection of finish not to be found in any other tree in the Sierra. The branches are whorled, in fives mostly, and stand out from the straight red purple bole in level or, on old trees, in drooping collars, every branch regularly pinnated like fern fronds, and clad with silvery needles, making broad plumes singularly rich and sumptuous.

The flowers are in their prime about the middle of June: the staminate red, growing on the underside of the branchlets in crowded profusion, giving a rich color to nearly all the tree; the pistillate greenish yellow tinged with pink, standing erect on the upper side of the topmost branches; while the tufts of young leaves, about as brightly colored as those of the Douglas spruce, push out their fragrant brown buds a few weeks later, making another grand show.

The cones mature in a single season from the flowers. When full grown they are about six to eight inches long, three or four in diameter, blunt, massive, cylindrical, greenish gray in color, covered with a fine silvery down, and beaded with transparent balsam, very rich and precious-looking, standing erect like casks on the topmost branches. If possible, the inside of the cone is still more beautiful. The scales and bracts are tinged with red, and the seed wings are purple with bright iridescence.

Abies concolor, the white silver fir, grows best about two thousand feet lower than the magnifica. It is nearly as large, but the branches are less regularly pinnated and whorled, the leaves are longer, and instead of standing out around the branchlets or turning up and clasping them they are mostly arranged in two horizontal or ascending rows, and the cones are less than half as large. The bark of the magnifica is reddish purple and closely furrowed, that of the concolor is gray and widely furrowed,—a noble pair, rivaled only by the Abies grandis, amabilis, and nobilis of the forests of Oregon, Washington, and the Northern California Coast Range. But none of these northern species form pure forests that in extent and beauty approach those of the Sierra.

The seeds of the conifers are curiously formed and colored, white, brown, purple, plain or spotted like birds eggs, and excepting the juniper they are all handsomely and ingeniously winged with reference to their distribution. They are a sort of cunningly devised flying machines,—one-winged birds, birds with but one feather,—and they take but one flight, all save those which, after flying from the cone-nest in calm weather, chance to alight on branches where they have to wait for a wind. And though these seed wings are intended for only a moment's use, they are as thoughtfully colored and fashioned as the wings of birds, and require from one to two seasons to grow. Those of the pine, fir, hemlock, and spruce are curved in such manner that, in being dragged through the air by the seeds, they are made to revolve, whirling the seeds in a close spiral, and sustaining them long enough to allow the winds to carry them to considerable distances,—a style of flying full of quick merry motion, strikingly contrasted to the sober dignified sailing of seeds on tufts of feathery pappus. Surely no merrier adventurers ever set out to seek their fortunes. Only in the fir woods are large flocks seen; for, unlike the cones of the pine, spruce, hemlock, etc., which let the seeds escape slowly, one or two at a time, by spreading the scales, the fir cones when ripe fall to pieces, and let nearly all go at once in favorable weather. All along the Sierra for hundreds of miles, on dry breezy autumn days, the sunny spaces in the woods among the colossal spires are in a whirl with these shining purplewinged wanderers, notwithstanding the harvesting squirrels have been working at the top of their speed for weeks trying to cut off every cone before the seeds were ready to swarm and fly. Sequoia seeds have flat wings, and glint and glance in their flight like a boy's kite. The dispersal of juniper seeds is effected by the plum and cherry plan of hiring birds at the cost of their board, and thus obtaining the use of a pair of extra good wings.

Above the great fir belt, and below the ragged beds and fringes of the dwarf pine, stretch the broad dark forests of Pinus contorta, var. Murrayana, usually called tamarack pine. On broad fields of moraine material it forms nearly pure forests at an elevation of about eight or nine thousand feet above the sea, where it is a small, well proportioned tree, fifty or sixty feet high and one or two in diameter, with thin gray bark, crooked much-divided straggling branches, short needles in clusters of two, bright yellow and crimson flowers, and small prickly cones. The very largest I ever measured was ninety feet in height, and a little over six feet in diameter four feet above the ground. On moist well-drained soil in sheltered hollows along streamsides it grows tall and slender with ascending branches, making graceful arrowy spires fifty to seventy-five feet high, with stems only five or six inches thick.

The most extensive forest of this pine in the park lies to the north of the Big Tuolumne Meadows,—a famous deer pasture and hunting ground of the Mono Indians. For miles over wide moraine beds there is an even, nearly pure growth, broken only by glacier meadows, around which the trees stand in trim array, their sharp spires showing on fine advantage both in green flowery summer and white winter. On account of the closeness of its growth in many places, and the thinness and gumminess of its bark, it is easily killed by running fires, which work wide-spread destruction in its ranks; but a new generation rises quickly from the ashes, for all or a part of its seeds are held in reserve for a year or two or many years, and when the tree is killed the cones open and the seeds are scattered over the burned ground like those of the attenuata.

Next to the mountain hemlock and the dwarf pine this species best endures burial in heavy snow, while in braving hunger and cold on rocky ridgetops it is not surpassed by any. It is distributed from Alaska to Southern California, and inland across the Rocky Mountains, taking many forms in accordance with demands of climate, soil, rivals, and enemies; growing patiently in bogs and on sand dunes beside the sea where it is pelted with salt scud, on high snowy mountains and down in the throats of extinct volcanoes; springing up with invincible vigor after every devastating fire and extending its conquests farther.

The sturdy storm-enduring red cedar (*Juniperus occidentalis*) delights to dwell on the tops of granite domes and ridges and glacier pavements of the upper pine belt, at an elevation of seven to ten thousand feet, where it can get plenty of sunshine and snow and elbow-room without encountering quick-growing overshadowing rivals. They never make anything like a forest, seldom come together even in groves, but stand out separate and independent in the wind, clinging by slight joints to the rock, living chiefly on snow and thin air, and maintaining tough health on this diet for two thousand years or more, every feature and gesture expressing steadfast dogged endurance. The largest are usually about six or eight feet in diameter, and fifteen or twenty in height. A very few are ten feet in diameter, and on isolated moraine heaps forty to sixty feet in height. Many are mere stumps, as broad as high, broken by avalanches and lightning, picturesquely tufted with dense gray scalelike foliage, and giving no hint of dying. The staminate flowers are like those of the libocedrus, but smaller; the pistillate are inconspicuous. The wood is red, fine-grained, and fragrant; the bark bright cinnamon and red, and in thrifty trees is strikingly braided and reticulated, flaking off in thin lustrous ribbons, which the Indians used to weave into matting and coarse cloth. These brown unshakable pillars, standing solitary on polished pavements with bossy masses of foliage in their arms, are exceedingly picturesque, and never fail to catch the eye of the artist. They seem sole survivors of some ancient race, wholly unacquainted with their neighbors.

I have spent a good deal of time, trying to determine their age, but on account of dry rot which honeycombs most of the old ones, I never got a complete count of the largest. Some are undoubtedly more than two thousand years old; for though on good moraine soil they grow about as fast as oaks, on bare pavements and smoothly glaciated overswept granite ridges in the dome region they grow extremely slowly. One on the Starr King ridge, only two feet eleven inches in diameter, was eleven hundred and forty years old. Another on the same ridge, only one foot seven and a half inches in diameter, had reached the age of eight hundred and thirty-four years. The first fifteen inches from the bark of a medium-sized tree—six feet in diameter—on the north Tenaya pavement had eight hundred and fifty-nine layers of wood, or fifty-seven to the inch. Beyond this the count was stopped by dry rot and scars of old wounds. The largest I examined was thirty-three feet in girth, or nearly ten in diameter; and though I failed to get anything like a complete count, I learned enough from this and many other specimens to convince me that most of the trees eight to ten feet thick standing on pavements are more than twenty centuries of age rather than less. Barring accidents, for all I can see, they would live forever. When killed, they waste out of existence about as slowly as granite. Even when overthrown by avalanches, after standing so long, they refuse to lie at rest, leaning stubbornly on their big elbows as if anxious to rise, and while a single root holds to the rock putting forth fresh leaves with a grim never-say-die and never-lie-down expression.

As the juniper is the most stubborn and unshakable of trees, the mountain hemlock (*Tsuga Mertensiana*) is the most graceful and pliant and sensitive, responding to the slightest touches of the wind. Until it reaches a height of fifty or sixty feet it is sumptuously clothed down to the ground with drooping branches, which are divided into countless delicate waving sprays, grouped and arranged in most indescribably beautiful ways, and profusely sprinkled with handsome brown cones. The flowers also are peculiarly beautiful and effective; the pistillate very dark rich purple; the staminate blue of so fine and pure a tone that the best azure of the high sky seems to be condensed in them.

Though apparently the most delicate and feminine of all the mountain trees, it grows best where the snow lies deepest, at an elevation of from nine thousand to nine thousand five hundred feet, in hollows on the northern slopes of mountains and ridges. But under all circumstances and conditions of weather and soil, sheltered from the main currents of the winds or in blank exposure to them, well fed or starved, it is always singularly graceful in habit. Even at its highest limit in the park, ten thousand five hundred feet above the sea on exposed ridgetops, where it crouches and huddles close together in low thickets like those of the dwarf pine, it still contrives to put forth its sprays and branches in forms of irrepressible beauty, while on moist well-drained moraines it displays a perfectly tropical luxuriance of foliage, flower, and fruit.

In the first winter storms the snow is oftentimes soft, and lodges in the dense leafy branches, pressing them down against the trunk, and the slender drooping axis bends lower and lower as the load increases, until the top touches the ground and an ornamental arch is made. Then, as storm succeeds storm and snow is heaped on snow, the whole tree is at last buried, not again to see the light or move leaf or limb until set free by the spring thaws in June or July. Not the young saplings only are thus carefully covered and put to sleep in the whitest of white beds for five or six months of the year, but trees thirty and forty feet high. From April to May, when the snow is compacted, you may ride over the prostrate groves without seeing a single branch or leaf of them. In the autumn they are full of merry life, when Clark crows, squirrels, and chipmunks are gathering the abundant crop of seeds while the deer rest beneath the thick concealing branches. The finest grove in the park is near Mount Conness, and the trail from the Tuolumne soda springs to the mountain runs through it. Many of the trees in this grove are three to four or five feet in diameter and about a hundred feet high.

The mountain hemlock is widely distributed from near the south extremity of the high Sierra northward along the Cascade Mountains of Oregon and Washington and the coast ranges of British Columbia to Alaska, where it was first discovered in 1827. Its northmost limit, so far as I have observed, is in the icy fiords of Prince William's Sound in latitude 61, where it forms pure forests at the level of the sea, growing tall and majestic on the banks of the great glaciers, waving in accord with the mountain winds and the thunder of the falling icebergs. Here as in the Sierra it is ineffably beautiful, the very loveliest evergreen in America.

Of the round-headed dicotyledonous trees in the park the most influential are the black and goldcup oaks. They occur in some parts of the main forest belt, scattered among the big pines like a heavier chaparral, but form extensive groves and reach perfect development only in the Yosemite valleys and flats of the main cañons. The California black oak (*Quercus Californica*) is one of the largest and most beautiful of the Western oaks, attaining under favorable conditions a height of sixty to a hundred feet, with a trunk three to seven feet in diameter, wide-spreading picturesque branches, and smooth lively green foliage handsomely scalloped, purple in the spring, yellow and red in autumn. It grows best in sunny open groves on ground covered with ferns, chokecherry, brier rose, rubus, mints, goldenrods, etc. Few, if any, of the famous oak groves of Europe, however extensive, surpass these in the size and strength and bright, airy beauty of the trees, the color and fragrance of the vegetation beneath them, the quality of the light that fills their leafy arches, and in the grandeur of the surrounding scenery. The finest grove in the park is in one of the little Yosemite valleys of the Tuolumne Cañon, a few miles above Hetch-Hetchy.

The mountain live-oak, or goldcup oak (*Quercus chrysolepis*), forms extensive groves on earthquake and avalanche taluses and terraces in cañons and Yosemite valleys, from about three to five thousand feet above the sea. In tough, sturdy, unwedgeable strength this is the oak of oaks. In general appearance it resembles the great live-oak of the Southern states. It has pale gray bark, a short, uneven, heavily buttressed trunk which usually divides a few feet above the ground into strong wide-reaching limbs, forming noble arches, and ending in an intricate maze of small branches and sprays, the outer ones frequently drooping in long tresses to the ground like those of the weeping willow, covered with small simple polished leaves, making a canopy broad and bossy, on which the sunshine falls in glorious brightness. The acorn cups are shallow, thick-walled, and covered with yellow fuzzy dust. The flowers appear in May and June with a profusion of pollened tresses, followed by the bronze-colored young leaves.

No tree in the park is a better measure of altitude. In cañons, at an elevation of four thousand, feet you may easily find a tree six or eight feet in diameter; and at the head of a side cañon, three thousand feet higher, up which you can climb in less than two hours, you find the knotty giant dwarfed to a slender shrub, with leaves like those of huckleberry bushes, still bearing acorns, and seemingly contented, forming dense patches of chaparral, on the top of which you may make your bed and sleep softly like a Highlander in heather. About a thousand feet higher it is still smaller, making fringes about a foot high around boulders and along seams in pavements and the brows of cañons, giving hand-holds here and there on cliffs hard to climb. The largest I have measured were from twenty-five to twenty-seven feet in girth, fifty to sixty feet high, and the spread of the limbs was about double the height.

The principal riverside trees are poplar, alder, willow, broad-leaved maple, and Nuttall's flowering dogwood. The poplar (*Populus trichocarpa*), often called balm of Gilead from the gum on its buds, is a tall, stately tree, towering above its companions and gracefully embowering the banks of the main streams at an elevation of about four thousand feet. Its abundant foliage turns bright yellow in the fall, and the Indian-summer sunshine sifts through it in delightful tones over the slow-gliding waters when they are at their lowest ebb.

The flowering dogwood is brighter still in these brooding days, for every branch of its broad head is then a brilliant crimson flame. In the spring, when the streams are in flood, it is the whitest of trees, white as a snow bank with its magnificent flowers four to eight inches in width, making a wonderful show, and drawing swarms of moths and butterflies.

The broad-leaved maple is usually found in the coolest boulder-choked cañons, where the streams are gray and white with foam, over which it spreads its branches in beautiful arches from bank to bank, forming leafy tunnels full of soft green light and spray,—favorite homes of the water ousel. Around the glacier lakes, two or three thousand feet higher, the common aspen grows in fringing lines and groves which are brilliantly colored in autumn, reminding you of the color glory of the Eastern woods.

Scattered here and there or in groves the botanist will find a few other trees, mostly small,—the mountain mahogany, cherry, chestnut-oak, laurel, and nutmeg. The California nutmeg (*Tumion Californicum*) is a handsome evergreen, belonging to the yew family, with pale bark, prickly leaves, fruit like a green-gage plum, and seed like a nutmeg. One of the best groves of it in the park is at the Cascades below Yosemite.

But the noble oaks and all these rock-shading, stream-embowering trees are as nothing amid the vast abounding billowy forests of conifers. During my first years in the Sierra I was ever calling on everybody within reach to admire them, but I found no one half warm enough until Emerson came. I had read his essays, and felt sure that of all men he would best interpret the sayings of these noble mountains and trees. Nor was my faith weakened when I met him in Yosemite. He seemed as serene as a sequoia, his head in the empyrean; and forgetting his age, plans, duties, ties of every sort, I proposed an immeasurable camping trip back in the heart of the mountains. He seemed anxious to go, but considerately mentioned his party. I said: "Never mind. The mountains are calling; run away, and let plans and parties and dragging lowland duties all gang tapsal-teerie. We'll go up a cañon singing your own song, 'Good-by, proud world! I'm going home,' in divine earnest. Up there lies a new heaven and a new earth; let us go to the show." But alas, it was too late,—too near the sundown of his life. The shadows were growing long, and he leaned on his friends. His party, full of indoor philosophy, failed to see the natural beauty and fullness of promise of my wild plan, and laughed at it in good-natured ignorance, as if it were necessarily amusing to imagine that Boston people might be led to accept Sierra manifestations of God at the price of rough camping. Anyhow, they would have none of it, and held Mr. Emerson to the hotels and trails.

After spending only five tourist days in Yosemite he was led away, but I saw him two days more; for I was kindly invited to go with the party as far as the Mariposa big trees. I told Mr. Emerson that I would gladly go to the sequoias with him, if he would camp in the grove. He consented heartily, and I felt sure that we would have at least one good wild memorable night around a sequoia camp-fire. Next day we rode through the magnificent forests of the Merced basin, and I kept calling his attention to the sugar pines, quoting his wood-notes, "Come listen what the pine tree saith," etc., pointing out the noblest as kings and high priests, the most eloquent and commanding preachers of all the mountain forests, stretching forth their century-old arms in benediction over the worshiping congregations crowded about them. He gazed in devout admiration, saying but little, while his fine smile faded away.

Early in the afternoon, when we reached Clark's Station, I was surprised to see the party dismount. And when I asked if we were not going up into the grove to camp they said: "No; it would never do to lie out in the night air. Mr. Emerson might take cold; and you know, Mr. Muir, that would be a dreadful thing." In vain I urged, that only in homes and hotels were colds caught, that nobody ever was known to take cold camping in these woods, that there was not a single cough or sneeze in all the Sierra. Then I pictured the big climate-changing, inspiring fire I would make, praised the beauty and fragrance of sequoia flame, told how the great trees would stand about us transfigured in the purple light, while the stars looked down between the great domes; ending by urging them to come on and make an immortal Emerson night of it. But the house habit was not to be overcome, nor the strange dread of pure night air, though it is only cooled day air with a little dew in it. So the carpet dust and unknowable reeks were preferred. And to think of this being a Boston choice! Sad commentary on culture and the glorious transcendentalism.

Accustomed to reach whatever place I started for, I was going up the mountain alone to camp, and wait the coming of the party next day. But since Emerson was so soon to vanish, I concluded to stop with him. He hardly spoke a word all the evening, yet it was a great pleasure simply to be near him, warming in the light of his face as at a fire. In the morning we rode up the trail through a noble forest of pine and fir into the famous Mariposa Grove, and stayed an hour or two, mostly in ordinary tourist fashion,—looking at the biggest giants, measuring them with a tape line, riding through prostrate fire-bored trunks, etc., though Mr. Emerson was alone occasionally, sauntering about as if under a spell. As we walked through a fine group, he quoted, "There were giants in those days," recognizing the antiquity of the race. To commemorate his visit, Mr. Galen Clark, the guardian of the grove, selected the finest of the unnamed trees and requested him to give it a name. He named it Samoset, after the New England sachem, as the best that occurred to him.

The poor bit of measured time was soon spent, and while the saddles were being adjusted I again urged Emerson to stay. "You are yourself a sequoia," I said. "Stop and get acquainted with your big brethren." But he was past his prime, and was now as a child in the hands of his affectionate but sadly civilized friends, who seemed as full of old-fashioned conformity as of bold intellectual independence. It was the afternoon of the day and the afternoon of his life, and his course was now westward down all the mountains into the sunset. The party mounted and rode away in wondrous contentment, apparently, tracing the trail through ceanothus and dogwood bushes, around the bases of the big trees, up the slope of the sequoia basin, and over the divide. I followed to the edge of the grove. Emerson lingered in the rear of the train, and when he reached the top of the ridge, after all the rest of the party were over and out of sight, he turned his horse, took off his hat and waved me a last good-by. I felt lonely, so sure had I been that Emerson of all men would be the quickest to see the mountains and sing them. Gazing awhile on the spot where he vanished, I sauntered back into the heart of the grove, made a bed of sequoia plumes and ferns by the side of a stream, gathered a store of firewood, and then walked about until sundown. The birds, robins, thrushes, warblers, etc., that had kept out of sight, came about me, now that all was quiet, and made cheer. After sundown I built a great fire, and as usual had it all to myself. And though lonesome for the first time in these forests, I quickly took heart again,—the trees had not gone to Boston, nor the birds; and as I sat by the fire, Emerson was still with me in spirit, though I never again saw him in the flesh. He sent books and wrote, cheering me on; advised me not to stay too long in solitude. Soon he hoped that my guardian angel would intimate that my probation was at a close. Then I was to roll up my herbariums, sketches, and poems (though I never knew I had any poems), and come to his house; and when I tired of him and his humble surroundings, he would show me to better people.

But there remained many a forest to wander through, many a mountain and glacier to cross, before I was to see his Wachusett and Monadnock, Boston and Concord. It was seventeen years after our parting on the Wawona ridge that I stood beside his grave under a pine tree on the hill above Sleepy Hollow. He had gone to higher Sierras, and, as I fancied, was again waving his hand in friendly recognition.

V

THE WILD GARDENS OF THE YOSEMITE PARK

When California was wild, it was the floweriest part of the continent. And perhaps it is so still, notwithstanding the lowland flora has in great part vanished before the farmers' flocks and ploughs. So exuberant was the bloom of the main valley of the state, it would still have been extravagantly rich had ninety-nine out of every hundred of its crowded flowers been taken away,—far flowerier than the beautiful prairies of Illinois and Wisconsin, or the savannas of the Southern states. In the early spring it was a smooth, evenly planted sheet of purple and gold, one mass of bloom more than four hundred miles long, with scarce a green leaf in sight.

Still more interesting is the rich and wonderfully varied flora of the mountains. Going up the Sierra across the Yosemite Park to the Summit peaks, thirteen thousand feet high, you find as much variety in the vegetation as in the scenery. Change succeeds change with bewildering rapidity, for in a few days you pass through as many climates and floras, ranged one above another, as you would in walking along the lowlands to the Arctic Ocean.

And to the variety due to climate there is added that caused by the topographical features of the different regions. Again, the vegetation is profoundly varied by the peculiar distribution of the soil and moisture. Broad and deep moraines, ancient and well weathered, are spread over the lower regions, rough and comparatively recent and unweathered moraines over the middle and upper regions, alternating with bare ridges and domes and glacier-polished pavements, the highest in the icy recesses of the peaks, raw and shifting, some of them being still in process of formation, and of course scarcely planted as yet.

Besides these main soilbeds there are many others comparatively small, reformations of both glacial and weather soils, sifted, sorted out, and deposited by running water and the wind on gentle slopes and in all sorts of hollows, potholes, valleys, lake basins, etc.,—some in dry and breezy situations, others sheltered and kept moist by lakes, streams, and waftings of waterfall spray, making comfortable homes for plants widely varied. In general, glaciers give soil to high and low places almost alike, while water currents are dispensers of special blessings, constantly tending to make the ridges poorer and the valleys richer. Glaciers mingle all kinds of material together, mud particles and boulders fifty feet in diameter: water, whether in oozing currents or passionate torrents, discriminates both in the size and shape of the material it carries. Glacier mud is the finest meal ground for any use in the Park, and its transportation into lakes and as foundations for flowery garden meadows was the first work that the young rivers were called on to do. Bogs occur only in shallow alpine basins where the climate is cool enough for sphagnum, and where the surrounding topographical conditions are such that they are safe, even in the most copious rains and thaws, from the action of flood currents capable of carrying rough gravel and sand, but where the water supply is nevertheless constant. The mosses dying from year to year gradually give rise to those rich spongy peat-beds in which so many of our best alpine plants delight to dwell. The strong winds that occasionally sweep the high Sierra play a more important part in the distribution of special soil-beds than is at first sight recognized, carrying forward considerable quantities of sand gravel, flakes of mica, etc., and depositing them in fields and beds beautifully ruffled and embroidered and adapted to the wants of some of the hardiest and handsomest of the alpine shrubs and flowers. The more resisting of the smooth, solid, glacier-polished domes and ridges can hardly be said to have any soil at all, while others beginning to give way to the weather are thinly sprinkled with coarse angular gravel. Some of them are full of crystals, which as the surface of the rock is decomposed are set free, covering the summits and rolling down the sides in minute avalanches, giving rise to zones and beds of crystalline soil. In some instances the various crystals occur only here and there, sprinkled in the gray gravel like daisies in a sod; but in others half or more is made up of crystals, and the glow of the imbedded or loosely strewn gems and their colored gleams and glintings at different times of the day when the sun is shining might well exhilarate the flowers that grow among them, and console them for being so completely outshone.

These radiant sheets and belts and dome-encircling rings of crystals are the most beautiful of all the Sierra soil-beds, while the huge taluses ranged along the walls of the great cañons are the deepest and roughest. Instead of being slowly weathered and accumulated from the cliffs overhead like common taluses, they were all formed suddenly and simultaneously by an earthquake that occurred at least three centuries ago. Though thus hurled into existence at a single effort, they are the least changeable and destructible of all the soil formations in the range. Excepting those which were launched directly into the channels of rivers, scarcely one of their wedged and interlocked boulders has been moved since the day of their creation, and though mostly made up of huge angular blocks of granite, many of them from ten to fifty feet cube, trees and shrubs make out to live and thrive on them, and even delicate herbaceous plants,—draperia, collomia, zauschneria, etc.,—soothing their rugged features with gardens and groves. In general views of the Park scarce a hint is given of its floral wealth. Only by patiently, lovingly sauntering about in it will you discover that it is all more or less flowery, the forests as well as the open spaces, and the mountain tops and rugged slopes around the glaciers as well as the sunny meadows.

Even the majestic cañon cliffs, seemingly absolutely flawless for thousands of feet and necessarily doomed to eternal sterility, are cheered with happy flowers on invisible niches and ledges wherever the slightest grip for a root can be found; as if Nature, like an enthusiastic gardener, could not resist the temptation to plant flowers everywhere. On high, dry rocky summits and plateaus, most of the plants are so small they make but little show even when in bloom. But in the opener parts of the main forests, the meadows, stream banks, and the level floors of Yosemite valleys the vegetation is exceedingly rich in flowers, some of the lilies and larkspurs being from eight to ten feet high. And on the upper meadows there are miles of blue gentians and daisies, white and blue violets; and great breadths of rosy purple heathworts covering rocky moraines with a marvelous abundance of bloom, enlivened by humming-birds, butterflies and a host of other insects as beautiful as flowers. In the lower and middle regions, also, many of the most extensive beds of bloom are in great part made by shrubs,— adenostoma, manzanita, ceanothus, chamæbatia, cherry, rose rubus, spiræa, shad, laurel, azalea, honeysuckle, calycanthus, ribes, philadelphus, and many others, the sunny spaces about them bright and fragrant with mints, lupines, geraniums, lilies, daisies, goldenrods, castilleias, gilias, pentstemons, etc.

Adenostoma fasciculatum is a handsome, hardy, heath-like shrub belonging to the rose family, flourishing on dry ground below the pine belt, and often covering areas of twenty or thirty square miles of rolling sun-beaten hills and dales with a dense, dark green, almost impenetrable chaparral, which in the distance looks like Scotch heather. It is about six to eight feet high, has slender elastic branches, red shreddy bark, needle-shaped leaves, and small white flowers in panicles about a foot long, making glorious sheets of fragrant bloom in the spring. To running fires it offers no resistance, vanishing with the few other flowery shrubs and vines and liliaceous plants that grow with it about as fast as dry grass, leaving nothing but ashes. But with wonderful vigor it rises again and again in fresh beauty from the root, and calls back to its hospitable mansions the multitude of wild animals that had to flee for their lives.

As soon as you enter the pine woods you meet the charming little Chamæbatia foliolosa, one of the handsomest of the Park shrubs, next in fineness and beauty to the heathworts of the alpine regions. Like adenostoma it belongs to the rose family, is from twelve to eighteen inches high, has brown bark, slender branches, white flowers like those of the strawberry, and thricepinnate glandular, yellow-green leaves, finely cut and fernlike, as if unusual pains had been taken in fashioning them. Where there is plenty of sunshine at an elevation of three thousand to six thousand feet, it makes a close, continuous growth, leaf touching leaf over hundreds of acres, spreading a handsome mantle beneath the yellow and sugar pines. Here and there a lily rises above it, an arching bunch of tall bromus, and at wide intervals a rosebush or clump of ceanothus or manzanita, but there are no rough weeds mixed with it—no roughness of any sort.

Perhaps the most widely distributed of all the Park shrubs and of the Sierra in general, certainly the most strikingly characteristic, are the many species of manzanita (*Arctostaphylos*). Though one species, the Uva-ursa, or bearberry,—the kinikinic of the Western Indians,—extends around the world, the greater part of them are Californian. They are mostly from four to ten feet high, round-headed, with innumerable branches, brown or red bark, pale green leaves set on edge, and a rich profusion of small, pink, narrow-throated, urn-shaped flowers like those of arbutus. The branches are knotty, zigzaggy, and about as rigid as bones, and the bark is so thin and smooth, both trunk and branches seem to be naked, looking as if they had been peeled, polished, and painted red. The wood also is red, hard, and heavy.

These grand bushes seldom fail to engage the attention of the traveler and hold it, especially if he has to pass through closely planted fields of them such as grow on moraine slopes at an elevation of about seven thousand feet, and in cañons choked with earthquake boulders; for they make the most uncompromisingly stubborn of all chaparral. Even bears take pains to go around the stoutest patches if possible, and when compelled to force a passage leave tufts of hair and broken branches to mark their way, while less skillful mountaineers under like circumstances sometimes lose most of their clothing and all their temper.

The manzanitas like sunny ground. On warm ridges and sandy flats at the foot of sun-beaten cañon cliffs, some of the tallest specimens have well-defined trunks six inches to a foot or more thick, and stand apart in orchard-like growths which in bloomtime are among the finest garden sights in the Park. The largest I ever saw had a round, slightly fluted trunk nearly four feet in diameter, which at a height of only eighteen inches from the ground dissolved into a wilderness of branches, rising and spreading to a height and width of about twelve feet. In spring every bush over all the mountains is covered with rosy flowers, in autumn with fruit. The red pleasantly acid berries, about the size of peas, are like little apples, and the hungry mountaineer is glad to eat them, though half their bulk is made up of hard seeds. Indians, bears, coyotes, foxes, birds, and other mountain people live on them for months.

Associated with manzanita there are six or seven species of ceanothus, flowery, fragrant, and altogether delightful shrubs, growing in glorious abundance in the forests on sunny or half-shaded ground, up to an elevation of about nine thousand feet above the sea. In the sugar-pine woods the most beautiful species is C. integerrimus, often called California lilac, or deer brush. It is five or six feet high, smooth, slender, willowy, with bright foliage and abundance of blue flowers in close, showy panicles. Two species, prostatus and procumbens, spread handsome blue-flowered mats and rugs on warm ridges beneath the pines, and offer delightful beds to the tired mountaineers. The commonest species, C. cordulatus, is mostly restricted to the silver fir belt. It is white-flowered and thorny, and makes extensive thickets of tangled chaparral, far too dense to wade through, and too deep and loose to walk on, though it is pressed flat every winter by ten or fifteen feet of snow.

Above these thorny beds, sometimes mixed with them, a very wild, red-fruited cherry grows in magnificent tangles, fragrant and white as snow when in bloom. The fruit is small and rather bitter, not so good as the black, puckery chokecherry that grows in the cañons, but thrushes, robins, chipmunks like it. Below the cherry tangles, chinquapin and goldcup oak spread generous mantles of chaparral, and with hazel and ribes thickets in adjacent glens help to clothe and adorn the rocky wilderness, and produce food for the many mouths Nature has to fill. Azalea occidentalis is the glory of cool streams and meadows. It is from two to five feet high, has bright green leaves and a rich profusion of large, fragrant white and yellow flowers, which are in prime beauty in June, July, and August, according to the elevation (from three thousand to six thousand feet.) Only the purple-flowered rhododendron of the redwood forests rivals or surpasses it in superb abounding bloom.

Back a little way from the azalea-bordered streams, a small wild rose makes thickets, often several acres in extent, deliciously fragrant on dewy mornings and after showers, the fragrance mingled with the music of birds nesting in them. And not far from these rose gardens Rubus Nutkanus covers the ground with broad velvety leaves and pure white flowers as large as those of its neighbor the rose, and finer in texture; followed at the end of summer by soft red berries good for bird and beast and man also. This is the commonest and the most beautiful of the whole blessed flowery fruity genus.

The glory of the alpine region in bloomtime are the heathworts, cassiope, bryanthus, kalmia, and vaccinium, enriched here and there by the alpine honeysuckle, Lonicera conjugialis, and by the purple-flowered Primula suffruticosa, the only primrose discovered in California, and the only shrubby species in the genus. The lowly, hardy, adventurous cassiope has exceedingly slender creeping branches, scalelike leaves, and pale pink or white waxen bell flowers. Few plants, large or small, so well endure hard weather and rough ground over so great a range. In July it spreads a wavering, interrupted belt of the loveliest bloom around glacier lakes and meadows and across wild moory expanses, between roaring streams, all along the Sierra, and northward beneath cold skies by way of the mountain chains of

Oregon, Washington, British Columbia, and Alaska, to the Arctic regions; gradually descending, until at the north end of the continent it reaches the level of the sea; blooming as profusely and at about the same time on mossy frozen tundras as on the high Sierra moraines.

Bryanthus, the companion of cassiope, accompanies it as far north as southeastern Alaska, where together they weave thick plushy beds on rounded mountain tops above the glaciers. It grows mostly at slightly lower elevations; the upper margin of what may be called the bryanthus belt in the Sierra uniting with and overlapping the lower margin of the cassiope. The wide bell-shaped flowers are bright purple, about three fourths of an inch in diameter, hundreds to the square yard, the young branches, mostly erect, being covered with them. No Highlander in heather enjoys more luxurious rest than the Sierra mountaineer in a bed of blooming bryanthus. And imagine the show on calm dewy mornings, when there is a radiant globe in the throat of every flower, and smaller gems on the needle-shaped leaves, the sunbeams pouring through them.

In the same wild, cold region the tiny Vaccinium myrtillus, mixed with kalmia and dwarf willows, spreads thinner carpets, the downpressed matted leaves profusely sprinkled with pink bells; and on higher sandy slopes you will find several alpine species of eriogonum with gorgeous bossy masses of yellow bloom, and the lovely Arctic daisy with many blessed companions; charming plants, gentle mountaineers, Nature's darlings, which seem always the finer the higher and stormier their homes.

Many interesting ferns are distributed over the Park from the foothills to a little above the timber line. The greater number are rock ferns, pellæa, cheilanthes, polypodium, adiantum, woodsia, cryptogramme, etc., with small tufted fronds, lining glens and gorges and fringing the cliffs and moraines. The most important of the larger species are woodwardia, aspidium, asplenium, and the common pteris. Woodwardia radicans is a superb fern five to eight feet high, growing in vaselike clumps where the ground is level, and on slopes in a regular thatch, frond over frond, like shingles

on a roof. Its range in the Park is from the western boundary up to about five thousand feet, mostly on benches of the
north walls of cañons watered by small outspread streams.
It is far more abundant in the Coast Mountains beneath the
noble redwoods, where it attains a height of ten to twelve
feet. The aspidiums are mostly restricted to the moist parts
of the lower forests, Asplenium filix-fœmina to marshy
streams. The hardy, broad-shouldered Pteris aquilina, the
commonest of ferns, grows tall and graceful on sunny flats
and hillsides, at elevations between three thousand and six
thousand feet. Those who know it only in the Eastern states
can form no fair conception of its stately beauty in the sunshine
of the Sierra. On the level sandy floors of Yosemite valleys it
often attains a height of six to eight feet in fields thirty or
forty acres in extent, the magnificent fronds outspread in a
nearly horizontal position, forming a ceiling beneath which
one may walk erect in delightful mellow shade. No other
fern does so much for the color glory of autumn, with its
browns and reds and yellows changing and interblending.
Even after lying dead all winter beneath the snow it spreads
a lively brown mantle over the desolate ground, until the
young fronds with a noble display of faith and hope come
rolling up into the light through the midst of the beautiful ruins. A few weeks suffice for their development, then,
gracefully poised each in its place, they manage themselves
in every exigency of weather as if they had passed through
a long course of training. I have seen solemn old sugar pines
thrown into momentary confusion by the sudden onset of a
storm, tossing their arms excitedly as if scarce awake, and
wondering what had happened, but I never noticed surprise
or embarrassment in the behavior of this noble pteris.

Of five species of pellæa in the Park, the handsome
andromedæfolia, growing in brushy foothills with Adiantum
emarginatum, is the largest. P. Breweri, the hardiest and at
the same time the most fragile of the genus, grows in dense
tufts among rocks on storm-beaten mountain sides along
the upper margin of the fern line. It is a charming little fern,
four or five inches high, has shining bronze-colored stalks
which are about as brittle as glass, and pale green pinnate

fronds. Its companions on the lower part of its range are Cryptogramme acrostichoides and Phegopteris alpestris, the latter soft and tender, not at all like a rock fern, though it grows on rocks where the snow lies longest. P. Bridgesii, with blue-green, narrow, simply pinnate fronds, is about the same size as Breweri and ranks next to it as a mountaineer, growing in fissures and round boulders on glacier pavements. About a thousand feet lower we find the smaller and more abundant P. densa, on ledges and boulder-strewn fissured pavements, watered until late in summer by oozing currents from snow-banks or thin outspread streams from moraines, growing in close sods,—its little bright green triangular tripinnate fronds, about an inch in length, as innumerable as leaves of grass. P. ornithopus has twice or thrice pinnate fronds, is dull in color, and dwells on hot rocky hillsides among chaparral.

Three species of Cheilanthes,—Californica, gracillima, and myriophylla, with beautiful two to four pinnate fronds, an inch to five inches long, adorn the stupendous walls of the cañons, however dry and sheer. The exceedingly delicate and interesting Californica is rare, the others abundant at from three thousand to seven thousand feet elevation, and are often accompanied by the little gold fern, Gymnogramme triangularis, and rarely by the curious little Botrychium simplex, the smallest of which are less than an inch high.

The finest of all the rock ferns is *Adiantum pedatum*, lover of waterfalls and the lightest waftings of irised spray. No other Sierra fern is so constant a companion of white spray-covered streams, or tells so well their wild thundering music. The homes it loves best are cave-like hollows beside the main falls, where it can float its plumes on their dewy breath, safely sheltered from the heavy spray-laden blasts. Many of these moss-lined chambers, so cool, so moist, and brightly colored with rainbow light, contain thousands of these happy ferns, clinging to the emerald walls by the slightest holds, reaching out the most wonderfully delicate fingered fronds on dark glossy stalks, sensitive, tremulous, all alive, in an attitude of eager attention; throbbing in unison with every motion and tone of the resounding waters, compliant to their faintest impulses, moving each division of the frond separately at times as if fingering the music, playing on invisible keys.

Considering the lilies as you go up the mountains, the first you come to is L. Pardalinum, with large orange-yellow, purple-spotted flowers big enough for babies bonnets. It is seldom found higher than thirty-five hundred feet above the sea, grows in magnificent groups of fifty to a hundred or more, in romantic waterfall dells in the pine woods shaded by overarching maple and willow, alder and dogwood, with bushes in front of the embowering trees for a border, and ferns and sedges in front of the bushes; while the bed of black humus in which the bulbs are set is carpeted with mosses and liverworts. These richly furnished lily gardens are the pride of the falls on the lower tributaries of the Tuolumne and Merced rivers, falls not like those of Yosemite valleys,—coming from the sky with rock-shaking thunder tones,—but small, with low, kind voices cheerily singing in calm leafy bowers, self-contained, keeping their snowy skirts well about them, yet furnishing plenty of spray for the lilies.

The Washington lily (*L. Washingtonianum*) is white, deliciously fragrant, moderate in size, with three to ten flowered racemes. The largest I ever measured was eight feet high, the raceme two feet long, with fifty-two flowers, fifteen of them open; the others had faded or were still in the bud. This famous lily is distributed over the sunny portions of the sugar-pine woods, never in large garden companies like pardalinum, but widely scattered, standing up to the waist in dense ceanothus and manzanita chaparral, waving its lovely flowers above the blooming wilderness of brush, and giving their fragrance to the breeze. These stony, thorny jungles are about the last places in the mountains in which one would look for lilies. But though they toil not nor spin, like other people under adverse circumstances, they have to do the best they can. Because their large bulbs are good to eat they are dug up by Indians and bears; therefore, like hunted animals, they seek refuge in the chaparral, where among the boulders and tough tangled roots they are comparatively safe. This is the favorite Sierra lily, and it is now growing in all the best parks and gardens of the world.

The showiest gardens in the Park lie imbedded in the silver fir forests on the top of the main dividing ridges or hang likely gayly colored scarfs down their sides. Their wet places are in great part taken up by veratrum, a robust broad-leaved plant determined to be seen, and habenaria and spiranthes; the drier parts by tall columbines, larkspurs, castilleias, lupines, hosackias, erigerons, valerian, etc., standing deep in grass, with violets here and there around the borders. But the finest feature of these forest gardens is Lilium parvum. It varies greatly in size, the tallest being from six to nine feet high, with splendid racemes of ten to fifty small orange-colored flowers, which rock and wave with great dignity above the other flowers in the infrequent winds that fall over the protecting wall of trees. Though rather frail-looking it is strong, reaching prime vigor and beauty eight thousand feet above the sea, and in some places venturing as high as eleven thousand.

Calochortus, or Mariposa tulip, is a unique genus of many species confined to the California side of the continent; charming plants, somewhat resembling the tulips of Europe, but far finer. The richest calochortus region lies below the western boundary of the Park; still five or six species are included. C. Nuttallii is common on moraines in the forests of the two-leaved pine; and C. cæruleus and nudus, very slender, lowly species, may be found in moist garden spots near Yosemite. C. albus, with pure white flowers, growing in shady places among the foothill shrubs, is, I think, the very loveliest of all the lily family,—a spotless soul, plant saint, that every one must love and so be made better. It puts the wildest mountaineer on his good behavior. With this plant the whole world would seem rich though none other existed. Next after Calochortus, Brodiæa is the most interesting genus. Nearly all the many species have beautiful showy heads of blue, lilac, and yellow flowers, enriching the gardens of the lower pine region. Other liliaceous plants likely to attract attention are the blue-flowered camassia, the bulbs of which are prized as food by Indians;

fritillaria, smilacina, chloragalum, and the twining climb-ing stropholirion.

The common orchidaceous plants are corallorhiza, goodyera, spiranthes, and habenaria. Cypripedium mon-tanum, the only moccasin flower I have seen in the Park, is a handsome, thoughtful-looking plant living beside cool brooks. The large oval lip is white, delicately veined with purple; the other petals and sepals purple, strap-shaped, and elegantly curved and twisted.

To tourists the most attractive of all the flowers of the forest is the snow plant (*Sarcodes sanguinea*). It is a bright red, fleshy, succulent pillar that pushes up through the dead needles in the pine and fir woods like a gigantic asparagus shoot. The first intimation of its coming is a loosening and upbulging of the brown stratum of decomposed needles on the forest floor, in the cracks of which you notice fiery gleams; presently a blunt dome-shaped head an inch or two in diameter appears, covered with closely imbricated scales and bracts. In a week or so it grows to a height of six to twelve inches. Then the long fringed bracts spread and curl aside, allowing the twenty or thirty five-lobed bell-shaped flowers to open and look straight out from the fleshy axis. It is said to grow up through the snow; on the contrary it always waits until the ground is warm, though with other early flowers it is occasionally buried or half buried for a day or two by spring storms. The entire plant—flowers, bracts, stem, scales, and roots—is red. But notwithstand-ing its glowing color and beautiful flowers, it is singularly unsympathetic and cold. Everybody admires it as a won-derful curiosity, but nobody loves it. Without fragrance, rooted in decaying vegetable matter, it stands beneath the pines and firs lonely, silent, and about as rigid as a graveyard monument.

Down in the main cañons adjoining the azalea and rose gardens there are fine beds of herbaceous plants,—tall mints and sunflowers, iris, œnothera, brodiæa, and bright beds of erythræa on the ferny meadows. Bolandera, sedum, and airy, feathery, purple-flowered heuchera adorn mossy nooks near falls, the shading trees wreathed and festooned with wild grapevines and clematis; while lightly shaded flats are covered with gilia and eunanus of many species, hosackia, arnica, chænactis, gayophytum, gnaphalium, monardella, etc.

Thousands of the most interesting gardens in the Park are never seen, for they are small and lie far up on ledges and terraces of the sheer cañon walls, wherever a strip of soil, however narrow and shallow, can rest. The birds, winds, and down-washing rains have planted them with all sorts of hardy mountain flowers, and where there is sufficient moisture they flourish in profusion. Many of them are watered by little streams that seem lost on the tremendous precipices, clinging to the face of the rock in lacelike strips, and dripping from ledge to ledge, too silent to be called falls, pathless wanderers from the upper meadows, which for centuries have been seeking a way down to the rivers they belong to, without having worn as yet any appreciable channel, mostly evaporated or given to the plants they meet before reaching the foot of the cliffs. To these unnoticed streams the finest of the cliff gardens owe their luxuriance and freshness of beauty. In the larger ones ferns and showy flowers flourish in wonderful profusion,—woodwardia, columbine, collomia, castilleia, draperia, geranium, erythræa, pink and scarlet mimulus, hosackia, saxifrage, sunflowers and daisies, with azalea, spiræa, and calycanthus, a few specimens of each that seem to have been culled from the large gardens above and beneath them. Even lilies are occasionally found in these irrigated cliff gardens, swinging their bells over the giddy precipices, seemingly as happy as their relatives down in the waterfall dells. Most of the cliff gardens, however, are dependent on summer showers, and though from the shallowness of the soil beds they are often dry, they still display a surprising number of bright flowers,—scarlet zauschneria, purple bush penstemon, mints, gilias, and bosses of glowing golden bahia. Nor is there any lack of commoner plants; the homely yarrow is often found in them, and sweet clover and honeysuckle for the bees.

In the upper cañons, where the walls are inclined at so low an angle that they are loaded with moraine material, through which perennial streams percolate in broad diffused currents, there are long wavering garden beds, that seem to be descending through the forest like cascades, their fluent lines suggesting motion, swaying from side to side of the forested banks, surging up here and there over island-like boulder piles, or dividing and flowing around them. In some of these floral cascades the vegetation is chiefly sedges and grasses ruffled with willows; in others, showy flowers like those of the lily gardens on the main divides. Another curious and picturesque series of wall gardens are made by thin streams that ooze slowly from moraines and slip gently over smooth glaciated slopes. From particles of sand and mud they carry, a pair of lobe-shaped sheets of soil an inch or two thick are gradually formed, one of them hanging down from the brow of the slope, the other leaning up from the foot of it like stalactite and stalagmite, the soil being held together by the flowery, moisture-loving plants growing in it.

Along the rocky parts of the cañon bottoms between lake basins, where the streams flow fast over glacier-polished granite, there are rows of pothole gardens full of ferns, daisies, golden-rods, and other common plants of the neighborhood nicely arranged like bouquets, and standing out in telling relief on the bare shining rock banks. And all the way up the cañons to the Summit mountains, wherever there is soil of any sort, there is no lack of flowers, however short the summer may be. Within eight or ten feet of a snow bank lingering beneath a shadow, you may see belated ferns unrolling their fronds in September, and sedges hurrying up their brown spikes on ground that has been free from snow only eight or ten days, and likely to be covered again within a few weeks; the winter in the coolest of these shadow gardens being about eleven months long, while spring, summer, and autumn are hurried and crowded into one month. Again, under favorable conditions, alpine gardens three or four thousand feet higher than the last are in their prime in June. Between the Summit peaks at the head of the cañons surprising effects are produced where the sunshine falls direct on rocky slopes and reverberates among boulders. Toward the end of August, in one of these natural hothouses on the north shore of a glacier lake 11,500 feet above the sea, I found a luxuriant growth of hairy lupines, thistles, goldenrods, shrubby potentilla, spraguea, and the mountain epilobium with thousands of purple flowers an inch wide, while the opposite shore, at a distance of only three hundred yards, was bound in heavy avalanche snow,—flowery summer on one side, winter on the other. And I know a bench garden on the north wall of Yosemite in which a few flowers are in bloom all winter; the massive rocks about it storing up sunshine enough in summer to melt the snow about as fast as it falls. When tired of the confinement of my cabin I used to camp out in it in January, and never failed to find flowers, and butterflies also, except during snowstorms and a few days after.

From Yosemite one can easily walk in a day to the top of Mount Hoffman, a massive gray mountain that rises in the centre of the Park, with easy slopes adorned with castellated piles and crests on the south side, rugged precipices banked with perpetual snow on the north. Most of the broad summit is comparatively level and smooth, and covered with crystals of quartz, mica, hornblende, feldspar, garnet, zircon, tourmaline, etc., weathered out and strewn loosely as if sown broadcast; their radiance so dazzling in some places as to fairly hide the multitude of small flowers that grow among them; myriads of keen lance rays infinitely fine, white or colored, making an almost continuous glow over all the ground, with here and there throbbing, spangling lilies of light, on the larger gems. At first sight only these crystal sunflowers are noticed, but looking closely you discover minute gilias, ivesias, eunanus, phloxes, etc., in thousands, showing more petals than leaves; and larger plants in hollows and on the borders of rills,—lupines, potentillas, daisies, harebells, mountain columbine, astragalus, fringed with heathworts. You wander about from garden to garden enchanted, as if walking among stars, gathering the brightest gems, each and all apparently doing their best with eager enthusiasm, as if everything depended on faithful shining; and considering the flowers basking in the glorious light, many of them looking like swarms of small moths and butterflies that were resting after long dances in the sunbeams. Now your attention is called to colonies of wood-chucks and pikas, the mounds in front of their burrows glittering like heaps of jewelry,—romantic ground to live in or die in. Now you look abroad over the vast round landscape bounded by the down-curving sky, nearly all the Park in it displayed like a map,—forests, meadows, lakes, rock waves, and snowy mountains. Northward lies the basin of Yosemite Creek, paved with bright domes and lakes like larger crystals; eastward, the meadowy, billowy Tuolumne region and the Summit peaks in glorious array; southward, Yosemite; and westward, the boundless forests. On no other mountain that I know of are you more likely to linger. It is a magnificent camp ground. Clumps of dwarf pine furnish rosiny roots and branches for fuel, and the rills pure water. Around your camp fire the flowers seem to be looking eagerly at the light, and the crystals shine unweariedly, making fine company as you lie at rest in the very heart of the vast, serene, majestic night.

The finest of the glacier meadow gardens lie at an elevation of about nine thousand feet, imbedded in the upper pine forests like lakes of light. They are smooth and level, a mile or two long, and the rich, well-drained ground is completely covered with a soft, silky, plushy sod enameled with flowers, not one of which is in the least weedy or coarse. In some places the sod is so crowded with showy flowers that the grasses are scarce noticed, in others they are rather sparingly scattered; while every leaf and flower seems to have its winged representative in the swarms of happy flower-like insects that enliven the air above them.

With the winter snowstorms wings and petals are folded, and for more than half the year the meadows are snow-buried ten or fifteen feet deep. In June they begin to thaw out, small patches of the dead sloppy sod appear, gradually increasing in size until they are free and warm again, face to face with the sky; myriads of growing points push through the steaming mould, frogs sing cheeringly, soon joined by the birds, and the merry insects come back as if suddenly raised from the dead. Soon the ground is green with mosses and liverworts and dotted with small fungi, making the first crop of the season. Then the grass leaves weave a new sod, and the exceedingly slender panicles rise above it like a purple mist, speedily followed by potentilla, ivesia, bossy orthocarpus, yellow and purple, and a few pentstemons. Later come the daisies and goldenrods, asters and gentians. Of the last there are three species, small and fine, with varying tones of blue, and in glorious abundance, coloring extensive patches where the sod is shallowest. Through the midst flows a stream only two or three feet wide, silently gliding as if careful not to disturb the hushed calm of the solitude, its banks embossed by the common sod bent down to the water's edge, and trimmed with mosses and violets; slender grass panicles lean over like miniature pine trees, and here and there on the driest places small mats of heathworts are neatly spread, enriching without roughening the bossy down-curling sod. In spring and summer the weather is mostly crisp, exhilarating sunshine, though magnificent mountain ranges of cumuli are often upheaved about noon, their shady hollows tinged with purple ineffably fine, their snowy sun-beaten bosses glowing against the sky, casting cooling shadows for an hour or two, then dissolving in a quick washing rain. But for days in succession there are no clouds at all, or only faint wisps and pencilings scarcely discernible.

Toward the end of August the sunshine grows hazy, announcing the coming of Indian summer, the outlines of the landscapes are softened and mellowed, and more and more plainly are the mountains clothed with light, white tinged with pale purple, richest in the morning and evening. The warm, brooding days are full of life and thoughts of life to come, ripening seeds with next summer in them or a hundred summers. The nights are unspeakably impressive and calm; frost crystals of wondrous beauty grow on the grass,—each carefully planned and finished as if intended to endure forever. The sod becomes yellow and brown, but the late asters and gentians, carefully closing their flower at night, do not seem to feel the frost; no nipped, wilted plants of any kind are to be seen; even the early snowstorms fail to blight them. At last the precious seeds are ripe, all the work of the season is done, and the sighing pines tell the coming of winter and rest.

Ascending the range you find that many of the higher meadows slope considerably, from the amount of loose material washed into their basins; and sedges and rushes are mixed with the grasses or take their places, though all are still more or less flowery and bordered with heathworts, sibbaldea, and dwarf willows. Here and there you come to small bogs, the wettest smooth and adorned with parnassia and butter-cups, others tussocky and ruffled like bits of Arctic tundra, their mosses and lichens interwoven with dwarf shrubs. On boulder piles the red iridescent oxyria abounds, and on sandy, gravelly slopes several species of shrubby, yellow-flowered eriogonum, some of the plants, less than a foot high, being very old, a century or more as is shown by the rings made by the annual whorls of leaves on the big roots. Above these flower-dotted slopes the gray, savage wilderness of crags and peaks seems lifeless and bare. Yet all the way up to the tops of the highest mountains, commonly supposed to be covered with eternal snow, there are bright garden spots crowded with flowers, their warm colors calling to mind the sparks and jets of fire on polar volcanoes rising above a world of ice. The principal mountain-top plants are phloxes, drabas, saxifrages, silene, cymopterus, hulsea, and polemonium, growing in detached stripes and mats,—the highest streaks and splashes of the summer wave as it breaks against these wintry heights. The most beautiful are the phloxes (douglasii and cæspitosum), and the red-flowered silene, with innumerable flowers hiding the leaves. Though herbaceous plants, like the trees and shrubs, are dwarfed as they ascend, two of these mountain dwellers, Hulsea algida and Polemonium confertum, are notable exceptions. The yellow-flowered hulsea is eight to twelve inches high, stout, erect,—the leaves, three to six inches long, secreting a rosiny, fragrant gum, standing up boldly on the grim lichen-stained crags, and never looking in the least tired or discouraged. Both the ray and disk flowers are yellow; the heads are nearly two inches wide, and are eagerly sought for by roving bee mountaineers. The polemonium is quite as luxuriant and tropical-looking as its companion, about the same height, glandular, fragrant, its blue flowers closely packed in eight or ten heads, twenty to forty in head. It is never far from hulsea, growing at elevations of between eleven and thirteen thousand feet wherever a little hollow or crevice favorably situated with a handful of wind-driven soil can be found.

From these frosty Arctic sky gardens you may descend in one straight swoop to the abronia, mentzelia, and œnothera gardens of Mono, where the sunshine is warm enough for palms.

But the greatest of all the gardens is the belt of forest trees, profusely covered in the spring with blue and purple, red and yellow blossoms, each tree with a gigantic panicle of flowers fifty to a hundred feet long. Yet strange to say they are seldom noticed. Few travel through the woods when they are in bloom, the flowers of some of the showiest species opening before the snow is off the ground. Nevertheless, one would think the news of such gigantic flowers would quickly spread, and travelers from all the world would make haste to the show. Eager inquiries are made for the bloomtime of rhododendron-covered mountains and for the bloomtime of Yosemite streams, that they may be enjoyed in their prime; but the far grander outburst of tree bloom covering a thousand mountains—who inquires about that? That the pistillate flowers of the pines and firs should escape the eyes of careless lookers is less to be wondered at, since they mostly grow aloft on the topmost branches, and can hardly be seen from the foot of the trees. Yet even these make a magnificent show from the top of an overlooking ridge when the sunbeams are pouring through them. But the far more numerous staminate flowers of the pines in large rosy clusters, and those of the silver firs in countless thousands on the under side of the branches, cannot be hid, stand where you may. The mountain hemlock also is gloriously colored with a profusion of lovely blue and purple flowers, a spectacle to gods and men. A single pine or hemlock or silver fir in the prime of its beauty about the middle of June is well worth the pains of the longest journey; how much more broad forests of them thousands of miles long!

One of the best ways to see tree flowers is to climb one of the tallest trees and to get into close tingling touch with them, and then look abroad. Speaking of the benefits of tree climbing, Thoreau says: "I found my account in climbing a tree once. It was a tall white pine, on the top of a hill; and though I got well pitched, I was well paid for it, for I discovered new mountains in the horizon which I had never seen before. I might have walked about the foot of the tree for threescore years and ten, and yet I certainly should never have seen them. But, above all, I discovered around me,—it was near the middle of June,—on the ends of the topmost branches, a few minute and delicate red conelike blossoms, the fertile flower of the white pine looking heavenward. I carried straightway to the village the topmost spire, and showed it to stranger jurymen who walked the streets,— for it was court week,—and to farmers and lumbermen and woodchoppers and hunters, and not one had ever seen the like before, but they wondered as at a star dropped down."

The same marvelous blindness prevails here, although the blossoms are a thousandfold more abundant and telling. Once when I was collecting flowers of the red silver fir near a summer tourist resort on the mountains above Lake Tahoe, I carried a handful of flowery branches to the boarding house, where they quickly attracted a wondering, admiring crowd of men, women, and children. "Oh, where did you get these?" they cried. "How pretty they are—mighty handsome—just too lovely for anything—where do they grow?" "On the commonest trees about you," I replied. "You are now standing beside one of them, and it is in full bloom; look up." And I pointed to a blossom-laden Abies magnifica, about a hundred and twenty feet high, in front of the house, used as a hitching post. And seeing its beauty for the first time, their wonder could hardly have been greater or more sincere had their silver fir hitching post blossomed for them at that moment as suddenly as Aaron's rod.

The mountain hemlock extends an almost continuous belt along the Sierra and northern ranges to Prince William's

Sound, accompanied part of the way by the pines; our two silver firs, to Mount Shasta, thence the fir belt is continued through Oregon, Washington, and British Columbia by four other species, Abies nobilis, grandis, amabilis, and lasiocarpa; while the magnificent Sitka spruce, with large, bright, purple flowers, adorns the coast region from California to Cook's Inlet and Kodiak. All these, interblending, form one flowery belt-one garden blooming in June, rocking its myriad spires in the hearty weather, bowing and swirling, enjoying clouds and the winds and filling them with balsam; covering thousands of miles of the wildest mountains, clothing the long slopes by the sea, crowning bluffs and headlands and innumerable islands, and, fringing the banks of the glaciers, one wild wavering belt of the noblest flowers in the world, worth a lifetime of love work to know it.

VI

AMONG THE ANIMALS OF THE YOSEMITE

The Sierra bear, brown or gray, the sequoia of the animals, tramps over all the park, though few travelers have the pleasure of seeing him. On he fares through the majestic forests and cañons, facing all sorts of weather, rejoicing in his strength, everywhere at home, harmonizing with the trees and rocks and shaggy chaparral. Happy fellow! his lines have fallen in pleasant places,—lily gardens in silver-fir forests, miles of bushes in endless variety and exuberance of bloom over hill-waves and valleys and along the banks of streams, cañons full of music and waterfalls, parks fair as Eden,—places in which one might expect to meet angels rather than bears.

In this happy land no famine comes nigh him. All the year round his bread is sure, for some of the thousand kinds that he likes are always in season and accessible, ranged on the shelves of the mountains like stores in a pantry. From one to another, from climate to climate, up and down he climbs, feasting on each in turn,—enjoying as great variety as if he traveled to far-off countries north and south. To him almost every thing is food except granite. Every tree helps to feed him, every bush and herb, with fruits and flowers, leaves and bark; and all the animals he can catch,—badgers, gophers, ground squirrels, lizards, snakes, etc., and ants, bees, wasps, old and young, together with their eggs and larvæ and nests. Craunched and hashed, down all go to his marvelous stomach, and vanish as if cast into a fire.

What digestion! A sheep or a wounded deer or a pig he eats warm, about as quickly as a boy eats a buttered muffin; or should the meat be a month old, it still is welcomed with tremendous relish. After so gross a meal as this, perhaps the next will be strawberries and clover, or raspberries with mushrooms and nuts, or puckery acorns and chokecherries. And as if fearing that anything eatable in all his dominions should escape being eaten, he breaks into cabins to look after sugar, dried apples, bacon, etc. Occasionally he eats the mountaineer's bed; but when he has had a full meal of more tempting dainties he usually leaves it undisturbed, though he has been known to drag it up through a hole in the roof, carry it to the foot of a tree, and lie down on it to enjoy a siesta. Eating everything, never is he himself eaten except by man, and only man is an enemy to be feared. "B'ar meat," said a hunter from whom I was seeking information, "b'ar meat is the best meat in the mountains; their skins make the best beds, and their grease the best butter. Biscuit shortened with b'ar grease goes as far as beans; a man will walk all day on a couple of them biscuit."

It my first interview with a Sierra bear we were frightened and embarrassed, both of us, but the bear's behavior was better than mine. When I discovered him, he was standing in a narrow strip of meadow, and I was concealed behind a tree on the side of it. After studying this appearance as he stood at rest, I rushed toward him to frighten him, that I might study his gait in running. But, contrary to all I had heard about the shyness of bears, he did not run at all; and when I stopped short within a few steps of him, as he held his ground in a fighting attitude, my mistake was monstrously plain. I was then put on my good behavior, and never afterward forgot the right manners of the wilderness.

This happened on my first Sierra excursion in the forest to the north of Yosemite Valley. I was eager to meet the animals, and many of them came to me as if willing to show themselves and make my acquaintance; but the bears kept out of my way.

An old mountaineer, in reply to my questions, told me that bears were very shy, all save grim old grizzlies, and that

I might travel the mountains for years without seeing one, unless I gave my mind to them and practiced the stealthy ways of hunters. Nevertheless, it was only a few weeks after I had received this information that I met the one mentioned above, and obtained instruction at first-hand.

I was encamped in the woods about a mile back of the rim of Yosemite, beside a stream that falls into the valley by the way of Indian Cañon. Nearly every day for weeks I went to the top of the North Dome to sketch; for it commands a general view of the valley, and I was anxious to draw every tree and rock and waterfall. Carlo, a St. Bernard dog, was my companion,—a fine, intelligent fellow that belonged to a hunter who was compelled to remain all summer on the hot plains, and who loaned him to me for the season for the sake of having him in the mountains, where he would be so much better off. Carlo knew bears through long experience, and he it was who led me to my first interview, though he seemed as much surprised as the bear at my unhunter-like behavior. One morning in June, just as the sunbeams began to stream through the trees, I set out for a day's sketching on the dome; and before we had gone half a mile from camp Carlo snuffed the air and looked cautiously ahead, lowered his bushy tail, drooped his ears, and began to step softly like a cat, turning every few yards and looking me in the face with a telling expression, saying plainly enough, "There is a bear a little way ahead." I walked carefully in the indicated direction, until I approached a small flowery meadow that I was familiar with, then crawled to the foot of a tree on its margin, bearing in mind what I had been told about the shyness of bears. Looking out cautiously over the instep of the tree, I saw a big, burly cinnamon bear about thirty yards off, half erect, his paws resting on the trunk of a fir that had fallen into the meadow, his hips almost buried in grass and flowers. He was listening attentively and trying to catch the scent, showing that in some way he was aware of our approach. I watched his gestures, and tried to make the most of my opportunity to learn what I could about him, fearing he would not stay long. He made a fine picture, standing alert in the sunny garden walled in by the most beautiful firs in the world.

After examining him at leisure, noting the sharp muzzle thrust inquiringly forward, the long shaggy hair on his broad chest, the stiff ears nearly buried in hair, and the slow, heavy way in which he moved his head, I foolishly made a rush on him, throwing up my arms and shouting to frighten him, to see him run. He did not mind the demonstration much; only pushed his head farther forward, and looked at me sharply as if asking, "What now? If you want to fight, I'm ready." Then I began to fear that on me would fall the work of running. But I was afraid to run, lest he should be encouraged to pursue me; therefore I held my ground, staring him in the face within a dozen yards or so, putting on as bold a look as I could, and hoping the influence of the human eye would be as great as it is said to be. Under these strained relations the interview seemed to last a long time. Finally, the bear, seeing how still I was, calmly withdrew his huge paws from the log, gave me a piercing look, as if warning me not to follow him, turned, and walked slowly up the middle of the meadow into the forest; stopping every few steps and looking back to make sure that I was not trying to take him at a disadvantage in a rear attack. I was glad to part with him, and greatly enjoyed the vanishing view as he waded through the lilies and columbines.

Thenceforth I always tried to give bears respectful notice of my approach, and they usually kept well out of my way. Though they often came around my camp in the night, only once afterward, as far as I know, was I very near one of them in daylight. This time it was a grizzly I met; and as luck would have it, I was even nearer to him than I had been to the big cinnamon. Though not a large specimen, he seemed formidable enough at a distance of less than a dozen yards. His shaggy coat was well grizzled, his head almost white. When I first caught sight of him he was eating acorns under a Kellogg oak, at a distance of perhaps seventy-five yards, and I tried to slip past without disturbing him. But he had either heard my steps on the gravel or caught my scent, for he came straight toward me, stopping every rod or so to look and listen: and as I was afraid to be seen running, I crawled on my hands and knees a little way to one side and hid behind a libocedrus, hoping he would pass me unnoticed. He soon came up opposite me, and stood looking ahead, while I looked at him, peering past the bulging trunk of the tree. At last, turning his head, he caught sight of mine, stared sharply a minute or two, and then, with fine dignity, disappeared in a manzanita-covered earthquake talus.

Considering how heavy and broad-footed bears are, it is wonderful how little harm they do in the wilderness. Even in the well-watered gardens of the middle region, where the flowers grow tallest, and where during warm weather the bears wallow and roll, no evidence of destruction is visible. On the contrary, under nature's direction, the massive beasts act as gardeners. On the forest floor, carpeted with needles and brush, and on the tough sod of glacier meadows, bears make no mark; but around the sandy margin of lakes their magnificent tracks form grand lines of embroidery. Their well-worn trails extend along the main cañons on either side, and though dusty in some places make no scar on the landscape. They bite and break off the branches of some of the pines and oaks to get the nuts, but this pruning is so light that few mountaineers ever notice it; and though they interfere with the orderly lichen-veiled decay of fallen trees, tearing them to pieces to reach the colonies of ants that inhabit them, the scattered ruins are quickly pressed back into harmony by snow and rain and over-leaning vegetation.

The number of bears that make the Park their home may be guessed by the number that have been killed by the two best hunters, Duncan and old David Brown. Duncan began to be known as a bear-killer about the year 1865. He was then roaming the woods, hunting and prospecting on the south fork of the Merced. A friend told me that he killed his first bear near his cabin at Wawona; that after mustering courage to fire he fled, without waiting to learn the effect of his shot. Going back in a few hours he found poor Bruin dead, and gained courage to try again. Duncan confessed to me, when we made an excursion together in 1875, that he was at first mortally afraid of bears, but after killing a half dozen he began to keep count of his victims, and became ambitious to be known as a great bear-hunter. In nine years he had killed forty-nine, keeping count by notches cut on one of the timbers of his cabin on the shore of Crescent Lake, near the south boundary of the Park. He said the more he knew about bears, the more he respected them and the less he feared them. But at the same time he grew more and more cautious, and never fired until he had every advantage, no matter how long he had to wait and how far he had to go before he got the bear just right as to the direction of the wind, the distance, and the way of escape in case of accident; making allowance also for the character of the animal, old or young, cinnamon or grizzly. For old grizzlies, he said, he had no use whatever, and he was mighty careful to avoid their acquaintance. He wanted to kill an even hundred; then he was going to confine himself to safer game. There was not much money in bears, anyhow, and a round hundred was enough for glory.

I have not seen or heard of him lately, and do not know how his bloody count stands. On my excursions, I occasionally passed his cabin. It was full of meat and skins hung in bundles from the rafters, and the ground about it was strewn with bones and hair,—infinitely less tidy than a bear's den. He went as hunter and guide with a geological survey party for a year or two, and was very proud of the scientific knowledge, he picked up. His admiring fellow mountaineers, he said, gave him credit for knowing not only the botanical names of all the trees and bushes, but also the "botanical names of the bears."

The most famous hunter of the region was David Brown, an old pioneer, who early in the gold period established his main camp in a little forest glade on the north fork of the Merced, which is still called "Brown's Flat." No finer solitude for a hunter and prospector could be found; the climate is delightful all the year, and the scenery of both earth and sky is a perpetual feast. Though he was not much of a "scenery fellow," his friends say that he knew a pretty place when he saw it as well as any one, and liked mightily to get on the top of a commanding ridge to "look off."

When out of provisions, he would take down his old-fashioned long-barreled rifle from its deer-horn rest over the fireplace and set out in search of game. Seldom did he have to go far for venison, because the deer liked the wooded slopes of Pilot Peak ridge, with its open spots where they could rest and look about them, and enjoy the breeze from the sea in warm weather, free from troublesome flies, while they found hiding-places and fine aromatic food in the deer-brush chaparral. A small, wise dog was his only companion, and well the little mountaineer understood the object of every hunt, whether deer or bears, or only grouse hidden in the fir-tops. In deer-hunting Sandy had little to do, trotting behind his master as he walked noiselessly through the fragrant woods, careful not to step heavily on dry twigs, scanning open spots in the chaparral where the deer feed in the early morning and toward sunset, peering over ridges and swells as new outlooks were reached, and along alder and willow fringed flats and streams, until he found a young buck, killed it, tied its legs together, threw it on his shoulder, and so back to camp. But when bears were hunted, Sandy played an important part as leader, and several times saved his master's life; and it was as a bear-hunter that David Brown became famous. His method, as I had it from a friend who had passed many an evening in his cabin listening to his long stories of adventure, was simply to take a few pounds of flour and his rifle, and go slowly and silently over hill and valley in the loneliest part of the wilderness, until little Sandy came upon the fresh track of a bear, then follow it to the death, paying no heed to time. Wherever the bear went he went, however rough the ground, led by Sandy, who looked back from time to time to see how his master was coming on, and regulated his pace accordingly, never growing weary or allowing any other track to divert him. When high ground was reached a halt was made, to scan the openings in every direction, and perchance Bruin would be discovered sitting upright on his haunches, eating manzanita berries; pulling down the fruit-laden branches with his paws and pressing them together, so as to get substantial mouthfuls, however mixed with leaves and twigs.

The time of year enabled the hunter to determine approximately where the game would be found: in spring and early summer, in lush grass and clover meadows and in berry tangles along the banks of streams, or on pea-vine and lupine clad slopes; in late summer and autumn, beneath the pines, eating the cones cut off by the squirrels, and in oak groves at the bottom of cañons, munching acorns, manzanita berries, and cherries; and after snow had fallen, in alluvial bottoms, feeding on ants and yellow-jacket wasps. These food places were always cautiously approached, so as to avoid the chance of sudden encounters.

"Whenever," said the hunter, "I saw a bear before he saw me, I had no trouble in killing him. I just took lots of time to learn what he was up to and how long he would be likely to stay, and to study the direction of the wind and the lay of the land. Then I worked round to leeward of him, no matter how far I had to go; crawled and dodged to within a hundred yards, near the foot of a tree that I could climb, but which was too small for a bear to climb. There I looked well to the priming of my rifle, took off my boots so as to climb quickly if necessary, and, with my rifle in rest and Sandy behind me, waited until my bear stood right, when I made a sure, or at least a good shot back of the fore leg. In case he showed fight, I got up the tree I had in mind, before he could reach me. But bears are slow and awkward with their eyes, and being to windward they could not scent me, and often I got in a second shot before they saw the smoke. Usually, however, they tried to get away when they were hurt, and I let them go a good safe while before I ventured into the brush after them. Then Sandy was pretty sure to find them dead; if not, he barked bold as a lion to draw attention, or rushed in and nipped them behind, enabling me to get to a safe distance and watch a chance for a finishing shot.

"Oh yes, bear-hunting is a mighty interesting business, and safe enough if followed just right, though, like every other business, especially the wild kind, it has its accidents, and Sandy and I have had close calls at times. Bears are nobody's fools, and they know enough to let men alone as a general thing, unless they are wounded, or cornered, or have cubs. In my opinion, a hungry old mother would catch and eat a man, if she could; which is only fair play, anyhow, for we eat them. But nobody, as far as I know, has been eaten up in these rich mountains. Why they never tackle a fellow when he is lying asleep I never could understand. They could gobble us mighty handy, but I suppose it's nature to respect a sleeping man."

Sheep-owners and their shepherds have killed a great many bears, mostly by poison and traps of various sorts. Bears are fond of mutton, and levy heavy toll on every flock driven into the mountains. They usually come to the corral at night, climb in, kill a sheep with a stroke of the paw, carry it off a little distance, eat about half of it, and return the next night for the other half; and so on all summer, or until they are themselves killed. It is not, however, by direct killing, but by suffocation through crowding against the corral wall in fright, that the greatest losses are incurred. From ten to fifteen sheep are found dead, smothered in the corral, after every attack; or the walls are broken, and the flock is scattered far and wide. A flock may escape the attention of these marauders for a week or two in the spring; but after their first taste of the fine mountain-fed meat the visits are persistently kept up, in spite of all precautions. Once I spent a night with two Portuguese shepherds, who were greatly troubled with bears, from two to four or five visiting them almost every night. Their camp was near the middle of the Park, and the wicked bears, they said, were getting worse and worse. Not waiting now until dark, they came out of the brush in broad daylight, and boldly carried off as many sheep as they liked. One evening, before sundown, a bear, followed by two cubs, came for an early supper, as the flock was being slowly driven toward the camp. Joe, the elder of the shepherds, warned by many exciting experiences, promptly climbed a tall tamarack pine, and left the freebooters to help themselves; while Antone, calling him a coward, and declaring that he was not going to let bears eat up his sheep before his face, set the dogs on them, and rushed toward them with a great noise and a stick. The frightened cubs ran up a tree, and the mother ran to meet the shepherd and dogs. Antone stood astonished for a moment, eying the oncoming bear; then fled faster than Joe had, closely pursued. He scrambled to the roof of their little cabin, the only refuge quickly available; and fortunately, the bear, anxious about her young, did not climb after him,—only held him in mortal terror a few minutes, glaring and threatening, then hastened back to her cubs, called them down, went to the frightened, huddled flock, killed a sheep, and feasted in peace. Antone piteously entreated cautious Joe to show him a good safe tree, up which he climbed like a sailor climbing a mast, and held on as long as he could with legs crossed, the slim pine recommended by Joe being nearly branchless. "So you, too, are a bear coward as well as Joe," I said, after hearing the story. "Oh, I tell you," he replied, with grand solemnity, "bear face close by look awful; she just as soon eat me as not. She do so as eef all my sheeps b'long every one to her own self. I run to bear no more. I take tree every time."

After this the shepherds corraled the flock about an hour before sundown, chopped large quantities of dry wood and made a circle of fires around the corral every night, and one with a gun kept watch on a stage built in a pine by the side of the cabin, while the other slept. But after the first night or two this fire fence did no good, for the robbers seemed to regard the light as an advantage, after becoming used to it.

On the night I spent at their camp the show made by the wall of fire when it was blazing in its prime was magnificent,—the illumined trees around about relieved against solid darkness, and the two thousand sheep lying down in one gray mass, sprinkled with gloriously brilliant gems, the effect of the firelight in their eyes. It was nearly midnight when a pair of the freebooters arrived. They walked boldly through a gap in the fire circle, killed two sheep, carried them out, and vanished in the dark woods, leaving ten dead in a pile, trampled down and smothered against the corral fence; while the scared watcher in the tree did not fire a single shot, saying he was afraid he would hit some of the sheep, as the bears got among them before he could get a good sight.

In the morning I asked the shepherds why they did not move the flock to a new pasture. "Oh, no use!" cried Antone. "Look my dead sheeps. We move three four time before, all the same bear come by the track. No use. To-morrow we go home below. Look my dead sheeps. Soon all dead."

Thus were they driven out of the mountains more than a month before the usual time. After Uncle Sam's soldiers, bears are the most effective forest police, but some of the shepherds are very successful in killing them. Altogether, by hunters, mountaineers, Indians, and sheepmen, probably five or six hundred have been killed within the bounds of the Park, during the last thirty years. But they are not in danger of extinction. Now that the Park is guarded by soldiers, not only has the vegetation in great part come back to the desolate ground, but all the wild animals are increasing in numbers. No guns are allowed in the Park except under certain restrictions, and after a permit has been obtained from the officer in charge. This has stopped the barbarous slaughter of bears, and especially of deer, by shepherds, hunters, and hunting tourists, who, it would seem, can find no pleasure without blood.

The Sierra deer—the blacktail—spend the winters in the brushy and exceedingly rough region just below the main timber-belt, and are less accessible to hunters there than when they are passing through the comparatively open forests to and from their summer pastures near the summits of the range. They go up the mountains early in the spring as the snow melts, not waiting for it all to disappear; reaching the high Sierra about the first of June, and the coolest recesses at the base of the peaks a month or so later. I have tracked them for miles over compacted snow from three to ten feet deep.

Deer are capital mountaineers, making their way into the heart of the roughest mountains; seeking not only pasturage, but a cool climate, and safe hidden places in which to bring forth their young. They are not supreme as rock-climbing animals; they take second rank, yielding the first to the mountain sheep, which dwell above them on the highest crags and peaks. Still, the two meet frequently; for the deer climbs all the peaks save the lofty summits above the glaciers, crossing piles of angular boulders, roaring swollen streams, and sheer-walled cañons by fords and passes that would try the nerves of the hardiest mountaineers,—climbing with graceful ease and reserve of strength that cannot fail to arouse admiration. Everywhere some species of deer seems to be at home,—on rough or smooth ground, lowlands or highlands, in swamps and barrens and the densest woods, in varying climates, hot or cold, over all the continent; maintaining glorious health, never making an awkward step. Standing, lying down, walking, feeding, running even for life, it is always invincibly graceful, and adds beauty and animation to every landscape,—a charming animal, and a great credit to nature.

I never see one of the common blacktail deer, the only species in the Park, without fresh admiration; and since I never carry a gun I see them well: lying beneath a juniper or dwarf pine, among the brown needles on the brink of some cliff or the end of a ridge commanding a wide outlook; feeding in sunny openings among chaparral, daintily selecting aromatic leaves and twigs; leading their fawns out of my way, or making them lie down and hide; bounding past through the forest, or curiously advancing and retreating again and again.

One morning when I was eating breakfast in a little garden spot on the Kaweah, hedged around with chaparral, I noticed a deer's head thrust through the bushes, the big beautiful eyes gazing at me. I kept still, and the deer ventured forward a step, then snorted and withdrew. In a few minutes she returned, and came into the open garden, stepping with infinite grace, followed by two others. After showing themselves for a moment, they bounded over the hedge with sharp, timid snorts and vanished. But curiosity brought them back with still another, and all four came into my garden, and, satisfied that I meant them no ill, began to feed, actually eating breakfast with me, like tame, gentle sheep around a shepherd,—rare company, and the most graceful in movements and attitudes. I eagerly watched them while they fed on ceanothus and wild cherry, daintily culling single leaves here and there from the side of the hedge, turning now and then to snip a few leaves of mint from the midst of the garden flowers. Grass they did not eat at all. No wonder the contents of the deer's stomach are eaten by the Indians.

While exploring the upper cañon of the north fork of the San Joaquin, one evening, the sky threatening rain, I searched for a dry bed, and made choice of a big juniper that had been pushed down by a snow avalanche, but was resting stubbornly on its knees high enough to let me lie under its broad trunk. Just below my shelter there was another juniper on the very brink of a precipice, and, examining it, I found a deer-bed beneath it, completely protected and concealed by drooping branches,—a fine refuge and lookout as well as resting-place. About an hour before dark I heard the clear, sharp snorting of a deer, and looking down on the brushy, rocky cañon bottom, discovered an anxious doe that no doubt had her fawns concealed near by. She bounded over the chaparral and up the farther slope of the wall, often stopping to look back and listen,—a fine picture of vivid, eager alertness. I sat perfectly still, and as my shirt was colored like the juniper bark I was not easily seen. After a little she came cautiously toward me, sniffing the air and grazing, and her movements, as she descended the cañon side over boulder piles and brush and fallen timber, were admirably strong and beautiful; she never strained or made apparent efforts, although jumping high here and there. As she drew nigh she sniffed anxiously, trying the air in different directions until she caught my scent; then bounded off, and vanished behind a small grove of firs. Soon she came back with the same caution and insatiable curiosity,—coming and going five or six times. While I sat admiring her, a Douglas squirrel, evidently excited by her noisy alarms, climbed a boulder beneath me, and witnessed her performances as attentively as I did, while a risky chipmunk, too restless or hungry for such shows, busied himself about his supper in a thicket of shadbushes, the fruit of which was then ripe, glancing about on the slender twigs lightly as a sparrow.

Toward the end of the Indian summer, when the young are strong, the deer begin to gather in little bands of from six to fifteen or twenty, and on the approach of the first snowstorm they set out on their march down the mountains to their winter quarters; lingering usually on warm hillsides and spurs eight or ten miles below the summits, as if loath to leave. About the end of November, a heavy, far-reaching storm drives them down in haste along the dividing ridges between the rivers, led by old experienced bucks whose knowledge of the topography is wonderful.

It is when the deer are coming down that the Indians set out on their grand fall hunt. Too lazy to go into the recesses of the mountains away from trails, they wait for the deer to come out, and then waylay them. This plan also has the advantage of finding them in bands. Great preparations are made. Old guns are mended, bullets moulded, and the hunters wash themselves and fast to some extent, to insure good luck, as they say. Men and women, old and young, set forth together. Central camps are made on the well-known highways of the deer, which are soon red with blood. Each hunter comes in laden, old crones as well as maidens smiling on the luckiest. All grow fat and merry. Boys, each armed with an antlered head, play at buck-fighting, and plague the industrious women, who are busily preparing the meat for transportation, by stealing up behind them and throwing fresh hides over them. But the Indians are passing away here as everywhere, and their red camps on the mountains are fewer every year.

There are panthers, foxes, badgers, porcupines, and coyotes in the Park, but not in large numbers. I have seen coyotes well back in the range at the head of the Tuolumne Meadows as early as June 1st, before the snow was gone, feeding on marmots; but they are far more numerous on the inhabited lowlands around ranches, where they enjoy life on chickens, turkeys, quail eggs, ground squirrels, hares, etc., and all kinds of fruit. Few wild sheep, I fear, are left hereabouts; for, though safe on the high peaks, they are driven down the eastern slope of the mountains when the deer are driven down the western, to ridges and outlying spurs where the snow does not fall to a great depth, and there they are within reach of the cattlemen's rifles.

The two squirrels of the Park, the Douglas and the California gray, keep all the woods lively. The former is far more abundant and more widely distributed, being found all the way up from the foothills to the dwarf pines on the Summit peaks. He is the most influential of the Sierra animals, though small, and the brightest of all the squirrels I know,—a squirrel of squirrels, quick mountain vigor and valor condensed, purely wild, and as free from disease as a sunbeam. One cannot think of such an animal ever being weary or sick. He claims all the woods, and is inclined to drive away even men as intruders. How he scolds, and what faces he makes! If not so comically small he would be a dreadful fellow. The gray, Sciurus fossor, is the handsomest, I think, of all the large American squirrels. He is something like the Eastern gray, but is brighter and clearer in color, and more lithe and slender. He dwells in the oak and pine woods up to a height of about five thousand feet above the sea, is rather common in Yosemite Valley, Hetch-Hetchy, Kings River Cañon, and indeed in all the main cañons and Yosemites, but does not like the high fir-covered ridges. Compared with the Douglas, the gray is more than twice as large; nevertheless, he manages to make his way through the trees with less stir than his small, peppery neighbor, and is much less influential in every way. In the spring, before the pine-nuts and hazel-nuts are ripe, he examines last year's cones for the few seeds that may be left in them between the half-open scales, and gleans fallen nuts and seeds on the ground among the leaves, after making sure that no enemy is nigh. His fine tail floats, now behind, now above him, level or gracefully curled, light and radiant as dry thistledown. His body seems hardly more substantial than his tail. The Douglas is a firm, emphatic bolt of life, fiery, pungent, full of brag and show and fight, and his movements have none of the elegant deliberation of the gray. They are so quick and keen they almost sting the onlooker,and the acrobatic harlequin gyrating show he makes of himself turns one giddy to see. The gray is shy and oftentimes stealthy, as if half expecting to find an enemy in every tree and bush and behind every log; he seems to wish to be let alone, and manifests no desire to be seen, or admired, or feared. He is hunted by the Indians, and this of itself is cause enough for caution. The Douglas is less attractive for game, and probably increasing in numbers in spite of every enemy. He goes his ways bold as a lion, up and down and across, round and round, the happiest, merriest of all the hairy tribe, and at the same time tremendously earnest and solemn, sunshine incarnate, making every tree tingle with his electric toes. If you prick him, you cannot think he will bleed. He seems above the chance and change that beset common mortals, though in busily gathering burs and nuts he shows that he has to work for a living, like the rest of us. I never found a dead Douglas. He gets into the world and out of it without being noticed; only in prime is he seen, like some little plants that are visible only when in bloom.

The little striped Tamias quadrivittatus is one of the most amiable and delightful of all the mountain tree-climbers. A brighter, cheerier chipmunk does not exist. He is smarter, more arboreal and squirrel-like, than the familiar Eastern species, and is distributed as widely on the Sierra as the Douglas. Every forest, however dense or open, every hilltop and cañon, however brushy or bare, is cheered and enlivened by this happy little animal. You are likely to notice him first on the lower edge of the coniferous belt, where the Sabine and yellow pines meet; and thence upward, go where you may, you will find him every day, even in winter, unless the weather is stormy. He is an exceedingly interesting little fellow, full of odd, quaint ways, confiding, thinking no evil; and without being a squirrel—a true shadow-tail—he lives the life of a squirrel, and has almost all squirrelish accomplishments without aggressive quarrelsomeness.

I never weary of watching him as he frisks about the bushes, gathering seeds and berries; poising on slender twigs of wild cherry, shad, chinquapin, buckthorn, bramble; skimming along prostrate trunks or over the grassy, needle-strewn forest floor; darting from boulder to boulder on glacial pavements and the tops of the great domes. When the seeds of the conifers are ripe, he climbs the trees and cuts off the cones for a winter store, working diligently, though not with the tremendous lightning energy of the Douglas, who frequently drives him out of the best trees. Then he lies in wait, and picks up a share of the burs cut off by his domineering cousin, and stores them beneath logs and in hollows. Few of the Sierra animals are so well liked as this little airy, fluffy half squirrel, half spermophile. So gentle, confiding, and busily cheery and happy, he takes one's heart and keeps his place among the best-loved of the mountain darlings. A diligent collector of seeds, nuts, and berries, of course he is well fed, though never in the least dumpy with fat. On the contrary, he looks like a mere fluff of fur, weighing but little more than a field mouse, and of his frisky, birdlike liveliness without haste there is no end. Douglas can bark with his mouth closed, but little quad always opens his when he talks or sings. He has a considerable variety of notes which correspond with his movements, some of them sweet and liquid, like water dripping into a pool with tinkling sound. His eyes are black and animated, shining like dew. He seems dearly to like teasing a dog, venturing within a few feet of it, then frisking away with a lively chipping and low squirrelish churring; beating time to his music, such as it is, with his tail, which at each chip and churr describes a half circle. Not even Douglas is surer footed or takes greater risks. I have seen him running about on sheer Yosemite cliffs, holding on with as little effort as a fly and as little thought of danger, in places where, if he had made the least slip, he would have fallen thousands of feet. How fine it would be could mountaineers move about on precipices with the same sure grip!

Before the pine-nuts are ripe, grass seeds and those of the many species of ceanothus, with strawberries, raspberries, and the soft red thimbleberries of Rubus nutkanus, form the bulk of his food, and a neater eater is not to be found in the mountains. Bees powdered with pollen, poking their blunt noses into the bells of flowers, are comparatively clumsy and boorish. Frisking along some fallen pine or fir, when the grass seeds are ripe, he looks about him, considering which of the tufts he sees is likely to have the best, runs out to it, selects what he thinks is sure to be a good head, cuts it off, carries it to the top of the log, sits upright and nibbles out the grain without getting awns in his mouth, turning the head round, holding it and fingering it as if playing on a flute; then skips for another and another, bringing them to the same dining-log.

The woodchuck (*Arctomys monax*) dwells on high bleak ridges and boulder piles; and a very different sort of mountaineer is he,—bulky, fat, aldermanic, and fairly bloated at times by hearty indulgence in the lush pastures of his airy home. And yet he is by no means a dull animal. In the midst of what we regard as storm-beaten desolation, high in the frosty air, beside the glaciers he pipes and whistles right cheerily and lives to a good old age. If you are as early a riser as he is, you may oftentimes see him come blinking out of his burrow to meet the first beams of the morning and take a sunbath on some favorite flat-topped boulder. Afterward, well warmed, he goes to breakfast in one of his garden hollows, eats heartily like a cow in clover until comfortably swollen, then goes a-visiting, and plays and loves and fights.

In the spring of 1875, when I was exploring the peaks and glaciers about the head of the middle fork of the San Joaquin, I had crossed the range from the head of Owen River, and one morning, passing around a frozen lake where the snow was perhaps ten feet deep, I was surprised to find the fresh track of a woodchuck plainly marked, the sun having softened the surface. What could the animal be thinking of, coming out so early while all the ground was snow-buried? The steady trend of his track showed he had a definite aim, and fortunately it was toward a mountain thirteen thousand feet high that I meant to climb. So I followed to see if I could find out what he was up to. From the base of the mountain the track pointed straight up, and I knew by the melting snow that I was not far behind him. I lost the track on a crumbling ridge, partly projecting through the snow, but soon discovered it again. Well toward the summit of the mountain, in an open spot on the south side, nearly inclosed by disintegrating pinnacles among which the sun heat reverberated, making an isolated patch of warm climate, I found a nice garden, full of rock cress, phlox, silene, draba, etc., and a few grasses; and in this garden I overtook the wanderer, enjoying a fine fresh meal, perhaps the first of the season. How did he know the way to this one garden spot, so high and far off, and what told him that it was in bloom while yet the snow was ten feet deep over his den? For this it would seem he would need more botanical, topographical, and climatological knowledge than most mountaineers are possessed of.

The shy, curious mountain beaver, Haplodon, lives on the heights, not far from the woodchuck. He digs canals and controls the flow of small streams under the sod. And it is startling when one is camped on the edge of a sloping meadow near the homes of these industrious mountaineers, to be awakened in the still night by the sound of water rushing and gurgling under one's head in a newly formed canal. Pouched gophers also have a way of awakening nervous campers that is quite as exciting as the Haplodon's pain; that is, by a series of firm upward pushes when they are driving tunnels and shoving up the dirt. One naturally cries out, "Who's there?" and then discovering the cause, "All right. Go on. Good-night." and goes to sleep again.

The haymaking pika, bob-tailed spermophile, and wood-rat are also among the most interesting of the Sierra animals. The last Neotoma is scarcely at all like the common rat, is nearly twice as large, has a delicate, soft, brownish fur, white on the belly, large ears thin and translucent, eyes full and liquid and mild in expression, nose blunt and squirrelish, slender claws sharp as needles, and as his limbs are strong he can climb about as well as a squirrel; while no rat or squirrel has so innocent a look, is so easily approached, or in general expresses so much confidence in one's good intentions. He seems too fine for the thorny thickets he inhabits, and his big, rough hut is as unlike himself as possible. No other animal in these mountains makes nests so large and striking in appearance as his. They are built of all kinds of sticks (broken branches, and old rotten moss-grown chunks and green twigs, smooth or thorny, cut from the nearest bushes), mixed with miscellaneous rubbish and curious odds and ends,—bits of cloddy earth, stones, bones, bits of deer-horn, etc.: the whole simply piled in conical masses on the ground in chaparral thickets. Some of these cabins are five or six feet high, and occasionally a dozen or more are grouped together; less, perhaps, for society's sake than for advantages of food and shelter.

Coming through deep, stiff chaparral in the heart of the wilderness, heated and weary in forcing a way, the solitary explorer, happening into one of these curious neotoma villages, is startled at the strange sight, and may imagine he is in an Indian village, and feel anxious as to the reception he will get in a place so wild. At first, perhaps, not a single inhabitant will be seen, or at most only two or three seated on the tops of their huts as at the doors, observing the stranger with the mildest of mild eyes. The nest in the centre of the cabin is made of grass and films of bark chewed to tow, and lined with feathers and the down of various seeds. The thick, rough walls seem to be built for defense against enemies—fox, coyote, etc.—as well as for shelter, and the delicate creatures in their big, rude homes, suggest tender flowers, like those of Salvia carduacea, defended by thorny involucres.

Sometimes the home is built in the forks of an oak, twenty or thirty feet from the ground, and even in garrets. Among housekeepers who have these bushmen as neighbors or guests they are regarded as thieves, because they carry away and pile together everything transportable (knives, forks, tin cups, spoons, spectacles, combs, nails, kindling-wood, etc., as well as eatables of all sorts), to strengthen their fortifications or to shine among rivals. Once, far back in the high Sierra, they stole my snow-goggles, the lid of my teapot, and my aneroid barometer; and one stormy night, when encamped under a prostrate cedar, I was awakened by a gritting sound on the granite, and by the light of my fire I discovered a handsome neotoma beside me, dragging away my ice-hatchet, pulling with might and main by a buckskin string on the handle. I threw bits of bark at him and made a noise to frighten him, but he stood scolding and chattering back at me, his fine eyes shining with an air of injured innocence.

A great variety of lizards enliven the warm portions of the Park. Some of them are more than a foot in length, others but little larger than grasshoppers. A few are snaky and repulsive at first sight, but most of the species are handsome and attractive, and bear acquaintance well; we like them better the farther we see into their charming lives. Small fellow mortals, gentle and guileless, they are easily tamed, and have beautiful eyes, expressing the clearest innocence, so that, in spite of prejudices brought from cool, lizardless countries, one must soon learn to like them. Even the horned toad of the plains and foothills, called horrid, is mild and gentle, with charming eyes, and so are the snake-like species found in the underbrush of the lower forests. These glide in curves with all the ease and grace of snakes, while their small, undeveloped limbs drag for the most part as useless appendages. One specimen that I measured was fourteen inches long, and as far as I saw it made no use whatever of its diminutive limbs.

Most of them glint and dart on the sunny rocks and across open spaces from bush to bush, swift as dragonflies and humming-birds, and about as brilliantly colored. They never make a long-sustained run, whatever their object, but dart direct as arrows for a distance of ten or twenty feet, then suddenly stop, and as suddenly start again. These stops are necessary as rests, for they are short-winded, and when pursued steadily are soon run out of breath, pant pitifully, and may easily be caught where no retreat in bush or rock is quickly available.

If you stay with them a week or two and behave well, these gentle saurians, descendants of an ancient race of giants, will soon know and trust you, come to your feet, play, and watch your every motion with cunning curiosity. You will surely learn to like them, not only the bright one, gorgeous as the rainbow, but the little ones, gray as lichened granite, and scarcely bigger than grasshoppers; and they will teach you that scales may cover as fine a nature as hair or feathers or anything tailored.

There are many snakes in the cañons and lower forests, but they are mostly handsome and armless. Of all the tourists and travelers who have visited Yosemite and the adjacent mountains, not one has been bitten by a snake of any sort, while thousands have been charmed by them. Some of them vie with the lizards in beauty of color and dress patterns. Only the rattlesnake is venomous, and he carefully keeps his venom to himself as far as man is concerned, unless his life is threatened.

Before I learned to respect rattlesnakes I killed two, the first on the San Joaquin plain. He was coiled comfortably around a tuft of bunch-grass, and I discovered him when he was between my feet as I was stepping over him. He held his head down and did not attempt to strike, although in danger of being trampled. At that time, thirty years ago, I imagined that rattlesnakes should be killed wherever found. I had no weapon of any sort, and on the smooth plain there was not a stick or a stone within miles; so I crushed him by jumping on him, as the deer are said to do. Looking me in the face he saw I meant mischief, and quickly cast himself into a coil, ready to strike in defense. I knew he could not strike when traveling, therefore I threw handfuls of dirt and grass sods at him, to tease him out of coil. He held his ground a few minutes, threatening and striking, and then started off to get rid of me. I ran forward and jumped on him; but he drew back his head so quickly my heel missed, and he also missed his stroke at me. Persecuted, tormented, again and again he tried to get away, bravely striking out to protect himself; but at last my heel came squarely down, sorely wounding him, and a few more brutal stampings crushed him. I felt degraded by the killing business, farther from heaven, and I made up my mind to try to be at least as fair and charitable as the snakes themselves, and to kill no more save in self-defense.

The second killing might also, I think, have been avoided, and I have always felt somewhat sore and guilty about it. I had built a little cabin in Yosemite, and for convenience in getting water, and for the sake of music and society, I led a small stream from Yosemite Creek into it.

Running along the side of the wall it was not in the way, and it had just fall enough to ripple and sing in low, sweet tones, making delightful company, especially at night when I was lying awake. Then a few frogs came in and made merry with the stream,—and one snake, I suppose to catch the frogs.

Returning from my long walks, I usually brought home a large handful of plants, partly for study, partly for ornament, and set them in a corner of the cabin, with their stems in the stream to keep them fresh. One day, when I picked up a handful that had begun to fade, I uncovered a large coiled rattler that had been hiding behind the flowers. Thus suddenly brought to light face to face with the rightful owner of the place, the poor reptile was desperately embarrassed, evidently realizing that he had no right in the cabin. It was not only fear that he showed, but a good deal of downright bashfulness and embarrassment, like that of a more than half honest person caught under suspicious circumstances behind a door. Instead of striking or threatening to strike, though coiled and ready, he slowly drew his head down as far as he could, with awkward, confused kinks in his neck and a shamefaced expression, as if wishing the ground would open and hide him. I have looked into the eyes of so many wild animals that I feel sure I did not mistake the feelings of this unfortunate snake. I did not want to kill him, but I had many visitors, some of them children, and I oftentimes came in late at night; so I judged he must die.

Since then I have seen perhaps a hundred or more in these mountains, but I have never intentionally disturbed them, nor have they disturbed me to any great extent, even by accident, though in danger of being stepped on. Once, while I was on my knees kindling a fire, one glided under the arch made by my arm. He was only going away from the ground I had selected for a camp, and there was not the slightest danger, because I kept still and allowed him to go in peace. The only time I felt myself in serious danger was when I was coming out of the Tuolumne Cañon by a steep side cañon toward the head of Yosemite Creek. On an earthquake talus, a boulder in my way presented a front so high that I could just reach the upper edge of it while standing on the next below it. Drawing myself up, as soon as my head was above the flat top of it I caught sight of a coiled rattler. My hands had alarmed him, and he was ready for me; but even with this provocation, and when my head came in sight within a foot of him, he did not strike. The last time I sauntered through the big cañon I saw about two a day. One was not coiled, but neatly folded in a narrow space between two cobble-stones on the side of the river, his head below the level of them, ready to shoot up like a Jack-in-the-box for frogs or birds. My foot spanned the space above within an inch or two of his head, but he only held it lower. In making my way through a particularly tedious tangle of buckthorn, I parted the branches on the side of an open spot and threw my bundle of bread into it; and when, with my arms free, I was pushing through after it, I saw a small rattlesnake dragging his tail from beneath my bundle. When he caught sight of me he eyed me angrily, and with an air of righteous indignation seemed to be asking why I had thrown that stuff on him. He was so small that I was inclined to slight him, but he struck out so angrily that I drew back, and approached the opening from the other side. But he had been listening, and when I looked through the brush I found him confronting me, still with a come-in-if-you-dare expression. In vain I tried to explain that I only wanted my bread; he stoutly held the ground in front of it; so I went back a dozen rods and kept still for half an hour, and when I returned he had gone.

One evening, near sundown, in a very rough, boulder-choked portion of the cañon, I searched long for a level spot for a bed, and at last was glad to find a patch of flood-sand on the river-bank, and a lot of driftwood close by for a campfire. But when I threw down my bundle, I found two snakes in possession of the ground. I might have passed the night even in this snake den without danger, for I never knew a single instance of their coming into camp in the night; but fearing that, in so small a space, some late comers, not aware of my presence, might get stepped on when I was replenishing the fire, to avoid possible crowding I encamped on one of the earthquake boulders.

There are two species of Crotalus in the Park, and when I was exploring the basin of Yosemite Creek I thought I had discovered a new one. I saw a snake with curious divided appendages on its head. Going nearer, I found that the strange headgear was only the feet of a frog. Cutting a switch, I struck the snake lightly until he disgorged the poor frog, or rather allowed it to back out. On its return to the light from one of the very darkest of death valleys, it blinked a moment with a sort of dazed look, then plunged into a stream, apparently happy and well.

Frogs abound in all the bogs, marshes, pools, and lakes, however cold and high and isolated. How did they manage to get up these high mountains? Surely not by jumping. Long and dry excursions through weary miles of boulders and brush would be trying to frogs. Most likely their stringy spawn is carried on the feet of ducks, cranes, and other waterbirds. Anyhow, they are most thoroughly distributed, and flourish famously. What a cheery, hearty set they are, and how bravely their krink and tronk concerts enliven the rocky wilderness!

None of the high-lying mountain lakes or branches of the rivers above sheer falls had fish of any sort until stocked by the agency of man. In the high Sierra, the only river in which trout exist naturally is the middle fork of Kings River. There are no sheer falls on this stream; some of the rapids, however, are so swift and rough, even at the lowest stage of water, that it is surprising any fish can climb them. I found trout in abundance in this fork up to seventy-five hundred feet. They also run quite high on the Kern. On the Merced they get no higher than Yosemite Valley, four thousand feet, all the forks of the river being barred there by sheer falls, and on the main Tuolumne they are stopped by a fall below Hetch-Hetchy, still lower than Yosemite. Though these upper waters are inaccessible to the fish, one would suppose their eggs might have been planted there by some means. Nature has so many ways of doing such things. In this case she waited for the agency of man, and now many of these hitherto fishless lakes and streams are full of fine trout, stocked by individual enterprise, Walton clubs etc., in great part under the auspices of the United States Fish Commission. A few trout carried into Hetch-Hetchy in a common water-bucket have multiplied wonderfully fast. Lake Tenaya, at an elevation of over eight thousand feet, was stocked eight years ago by Mr. Murphy, who carried a few trout from Yosemite. Many of the small streams of the eastern slope have also been stocked with trout transported over the passes in tin cans on the backs of mules. Soon, it would seem, all the streams of the range will be enriched by these lively fish, and will become the means of drawing thousands of visitors into the mountains. Catching trout with a bit of bent wire is a rather trivial business, but fortunately people fish better than they know. In most cases it is the man who is caught. Trout-fishing regarded as bait for catching men, for the saving of both body and soul, is important, and deserves all the expense and care bestowed on it.

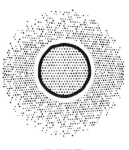

VII

AMONG THE BIRDS OF THE YOSEMITE

Travelers in the Sierra forests usually complain of the want of life. "The trees," they say, "are fine, but the empty stillness is deadly; there are no animals to be seen, no birds. We have not heard a song in all the woods." And no wonder! They go in large parties with mules and horses; they make a great noise; they are dressed in outlandish unnatural colors; every animal shuns them. Even the frightened pines would run away if they could. But Nature-lovers, devout, silent, open-eyed, looking and listening with love, find no lack of inhabitants in these mountain mansions, and they come to them gladly. Not to mention the large animals or the small insect people, every waterfall has its ouzel and every tree its squirrel or tamias or bird: tiny nuthatch threading the furrows of the bark, cheerily whispering to itself as it deftly pries off loose scales and examines the curled edges of lichens; or Clarke crow or jay examining the cones; or some singer—oriole, tanager, warbler—resting, feeding, attending to domestic affairs. Hawks and eagles sail overhead, grouse walk in happy flocks below, and song sparrows sing in every bed of chaparral. There is no crowding, to be sure. Unlike the low Eastern trees, those of the Sierra in the main forest belt average nearly two hundred feet in height, and of course many birds are required to make much show in them, and many voices to fill them. Nevertheless, the whole range, from foothills to snowy summits, is shaken into song every summer; and though low and thin in winter, the music never ceases.

The sage cock (*Centrocercus urophasianus*) is the largest of the Sierra game-birds and the king of American grouse. It is admirably strong, hardy, handsome, independent bird, able with comfort to bid defiance to heat, cold, drought, hunger, and all sorts of storms, living on whatever seeds or insects chance to come in its way, or simply on the leaves of sage-brush, everywhere abundant on its desert range. In winter, when the temperature is oftentimes below zero, and heavy snowstorms are blowing, he sits beneath a sage bush and allows himself to be covered, poking his head now and then through the snow to feed on the leaves of his shelter. Not even the Arctic ptarmigan is hardier in braving frost and snow and wintry darkness. When in full plumage he is a beautiful bird, with a long, firm, sharp-pointed tail, which in walking is slightly raised and swings sidewise back and forth with each step. The male is handsomely marked with black and white on the neck, back, and wings, weighs five or six pounds, and measures about thirty inches in length. The female is clad mostly in plain brown, and is not so large. They occasionally wander from the sage plains into the open nut-pine and juniper woods, but never enter the main coniferous forest. It is only in the broad, dry, half-desert sage plains that they are quite at home, where the weather is blazing hot in summer, cold in winter. If any one passes through a flock, all squat on the gray ground and hold their heads low, hoping to escape observation; but when approached within a rod or so, they rise with a magnificent burst of wing-beats, looking about as big as turkeys and making a noise like a whirlwind.

On the 28th of June, at the head of Owen's Valley, I caught one of the young that was then just able to fly. It was seven inches long, of a uniform gray color, blunt-billed, and when captured cried lustily in a shrill piping voice, clear in tone as a boy's small willow whistle. I have seen flocks of from ten to thirty or forty on the east margin of the Park, where the Mono Desert meets the gray foothills of the Sierra; but since cattle have been pastured there they are becoming rarer every year.

Another magnificent bird, the blue or dusky grouse, next in size to the sage cock, is found all through the main forest belt, though not in great numbers. They like best the heaviest silver-fir woods near garden and meadow openings, where there is but little underbrush to cover the approach of enemies. When a flock of these brave birds, sauntering and feeding on the sunny, flowery levels of some hidden meadow or Yosemite valley far back in the heart of the mountains, see a man for the first time in their lives, they rise with hurried notes of surprise and excitement and alight on the lowest branches of the trees, wondering what the wanderer may be, and showing great eagerness to get a good view of the strange vertical animal. Knowing nothing of guns, they allow you to approach within a half dozen paces, then quietly hop a few branches higher or fly to the next tree without a thought of concealment, so that you may observe them as long as you like, near enough to see the fine shading of their plumage, the feathers on their toes, and the innocent wonderment in their beautiful wild eyes. But in the neighborhood of roads and trails they soon become shy, and when disturbed fly into the highest, leafiest trees, and suddenly become invisible, so well do they know how to hide and keep still and make use of their protective coloring. Nor can they be easily dislodged ere they are ready to go. In vain the hunter goes round and round some tall pine or fir into which he has perhaps seen a dozen enter, gazing up through the branches, straining his eyes while his gun is held ready; not a feather can he see unless his eyes have been sharpened by long experience and knowledge of the blue grouse's habits. Then, perhaps, when he is thinking that the tree must be hollow and that the birds have all gone inside, they burst forth with a startling whir of wing-beats, and after gaining full speed go skating swiftly away through the forest arches in a long, silent, wavering slide, with wings held steady.

During the summer they are most of the time on the ground, feeding on insects, seeds, berries, etc., around the margins of open spots and rocky moraines, playing and sauntering, taking sun baths and sand baths, and drinking at little pools and rills during the heat of the day. In winter they live mostly in the trees, depending on buds for food, sheltering beneath dense overlapping branches at night and during storms on the leeside of the trunk, sunning themselves on the southside limbs in fine weather, and sometimes diving into the mealy snow to flutter and wallow, apparently for exercise and fun.

I have seen young broods running beneath the firs in June at a height of eight thousand feet above the sea. On the approach of danger, the mother with a peculiar cry warns the helpless midgets to scatter and hide beneath leaves and twigs, and even in plain open places it is almost impossible to discover them. In the meantime the mother feigns lameness, throws herself at your feet, kicks and gasps and flutters, to draw your attention from the chicks. The young are generally able to fly about the middle of July; but even after they can fly well they are usually advised to run and hide and lie still, no matter how closely approached, while the mother goes on with her loving, lying acting, apparently as desperately concerned for their safety as when they were featherless infants. Sometimes, however, after carefully studying the circumstances, she tells them to take wing; and up and away in a blurry birr and whir they scatter to all points of the compass, as if blown up with gunpowder, dropping cunningly out of sight three or four hundred yards off, and keeping quiet until called, after the danger is supposed to be past. If you walk on a little way without manifesting any inclination to hunt them, you may sit down at the foot of a tree near enough to see and hear the happy reunion. One touch of nature makes the whole world kin; and it is truly wonderful how love-telling the small voices of these birds are, and how far they reach through the woods into one another's hearts and into ours. The tones are so perfectly human and so full of anxious affection, few mountaineers can fail to be touched by them.

They are cared for until full grown. On the 20th of August, as I was passing along the margin of a garden spot on the head-waters of the San Joaquin, a grouse rose from the ruins of an old juniper that had been uprooted and brought down by an avalanche from a cliff overhead. She threw herself at my feet, limped and fluttered and gasped, showing, as I thought, that she had a nest and was raising a second brood. Looking for the eggs, I was surprised to see a strong-winged flock nearly as large as the mother fly up around me.

Instead of seeking a warmer climate when the winter storms set in, these hardy birds stay all the year in the high Sierra forests, and I have never known them to suffer in any sort of weather. Able to live on the buds of pine, spruce, and fir, they are forever independent in the matter of food supply, which gives so many of us trouble, dragging us here and there away from our best work. How gladly I would live on pine buds, however pitchy, for the sake of this grand independence! With all his superior resources, man makes more distracting difficulty concerning food than any other of the family.

The mountain quail, or plumed partridge (*Oreortyx pictus plumiferus*) is common in all the upper portions of the Park, though nowhere in numbers. He ranges considerably higher than the grouse in summer, but is unable to endure the heavy storms of winter. When his food is buried, he descends the range to the brushy foothills, at a height of from two to three thousand feet above sea; but like every true mountaineer, he is quick to follow the spring back into the highest mountains. I think he is the very handsomest and most interesting of all the American partridges, larger and handsomer than the famous Bob White, or even the fine California valley quail, or the Massena partridge of Arizona and Mexico. That he is not so regarded, is because as a lonely mountaineer he is not half known.

His plumage is delicately shaded, brown above, white and rich chestnut below and on the sides, with many dainty markings of black and white and gray here and there, while his beautiful head plume, three or four inches long, nearly straight, composed of two feathers closely folded so as to appear as one, is worn jauntily slanted backward like a single feather in a boy's cap, giving him a very marked appearance. They wander over the lonely mountains in family flocks of from six to fifteen, beneath ceanothus, manzanita, and wild cherry thickets, and over dry sandy flats, glacier meadows, rocky ridges, and beds of Bryanthus around glacier lakes, especially in autumn, when the berries of the upper gardens are ripe, uttering low clucking notes to enable them to keep together. When they are so suddenly disturbed that they are afraid they cannot escape the danger by running into thickets, they rise with a fine hearty whir and scatter in the brush over an area of half a square mile or so, a few of them diving into leafy trees. But as soon as the danger is past, the parents with a clear piping note call them together again. By the end of July the young are two thirds grown and fly well, though only dire necessity can compel them to try their wings. In gait, gestures, habits, and general behavior they are like domestic chickens, but infinitely finer, searching for insects and seeds, looking to this side and that, scratching among fallen leaves, jumping up to pull down grass heads, and clucking and muttering in low tones.

Once when I was seated at the foot of a tree on the head-waters of the Merced, sketching, I heard a flock up the valley behind me, and by their voices gradually sounding nearer I knew that they were feeding toward me. I kept still, hoping to see them. Soon one came within three or four feet of me, without noticing me any more than if I were a stump or a bulging part of the trunk against which I was leaning, my clothing being brown, nearly like the bark. Presently along came another and another, and it was delightful to get so near a view of these handsome chickens perfectly undisturbed, observe their manners, and hear their low peaceful notes. At last one of them caught my eye, gazed in silent wonder for a moment, then uttered a peculiar cry, which was followed by a lot of hurried muttered notes that sounded like speech. The others, of course, saw me as soon as the alarm was sounded, and joined the wonder talk, gazing and chattering, astonished but not frightened. Then all with one accord ran back with the news to the rest of the flock. "What is it? what is it? Oh, you never saw the like," they seemed to be saying. "Not a deer, or a wolf, or a bear; come see, come see." "Where? where? "Down there by that tree." Then they approached cautiously, past the tree, stretching their necks, and looking up in turn as if knowing from the story told them just where I was. For fifteen or twenty minutes they kept coming and going, venturing within a few feet of me, and discussing the wonder in charming chatter. Their curiosity at last satisfied, they began to scatter and feed again, going back in the direction they had come from; while I, loath to part with them, followed noiselessly, crawling beneath the bushes, keeping them in sight for an hour or two, learning their habits, and finding out what seeds and berries they like best.

The valley quail is not a mountaineer, and seldom enters the Park except at a few of the lowest places on the western boundary. It belongs to the brushy foothills and plains, orchards and wheatfields, and is a hundred times more numerous than the mountain quail. It is a beautiful bird, about the size of the Bob White, and has a handsome crest of four or five feathers an inch long, recurved, standing nearly erect at times or drooping forward. The loud calls of these quails in the spring—Pe-check-ah, Pe-check-a, Hoy, Hoy—are heard far and near over all the lowlands. They have vastly increased in numbers since the settlement of the country, notwithstanding the immense numbers killed every season by boys and pot-hunters as well as the regular leggined sportsmen from the towns; for man's destructive action is more than counterbalanced by increased supply of food from cultivation, and by the destruction of their enemies—coyotes, skunks, foxes, hawks, owls, etc.—which not only kill the old birds, but plunder their nests. Where coyotes and skunks abound, scarce one pair in a hundred is successful in raising a brood. So well aware are these birds of the protection afforded by man, even now that the number of their wild enemies has been greatly diminished, that they prefer to nest near houses, notwithstanding they are so shy. Four or five pairs rear their young around our cottage every spring. One year a pair nested in a straw pile within four or five feet of the stable door, and did not leave the eggs when the men led the horses back and forth within a foot or two. For many seasons a pair nested in a tuft of pampas grass in the garden; another pair in an ivy vine on the cottage roof, and when the young were hatched, it was interesting to see the parents getting the fluffy dots down. They were greatly excited, and their anxious calls and directions to their many babes attracted our attention. They had no great difficulty in persuading the young birds to pitch themselves from the main roof to the porch roof among the ivy, but to get them safely down from the latter to the ground, a distance of ten feet, was most distressing. It seemed impossible the frail soft things could avoid being killed. The anxious parents led them to a point above a spiræa bush, that reached nearly to the eaves, which they seemed to know would break the fall. Anyhow they led their chicks to this point, and with infinite coaxing and encouragement got them to tumble themselves off. Down they rolled and sifted through the soft leaves and panicles to the pavement, and, strange to say, all got away unhurt except one that lay as if dead for a few minutes. When it revived, the joyful parents, with their brood fairly launched on the journey of life, proudly led them down the cottage hill, through the garden, and along an osage orange hedge into the cherry orchard. These charming birds even enter towns and villages, where the gardens are of good size and guns are forbidden, sometimes going several miles to feed, and returning every evening to their roosts in ivy or brushy trees and shrubs.

Geese occasionally visit the Park, but never stay long. Sometimes on their way across the range, a flock wanders into Hetch-Hetchy or Yosemite to rest or get something to eat, and if shot at, are often sorely bewildered in seeking a way out. I have seen them rise from the meadow or river, wheel round in a spiral until a height of four or five hundred feet was reached, then form ranks and try to fly over the wall. But Yosemite magnitudes seem to be as deceptive to geese as to men, for they would suddenly find themselves against the cliffs not a fourth of the way to the top. Then turning in confusion, and screaming at the strange heights, they would try the opposite side, and so until exhausted they were compelled to rest, and only after discovering the river cañon could they make their escape. Large, harrow-shaped flocks may often be seen crossing the range in the spring, at a height of at least fourteen thousand feet. Think of the strength of wing required to sustain so heavy a bird in air so thin. At this elevation it is but little over half as dense as at the sea level. Yet they hold bravely on in beautifully dressed ranks, and have breath enough to spare for loud honking. After the crest of the Sierra is passed it is only a smooth slide down the sky to the waters of Mono, where they may rest as long as they like.

Ducks of five or six species, among which are the mallard and wood duck, go far up into the heart of the mountains in the spring, and of course come down in the fall with the families they have reared. A few, as if loath to leave the mountains, pass the winter in the lower valleys of the Park at a height of three thousand to four thousand feet, where the main streams are never wholly frozen over, and snow never falls to a great depth or lies long. In summer they are found up to a height of eleven thousand feet on all the lakes and branches of the rivers except the smallest, and those beside the glaciers incumbered with drifting ice and snow. I found mallards and wood ducks at Lake Tenaya, June 1, before the ice-covering was half melted, and a flock of young ones in Bloody Cañon Lake, June 20. They are usually met in pairs, never in large flocks. No place is too wild or rocky or solitary for these brave swimmers, no stream too rapid. In the roaring, resounding cañon torrents, they seem as much at home as in the tranquil reaches and lakes of the broad glacial valleys. Abandoning themselves to the wild play of the waters, they go drifting confidingly through blinding, thrashing spray, dancing on boulder-dashed waves, tossing in beautiful security on rougher water than is usually encountered by sea birds when storms are blowing.

A mother duck with her family of ten little ones, waltzing round and round in a pot-hole ornamented with foam bells, huge rocks leaning over them, cascades above and below and beside them, made one of the most interesting bird pictures I ever saw.

I have never found the great northern diver in the Park lakes. Most of them are inaccessible to him. He might plump down into them, but would hardly be able to get out of them, since, with his small wings and heavy body, a wide expanse of elbow room is required in rising. Now and then one may be seen in the lower Sierra lakes to the northward about Lassens Butte and Shasta, at a height of four thousand to five thousand feet, making the loneliest places lonelier with the wildest of wild cries.

Plovers are found along the sandy shores of nearly all the mountain lakes, tripping daintily on the water's edge, picking up insects; and it is interesting to learn how few of these familiar birds are required to make a solitude cheerful.

Sandhill cranes are sometimes found in comparatively small marshes, mere dots in the mighty forest. In such spots, at an elevation of from six thousand to eight thousand feet above the sea, they are occasionally met in pairs as early as the end of May, while the snow is still deep in the surrounding fir and sugar-pine woods. And on sunny days in autumn, large flocks may be seen sailing at a great height above the forests, shaking the crisp air into rolling waves with their hearty koor-r-r, koor-r-r, uck-uck, soaring in circles for hours together on their majestic wings, seeming to float without effort like clouds, eying the wrinkled landscape outspread like a map mottled with lakes and glaciers and meadows and streaked with shadowy cañons and streams, and surveying every frog marsh and sandy flat within a hundred miles.

Eagles and hawks are oftentimes seen above the ridges and domes. The greatest height at which I have observed them was about twelve thousand feet, over the summits of Mount Hoffman, in the middle region of the Park. A few pairs had their nests on the cliffs of this mountain, and could be seen every day in summer, hunting marmots, mountain beavers, pikas, etc. A pair of golden eagles have made their home in Yosemite ever since I went there thirty years ago. Their nest is on the Nevada Fall Cliff, opposite the Liberty Cap. Their screams are rather pleasant to hear in the vast gulfs between the granite cliffs, and they help the owls in keeping the echoes busy.

But of all the birds of the high Sierra, the strangest, noisiest, and most notable is the Clarke crow (*Nucifraga columbiana*). He is a foot long and nearly two feet in extent of wing, ashy gray in general color, with black wings, white-tail, and a strong, sharp bill, with which he digs into the pine cones for the seeds on which he mainly subsists. He is quick, boisterous, jerky, and irregular in his movements and speech, and makes a tremendously loud and showy advertisement of himself,—swooping and diving in deep curves across gorges and valleys from ridge to ridge, alighting on dead spars, looking warily about him, and leaving his dry springy perches, trembling from the vigor of his kick as he launches himself for a new flight, screaming from time to time loud enough to be heard more than a mile in still weather. He dwells far back on the high stormbeaten margin of the forest, where the mountain pine, juniper, and hemlock grow wide apart on glacier pavements and domes and rough crumbling ridges, and the dwarf pine makes a low crinkled growth along the flanks of the Summit peaks. In so open a region, of course, he is well seen. Everybody notices him, and nobody at first knows what to make of him. One guesses he must be a woodpecker; another a crow or some sort of jay, another a magpie. He seems to be a pretty thoroughly mixed and fermented compound of all these birds, has all their strength, cunning, shyness, thievishness, and wary, suspicious curiosity combined and condensed. He flies like a woodpecker, hammers dead limbs for insects, digs big holes in pine cones to get at the seeds, cracks nuts held between his toes, cries like a crow or Stellar jay,—but in a far louder, harsher, and more forbidding tone of voice,—and besides his crow caws and screams, has a great variety of small chatter talk, mostly uttered in a fault-finding tone. Like the magpie, he steals articles that can be of no use to him. Once when I made my camp in a grove at Cathedral Lake, I chanced to leave a cake of soap on the shore where I had been washing, and a few minutes afterward I saw my soap flying past me through the grove, pushed by a Clarke crow.

In winter, when the snow is deep, the cones of the mountain pines are empty, and the juniper, hemlock, and dwarf pine orchard buried, he comes down to glean seeds in the yellow pine forests, startling the grouse with his loud screams. But even in winter, in calm weather, he stays in his high mountain home, defying the bitter frost. Once I lay snowbound through a three days storm at the timber-line on Mount Shasta; and while the roaring snow-laden blast swept by, one of these brave birds came to my camp, and began hammering at the cones on the topmost branches of half-buried pines, without showing the slightest distress. I have seen Clarke crows feeding their young as early as June 19, at a height of more than ten thousand feet, when nearly the whole landscape was snow-covered.

They are excessively shy, and keep away from the traveler as long as they think they are observed; but when one goes on without seeming to notice them, or sits down and keeps still, their curiosity speedily gets the better of their caution, and they come flying from tree to tree, nearer and nearer, and watch every motion. Few, I am afraid, will ever learn to like this bird, he is so suspicious and self-reliant, and his voice is so harsh that to most ears the scream of the eagle will seem melodious compared with it. Yet the mountaineer who has battled and suffered and struggled must admire his strength and endurance,—the way he faces the mountain weather, cleaves the icy blasts, cares for his young, and digs a living from the stern wilderness.

Higher yet than Nucifraga dwells the little dun-headed sparrow (*Leucosticte tephrocotis*). From early spring to late autumn he is to be found only on the snowy, icy peaks at the head of the glacier cirques and cañons. His feeding grounds in spring are the snow sheets between the peaks, and in midsummer and autumn the glaciers. Many bold insects go mountaineering almost as soon as they are born, ascending the highest summits on the mild breezes that blow in from the sea every day during steady weather; but comparatively few of these adventurers find their way down or see a flower bed again. Getting tired and chilly, they alight on the snow fields and glaciers, attracted perhaps by the glare, take cold, and die. There they lie as if on a white cloth purposely outspread for them, and the dun sparrows find them a rich and varied repast requiring no pursuit,—bees and butterflies on ice, and many spicy beetles, a perpetual feast, on tables big for guests so small, and in vast banqueting halls ventilated by cool breezes that ruffle the feathers of the fairy brownies. Happy fellows, no rivals come to dispute possession with them. No other birds, not even hawks, as far as I have noticed, live so high. They see people so seldom, they flutter around the explorer with the liveliest curiosity, and come down a little way, sometimes nearly a mile, to meet him and conduct him into their icy homes.

When I was exploring the Merced group, climbing up the grand cañon between the Merced and Red mountains into the fountain amphi-theatre of an ancient glacier, just as I was approaching the small active glacier that leans back in the shadow of Merced Mountain, a flock of twenty or thirty of these little birds, the first I had seen, came down the cañon to meet me, flying low, straight toward me as if they meant to fly in my face. Instead of attacking me or passing by, they circled round my head, chirping and fluttering for a minute or two, then turned and escorted me up the cañon, alighting on the nearest rocks on either hand, and flying ahead a few yards at a time to keep even with me.

I have not discovered their winter quarters. Probably they are in the desert ranges to the eastward, for I never saw any of them in Yosemite, the winter refuge of so many of the mountain birds.

Humming-birds are among the best and most conspicuous of the mountaineers, flashing their ruby throats in countless wild gardens far up the higher slopes, where they would be least expected. All one has to do to enjoy the company of these mountain-loving midgets is to display a showy blanket or handkerchief.

The arctic bluebird is another delightful mountaineer, singing a wild, cheery song and "carrying the sky on his back" over all the gray ridges and domes of the subalpine region.

A fine, hearty, good-natured lot of woodpeckers dwell in the Park, and keep it lively all the year round. Among the most notable of these are the magnificent log cock (*Ceophlus pileatus*), the prince of Sierra woodpeckers, and only second in rank, as far as I know, of all the woodpeckers of the world; the Lewis woodpecker, large, black, glossy, that flaps and flies like a crow, does but little hammering, and feeds in great part on wild cherries and berries; and the carpenter, who stores up great quantities of acorns in the bark of trees for winter use. The last-named species is a beautiful bird, and far more common than the others. In the woods of the West he represents the Eastern red-head. Bright, cheerful, industrious, not in the least shy, the carpenters give delightful animation to the open Sierra forests at a height of from three thousand to fifty-five hundred feet, especially in autumn, when the acorns are ripe. Then no squirrel works harder at his pine-nut harvest than these woodpeckers at their acorn harvest, drilling holes in the thick, corky bark of the yellow pine and incense cedar, in which to store the crop for winter use,—a hole for each acorn, so nicely adjusted as to size that when the acorn, point foremost, is driven in, it fits so well that it cannot be drawn out without digging around it. Each acorn is thus carefully stored in a dry bin, perfectly protected from the weather,—a most laborious method of stowing away a crop, a granary for each kernel. Yet the birds seem never to weary at the work, but go on so diligently that they seem determined to save every acorn in the grove. They are never seen eating acorns at the time they are storing them, and it is commonly believed that they never eat them or intend to eat them, but that the wise birds store them and protect them from the depredations of squirrels and jays, solely for the sake of the worms they are supposed to contain. And because these worms are too small for use at the time the acorns drop, they are shut up like lean calves and steers, each in a separate stall with abundance of food, to grow big and fat by the time they will be most wanted, that is, in winter, when insects are scarce and stall-fed worms most valuable. So these woodpeckers are supposed to be a sort of cattle-raisers, each with a drove of thousands, rivaling the ants that raise grain and keep herds of plant lice for milk cows. Needless to say the story is not true, though some naturalists, even, believe it. When Emerson was in the Park, having heard the worm story and seen the great pines plugged full of acorns, he asked (just to pump me, I suppose), "Why do the woodpeckers take the trouble to put acorns into the bark of the trees?" "For the same reason," I replied, "that bees store honey and squirrels nuts." "But they tell me, Mr. Muir, that woodpeckers don't eat acorns." "Yes, they do," I said, "I have seen them eating them. During snowstorms they seem to eat little besides acorns. I have repeatedly interrupted them at their meals, and seen the perfectly sound, half-eaten acorns. They eat them in the shell as some people eat eggs." "But what about the worms?" "I suppose," I said, "that when they come to a wormy one they eat both worm and acorn. Anyhow, they eat the sound ones when they can't find anything they like better, and from the time they store them until they are used they guard them, and woe to the squirrel or jay caught stealing." Indians, in times of scarcity, frequently resort to these stores and chop them out with hatchets; a bushel or more may be gathered from a single cedar or pine.

The common robin, with all his familiar notes and gestures, is found nearly everywhere throughout the Park,—in shady dells beneath dogwoods and maples, along the flowery banks of the streams, tripping daintily about the margins of meadows in the fir and pine woods, and far beyond on the shores of glacier lakes and the slopes of the peaks. How admirable the constitution and temper of this cheery, graceful bird, keeping glad health over so vast and varied a range. In all America he is at home, flying from plains to mountains, up and down, north and south, away and back, with the seasons and supply of food. Oftentimes in the High Sierra, as you wander through the solemn woods, awestricken and silent, you will hear the reassuring voice of this fellow wanderer ringing out sweet and clear as if saying, "Fear not, fear not. Only love is here." In the severest solitudes he seems as happy as in gardens and apple orchards.

The robins enter the Park as soon as the snow melts, and go on up the mountains, gradually higher, with the opening flowers, until the topmost glacier meadows are reached in June and July. After the short summer is done, they descend like most other summer visitors in concord with the weather, keeping out of the first heavy snows as much as possible, while lingering among the frost-nipped wild cherries on the slopes just below the glacier meadows.

Thence they go to the lower slopes of the forest region, compelled to make haste at times by heavy all-day storms, picking up seeds or benumbed insects by the way; and at last all, save a few that winter in Yosemite valleys, arrive in the vineyards and orchards and stubble-fields of the lowlands in November, picking up fallen fruit and grain, and awakening old-time memories among the white-headed pioneers, who cannot fail to recognize the influence of so homelike a bird. They are then in flocks of hundreds, and make their way into the gardens of towns as well as into the parks and fields and orchards about the bay of San Francisco, where many of the wanderers are shot for sport and the morsel of meat on their breasts. Man then seems a beast of prey. Not even genuine piety can make the robin-killer quite respectable. Saturday is the great slaughter day in the bay region. Then the city pot-hunters, with a rag-tag of boys, go forth to kill, kept in countenance by a sprinkling of regular sportsmen arrayed in self-conscious majesty and leggins, leading dogs and carrying hammerless, breech-loading guns of famous makers. Over the fine landscapes the killing goes forward with shameful enthusiasm. After escaping countless dangers, thousands fall, big bagfuls are gathered, many are left wounded to die slowly, no Red Cross Society to help them. Next day, Sunday, the blood and leggins vanish from the most devout of the bird-butchers, who go to church, carrying gold-headed canes instead of guns. After hymns, prayers, and sermon they go home to feast, to put God's song birds to use, put them in their dinners instead of in their hearts, eat them, and suck the pitiful little drumsticks. It is only race living on race, to be sure, but Christians singing Divine Love need not be driven to such straits while wheat and apples grow and the shops are full of dead cattle. Song birds for food! Compared with this, making kindlings of pianos and violins would be pious economy.

The larks come in large flocks from the hills and mountains in the fall, and are slaughtered as ruthlessly as the robins. Fortunately, most of our song birds keep back in leafy hidings, and are comparatively inaccessible.

The water ouzel, in his rocky home amid foaming waters, seldom sees a gun, and of all the singers I like him the best. He is a plainly dressed little bird, about the size of a robin, with short, crisp, but rather broad wings, and a tail of moderate length, slanted up, giving him, with his nodding, bobbing manners, a wrennish look. He is usually seen fluttering about in the spray of falls and the rapid cascading portions of the main branches of the rivers. These are his favorite haunts; but he is often seen also on comparatively level reaches and occasionally on the shores of mountain lakes, especially at the beginning of winter, when heavy snowfalls have blurred the streams with sludge. Though not a water-bird in structure, he gets his living in the water, and is never seen away from the immediate margin of streams. He dives fearlessly into rough, boiling eddies and rapids to feed at the bottom, flying under water seemingly as easily as in the air. Sometimes he wades in shallow places, thrusting his head under from time to time in a nodding, frisky way that is sure to attract attention. His flight is a solid whir of wing-beats like that of a partridge, and in going from place to place along his favorite string of rapids he follows the windings of the stream, and usually alights on some rock or snag on the bank or out in the current, or rarely on the dry limb of an overhanging tree, perching like a tree bird when it suits his convenience. He has the oddest, neatest manners imaginable, and all his gestures as he flits about in the wild, dashing waters bespeak the utmost cheerfulness and confidence. He sings both winter and summer, in all sorts of weather,—a sweet, fluty melody, rather low, and much less keen and accentuated than from the brisk vigor of his movements one would be led to expect.

How romantic and beautiful is the life of this brave little singer on the wild mountain streams, building his round bossy nest of moss by the side of a rapid or fall, where it is sprinkled and kept fresh and green by the spray! No wonder he sings well, since all the air about him is music; every breath he draws is part of a song, and he gets his first music lessons before he is born; for the eggs vibrate in time with the tones of the waterfalls. Bird and stream are inseparable, songful and wild, gentle and strong,—the bird ever in danger in the midst of the stream's mad whirlpools, yet seemingly immortal. And so I might go on, writing words, words, words; but to what purpose? Go see him and love him, and through him as through a window look into Nature's warm heart.

VIII

THE FOUNTAINS AND STREAMS OF THE YOSEMITE NATIONAL PARK

"Come let's to the fields, the meads, and the mountains,
The forests invite us, the streams and the fountains."
Carlyle, Translations, *vol. iii.*

The joyful, songful streams of the Sierra are among the most famous and interesting in the world, and draw the admiring traveler on and on through their wonderful cañons, year after year, unwearied. After long wanderings with them, tracing them to their fountains, learning their history and the forms they take in their wild works and ways throughout the different seasons of the year, we may then view them together in one magnificent show, outspread over all the range like embroidery, their silvery branches interlacing on a thousand mountains, singing their way home to the sea: the small rills, with hard roads to travel, dropping from ledge to ledge, pool to pool, like chains of sweet-toned bells, slipping gently over beds of pebbles and sand, resting in lakes, shining, spangling, shimmering, lapping the shores with whispering ripples, and shaking over-leaning bushes and grass; the larger streams and rivers in the cañons displaying noble purity and beauty with ungovernable energy, rushing down smooth inclines in wide foamy sheets fold over fold, springing up here and there in magnificent whirls, scattering crisp clashing spray for the sunbeams to iris, bursting with hoarse reverberating roar through rugged gorges and boulder dams, booming in falls, gliding, glancing with cool soothing murmuring, through long forested reaches richly embowered,—filling the grand cañons with glorious song, and giving life to all the landscape.

The present rivers of the Sierra are still young, and have made but little mark as yet on the grand cañons prepared for them by the ancient glaciers. Only a very short geological time ago they all lay buried beneath the glaciers they drained, singing in low smothered or silvery ringing tones in crystal channels, while the summer weather melted the ice and snow of the surface or gave showers. At first only in warm weather was any part of these buried rivers displayed in the light of day; for as soon as frost prevailed the surface rills vanished, though the streams beneath the ice and in the body of it flowed on all the year.

When, toward the close of the glacial period, the ice mantle began to shrink and recede from the lowlands, the lower portions of the rivers were developed, issuing from cavelike openings on the melting margin and growing longer as the ice withdrew; while for many a century the tributaries and upper portions of the trunks remained covered. In the fullness of time these also were set free in the sunshine, to take their places in the newborn landscapes; each tributary with its smaller branches being gradually developed like the main trunks, as the climatic changes went on. At first all of them were muddy with glacial detritus, and they became clear only after the glaciers they drained had receded beyond lake basins in which the sediments were dropped.

This early history is clearly explained by the present rivers of southeastern Alaska. Of those draining glaciers that discharge into arms of the sea, only the rills on the surface of the ice, and upboiling, eddying, turbid currents in the tide water in front of the terminal ice wall, are visible. Where glaciers, in the first stage of decadence, have receded from the shore, short sections of the trunks of the rivers that are to take their places may be seen rushing out from caverns and tunnels in the melting front,—rough, roaring, detritus-laden torrents, foaming and tumbling over outspread terminal moraines to the sea, perhaps without a single bush or flower to brighten their raw, shifting banks. Again, in some of the warmer cañons and valleys from which the trunk glaciers have been melted, the main trunks of the rivers are well developed, and their banks planted with fine forests, while their upper branches, lying high on the snowy mountains, are still buried beneath shrinking residual glaciers; illustrating every state of development, from icy darkness to light, and from muddiness to crystal clearness.

Now that the hard grinding sculpture work of the glacial period is done, the whole bright band of Sierra rivers run clear all the year, except when the snow is melting fast in the warm spring weather, and during extraordinary winter floods and the heavy thunderstorms of summer called cloud-bursts. Even then they are not muddy above the foothill mining region, unless the moraines have been loosened and the vegetation destroyed by sheep; for the rocks of the upper basins are clean, and the most able streams find but little to carry save the spoils of the forests,—trees, branches, flakes of bark, cones, leaves, pollen dust, etc.,—with scales of mica, sand grains, and boulders, which are rolled along the bottom of the steep parts of the main channels. Short sections of a few of the highest tributaries heading in glaciers are of course turbid with finely ground rock mud, but this is dropped in the first lakes they enter.

On the northern part of the range, mantled with porous fissured volcanic rocks, the fountain waters sink and flow below the surface for considerable distances, groping their way in the dark like the draining streams of glaciers, and at last bursting forth in big generous springs, filtered and cool and exquisitely clear. Some of the largest look like lakes, their waters welling straight up from the bottom of deep rock basins in quiet massive volume giving rise to young rivers. Others issue from horizontal clefts in sheer bluffs, with loud tumultuous roaring that may be heard half a mile or more. Magnificent examples of these great northern spring fountains, twenty or thirty feet deep and ten to nearly a hundred yards wide, abound on the main branches of the Feather, Pitt, McCloud, and Fall rivers.

The springs of the Yosemite Park, and the high Sierra in general, though many times more numerous, are comparatively small, oozing from moraines and snowbanks in thin, flat irregular currents which remain on the surface or near it, the rocks of the south half of the range being mostly flawless impervious granite; and since granite is but slightly soluble, the streams are particularly pure. Nevertheless, though they are all clear, and in the upper and main central forest regions delightfully lively and cool, they vary somewhat in color and taste as well as temperature, on account of differences, however slight, in exposure, and in the rocks and vegetation with which they come in contact. Some are more exposed than others to winds and sunshine in their falls and thin plumelike cascades; the amount of dashing, mixing, and airing the waters of each receive varies considerably; and there is always more or less variety in the kind and quantity of the vegetation they flow through, and in the time they lie in shady or sunny lakes and bogs.

The water of one of the branches of the north fork of Owens River, near the southeastern boundary of the Park, at an elevation of ninety-five hundred feet above the sea, is the best I ever found. It is not only delightfully cool and bright, but brisk, sparkling, exhilarating, and so positively delicious to the taste that a party of friends I led to it twenty-five years ago still praise it, and refer to it as "that wonderful champagne water;" though, comparatively, the finest wine is a coarse and vulgar drink. The party camped about a week in a pine grove on the edge of a little round sedgy meadow through which the stream ran bank full, and drank its icy water on frosty mornings, before breakfast, and at night about as eagerly as in the heat of the day; lying down and taking massy draughts direct from the brimming flood, lest the touch of a cup might disturb its celestial flavor. On one of my excursions I took pains to trace this stream to its head springs. It is mostly derived from snow that lies in heavy drifts and avalanche heaps on or near the axis of the range. It flows first in flat sheets over coarse sand or shingle derived from a granite ridge and the metamorphic slates of Red Mountain. Then, gathering its many small branches, it runs through beds of moraine material, and a series of lakelets and meadows and frosty juicy bogs bordered with heathworts and linked together by short bouldery reaches. Below these, growing strong with tribute drawn from many a snowy fountain on either side, the glad stream goes dashing and swirling through clumps of the white-barked pine, and tangled willow and alder thickets enriched by the fragrant herbaceous vegetation usually found about them. And just above the level camp meadow it is chafed and churned and beaten white over and over again in crossing a talus of big earthquake boulders, giving it a very thorough airing. But to what the peculiar indefinable excellence of this water is due I don't know; for other streams in adjacent cañons are aired in about the same way, and draw traces of minerals and plant essences from similar sources. The best mineral water yet discovered in the Park flows from the Tuolumne soda springs, on the north side of the Big Meadow. Mountaineers like it and ascribe every healing virtue to it, but in no way can any of these waters be compared with the Owens River champagne.

It is a curious fact that the waters of some of the Sierra lakes and streams are invisible, or nearly so, under certain weather conditions. This is noticed by mountaineers, hunters, and prospectors, wide-awake, sharp-eyed observers, little likely to be fooled by fine whims. One of these mountain men, whom I had nursed while a broken leg was mending, always gratefully reported the wonders he found. One, returning from a trip on the head waters of the Tuolumne, he came running eagerly, crying: "Muir, I've found the queerest lake in the mountains! It's high up where nothing grows; and when it isn't shiny you can't see it, and you walk right into it as if there was nothing there. The first you know of that lake you are in it, and get tripped up by the water, and hear the splash." The waters of Illilouette Creek are nearly invisible in the autumn; so that, in following the channel, jumping from boulder to boulder after a shower, you will frequently drag your feet in the apparently surfaceless pools.

Excepting a few low, warm slopes, fountain snow usually covers all the Yosemite Park from November or December to May, most of it until June or July, while on the coolest parts of the north slopes of the mountains, at a height of eleven to thirteen thousand feet, it is perpetual. It seldom lies at a greater depth than two or three feet on the lower margin, ten feet over the middle forested region, or fifteen to twenty feet in the shadowy cañons and cirques among the peaks of the Summit, except where it is drifted, or piled in avalanche heaps at the foot of long converging slopes to form perennial fountains.

The first crop of snow crystals that whitens the mountains and refreshes the streams usually falls in September or October, in the midst of charming Indian summer weather, often while the goldenrods and gentians are in their prime; but these Indian summer snows, like some of the late ones that bury the June gardens, vanish in a day or two, and garden work goes on with accelerated speed. The grand winter storms that load the mountains with enduring fountain snow seldom set in before the end of November. The fertile clouds, descending, glide about and hover in brooding silence, as if thoughtfully examining the forests and streams with reference to the work before them; then small flakes or single crystals appear, glinting and swirling in zigzags and spirals; and soon the thronging feathery masses fill the sky and make darkness like night, hurrying wandering mountaineers to their winter quarters. The first fall is usually about two to four feet deep. Then, with intervals of bright weather, not very cold, storm succeeds storm, heaping snow on snow, until from thirty to fifty or sixty feet has fallen; but on account of heavy settling and compacting, and the waste from evaporation and melting, the depth in the middle region, as stated above, rarely exceeds ten feet. Evaporation never wholly ceases, even in the coldest weather, and the sunshine between storms melts the surface more or less. Waste from melting also goes on at the bottom from summer heat stored in the rocks, as is shown by the rise of the streams after the first general storm, and their steady sustained flow all winter.

In the deep sugar-pine and silver-fir woods, up to a height of eight thousand feet, most of the snow lies where it falls, in one smooth universal fountain, until set free in the streams. But in the lighter forests of the two-leaved pine, and on the bleak slopes above the timber line, there is much wild drifting during storms accompanied by high winds, and for a day or two after they have fallen, when the temperature is low, and the snow dry and dusty. Then the trees, bending in the darkening blast, roar like feeding lions; the frozen lakes are buried; so also are the streams, which now flow in dark tunnels, as if another glacial period had come. On high ridges, where the winds have a free sweep, magnificent overcurling cornices are formed, which, with the avalanche piles, last as fountains almost all summer; and when an exceptionally high wind is blowing from the north, the snow, rolled, drifted, and ground to dust, is driven up the converging northern slopes of the peaks and sent flying for miles in the form of bright wavering banners, displayed in wonderful clearness and beauty against the sky.

The greatest storms, however, are usually followed by a deep, peculiar silence, especially profound and solemn in the forests; and the noble trees stand hushed and motionless, as if under a spell, until the morning sunbeams begin to sift through their laden spires. Then the snow, shifting and falling from the top branches, strikes the lower ones in succession, and dislodges bossy masses all the way down. Thus each tree is enveloped in a hollow conical avalanche of fairy fineness, silvery white, irised on the outside; while the relieved branches spring up and wave with startling effect in the general stillness, as if moving of their own volition. These beautiful tree avalanches, hundreds of which may be seen falling at once on fine mornings after storms, pile their snow in raised rings around corresponding hollows beneath the trees, making the forest mantle somewhat irregular, but without greatly influencing its duration and the flow of the streams.

The large storm avalanches are most abundant on the Summit peaks of the range. They descend the broad, steep slopes, as well as narrow gorges and couloirs, with grand roaring and booming, and glide in graceful curves out on the glaciers they so bountifully feed.

Down in the main cañons of the middle region broad masses are launched over the brows of cliffs three or four thousand feet high, which, worn to dust by friction in falling so far through the air, oftentimes hang for a minute or two in front of the tremendous precipices like gauzy half-transparent veils, gloriously beautiful when the sun is shining through them. Most of the cañon avalanches, however, flow in regular channels, like the cascades of tributary streams. When the snow first gives way on the upper slopes of their basins a dull muffled rush and rumble is heard, which, increasing with heavy deliberation, seems to draw rapidly nearer with appalling intensity of tone. Presently the wild floods comes in sight, bounding out over bosses and sheer places, leaping from bench to bench, spreading and narrowing and throwing off clouds of whirling diamond dust like a majestic foamy cataract. Compared with cascades and falls, avalanches are short-lived, and the sharp clashing sounds so common in dashing water are usually wanting; but in their deep thunder tones and pearly purple-tinged whiteness, and in dress, gait, gestures, and general behavior, they are much alike.

Besides these common storm avalanches there are two other kinds, the annual and the century, which still further enrich the scenery, though their influence on fountains is comparatively small. Annual avalanches are composed of heavy compacted snow which has been subjected to frequent alternations of frost and thaw. They are developed on cañon and mountain sides, the greater number of them, at elevations of from nine to ten thousand feet, where the slopes are so inclined that the dry snows of winter accumulate and hold fast until the spring thaws sap their foundations and make them slippery. Then away in grand style go the ponderous icy masses, adorned with crystalline spray without any cloudy snow dust; some of the largest descending more than a mile with even, sustained energy and directness like thunderbolts. The grand century avalanches, that mow wide swaths through the upper forests, occur on shady mountain sides about ten to twelve thousand feet high, where, under ordinary conditions, the snow accumulated from winter to winter lies at rest for many years, allowing trees fifty to a hundred feet high to grow undisturbed on the slopes below them. On their way through the forests they usually make a clean sweep, stripping off the soil as well as the trees, clearing paths two or three hundred yards wide from the timber line to the glacier meadows, and piling the uprooted trees, head downward, in windrows along the sides like lateral moraines. Scars and broken branches on the standing trees bordering the gaps record the side depth of the overwhelming flood; and when we come to count the annual wood rings of the uprooted trees, we learn that some of these colossal avalanches occur only once in about a century, or even at still wider intervals.

Few mountaineers go far enough, during the snowy months, to see many avalanches, and fewer still know the thrilling exhilaration of riding on them. In all my wild mountaineering I have enjoyed only one avalanche ride; and the start was so sudden, and the end came so soon, I thought but little of the danger that goes with this sort of travel, though one thinks fast at such times. One calm, bright morning in Yosemite, after a hearty storm had given three or four feet of fresh snow to the mountains, being eager to see as many avalanches as possible, and gain wide views of the peaks and forests arrayed in their new robes, before the sunshine had time to change or rearrange them, I set out early to climb by a side cañon to the top of a commanding ridge a little over three thousand feet above the valley. On account of the looseness of the snow that blocked the cañon I knew the climb would be trying, and estimated it might require three or four hours. But it proved far more difficult than I had foreseen. Most of the way I sank waist-deep, in some places almost out of sight; and after spending the day to within half an hour of sundown in this loose, baffling snow work, I was still several hundred feet below the summit. Then my hopes were reduced to getting up in time for the sunset, and a quick, sparkling home-going beneath the stars. But I was not to get top views of any sort that day; for deep trampling near the cañon head, where the snow was strained, started an avalanche, and I was swished back down to the foot of the cañon as if by enchantment. The plodding, wallowing ascent of about a mile had taken all day, the undoing descent perhaps a minute.

When the snow suddenly gave way, I instinctively threw myself on my back and spread my arms, to try to keep from sinking. Fortunately, though the grade of the cañon was steep, it was not interrupted by step levels or precipices big enough to cause outbounding or free plunging. On no part of the rush was I buried. I was only moderately imbedded on the surface or a little below it, and covered with a hissing back-streaming veil of dusty snow particles; and as the whole mass beneath or about me joined in the flight I felt no friction, though tossed here and there, and lurched from side to side. And when the torrent swedged and came to rest, I found myself on the top of the crumpled pile, without a single bruise or scar. Hawthorne says that steam has spiritualized travel, notwithstanding the smoke, friction, smells, and clatter of boat and rail riding. This flight in a milky way of snow flowers was the most spiritual of all my travels; and, after many years, the mere thought of it is still an exhilaration.

In the spring, after all the avalanches are down and the snow is melting fast, it is glorious to hear the streams sing out on the mountains. Every fountain swelling, countless rills hurry together to the rivers at the call of the sun,— beginning to run and sing soon after sunrise, increasing until toward sundown, then gradually failing through the cold frosty hours of the night. Thus the volume of the upper rivers, even in flood time, is nearly doubled during the day, rising and falling as regularly as the tides of the sea. At the height of flood, in the warmest June weather, they seem fairly to shout for joy, and clash their upleaping waters together like clapping of hands; racing down the cañons with white manes flying in glorious exuberance of strength, compelling huge sleeping boulders to wake up and join in the dance and song to swell their chorus.

Then the plants also are in flood; the hidden sap singing into leaf and flower, responding as faithfully to the call of the sun as the streams from the snow, gathering along the outspread roots like rills in their channels on the mountains, rushing up the stems of herb and tree, swirling in their myriad cells like streams in potholes, spreading along the branches and breaking into foamy bloom, while fragrance, like a finer music, rises and flows with the winds.

About the same may be said of the spring gladness of blood when the red streams surge and sing in accord with the swelling plants and rivers, inclining animals and everybody to travel in hurrahing crowds like floods, while exhilarating melody in color and fragrance, form and motion, flows to the heart through all the quickening senses.

In early summer the streams are in bright prime, running crystal clear, deep and full, but not overflowing their banks,—about as deep through the night as the day, the variation so marked in spring being now too slight to be noticed. Nearly all the weather is cloudless sunshine, and everything is at its brightest,—lake, river, garden, and forest, with all their warm, throbbing life. Most of the plants are in full leaf and flower; the blessed ousels have built their mossy huts, and are now singing their sweetest song on spray-sprinkled ledges beside the waterfalls.

In tranquil, mellow autumn, when the year's work is about done, when the fruits are ripe, birds and seeds out of their nests, and all the landscape is glowing like a benevolent countenance at rest, then the streams are at their lowest ebb,—their wild rejoicing soothed to thoughtful calm. All the smaller tributaries whose branches do not reach back to the perennial fountains of the Summit peaks shrink to whispering, tinkling currents. The snow of their basins gone, they are now fed only by small moraine springs, whose waters are mostly evaporated in passing over warm pavements, and in feeling their way from pool to pool through the midst of boulders and sand. Even the main streams are so low they may be easily forded, and their grand falls and cascades, now gentle and approachable, have waned to sheets and webs of embroidery, falling fold over fold in new and ever changing beauty.

Two of the most songful of the rivers, the Tuolumne and Merced, water nearly all the Park, spreading their branches far and wide, like broad-headed oaks; and the highest branches of each draw their sources from one and the same foundation on Mount Lyell, at an elevation of about thirteen thousand feet above the sea. The crest of the mountain, against which the head of the glacier rests, is worn to a thin blade full of joints, through which a part of the glacial water flows southward, giving rise to the highest trickling affluents of the Merced; while the main drainage, flowing northward, gives rise to those of the Tuolumne. After diverging for a distance of ten or twelve miles, these twin rivers flow in a general westerly direction, descending rapidly for the first thirty miles, and rushing in glorious apron cascades and falls from one Yosemite valley to another. Below the Yosemites they descend in gray rapids and swirling, swaying reaches, through the chaparral-clad cañons of the foothills and across the golden California plain, to their confluence with the San Joaquin, where, after all their long wanderings, they are only about ten miles apart.

The main cañons are from fifty to seventy miles long, and from two to four thousand feet deep, carved in the solid flank of the range. Though rough in some places and hard to travel, they are the most delightful of roads, leading through the grandest scenery, full of life and motion, and offering most telling lessons in earth sculpture. The walls, far from being unbroken, featureless cliffs, seem like ranges of separate mountains, so deep and varied is their sculpture; rising in lordly domes, towers, round-browed outstanding headlands, and clustering spires, with dark, shadowy side cañons between. But, however wonderful in height and mass and fineness of finish, no anomalous curiosities are presented, no "freaks of nature." All stand related in delicate rhythm, a grand glacial rock song.

Among the interesting and influential of the secondary features of cañon scenery are the great avalanche taluses, that lean against the walls at intervals of a mile or two. In the middle Yosemite region they are usually from three to five hundred feet high, and are made up of huge, angular, well-preserved, unshifting boulders, overgrown with gray lichens, trees shrubs, and delicate flowering plants. Some of the largest of the boulders are forty or fifty feet cube, weighing from five to ten thousand tons; and where the cleavage joints of the granite are exceptionally wide apart a few blocks may be found nearly a hundred feet in diameter. These wonderful boulder piles are distributed throughout all the cañons of the range, completely choking them in some of the narrower portions, and no mountaineer will be likely to forget the savage roughness of the roads they make. Even the swift, overbearing rivers, accustomed to sweep everything out of their way, are in some places bridled and held in check by them. Foaming, roaring, in glorious majesty of flood, rushing off long rumbling trains of ponderous blocks without apparent effort, they are not able to move the largest, which, withstanding all assaults for centuries, are left at rest in the channels like islands, with gardens on their tops, fringed with foam below, with flowers above.

On some points concerning the origin of these taluses I was long in doubt. Plainly enough they were derived from the cliffs above them, the size of each talus being approximately measured by a scar on the wall, the rough angular surface of which contrasts with the rounded, glaciated, unfractured parts. I saw also that, instead of being slowly accumulated material, weathered off, boulder by boulder, in the ordinary way, almost every talus had been formed suddenly, in a single avalanche, and had not been increased in size during the last three or four centuries; for trees three or four hundred years old were growing on them, some standing at the top close to the wall, without a bruise or broken branch, showing that scarcely a single boulder had fallen among them since they were planted. Furthermore, all the taluses throughout the range seemed, by the trees and lichens growing on them, to be of the same age. All the phenomena pointed straight to a grand ancient earthquake. But I left the question open for years, and went on from cañon to cañon, observing again and again; measuring the heights of taluses throughout the range on both flanks, and the variations in the angles of their surface slopes; studying the way their boulders were assorted and related and brought to rest, and the cleavage joints of the cliffs from whence they were derived, cautious about making up my mind. Only after I had seen one made did all doubt as to their formation vanish.

In Yosemite Valley, one morning about two o'clock, I was aroused by an earthquake; and though I had never before enjoyed a storm of this sort, the strange, wild thrilling motion and rumbling could not be mistaken, and I ran out of my cabin, near the Sentinel Rock, both glad and frightened, shouting, "A noble earthquake!" feeling sure I was going to learn something. The shocks were so violent and varied, and succeeded one another so closely, one had to balance in walking as if on the deck of a ship among the waves, and it seemed impossible the high cliffs should escape being shattered. In particular, I feared that the sheer-fronted Sentinel Rock, which rises to a height of three thousand feet, would be shaken down, and I took shelter back of a big pine, hoping I might be protected from outbounding boulders, should any come so far. I was now convinced that an earthquake had been the maker of the taluses, and positive proof soon came. It was a calm moonlight night, and no sound was heard for the first minute or two save a low muffled underground rumbling and a slight rustling of the agitated trees, as if, in wrestling with the mountains, Nature were holding her breath. Then, suddenly, out of the strange silence and strange motion there came a tremendous roar. The Eagle Rock, a short distance up the valley, had given way, and I saw it falling in thousands of the great boulders I had been studying so long, pouring to the valley floor in a free curve luminous from friction, making a terribly sublime and beautiful spectacle,—an arc of the fifteen hundred feet span, as true in form and as steady as a rainbow, in the midst of the stupendous roaring rock storm. The sound was inconceivably deep and broad and earnest, as if the whole earth, like a living creature, had at last found a voice and were calling to her sister planets. It seemed to me that if all the thunder I ever heard were condensed into one roar it would not equal this rock roar at the birth of a mountain talus. Think, then, of the roar that arose to heaven when all the thousands of ancient cañon taluses throughout the length and breadth of the range were simultaneously given birth.

The main storm was soon over, and, eager to see the new-born talus, I ran up the valley in the moonlight and climbed it before the huge blocks, after their wild fiery flight, had come to complete rest. They were slowly settling into their places, chafing, grating against one another, groaning, and whispering; but no motion was visible except in a stream of small fragments pattering down the face of the cliff at the head of the talus. A cloud of dust particles, the smallest of the boulders, floated out across the whole breadth of the valley and formed a ceiling that lasted until after sunrise; and the air was loaded with the odor of crushed Douglas spruces, from a grove that had been mowed down and mashed like weeds.

Sauntering about to see what other changes had been made, I found the Indians in the middle of the valley, terribly frightened, of course, fearing the angry spirits of the rocks were trying to kill them, The few whites wintering in the valley were assembled in front of the old Hutchings Hotel, comparing notes and meditating flight to steadier ground, seemingly as sorely frightened as the Indians. It is always interesting to see people in dead earnest, from whatever cause, and earthquakes make everybody earnest. Shortly after sunrise, a low blunt muffled rumbling, like distant thunder, was followed by another series of shocks, which, though not nearly so severe as the first, made the cliffs and domes tremble like jelly, and the big pines and oaks thrill and swish and wave their branches with startling effect. Then the groups of talkers were suddenly hushed, and the solemnity on their faces was sublime. One in particular of these winter neighbors, a rather thoughtful, speculative man, with whom I had often conversed, was a firm believer in the cataclysmic origin of the valley; and I now jokingly remarked that his wild tumble-down-and-engulfment hypothesis might soon be proved, since these underground rumblings and shakings might be the forerunners of another Yosemite-making cataclysm, which would perhaps double the depth of the valley by swallowing the floor, leaving the ends of the wagon roads and trails three or four thousand feet in the air. Just then came the second series of shocks, and it was fine to see how awfully silent and solemn he became. His belief in the existence of a mysterious abyss, into which the suspended floor of the valley and all the domes and battlements of the walls might at any moment go roaring down, mightily troubled him. To cheer and tease him into another view of the case, I said: "Come, cheer up; smile a little and clap your hands, now that kind Mother Earth is trotting us on her knee to amuse us and make us good." But the well-meant joke seemed irreverent and utterly failed, as if only prayerful terror could rightly belong to the wild beauty-making business. Even after all the heavier shocks were over, I could do nothing to reassure him. On the contrary, he handed me the keys of his little store, and, with a companion of like mind, fled to the lowlands. In about a month he returned; but a sharp shock occurred that very day, which sent him flying again.

The rocks trembled more or less every day for over two months, and I kept a bucket of water on my table to learn what I could of the movements. The blunt thunder-tones in the depths of the mountains were usually followed by sudden jarring, horizontal thrusts from the northward, often succeeded by twisting, upjolting movements. Judging by its effects, this Yosemite, or Inyo earthquake, as it is sometimes called, was gentle as compared with the one that gave rise to the grand talus system of the range and did so much for the cañon scenery. Nature, usually so deliberate in her operations, then created, as we have seen, a new set of features, simply by giving the mountains a shake,—changing not only the high peaks and cliffs, but the streams. As soon as these rock avalanches fell every stream began to sing new songs; for in many places thousands of boulders were hurled into their channels, roughening and half damming them, compelling the waters to surge and roar in rapids where before they were gliding smoothly. Some of the streams were completely dammed, driftwood, leaves, etc., filling the interstices between the boulders, thus giving rise to lakes and level reaches; and these, again, after being gradually filled in, to smooth meadows, through which the streams now silently meander; while at the same time some of the taluses took the places of old meadows and groves. Thus rough places were made smooth, and smooth places rough. But on the whole, by what at first sight seemed pure confusion and ruin, the landscapes were enriched; for gradually every talus, however big the boulders composing it, was covered with groves and gardens, and made a finely proportioned and ornamental base for the sheer cliffs. In this beauty work, every boulder is prepared and measured and put in its place more thoughtfully than are the stones of temples. If for a moment you are inclined to regard these taluses as mere draggled, chaotic dumps, climb to the top of one of them, tie your mountain shoes firmly over the instep, and with braced nerves run down without any haggling, puttering hesitation, boldly jumping from boulder to boulder with even speed. You will then find your feet playing a tune, and quickly discover the music and poetry of rock piles,—a fine lesson; and all nature's wildness tells the same story. Storms of every sort, torrents, earthquakes, cataclysms, "convulsions of nature," etc., however mysterious and lawless at first sight they may seem, are only harmonious notes in the song of creation, varied expressions of God's love.

IX

THE SEQUOIA AND GENERAL GRANT NATIONAL PARKS

The Big Tree (*Sequoia gigantea*) is Nature's forest masterpiece, and, so far as I know, the greatest of living things. It belongs to an ancient stock, as its remains in old rocks show, and has a strange air of other days about it, a thoroughbred look inherited from the long ago—the auld lang syne of trees. Once the genus was common, and with many species flourished in the now desolate Arctic regions, in the interior of North America, and in Europe, but in long, eventful wanderings from climate to climate only two species have survived the hardships they had to encounter, the gigantea and sempervirens, the former now restricted to the western slopes of the Sierra, the other to the Coast Mountains, and both to California, excepting a few groves of Redwood which extend into Oregon. The Pacific Coast in general is the paradise of conifers. Here nearly all of them are giants, and display a beauty and magnificence unknown elsewhere. The climate is mild, the ground never freezes, and moisture and sunshine abound all the year. Nevertheless it is not easy to account for the colossal size of the Sequoias. The largest are about three hundred feet high and thirty feet in diameter. Who of all the dwellers of the plains and prairies and fertile home forests of round-headed oak and maple, hickory and elm, ever dreamed that earth could bear such growths,—trees that the familiar pines and firs seem to know nothing about, lonely, silent, serene, with a physiognomy almost godlike; and so old, thousands of them still living had already counted their years by tens of centuries when Columbus set sail from Spain and were in the vigor of youth or middle age when the star led the Chaldean sages to the infant Saviour's cradle! As far as man is concerned they are the same yesterday, to-day, and forever, emblems of permanence.

No description can give any adequate idea of their singular majesty, much less their beauty. Excepting the sugar-pine, most of their neighbors with pointed tops seem to be forever shouting Excelsior, while the Big Tree, though soaring above them all, seems satisfied, its rounded head, poised lightly as a cloud, giving no impression of trying to go higher. Only in youth does it show like other conifers a heavenward yearning, keenly aspiring with a long quick-growing top. Indeed the whole tree for the first century or two, or until a hundred to a hundred and fifty feet high, is arrowhead in form, and, compared with the solemn rigidity of age, is as sensitive to the wind as a squirrel tail. The lower branches are gradually dropped as it grows older, and the upper ones thinned out until comparatively few are left. These, however, are developed to great size, divide again and again, and terminate in bossy rounded masses of leafy branchlets, while the head becomes dome-shaped. Then poised in fullness of strength and beauty, stern and solemn in mien, it glows with eager, enthusiastic life, quivering to the tip of every leaf and branch and far-reaching root, calm as a granite dome, the first to feel the touch of the rosy beams of the morning, the last to bid the sun good-night.

Perfect specimens, unhurt by running fires or lightning, are singularly regular and symmetrical in general form, though not at all conventional, showing infinite variety in sure unity and harmony of plan. The immensely strong, stately shafts, with rich purplish brown bark, are free of limbs for a hundred and fifty feet or so, though dense tufts of sprays occur here and there, producing an ornamental effect, while long parallel furrows give a fluted columnar appearance. It shoots forth its limbs with equal boldness in every direction, showing no weather side. On the old trees the main branches are crooked and rugged, and strike rigidly outward mostly at right angles from the trunk, but there is always a certain measured restraint in their reach which keeps them within bounds. No other Sierra tree has foliage so densely massed or outline so finely, firmly drawn and so obediently subordinate to an ideal type. A particularly knotty, angular, ungovernable-looking branch, five to eight feet in diameter and perhaps a thousand years old, may occasionally be seen pushing out from the trunk as if determined to break across the bounds of the regular curve, but like all the others, as soon as the general outline is approached the huge limb dissolves into massy bosses of branchlets and sprays, as if the tree were growing beneath an invisible bell glass against the sides of which the branches were moulded, while many small, varied departures from the ideal form give the impression of freedom to grow as they like.

Except in picturesque old age, after being struck by lightning and broken by a thousand snowstorms, this regularity of form is one of the Big Tree's most distinguishing characteristics. Another is the simple sculptural beauty of the trunk and its great thickness as compared with its height and the width of the branches, many of them being from eight to ten feet in diameter at a height of two hundred feet from the ground, and seeming more like finely modeled and sculptured architectural columns than the stems of trees, while the great strong limbs are like rafters supporting the magnificent dome head.

The root system corresponds in magnitude with the other dimensions of the tree, forming a flat far-reaching spongy network two hundred feet or more in width without any taproot, and the instep is so grand and fine, so suggestive of endless strength, it is long ere the eye is released to look above it. The natural swell of the roots, though at first sight excessive, gives rise to buttresses no greater than are required for beauty as well as strength, as at once appears when you stand back far enough to see the whole tree in its true proportions. The fineness of the taper of the trunk is shown by its thickness at great heights—a diameter of ten feet at a height of two hundred being, as we have seen, not uncommon. Indeed the boles of but few trees hold their thickness as well as Sequoia. Resolute, consummate, determined in form, always beheld with wondering admiration, the Big Tree always seems unfamiliar, standing alone, unrelated, with peculiar physiognomy, awfully solemn and earnest. Nevertheless, there is nothing alien in its looks. The Madrona, clad in thin, smooth, red and yellow bark and big glossy leaves, seems, in the dark coniferous forests of Washington and Vancouver Island, like some lost wanderer from the magnolia groves of the South, while the Sequoia, with all its strangeness, seems more at home than any of its neighbors, holding the best right to the ground as the oldest, strongest inhabitant. One soon becomes acquainted with new species of pine and fir spruce as with friendly people, shaking their outstretched branches like shaking hands, and fondling their beautiful little ones; while the venerable aboriginal Sequoia, ancient of other days, keeps you at a distance, taking no notice of you, speaking only to the winds, thinking only of the sky, looking as strange in aspect and behavior among the neighboring trees as would the mastodon or hairy elephant among the homely bears and deer. Only the Sierra Juniper is at all like it, standing rigid and unconquerable on glacial pavements for thousands of years, grim, rusty, silent, uncommunicative, with an air of antiquity about as pronounced as that so characteristic of Sequoia.

The bark of full grown trees is from one to two feet thick, rich cinnamon brown, purplish on young trees and shady parts of the old, forming magnificent masses of color with the underbrush and beds of flowers. Toward the end of winter the trees themselves bloom while the snow is still eight or ten feet deep. The pistillate flowers are about three eighths of an inch long, pale green, and grow in countless thousands on the ends of the sprays. The staminate are still more abundant, pale yellow, a fourth of an inch long; and when the golden pollen is ripe they color the whole tree and dust the air and the ground far and near.

The cones are bright grass-green in color, about two and a half inches long, one and a half wide, and are made up of thirty or forty strong, closely packed, rhomboidal scales with four to eight seeds at the base of each. The seeds are extremely small and light, being only from an eighth to a fourth of an inch long and wide, including a filmy surrounding wing, which causes them to glint and waver in falling and enables the wind to carry them considerable distances from the tree.

The faint lisp of snowflakes as they alight is one of the smallest sounds mortal can hear. The sound of falling Sequoia seeds, even when they happen to strike on flat leaves or flakes of bark, is about as faint. Very different is the bumping and thudding of the falling cones. Most of them are cut off by the Douglas squirrel and stored for the sake of the seeds, small as they are. In the calm Indian summer these busy harvesters with ivory sickles go to work early in the morning, as soon as breakfast is over, and nearly all day the ripe cones fall in a steady pattering, bumping shower. Unless harvested in this way they discharge their seeds and remain on the trees for many years. In fruitful seasons the trees are fairly laden. On two small specimen branches one and a half and two inches in diameter I counted four hundred and eighty cones. No other California conifer produces nearly so many seeds, excepting perhaps its relative, the Redwood of the Coast Mountains. Millions are ripened annually by a single tree, and the product of one of the main groves in a fruitful year would suffice to plant all the mountain ranges of the world.

The dense tufted sprays make snug nesting places for birds, and in some of the loftiest, leafiest towers of verdure thousands of generations have been reared, the great solemn trees shedding off flocks of merry singers every year from nests, like the flocks of winged seeds from the cones.

The Big Tree keeps its youth far longer than any of its neighbors. Most silver firs are old in their second or third century, pines in their fourth or fifth, while the Big Tree growing beside them is still in the bloom of its youth, juvenile in every feature at the age of old pines, and cannot be said to attain anything like prime size and beauty before its fifteen hundredth year, or under favorable circumstances become old before its three thousandth. Many, no doubt, are much older than this. On one of the Kings River giants, thirty-five feet and eight inches in diameter exclusive of bark, I counted upwards of four thousand annual wood-rings, in which there was no trace of decay after all these centuries of mountain weather. There is no absolute limit to the existence of any tree. Their death is due to accidents, not, as of animals, to the wearing out of organs. Only the leaves die of old age, their fall is foretold in their structure; but the leaves are renewed every year and so also are the other essential organs—wood, roots, bark, buds. Most of the Sierra trees die of disease. Thus the magnificent silver firs are devoured by fungi, and comparatively few of them live to see their three hundredth birth year. But nothing hurts the Big Tree. I never saw one that was sick or showed the slightest sign of decay. It lives on through indefinite thousands of years until burned, blown down, undermined, or shattered by some tremendous lightning stroke. No ordinary bolt ever seriously hurts Sequoia. In all my walks I have seen only one that was thus killed outright. Lightning, though rare in the California lowlands, is common on the Sierra. Almost every day in June and July small thunderstorms refresh the main forest belt. Clouds like snowy mountains of marvelous beauty grow rapidly in the calm sky about midday and cast cooling shadows and showers that seldom last more than an hour. Nevertheless these brief, kind storms wound or kill a good many trees. I have seen silver firs two hundred feet high split into long peeled rails and slivers down to the roots, leaving not even a stump, the rails radiating like the spokes of a wheel from a hole in the ground where the tree stood. But the Sequoia, instead of being split and slivered, usually has forty or fifty feet of its brash knotty top smashed off in short chunks about the size of cord-wood, the beautiful rosy red ruins covering the ground in a circle a hundred feet wide or more. I never saw any that had been cut down to the ground or even to below the branches except one in the Stanislaus Grove, about twelve feet in diameter, the greater part of which was smashed to fragments, leaving only a leafless stump about seventy-five feet high. It is a curious fact that all the very old Sequoias have lost their heads by lightning. "All things come to him who waits." But of all living things Sequoia is perhaps the only one able to wait long enough to make sure of being struck by lightning. Thousands of years it stands ready and waiting, offering its head to every passing cloud as if inviting its fate, praying for heaven's fire as a blessing; and when at last the old head is off, another of the same shape immediately begins to grow on. Every bud and branch seems excited, like bees that have lost their queen, and tries hard to repair the damage. Branches that for many centuries have been growing out horizontally at once turn upward and all their branchlets arrange themselves with reference to a new top of the same peculiar curve as the old one. Even the small subordinate branches halfway down the trunk do their best to push up to the top and help in this curious head-making.

The great age of these noble trees is even more wonderful than their huge size, standing bravely up, millennium in, millennium out, to all that fortune may bring them, triumphant over tempest and fire and time, fruitful and beautiful, giving food and shelter to multitudes of small fleeting creatures dependent on their bounty. Other trees may claim to be about as large or as old: Australian Gums, Senegal Baobabs, Mexican Taxodiums, English Yews, and venerable Lebanon Cedars, trees of renown, some of which are from ten to thirty feet in diameter. We read of oaks that are supposed to have existed ever since the creation, but strange to say I can find no definite accounts of the age of any of these trees, but only estimates based on tradition and assumed average rates of growth. No other known tree approaches the Sequoia in grandeur, height and thickness being considered, and none as far as I know has looked down on so many centuries or opens such impressive and suggestive views into history. The majestic monument of the Kings River Forest is, as we have seen, fully four thousand years old, and measuring the rings of annual growth we find it was no less than twenty-seven feet in diameter at the beginning of the Christian era, while many observations lead me to expect the discovery of others ten or twenty centuries older. As to those of moderate age, there are thousands, mere youth as yet, that—

> *"Saw the light that shone*
> *On Mahomet's uplifted crescent,*
> *On many a royal gilded throne*
> *And deed forgotten in the present,*
> *. . . saw the age of sacred trees*
> *And Druid groves and mystic larches,*
> *And saw from forest domes like these*
> *The builder bring his Gothic arches."*

Great trees and groves used to be venerated as sacred monuments and halls of council and worship. But soon after the discovery of the Calaveras Grove one of the grandest trees was cut down for the sake of a stump! The laborious vandals had seen "the biggest tree in the world," then, forsooth, they must try to see the biggest stump and dance on it.

The growth in height for the first two centuries is usually at the rate of eight to ten inches a year. Of course all very large trees are old, but those equal in size may vary greatly in age on account of variations in soil, closeness or openness of growth, etc. Thus a tree about ten feet in diameter that grew on the side of a meadow was, according to my own count of the wood-rings, only two hundred and fifty-nine years old at the time it was felled, while another in the same grove, of almost exactly the same size but less favorably situated, was fourteen hundred and forty years old. The Calaveras tree cut for a dance floor was twenty-four feet in diameter and only thirteen hundred years old, another about the same size was a thousand years older.

The following Sequoia notes and measurements are copied from my notebooks:—

Diameter.		Height in Feet.	Age. Years.
Feet.	Inches.		
0	1 3-4	10	7
0	5	24	20
0	5	25	41
0	6	25	66
0	6	28 1-2	39
0	8	25	29
0	11	45	71
1	0	60	71
3	2	156	260
6	0	192	240
7	3	195	339
7	3	255	506
7	6	240	493
7	7	207	424
9	0	243	259
9	3	222	280
10	6		1440
12			1825[1]
15			2150[2]
24			1300
25			2300
35	8 inside bark		over 4000

[1] 16 feet in diameter at height of 200 feet.

[2] 27 feet in diameter at height of 200 feet.

Little, however, is to be learned in confused, hurried tourist trips, spending only a poor noisy hour in a branded grove with a guide. You should go looking and listening alone on long walks through the wild forests and groves in all the seasons of the year. In the spring the winds are balmy and sweet, blowing up and down over great beds of chaparral and through the woods now rich in softening balsam and rosin and the scent of steaming earth. The sky is mostly sunshine, oftentimes tempered by magnificent clouds, the breath of the sea built up into new mountain ranges, warm during the day, cool at night, good flower-opening weather. The young cones of the Big Trees are showing in clusters, their flower time already past, and here and there you may see the sprouting of their tiny seeds of the previous autumn, taking their first feeble hold of the ground and unpacking their tender whorls of cotyledon leaves. Then you will naturally be led on to consider their wonderful growth up and up through the mountain weather, now buried in snow bent and crinkled, now straightening in summer sunshine like uncoiling ferns, shooting eagerly aloft in youth's joyful prime, and towering serene and satisfied through countless years of calm and storm, the greatest of plants and all but immortal.

Under the huge trees up come the small plant people, putting forth fresh leaves and blossoming in such profusion that the hills and valleys would still seem gloriously rich and glad were all the grand trees away. By the side of melting snowbanks rise the crimson sarcodes, round-topped and massive as the Sequoias themselves, and beds of blue violets and larger yellow one with leaves curiously lobed; azalea and saxifrage, daisies and lilies on the mossy banks of the streams; and a little way back of them, beneath the trees and on sunny spots on the hills around the groves, wild rose and rubus, spiræa and ribes, mitella, tiarella, campanula, monardella, forget-me-not, etc., many of them as worthy of lore immortality as the famous Scotch daisy, wanting only a Burns to sing them home to all hearts.

In the midst of this glad plant work the birds are busy nesting, some singing at their work, some silent, others, especially the big pileated woodpeckers, about as noisy as backwoodsmen building their cabins. Then every bower in the groves is a bridal bower, the winds murmur softly overhead, the streams sing with the birds, while from far-off waterfalls and thunder-clouds come deep rolling organ notes.

In summer the days go by in almost constant brightness, cloudless sunshine pouring over the forest roof, while in the shady depths there is the subdued light of perpetual morning. The new leaves and cones are growing fast and make a grand show, seeds are ripening, young birds learning to fly, and with myriads of insects glad as birds keep the air whirling, joy in every wingbeat, their humming and singing blending with the gentle ah-ing of the winds; while at evening every thicket and grove is enchanted by the tranquil chirping of the blessed hylas, the sweetest and most peaceful of sounds, telling the very heart-joy of earth as it rolls through the heavens.

In the autumn the sighing of the winds is softer than ever, the gentle ah-ah-ing filling the sky with a fine universal mist of music, the birds have little to say, and there is no appreciable stir or rustling among the trees save that caused by the harvesting squirrels. Most of the seeds are ripe and away, those of the trees mottling the sunny air, glinting, glancing through the midst of the merry insect people, rocks and trees, everything alike drenched in gold light, heaven's colors coming down to the meadows and groves, making every leaf a romance, air, earth, and water in peace beyond thought, the great brooding days opening and closing in divine psalms of color.

Winter comes suddenly, arrayed in storms, though to mountaineers silky streamers on the peaks and the tones of the wind give sufficient warning. You hear strange whisperings among the tree-tops, as if the giants were taking counsel together. One after another, nodding and swaying, calling and replying, spreads the news, until all with one accord break forth into glorious song, welcoming the first grand snowstorm of the year, and looming up in the dim clouds and snowdrifts like lighthouse towers in flying scud and spray. Studying the behavior of the giants from some friendly shelter, you will see that even in the glow of their wildest enthusiasm, when the storm roars loudest, they never lose their god-like composure, never toss their arms or bow or wave like the pines, but only slowly, solemnly nod and sway, standing erect, making no sign of strife, none of rest, neither in alliance nor at war with the winds, too calmly, unconsciously noble and strong to strive with or bid defiance to anything. Owing to the density of the leafy branchlets and great breadth of head the Big Tree carries a much heavier load of snow than any of its neighbors, and after a storm, when the sky clears, the laden trees are a glorious spectacle, worth any amount of cold camping to see. Every bossy limb and crown is solid white, and the immense height of the giants becomes visible as the eye travels the white steps of the colossal tower, each relieved by a mass of blue shadow.

In midwinter the forest depths are as fresh and pure as the crevasses and caves of glaciers. Grouse, nuthatches, a few woodpeckers, and other hardy birds dwell in the groves all winter, and the squirrels may be seen every clear day frisking about, lively as ever, tunneling to their stores, never coming up empty-mouthed, dividing in the loose snow about as quickly as ducks in water, while storms and sunshine sing to each other.

One of the noblest and most beautiful of the late winter sights is the blossoming of the Big Tree like gigantic goldenrods and the sowing of their pollen over all the forest and the snow-covered ground—a most glorious view of Nature's immortal virility and flower-love.

One of my own best excursions among the Sequoias was made in the autumn of 1875, when I explored the then unknown or little known Sequoia region south of the Mariposa Grove for comprehensive views of the belt, and to learn what I could of the peculiar distribution of the species and its history in general. In particular I was anxious to try to find out whether it had ever been more widely distributed since the glacial period; what conditions favorable or otherwise were affecting it; what were its relations to climate, topography, soil, and the other trees growing with it, etc.;

and whether, as was generally supposed, the species was nearing extinction. I was already acquainted in a general way with the northern groves, but excepting some passing glimpses gained on excursions into the high Sierra about the head-waters of Kings and Kern rivers I had seen nothing of the south end of the belt.

Nearly all my mountaineering has been done on foot, carrying as little as possible, depending on camp-fires for warmth, that so I might be light and free to go wherever my studies might lead. On this Sequoia trip, which promised to be long, I was persuaded to take a small wild mule with me to carry provisions and a pair of blankets. The friendly owner of the animal, having noticed that I sometimes looked tired when I came down from the peaks to replenish my bread sack, assured me that his "little Brownie mule" was just what I wanted, tough as a knot, perfectly untirable, low and narrow, just right for squeezing through brush, able to climb like a chipmunk, jump from boulder to boulder like a wild sheep, and go anywhere a man could go. But tough as he was and accomplished as a climber, many a time in the course of our journey when he was jaded and hungry, wedged fast in rocks or struggling in chaparral like a fly in a spiderweb, his troubles were sad to see, and I wished he would leave me and find his way home alone.

We set out from Yosemite about the end of August, and our first camp was made in the well-known Mariposa Grove. Here and in the adjacent pine woods I spent nearly a week, carefully examining the boundaries of the grove for traces of its greater extension without finding any. Then I struck out into the majestic trackless forest to the south-eastward, hoping to find new groves or traces of old ones in the dense silver fir and pine woods about the head of Big Creek, where soil and climate seemed most favorable to their growth, but not a single tree or old monument of any sort came to light until I climbed the high rock called Wamellow by the Indians. Here I obtained telling views of the fertile forest-filled basin of the upper Fresno. Innumerable spires of the noble yellow pine were displayed rising above one another on the braided slopes, and yet nobler sugar pines with superb arms outstretched in the rich autumn light, while away toward the southwest, on the verge of the glowing horizon, I discovered the majestic dome-like crowns of Big Trees towering high over all, singly and in close grove congregations. There is something wonderfully attractive in this king tree, even when beheld from afar, that draws us to it with indescribable enthusiasm; its superior height and massive smoothly rounded outlines proclaiming its character in any company; and when one of the oldest attains full stature on some commanding ridge it seems the very god of the woods. I ran back to camp, packed Brownie, steered over the divide and down into the heart of the Fresno Grove. Then choosing a camp on the side of a brook where the grass was good, I made a cup of tea, and set off free among the brown giants, glorying in the abundance of new work about me. One of the first special things that caught my attention was an extensive landslip. The ground on the side of a stream had given way to a depth of about fifty feet and with all its trees had been launched into the bottom of the stream ravine. Most of the trees—pines, firs, incense cedar, and Sequoia—were still standing erect and uninjured, as if unconscious that anything out of the common had happened. Tracing the ravine alongside the avalanche, I saw many trees whose roots had been laid bare, and in one instance discovered a Sequoia about fifteen feet in diameter growing above an old prostrate trunk that seemed to belong to a former generation. This slip had occurred seven or eight years ago, and I was glad to find that not only were most of the Big Trees uninjured, but that many companies of hopeful seedlings and saplings were growing confidently on the fresh soil along the broken front of the avalanche. These young trees were already eight or ten feet high, and were shooting up vigorously, as if sure of eternal life, though young pines, firs, and libocedrus were running a race with them for the sunshine with an even start. Farther down the ravine I counted five hundred and thirty-six promising young Sequoias on a bed of rough bouldery soil not exceeding two acres in extent.

The Fresno Big Trees covered an area of about four square miles, and while wandering about surveying the boundaries of the grove, anxious to see every tree, I came suddenly on a handsome log cabin, richly embowered and so fresh and unweathered it was still redolent of gum and balsam like a newly felled tree. Strolling forward, wondering who could have built it, I found an old, weary-eyed, speculative, gray-haired man on a bark stool by the door, reading a book. The discovery of his hermitage by a stranger seemed to surprise him, but when I explained that I was only a tree-lover sauntering along the mountains to study Sequoia, he bade me welcome, made me bring my mule down to a little slanting meadow before his door and camp with him, promising to show me his pet trees and many curious things bearing on my studies.

After supper, as the evening shadows were falling, the good hermit sketched his life in the mines, which in the main was like that of most other pioneer gold-hunters—a succession of intense experiences full of big ups and downs like the mountain topography. Since "'49" he had wandered over most of the Sierra, sinking innumerable prospect holes like a sailor making soundings, digging new channels for streams, sifting gold-sprinkled boulder and gravel beds with unquenchable energy, life's noon the mean-while passing unnoticed into late afternoon shadows. Then, health and gold gone, the game played and lost, like a wounded deer creeping into this forest solitude, he awaits the sundown call. How sad the undertones of many a life here, now the noise of the first big gold battles has died away! How many interesting wrecks lie drifted and stranded in hidden nooks of the gold region! Perhaps no other range contains the remains of so many rare and interesting men. The name of my hermit friend is John A. Nelder, a fine kind man, who in going into the woods has at last gone home; for he loves nature truly, and realizes that these last shadowy days with scarce a glint of gold in them are the best of all. Birds, squirrels, plants get loving, natural recognition, and delightful it was to see how sensitively he responds to the silent influences of the woods. His eyes brightened as he gazed on the trees that stand guard around his little home; squirrels and mountain quail came to his call to be fed, and he tenderly stroked the little snowbent sapling Sequoias, hoping they yet might grow straight to the sky and rule the grove. One of the greatest of his trees stands a little way back of his cabin, and he proudly led me to it, bidding me admire its colossal proportions and measure it to see if in all the forest there could be another so grand. It proved to be only twenty-six feet in diameter, and he seemed distressed to learn that the Mariposa Grizzly Giant was larger. I tried to comfort him by observing that his was the taller, finer formed, and perhaps the more favorably situated. Then he led me to some noble ruins, remnants of gigantic trunks of trees that he supposed must have been larger than any now standing, and though they had lain on the damp ground exposed to fire and the weather for centuries, the wood was perfectly sound. Sequoia timber is not only beautiful in color, rose red when fresh, and as easily worked as pine, but it is almost absolutely unperishable. Build a house of Big Tree logs on granite and that house will last about as long as its foundation. Indeed fire seems to be the only agent that has any appreciable effect on it. From one of these ancient trunk remnants I cut a specimen of the wood, which neither in color, strength, nor soundness could be distinguished from specimens cut from living trees, although it had certainly lain on the damp forest floor for more than three hundred and eighty years, probably more than thrice as long. The time in this instance was determined as follows: When the tree from which the specimen was derived fell it sunk itself into the ground, making a ditch about two hundred feet long and five or six feet deep; and in the middle of this ditch, where a part of the fallen trunk had been burned, a silver fir four feet in diameter and three hundred and eighty years old was growing, showing that the Sequoia trunk had lain on the ground three hundred and eighty years plus the unknown time that it lay before the part whose place had been taken by the fir was burned out of the way, and that which had elapsed ere the seed from which the monumental fir sprang fell into the prepared soil and took root. Now because Sequoia trunks are never wholly consumed in one forest fire and these fires recur only at considerable intervals, and because Sequoia ditches, after being cleared, are often left unplanted for centuries, it becomes evident that the trunk remnant in question may have been on the ground a thousand years or more. Similar vestiges are common, and together with the root-bowls and long straight ditches of the fallen monarchs, throw a sure light back on the post-glacial history of the species, bearing on its distribution. One of the most interesting features of this grove is the apparent ease and strength and comfortable independence in which the trees occupy their place in the general forest. Seedlings, saplings, young and middle-aged trees are grouped promisingly around the old patriarchs, betraying no sign of approach to extinction. On the contrary, all seem to be saying, "Everything is to our mind and we mean to live forever." But, sad to tell, a lumber company was building a large mill and flume near by, assuring widespread destruction.

In the cones and sometimes in the lower portion of the trunk and roots there is a dark gritty substance which dissolves readily in water and yields a magnificent purple color. It is a strong astringent, and is said to be used by the Indians as a big medicine. Mr. Nelder showed me specimens of ink he had made from it, which I tried and found good, flowing freely and holding its color well. Indeed everything about the tree seems constant. With these interesting trees, forming the largest of the northern groves, I stopped only a week, for I had far to go before the fall of the snow. The hermit seemed to cling to me and tried to make me promise to winter with him after the season's work was done. Brownie had to be got home, however, and other work awaited me, therefore I could only promise to stop a day or two on my way back to Yosemite and give him the forest news.

The next two weeks were spent in the wide basin of the San Joaquin, climbing, innumerable ridges and surveying the far-extending sea of pines and firs. But not a single Sequoia crown appeared among them all, nor any trace of a fallen trunk, until I had crossed the south divide of the basin, opposite Dinky Creek, one of the northmost tributaries of

Kings River. On this stream there is a small grove, said to have been discovered a few years before my visit by two hunters in pursuit of a wounded bear. Just as I was fording one of the branches of Dinky Creek I met a shepherd, and when I asked him whether he knew anything about the Big Trees of the neighborhood he replied, "I know all about them, for I visited them only a few days ago and pastured my sheep in the grove." He was fresh from the East, and as this was his first summer in the Sierra I was curious to learn what impression the Sequoias had made on him. When I asked whether it was true that the Big Trees were really so big as people say, he warmly replied, "Oh, yes sir, you bet. They're whales. I never used to believe half I heard about the awful size of California trees, but they're monsters and no mistake. One of them over here, they tell me, is the biggest tree in the whole world, and I guess it is, for it's forty foot through and as many good long paces around." He was very earnest, and in fullness of faith offered to guide me to the grove that I might not miss seeing this biggest tree. A fair measurement four feet from the ground, above the main swell of the roots, showed a diameter of only thirty-two feet, much to the young man's disgust. "Only thirty-two feet," he lamented, "only thirty-two, and I always thought it was forty!" Then with a sigh of relief, "No matter, that's a big tree, anyway; no fool of a tree, sir, that you can cut a plank out of thirty feet broad, straight-edged, no bark, all good wood, sound and solid. It would make the brag white pine planks from old Maine look like laths." A good many other fine specimens are distributed along three small branches of the creek, and I noticed several thrifty moderate-sized Sequoias growing on a granite ledge, apparently as independent of deep soil as the pines and firs, clinging to seams and fissures and sending their roots far abroad in search of moisture.

The creek is very clear and beautiful, gliding through tangles of shrubs and flower beds, gay bee and butterfly pastures, the grove's own stream, pure Sequoia water. flowing all the year, every drop filtered through moss and leaves and the myriad spongy rootlets of the giant trees. One of the most interesting features of the grove is a small waterfall with a flowery, ferny, clear brimming pool at the foot of it. How cheerily it sings the songs of the wilderness, and how sweet it tones! You seem to taste as well as hear them, while only the subdued roar of the river in the deep cañon reaches up into the grove, sounding like the sea and the winds. So charming a fall and pool in the heart of so glorious a forest good pagans would have consecrated to some lovely nymph.

Hence down into the main Kings River cañon, a mile deep, I led and dragged and shoved my patient, much-enduring mule through miles and miles of gardens and brush, fording innumerable streams, crossing savage rock slopes and taluses, scrambling, sliding through gulches and gorges, then up into the grand Sequoia forests of the south side, cheered by the royal crowns displayed on the narrow horizon. In a day and a half we reached the Sequoia woods in the neighborhood of the old Thomas Mill Flat. Thence striking off northeastward I found a magnificent forest nearly six miles long by two in width, composed mostly of Big Trees, with outlying groves as far east as Boulder Creek. Here five or six days were spent, and it was delightful to learn from countless trees, old and young, how comfortably they were settled down in concordance with climate and soil and their noble neighbors.

Imbedded in these majestic woods there are numerous meadows, around the sides of which the Big Trees press close together in beautiful lines, showing their grandeur openly from the ground to their domed heads in the sky. The young trees are still more numerous and exuberant than in the Fresno and Dinky groves, standing apart in beautiful family groups, or crowding around the old giants. For every venerable lightning-stricken tree, there is one or more in all the glory of prime, and for each of these, many young trees and crowds of saplings. The young trees express the grandeur of their race in a way indefinable by any words at my command. When they are five or six feet in diameter and a hundred and fifty feet high, they seem like mere baby saplings as many inches in diameter, their juvenile habit and gestures completely veiling their real size, even to those

who, from long experience, are able to make fair approximation in their measurements of common trees. One morning
I noticed three airy, spiry, quick-growing babies on the side
of a meadow, the largest of which I took to be about eight
inches in diameter. On measuring it, I found to my astonishment it was five feet six inches in diameter, and about a
hundred and forty feet high.

On a bed of sandy ground fifteen yards square,
which had been occupied by four sugar pines, I counted
ninety-four promising seedlings, an instance of Sequoia
gaining ground from its neighbors. Here also I noted eighty-
six young Sequoias from one to fifty feet high on less than
half an acre of ground that had been cleared and prepared
for their reception by fire. This was a small bay burned into
dense chaparral, showing that fire, the great destroyer of
tree life, is sometimes followed by conditions favorable for
new growths. Sufficient fresh soil, however, is furnished for
the constant renewal of the forest by the fall of old trees
without the help of any other agent,—burrowing animals,
fire, flood, landslip, etc.,—for the ground is thus turned and
stirred as well as cleared, and in every roomy, shady hollow
beside the walls of upturned roots many hopeful seedlings
spring up.

The largest, and as far as I know the oldest, of all the
Kings River trees that I saw is the majestic stump, already
referred to, about a hundred and forty feet high, which
above the swell of the roots is thirty-five feet and eight
inches inside the bark, and over four thousand years old.
It was burned nearly half through at the base, and I spent
a day in chopping off the charred surface, cutting into the
heart, and counting the wood-rings with the aid of a lens.
I made out a little over four thousand without difficulty
or doubt, but I was unable to get a complete count, owing
to confusion in the rings where wounds had been healed
over. Judging by what is left of it, this was a fine, tall, symmetrical tree nearly forty feet in diameter before it lost its
bark. In the last sixteen hundred and seventy-two years the
increase in diameter was ten feet. A short distance south of
this forest lies a beautiful grove, now mostly included in the

General Grant National Park. I found many shake-makers at work in it, access to these magnificent woods having been made easy by the old mill wagon road. The Park is only two miles square, and the largest of its many fine trees is the General Grant, so named before the date of my first visit, twenty-eight years ago, and said to be the largest tree in the world, though above the craggy bulging base the diameter is less than thirty feet. The Sanger Lumber Company owns nearly all the Kings River groves outside the Park, and for many years the mills have been spreading desolation without any advantage.

One of the shake-makers directed me to an "old snag biggeren Grant." It proved to be a huge black charred stump thirty-two feet in diameter, the next in size to the grand monument mentioned above.

I found a scattered growth of Big Trees extending across the main divide to within a short distance of Hyde's Mill, on a tributary of Dry Creek. The mountain ridge on the south side of the stream was covered from base to summit with a most superb growth of Big Trees. What a picture it made! In all my wide forest wanderings I had seen none so sublime. Every tree of all the mighty host seemed perfect in beauty and strength, and their majestic domed heads, rising above one another on the mountain slope, were most imposingly displayed, like a range of bossy upswelling cumulus clouds on a calm sky.

In this glorious forest the mill was busy, forming a sore, sad centre of destruction, though small as yet, so immensely heavy was the growth. Only the smaller and most accessible of the trees were being cut. The logs, from three to ten or twelve feet in diameter, were dragged or rolled with long strings of oxen into a chute and sent flying down the steep mountain side to the mill flat, where the largest of them were blasted into manageable dimensions for the saws. And as the timber is very brash, by this blasting and careless felling on uneven ground, half or three fourths of the timber was wasted.

I spent several days exploring the ridge and counting the annual wood rings on a large number of stumps in the clearings, then replenished my bread sack and pushed on southward. All the way across the broad rough basins of the Kaweah and Tule rivers Sequoia ruled supreme, forming an almost continuous belt for sixty or seventy miles, waving up and down in huge massy mountain billows in compliance with the grand glacier-ploughed topography.

Day after day, from grove to grove, cañon to cañon, I made a long, wavering way, terribly rough in some places for Brownie, but cheery for me, for Big Trees were seldom out of sight. We crossed the rugged, picturesque basins of Redwood Creek, the North Fork of the Kaweah, and Marble Fork gloriously forested, and full of beautiful cascades and falls, sheer and slanting, infinitely varied with broad curly foam fleeces and strips of embroidery in which the sunbeams revel. Thence we climbed into the noble forest on the Marble and Middle Fork Divide. After a general exploration of the Kaweah basin, this part of the Sequoia belt seemed to me the finest, and I then named it "the Giant Forest." It extends, a magnificent growth of giants grouped in pure temple groves, ranged in colonnades along the sides of meadows, or scattered among the other trees, from the granite headlands overlooking the hot foothills and plains of the San Joaquin back to within a few miles of the old glacier fountains at an elevation of 5000 to 8400 feet above the sea.

When I entered this sublime wilderness the day was nearly done, the trees with rosy, glowing countenances seemed to be hushed and thoughtful, as if waiting in conscious religious dependence on the sun, and one naturally walked softly and awe-stricken among them. I wandered on, meeting nobler trees where all are noble, subdued in the general calm, as if in some vast hall pervaded by the deepest sanctities and solemnities that sway human souls. At sundown the trees seemed to cease their worship and breathe free. I heard the birds going home. I too sought a home for the night on the edge of a level meadow where there is a long, open view between the evenly ranked trees standing guard along its sides. Then after a good place was found for poor Brownie, who had had a hard, weary day sliding and scrambling across the Marble Cañon, I made my bed and supper and lay on my back looking up to the stars through pillared arches finer far than the pious heart of man, telling its love, ever reared. Then I took a walk up the meadow to see the trees in the pale light. They seemed still more marvelously massive and tall than by day, heaving their colossal heads into the depths of the sky, among the stars, some of which appeared to be sparkling on their branches like flowers. I built a big fire that vividly illumined the huge brown boles of the nearest trees and the little plants and cones and fallen leaves at their feet, keeping up the show until I fell asleep to dream of boundless forests and trail-building for Brownie.

Joyous birds welcomed the dawn; and the squirrels, now their food cones were ripe and had to be quickly gathered and stored for winter, began their work before sunrise. My tea-and-bread-crumb breakfast was soon done, and leaving jaded Brownie to feed and rest I sauntered forth to my studies. In every direction Sequoia ruled the woods. Most of the other big conifers were present here and there, but not as rivals or companions. They only served to thicken and enrich the general wilderness. Trees of every age cover craggy ridges as well as the deep moraine-soiled slopes, and plant their magnificent shafts along every brookside and meadow. Bogs and meadows are rare or entirely wanting in the isolated groves north of Kings River; here there is a beautiful series of them lying on the broad top of the main dividing ridge, imbedded in the very heart of the mammoth woods as if for ornament, their smooth, plushy bosoms kept bright and fertile by streams and sunshine.

Resting awhile on one of the most beautiful of them when the sun was high, it seemed impossible that any other forest picture in the world could rival it. There lay the grassy, flowery lawn, three fourths of a mile long, smoothly outspread, basking in mellow autumn light, colored brown and yellow and purple, streaked with lines of green along the streams, and ruffled here and there with patches of ledum and scarlet vaccinium. Around the margin there is first a fringe of azalea and willow bushes, colored orange yellow, enlivened with vivid dashes of red cornel, as if painted. Then up spring the mighty walls of verdure three hundred feet high, the brown fluted pillars so thick and tall and strong they seem fit to uphold the sky; the dense foliage, swelling forward in rounded bosses on the upper half, variously shaded and tinted, that of the young trees dark green, of the old yellowish. An aged lightning-smitten patriarch standing a little forward beyond the general line with knotty arms outspread was covered with gray and yellow lichens and surrounded by a group of saplings whose slender spires seemed to lack not a single leaf or spray in their wondrous perfection. Such was the Kaweah meadow picture that golden afternoon, and as I gazed every color seemed to deepen and glow as if the progress of the fresh sun-work were visible from hour to hour, while every tree seemed religious and conscious of the presence of God. A free man revels in a scene like this and time goes by unmeasured. I stood fixed in silent wonder or sauntered about shifting my points of view, studying the physiognomy of separate trees, and going out to the different color patches to see how they were put on and what they were made of, giving free expression to my joy, exulting in Nature's wild immortal vigor and beauty, never dreaming any other human being was near. Suddenly the spell was broken by dull bumping, thudding sounds, and a man and horse came in sight at the farther end of the meadow, where they seemed sadly out of place. A good big bear or mastodon or megatherium would have been more in keeping with the old mammoth forest. Nevertheless, it is always pleasant to meet one of our own species after solitary rambles, and I stepped out where I could be seen and shouted, when the rider reined in his galloping mustang and waited my approach. He seemed too much surprised to speak until, laughing in his puzzled face, I said I was glad to meet a fellow mountaineer in so lonely a place. Then he abruptly asked, "What are you doing? How did you get here?" I explained that I came across the cañons from Yosemite and was only looking at the trees. "Oh then, I know," he said, greatly to my surprise, "you must be John Muir." He was herding a band of horses that had been driven up a rough trail from the lowlands to feed on these forest meadows. A few handfuls of crumb detritus was all that was left in my bread sack, so I told him that I was nearly out of provision and asked whether he could spare me a little flour. "Oh yes, of course you can have anything I've got," he said. "Just take my track and it will lead you to my camp in a big hollow log on the side of a meadow two or three miles from here. I must ride after some strayed horses, but I'll be back before night; in the mean time make yourself at home." He galloped away to the northward, I returned to my own camp, saddled Brownie, and by the middle of the afternoon discovered his noble den in a fallen Sequoia hollowed by fire—a spacious loghouse of one log, carbon-lined, centuries old yet sweet and fresh, weather proof, earthquake proof, likely to outlast the most durable stone castle, and commanding views of garden and grove grander far than the richest king ever enjoyed. Brownie found plenty of grass and I found bread, which I ate with views from the big round, ever-open door. Soon the good Samaritan mountaineer came in, and I enjoyed a famous rest listening to his observations on trees, animals, adventures, etc., while he was busily preparing supper. In answer to inquiries concerning the distribution of the Big Trees he gave a good deal of particular information of the forest we were in, and he had heard that the species extended a long way south, he knew not now far. I wandered about for several days within a radius of six or seven miles of the camp, surveying boundaries, measuring trees, and climbing the highest points for general views. From the south side of the divide I saw telling ranks of Sequoia-crowned headlands stretching far into the hazy distance, and plunging vaguely down into profound cañon depths foreshadowing weeks of good work. I had now been out on the trip more than a month, and I began to fear my studies would be interrupted by snow, for winter was drawing nigh. "Where there isn't a way make a way," is easily said when no way at the time is needed, but to the Sierra explorer with a mule traveling across the cañon lines of drainage the brave old phrase becomes heavy with meaning. There are ways across the Sierra graded by glaciers, well marked, and followed by men and beasts and birds, and one of them even by locomotives; but none natural or artificial along the range, and the explorer who would thus travel at right angles to the glacial ways must traverse cañons and ridges extending side by side in endless succession, roughened by side gorges and gulches and stubborn chaparral, and defended by innumerable sheer-fronted precipices. My own ways are easily made in any direction, but Brownie, though one of the toughest and most skillful of his race, was oftentimes discouraged for want of hands, and caused endless work. Wild at first, he was tame enough now; and when turned loose he not only refused to run away, but as his troubles increased came to depend on me in such a pitiful, touching way, I became attached to him and helped him as if he were a good-natured boy in distress, and then the labor grew lighter. Bidding good-by to the kind Sequoia cave-dweller, we vanished again in the wilderness, drifting slowly southward, Sequoias on every ridge-top beckoning and pointing the way.

In the forest between the Middle and East forks of the Kaweah, I met a great fire, and as fire is the master scourge and controller of the distribution of trees, I stopped to watch it and learn what I could of its works and ways with the giants. It came racing up the steep chaparral-covered slopes of the East Fork cañon with passionate enthusiasm in a broad cataract of flames, now bending down low to feed on the green bushes, devouring acres of them at a breath, now towering high in the air as if looking abroad to choose a way, then stooping to feed again, the lurid flapping surges and the smoke and terrible rushing and roaring hiding all that is gentle and orderly in the work. But as soon as the deep forest was reached the ungovernable flood became calm like a torrent entering a lake, creeping and spreading beneath the trees where the ground was level or sloped gently, slowly nibbling the cake of compressed needles and scales with flames an inch high, rising here and there to a foot or two on dry twigs and clumps of small bushes and brome grass. Only at considerable intervals were fierce bonfires lighted, where heavy branches broken off by snow had accumulated, or around some venerable giant whose head had been stricken off by lightning.

I tethered Brownie on the edge of a little meadow beside a stream a good safe way off, and then cautiously chose a camp for myself in a big stout hollow trunk not likely to be crushed by the fall of burning trees, and made a bed of ferns and boughs in it. The night, however, and the strange wild fireworks were too beautiful and exciting to allow much sleep. There was no danger of being chased and hemmed in, for in the main forest belt of the Sierra, even when swift winds are blowing, fires seldom or never sweep over the trees in broad all-embracing sheets as they do in the dense Rocky Mountain woods and in those of the Cascade Mountains of Oregon and Washington. Here they creep from tree to tree with tranquil deliberation, allowing close observation, though caution is required in venturing around the burning giants to avoid falling limbs and knots and fragments from dead shattered tops. Though the day was best for study, I sauntered about night after night, learning what I could and admiring the wonderful show vividly displayed in the lonely darkness, the ground-fire advancing in long crooked lines gently grazing and smoking on the close-pressed leaves, springing up in thousands of little jets of pure flame on dry tassels and twigs, and tall spires and flat sheets with jagged flapping edges dancing here and there on grass tufts and bushes, big bonfires blazing in perfect storms of energy where heavy branches mixed with small ones lay smashed together in hundred cord piles, big red arches between spreading root-swells and trees growing close together, huge fire-mantled trunks on the hill slopes glowing like bars of hot iron, violet-colored fire running up the tall trees, tracing the furrows of the bark in quick quivering rills, and lighting magnificent torches on dry shattered tops, and ever and anon, with a tremendous roar and burst of light, young trees clad in low-descending feathery branches vanishing in one flame two or three hundred feet high.

One of the most impressive and beautiful sights was made by the great fallen trunks lying on the hillsides all red and glowing like colossal iron bars fresh from a furnace, two hundred feet long some of them, and ten to twenty feet thick. After repeated burnings have consumed the bark and sapwood, the sound charred surface, being full of cracks and sprinkled with leaves, is quickly overspread with a pure, rich, furred, ruby glow almost flameless and smokeless, producing a marvelous effect in the night. Another grand and interesting sight are the fires on the tops of the largest living trees flaming above the green branches at a height of perhaps two hundred feet, entirely cut off from the ground-fires, and looking like signal beacons on watch towers. From one standpoint I sometimes saw a dozen or more, those in the distance looking like great stars above the forest roof. At first I could not imagine how these Sequoia lamps were lighted, but the very first night, strolling about waiting and watching, I saw the thing done again and again. The thick, fibrous bark of old trees is divided by deep, nearly continuous furrows, the sides of which are bearded with the bristling ends of fibres broken by the growth swelling of the trunk, and when the fire comes creeping around the feet of the trees, it runs up these bristly furrows in lovely pale blue quivering, bickering rills of flame with a low, earnest whispering sound to the lightning-shattered top of the trunk, which, in the dry Indian summer, with perhaps leaves and twigs and squirrel-gnawed cone-scales and seed-wings lodged in it, is readily ignited. These lamp-lighting rills, the most beautiful fire streams I ever saw, last only a minute or two, but the big lamps burn with varying brightness for days and weeks, throwing off sparks like the spray of a fountain, while ever and anon a shower of red coals comes sifting down through the branches, followed at times with startling effect by a big burned-off chunk weighing perhaps half a ton.

The immense bonfires where fifty or a hundred cords of peeled, split, smashed wood has been piled around some old giant by a single stroke of lightning is another grand sight in the night. The light is so great I found I could read common print three hundred yards from them, and the illumination of the circle of onlooking trees is indescribably impressive. Other big fires, roaring and booming like waterfalls, were blazing on the upper sides of trees on hillslopes, against which limbs broken off by heavy snow had rolled, while branches high overhead, tossed and shaken by the ascending air current, seemed to be writhing in pain. Perhaps the most starting phenomenon of all was the quick death of childlike Sequoias only a century or two of age. In the midst of the other comparatively slow and steady fire work one of these tall, beautiful saplings, leafy and branchy, would be seen blazing up suddenly, all in one heaving, booming, passionate flame reaching from the ground to the top of the tree and fifty to a hundred feet or more above it, with a smoke column bending forward and streaming away on the upper, free-flowing wind. To burn these green trees a strong fire of dry wood beneath them is required, to send up a current of air hot enough to distill inflammable gases from the leaves and sprays; then instead of the lower limbs gradually catching fire and igniting the next and next in succession, the whole tree seems to explode almost simultaneously, and with awful roaring and throbbing a round, tapering flame shoots up two or three hundred feet, and in a second or two is quenched, leaving the green spire a black, dead mast, bristled and roughened with down-curling boughs. Nearly all the trees that have been burned down are lying with their heads uphill, because they are burned far more deeply on the upper side, on account of broken limbs rolling down against them to make hot fires, while only leaves and twigs accumulate on the lower side and are quickly consumed without injury to the tree. But green, resinless Sequoia wood burns very slowly, and many successive fires are required to burn down a large tree. Fires can run only at intervals of several years, and when the ordinary amount of firewood that has rolled against the gigantic trunk is consumed, only a shallow scar is made, which is slowly deepened by recurring fires until far beyond the centre of gravity, and when at last the tree falls, it of course falls uphill. The healing folds of wood layers on some of the deeply burned trees show that centuries have elapsed since the last wounds were made.

When a great Sequoia falls, its head is smashed into fragments about as small as those made by lightning, which are mostly devoured by the first running, hunting fire that finds them, while the trunk is slowly wasted away by centuries of fire and weather. One of the most interesting fire actions on the trunk is the boring of those great tunnel-like hollows through which horsemen may gallop. All of these famous hollows are burned out of the solid wood, for no Sequoia is ever hollowed by decay. When the tree falls the brash trunk is often broken straight across into sections as if sawed; into these joints the fire creeps, and, on account of the great size of the broken ends, burns for weeks for even months without being much influenced by the weather. After the great glowing ends fronting each other have burned so far apart that their rims cease to burn, the fire continues to work on in the centres, and the ends become deeply concave. Then heat being radiated from side to side, the burning goes on in each section of the trunk independent of the other, until the diameter of the bore is so great that the heat radiated across from side to side is not sufficient to keep them burning. It appears, therefore, that only very large trees can receive the fire-auger and have any shell rim left.

Fire attacks the large trees only at the ground, consuming the fallen leaves and humus at their feet, doing them but little harm unless considerable quantities of fallen limbs happen to be piled about them, their thick mail of spongy, unpitchy, almost unburnable bark affording strong protection. Therefore the oldest and most perfect unscarred trees are found on ground that is nearly level, while those growing on hillsides, against which falling branches roll, are always deeply scarred on the upper side, and as we have seen are sometimes burned down. The saddest thing of all was to see the hopeful seedlings, many of them crinkled and bent with the pressure of winter snow, yet bravely aspiring at the top, helplessly perishing, and young trees, perfect spires of verdure and naturally immortal, suddenly changed to dead masts. Yet the sun looked cheerily down the openings in the forest roof, turning the black smoke to a beautiful brown, as if all was for the best.

Beneath the smoke-clouds of the suffering forest we again pushed southward, descending a side-gorge of the East Fork cañon and climbing another into new forests and groves not a whit less noble. Brownie, the meanwhile, had been resting, while I was weary and sleepy with almost ceaseless wanderings, giving only an hour or two each night or day to sleep in my log home. Way-making here seemed to become more and more difficult, "impossible," in common phrase, for four-legged travelers. Two or three miles was all the day's work as far as distance was concerned. Nevertheless, just before sundown we found a charming camp ground with plenty of grass, and a forest to study that had felt no fire for many a year. The camp hollow was evidently a favorite home of bears. On many of the trees, at a height of six or eight feet, their autographs were inscribed in strong, free, flowing strokes on the soft bark where they had stood up like cats to stretch their limbs. Using both hands, every claw a pen, the handsome curved lines of their writing take the form of remarkably regular interlacing pointed arches, producing a truly ornamental effect. I looked and listened, half expecting to see some of the writers alarmed and withdrawing from the unwonted disturbance. Brownie also looked and listened, for mules fear bears instinctively and have a very keen nose for them. When I turned him loosed, instead of going to the best grass, he kept cautiously near the camp-fire for protection, but was careful not to step on me. The great starry night passed away in deep peace and the rosy morning sunbeams were searching the grove ere I woke from a long, blessed sleep.

The breadth of the Sequoia belt here is about the same as on the north side of the river, extending, rather thin and scattered in some places, among the noble pines from near the main forest belt of the range well back towards the frosty peaks, where most of the trees are growing on moraines but little changed as yet.

Two days scramble above Bear Hollow I enjoyed an interesting interview with deer. Soon after sunrise a little company of four came to my camp in a wild garden imbedded in chaparral, and after much cautious observation quietly began to eat breakfast with me. Keeping perfectly still I soon had their confidence, and they came so near I found no difficulty, while admiring their graceful manners and gestures, in determining what plants they were eating, thus gaining a far finer knowledge and sympathy than comes by killing and hunting.

Indian summer gold with scarce a whisper of winter in it was painting the glad wilderness in richer and yet richer colors as we scrambled across the South cañon into the basin of the Tule. Here the Big Tree forests are still more extensive, and furnished abundance of work in tracing boundaries and gloriously crowned ridges up and down, back and forth, exploring, studying, admiring, while the great measureless days passed on and away uncounted. But in the calm of the camp-fire the end of the season seemed near. Brownie too often brought snow-storms to mind. He became doubly jaded, though I never rode him, and always left him in camp to feed and rest while I explored. The invincible bread business also troubled me again; the last mealy crumbs were consumed, and grass was becoming scarce even in the roughest rock-piles naturally inaccessible to sheep. One afternoon, as I gazed over the rolling bossy Sequoia billows stretching interminably southward, seeking a way and counting how far I might go without food, a rifle shot rang out sharp and clear. Marking the direction I pushed gladly on, hoping to find some hunter who could spare a little food. Within a few hundred rods I struck the track of a shod horse, Which led to the camp of two Indian shepherds. One of them was cooking supper when I arrived. Glancing curiously at me he saw that I was hungry, and gave me some mutton and bread, and said encouragingly as he pointed to the west, "Putty soon Indian come, heap speak English." Toward sundown two thousand sheep beneath a cloud of dust came streaming through the grand Sequoias to a meadow below the camp, and presently the English-speaking shepherd came in, to whom I explained my wants and what I was doing. Like most white men, he could not conceive how anything other than gold could be the object of such rambles as mine, and asked repeatedly whether I had discovered any mines. I tried to make him talk about trees and the wild animals, but unfortunately he proved to be a tame Indian from the Tule Reservation, had been to school, claimed to be civilized, and spoke contemptuously of "wild Indians," and so of course his inherited instincts were blurred or lost. The Big Trees, he said, grew far south, for he had seen them in crossing the mountains from Porterville to Lone Pine. In the morning he kindly gave me a few pounds of flour, and assured me that I would get plenty more at a sawmill on the South Fork if I reached it before it was shut down for the season.

Of all the Tule basin forest the section on the North Fork seemed the finest, surpassing, I think, even the Giant Forest of the Kaweah. Southward from here, though the width and general continuity of the belt is well sustained, I thought I could detect a slight falling off in the height of the trees and in closeness of growth. All the basin was swept by swarms of hoofed locusts, the southern part over and over again, until not a leaf within the reach was left on the wettest bogs, the outer edges of the thorniest chaparral beds, or even on the young conifers, which unless under the stress of dire famine, sheep never touch. Of course Brownie suffered, though I made diligent search for grassy sheep-proof spots. Turning him loose one evening on the side of a carex bog, he dolefully prospected the desolate neighborhood without finding anything that even a starving mule could eat. Then, utterly discouraged, he stole up behind me while I was bent over on my knees making a fire for tea, and in a pitiful mixture of bray and neigh, begged for help. It was a mighty touching prayer, and I answered it as well as I could with half of what was left of a cake made from the last of the flour given me by the Indians, hastily passing it over my shoulder, and saying, "Yes, poor fellow, I know, but soon you'll have plenty. To-morrow down we go to alfalfa and barley," speaking to him as if he were human, as through stress of trouble plainly he was. After eating his portion of bread he seemed content, for he said no more, but patiently turned away to gnaw leafless ceanothus stubs. Such clinging, confiding dependence after all our scrambles and adventures together was very touching, and I felt conscience-stricken for having led him so far in so rough and desolate a country. "Man," says Lord Bacon, "is the god of the dog." So, also, he is of the mule and many other dependent fellow mortals.

Next morning I turned westward, determined to force a way straight to pasture, letting Sequoia wait. Fortunately ere we had struggled down through half a mile of chaparral we heard a mill whistle, for which we gladly made a bee line. At the sawmill we both got a good meal, then taking the dusty lumber road pursued our way to the lowlands. The nearest good pasture I counted might be thirty or forty miles away. But scarcely had we gone ten when I noticed a little log cabin a hundred yards or so back from the road, and a tall man straight as a pine standing in front of it observing us as we came plodding down through the dust. Seeing no sign of grass or hay, I was going past without stopping, when he shouted, "Travelin'?" Then drawing nearer, "Where have you come from? I didn't notice you go up." I replied I had come through the woods from the north, looking at the trees. "Oh, then, you must be John Muir. Halt, you're tired; come and rest and I'll cook for you." Then I explained that I was tracing the Sequoia belt, that on account of sheep my mule was starving, and therefore must push on to the lowlands. "No, no," he said, "that corral over there is full of hay and grain. Turn your mule into it. I don't own it, but the fellow who does is hauling lumber, and it will be all right. He's a white man. Come and rest. How tired you must be! The Big Trees don't go much farther south, nohow. I know the country up there, have hunted all over it. Come and rest, and let your little doggone rat of a mule rest. How in heavens did you get him across the cañons—roll him? or carry him? He's poor, but he'll get fat, and I'll give you a horse and go with you up the mountains, and while you're looking at the trees I'll go hunting. It will be a short job, for the end of the Big Trees is not far." Of course I stopped. No true invitation is ever declined. He had been hungry and tired himself many a time in the Rocky Mountains as well as in the Sierra. Now he owned a band of cattle and lived alone. His cabin was about eight by ten feet, the door at one end, a fireplace at the other, and a bed on one side fastened to the logs. Leading me in without a word of mean apology, he made me lie down on the bed, then reached under it, brought forth a sack of apples and advised me to keep "chawing" at them until he got supper ready. Finer, braver hospitality I never found in all this good world so often called selfish.

Next day with hearty, easy alacrity the mountaineer procured horses, prepared and packed provisions, and got everything ready for an early start the following morning. Well mounted, we pushed rapidly upon the South Fork of the river and soon after noon were among the giants once more. On the divide between the Tule and Deer Creek a central camp was made, and the mountaineer spent his time in deer-hunting, while with provisions for two or three days I explored the woods, and in accordance with what I had been told soon reached the southern extremity of the belt on the South Fork of Deer Creek. To make sure, I searched the woods a considerable distance south of the last Deer Creek grove, passed over into the basin of the Kern, and climbed several high points commanding extensive views over the sugar-pine woods, without seeing a single Sequoia crown in all the wide expanse to the southward. On the way back to camp, however, I was greatly interested in a grove I discovered on the east side of the Kern River divide, opposite the North Fork of Deer Creek. The height of the pass where the species crossed over is about 7000 feet, and I heard of still another grove whose waters drain into the upper Kern opposite the Middle Fork of the Tule.

It appears, therefore, that though the Sequoia belt is two hundred and sixty miles long, most of the trees are on a section to the south of Kings River only about seventy miles in length. But though the area occupied by the species increases so much to the southward, there is but little difference in the size of the trees. A diameter of twenty feet and height of two hundred and seventy-five is perhaps about the average for anything like mature and favorably situated trees. Specimens twenty-five feet in diameter are not rare, and a good many approach a height of three hundred feet. Occasionally one meets a specimen thirty feet in diameter, and rarely one that is larger. The majestic stump on Kings River is the largest I saw and measured on the entire trip. Careful search around the boundaries of the forests and groves and in the gaps of the belt failed to discover any trace of the former existence of the species beyond its present limits. On the contrary, it seems to be slightly extending its boundaries; for the outstanding stragglers, occasionally met a mile or two from the main bodies, are young instead of old monumental trees. Ancient ruins and the ditches and root-bowls the big trunks make in falling were found in all the groves, but none outside of them. We may therefore conclude that the area covered by the species has not been diminished during the last eight or ten thousand years, and probably not at all in post-glacial times. For admitting that upon those areas supposed to have been once covered by Sequoia every tree may have fallen, and that fire and the weather had left not a vestige of them, many of the ditches made by the fall of the ponderous trunks, weighing five hundred to nearly a thousand tons, and the bowls made by their up-turned roots would remain visible for thousands of years after the last remnants of the trees had vanished. Some of these records would doubtless be effaced in a comparatively short time by the inwashing of sediments, but no inconsiderable part of them would remain enduringly engraved on flat ridge tops, almost wholly free from such action.

In the northern groves, the only ones that at first came under the observation of students, there are but few seedlings and young trees to take the places of the old ones. Therefore the species was regarded as doomed to speedy extinction, as being only an expiring remnant vanquished in the so-called struggle for life, and shoved into its last strongholds in moist glens where conditions are exceptionally favorable. But the majestic continuous forests of the south end of the belt create a very different impression. Here, as we have seen, no tree in the forest is more enduringly established. Nevertheless it is oftentimes vaguely said that the Sierra climate is drying out, and that this oncoming, constantly increasing drought will of itself surely extinguish King Sequoia, though sections of wood-rings show that there has been no appreciable change of climate during the last forty centuries. Furthermore, that Sequoia can grow and is growing on as dry ground as any of its neighbors or rivals, we have seen proved over and over again. "Why, then," it will be asked, "are the Big Tree groves always found on well-watered spots?" Simply because Big Trees give rise to streams. It is a mistake to suppose that the water is the cause of the groves being there. On the contrary, the groves are the cause of the water being there. The roots of this immense tree fill the ground, forming a sponge which hoards the bounty of the clouds and sends it forth in clear perennial streams instead of allowing it to rush headlong in short-lived destructive floods. Evaporation is also checked, and the air kept still in the shady Sequoia depths, while thirsty robber winds are shut out.

Since, then, it appears that Sequoia can and does grow on as dry ground as its neighbors and that the greater moisture found with it is an effect rather than a cause of its presence, the notions as to the former greater extension of the species and its near approach to extinction, based on its supposed dependence on greater moisture, are seen to be erroneous. Indeed, all my observations go to show that in case of prolonged drought the sugar pines and firs would die before Sequoia. Again, if the restricted and irregular distribution of the species be interpreted as the result of the desiccation of the range, then, instead of increasing in individuals toward the south, where the rainfall is less, it should diminish.

If, then, its peculiar distribution has not been governed by superior conditions of soil and moisture, by what has it been governed? Several years before I made this trip, I noticed that the northern groves were located on those parts of the Sierra soil-belt that were first laid bare and opened to preëmption when the ice-sheet began to break up into individual glaciers. And when I was examining the basin of the San Joaquin and trying to account for the absence of Sequoia, when every condition seemed favorable for its growth, it occurred to me that this remarkable gap in the belt is located in the channel of the great ancient glacier of the San Joaquin and Kings River basins, which poured its frozen floods to the plain, fed by the snows that fell on more than fifty miles of the Summit peaks of the range. Constantly brooding on the question, I next perceived that the great gap in the belt to the northward, forty miles wide, between the Stanislaus and Tuolumne groves, occurs in the channel of the great Stanislaus and Tuolumne glacier, and that the smaller gap between the Merced and Mariposa groves occurs in the channel of the smaller Merced glacier. The wider the ancient glacier, the wider the gap in the Sequoia belt, while the groves and forests attain their greatest development in the Kaweah and Tule River basins, just where, owing to topographical conditions, the region was first cleared and warmed, while protected from the main ice-rivers, that flowed past to right and left down the Kings and Kern valleys. In general, where the ground on the belt was first cleared of ice, there the Sequoia now is, and where at the same elevation and time the ancient glaciers lingered, there the Sequoia is not. What the other conditions may have been which enabled the Sequoia to establish itself upon these oldest and warmest parts of the main soil-belt I cannot say. I might venture to state, however, that since the Sequoia forests present a more and more ancient and long established aspect to the southward, the species was probably distributed from the south toward the close of the glacial period, before the arrival of other trees. About this branch of the question, however, there is at present much fog, but the general relationship we have pointed out between the distribution of the Big Tree and the ancient glacial system is clear. And when we bear in mind that all the existing forests of the Sierra are growing on comparatively fresh moraine soil, and that the range itself has been recently sculptured and brought to light from beneath the ice-mantle of the glacial winter, then many lawless mysteries vanish, and harmonies take their places.

But notwithstanding all the observed phenomena bearing on the post-glacial history of this colossal tree, point to the conclusion that it never was more widely distributed on the Sierra since the close of the glacial epoch; that its present forests are scarcely past prime; if, indeed, they have reached prime; that the post-glacial day of the species is probably not half done; yet, when from a wider outlook the vast antiquity of the genus is considered, and its ancient richness in species and individuals, comparing our Sierra giant and Sequoia sempervirens of the coast, the only other living species, with the many fossil species already discovered, and described by the Heer and Lesquereux, some of which flourished over large areas around the Arctic Circle, and in Europe and our own territories, during tertiary and cretaceous times,—then, indeed, it becomes plain that our two surviving species, restricted to narrow belts within the limits of California, are mere remnants of the genus both as to species and individuals, and that they probably are verging to extinction. But the verge of a period beginning in cretaceous times may have a breadth of tens of thousands of years, not to mention the possible existence of conditions calculated to multiply and reëxtend both species and individuals. No unfavorable change of climate, so far as I can see, no disease, but only fire and the axe and the ravages of flocks and herds threaten the existence of these noblest of God's trees. In Nature's keeping they are safe, but through man's agency destruction is making rapid progress, while in the work of protection only a beginning has been made. The Mariposa Grove belongs to and is guarded by the State; the General Grant and Sequoia National Parks, established ten years ago, are efficiently guarded by a troop of cavalry under the direction of the Secretary of the Interior; so also are the small Tuolumne and Merced groves, which are included in the Yosemite National Park, while a few scattered patches and fringes, scarce at all protected, though belonging to the national government, are in the Sierra Forest Reservation.

Perhaps more than half of all the Big Trees have been sold, and are now in the hands of speculators and mill men. Even the beautiful little Calaveras Grove of ninety trees, so historically interesting from its being the first discovered, is now owned, together with the much larger South or Stanislaus Grove, by a lumber company.

Far the largest and most important section of protected Big Trees is in the grand Sequoia National Park, now easily accessible by stage from Visalia. It contains seven townships and extends across the whole breadth of the magnificent Kaweah basin. But large as it is, it should be made much larger. Its natural eastern boundary is the high Sierra, and the northern and southern boundaries, and the Kings and

Kern rivers, and thus including the sublime scenery on the headwaters of these rivers and perhaps nine tenths of all the Big Trees in existence. Private claims cut and blotch both of the Sequoia parks as well as all the best of the forests, every one of which the government should gradually extinguish by purchase, as it readily may, for none of these holdings are of much value to their owners. Thus as far as possible the grand blunder of selling would be corrected. The value of these forests in storing and dispensing the bounty of the mountain clouds is infinitely greater than lumber or sheep. To the dwellers of the plain, dependent on irrigation, the Big Tree, leaving all its higher uses out of the count, is a tree of life, a never-failing spring, sending living water to the lowlands all through the hot, rainless summer. For every grove cut down a stream is dried up. Therefore, all California is crying, "Save the trees of the fountains," nor, judging by the signs of the times, it is likely that the cry will cease until the salvation of all that is left of Sequoia gigantea is sure.

X

THE AMERICAN FORESTS

The forests of America, however slighted by man, must have been a great delight to God; for they were the best he ever planted. The whole continent was a garden, and from the beginning it seemed to be favored above all the other wild parks and gardens of the globe. To prepare the ground, it was rolled and sifted in seas with infinite loving deliberation and fore-thought, lifted into the light, submerged and warmed over and over again, pressed and crumpled into folds and ridges, mountains, and hills, subsoiled with heaving volcanic fires, ploughed and ground and sculptured into scenery and soil with glaciers and rivers,—every feature growing and changing from beauty to beauty, higher and higher. And in the fullness of time it was planted in groves, and belts, and broad, exuberant, mantling forests, with the largest, most varied, most fruitful, and most beautiful trees in the world. Bright seas made its border, with wave embroidery and icebergs; gray deserts were outspread in the middle of it, mossy tundras on the north, savannas on the south, and blooming prairies and plains; while lakes and rivers shone through all the vast forests and openings, and happy birds and beasts gave delightful animation. Everywhere, everywhere over all the blessed continent, there were beauty and melody and kindly, wholesome, foodful abundance.

These forests were composed of about five hundred species of trees, all of them in some way useful to man, ranging in size from twenty-five feet in height and less than one foot in diameter at the ground to four hundred feet in height and more than twenty feet in diameter,—lordly monarchs proclaiming the gospel of beauty like apostles. For many a century after the ice-ploughs were melted, nature fed them and dressed them every day,—working like a man, a loving, devoted, painstaking gardener; fingering every leaf and flower and mossy furrowed bole; bending, trimming, modeling, balancing; painting them with the loveliest colors; bringing over them now clouds with cooling shadows and showers, now sunshine; fanning them with gentle winds and rustling their leaves; exercising them in every fibre with storms, and pruning them; loading them with flowers and fruit, loading them with snow, and ever making them more beautiful as the years rolled by. Wide-branching oak and elm in endless variety, walnut and maple, chestnut and beech, ilex and locust, touching limb to limb, spread a leafy translucent canopy along the coast of the Atlantic over the wrinkled folds and ridges of the Alleghanies,—a green billowy sea in summer, golden and purple in autumn, pearly gray like a steadfast frozen mist of interlacing branches and sprays in leafless, restful winter.

To the southward stretched dark, level-topped cypresses in knobby, tangled swamps, grassy savannas in the midst of them like lakes of light, groves of gay, sparkling spice-trees, magnolias and palms, glossy-leaved and blooming and shining continually. To the northward, over Maine and Ottawa, rose hosts of spiry, rosiny evergreens,—white pine and spruce, hemlock and cedar, shoulder to shoulder, laden with purple cones, their myriad needles sparkling and shimmering, covering hills and swamps, rocky headlands and domes, ever bravely aspiring and seeking the sky; the ground in their shade now snow-clad and frozen, now mossy and flowery; beaver meadows here and there, full of lilies and grass; lakes gleaming like eyes, and a silvery embroidery of rivers and creeks watering and brightening all the vast glad wilderness.

Thence westward were oak and elm, hickory and tupelo, gum and liriodendron, sassafras and ash, linden and laurel, spreading on ever wider in glorious exuberance over the great fertile tile basin of the Mississippi, over damp level bottoms, low dimpling hollows, and round dotting hills, embosoming sunny prairies and cheery park openings, half sunshine, half shade; while a dark wilderness of pines covered the region around the Great Lakes. Thence still westward swept the forests to right and left around grassy plains and deserts a thousand miles wide: irrepressible hosts of spruce and pine, aspen and willow, nut-pine and juniper, cactus and yucca, caring nothing for drought, extending undaunted from mountain to mountain, over mesa and desert, to join the darkening multitudes of pines that covered the high Rocky ranges and the glorious forests along the coast of the moist and balmy Pacific, where new species of pine, giant cedars and spruces, silver firs and Sequoias, kings of their race, growing close together like grass in a meadow, poised their brave domes and spires in the sky, three hundred feet above the ferns and the lilies that enameled the ground; towering serene through the long centuries, preaching God's forestry fresh from heaven.

Here the forests reached their highest development. Hence they went wavering northward over icy Alaska, brave spruce and fir, poplar and birch, by the coasts and the rivers, to within sight of the Arctic Ocean. American forests! the glory of the world! Surveyed thus from the east to the west, from the north to the south, they are rich beyond thought, immortal, immeasurable, enough and to spare for every feeding, sheltering beast and bird, insect and son of Adam; and nobody need have cared had there been no pines in Norway, no cedars and deodars on Lebanon and the Himalayas, no vine-clad selvas in the basin of the Amazon. With such variety, harmony, and triumphant exuberance, even nature, it would seem, might have rested content with the forests of North America, and planted no more.

So they appeared a few centuries ago when they were rejoicing in wildness. The Indians with stone axes could do them no more harm than could gnawing beavers and browsing moose. Even the fires of the Indians and the fierce shattering lightning seemed to work together only for good in clearing spots here and there for smooth garden prairies, and openings for sunflowers seeking the light. But when the steel axe of the white man rang out on the startled air their doom was sealed. Every tree heard the bodeful sound, and pillars of smoke gave the sign in the sky.

I suppose we need not go mourning the buffaloes. In the nature of things they had to give place to better cattle, though the change might have been made without barbarous wickedness. Likewise many of nature's five hundred kinds of wild trees had to make way for orchards and cornfields. In the settlement and civilization of the country, bread more than timber or beauty was wanted; and in the blindness of hunger, the early settlers, claiming Heaven as their guide, regarded God's trees as only a larger kind of pernicious weeds, extremely hard to get rid of. Accordingly, with no eye to the future, these pious destroyers waged interminable forest wars; chips flew thick and fast; trees in their beauty fell crashing by millions, smashed to confusion, and the smoke of their burning has been rising to heaven more than two hundred years. After the Atlantic coast from Maine to Georgia had been mostly cleared and scorched into melancholy ruins, the overflowing multitude of bread and money seekers poured over the Alleghanies into the fertile middle West, spreading ruthless devastation ever wider and farther over the rich valley of the Mississippi and the vast shadowy pine region about the Great Lakes. Thence still westward, the invading horde of destroyers called settlers made its fiery way over the broad Rocky Mountains, felling and burning more fiercely than ever, until at last it has reached the wild side of the continent, and entered the last of the great aboriginal forests on the shores of the Pacific.

Surely, then, it should not be wondered at that lovers of their country, bewailing its baldness, are now crying aloud, "Save what is left of the forests!" Clearing has surely now gone far enough; soon timber will be scarce, and not a grove will be left to rest in or pray in. The remnant protected will yield plenty of timber, a perennial harvest for every right use, without further diminution of its area, and will continue to cover the springs of the rivers that rise in the mountains and give irrigating waters to the dry valleys at their feet, prevent wasting floods and be a blessing to everybody forever.

Every other civilized nation in the world has been compelled to care for its forests, and so must we if waste and destruction are not to go on to the bitter end, leaving America as barren as Palestine or Spain. In its calmer moments, in the midst of bewildering hunger and war and restless over-industry, Prussia has learned that the forest plays an important part in human progress, and that the advance in civilization only makes it more indispensable. It has, therefore, as shown by Mr. Pinchot, refused to deliver its forests to more or less speedy destruction by permitting them to pass into private ownership. But the state woodlands are not allowed to lie idle. On the contrary, they are made to produce as much timber as is possible without spoiling them. In the administration of its forests, the state righteously considers itself bound to treat them as a trust for the nation as a whole, and to keep in view the common good of the people for all time.

In France no government forests have been sold since 1870. On the other hand, about one half of the fifty million francs spent on forestry has been given to engineering works, to make the replanting of denuded areas possible. The disappearance of the forests in the first place, it is claimed, may be traced in most cases directly to mountain pasturage. The provisions of the Code concerning private woodlands are substantially these: no private owner may clear his woodlands without giving notice to the government at least four months in advance, and the forest service may forbid the clearing on the following grounds,—to maintain the soil on mountains, to defend the soil against erosion and flooding by rivers or torrents, to insure the existence of springs or watercourses, to protect the dunes and seashore, etc. A proprietor who has cleared his forest without permission is subject to heavy fine, and in addition may be made to replant the cleared area.

In Switzerland, after many laws like our own had been found wanting, the Swiss forest school was established in

1865, and soon after the federal forest law was enacted, which is binding over nearly two thirds of the country. Under its provisions, the cantons must appoint and pay the number of suitably educated foresters required for the fulfillment of the forest law; and in the organization of a normally stocked forest, the object of first importance must be the cutting each year of an amount of timber equal to the total annual increase, and no more.

The Russian government passed a law in 1888, declaring that clearing is forbidden in protected forests, and is allowed in others "only when its effects will not be to disturb the suitable relations which should exist between forest and agricultural lands."

Even Japan is ahead of us in the management of her forests. They cover an area of about twenty-nine million acres. The feudal lords valued the woodlands, and enacted vigorous protective laws; and when, in the latest civil war, the Mikado government destroyed the feudal system, it declared the forests that had belonged to the feudal lords to be the property of the state, promulgated a forest law binding on the whole kingdom, and founded a school of forestry in Tokio. The forest service does not rest satisfied with the present proportion of woodland, but looks to planting the best forest trees it can find in any country, if likely to be useful and to thrive in Japan.

In India systematic forest management was begun about forty years ago, under difficulties—presented by the character of the country, the prevalence of running fires, opposition from lumbermen, settlers, etc.—not unlike those which confront us now. Of the total area of government forests, perhaps seventy million acres, fifty-five million acres have been brought under the control of the forestry department,—a larger area than that of all our national parks and reservations. The chief aims of the administration are effective protection of the forests from fire, an efficient system of regeneration, and cheap transportation of the forest products; the results so far have been most beneficial and encouraging.

It seems, therefore, that almost every civilized nation can give us a lesson on the management and care of forests.

So far our government has done nothing effective with its forests, though the best in the world, but is like a rich and foolish spendthrift who has inherited a magnificent estate in perfect order, and then has left his fields and meadows, forests and parks, to be sold and plundered and wasted at will, depending on their inexhaustible abundance. Now it is plain that the forests are not inexhaustible, and that quick measures must be taken if ruin is to be avoided. Year by year the remnant is growing smaller before the axe and fire, while the laws in existence provide neither for the protection of the timber from destruction nor for its use where it is most needed.

As is shown by Mr. E. A. Bowers, formerly Inspector of the Public Land Service, the foundation of our protective policy, which has never protected, is an act passed March 1, 1817, which authorized the Secretary of the Navy to reserve lands producing live-oak and cedar, for the sole purpose of supplying timber for the navy of the United States. An extension of this law by the passage of the act of March 2, 1831, provided that if any person should cut live-oak or red cedar trees or *other timber* from the lands of the United States for any other purpose than the construction of the navy, such person should pay a fine not less than triple the value of the timber cut, and be imprisoned for a period not exceeding twelve months. Upon this old law, as Mr. Bowers points out, having the construction of a wooden navy in view, the United States government has to-day chiefly to rely in protecting its timber throughout the arid regions of the West, where none of the naval timber which the law had in mind is to be found.

By the act of June 3, 1878, timber can be taken from public lands not subject to entry under any existing laws except for minerals, by bona fide residents of the Rocky Mountain states and territories and the Dakotas. Under the timber and stone act, of the same date, land in the Pacific States and Nevada, valuable mainly for timber, and unfit for cultivation if the timber is removed, can be purchased for two dollars and a half an acre, under certain restrictions. By the act of March 3, 1875, all land-grant and right-of-way railroads are authorized to take timber from the public lands adjacent to their lines for construction purposes; and they have taken it with a vengeance, destroying a hundred times more than they have used, mostly by allowing fires to run in the woods. The settlement laws, under which a settler may enter lands valuable for timber as well as for agriculture, furnish another means of obtaining title to public timber.

With the exception of the timber culture act, under which, in consideration of planting a few acres of seedlings, settlers on the treeless plains got 160 acres each, the above is the only legislation aiming to protect and promote the planting of forests. In no other way than under some one of these laws can a citizen of the United States make any use of the public forests. To show the results of the timber-planting act, it need only be stated that of the thirty-eight million acres entered under it, less than one million acres have been patented. This means that less than fifty thousand acres have been planted with stunted, woebegone, almost hopeless sprouts of trees, while at the same time the government has allowed millions of acres of the grandest forest trees to be stolen or destroyed, or sold for nothing. Under the act of June 3, 1878, settlers in Colorado and the Territories were allowed to cut timber for mining and educational purposes from mineral land, which in the practical West means both cutting and burning anywhere and everywhere, for any purpose, on any sort of public land. Thus, the prospector, the miner, and mining and railroad companies are allowed by law to take all the timber they like for their mines and roads, and the forbidden settler, if there are no mineral lands near his farm or stock-ranch, or none that he knows of, can hardly be expected to forbear taking what he needs wherever he can find it. Timber is as necessary as bread, and no scheme of management failing to recognize and properly provide for this want can possibly be maintained. In any case, it will be hard to teach the pioneers that it is wrong to steal government timber. Taking from the government is with them the same as taking from nature, and their consciences flinch no more in cutting timber from the wild forests than in drawing water from a lake or river. As for reservation and protection of forests, it seems as silly and needless to them as protection and reservation of the ocean would be, both appearing to be boundless and inexhaustible.

The special land agents employed by the General Land Office to protect the public domain from timber depredations are supposed to collect testimony to sustain prosecution and to superintend such prosecution on behalf of the government, which is represented by the district attorneys. But timber thieves of the Western class are seldom convicted, for the good reason that most of the jurors who try such cases are themselves as guilty as those on trial. The effect of the present confused, discriminating, and unjust system has been to place almost the whole population in opposition to the government; and as conclusive of its futility, as shown by Mr. Bowers, we need only state that during the seven years from 1881 to 1887 inclusive, the value of the timber reported stolen from the government lands was $36,719,935, and the amount recovered was $478,073, while the cost of the services of special agents alone was $455,000, to which must be added the expense of the trials. Thus for nearly thirty-seven million dollars worth of timber the government got less than nothing; and the value of that consumed by running fires during the same period, without benefit even to thieves, was probably over two hundred millions of dollars. Land commissioners and Secretaries of the Interior have repeatedly called attention to this ruinous state of affairs, and asked Congress to enact the requisite legislation for reasonable reform. But, busied with tariffs, etc., Congress has given no heed to these or other appeals, and our forests, the most valuable and the most destructible of all the natural resources of the country, are being robbed and burned more rapidly than ever. The annual appropriation for so-called "protection service" is hardly sufficient to keep twenty-five timber agents in the field, and as far as any efficient protection of timber is concerned these agents themselves night as well be timber.[1]

That a change from robbery and ruin to a permanent rational policy is urgently needed nobody with the slightest knowledge of American forests will deny. In the East and along the northern Pacific coast, where the rainfall is abundant, comparatively few care keenly what becomes of the trees so long as fuel and lumber are not noticeably dear. But in the Rocky Mountains and California and Arizona, where the forests are inflammable, and where the fertility of the lowlands depends upon irrigation, public opinion is growing stronger every year in favor of permanent protection by the federal government of all the forests that cover the sources of the streams. Even lumbermen in these regions, long accustomed to steal, are now willing and anxious to buy lumber for their mills under cover of law: some possibly from a late second growth of honesty, but most, especially the small mill-owners, simply because it no longer pays to steal where all may not only steal, but also destroy, and in particular because it costs about as much to steal timber for one mill as for ten, and, therefore, the ordinary lumberman can no longer compete with the large corporations. Many of the miners find that timber is already becoming scarce and dear on the denuded hills around their mills, and they, too, are asking for protection of forests, at least against fire. The slow-going, unthrifty farmers, also, are beginning to realize that when the timber is stripped from the mountains the irrigating streams dry up in summer, and are destructive in winter; that soil, scenery, and everything slips off with the trees: so of course they are coming into the ranks of tree-friends.

Of all the magnificent coniferous forests around the Great Lakes, once the property of the United States, scarcely any belong to it now. They have disappeared in lumber and smoke, mostly smoke, and the government got not one cent for them; only the land they were growing on was considered valuable, and two and a half dollars an acre was charged for it. Here and there in the Southern States there are still considerable areas of timbered government land, but these are comparatively unimportant. Only the forests of the West are significant in size and value, and these, although still great, are rapidly vanishing. Last summer, of the unrivaled red-wood forests of the Pacific Coast Range, the United States Forestry Commission could not find a single quarter-section that remained in the hands of the government.[2]

Under the timber and stone act of 1878, which might well have been called the "dust and ashes act," any citizen of the United States could take up one hundred and sixty acres of timber land, and by paying two dollars and a half an acre for it obtain title. There was some virtuous effort made with a view to limit the operations of the act by requiring that the purchaser should make affidavit that he was entering the land exclusively for his own use, and by not allowing any association to enter more than one hundred and sixty acres. Nevertheless, under this act wealthy corporations have fraudulently obtained title to from ten thousand to twenty thousand acres or more. The plan was usually as follows: A mill company, desirous of getting title to a large body of red-wood or sugar-pine land, first blurred the eyes and ears of the land agents, and then hired men to enter the land they wanted, and immediately deed it to the company after a nominal compliance with the law; false swearing in the wilderness against the government being held of no account. In one case which came under the observation of Mr. Bowers, it was the practice of a lumber company to hire the entire crew of every vessel which might happen to touch at any port in the red-wood belt, to enter one hundred and sixty acres each and immediately deed the land to the company, in consideration of the company's paying all expenses and giving the jolly sailors fifty dollars apiece for their trouble.

By such methods have our magnificent redwoods and much of the sugar-pine forests of the Sierra Nevada been absorbed by foreign and resident capitalists. Uncle Sam is not often called a fool in business matters, yet he has sold millions of acres of timber land at two dollars and a half an acre on which a single tree was worth more than a hundred dollars. But this priceless land has been patented, and nothing can be done now about the crazy bargain. According to the everlasting law of righteousness, even the fraudulent buyers at less than one per cent of its value are making little or nothing, on account of fierce competition. The trees are felled, and about half of each giant is left on the ground to be converted into smoke and ashes; the better half is sawed into choice lumber and sold to citizens of the United States or to foreigners: thus robbing the country of its glory and impoverishing it without right benefit to anybody,—a bad, black business from beginning to end.

The redwood is one of the few conifers that sprout from the stump and roots, and it declares itself willing to begin immediately to repair the damage of the lumberman and also that of the forest-burner. As soon as a redwood is cut down or burned it sends up a crowd of eager, hopeful shoots, which, if allowed to grow, would in a few decades attain a height of a hundred feet, and the strongest of them would finally become giants as great as the original tree. Gigantic second and third growth trees are found in the redwoods, forming magnificent temple-like circles around charred ruins more than a thousand years old. But not one denuded acre in a hundred is allowed to raise a new forest growth. On the contrary, all the brains, religion, and superstition of the neighborhood are brought into play to prevent a new growth. The sprouts from the roots and stumps are cut off again and again, with zealous concern as to the best time and method of making death sure. In the clearings of one of the largest mills on the coast we found thirty men at work, last summer, cutting off redwood shoots "in the dark of the moon," claiming that all the stumps and roots cleared at this auspicious time would send up no more shoots. Anyhow, these vigorous, almost immortal trees are killed at last, and black stumps are now their only monuments over most of the chopped and burned areas.

The redwood is the glory of the Coast Range. It extends along the western slope, in a nearly continuous belt about ten miles wide, from beyond the Oregon boundary to the south of Santa Cruz, a distance of nearly four hundred miles, and in massive, sustained grandeur and closeness of growth surpasses all the other timber woods of the world. Threes from ten to fifteen feet in diameter and three hundred feet high are not uncommon, and a few attain a height of three hundred and fifty feet or even four hundred, with a diameter at the base of fifteen to twenty feet or more, while the ground beneath them is a garden of fresh, exuberant ferns, lilies, gaultheria, and rhododendron. This grand tree, Sequoia sempervirens, is surpassed in size only by its near relative, Sequoia gigantea, or Big Tree, of the Sierra Nevada, if, indeed, it is surpassed. The sempervirens is certainly the taller of the two. The gigantea attains a greater girth, and is heavier, more noble in port, and more sublimely beautiful. These two Sequoia are all that are known to exist in the world, though in former geological times the genus was common and had many species. The redwood is restricted to the Coast Range, and the Big Tree to the Sierra.

As timber the redwood is too good to live. The largest sawmills ever built are busy along its seaward border, "with all the modern improvements," but so immense is the yield per acre it will be long ere the supply is exhausted. The Big Tree is also, to some extent, being made into lumber. It is far less abundant than the redwood, and is, fortunately, less accessible, extending along the western flank of the Sierra in a partially interrupted belt, about two hundred and fifty miles long, at a height of from four to eight thousand feet above the sea. The enormous logs, too heavy to handle, are blasted into manageable dimensions with gunpowder. A large portion of the best timber is thus shattered and destroyed, and, with the huge, knotty tops, is left in ruins for tremendous fires that kill every tree within their range, great and small. Still, the species is not in danger of extinction. It has been planted and is flourishing over a great part of Europe, and magnificent sections of the aboriginal forests have been reserved as national and State parks,— the Mariposa Sequoia Grove, near Yosemite, managed by the State of California, and the General Grant and Sequoia national parks on the Kings, Kaweah, and Tule rivers, efficiently guarded by a small troop of United States cavalry under the direction of the Secretary of the interior. But there is not a single specimen of the redwood in any national park. Only by gift or purchase, so far as I know, can the government get back into its possession a single acre of this wonderful forest.

The legitimate demands on the forests that have passed into private ownership, as well as those in the hands of the government, are increasing every year with the rapid settlement and up-building of the country, but the methods of lumbering are as yet grossly wasteful. In most mills only the best portions of the best trees are used, while the ruins are left on the ground to feed great fires, which kill much of what is left of the less desirable timber, together with the seedlings, on which the permanence of the forest depends. Thus every mill is a centre of destruction far more severe from waste and fire than from use. The same thing is true of the mines, which consume and destroy indirectly immense quantities of timber with their innumerable fires, accidental or set to make open ways, and often without regard to how far they run. The prospector deliberately sets fires to clear off the woods just where they are densest, to lay the rocks bare and make the discovery of mines easier. Sheep-owners and their shepherds also set fires everywhere through the woods in the fall to facilitate the march of their countless flocks the next summer, and perhaps in some places to improve the pasturage. The axe is not yet at the root of every tree, but the sheep is,or was before the national parks were established and guarded by the military, the only effective and reliable arm of the government free from the blight of politics. Not only do the shepherds, at the driest time of the year, set fire to everything that will burn, but the sheep consume every green leaf, not sparing even the young conifers, where they are in a starving condition from crowding, and they rake and dibble the loose soil of the mountain sides for the spring floods to wash away, and thus at last leave the ground barren.

Of all the destroyers that infest the woods, the shake-maker seems the happiest. Twenty or thirty years ago, shakes, a kind of long, board-like shingles split with a mallet and a frow, were in great demand for covering barns and sheds, and many are used still in preference to common shingles, especially those made from the sugar-pine, which do not warp or crack in the hottest sunshine. Drifting adventurers in California, after harvest and threshing are over, oftentimes meet to discuss their plans for the winter, and their talk is interesting. Once, in a company of this kind, I heard a man say, as he peacefully smoked his pipe: "Boys, as soon as this job's done I'm goin' into the duck business. There's big money in it, and your grub costs nothing. Tule Joe made five hundred dollars last winter on mallard and teal. Shot 'em on the Joaquin, tied 'em in dozens by the neck, and shipped 'em to San Francisco. And when he was tired wading in the sloughs and touched with rheumatiz, he just knocked off on ducks, and went to the Contra Costa hills for dove and quail. It's a mighty good business, and you're your own boss, and the whole thing's fun."

Another of the company, a bushy-bearded fellow, with a trace of brag in his voice, drawled out: "Bird business is well enough for some, but bear is my game, with a deer and a California lion thrown in now and then for change. There's always market for bear grease, and sometimes you can sell the hams. They're good as hog hams any day. And you are your own boss in my business, too, if the bears ain't too big and too many for you. Old grizzlies I despise,—they want cannon to kill 'em; but the blacks and browns are beauties for grease, and when once I get 'em just right, and draw a bead on 'em, I fetch 'em every time." Another said he was going to catch up a lot of mustangs as soon as the rains set in, hitch them to a gang-plough, and go to farming on the San Joaquin plains for wheat. But most preferred the shake business, until something more profitable and as sure could be found, with equal comfort and independence.

With a cheap mustang or mule to carry a pair of blankets, a sack of flour, a few pounds of coffee, and an axe, a frow, and a cross-cut saw, the shake-maker ascends the mountains to the pine belt where it is most accessible, usually by some mine or mill road. Then he strikes off into the virgin woods, where the sugar pine, king of all the hundred species of pines in the world in size and beauty, towers on the open sunny slopes of the Sierra in the fullness of its glory. Selecting a favorable spot for a cabin near a meadow with a stream, he unpacks his animal and stakes it out on the meadow. Then he chops into one after another of the pines, until he finds one that he feels sure will split freely, cuts this down, saws off a section four feet long, splits it, and from this first cut, perhaps seven feet in diameter, he gets shakes enough for a cabin and its furniture,—walls, roof, door, bedstead, table, and stool. Besides his labor, only a few pounds of nails are required. Sapling poles form the frame of the airy building, usually about six feet by eight in size, on which the shakes are nailed, with the edges overlapping. A few bolts from the same section that the shakes were made from are split into square sticks and built up to form a chimney, the inside and interspaces being plastered and filled in with mud. Thus, with abundance of fuel, shelter and comfort by his own fireside are secured. Then he goes to work sawing and splitting for the market, tying the shakes in bundles of fifty or a hundred. They are four feet long, four inches wide, and about one fourth of an inch thick. The first few thousands he sells or trades at the nearest mill or store, getting provisions in exchange. Then he advertises, in whatever way he can, that he has excellent sugar-pine shakes for sale, easy of access and cheap.

Only the lower, perfectly clear, free-splitting portions of the giant pines are used,—perhaps ten to twenty feet from a tree two hundred and fifty in height; all the rest is left a mass of ruins, to rot or to feed the forest fires, while thousands are hacked deeply and rejected in proving the grain. Over nearly all of the more accessible slopes of the Sierra and Cascade mountains in southern Oregon, at a height of from three to six thousand feet above the sea, and for a distance of about six hundred miles, this waste and confusion extends. Happy robbers! dwelling in the most beautiful woods, in the most salubrious climate, breathing delightful odors both day and night, drinking cool living water,—roses and lilies at their feet in the spring, shedding fragrance and ringing bells as if cheering them on in their desolating work. There is none to say them nay. They buy no land, pay no taxes, dwell in a paradise with no forbidding angel either from Washington or from heaven. Every one of the frail shake shanties is a centre of destruction, and the extent of the ravages wrought in this quiet way is in the aggregate enormous.

It is not generally known that, notwithstanding the immense quantities of timber cut every year for foreign and home markets and mines, from five to ten times as much is destroyed as is used, chiefly by running forest fires that only the federal government can stop. Travelers through the West in summer are not likely to forget the fire-work displayed along the various railway tracks. Thoreau, when contemplating the destruction of the forests on the east side of the continent, said that soon the country would be so bald that every man would have to grow whiskers to hide its nakedness, but he thanked God that at least the sky was safe. Had he gone West he would have found out that the sky was not safe; for all through the summer months, over most of the mountain regions, the smoke of mill and forest fires is so thick and black that no sunbeam can pierce it. The whole sky, with clouds, sun, moon, and stars, is simply blotted out. There is no real sky and no scenery. Not a mountain is left in the landscape. At least none is in sight from the lowlands, and they all might as well be on the moon, as far as scenery is concerned.

The half-dozen transcontinental railroad companies advertise the beauties of their lines in gorgeous many-colored folders, each claiming its as the "scenic route." "The route of superior desolation"—the smoke, dust, and ashes route—would be a more truthful description. Every train rolls on through dismal smoke and barbarous, melancholy ruins; and the companies might well cry in their advertisements: "Come! travel our way. Ours is the blackest. It is the only genuine Erebus route. The sky is black and the ground is black, and on either side there is a continuous border of black stumps and logs and blasted trees appealing to heaven for help as if still half alive, and their mute eloquence is most interestingly touching. The blackness is perfect. On account of the superior skill of our workmen, advantages of climate, and the kind of trees, the charring is generally deeper along our line, and the ashes are deeper, and the confusion and desolation displayed can never be rivaled. No other route on this continent so fully illustrates the abomination of desolation." Such a claim would be reasonable, as each seems the worst, whatever route you chance to take.

Of course a way had to be cleared through the woods. But the felled timber is not worked up into firewood for the engines and into lumber for the company's use; it is left lying in vulgar confusion, and is fired from time to time by sparks from locomotives or by the workmen camping along the line. The fires, whether accidental or set, are allowed to run into the woods as far as they may, thus assuring comprehensive destruction. The directors of a line that guarded against fires, and cleared a clean gap edged with living trees, and fringed and mantled with the grass and flowers and beautiful seedlings that are ever ready and willing to spring up, might justly boast of the beauty of their road; for nature is always ready to heal every scar. But there is no such road on the western side of the continent. Last summer, in the Rocky Mountains, I saw six fires started by sparks from a locomotive within a distance of three miles, and nobody was in sight to prevent them from spreading. They might run into the adjacent forests and burn the timber from hundreds of square miles; not a man in the State would care to spend an hour in fighting them, as long as his own fences and buildings were not threatened.

Notwithstanding all the waste and use which have been going on unchecked like a storm for more than two centuries, it is not yet too late—though it is high time-for the government to begin a rational administration of its forests. About seventy million acres it still owns,—enough for all the country, if wisely used. These residual forests are generally on mountain slopes, just where they are doing the most good, and where their removal would be followed by the greatest number of evils; the lands they cover are too rocky and high for agriculture, and can never be made as valuable for any other crop as for present crop of trees. It has been shown over and over again that if these mountains were to be stripped of their trees and underbrush, and kept bare and sodless by hordes of sheep and the innumerable fires the shepherds set, besides those of the millmen, prospectors shake-makers, and all sorts of adventurers, both lowlands and mountains would speedily become little better than desert, compared with their present beneficent fertility. During heavy rainfalls and while the winter accumulations of snow were melting, the large streams would swell into destructive torrents, cutting deep, rugged-edged gullies, carrying away the fertile humus and soil as well as sand and rocks, filling up and overflowing their lower channels, and covering the lowland fields with raw detritus. Drought and barrenness would follow.

In their natural condition, or under wise management, keeping out destructive sheep, preventing fires, selecting the trees that should be cut for lumber, and preserving the young ones and the shrubs and sod of herbaceous vegetation, these forests would be a never failing fountain of wealth and beauty. The cool shades of the forest give rise to moist beds and currents of air, and the sod of grasses and the various flowering plants and shrubs thus fostered, together with the network and sponge of tree roots, absorb and hold back the rain and the waters from melting snow, compelling them to ooze and percolate and flow gently through the soil in streams that never dry. All the pine needles and rootlets and blades of grass, and the fallen, decaying trunks of trees, are dams, storing the bounty of the clouds and dispensing it in perennial life-giving streams, instead of allowing it to gather suddenly and rush headlong in short-lived devastating floods. Everybody on the dry side of the continent is beginning to find this out, and, in view of the waste going on, is growing more and more anxious for government protection. The outcries we hear against forest reservations come mostly from thieves who are wealthy and steal timber by wholesale. They have so long been allowed to steal and destroy in peace that any impediment to forest robbery is denounced as a cruel and irreligious interference with "vested rights," likely to endanger the repose of all ungodly welfare.

Gold, gold, gold! How strong a voice that metal has!

"O wae for the siller, it is sae preva'lin'!"

Even in Congress a sizable chunk of gold, carefully concealed, will outtalk and outfight all the nation on a subject like forestry, well smothered in ignorance, and in which the money interests of only a few are conspicuously involved. Under these circumstances, the bawling, blethering oratorical stuff drowns the voice of God himself. Yet the dawn of a new day in forestry is breaking. Honest citizens see that only the rights of the government are being trampled, not those of the settlers. Only what belongs to all alike is reserved, and every acre that is left should be held together under the federal government as a basis for a general policy of administration for the public good. The people will not always be deceived by selfish opposition, whether from lumber and mining corporations or from sheepmen and prospectors, however cunningly brought forward underneath fables and gold.

Emerson says that things refuse to be mismanaged long. An exception would seem to be found in the case of our forests, which have been mismanaged rather long, and now come desperately near being like smashed eggs and spilt milk. Still, in the long run the world does not move backward. The wonderful advance made in the last few years, in creating four national parks in the West, and thirty forest reservations, embracing nearly forty million acres; and in the planting of the borders of streets and highways and spacious parks in all the great cities, to satisfy the natural taste and hunger for landscape beauty and righteousness that God has put, in some measure, into every human being and animal, shows the trend of awakening public opinion. The making of the far-famed New York Central Park was opposed by even good men, with misguided pluck, perseverance, and ingenuity; but straight right won its way, and now that park is appreciated. So we confidently believe it will be with our great national parks and forest reservations. There will be a period of indifference on the part of the rich, sleepy with wealth, and of the toiling millions, sleepy with poverty, most of whom never saw a forest; a period of screaming protest and objection from the plunderers, who are as unconscionable and enterprising as Satan. But light is surely coming, and the friends of destruction will preach and bewail in vain.

The United States government has always been proud of the welcome it has extended to good men of every nation, seeking freedom and homes and bread. Let them be welcomed still as nature welcomes them, to the woods as well as to the prairies and plains. No place is too good for good men, and still there is room. They are invited to heaven, and may well be allowed in America. Every place is made better by them. Let them be as free to pick gold and gems from the hills, to cut and hew, dig and plant, for homes and bread, as the birds are to pick berries from the wild bushes, and moss and leaves for nests. The ground will be glad to feed them, and the pines will come down from the mountains for their homes as willingly as the cedars came from Lebanon for Solomon's temple. Nor will the woods be the worse for this use, or their benign influences be diminished any more than the sun is diminished by shining. Mere destroyers, however, tree-killers, wool and mutton men, spreading death and confusion in the fairest groves and gardens ever planted,—let the government hasten to cast them out and make an end of them. For it must be told again and again, and be burningly borne in mind, that just now, while protective measures are being deliberated languidly, destruction and use are speeding on faster and farther every day. The axe and saw are insanely busy, chips are flying thick as snowflakes, and every summer thousands of acres of priceless forests, with their underbrush, soil, springs, climate, scenery, and religion, are vanishing away in clouds of smoke, while, except in the national parks, not one forest guard is employed.

All sorts of local laws and regulations have been tried and found wanting, and the costly lessons of our own experience, as well as that of every civilized nation, show conclusively that the fate of the remnant of our forests is in the hands of the federal government, and that if the remnant is to be saved at all, it must be saved quickly.

Any fool can destroy trees. They cannot run away; and if they could, they would still be destroyed,—chased and hunted down as long as fun or a dollar could be got out of their bark hides, branching horns, or magnificent bole backbones. Few that fell trees plant them; nor would planting avail much towards getting back anything like the noble primeval forests. During a man's life only saplings can be grown, in the place of the old trees—tens of centuries old—that have been destroyed. It took more than three thousand years to make some of the trees in these Western woods,—trees that are still standing in perfect strength and beauty, waving and singing in the mighty forests of the Sierra. Through all the wonderful, eventful centuries since Christ's time—and long before that—God has cared for these trees, saved them from drought, disease, avalanches, and a thousand straining, leveling tempests and floods; but he cannot save them from fools,—only Uncle Sam can do that.

[1] A change for the better, compelled by public opinion, is now going on,—1901.

[2] The State of California recently appropriated two hundred and fifty thousand dollars to buy a block of redwood land near Santa Cruz for a state park. A much larger national park should be made in Humboldt or Mendocino county.

MY FIRST
SUMMER IN THE
SIERRA

JOHN MUIR

MY FIRST SUMMER IN THE SIERRA

GIBBS SMITH
TO ENRICH AND INSPIRE HUMANKIND

Published by
Gibbs Smith
P.O. Box 667
Layton, Utah 84041

1.800.835.4993 orders
www.gibbs-smith.com

Cover art by Seth Lucas
Printed and bound in China

Gibbs Smith books are printed on either recycled, 100% post-consumer waste, FSC-certified papers or on paper produced from sustainable PEFC-certified forest/controlled wood source. Learn more at www.pefc.org.

Library of Congress Cataloging-in-Publication Data

Names: Muir, John, 1838–1914, author.
Title: My first summer in the Sierra / John Muir.
Identifiers: LCCN 2017031769 | ISBN 9781423649120 (hardcover)
Subjects: LCSH: Muir, John, 1838–1914. | Natural history—Sierra
    Nevada (Calif. and Nev.) | Naturalists—United States—Biography.
Classification: LCC QH31.M9 A3 2018 | DDC 508.092 [B]—dc23
LC record available at https://lccn.loc.gov/2017031769

26 25 24 23 22   10 9 8 7 6

CONTENTS

THROUGH THE FOOTHILLS WITH A
FLOCK OF SHEEP

1869

In the great Central Valley of California there are only two seasons—spring and summer. The spring begins with the first rainstorm, which usually falls in November. In a few months the wonderful flowery vegetation is in full bloom, and by the end of May it is dead and dry and crisp, as if every plant had been roasted in an oven.

Then the lolling, panting flocks and herds are driven to the high, cool, green pastures of the Sierra. I was longing for the mountains about this time, but money was scarce and I couldn't see how a bread supply was to be kept up. While I was anxiously brooding on the bread problem, so troublesome to wanderers, and trying to believe that I might learn to live like the wild animals, gleaning nourishment here and there from seeds, berries, etc., sauntering and climbing in joyful independence of money or baggage, Mr. Delaney, a sheep-owner, for whom I had worked a few weeks, called on me, and offered to engage me to go with his shepherd and flock to the headwaters of the Merced and Tuolumne rivers—the very region I had most in mind. I was in the mood to accept work of any kind that would take me into the mountains whose treasures I had tasted last summer in the Yosemite region. The flock, he explained, would be moved gradually higher through the successive forest belts as the snow melted, stopping for a few weeks at the best places we came to. These I thought would be good centers of observation from which I might be able to make many telling excursions within a radius of eight or ten miles of the camps to learn something of the plants, animals, and rocks; for he assured me that I should be left perfectly free to follow my studies. I judged, however, that I was in no way the right man for the place, and freely explained my shortcomings, confessing that I was wholly unacquainted with the topography of the upper mountains, the streams that would have to be crossed, and the wild sheep-eating animals, etc.; in short that, what with bears, coyotes, rivers, cañons, and thorny, bewildering chaparral, I feared that half or more of his flock would be lost. Fortunately these shortcomings seemed insignificant to Mr. Delaney. The main thing, he said, was to have a man about the camp whom he could trust to see that the shepherd did his duty, and he assured me that the difficulties that seemed so formidable at a distance would vanish as we went on; encouraging me further by saying that the shepherd would do all the herding, that I could study plants and rocks and scenery as much as I liked, and that he would himself accompany us to the first main camp and make occasional visits to our higher ones to replenish our store of provisions and see how we prospered. Therefore I concluded to go, though still fearing, when I saw the silly sheep bouncing one by one through the narrow gate of the home corral to be counted, that of the two thousand and fifty many would never return.

I was fortunate in getting a fine St. Bernard dog for a companion. His master, a hunter with whom I was slightly acquainted, came to me as soon as he heard that I was going to spend the summer in the Sierra and begged me to take his favorite dog, Carlo, with me, for he feared that if he were compelled to stay all summer on the plains the fierce heat might be the death of him. "I think I can trust you to be kind to him," he said, "and I am sure he will be good to you. He knows all about the mountain animals, will guard the camp, assist in managing the sheep, and in every way be found able and faithful." Carlo knew we were talking about him, watched our faces, and listened so attentively that I fancied he understood us. Calling him by name, I asked him if he was willing to go with me. He looked me in the face with eyes expressing wonderful intelligence, then turned to his master, and after permission was given by a wave of the hand toward me and a farewell patting caress, he quietly followed me as if he perfectly understood all that had been said and had known me always.

June 3, 1869. This morning provisions, camp-kettles, blankets, plant-press, etc., were packed on two horses, the flock headed for the tawny foothills, and away we sauntered in a cloud of dust: Mr. Delaney, bony and tall, with sharply hacked profile like Don Quixote, leading the pack-horses, Billy, the proud shepherd, a Chinaman and a Digger Indian to assist in driving for the first few days in the brushy foothills, and myself with notebook tied to my belt.

The home ranch from which we set out is on the south side of the Tuolumne River near French Bar, where the foothills of metamorphic gold-bearing slates dip below the stratified deposits of the Central Valley. We had not gone more than a mile before some of the old leaders of the flock showed by the eager, inquiring way they ran and looked ahead that they were thinking of the high pastures they had enjoyed last summer. Soon the whole flock seemed to be hopefully excited, the mothers calling their lambs, the lambs replying in tones wonderfully human, their fondly quavering calls interrupted now and then by hastily snatched mouthfuls of withered grass. Amid all this seeming babel of baas as they streamed over the hills every mother and child recognized each other's voice. In case a tired lamb, half asleep in the smothering dust, should fail to answer, its mother would come running back through the flock toward the spot whence its last response was heard, and refused to be comforted until she found it, the one of a thousand, though to our eyes and ears all seemed alike.

The flock traveled at the rate of about a mile an hour, outspread in the form of an irregular triangle, about a hundred yards wide at the base, and a hundred and fifty yards long, with a crooked, ever-changing point made up of the strongest foragers, called the "leaders," which, with the most active of those scattered along the ragged sides of the "main body," hastily explored nooks in the rocks and bushes for grass and leaves; the lambs and feeble old mothers dawdling in the rear were called the "tail end."

About noon the heat was hard to bear; the poor sheep panted pitifully and tried to stop in the shade of every tree they came to, while we gazed with eager longing through the dim burning glare toward the snowy mountains and streams, though not one was in sight. The landscape is only wavering foothills roughened here and there with bushes and trees and outcropping masses of slate. The trees, mostly the blue oak (*Quercus Douglasii*), are about thirty to forty feet high, with pale blue-green leaves and white bark, sparsely planted on the thinnest soil or in crevices of rocks beyond the reach of grass fires. The slates in many places rise abruptly through the tawny grass in sharp lichen-covered slabs like tombstones in deserted burying-grounds. With the exception of the oak and four or five species of manzanita and ceanothus, the vegetation of the foothills is mostly the same as that of the plains. I saw this region in the early spring, when it was a charming landscape garden full of birds and bees and flowers. Now the scorching weather makes everything dreary. The ground is full of cracks, lizards glide about on the rocks, and ants in amazing numbers, whose tiny sparks of life only burn the brighter with the heat, fairly quiver with unquenchable energy as they run in long lines to fight and gather food. How it comes that they do not dry to a crisp in a few seconds' exposure to such sun-fire is marvelous. A few rattlesnakes lie coiled in out-of-the-way places, but are seldom seen. Magpies and crows, usually so noisy, are silent now, standing in mixed flocks on the ground beneath the best shade trees, with bills wide open and wings drooped, too breathless to speak; the quails also are trying to keep in the shade about the few tepid alkaline water-holes; cottontail rabbits are running from shade to shade among the ceanothus brush, and occasionally the long-eared hare is seen cantering gracefully across the wider openings.

After a short noon rest in a grove, the poor dust-choked flock was again driven ahead over the brushy hills, but the dim roadway we had been following faded away just where it was most needed, compelling us to stop to look about us and get our bearings. The Chinaman seemed to think we were lost, and chattered in pidgin English concerning the abundance of "litty stick" (chaparral), while the Indian silently scanned the billowy ridges and gulches for openings. Pushing through the thorny jungle, we at length discovered a road trending toward Coulterville, which we followed until an hour before sunset, when we reached a dry ranch and camped for the night.

Camping in the foothills with a flock of sheep is simple and easy, but far from pleasant. The sheep were allowed to pick what they could find in the neighborhood until after sunset, watched by the shepherd, while the others gathered wood, made a fire, cooked, unpacked and fed the horses, etc. About dusk the weary sheep were gathered on the highest open spot near camp, where they willingly bunched close together, and after each mother had found her lamb and suckled it, all lay down and required no attention until morning.

Supper was announced by the call, "Grub!" Each with a tin plate helped himself direct from the pots and pans while chatting about such camp studies as sheep-feed, mines, coyotes, bears, or adventures during the memorable gold days of pay dirt. The Indian kept in the background, saying never a word, as if he belonged to another species. The meal finished, the dogs were fed, the smokers smoked by the fire, and under the influences of fullness and tobacco the calm that settled on their faces seemed almost divine, something like the mellow meditative glow portrayed on the countenances of saints. Then suddenly, as if awakening from a dream, each with a sigh or a grunt knocked the ashes out of his pipe, yawned, gazed at the fire a few moments, said, "Well, I believe I'll turn in," and straightway vanished beneath his blankets. The fire smouldered and flickered an hour or two longer; the stars shone brighter; coons, coyotes, and owls stirred the silence here and there, while crickets and hylas made a cheerful, continuous music, so fitting and full that it seemed a part of the very body of the night. The only discordance came from a snoring sleeper, and the coughing sheep with dust in their throats. In the starlight the flock looked like a big gray blanket.

June 4. The camp was astir at daybreak; coffee, bacon, and beans formed the breakfast, followed by quick dish-washing and packing. A general bleating began about sunrise. As soon as a mother ewe arose, her lamb came bounding and bunting for its breakfast, and after the thousand youngsters had been suckled the flock began to nibble and spread. The restless wethers with ravenous appetites were the first to move, but dared not go far from the main body. Billy and the Indian and the Chinaman kept them headed along the weary road, and allowed them to pick up what little they could find on a breadth of about a quarter of a mile. But as several flocks had already gone ahead of us, scarce a leaf, green or dry, was left; therefore the starving flock had to be hurried on over the bare, hot hills to the nearest of the green pastures, about twenty or thirty miles from here.

The pack-animals were led by Don Quixote, a heavy rifle over his shoulder intended for bears and wolves. This day has been as hot and dusty as the first, leading over gently sloping brown hills, with mostly the same vegetation, excepting the strange-looking Sabine pine

(*Pinus Sabiniana*), which here forms small groves or is scattered among the blue oaks. The trunk divides at a height of fifteen or twenty feet into two or more stems, outleaning or nearly upright, with many straggling branches and long gray needles, casting but little shade. In general appearance this tree looks more like a palm than a pine. The cones are about six or seven inches long, about five in diameter, very heavy, and last long after they fall, so that the ground beneath the trees is covered with them. They make fine resiny, light-giving camp-fires, next to ears of Indian corn the most beautiful fuel I've ever seen. The nuts, the Don tells me, are gathered in large quantities by the Digger Indians for food. They are about as large and hard-shelled as hazelnuts—food and fire fit for the gods from the same fruit.

June 5. This morning a few hours after setting out with the crawling sheep-cloud, we gained the summit of the first well-defined bench on the mountain-flank at Pino Blanco. The Sabine pines interest me greatly. They are so airy and strangely palm-like I was eager to sketch them, and was in a fever of excitement without accomplishing much. I managed to halt long enough, however, to make a tolerably fair sketch of Pino Blanco peak from the southwest side, where there is a small field and vineyard irrigated by a stream that makes a pretty fall on its way down a gorge by the roadside.

After gaining the open summit of this first bench, feeling the natural exhilaration due to the slight elevation of a thousand feet or so, and the hopes excited concerning the outlook to be obtained, a magnificent section of the Merced Valley at what is called Horseshoe Bend came full in sight—a glorious wilderness that seemed to be calling with a thousand songful voices. Bold, down-sweeping slopes, feathered with pines and clumps of manzanita with sunny, open spaces between them, make up most of the foreground; the middle and background present fold beyond fold of finely modeled hills and ridges rising into mountain-like masses in the distance, all covered with a shaggy growth of chaparral, mostly adenostoma, planted so marvelously close and even that it looks like soft, rich plush without a single tree or bare spot. As far as the eye can reach it extends, a heaving, swelling sea of green as regular and continuous as that produced by the heaths of Scotland. The sculpture of the landscape is as striking in its main lines as in its lavish richness of detail; a grand congregation of massive heights with the river shining between, each carved into smooth, graceful folds without leaving a single rocky angle exposed, as if the delicate fluting and ridging fashioned out of metamorphic slates had been carefully sandpapered. The whole landscape showed design, like man's noblest sculptures. How wonderful the power of its beauty! Gazing awe-stricken, I might have left everything for it. Glad, endless work would then be mine tracing the forces that have brought forth its features, its rocks and plants and animals and glorious weather. Beauty beyond thought everywhere, beneath, above, made and being made forever. I gazed and gazed and longed and admired until the dusty sheep and packs were far out of sight, made hurried notes and a sketch, though there was no need of either, for the colors and lines and expression of this divine landscape-countenance are so burned into mind and heart they surely can never grow dim.

The evening of this charmed day is cool, calm,

cloudless, and full of a kind of lightning I have never seen before—white glowing cloud-shaped masses down among the trees and bushes, like quick-throbbing fireflies in the Wisconsin meadows rather than the so-called "wild fire." The spreading hairs of the horses' tails and sparks from our blankets show how highly charged the air is.

June 6. We are now on what may be called the second bench or plateau of the Range, after making many small ups and downs over belts of hill-waves, with, of course, corresponding changes in the vegetation. In open spots many of the lowland compositæ are still to be found, and some of the Mariposa tulips and other conspicuous members of the lily family; but the characteristic blue oak of the foothills is left below, and its place is taken by a fine large species (*Quercus Californica*) with deeply lobed deciduous leaves, picturesquely divided trunk, and broad, massy, finely lobed and modeled head. Here also at a height of about twenty-five hundred feet we come to the edge of the great coniferous forest, made up mostly of yellow pine with just a few sugar pines. We are now in the mountains and they are in us, kindling enthusiasm, making every nerve quiver, filling every pore and cell of us. Our flesh-and-bone tabernacle seems transparent as glass to the beauty about us, as if truly an inseparable part of it, thrilling with the air and trees, streams and rocks, in the waves of the sun,—a part of all nature, neither old nor young, sick nor well, but immortal. Just now I can hardly conceive of any bodily condition dependent on food or breath any more than the ground or the sky. How glorious a conversion, so complete and wholesome it is, scarce memory enough of old bondage days left as a standpoint to view it from! In this new-ness of life we seem to have been so always.

Through a meadow opening in the pine woods I see snowy peaks about the headwaters of the Merced above Yosemite. How near they seem and how clear their outlines on the blue air, or rather *in* the blue air; for they seem to be saturated with it. How consuming strong the invitation they extend! Shall I be allowed to go to them? Night and day I'll pray that I may, but it seems too good to be true. Some one worthy will go, able for the Godful work, yet as far as I can I must drift about these love-monument mountains, glad to be a servant of servants in so holy a wilderness.

Found a lovely lily (*Calochortus albus*) in a shady adenostoma thicket near Coulterville, in company with *Adiantum Chilense.* It is white with a faint purplish tinge inside at the base of the petals, a most impressive plant, pure as a snow crystal, one of the plant saints that all must love and be made so much the purer by it every time it is seen. It puts the roughest mountaineer on his good behavior. With this plant the whole world would seem rich though none other existed. It is not easy to keep on with the camp cloud while such plant people are standing preaching by the wayside.

During the afternoon we passed a fine meadow bounded by stately pines, mostly the arrowy yellow pine, with here and there a noble sugar pine, its feath-ery arms outspread above the spires of its companion species in marked contrast; a glorious tree, its cones fifteen to twenty inches long, swinging like tassels at the ends of the branches with superb ornamental effect. Saw some logs of this species at the Greeley Mill. They are round and regular as if turned in a lathe, excepting the butt cuts, which have a few buttressing projections.

The fragrance of the sugary sap is delicious and scents the mill and lumber yard. How beautiful the ground beneath this pine thickly strewn with slender needles and grand cones, and the piles of cone-scales, seed-wings and shells around the instep of each tree where the squirrels have been feasting! They get the seeds by cutting off the scales at the base in regular order, following their spiral arrangement, and the two seeds at the base of each scale, a hundred or two in a cone, must make a good meal. The yellow pine cones and those of most other species and genera are held upside down on the ground by the Douglas squirrel, and turned around gradually until stripped, while he sits usually with his back to a tree, probably for safety. Strange to say, he never seems to get himself smeared with gum, not even his paws or whiskers—and how cleanly and beautiful in color the cone-litter kitchen-middens he makes.

We are now approaching the region of clouds and cool streams. Magnificent white cumuli appeared about noon above the Yosemite region,—floating fountains refreshing the glorious wilderness,—sky mountains in whose pearly hills and dales the streams take their rise,—blessing with cooling shadows and rain. No rock landscape is more varied in sculpture, none more delicately modeled than these landscapes of the sky; domes and peaks rising, swelling, white as finest marble and firmly outlined, a most impressive manifestation of world building. Every rain-cloud, however fleeting, leaves its mark, not only on trees and flowers whose pulses are quickened, and on the replenished streams and lakes, but also on the rocks are its marks engraved whether we can see them or not.

I have been examining the curious and influential shrub *Adenostoma fasciculata*, first noticed about

Horseshoe Bend. It is very abundant on the lower slopes of the second plateau near Coulterville, forming a dense, almost impenetrable growth that looks dark in the distance. It belongs to the rose family, is about six or eight feet high, has small white flowers in racemes eight to twelve inches long, round needle-like leaves, and reddish bark that becomes shreddy when old. It grows on sun-beaten slopes, and like grass is often swept away by running fires, but is quickly renewed from the roots. Any trees that may have established themselves in its midst are at length killed by these fires, and this no doubt is the secret of the unbroken character of its broad belts. A few manzanitas, which also rise again from the root after consuming fires, make out to dwell with it, also a few bush compositæ—baccharis and linosyris, and some liliaceous plants, mostly calochortus and brodiæa, with deepset bulbs safe from fire. A multitude of birds and "wee, sleekit, cow'rin', tim'rous beasties" find good homes in its deepest thickets, and the open bays and lanes that fringe the margins of its main belts offer shelter and food to the deer when winter storms drive them down from their high mountain pastures. A most admirable plant! It is now in bloom, and I like to wear its pretty fragrant racemes in my buttonhole.

Azalea occidentalis, another charming shrub, grows beside cool streams hereabouts and much higher in the Yosemite region. We found it this evening in bloom a few miles above Greeley's Mill, where we are camped for the night. It is closely related to the rhododendrons, is very showy and fragrant, and everybody must like it not only for itself but for the shady alders and willows, ferny meadows, and living water associated with it.

Another conifer was met to-day,—incense cedar (*Libocedrus decurrens*), a large tree with warm yellow-green foliage in flat plumes like those of arborvitæ, bark cinnamon-colored, and as the boles of the old trees are without limbs they make striking pillars in the woods where the sun chances to shine on them—a worthy companion of the kingly sugar and yellow pines. I feel strangely attracted to this tree. The brown close-grained wood, as well as the small scale-like leaves, is fragrant, and the flat overlapping plumes make fine beds, and must shed the rain well. It would be delightful to be storm-bound beneath one of these noble, hospitable, inviting old trees, its broad sheltering arms bent down like a tent, incense rising from the fire made from its dry fallen branches, and a hearty wind chanting overhead. But the weather is calm to-night, and our camp is only a sheep camp. We are near the North Fork of the Merced. The night wind is telling the wonders of the upper mountains, their snow fountains and gardens, forests and groves; even their topography is in its tones. And the stars, the everlasting sky lilies, how bright they are now that we have climbed above the lowland dust! The horizon is bounded and adorned by a spiry wall of pines, every tree harmoniously related to every other; definite symbols, divine hieroglyphics written with sunbeams. Would I could understand them! The stream flowing past the camp through ferns and lilies and alders makes sweet music to the ear, but the pines marshaled around the edge of the sky make a yet sweeter music to the eye. Divine beauty all. Here I could stay tethered forever with just bread and water, nor would I be lonely; loved friends and neighbors, as love for everything increased, would seem all the nearer however many the miles and mountains between us.

June 7. The sheep were sick last night, and many of them are still far from well, hardly able to leave camp, coughing, groaning, looking wretched and pitiful, all from eating the leaves of the blessed azalea. So at least say the shepherd and the Don. Having had but little grass since they left the plains, they are starving, and so eat anything green they can get. "Sheep men" call azalea "sheep-poison," and wonder what the Creator was thinking about when he made it,—so desperately does sheep business blind and degrade, though supposed to have a refining influence in the good old days we read of. The California sheep owner is in haste to get rich, and often does, now that pasturage costs nothing, while the climate is so favorable that no winter food supply, shelter-pens, or barns are required. Therefore large flocks may be kept at slight expense, and large profits realized, the money invested doubling, it is claimed, every other year. This quickly acquired wealth usually creates desire for more. Then indeed the wool is drawn close down over the poor fellow's eyes, dimming or shutting out almost everything worth seeing.

As for the shepherd, his case is still worse, especially in winter when he lives alone in a cabin. For, though stimulated at times by hopes of one day owning a flock and getting rich like his boss, he at the same time is likely to be degraded by the life he leads, and seldom reaches the dignity or advantage—or disadvantage—of ownership. The degradation in his case has for cause one not far to seek. He is solitary most of the year, and solitude to most people seems hard to bear. He seldom has much good mental work or recreation in the way of books. Coming into his dingy hovel-cabin at night, stupidly weary, he finds nothing to balance and

level his life with the universe. No, after his dull drag
all day after the sheep, he must get his supper; he is
likely to slight this task and try to satisfy his hunger with whatever comes handy. Perhaps no bread is
baked; then he just makes a few grimy flapjacks in his
unwashed frying-pan, boils a handful of tea, and perhaps fries a few strips of rusty bacon. Usually there
are dried peaches or apples in the cabin, but he hates
to be bothered with the cooking of them, just swallows
the bacon and flapjacks, and depends on the genial
stupefaction of tobacco for the rest. Then to bed, often
without removing the clothing worn during the day.
Of course his health suffers, reacting on his mind; and
seeing nobody for weeks or months, he finally becomes
semi-insane or wholly so.

The shepherd in Scotland seldom thinks of being
anything but a shepherd. He has probably descended
from a race of shepherds and inherited a love and
aptitude for the business almost as marked as that of
his collie. He has but a small flock to look after, sees
his family and neighbors, has time for reading in fine
weather, and often carries books to the fields with
which he may converse with kings. The oriental shepherd, we read, called his sheep by name; they knew
his voice and followed him. The flocks must have been
small and easily managed, allowing piping on the
hills and ample leisure for reading and thinking. But
whatever the blessings of sheep-culture in other times
and countries, the California shepherd, as far as I've
seen or heard, is never quite sane for any considerable
time. Of all Nature's voices baa is about all he hears.
Even the howls and ki-yis of coyotes might be blessings if well heard, but he hears them only through a
blur of mutton and wool, and they do him no good.

16

The sick sheep are getting well, and the shepherd is discoursing on the various poisons lurking in these high pastures—azalea, kalmia, alkali. After crossing the North Fork of the Merced we turned to the left toward Pilot Peak, and made a considerable ascent on a rocky, brush-covered ridge to Brown's Flat, where for the first time since leaving the plains the flock is enjoying plenty of green grass. Mr. Delaney intends to seek a permanent camp somewhere in the neighborhood, to last several weeks.

Before noon we passed Bower Cave, a delightful marble palace, not dark and dripping, but filled with sunshine, which pours into it through its wide-open mouth facing the south. It has a fine, deep, clear little lake with mossy banks embowered with broad-leaved maples, all under ground, wholly unlike anything I have seen in the cave line even in Kentucky, where a large part of the State is honeycombed with caves. This curious specimen of subterranean scenery is located on a belt of marble that is said to extend from the north end of the Range to the extreme south. Many other caves occur on the belt, but none like this, as far as I have learned, combining as it does sunny outdoor brightness and vegetation with the crystalline beauty of the under world. It is claimed by a Frenchman, who has fenced and locked it, placed a boat on the lakelet and seats on the mossy bank under the maple trees, and charges a dollar admission fee. Being on one of the ways to the Yosemite Valley, a good many tourists visit it during the travel months of summer, regarding it as an interesting addition to their Yosemite wonders.

Poison oak or poison ivy (*Rhus diversiloba*), both as a bush and a scrambler up trees and rocks, is common throughout the foothill region up to a height of at least three thousand feet above the sea. It is somewhat troublesome to most travelers, inflaming the skin and eyes, but blends harmoniously with its companion plants, and many a charming flower leans confidingly upon it for protection and shade. I have oftentimes found the curious twining lily (*Stropholirion Californicum*) climbing its branches, showing no fear but rather congenial companionship. Sheep eat it without apparent ill effects; so do horses to some extent, though not fond of it, and to many persons it is harmless. Like most other things not apparently useful to man, it has few friends, and the blind question, "Why was it made?" goes on and on with never a guess that first of all it might have been made for itself.

Brown's Flat is a shallow fertile valley on the top of the divide between the North Fork of the Merced and Bull Creek, commanding magnificent views in every direction. Here the adventurous pioneer David Brown made his headquarters for many years, dividing his time between gold-hunting and bear-hunting. Where could lonely hunter find a better solitude? Game in the woods, gold in the rocks, health and exhilaration in the air, while the colors and cloud furniture of the sky are ever inspiring through all sorts of weather. Though sternly practical, like most pioneers, old David seems to have been uncommonly fond of scenery. Mr. Delaney, who knew him well, tells me that he dearly loved to climb to the summit of a commanding ridge to gaze abroad over the forest to the snow-clad peaks and sources of the rivers, and over the foreground valleys and gulches to note where miners were at work or claims were abandoned, judging by smoke from cabins and camp-fires, the sounds of axes, etc.; and when a rifle-shot was heard, to guess who was the hunter,

whether Indian or some poacher on his wide domain.
His dog Sandy accompanied him everywhere, and well
the little hairy mountaineer knew and loved his master
and his master's aims. In deer-hunting he had but little to do, trotting behind his master as he slowly made
his way through the wood, careful not to step heavily
on dry twigs, scanning open spots in the chaparral,
where the game loves to feed in the early morning and
towards sunset; peering cautiously over ridges as new
outlooks were reached, and along the meadowy borders
of streams. But when bears were hunted, little Sandy
became more important, and it was as a bear-hunter
that Brown became famous. His hunting method, as
described by Mr. Delaney, who had passed many a night
with him in his lonely cabin and learned his stories,
was simply to go slowly and silently through the best
bear pastures, with his dog and rifle and a few pounds
of flour, until he found a fresh track and then follow
it to the death, paying no heed to the time required.
Wherever the bear went he followed, led by little Sandy,
who had a keen nose and never lost the track, however
rocky the ground. When high open points were reached,
the likeliest places were carefully scanned. The time of
year enabled the hunter to determine approximately
where the bear would be found,—in the spring and
early summer on open spots about the banks of streams
and springy places eating grass and clover and lupines,
or in dry meadows feasting on strawberries; toward the
end of summer, on dry ridges, feasting on manzanita
berries, sitting on his haunches, pulling down the laden
branches with his paws, and pressing them together so
as to get good compact mouthfuls however much mixed
with twigs and leaves; in the Indian summer, beneath
the pines, chewing the cones cut off by the squirrels,

or occasionally climbing a tree to gnaw and break off the fruitful branches. In late autumn, when acorns are ripe, Bruin's favorite feeding-grounds are groves of the California oak in park-like cañon flats. Always the cunning hunter knew where to look, and seldom came upon Bruin unawares. When the hot scent showed the dangerous game was nigh, a long halt was made, and the intricacies of the topography and vegetation leisurely scanned to catch a glimpse of the shaggy wanderer, or to at least determine where he was most likely to be.

"Whenever," said the hunter, "I saw a bear before it saw me I had no trouble in killing it. I just studied the lay of the land and got to leeward of it no matter how far around I had to go, and then worked up to within a few hundred yards or so, at the foot of a tree that I could easily climb, but too small for the bear to climb. Then I looked well to the condition of my rifle, took off my boots so as to climb well if necessary, and waited until the bear turned its side in clear view when I could make a sure or at least a good shot. In case it showed fight I climbed out of reach. But bears are slow and awkward with their eyes, and being to leeward of them they could not scent me, and I often got in a second shot before they noticed the smoke. Usually, however, they run when wounded and hide in the brush. I let them run a good safe time before I ventured to follow them, and Sandy was pretty sure to find them dead. If not, he barked and drew their attention, and occasionally rushed in for a distracting bite, so that I was able to get to a safe distance for a final shot. Oh yes, bear-hunting is safe enough when followed in a safe way, though like every other business it has its accidents, and little doggie and I have had some close calls. Bears like to keep out of the way of men as a general thing, but if an old, lean, hungry mother with cubs met a man on her own ground she would, in my opinion, try to catch and eat him. This would be only fair play anyhow, for we eat them, but nobody hereabout has been used for bear grub that I know of."

Brown had left his mountain home ere we arrived, but a considerable number of Digger Indians still linger in their cedar-bark huts on the edge of the flat. They were attracted in the first place by the white hunter whom they had learned to respect, and to whom they looked for guidance and protection against their enemies the Pah Utes, who sometimes made raids across from the east side of the Range to plunder the stores of the comparatively feeble Diggers and steal their wives.

IN CAMP ON THE NORTH FORK OF THE MERCED

June 8. The sheep, now grassy and good-natured, slowly nibbled their way down into the valley of the North Fork of the Merced at the foot of Pilot Peak Ridge to the place selected by the Don for our first central camp, a picturesque hopper-shaped hollow formed by converging hill slopes at a bend of the river. Here racks for dishes and provisions were made in the shade of the river-bank trees, and beds of fern fronds, cedar plumes, and various flowers, each to the taste of its owner, and a corral back on the open flat for the wool.

June 9. How deep our sleep last night in the mountain's heart, beneath the trees and stars, hushed by solemn-sounding waterfalls and many small soothing voices in sweet accord whispering peace! And our first pure mountain day, warm, calm, cloudless,—how immeasurable it seems, how serenely wild! I can scarcely remember its beginning. Along the river, over the hills, in the ground, in the sky, spring work is going on with joyful enthusiasm, new life, new beauty, unfolding, unrolling in glorious exuberant extravagance,—new birds in their nests, new winged creatures in the air, and new leaves, new flowers, spreading, shining, rejoicing everywhere.

The trees about the camp stand close, giving ample

shade for ferns and lilies, while back from the bank most of the sunshine reaches the ground, calling up the grasses and flowers in glorious array, tall bromus waving like bamboos, starry compositæ, monardella, Mariposa tulips, lupines, gilias, violets, glad children of light. Soon every fern frond will be unrolled, great beds of common pteris and woodwardia along the river, wreaths and rosettes of pellæa and cheilanthes on sunny rocks. Some of the woodwardia fronds are already six feet high.

A handsome little shrub, *Chamæbatia foliolosa*, belonging to the rose family, spreads a yellow-green mantle beneath the sugar pines for miles without a break, not mixed or roughened with other plants. Only here and there a Washington lily may be seen nodding above its even surface, or a bunch or two of tall bromus as if for ornament. This fine carpet shrub begins to appear at, say, twenty-five hundred or three thousand feet above sea level, is about knee high or less, has brown branches, and the largest stems are only about half an inch in diameter. The leaves, light yellow green, thrice pinnate and finely cut, give them a rich ferny appearance, and they are dotted with minute glands that secrete wax with a peculiar pleasant odor that blends finely with the spicy fragrance of the pines. The flowers are white, five-eighths of an inch in diameter, and look like those of the strawberry. Am delighted with this little bush. It is the only true carpet shrub of this part of the Sierra. The manzanita, rhamnus, and most of the species of ceanothus make shaggy rugs and border fringes rather than carpets or mantles.

The sheep do not take kindly to their new pastures, perhaps from being too closely hemmed in by the hills. They are never fully at rest. Last night they were frightened, probably by bears or coyotes prowling and planning for a share of the grand mass of mutton.

June 10. Very warm. We get water for the camp from a rock basin at the foot of a picturesque cascading reach of the river where it is well stirred and made lively without being beaten into dusty foam. The rock here is black metamorphic slate, worn into smooth knobs in the stream channels, contrasting with the fine gray and white cascading water as it glides and glances and falls in lace-like sheets and braided over-folding currents. Tufts of sedge growing on the rock knobs that rise above the surface produce a charming effect, the long elastic leaves arching over in every direction, the tips of the longest drooping into the current, which dividing against the projecting rocks makes still finer lines, uniting with the sedges to see how beautiful the happy stream can be made. Nor is this all, for the giant saxifrage also is growing on some of the knob rock islets, firmly anchored and displaying their broad, round, umbrella-like leaves in showy groups by themselves, or above the sedge tufts. The flowers of this species (*Saxifraga peltata*) are purple, and form tall glandular racemes that are in bloom before the appearance of the leaves. The fleshy root-stocks grip the rock in cracks and hollows, and thus enable the plant to hold on against occasional floods,—a marked species employed by Nature to make yet more beautiful the most interesting portions of these cool clear streams. Near camp the trees arch over from bank to bank, making a leafy tunnel full of soft subdued light, through which the young river sings and shines like a happy living creature.

Heard a few peals of thunder from the upper

Sierra, and saw firm white bossy cumuli rising back of the pines. This was about noon.

June 11. On one of the eastern branches of the river discovered some charming cascades with a pool at the foot of each of them. White dashing water, a few bushes and tufts of carex on ledges leaning over with fine effect, and large orange lilies assembled in superb groups on fertile soil-beds beside the pools.

There are no large meadows or grassy plains near camp to supply lasting pasture for our thousands of busy nibblers. The main dependence is ceanothus brush on the hills and tufted grass patches here and there, with lupines and pea-vines among the flowers on sunny open spaces. Large areas have already been stripped bare, or nearly so, compelling the poor hungry wool bundles to scatter far and wide, keeping the shepherds and dogs at the top of their speed to hold them within bounds. Mr. Delaney has gone back to the plains, taking the Indian and Chinaman with him, leaving instruction to keep the flock here or hereabouts until his return, which he promised would not be long delayed.

How fine the weather is! Nothing more celestial can I conceive. How gently the winds blow! Scarce can these tranquil air-currents be called winds. They seem the very breath of Nature, whispering peace to every living thing. Down in the camp dell there is no swaying of tree-tops; most of the time not a leaf moves. I don't remember having seen a single lily swinging on its stalk, though they are so tall the least breeze would rock them. What grand bells these lilies have! Some of them big enough for children's bonnets. I have been sketching them, and would fain draw every leaf of their wide shining whorls and every curved and spotted petal. More beautiful, better kept gardens cannot be imagined. The species is *Lilium pardalinum*, five to six feet high, leaf-whorls a foot wide, flowers about six inches wide, bright orange, purple spotted in the throat, segments revolute—a majestic plant.

June 12. A slight sprinkle of rain—large drops far apart, falling with hearty pat and plash on leaves and stones and into the mouths of the flowers. Cumuli rising to the eastward. How beautiful their pearly bosses! How well they harmonize with the upswelling rocks beneath them. Mountains of the sky, solid-looking, finely sculptured, their richly varied topography wonderfully defined. Never before have I seen clouds so substantial looking in form and texture. Nearly every day toward noon they rise with visible swelling motion as if new worlds were being created. And how fondly they brood and hover over the gardens and forests with their cooling shadows and showers, keeping every petal and leaf in glad health and heart. One may fancy the clouds themselves are plants, springing up in the sky-fields at the call of the sun, growing in beauty until they reach their prime, scattering rain and hail like berries and seeds, then wilting and dying.

The mountain live oak, common here and a thousand feet or so higher, is like the live oak of Florida, not only in general appearance, foliage, bark, and wide-branching habit, but in its tough, knotty, unwedgeable wood. Standing alone with plenty of elbow room, the largest trees are about seven to eight feet in diameter near the ground, sixty feet high, and as wide or wider across the head. The leaves are small and undivided, mostly without teeth or wavy edging, though on young

26

shoots some are sharply serrated, both kinds being found on the same tree. The cups of the medium-sized acorns are shallow, thick walled, and covered with a golden dust of minute hairs. Some of the trees have hardly any main trunk, dividing near the ground into large wide-spreading limbs, and these, dividing again and again, terminate in long, drooping, cord-like branchlets, many of which reach nearly to the ground, while a dense canopy of short, shining, leafy branchlets forms a round head which looks something like a cumulus cloud when the sunshine is pouring over it.

A marked plant is the bush poppy (*Dendromecon rigidum*), found on the hot hillsides near camp, the only woody member of the order I have yet met in all my walks. Its flowers are bright orange yellow, an inch to two inches wide, fruit-pods three or four inches long, slender and curving,—height of bushes about four feet, made up of many slim, straight branches, radiating from the root,—a companion of the manzanita and other sun-loving chaparral shrubs.

June 13. Another glorious Sierra day in which one seems to be dissolved and absorbed and sent pulsing onward we know not where. Life seems neither long nor short, and we take no more heed to save time or make haste than do the trees and stars. This is true freedom, a good practical sort of immortality. Yonder rises another white skyland. How sharply the yellow pine spires and the palm-like crowns of the sugar pines are outlined on its smooth white domes. And hark! the grand thunder billows booming, rolling from ridge to ridge, followed by the faithful shower.

A good many herbaceous plants come thus far up the mountains from the plains, and are now in flower, two months later than their lowland relatives. Saw a few columbines to-day. Most of the ferns are in their prime,—rock ferns on the sunny hillsides, cheilanthes, pellæa, gymnogramme; woodwardia, aspidium, woodsia along the stream banks, and the common *Pteris aquilina* on sandy flats. This last, however common, is here making shows of strong, exuberant, abounding beauty to set the botanist wild with admiration. I measured some scarce full grown that are more than seven feet high. Though the commonest and most widely distributed of all the ferns, I might almost say that I never saw it before. The broad-shouldered fronds held high on smooth stout stalks growing close together, overleaning and overlapping, make a complete ceiling, beneath which one may walk erect over several acres without being seen, as if beneath a roof. And how soft and lovely the light streaming through this living ceiling, revealing the arching branching ribs and veins of the fronds as the framework of countless panes of pale green and yellow plant-glass nicely fitted together—a fairyland created out of the commonest fern-stuff.

The smaller animals wander about as if in a tropical forest. I saw the entire flock of sheep vanish at one side of a patch and reappear a hundred yards farther on at the other, their progress betrayed only by the jerking and trembling of the fronds; and strange to say very few of the stout woody stalks were broken. I sat a long time beneath the tallest fronds, and never enjoyed anything in the way of a bower of wild leaves more strangely impressive. Only spread a fern frond over a man's head and worldly cares are cast out, and freedom and beauty and peace come in. The waving of a pine tree on the top of a mountain,—a magic wand in Nature's hand,—every devout mountaineer knows its power; but the marvelous beauty value of what the Scotch call a breckan in a still dell, what poet has sung this? It would seem impossible that any one, however incrusted with care, could escape the Godful influence of these sacred fern forests. Yet this very day I saw a shepherd pass through one of the finest of them without betraying more feeling than his sheep. "What do you think of these grand ferns?" I asked. "Oh, they're only d——d big brakes," he replied.

Lizards of every temper, style, and color dwell here, seemingly as happy and companionable as the birds and squirrels. Lowly, gentle fellow mortals, enjoying God's sunshine, and doing the best they can in getting a living, I like to watch them at their work and play. They bear acquaintance well, and one likes them the better the longer one looks into their beautiful, innocent eyes. They are easily tamed, and one soon learns to love them, as they dart about on the hot rocks, swift as dragon-flies. The eye can hardly follow them; but they never make long-sustained runs, usually only about ten or twelve feet, then a sudden stop, and as sudden a start again; going all their journeys by quick, jerking impulses. These many stops I find are necessary as rests, for they are short-winded, and when pursued steadily are soon out of breath, pant pitifully, and are easily caught. Their bodies are more than half tail, but these tails are well managed, never heavily dragged nor curved up as if hard to carry; on the contrary, they seem to follow the body lightly of their own will. Some are colored like the sky, bright as bluebirds, others gray like the lichened rocks on which they hunt and bask. Even the horned toad of the plains is a mild, harmless creature, and so are the snake-like species which glide in curves with true snake motion, while their small, undeveloped limbs drag as useless appendages. One specimen fourteen inches long which I observed closely made no use whatever of its tender, sprouting limbs, but glided with all the soft, sly ease and grace of a snake. Here comes a little, gray, dusty fellow who seems to know and trust me, running about my feet, and looking up cunningly into my face. Carlo is watching, makes a quick pounce on him, for the fun of the thing I suppose; but Liz has shot away from his paws like an arrow, and is safe in the recesses of a clump of chaparral. Gentle saurians, dragons, descendants of an ancient and mighty race, Heaven bless you all and make your virtues known! for few of us know as yet that scales may cover fellow creatures as gentle and lovable as feathers, or hair, or cloth.

Mastodons and elephants used to live here no great geological time ago, as shown by their bones, often discovered by miners in washing gold-gravel. And bears of at least two species are here now, besides the California lion or panther, and wild cats, wolves, foxes, snakes, scorpions, wasps, tarantulas; but one is almost tempted at times to regard a small savage black ant as the master existence of this vast mountain world. These fearless, restless, wandering imps, though only about a quarter of an inch long, are fonder of fighting and biting than any beast I know. They attack every living thing around their homes, often without cause as far as I can see. Their bodies are mostly jaws curved like ice-hooks, and to get work for these weapons seems to be their chief aim and pleasure. Most of their colonies are established in living oaks somewhat decayed or hollowed, in which they can conveniently build their cells. These are chosen probably because of their strength as opposed to the attacks of animals and storms. They work both day and night, creep into dark caves, climb the highest trees, wander and hunt through cool ravines as well as on hot, unshaded ridges, and extend their highways and byways over everything but water and sky. From the foothills to a mile above the level of the sea nothing can stir without their knowledge; and alarms are spread in an incredibly short time, without any howl or cry that we can hear. I can't understand the need of their ferocious courage; there seems to be no common sense in it. Sometimes, no doubt, they fight in defense of their homes, but they fight anywhere and always wherever they can find anything to bite. As soon as a vulnerable spot is discovered on man or beast, they stand on their heads and sink their jaws, and though torn limb from limb, they will yet hold on and die biting deeper. When I contemplate this fierce creature so widely distributed and strongly intrenched, I see that much remains to be done ere the world is brought under the rule of universal peace and love.

On my way to camp a few minutes ago, I passed a dead pine nearly ten feet in diameter. It has been enveloped in fire from top to bottom so that now it looks like a grand black pillar set up as a monument. In this noble shaft a colony of large jet-black ants have established themselves, laboriously cutting tunnels and cells through the wood, whether sound or decayed. The entire trunk seems to have been honeycombed, judging by the size of the talus of gnawed chips like sawdust piled up around its base. They are more intelligent looking than their small, belligerent, strong-scented brethren, and have better manners, though quick to fight when required. Their towns are

carved in fallen trunks as well as in those left standing, but never in sound, living trees or in the ground.
When you happen to sit down to rest or take notes near
a colony, some wandering hunter is sure to find you
and come cautiously forward to discover the nature of
the intruder and what ought to be done. If you are not
too near the town and keep perfectly still he may run
across your feet a few times, over your legs and hands
and face, up your trousers, as if taking your measure
and getting comprehensive views, then go in peace
without raising an alarm. If, however, a tempting spot
is offered or some suspicious movement excites him,
a bite follows, and such a bite! I fancy that a bear or
wolf bite is not to be compared with it. A quick electric
flame of pain flashes along the outraged nerves, and
you discover for the first time how great is the capacity
for sensation you are possessed of. A shriek, a grab for
the animal, and a bewildered stare follow this bite of
bites as one comes back to consciousness from sudden
eclipse. Fortunately, if careful, one need not be bitten
oftener than once or twice in a lifetime. This wonderful
electric species is about three fourths of an inch long.
Bears are fond of them, and tear and gnaw their home-
logs to pieces, and roughly devour the eggs, larvæ,
parent ants, and the rotten or sound wood of the cells,
all in one spicy acid hash. The Digger Indians also are
fond of the larvæ and even of the perfect ants, so I have
been told by old mountaineers. They bite off and reject
the head, and eat the tickly acid body with keen relish.
Thus are the poor biters bitten, like every other biter,
big or little, in the world's great family.

There is also a fine, active, intelligent-looking
red species, intermediate in size between the above.
They dwell in the ground, and build large piles of seed

husks, leaves, straw, etc., over their nests. Their food seems to be mostly insects and plant leaves, seeds and sap. How many mouths Nature has to fill, how many neighbors we have, how little we know about them, and how seldom we get in each other's way! Then to think of the infinite numbers of smaller fellow mortals, invisibly small, compared with which the smallest ants are as mastodons.

June 14. The pool-basins below the falls and cascades hereabouts, formed by the heavy down-plunging currents, are kept nicely clean and clear of detritus. The heavier parts of the material swept over the falls are heaped up a short distance in front of the basins in the form of a dam, thus tending, together with erosion, to increase their size. Sudden changes, however, are effected during the spring floods, when the snow is melting and the upper tributaries are roaring loud from "bank to brae." Then boulders that have fallen into the channels, and which the ordinary summer and winter currents were unable to move, are suddenly swept forward as by a mighty besom, hurled over the falls into these pools, and piled up in a new dam together with part of the old one, while some of the smaller boulders are carried further down stream and variously lodged according to size and shape, all seeking rest where the force of the current is less than the resistance they are able to offer. But the greatest changes made in these relations of fall, pool, and dam are caused, not by the ordinary spring floods, but by extraordinary ones that occur at irregular intervals. The testimony of trees growing on flood boulder deposits shows that a century or more has passed since the last master flood came to awaken everything movable to go swirling and dancing on wonderful journeys. These floods may occur during the summer, when heavy thunder-showers, called "cloud-bursts," fall on wide, steeply inclined stream basins furrowed by converging channels, which suddenly gather the waters together into the main trunk in booming torrents of enormous transporting power, though short lived.

One of these ancient flood boulders stands firm in the middle of the stream channel, just below the lower edge of the pool dam at the foot of the fall nearest our camp. It is a nearly cubical mass of granite about eight feet high, plushed with mosses over the top and down the sides to ordinary high-water mark. When I climbed on top of it to-day and lay down to rest, it seemed the most romantic spot I had yet found—the one big stone with its mossy level top and smooth sides standing square and firm and solitary, like an altar, the fall in front of it bathing it lightly with the finest of the spray, just enough to keep its moss cover fresh; the clear green pool beneath, with its foam-bells and its half circle of lilies leaning forward like a band of admirers, and flowering dogwood and alder trees leaning over all in sun-sifted arches. How soothingly, restfully cool it is beneath that leafy, translucent ceiling, and how delightful the water music—the deep bass tones of the fall, the clashing, ringing spray, and infinite variety of small low tones of the current gliding past the side of the boulder-island, and glinting against a thousand smaller stones down the ferny channel! All this shut in; every one of these influences acting at short range as if in a quiet room. The place seemed holy, where one might hope to see God.

After dark, when the camp was at rest, I groped my

way back to the altar boulder and passed the night on it,—above the water, beneath the leaves and stars,— everything still more impressive than by day, the fall seen dimly white, singing Nature's old love song with solemn enthusiasm, while the stars peering through the leaf-roof seemed to join in the white water's song. Precious night, precious day to abide in me forever. Thanks be to God for this immortal gift.

June 15. Another reviving morning. Down the long mountain-slopes the sunbeams pour, gilding the awakening pines, cheering every needle, filling every living thing with joy. Robins are singing in the alder and maple groves, the same old song that has cheered and sweetened countless seasons over almost all of our blessed continent. In this mountain hollow they seem as much at home as in farmers' orchards. Bullock's oriole and the Louisiana tanager are here also, with many warblers and other little mountain troubadours, most of them now busy about their nests.

Discovered another magnificent specimen of the goldcup oak six feet in diameter, a Douglas spruce seven feet, and a twining lily (*Stropholirion*), with stem eight feet long, and sixty rose-colored flowers.

Sugar pine cones are cylindrical, slightly tapered at the end and rounded at the base. Found one to-day nearly twenty-four inches long and six in diameter, the scales being open. Another specimen nineteen inches long; the average length of full-grown cones on trees favorably situated is nearly eighteen inches. On the lower edge of the belt at a height of about twenty-five hundred feet above the sea they are smaller, say a foot to fifteen inches long, and at a height of seven thousand feet or more near the upper limits of its growth in the Yosemite region they are about the same size. This noble tree is an inexhaustible study and source of pleasure. I never weary of gazing at its grand tassel cones, its perfectly round bole one hundred feet or more without a limb, the fine purplish color of its bark, and its magnificent outsweeping, down-curving feathery arms forming a crown always bold and striking and exhilarating. In habit and general port it looks somewhat like a palm, but no palm that I have yet seen displays such majesty of form and behavior either when poised silent and thoughtful in sunshine, or wide-awake waving in storm winds with every needle quivering. When young it is very straight and regular in form like most other conifers; but at the age of fifty to one hundred years it begins to acquire individuality, so that no two are alike in their prime or old age. Every tree calls for special admiration. I have been making many sketches, and regret that I cannot draw every needle. It is said to reach a height of three hundred feet, though the tallest I have measured falls short of this stature sixty feet or more. The diameter of the largest near the ground is about ten feet, though I've heard of some twelve feet thick or even fifteen. The diameter is held to a great height, the taper being almost imperceptibly gradual. Its companion, the yellow pine, is almost as large. The long silvery foliage of the younger specimens forms magnificent cylindrical brushes on the top shoots and the ends of the upturned branches, and when the wind sways the needles all one way at a certain angle every tree becomes a tower of white quivering sun-fire. Well may this shining species be called the silver pine. The needles are sometimes more than a foot long, almost as long as those of the long-leaf pine of Florida. But though in size the yellow pine almost equals the sugar pine, and in rugged enduring strength seems to surpass it, it is far less marked in general habit and expression, with its regular conventional spire and its comparatively small cones clustered stiffly among the needles. Were there no sugar pine, then would this be the king of the world's eighty or ninety species, the brightest of the bright, waving, worshiping multitude. Were they mere mechanical sculptures, what noble objects they would still be! How much more throbbing, thrilling, overflowing, full of life in every fiber and cell, grand glowing silver-rods—the very gods of the plant kingdom, living their sublime century lives in sight of Heaven, watched and loved and admired from generation to generation! And how many other radiant resiny sun trees are here and higher up,—libocedrus, Douglas spruce, silver fir, sequoia. How rich our inheritance in these blessed mountains, the tree pastures into which our eyes are turned!

Now comes sundown. The west is all a glory of color transfiguring everything. Far up the Pilot Peak Ridge the radiant host of trees stand hushed and thoughtful, receiving the Sun's good-night, as solemn and impressive a leave-taking as if sun and trees were to meet no more. The daylight fades, the color spell is broken, and the forest breathes free in the night breeze beneath the stars.

June 16. One of the Indians from Brown's Flat got right into the middle of the camp this morning, unobserved. I was seated on a stone, looking over my notes and sketches, and happening to look up, was startled to see him standing grim and silent within a few steps of me, as motionless and weather-stained as an old tree-stump that had stood there for centuries. All Indians seem to have learned this wonderful way of walking unseen,—making themselves invisible like certain spiders I have been observing here, which, in case of alarm, caused, for example, by a bird alighting on the bush their webs are spread upon, immediately bounce themselves up and down on their elastic threads so rapidly that only a blur is visible. The wild Indian power of escaping observation, even where there is little or no cover to hide in, was probably slowly acquired in hard hunting and fighting lessons while trying to approach game, take enemies by surprise, or get safely away when compelled to retreat. And this experience transmitted through many generations seems at length to have become what is vaguely called instinct.

How smooth and changeless seems the surface of the mountains about us! Scarce a track is to be found beyond the range of the sheep except on small open spots on the sides of the streams, or where the forest carpets are thin or wanting. On the smoothest of these open strips and patches deer tracks may be seen, and the great suggestive footprints of bears, which, with those of the many small animals, are scarce enough to answer as a kind of light ornamental stitching or embroidery. Along the main ridges and larger branches of the river Indian trails may be traced, but they are not nearly as distinct as one would expect to find them. How many centuries Indians have roamed these woods nobody knows, probably a great many, extending far beyond the time that Columbus touched our shores, and it seems strange that heavier marks have not been made. Indians walk softly and hurt the landscape hardly more than the birds and squirrels, and their brush and bark huts last hardly longer than those of wood rats, while their more enduring monuments, excepting those wrought on the forests by the fires they made to improve their hunting grounds, vanish in a few centuries.

How different are most of those of the white man, especially on the lower gold region—roads blasted in the solid rock, wild streams dammed and tamed and turned out of their channels and led along the sides of cañons and valleys to work in mines like slaves. Crossing from ridge to ridge, high in the air, on long straddling trestles as if flowing on stilts, or down and up across valleys and hills, imprisoned in iron pipes to strike and wash away hills and miles of the skin of the mountain's face, riddling, stripping every gold gully and flat. These are the white man's marks made in a few feverish years, to say nothing of mills, fields, villages, scattered hundreds of miles along the flank of the Range. Long will it be ere these marks are effaced, though Nature is doing what she can, replanting, gardening, sweeping away old dams and flumes, leveling gravel and boulder piles, patiently trying to heal every raw scar. The main gold storm is over. Calm enough are the gray old miners scratching a bare living in waste diggings here and there. Thundering underground blasting is still going on to feed the pounding quartz mills, but their influence on the landscape is light as compared with that of the pick-and-shovel storms waged a few years ago. Fortunately for Sierra scenery the gold-bearing slates are mostly restricted to the foothills. The region about our camp is still wild, and higher lies the snow about as trackless as the sky.

Only a few hills and domes of cloudland were

built yesterday and none at all to-day. The light is peculiarly white and thin, though pleasantly warm. The serenity of this mountain weather in the spring, just when Nature's pulses are beating highest, is one of its greatest charms. There is only a moderate breeze from the summits of the Range at night, and a slight breathing from the sea and the lowland hills and plains during the day, or stillness so complete no leaf stirs. The trees hereabouts have but little wind history to tell.

Sheep, like people, are ungovernable when hungry. Excepting my guarded lily gardens, almost every leaf that these hoofed locusts can reach within a radius of a mile or two from camp has been devoured. Even the bushes are stripped bare, and in spite of dogs and shepherds the sheep scatter to all points of the compass and vanish in dust. I fear some are lost, for one of the sixteen black ones is missing.

June 17. Counted the wool bundles this morning as they bounced through the narrow corral gate. About three hundred are missing, and as the shepherd could not go to seek them, I had to go. I tied a crust of bread to my belt, and with Carlo set out for the upper slopes of the Pilot Peak Ridge, and had a good day, notwithstanding the care of seeking the silly runaways. I went out for wool, and did not come back shorn. A peculiar light circled around the horizon, white and thin like that often seen over the auroral corona, blending into the blue of the upper sky. The only clouds were a few faint flossy pencilings like combed silk. I pushed direct to the boundary of the usual range of the flock, and around it until I found the outgoing trail of the wanderers. It led far up the ridge into an open place surrounded by a hedge-like growth of ceanothus chaparral. Carlo knew what I was about, and eagerly followed the scent until we came up to them, huddled in a timid, silent bunch. They had evidently been here all night and all the forenoon, afraid to go out to feed. Having escaped restraint, they were, like some people we know of, afraid of their freedom, did not know what to do with it, and seemed glad to get back into the old familiar bondage.

June 18. Another inspiring morning, nothing better in any world can be conceived. No description of Heaven that I have ever heard or read of seems half so fine. At noon the clouds occupied about .05 of the sky, white filmy touches drawn delicately on the azure.

The high ridges and hilltops beyond the woolly locusts are now gay with monardella, clarkia, coreopsis, and tall tufted grasses, some of them tall enough to wave like pines. The lupines, of which there are many ill-defined species, are now mostly out of flower, and many of the compositæ are beginning to fade, their radiant corollas vanishing in fluffy pappus like stars in mist.

We had another visitor from Brown's Flat to-day, an old Indian woman with a basket on her back. Like our first caller from the village, she got fairly into camp and was standing in plain view when discovered. How long she had been quietly looking on, I cannot say. Even the dogs failed to notice her stealthy approach. She was on her way, I suppose, to some wild garden, probably for lupine and starchy saxifrage leaves and rootstocks. Her dress was calico rags, far from clean. In every way she seemed sadly unlike Nature's neat well-dressed animals, though living like them on the bounty of the wilderness. Strange that mankind alone is dirty. Had she been clad in fur, or cloth woven of grass or shreddy bark, like the juniper and libocedrus mats, she might then have seemed a rightful part of the wilderness; like a good wolf at least, or bear. But from no point of view that I have found are such debased fellow beings a whit more natural than the glaring tailored tourists we saw that frightened the birds and squirrels.

June 19. Pure sunshine all day. How beautiful a rock is made by leaf shadows! Those of the live oak are particularly clear and distinct, and beyond all art in grace and delicacy, now still as if painted on stone, now gliding softly as if afraid of noise, now dancing, waltzing in swift, merry swirls, or jumping on and off sunny rocks in quick dashes like wave embroidery on seashore cliffs. How true and substantial is this shadow beauty, and with what sublime extravagance is beauty thus multiplied! The big orange lilies are now arrayed in all their glory of leaf and flower. Noble plants, in perfect health, Nature's darlings.

June 20. Some of the silly sheep got caught fast in a tangle of chaparral this morning, like flies in a spider's web, and had to be helped out. Carlo found them and tried to drive them from the trap by the easiest way. How far above sheep are intelligent dogs! No friend and helper can be more affectionate and constant than Carlo. The noble St. Bernard is an honor to his race.

The air is distinctly fragrant with balsam and resin and mint,—every breath of it a gift we may well thank God for. Who could ever guess that so rough a wilderness should yet be so fine, so full of good things. One seems to be in a majestic domed pavilion in which a grand play is being acted with scenery and music and incense,—all the furniture and action so interesting we are in no danger of being called on to endure one dull moment. God himself seems to be always doing his best here, working like a man in a glow of enthusiasm.

June 21. Sauntered along the river-bank to my lily gardens. The perfection of beauty in these lilies of the wilderness is a never-ending source of admiration and wonder. Their rhizomes are set in black mould accumulated in hollows of the metamorphic slates beside the pools, where they are well watered without being subjected to flood action. Every leaf in the level whorls around the tall polished stalks is as finely finished as the petals, and the light and heat required are measured for them and tempered in passing through the branches of over-leaning trees. However strong the winds from the noon rainstorms, they are securely sheltered. Beautiful hypnum carpets bordered with ferns are spread beneath them, violets too, and a few daisies. Everything around them sweet and fresh like themselves.

Cloudland to-day is only a solitary white mountain; but it is so enriched with sunshine and shade, the tones of color on its big domed head and bossy out-bulging ridges, and in the hollows and ravines between them, are ineffably fine.

June 22. Unusually cloudy. Besides the periodical shower-bearing cumuli there is a thin, diffused, fog-like cloud overhead. About .75 in all.

June 23. Oh, these vast, calm, measureless mountain days, inciting at once to work and rest! Days in whose light everything seems equally divine, opening a thousand windows to show us God. Nevermore, however weary, should one faint by the way who gains the blessings of one mountain day; whatever his fate, long life, short life, stormy or calm, he is rich forever.

June 24. Our regular allowance of clouds and thunder. Shepherd Billy is in a peck of trouble about the sheep; he declares that they are possessed with more of the evil one than any other flock from the beginning of the invention of mutton and wool to the last batch of it. No matter how many are missing, he will not, he says, go a step to seek them, because, as he reasons, while getting back one wanderer he would probably lose ten. Therefore runaway hunting must be Carlo's and mine. Billy's little dog Jack is also giving trouble by leaving camp every night to visit his neighbors up the mountain at Brown's Flat. He is a common-looking cur of no particular breed, but tremendously enterprising in love and war. He has cut all the ropes and leather straps he has been tied with, until his master in desperation, after climbing the brushy mountain again and again to drag him back, fastened him with a pole attached to his collar under his chin at one end, and to a stout sapling at the other. But the pole gave good leverage, and by constant twisting during the night, the fastening at the sapling end was chafed off, and he set out on his usual journey, dragging the pole through the brush, and reached the Indian settlement in safety. His master followed, and making no allowance, gave him a beating, and swore in bad terms that next evening he would "fix that infatuated pup" by anchoring him unmercifully to the heavy cast-iron lid of our Dutch oven, weighing about as much as the dog. It was linked directly to his collar close up under the chin, so that the poor fellow seemed unable to stir. He stood quite discouraged until after dark, unable to look about him, or even to lie down unless he stretched himself out with his front feet across the lid, and his head close down between his paws. Before morning, however, Jack was heard far up the height howling Excelsior, cast-iron anchor to the contrary notwithstanding. He must have walked, or rather climbed, erect on his hind legs, clasping the heavy lid like a shield against his breast, a formidable iron-clad condition in which to meet his rivals. Next night, dog, pot-lid, and all, were tied up in an old bean-sack, and thus at last angry Billy gained the victory. Just before leaving home, Jack was bitten in the lower jaw by a rattlesnake, and for a week or so his head and neck were swollen to more than double the normal size; nevertheless he ran about as brisk and lively as ever, and is now completely recovered. The only treatment he got was fresh milk—a gallon or two at a time forcibly poured down his sore, poisoned throat.

June 25. Though only a sheep camp, this grand mountain hollow is home, sweet home, every day growing sweeter, and I shall be sorry to leave it. The lily gardens are safe as yet from the trampling flock. Poor, dusty, raggedy, famishing creatures, I heartily pity them. Many a mile they must go every day to gather their fifteen or twenty tons of chaparral and grass.

June 26. Nuttall's flowering dogwood makes a fine

show when in bloom. The whole tree is then snowy white. The involucres are six to eight inches wide. Along the streams it is a good-sized tree thirty to fifty feet high, with a broad head when not crowded by companions. Its showy involucres attract a crowd of moths, butterflies, and other winged people about it for their own and, I suppose, the tree's advantage. It likes plenty of cool water, and is a great drinker like the alder, willow, and cottonwood, and flourishes best on stream banks, though it often wanders far from streams in damp shady glens beneath the pines, where it is much smaller. When the leaves ripen in the fall, they become more beautiful than the flowers, displaying charming tones of red, purple, and lavender. Another species grows in abundance as a chaparral shrub on the shady sides of the hills, probably *Cornus sessilis*. The leaves are eaten by the sheep.—Heard a few lightning strokes in the distance, with rumbling, mumbling reverberations.

June 27. The beaked hazel (*Corylus rostrata*, var. *Californica*) is common on cool slopes up toward the summit of the Pilot Peak Ridge. There is something peculiarly attractive in the hazel, like the oaks and heaths of the cool countries of our forefathers, and through them our love for these plants has, I suppose, been transmitted. This species is four or five feet high, leaves soft and hairy, grateful to the touch, and the delicious nuts are eagerly gathered by Indians and squirrels. The sky as usual adorned with white noon clouds.

June 28. Warm, mellow summer. The glowing sunbeams make every nerve tingle. The new needles of the pines and firs are nearly full grown and shine gloriously. Lizards are glinting about on the hot rocks; some that live near the camp are more than half tame. They seem attentive to every movement on our part, as if curious to simply look on without suspicion of harm, turning their heads to look back, and making a variety of pretty gestures. Gentle, guileless creatures with beautiful eyes, I shall be sorry to leave them when we leave camp.

June 29. I have been making the acquaintance of a very interesting little bird that flits about the falls and rapids of the main branches of the river. It is not a water-bird in structure, though it gets its living in the water, and never leaves the streams. It is not web-footed, yet it dives fearlessly into deep swirling rapids, evidently to feed at the bottom, using its wings to swim with under water just as ducks and loons do. Sometimes it wades about in shallow places, thrusting its head under from time to time in a jerking, nodding, frisky way that is sure to attract attention. It is about the size of a robin, has short crisp wings serviceable for flying either in water or air, and a tail of moderate size slanted upward, giving it, with its nodding, bobbing manners, a wrennish look. Its color is plain bluish ash, with a tinge of brown on the head and shoulders. It flies from fall to fall, rapid to rapid, with a solid whir of wing-beats like those of a quail, follows the windings of the stream, and usually alights on some rock jutting up out of the current, or on some stranded snag, or rarely on the dry limb of an overhanging tree, perching like regular tree birds when it suits its convenience. It has the oddest, daintiest mincing manners imaginable; and the little fellow can sing too, a sweet, thrushy, fluty song, rather low, not the least boisterous, and much less keen and accentuated than from its vigorous briskness one would be led to look for. What a romantic life this little bird leads on the most beautiful portions of the streams, in a genial climate with shade and cool water and spray to temper the summer heat. No wonder it is a fine singer, considering the stream songs it hears day and night. Every breath the little poet draws is part of a song, for all the air about the rapids and falls is beaten into music, and its first lessons must begin before it is born by the thrilling and quivering of the eggs in unison with the tones of the falls. I have not yet found its nest, but it must be near the streams, for it never leaves them.

June 30. Half cloudy, half sunny, clouds lustrous white. The tall pines crowded along the top of the Pilot Peak Ridge look like six-inch miniatures exquisitely outlined on the satiny sky. Average cloudiness for the day about .25. No rain. And so this memorable month ends, a stream of beauty unmeasured, no more to be sectioned off by almanac arithmetic than sun-radiance or the currents of seas and rivers—a peaceful, joyful stream of beauty. Every morning, arising from the death of sleep, the happy plants and all our fellow animal creatures great and small, and even the rocks, seemed to be shouting, "Awake, awake, rejoice, rejoice, come love us and join in our song. Come! Come!" Looking back through the stillness and romantic enchanting beauty and peace of the camp grove, this June seems the greatest of all the months of my life, the most truly, divinely free, boundless like eternity, immortal. Everything in it seems equally divine—one smooth, pure, wild glow of Heaven's love, never to be blotted or blurred by anything past or to come.

July 1. Summer is ripe. Flocks of seeds are already out of their cups and pods seeking their predestined places. Some will strike root and grow up beside their parents, others flying on the wings of the wind far from them, among strangers. Most of the young birds are full feathered and out of their nests, though still looked after by both father and mother, protected and fed and to some extent educated. How beautiful the home life of birds! No wonder we all love them.

I like to watch the squirrels. There are two species here, the large California gray and the Douglas. The latter is the brightest of all the squirrels I have ever seen, a hot spark of life, making every tree tingle with his prickly toes, a condensed nugget of fresh mountain vigor and valor, as free from disease as a sunbeam. One cannot think of such an animal ever being weary or sick. He seems to think the mountains belong to him, and at first tried to drive away the whole flock of sheep as well as the shepherd and dogs. How he scolds, and what faces he makes, all eyes, teeth, and whiskers! If not so comically small, he would indeed be a dreadful fellow. I should like to know more about his bringing up, his life in the home knot-hole, as well as in the tree-tops, throughout all seasons. Strange that I have not yet found a nest full of young ones. The Douglas is nearly allied to the red squirrel of the Atlantic slope, and may have been distributed to this side of the continent by way of the great unbroken forests of the north.

The California gray is one of the most beautiful, and, next to the Douglas, the most interesting of our hairy neighbors. Compared with the Douglas he is twice as large, but far less lively and influential as a worker in the woods and he manages to make his way through leaves and branches with less stir than his small brother. I have never heard him bark at anything except our dogs. When in search of food he glides silently from branch to branch, examining last year's cones, to see whether some few seeds may not be left between the scales, or gleans fallen ones among the leaves on the ground, since none of the present season's crop is yet available. His tail floats now behind him, now above him, level or gracefully curled like a wisp of cirrus cloud, every hair in its place, clean and shining and radiant as thistle-down in spite of rough, gummy work. His whole body seems about as unsubstantial as his tail. The little Douglas is fiery, peppery, full of brag and fight and show, with movements so quick and keen they almost sting the onlooker, and the harlequin gyrating show he makes of himself turns one giddy to see. The gray is shy, and oftentimes stealthy in his movements, as if half expecting an enemy in every tree and bush, and back of every log, wishing only to be let alone apparently, and manifesting no desire to be seen or admired or feared. The Indians hunt this species for food, a good cause for caution, not to mention other enemies—hawks, snakes, wild cats. In woods where food is abundant they wear paths through sheltering thickets and over prostrate trees to some favorite pool where in hot and dry weather they drink at nearly the same hour every day. These pools are said to be narrowly watched, especially by the boys, who lie in ambush with bow and arrow, and kill without noise. But, in spite of enemies, squirrels are happy fellows, forest favorites, types of tireless life. Of all Nature's wild beasts, they seem to me the wildest. May we come to know each other better.

The chaparral-covered hill-slope to the south of

the camp, besides furnishing nesting-places for countless merry birds, is the home and hiding-place of the curious wood rat (*Neotoma*), a handsome, interesting animal, always attracting attention wherever seen. It is more like a squirrel than a rat, is much larger, has delicate, thick, soft fur of a bluish slate color, white on the belly; ears large, thin, and translucent; eyes soft, full, and liquid; claws slender, sharp as needles; and as his limbs are strong, he can climb about as well as a squirrel. No rat or squirrel has so innocent a look, is so easily approached, or expresses such confidence in one's good intentions. He seems too fine for the thorny thickets he inhabits, and his hut also is as unlike himself as may be, though softly furnished inside. No other animal inhabitant of these mountains builds houses so large and striking in appearance. The traveler coming suddenly upon a group of them for the first time will not be likely to forget them. They are built of all kinds of sticks, old rotten pieces picked up anywhere, and green prickly twigs bitten from the nearest bushes, the whole mixed with miscellaneous odds and ends of everything movable, such as bits of cloddy earth, stones, bones, deerhorn, etc., piled up in a conical mass as if it were got ready for burning. Some of these curious cabins are six feet high and as wide at the base, and a dozen or more of them are occasionally grouped together, less perhaps for the sake of society than for advantages of food and shelter. Coming through the dense shaggy thickets of some lonely hillside, the solitary explorer happening into one of these strange villages is startled at the sight, and may fancy himself in an Indian settlement, and begin to wonder what kind of reception he is likely to get. But no savage face will he see, perhaps not a single inhabitant, or at most two or three seated on top of their wigwams, looking at the stranger with the mildest of wild eyes, and allowing a near approach. In the centre of the rough spiky hut a soft nest is made of the inner fibres of bark chewed to tow, and lined with feathers and the down of various seeds, such as willow and milkweed. The delicate creature in its prickly, thick-walled home suggests a tender flower in a thorny involucre. Some of the nests are built in trees thirty or forty feet from the ground, and even in garrets, as if seeking the company and protection of man, like swallows and linnets, though accustomed to the wildest solitude. Among housekeepers Neotoma has the reputation of a thief, because he carries away everything transportable to his queer hut,—knives, forks, combs, nails, tin cups, spectacles, etc.,—merely, however, to strengthen his fortifications, I guess. His food at home, as far as I have learned, is nearly the same as that of the squirrels,—nuts, berries, seeds, and sometimes the bark and tender shoots of the various species of ceanothus.

July 2. Warm, sunny day, thrilling plant and animals and rocks alike, making sap and blood flow fast, and making every particle of the crystal mountains throb and swirl and dance in glad accord like stardust. No dullness anywhere visible or thinkable. No stagnation, no death. Everything kept in joyful rhythmic motion in the pulses of Nature's big heart.

Pearl cumuli over the higher mountains—clouds, not with a silver lining, but all silver. The brightest, crispest, rockiest-looking clouds, most varied in features and keenest in outline I ever saw at any time of year in any country. The daily building and unbuilding of these snowy cloud-ranges—the highest Sierra—is a prime marvel to me, and I gaze at the stupendous white domes, miles high, with ever fresh admiration. But in the midst of these sky and mountain affairs a change of diet is pulling us down. We have been out of bread a few days, and begin to miss it more than seems reasonable for we have plenty of meat and sugar and tea. Strange we should feel food-poor in so rich a wilderness. The Indians put us to shame, so do the squirrels,—starchy roots and seeds and bark in abundance, yet the failure of the meal sack disturbs our bodily balance, and threatens our best enjoyments.

July 3. Warm. Breeze just enough to sift through the woods and waft fragrance from their thousand fountains. The pine and fir cones are growing well, resin and balsam dripping from every tree, and seeds are ripening fast, promising a fine harvest. The squirrels will have bread. They eat all kinds of nuts long before they are ripe, and yet never seem to suffer in stomach.

A BREAD FAMINE

July 4. The air beyond the flock range, full of the essences of the woods, is growing sweeter and more fragrant from day to day, like ripening fruit.

Mr. Delaney is expected to arrive soon from the lowlands with a new stock of provisions, and as the flock is to be moved to fresh pastures we shall all be well fed. In the mean time our stock of beans as well as flour has failed—everything but mutton, sugar, and tea. The shepherd is somewhat demoralized, and seems to care but little what becomes of his flock. He says that since the boss has failed to feed him he is not rightly bound to feed the sheep, and swears that no decent white man can climb these steep mountains on mutton alone. "It's not fittin' grub for a white man really white. For dogs and coyotes and Indians it's different. Good grub, good sheep. That's what I say." Such was Billy's Fourth of July oration.

July 5. The clouds of noon on the high Sierra seem yet more marvelously, indescribably beautiful from day to day as one becomes more wakeful to see them. The smoke of the gunpowder burned yesterday on the lowlands, and the eloquence of the orators has probably settled or been blown away by this time. Here every day is a holiday, a jubilee ever sounding with serene enthusiasm, without wear or waste or cloying weariness. Everything rejoicing. Not a single cell or crystal unvisited or forgotten.

July 6. Mr. Delaney has not arrived, and the bread famine is sore. We must eat mutton a while longer, though it seems hard to get accustomed to it. I have heard of Texas pioneers living without bread or anything made from the cereals for months without suffering, using the breast-meat of wild turkeys for bread. Of this kind they had plenty in the good old days when life, though considered less safe, was fussed over the less. The trappers and fur traders of early days in the Rocky Mountain regions lived on bison and beaver meat for months. Salmon-eaters, too, there are among both Indians and whites who seem to suffer little or not at all from the want of bread. Just at this moment mutton seems the least desirable of food, though of good quality. We pick out the leanest bits, and down they go against heavy disgust, causing nausea and an effort to reject the offensive stuff. Tea makes matters worse, if possible. The stomach begins to assert itself as an independent creature with a will of its own. We should boil lupine leaves, clover, starchy petioles, and saxifrage rootstocks like the Indians. We try to ignore our gastric troubles, rise and gaze about us, turn our eyes to the mountains, and climb doggedly up through brush and rocks into the heart of the scenery. A stifled calm comes on, and the day's duties and even enjoyments are languidly got through with. We chew a few leaves of ceanothus by way of luncheon, and smell or chew the spicy monardella for the dull headache and stomach-ache that now lightens, now comes muffling down upon us and into us like fog. At night more mutton, flesh to flesh, down with it, not too much, and there are the stars shining through the cedar plumes and branches above our beds.

July 7. Rather weak and sickish this morning, and all about a piece of bread. Can scarce command attention to my best studies, as if one couldn't take a few days' saunter in the Godful woods without maintaining a base on a wheat-field and gristmill. Like caged parrots we want a cracker, any of the hundred kinds— the remainder biscuit of a voyage around the world would answer well enough, nor would the wholesomeness of saleratus biscuit be questioned. Bread without flesh is a good diet, as on many botanical excursions I have proved. Tea also may easily be ignored. Just bread and water and delightful toil is all I need,— not unreasonably much, yet one ought to be trained and tempered to enjoy life in these brave wilds in full independence of any particular kind of nourishment. That this may be accomplished is manifest, as far as bodily welfare is concerned, in the lives of people of other climes. The Eskimo, for example, gets a living far north of the wheat line, from oily seals and whales. Meat, berries, bitter weeds, and blubber, or only the last, for months at a time; and yet these people all around the frozen shores of our continent are said to be hearty, jolly, stout, and brave. We hear, too, of fish-eaters, carnivorous as spiders, yet well enough as far as stomachs are concerned, while we are so ridiculously helpless, making wry faces over our fare, looking sheepish in digestive distress amid rumbling, grumbling sounds that might well pass for smothered baas. We have a large supply of sugar, and this evening it occurred to me that these belligerent stomachs might possibly, like complaining children, be coaxed with candy. Accordingly the frying-pan was cleansed, and a lot of sugar cooked in it to a sort of wax, but this stuff only made matters worse.

Man seems to be the only animal whose food soils him, making necessary much washing and shield-like bibs and napkins. Moles living in the earth and eating slimy worms are yet as clean as seals or fishes, whose lives are one perpetual wash. And, as we have seen, the squirrels in these resiny woods keep themselves clean in some mysterious way; not a hair is sticky, though they handle the gummy cones, and glide about apparently without care. The birds, too, are clean, though they seem to make a good deal of fuss washing and cleaning their feathers. Certain flies and ants I see are in a fix, entangled and sealed up in the sugar-wax we threw away, like some of their ancestors in amber. Our stomachs, like tired muscles, are sore with long squirming. Once I was very hungry in the Bonaventure graveyard near Savannah, Georgia, having fasted for several days; then the empty stomach seemed to chafe in much the same way as now, and a somewhat similar tenderness and aching was produced, hard to bear, though the pain was not acute. We dream of bread, a sure sign we need it. Like the Indians, we ought to know how to get the starch out of fern and saxifrage stalks, lily bulbs, pine bark, etc. Our education has been sadly neglected for many generations. Wild rice would be good. I noticed a leersia in wet meadow edges, but the seeds are small. Acorns are not ripe, nor pine nuts, nor filberts. The inner bark of pine or spruce might be tried. Drank tea until half intoxicated. Man seems to crave a stimulant when anything extraordinary is going on, and this is the only one I use. Billy chews great quantities of tobacco, which I suppose helps to stupefy and moderate his misery. We look and listen for the Don every hour. How beautiful upon the mountains his big feet would be!

In the warm, hospitable Sierra, shepherds and mountain men in general, as far as I have seen, are easily satisfied as to food supplies and bedding. Most of them are heartily content to "rough it," ignoring Nature's fineness as bothersome or unmanly. The shepherd's bed is often only the bare ground and a pair of blankets, with a stone, a piece of wood, or a pack-saddle for a pillow. In choosing the spot, he shows less care than the dogs, for they usually deliberate before making up their minds in so important an affair, going from place to place, scraping away loose sticks and pebbles, and trying for comfort by making many changes, while the shepherd casts himself down anywhere, seemingly the least skilled of all rest seekers. His food, too, even when he has all he wants, is usually far from delicate, either in kind or cooking. Beans, bread of any sort, bacon, mutton, dried peaches, and sometimes potatoes and onions, make up his bill-of-fare, the two latter articles being regarded as luxuries on account of their weight as compared with the nourishment they contain; a half-sack or so of each may be put into the pack in setting out from the home ranch and in a few days they are done. Beans are the main standby, portable, wholesome, and capable of going far, besides being easily cooked, although curiously enough a great deal of mystery is supposed to lie about the bean-pot. No two cooks quite agree on the methods of making beans do their best, and, after petting and coaxing and nursing the savory mess,—well oiled and mellowed with bacon boiled into the heart of it,—the proud cook will ask, after dishing out a quart or two for trial, "Well, how do you like *my* beans?" as if by no possibility could they be like any other beans cooked in the same way, but must needs possess some special virtue of which he alone is master. Molasses, sugar, or pepper may be used to give desired flavors; or the first water may be poured off and a spoonful or two of ashes or soda added to dissolve or soften the skins more fully, according to various tastes and notions. But, like casks of wine, no two potfuls are exactly alike to every palate. Some are supposed to be spoiled by the moon, by some unlucky day, by the beans having been grown on soil not suitable; or the whole year may be to blame as not favorable for beans.

Coffee, too, has its marvels in the camp kitchen, but not so many, and not so inscrutable as those that beset the bean-pot. A low, complacent grunt follows a mouthful drawn in with a gurgle, and the remark cast forth aimlessly, "That's good coffee." Then another gurgling sip and repetition of the judgment, "*Yes, sir*, that *is* good coffee." As to tea, there are but two kinds, weak and strong, the stronger the better. The only remark heard is, "That tea's weak," otherwise it is good enough and not worth mentioning. If it has been boiled an hour or two or smoked on a pitchy fire, no matter,—who cares for a little tannin or creosote? they make the black beverage all the stronger and more attractive to tobacco-tanned palates.

Sheep-camp bread, like most California camp bread, is baked in Dutch ovens, some of it in the form of yeast powder biscuit, an unwholesome sticky compound leading straight to dyspepsia. The greater part, however, is fermented with sour dough, a handful from each batch being saved and put away in the mouth of the flour sack to inoculate the next. The oven is simply a cast-iron pot, about five inches deep and from twelve to eighteen inches wide. After the batch has been mixed and kneaded in a tin pan the oven is slightly heated and rubbed with a piece of tallow or pork rind. The dough is then placed in it, pressed out against the sides, and left to rise. When ready for baking a shovelful of coals is spread out by the side of the fire and the oven set upon them, while another shovelful is placed on top of the lid, which is raised from time to time to see that the requisite amount of heat is being kept up. With care good bread may be made in this way, though it is liable to be burned or to be sour, or raised too much, and the weight of the oven is a serious objection.

At last Don Delaney comes doon the lang glen—hunger vanishes, we turn our eyes to the mountains, and to-morrow we go climbing toward cloudland.

Never while anything is left of me shall this first camp be forgotten. It has fairly grown into me, not merely as memory pictures, but as part and parcel of mind and body alike. The deep hopper-like hollow, with its majestic trees through which all the wonderful nights the stars poured their beauty. The flowery wildness of the high steep slope toward Brown's Flat, and its bloom-fragrance descending at the close of the still days. The embowered river-reaches with their multitude of voices making melody, the stately flow and rush and glad exulting onsweeping currents caressing the dipping sedge-leaves and bushes and mossy stones, swirling in pools, dividing against little flowery islands, breaking gray and white here and there, ever rejoicing, yet with deep solemn undertones recalling the ocean—the brave little bird ever beside them, singing with sweet human tones among the waltzing foam-bells, and like a blessed evangel explaining God's love. And the Pilot Peak Ridge, its long withdrawing slopes gracefully modeled and braided, reaching from climate to climate, feathered with trees that are the kings of their race, their ranks nobly marshaled to view, spire above spire, crown above crown, waving their long, leafy arms, tossing their cones like ringing bells—blessed sun-fed mountaineers rejoicing in their strength, every tree tuneful, a harp for the winds and the sun. The hazel and buckthorn pastures of the deer, the sun-beaten brows purple and yellow with mint and golden-rods, carpeted with chamæbatia, humming with bees.

And the dawns and sunrises and sundowns of these mountain days,—the rose light creeping higher among the stars, changing to daffodil yellow, the level beams bursting forth, streaming across the ridges, touching pine after pine, awakening and warming all the mighty host to do gladly their shining day's work. The great sun-gold noons, the alabaster cloud-mountains, the landscape beaming with consciousness like the face of a god. The sunsets, when the trees stood hushed awaiting their good-night blessings. Divine, enduring, unwastable wealth.

TO THE HIGH MOUNTAINS

July 8. Now away we go toward the topmost mountains. Many still, small voices, as well as the noon thunder, are calling, "Come higher." Farewell, blessed dell, woods, gardens, streams, birds, squirrels, lizards, and a thousand others. Farewell. Farewell.

Up through the woods the hoofed locusts streamed beneath a cloud of brown dust. Scarcely were they driven a hundred yards from the old corral ere they seemed to know that at last they were going to new pastures, and rushed wildly ahead, crowding through gaps in the brush, jumping, tumbling like exulting hurrahing flood-waters escaping through a broken dam. A man on each flank kept shouting advice to the leaders, who in their famishing condition were behaving like Gadarene swine; two other drivers were busy with stragglers, helping them out of brush tangles; the Indian, calm, alert, silently watched for wanderers likely to be overlooked; the two dogs ran here and there, at a loss to know what was best to be done, while the Don, soon far in the rear, was trying to keep in sight of his troublesome wealth.

As soon as the boundary of the old eaten-out range was passed the hungry horde suddenly became calm, like a mountain stream in a meadow. Thenceforward they were allowed to eat their way as slowly as they wished, care being taken only to keep them headed toward the summit of the Merced and Tuolumne divide. Soon the two thousand flattened paunches were bulged out with sweet-pea vines and grass, and the gaunt, desperate creatures, more like wolves than sheep, became bland and governable, while the howling drivers changed to gentle shepherds, and sauntered in peace.

Toward sundown we reached Hazel Green, a charming spot on the summit of the dividing ridge between the basins of the Merced and Tuolumne, where there is a small brook flowing through hazel and dogwood thickets beneath magnificent silver firs and pines. Here, we are camped for the night, our big fire, heaped high with rosiny logs and branches, is blazing like a sunrise, gladly giving back the light slowly sifted from the sunbeams of centuries of summers; and in the glow of that old sunlight how impressively surrounding objects are brought forward in relief against the outer darkness! Grasses, larkspurs, columbines, lilies, hazel bushes, and the great trees form a circle around the fire like thoughtful spectators, gazing and listening with human-like enthusiasm. The night breeze is cool, for all day we have been climbing into the upper sky, the home of the cloud mountains we so long have admired. How sweet and keen the air! Every breath a blessing. Here the sugar pine reaches its fullest development in size and beauty and number of individuals, filling every swell and hollow and down-plunging ravine almost to the exclusion of other species. A few yellow pines are still to be found as companions, and in the coolest places silver firs; but noble as these are, the sugar pine is king, and spreads long protecting arms above them while they rock and wave in sign of recognition.

We have now reached a height of six thousand feet. In the forenoon we passed along a flat part of the dividing ridge that is planted with manzanita (*Arctostaphylos*), some specimens the largest I have seen. I measured one, the bole of which is four feet in diameter and only eighteen inches high from the ground, where it dissolves into many wide-spreading branches forming a broad round head about ten or twelve feet high, covered with clusters of small narrow-throated pink bells. The leaves are pale green, glandular, and set on edge by a twist of the petiole. The branches seem naked; for the chocolate-colored bark is very smooth and thin, and is shed off in flakes that curl when dry. The wood is red, close-grained, hard, and heavy. I wonder how old these curious tree-bushes are, probably as old as the great pines. Indians and bears and birds and fat grubs feast on the berries, which look like small apples, often rosy on one side, green on the other. The Indians are said to make a kind of beer or cider out of them. There are many species. This one, *Arctostaphylos pungens*, is common hereabouts. No need have they to fear the wind, so low they are and steadfastly rooted. Even the fires that sweep the woods seldom destroy them utterly, for they rise again from the root, and some of the dry ridges they grow on are seldom touched by fire. I must try to know them better.

I miss my river songs to-night. Here Hazel Creek at its topmost springs has a voice like a bird. The wind-tones in the great trees overhead are strangely impressive, all the more because not a leaf stirs below them. But it grows late, and I must to bed. The camp is silent; everybody asleep. It seems extravagant to spend hours so precious in sleep. "He giveth his beloved sleep." Pity the poor beloved needs it, weak, weary, forspent; oh, the pity of it, to sleep in the midst of eternal, beautiful motion instead of gazing forever, like the stars.

July 9. Exhilarated with the mountain air, I feel like shouting this morning with excess of wild animal joy. The Indian lay down away from the fire last night, without blankets, having nothing on, by way of clothing, but a pair of blue overalls and a calico shirt wet with sweat. The night air is chilly at this elevation, and we gave him some horse-blankets, but he didn't seem to care for them. A fine thing to be independent of clothing where it is so hard to carry. When food is scarce, he can live on whatever comes in his way—a few berries, roots, bird eggs, grasshoppers, black ants, fat wasp or bumblebee larvæ, without feeling that he is doing anything worth mention, so I have been told.

Our course to-day was along the broad top of the main ridge to a hollow beyond Crane Flat. It is scarce at all rocky, and is covered with the noblest pines and spruces I have yet seen. Sugar pines from six to eight feet in diameter are not uncommon, with a height of two hundred feet or even more. The silver firs (*Abies concolor* and *A. magnifica*) are exceedingly beautiful, especially the *magnifica*, which becomes more abundant the higher we go. It is of great size, one of the most notable in every way of the giant conifers of the Sierra. I saw specimens that measured seven feet in diameter and over two hundred feet in height, while the average size for what might be called full-grown mature trees can hardly be less than one hundred and eighty or two hundred feet high and five or six feet in diameter; and with these noble dimensions there is a symmetry and perfection of finish not to be seen in any other tree, hereabout at least. The branches are whorled in fives mostly, and stand out from the tall, straight, exquisitely tapered bole in level collars, each branch regularly pinnated like the fronds of ferns, and densely clad with leaves all around the branchlets, thus giving them a singularly rich and sumptuous appearance. The extreme top of the tree is a thick blunt shoot pointing straight to the zenith like an admonishing finger. The cones stand erect like casks on the upper branches. They are about six inches long, three in diameter, blunt, velvety, and cylindrical in form, and very rich and precious looking. The seeds are about three quarters of an inch long, dark reddish brown with brilliant iridescent purple wings, and when ripe, the cone falls to pieces, and the seeds thus set free at a height of one hundred and fifty or two hundred feet have a good send off and may fly considerable distances in a good breeze; and it is when a good breeze is blowing that most of them are shaken free to fly.

The other species, *Abies concolor*, attains nearly as great a height and thickness as the *magnifica*, but the branches do not form such regular whorls, nor are they so exactly pinnated or richly leaf-clad. Instead of growing all around the branchlets, the leaves are mostly arranged in two flat horizontal rows. The cones and seeds are like those of the *magnifica* in form but less than half as large. The bark of the *magnifica* is reddish purple and closely furrowed, that of the *concolor* gray and widely furrowed. A noble pair.

At Crane Flat we climbed a thousand feet or more in a distance of about two miles, the forest growing more dense and the silvery *magnifica* fir forming a still greater portion of the whole. Crane Flat is a meadow with a wide sandy border lying on the top of the divide. It is often visited by blue cranes to rest and feed on their long journeys, hence the name. It is about half a mile long, draining into the Merced, sedgy in the middle, with a margin bright with lilies, columbines, lark spurs, lupines, castilleia, then an outer zone of dry, gently sloping ground starred with a multitude of small flowers,—eunanus, mimulus, gilia, with rosettes of spraguea, and tufts of several species of eriogonum and the brilliant zauschneria. The noble forest wall about it is made up of the two silver firs and the yellow and sugar pines, which here seem to reach their highest pitch of beauty and grandeur; for the elevation, six thousand feet or a little more, is not too great for the sugar and yellow pines or too low for the *magnifica* fir, while the *concolor* seems to find this elevation the best possible. About a mile from the north end of the flat there is a grove of *Sequoia gigantea*, the king of all the conifers. Furthermore, the Douglas spruce (*Pseudotsuga Douglasii*) and *Libocedrus decurrens*, and a few two-leaved pines, occur here and there, forming a small part of the forest. Three pines, two silver firs, one Douglas spruce, one sequoia,—all of them, except the two-leaved pine, colossal trees,— are found here together, an assemblage of conifers unrivaled on the globe.

We passed a number of charming garden-like meadows lying on top of the divide or hanging like ribbons down its sides, imbedded in the glorious forest. Some are taken up chiefly with the tall white-flowered *Veratrum Californicum*, with boat-shaped leaves about a foot long, eight or ten inches wide, and veined like those of cypripedium,—a robust, hearty, liliaceous plant, fond of water and determined to be seen.

Columbine and larkspur grow on the dryer edges of the meadows, with a tall handsome lupine standing waist-deep in long grasses and sedges. Castilleias, too, of several species make a bright show with beds of violets at their feet. But the glory of these forest meadows is a lily (*L. parvum*). The tallest are from seven to eight feet high with magnificent racemes of ten to twenty or more small orange-colored flowers; they stand out free in open ground, with just enough grass and other companion plants about them to fringe their feet, and show them off to best advantage. This is a grand addition to my lily acquaintances,—a true mountaineer, reaching prime vigor and beauty at a height of seven thousand feet or thereabouts. It varies, I find, very much in size even in the same meadow, not only with the soil, but with age. I saw a specimen that had only one flower, and another within a stone's throw had twenty-five. And to think that the sheep should be allowed in these lily meadows! after how many centuries of Nature's care planting and watering them, tucking the bulbs in snugly below winter frost, shading the tender shoots with clouds drawn above them like curtains, pouring refreshing rain, making them perfect in beauty, and keeping them safe by a thousand miracles; yet, strange to say, allowing the trampling of devastating sheep. One might reasonably look for a wall of fire to fence such gardens. So extravagant is Nature with her choicest treasures, spending plant beauty as she spends sunshine, pouring it forth into land and sea, garden and desert. And so the beauty of lilies falls on angels and men, bears and squirrels, wolves and sheep, birds and bees, but as far as I have seen, man alone, and the animals he tames, destroy these gardens. Awkward, lumbering bears, the Don tells me, love to wallow in them in hot weather, and deer with their sharp feet cross them again and again, sauntering and feeding, yet never a lily have I seen spoiled by them. Rather, like gardeners, they seem to cultivate them, pressing and dibbling as required. Anyhow not a leaf or petal seems misplaced.

The trees round about them seem as perfect in beauty and form as the lilies, their boughs whorled like lily leaves in exact order. This evening, as usual, the glow of our camp-fire is working enchantment on everything within reach of its rays. Lying beneath the firs, it is glorious to see them dipping their spires in the starry sky, the sky like one vast lily meadow in bloom! How can I close my eyes on so precious a night?

July 10. A Douglas squirrel, peppery, pungent autocrat of the woods, is barking overhead this morning, and the small forest birds, so seldom seen when one travels noisily, are out on sunny branches along the edge of the meadow getting warm, taking a sun bath and dew bath—a fine sight. How charming the sprightly confident looks and ways of these little feathered people of the trees! They seem sure of dainty, wholesome breakfasts, and where are so many breakfasts to come from? How helpless should we find ourselves should we try to set a table for them of such buds, seeds, insects, etc., as would keep them in the pure wild health they enjoy! Not a headache or any other ache amongst them, I guess. As for the irrepressible Douglas squirrels, one never thinks of their breakfasts or the possibility of hunger, sickness or death; rather they seem like stars above chance or change, even though we may see them at times busy gathering burrs, working hard for a living.

On through the forest ever higher we go, a cloud of dust dimming the way, thousands of feet trampling leaves and flowers, but in this mighty wilderness they seem but a feeble band, and a thousand gardens will escape their blighting touch. They cannot hurt the trees, though some of the seedlings suffer, and should the woolly locusts be greatly multiplied, as on account of dollar value they are likely to be, then the forests, too, may in time be destroyed. Only the sky will then be safe, though hid from view by dust and smoke, incense of a bad sacrifice. Poor, helpless, hungry sheep, in great part misbegotten, without good right to be, semi-manufactured, made less by God than man, born out of time and place, yet their voices are strangely human and call out one's pity.

Our way is still along the Merced and Tuolumne divide, the streams on our right going to swell the songful Yosemite River, those on our left to the songful Tuolumne, slipping through sunny carex and lily meadows, and breaking into song down a thousand ravines almost as soon as they are born. A more tuneful set of streams surely nowhere exists, or more sparkling crystal pure, now gliding with tinkling whisper, now with merry dimpling rush, in and out through sunshine and shade, shimmering in pools, uniting their currents, bouncing, dancing from form to form over cliffs and inclines, ever more beautiful the farther they go until they pour into the main glacial rivers.

All day I have been gazing in growing admiration at the noble groups of the magnificent silver fir which more and more is taking the ground to itself. The woods above Crane Flat still continue comparatively open, letting in the sunshine on the brown needle-strewn ground. Not only are the individual trees admirable in symmetry and superb in foliage and port, but half a dozen or more often form temple groves in which the trees are so nicely graded in size and position as to seem one. Here, indeed, is the tree-lover's paradise. The dullest eye in the world must surely be quickened by such trees as these.

Fortunately the sheep need little attention, as they are driven slowly and allowed to nip and nibble as they like. Since leaving Hazel Green we have been following the Yosemite trail; visitors to the famous valley coming by way of Coulterville and Chinese Camp pass this way—the two trails uniting at Crane Flat—and enter the valley on the north side. Another trail enters on the south side by way of Mariposa. The tourists we saw were in parties of from three or four to fifteen or twenty, mounted on mules or small mustang ponies. A strange show they made, winding single file through the solemn woods in gaudy attire, scaring the wild creatures, and one might fancy that even the great pines would be disturbed and groan aghast. But what may we say of ourselves and the flock?

We are now camped at Tamarack Flat, within four or five miles of the lower end of Yosemite. Here is another fine meadow embosomed in the woods, with a deep, clear stream gliding through it, its banks rounded and beveled with a thatch of dipping sedges. The flat is named after the two-leaved pine (*Pinus contorta*, var. *Murrayana*), common here, especially around the cool margin of the meadow. On rocky ground it is a rough, thickset tree, about forty to sixty feet high and one to three feet in diameter, bark thin and gummy, branches rather naked, tassels, leaves, and cones small. But in damp, rich soil it grows close and slender, and reaches a height at times of nearly a hundred feet. Specimens only six inches in diameter at the ground are often fifty or sixty feet in height, as slender and sharp in outline as arrows, like the true tamarack (larch) of the Eastern States; hence the name, though it is a pine.

July 11. The Don has gone ahead on one of the pack animals to spy out the land to the north of Yosemite in search of the best point for a central camp. Much higher than this we cannot now go, for the upper pastures, said to be better than any hereabouts, are still buried in heavy winter snow. Glad I am that camp is to be fixed in the Yosemite region, for many a glorious ramble I'll have along the top of the walls, and then what landscapes I shall find with their new mountains and cañons, forests and gardens, lakes and streams and falls.

We are now about seven thousand feet above the sea, and the nights are so cool we have to pile coats and extra clothing on top of our blankets. Tamarack Creek is icy cold, delicious, exhilarating champagne water. It is flowing bank-full in the meadow with silent speed, but only a few hundred yards below our camp the ground is bare gray granite strewn with boulders, large spaces being without a single tree or only a small one here and there anchored in narrow seams and cracks. The boulders, many of them very large, are not in piles or scattered like rubbish among loose crumbling débris as if weathered out of the solid as boulders of disintegration; they mostly occur singly, and are lying on a clean pavement on which the sunshine falls in a glare that contrasts with the shimmer of light and shade we have been accustomed to in the leafy woods. And, strange to say, these boulders lying so still and deserted, with no moving force near them, no boulder carrier anywhere in sight, were nevertheless brought from a distance, as difference in color and composition shows, quarried and carried and laid down here each in its place; nor have they stirred, most of them, through calm and storm since first they arrived. They look lonely here, strangers in a strange land,—huge blocks, angular mountain chips, the largest twenty or thirty feet in diameter, the chips that Nature has made in modeling her landscapes, fashioning the forms of her mountains and valleys. And with what tool were they quarried and carried? On the pavement we find its marks. The most resisting unweathered portion of the surface is scored and striated in a rigidly parallel way, indicating that the region has been overswept by a glacier from the northeastward, grinding down the general mass of the mountains, scoring and polishing, producing a strange, raw, wiped appearance, and dropping whatever boulders it chanced to be carrying at the time it was melted at the close of the Glacial Period. A fine discovery this. As for the forests we have been passing through, they are probably growing on deposits of soil most of which has been laid down by this same ice agent in the form of moraines of different sorts, now in great part disintegrated and outspread by post-glacial weathering.

Out of the grassy meadow and down over this ice-planed granite runs the glad young Tamarack Creek, rejoicing, exulting, chanting, dancing in white, glowing, irised falls and cascades on its way to the Merced Cañon, a few miles below Yosemite, falling more than three thousand feet in a distance of about two miles.

All the Merced streams are wonderful singers, and Yosemite is the centre where the main tributaries meet. From a point about half a mile from our camp we can see into the lower end of the famous valley, with its wonderful cliffs and groves, a grand page of mountain manuscript that I would gladly give my life to be able to read. How vast it seems, how short human life when we happen to think of it, and how little we may learn, however hard we try! Yet why bewail our poor inevitable ignorance? Some of the external beauty is always in sight, enough to keep every fibre of us tingling, and this we are able to gloriously enjoy though the methods of its creation may lie beyond our ken. Sing on, brave Tamarack Creek, fresh from your snowy fountains, plash and swirl and dance to your fate in the sea; bathing, cheering every living thing along your way.

Have greatly enjoyed all this huge day, sauntering and seeing, steeping in the mountain influences, sketching, noting, pressing flowers, drinking ozone and Tamarack water. Found the white fragrant Washington lily, the finest of all the Sierra lilies. Its bulbs are buried in shaggy chaparral tangles, I suppose for safety from pawing bears; and its magnificent panicles sway and rock over the top of the rough snow-pressed bushes, while big, bold, blunt-nosed bees drone and mumble in its polleny bells. A lovely flower, worth going hungry and footsore endless miles to see. The whole world seems richer now that I have found this plant in so noble a landscape.

A log house serves to mark a claim to the Tamarack meadow, which may become valuable as a station in case travel to Yosemite should greatly increase. Belated parties occasionally stop here. A white man with an Indian woman is holding possession of the place.

Sauntered up the meadow about sundown, out of

74

sight of camp and sheep and all human mark, into the deep peace of the solemn old woods, everything glowing with Heaven's unquenchable enthusiasm.

July 12. The Don has returned, and again we go on pilgrimage. "Looking over the Yosemite Creek country," he said, "from the tops of the hills you see nothing but rocks and patches of trees; but when you go down into the rocky desert you find no end of small grassy banks and meadows, and so the country is not half so lean as it looks. There we'll go and stay until the snow is melted from the upper country."

I was glad to hear that the high snow made a stay in the Yosemite region necessary, for I am anxious to see as much of it as possible. What fine times I shall have sketching, studying plants and rocks, and scrambling about the brink of the great valley alone, out of sight and sound of camp!

We saw another party of Yosemite tourists to-day. Somehow most of these travelers seem to care but little for the glorious objects about them, though enough to spend time and money and endure long rides to see the famous valley. And when they are fairly within the mighty walls of the temple and hear the psalms of the falls, they will forget themselves and become devout. Blessed, indeed, should be every pilgrim in these holy mountains!

We moved slowly eastward along the Mono Trail, and early in the afternoon unpacked and camped on the bank of Cascade Creek. The Mono Trail crosses the range by the Bloody Cañon Pass to gold mines near the north end of Mono Lake. These mines were reported to be rich when first discovered, and a grand rush took place, making a trail necessary. A few small bridges were built over streams where fording was not practicable on account of the softness of the bottom, sections of fallen trees cut out, and lanes made through thickets wide enough to allow the passage of bulky packs; but over the greater part of the way scarce a stone or shovelful of earth has been moved.

The woods we passed through are composed almost wholly of *Abies magnifica*, the companion species, *concolor*, being mostly left behind on account of altitude, while the increasing elevation seems grateful to the charming *magnifica*. No words can do anything like justice to this noble tree. At one place many had fallen during some heavy wind-storm, owing to the loose sandy character of the soil, which offered no secure anchorage. The soil is mostly decomposed and disintegrated moraine material.

The sheep are lying down on a bare rocky spot such as they like, chewing the cud in grassy peace. Cooking is going on, appetites growing keener every day. No lowlander can appreciate the mountain appetite, and the facility with which heavy food called "grub" is disposed of. Eating, walking, resting, seem alike delightful, and one feels inclined to shout lustily on rising in the morning like a crowing cock. Sleep and digestion as clear as the air. Fine spicy plush boughs for bedding we shall have to-night, and a glorious lullaby from this cascading creek. Never was stream more fittingly named, for as far as I have traced it above and below our camp it is one continuous bouncing, dancing, white bloom of cascades. And at the very last unwearied it finishes its wild course in a grand leap of three hundred feet or more to the bottom of the main Yosemite cañon near the fall of Tamarack Creek, a few miles below the foot of the valley. These falls almost rival some of the far-famed Yosemite falls. Never shall I forget these glad cascade songs, the low booming, the roaring, the keen, silvery clashing of the cool water rushing exulting from form to form beneath irised spray; or in the deep still night seen white in the darkness, and its multitude of voices sounding still more impressively sublime. Here I find the little water ouzel as much at home as any linnet in a leafy grove, seeming to take the greater delight the more boisterous the stream. The dizzy precipices, the swift dashing energy displayed, and the thunder tones of the sheer falls are awe inspiring, but there is nothing awful about this little bird. Its song is sweet and low, and all its gestures, as it flits about amid the loud uproar, bespeak strength and peace and joy. Contemplating these darlings of Nature coming forth from spray-sprinkled nests on the brink of savage streams, Samson's riddle comes to mind, "Out of the strong cometh forth sweetness." A yet finer bloom is this little bird than the foam-bells in eddying pools. Gentle bird, a precious message you bring me. We may miss the meaning of the torrent, but thy sweet voice, only love is in it.

July 13. Our course all day has been eastward over the rim of Yosemite Creek basin and down about halfway to the bottom, where we have encamped on a sheet of glacier-polished granite, a firm foundation for beds. Saw the tracks of a very large bear on the trail, and the Don talked of bears in general. I said I should like to see the maker of these immense tracks as he marched along, and follow him for days, without disturbing him, to learn something of the life of this master beast of the wilderness. Lambs, the Don told me,

born in the lowland, that never saw or heard a bear,
snort and run in terror when they catch the scent,
showing how fully they have inherited a knowledge
of their enemy. Hogs, mules, horses, and cattle are
afraid of bears, and are seized with ungovernable terror when they approach, particularly hogs and mules.
Hogs are frequently driven to pastures in the foothills
of the Coast Range and Sierra where acorns are abundant, and are herded in droves of hundreds like sheep.
When a bear comes to the range they promptly leave
it, emigrating in a body, usually in the night time, the
keepers being powerless to prevent; they thus show
more sense than sheep, that simply scatter in the
rocks and brush and await their fate. Mules flee like
the wind with or without riders when they see a bear,
and, if picketed, sometimes break their necks in trying to break their ropes, though I have not heard of
bears killing mules or horses. Of hogs they are said
to be particularly fond, bolting small ones, bones and
all, without choice of parts. In particular, Mr. Delaney
assured me that all kinds of bears in the Sierra are
very shy, and that hunters found far greater difficulty in getting within gunshot of them than of deer
or indeed any other animal in the Sierra, and if I was
anxious to see much of them I should have to wait and
watch with endless Indian patience and pay no attention to anything else.

Night is coming on, the gray rock waves are growing dim in the twilight. How raw and young this region
appears! Had the ice sheet that swept over it vanished
but yesterday, its traces on the more resisting portions about our camp could hardly be more distinct
than they now are. The horses and sheep and all of us,
indeed, slipped on the smoothest places.

July 14. How deathlike is sleep in this mountain air, and quick the awakening into newness of life! A calm dawn, yellow and purple, then floods of sun-gold, making every thing tingle and glow.

In an hour or two we came to Yosemite Creek, the stream that makes the greatest of all the Yosemite falls. It is about forty feet wide at the Mono Trail crossing, and now about four feet in average depth, flowing about three miles an hour. The distance to the verge of the Yosemite wall, where it makes its tremendous plunge, is only about two miles from here. Calm, beautiful, and nearly silent, it glides with stately gestures, a dense growth of the slender two-leaved pine along its banks, and a fringe of willow, purple spirea, sedges, daisies, lilies, and columbines. Some of the sedges and willow boughs dip into the current, and just outside of the close ranks of trees there is a sunny flat of washed gravelly sand which seems to have been deposited by some ancient flood. It is covered with millions of erethrea, eriogonum, and oxytheca, with more flowers than leaves, forming an even growth, slightly dimpled and ruffled here and there by rosettes of *Spraguea umbellata.* Back of this flowery strip there is a wavy upsloping plain of solid granite, so smoothly ice-polished in many places that it glistens in the sun like glass. In shallow hollows there are patches of trees, mostly the rough form of the two-leaved pine, rather scrawny looking where there is little or no soil. Also a few junipers (*Juniperus occidentalis*), short and stout, with bright cinnamon-colored bark and gray foliage, standing alone mostly, on the sun-beaten pavement, safe from fire, clinging by slight joints,—a sturdy storm-enduring mountaineer of a tree, living on sunshine and snow, maintaining tough health on this diet for perhaps more than a thousand years.

Up towards the head of the basin I see groups of domes rising above the wavelike ridges, and some picturesque castellated masses, and dark strips and patches of silver fir, indicating deposits of fertile soil. Would that I could command the time to study them! What rich excursions one could make in this well-defined basin! Its glacial inscriptions and sculptures, how marvelous they seem, how noble the studies they offer! I tremble with excitement in the dawn of these glorious mountain sublimities, but I can only gaze and wonder, and, like a child, gather here and there a lily, half hoping I may be able to study and learn in years to come.

The drivers and dogs had a lively, laborious time getting the sheep across the creek, the second large stream thus far that they have been compelled to cross without a bridge; the first being the North Fork of the Merced near Bower Cave. Men and dogs, shouting and barking, drove the timid, water-fearing creatures in a close crowd against the bank, but not one of the flock would launch away. While thus jammed, the Don and the shepherd rushed through the frightened crowd to stampede those in front, but this would only cause a break backward, and away they would scamper through the stream-bank trees and scatter over the rocky pavement. Then with the aid of the dogs the runaways would again be gathered and made to face the stream, and again the compacted mass would break away, amid wild shouting and barking that might well have disturbed the stream itself and marred the music of its falls, to which visitors no doubt from all quarters of the globe were listening. "Hold them there! Now hold them there!" shouted the Don; "the front ranks will soon tire of the pressure, and be glad to take to the water, then all will jump in and cross in a hurry." But they did nothing of the kind; they only avoided the pressure by breaking back in scores and hundreds, leaving the beauty of the banks sadly trampled.

If only one could be got to cross over, all would make haste to follow; but that one could not be found. A lamb was caught, carried across, and tied to a bush on the opposite bank, where it cried piteously for its mother. But though greatly concerned, the mother only called it back. That play on maternal affection failed, and we began to fear that we should be forced to make a long roundabout drive and cross the widespread tributaries of the creek in succession. This would require several days, but it had its advantages, for I was eager to see the sources of so famous a stream. Don Quixote, however, determined that they must ford just here, and immediately began a sort of siege by cutting down slender pines on the bank and building a corral barely large enough to hold the flock when well pressed together. And as the stream would form one side of the corral he believed that they could easily be forced into the water.

In a few hours the inclosure was completed, and the silly animals were driven in and rammed hard against the brink of the ford. Then the Don, forcing a way through the compacted mass, pitched a few of the terrified unfortunates into the stream by main strength; but instead of crossing over, they swam about close to the bank, making desperate attempts to get back into the flock. Then a dozen or more were shoved off, and the Don, tall like a crane and a good natural wader, jumped in after them, seized a struggling wether, and dragged it to the opposite shore. But no sooner did he let it go than it jumped into the stream and swam back to its frightened companions in the corral, thus manifesting sheep-nature as unchangeable as gravitation. Pan with his pipes would have had no better luck, I fear. We were now pretty well baffled. The silly creatures would suffer any sort of death rather than cross that stream. Calling a council, the dripping Don declared that starvation was now the only likely scheme to try, and that we might as well camp here in comfort and let the besieged flock grow hungry and cool, and come to their senses, if they had any. In a few minutes after being thus let alone, an adventurer in the foremost rank plunged in and swam bravely to the farther shore. Then suddenly all rushed in pell-mell together, trampling one another under water, while we vainly tried to hold them back. The Don jumped into the thickest of the gasping, gurgling, drowning mass, and shoved them right and left as if each sheep was a piece of floating timber. The current also served to drift them apart; a long bent column was soon formed, and in a few minutes all were over and began baaing and feeding as if nothing out of the common had happened. That none were drowned seems wonderful. I fully expected that hundreds would gain the romantic fate of being swept into Yosemite over the highest waterfall in the world.

As the day was far spent, we camped a little way back from the ford, and let the dripping flock scatter and feed until sundown. The wool is dry now, and calm, cud-chewing peace has fallen on all the comfortable band, leaving no trace of the watery battle. I have seen fish driven out of the water with less ado than was made in driving these animals into it. Sheep brain must surely be poor stuff. Compare today's exhibition with the performances of deer swimming quietly across broad and rapid rivers, and from island to island in seas and lakes; or with dogs, or even with the squirrels that, as the story goes, cross the Mississippi River on selected chips, with tails for sails comfortably trimmed to the breeze. A sheep can hardly be called an animal; an entire flock is required to make one foolish individual.

THE YOSEMITE

July 15. Followed the Mono Trail up the eastern rim of the basin nearly to its summit, then turned off southward to a small shallow valley that extends to the edge of the Yosemite, which we reached about noon, and encamped. After luncheon I made haste to high ground, and from the top of the ridge on the west side of Indian Cañon gained the noblest view of the summit peaks I have ever yet enjoyed. Nearly all the upper basin of the Merced was displayed, with its sublime domes and cañons, dark upsweeping forests, and glorious array of white peaks deep in the sky, every feature glowing, radiating beauty that pours into our flesh and bones like heat rays from fire. Sunshine over all; no breath of wind to stir the brooding calm. Never before had I seen so glorious a landscape, so boundless an affluence of sublime mountain beauty. The most extravagant description I might give of this view to any one who has not seen similar landscapes with his own eyes would not so much as hint its grandeur and the spiritual glow that covered it. I shouted and gesticulated in a wild burst of ecstasy, much to the astonishment of St. Bernard Carlo, who came running up to me, manifesting in his intelligent eyes a puzzled concern that was very ludicrous, which had the effect of bringing me to my senses. A brown bear, too, it would seem, had been a spectator of the show I had made of myself, for I had gone but a few yards when I started one from a thicket of brush. He evidently considered me dangerous, for he ran away very fast, tumbling over the tops of the tangled manzanita bushes in his haste. Carlo drew back, with his ears depressed as if afraid, and kept looking me in the face, as if expecting me to pursue and shoot, for he had seen many a bear battle in his day.

Following the ridge, which made a gradual descent to the south, I came at length to the brow of that massive cliff that stands between Indian Cañon and Yosemite Falls, and here the far-famed valley came suddenly into view throughout almost its whole extent. The noble walls—sculptured into endless variety of domes and gables, spires and battlements and plain mural precipices—all a-tremble with the thunder tones of the falling water. The level bottom seemed to be dressed like a garden—sunny meadows here and there, and groves of pine and oak; the river of Mercy sweeping in majesty through the midst of them and flashing back the sunbeams. The great Tissiack, or Half-Dome, rising at the upper end of the valley to a height of nearly a mile, is nobly proportioned and life-like, the most impressive of all the rocks, holding the eye in devout admiration, calling it back again and again from falls or meadows, or even the mountains beyond,—marvelous cliffs, marvelous in sheer dizzy depth and sculpture, types of endurance. Thousands of years have they stood in the sky exposed to rain, snow, frost, earthquake and avalanche, yet they still wear the bloom of youth.

I rambled along the valley rim to the westward; most of it is rounded off on the very brink, so that it is not easy to find places where one may look clear down the face of the wall to the bottom. When such places were found, and I had cautiously set my feet and drawn my body erect, I could not help fearing a little that the rock might split off and let me down, and what a down!—more than three thousand feet. Still my limbs did not tremble, nor did I feel the least uncertainty as to the reliance to be placed on them. My only fear was that a flake of the granite, which in some places showed joints more or less open and running parallel with the face of the cliff, might give way. After withdrawing from such places, excited with the view I had got, I would say to myself, "Now don't go out on the verge again." But in the face of Yosemite scenery cautious remonstrance is vain; under its spell one's body seems to go where it likes with a will over which we seem to have scarce any control.

After a mile or so of this memorable cliff work I approached Yosemite Creek, admiring its easy, graceful, confident gestures as it comes bravely forward in its narrow channel, singing the last of its mountain songs on its way to its fate—a few rods more over the shining granite, then down half a mile in showy foam to another world, to be lost in the Merced, where climate, vegetation, inhabitants, all are different. Emerging from its last gorge, it glides in wide lace-like rapids down a smooth incline into a pool where it seems to rest and compose its gray, agitated waters before taking the grand plunge, then slowly slipping over the lip of the pool basin, it descends another glossy slope with rapidly accelerated speed to the brink of the tremendous cliff, and with sublime, fateful confidence springs out free in the air.

I took off my shoes and stockings and worked my way cautiously down alongside the rushing flood, keeping my feet and hands pressed firmly on the polished rock. The booming, roaring water, rushing past close to my head, was very exciting. I had expected that the sloping apron would terminate with the perpendicular wall of the valley, and that from the foot of it, where it is less steeply inclined, I should be able to lean far enough out to see the forms and behavior of the fall all the way down to the bottom. But I found that there was yet another small brow over which I could not see, and which appeared to be too steep for mortal feet. Scanning it keenly, I discovered a narrow shelf about three inches wide on the very brink, just wide enough for a rest for one's heels. But there seemed to be no way of reaching it over so steep a brow. At length, after careful scrutiny of the surface, I found an irregular edge of a flake of the rock some distance back from the margin of the torrent. If I was to get down to the brink at all that rough edge, which might offer slight finger-holds, was the only way. But the slope beside it looked dangerously smooth and steep, and the swift roaring flood beneath, overhead, and beside me was very nerve-trying. I therefore concluded not to venture farther, but did nevertheless. Tufts of artemisia were growing in clefts of the rock near by, and I filled my mouth with the bitter leaves, hoping they might help to prevent giddiness. Then, with a caution not known in ordinary circumstances, I crept down safely to the little ledge, got my heels well planted on it, then shuffled in a horizontal direction twenty or thirty feet until close to the outplunging current, which, by the time it had descended thus far, was already white. Here I obtained a perfectly free view down into the heart of the snowy, chanting throng of comet-like streamers, into which the body of the fall soon separates.

While perched on that narrow niche I was not distinctly conscious of danger. The tremendous grandeur of the fall in form and sound and motion, acting at close range, smothered the sense of fear, and in such places one's body takes keen care for safety on its own account. How long I remained down there, or how I returned, I can hardly tell. Anyhow I had a glorious time, and got back to camp about dark, enjoying triumphant exhilaration soon followed by dull weariness. Hereafter I'll try to keep from such extravagant, nerve-straining places. Yet such a day is well worth venturing for. My first view of the High Sierra, first view looking down into Yosemite, the death song of Yosemite Creek, and its flight over the vast cliff, each one of these is of itself enough for a great life-long landscape fortune—a most memorable day of days—enjoyment enough to kill if that were possible.

July 16. My enjoyments yesterday afternoon, especially at the head of the fall, were too great for good sleep. Kept starting up last night in a nervous tremor, half awake, fancying that the foundation of the mountain we were camped on had given way and was falling into Yosemite Valley. In vain I roused myself to make a new beginning for sound sleep. The nerve strain had been too great, and again and again I dreamed I was rushing through the air above a glorious avalanche of water and rocks. One time, springing to my feet, I said, "This time it is real—all must die, and where could mountaineer find a more glorious death!"

Left camp soon after sunrise for an all-day ramble eastward. Crossed the head of Indian Basin, forested with *Abies magnifica*, underbrush mostly *Ceanothus cordulatus* and manzanita, a mixture not easily trampled over or penetrated, for the ceanothus is thorny and grows in dense snow-pressed masses, and the manzanita has exceedingly crooked, stubborn branches. From the head of the cañon continued on past North Dome into the basin of Dome or Porcupine Creek. Here are many fine meadows imbedded in the woods, gay with *Lilium parvum* and its companions; the elevation, about eight thousand feet, seems to be best suited for it—saw specimens that were a foot or two higher than my head. Had more magnificent views of the upper mountains, and of the great South Dome, said to be the grandest rock in the world. Well it may be, since it is of such noble dimensions and sculpture. A wonderfully impressive monument, its lines exquisite in fineness, and though sublime in size, is finished like the finest work of art, and seems to be alive.

July 17. A new camp was made to-day in a magnificent silver fir grove at the head of a small stream that flows into Yosemite by way of Indian Cañon. Here we intend to stay several weeks,—a fine location from which to make excursions about the great valley and its fountains. Glorious days I'll have sketching, pressing plants, studying the wonderful topography and the wild animals, our happy fellow mortals and neighbors. But the vast mountains in the distance, shall I ever know them, shall I be allowed to enter into their midst and dwell with them?

We were pelted about noon by a short, heavy rainstorm, sublime thunder reverberating among the mountains and cañons,—some strokes near, crashing, ringing in the tense crisp air with startling keenness, while the distant peaks loomed gloriously through the cloud fringes and sheets of rain. Now the storm is past, and the fresh washed air is full of the essences of the flower gardens and groves. Winter storms in Yosemite must be glorious. May I see them!

Have got my bed made in our new camp,— plushy, sumptuous, and deliciously fragrant, most of it *magnifica* fir plumes, of course, with a variety of sweet flowers in the pillow. Hope to sleep to-night without tottering nerve-dreams. Watched a deer eating ceanothus leaves and twigs.

July 18. Slept pretty well; the valley walls did not seem to fall, though I still fancied myself at the brink, alongside the white, plunging flood, especially when half asleep. Strange the danger of that adventure should be more troublesome now that I am in the bosom of the peaceful woods, a mile or more from the fall, than it was while I was on the brink of it.

Bears seem to be common here, judging by their tracks. About noon we had another rainstorm with keen startling thunder, the metallic, ringing, clashing, clanging notes gradually fading into low bass rolling and muttering in the distance. For a few minutes the rain came in a grand torrent like a waterfall, then hail; some of the hailstones an inch in diameter, hard, icy, and irregular in form, like those oftentimes seen in Wisconsin. Carlo watched them with intelligent astonishment as they came pelting and thrashing through the quivering branches of the trees. The cloud scenery sublime. Afternoon calm, sunful, and clear, with delicious freshness and fragrance from the firs and flowers and steaming ground.

July 19. Watching the daybreak and sunrise. The pale rose and purple sky changing softly to daffodil yellow and white, sunbeams pouring through the passes between the peaks and over the Yosemite domes, making their edges burn; the silver firs in the middle ground catching the glow on their spiry tops, and our camp grove fills and thrills with the glorious light. Everything awakening alert and joyful; the birds begin to stir and innumerable insect people. Deer quietly withdraw into leafy hiding-places in the chaparral; the dew vanishes, flowers spread their petals, every pulse beats high, every life cell rejoices, the very rocks seem to thrill with life. The whole landscape glows like a human face in a glory of enthusiasm, and the blue sky, pale around the horizon, bends peacefully down over all like one vast flower.

About noon, as usual, big bossy cumuli began to grow above the forest, and the rainstorm pouring from them is the most imposing I have yet seen. The silvery zigzag lightning lances are longer than usual, and the thunder gloriously impressive, keen, crashing, intensely concentrated, speaking with such tremendous energy it would seem that an entire mountain is being shattered at every stroke, but probably only a few trees are being shattered, many of which I have seen on my walks hereabouts strewing the ground. At last the clear ringing strokes are succeeded by deep low tones that grow gradually fainter as they roll afar into the recesses of the echoing mountains, where they seem to be welcomed home. Then another and another peal, or rather crashing, splintering stroke, follows in quick succession, perchance splitting some giant pine or fir from top to bottom into long rails and slivers, and scattering them to all points of the compass. Now comes the rain, with corresponding extravagant grandeur, covering the ground high and low with a sheet of flowing water, a transparent film fitted like a skin upon the rugged anatomy of the landscape, making the rocks glitter and glow, gathering in the ravines, flooding the streams, and making them shout and boom in reply to the thunder.

How interesting to trace the history of a single raindrop! It is not long, geologically speaking, as we have seen, since the first raindrops fell on the new-born leafless Sierra landscapes. How different the lot of these falling now! Happy the showers that fall on so fair a wilderness,—scarce a single drop can fail to find a beautiful spot,—on the tops of the peaks, on the shining glacier pavements, on the great smooth domes, on forests and gardens and brushy moraines, plashing, glinting, pattering, laving. Some go to the high snowy fountains to swell their well-saved stores; some into the lakes, washing the mountain windows, patting their smooth glassy levels, making dimples and bubbles and spray; some into the waterfalls and cascades, as if eager to join in their dance and song and beat their foam yet finer; good luck and good work for the happy mountain raindrops, each one of them a high waterfall in itself, descending from the cliffs and hollows of the clouds to the cliffs and hollows of the rocks, out of the sky-thunder into the thunder of the falling rivers. Some, falling on meadows and bogs, creep silently out of sight to the grass roots, hiding softly as in a nest, slipping, oozing hither, thither, seeking and finding their appointed work. Some, descending through the spires of the woods, sift spray through the shining needles, whispering peace and good cheer to each one of them. Some drops with happy aim glint on the sides of crystals,—quartz, hornblende, garnet, zircon, tourmaline, feldspar,—patter on grains of gold and heavy way-worn nuggets; some, with blunt plap-plap and low bass drumming, fall on the broad leaves of veratrum, saxifrage, cypripedium. Some happy drops fall straight into the cups of flowers, kissing the lips of lilies. How far they have to go, how many cups to fill, great and small, cells too small to be seen, cups holding half a drop as well as lake basins between the hills, each replenished with equal care, every drop in all the blessed throng a silvery newborn star with lake and river, garden and grove, valley and mountain, all that the landscape holds reflected in its crystal depths, God's messenger, angel of love sent on its way with majesty and pomp and display of power that make man's greatest shows ridiculous.

Now the storm is over, the sky is clear, the last rolling thunder-wave is spent on the peaks, and where are the raindrops now—what has become of all the shining throng? In winged vapor rising some are already hastening back to the sky, some have gone into the plants, creeping through invisible doors into the round rooms of cells, some are locked in crystals of ice, some in rock crystals, some in porous moraines to keep their small springs flowing, some have gone journeying on in the rivers to join the larger raindrop of the ocean. From form to form, beauty to beauty, ever changing, never resting, all are speeding on with love's enthusiasm, singing with the stars the eternal song of creation.

July 20. Fine calm morning; air tense and clear; not the slightest breeze astir; everything shining, the rocks with wet crystals, the plants with dew, each receiving its portion of irised dewdrops and sunshine like living creatures getting their breakfast, their dew manna coming down from the starry sky like swarms of smaller stars. How wondrous fine are the particles in showers of dew, thousands required for a single drop, growing in the dark as silently as the grass! What pains are taken to keep this wilderness in health,—showers of snow, showers of rain, showers of dew, floods of light, floods of invisible vapor, clouds, winds, all sorts of weather, interaction of plant on plant, animal on animal, etc., beyond thought! How fine Nature's methods! How deeply with beauty is beauty overlaid! the ground covered with crystals, the crystals with mosses and lichens and low-spreading grasses and flowers, these with larger plants leaf over leaf with ever-changing color and form, the broad palms of the firs outspread over these, the azure dome over all like a bell-flower, and star above star.

Yonder stands the South Dome, its crown high above our camp, though its base is four thousand feet below us; a most noble rock, it seems full of thought, clothed with living light, no sense of dead stone about it, all spiritualized, neither heavy looking nor light, steadfast in serene strength like a god.

Our shepherd is a queer character and hard to place in this wilderness. His bed is a hollow made in red dry-rot punky dust beside a log which forms a portion of the south wall of the corral. Here he lies with his wonderful everlasting clothing on, wrapped in a red blanket, breathing not only the dust of the decayed wood but also that of the corral, as if determined to take ammoniacal snuff all night after chewing tobacco all day. Following the sheep he carries a heavy six-shooter swung from his belt on one side and his luncheon on the other. The ancient cloth in which the meat, fresh from the frying-pan, is tied serves as a filter through which the clear fat and gravy juices drip down on his right hip and leg in clustering stalactites. This oleaginous formation is soon broken up, however, and diffused and rubbed evenly into his scanty apparel, by sitting down, rolling over, crossing his legs while resting on logs, etc., making shirt and trousers watertight and shiny. His trousers, in particular, have become so adhesive with the mixed fat and resin that pine needles, thin flakes and fibres of bark, hair, mica scales and minute grains of quartz, hornblende, etc., feathers, seed wings, moth and butterfly wings, legs and antennæ of innumerable insects, or even whole insects such as the small beetles, moths and mosquitoes, with flower petals, pollen dust and indeed bits of all plants, animals, and minerals of the region adhere to them and are safely imbedded, so that though far from being a naturalist he collects fragmentary specimens of everything and becomes richer than he knows. His specimens are kept passably fresh, too, by the purity of the air and the resiny bituminous beds into which they are pressed. Man is a microcosm, at least our shepherd is, or rather his trousers. These precious overalls are never taken off, and nobody knows how old they are, though one may guess by their thickness and concentric structure. Instead of wearing thin they wear thick, and in their stratification have no small geological significance.

Besides herding the sheep, Billy is the butcher, while I have agreed to wash the few iron and tin utensils and make the bread. Then, these small duties done, by the time the sun is fairly above the mountain-tops I am beyond the flock, free to rove and revel in the wilderness all the big immortal days.

Sketching on the North Dome. It commands views of nearly all the valley besides a few of the high mountains. I would fain draw everything in sight— rock, tree, and leaf. But little can I do beyond mere outlines,—marks with meanings like words, readable only to myself,—yet I sharpen my pencils and work on as if others might possibly be benefited. Whether these picture-sheets are to vanish like fallen leaves or go to friends like letters, matters not much; for little can they tell to those who have not themselves seen similar wildness, and like a language have learned it. No pain here, no dull empty hours, no fear of the past, no fear of the future. These blessed mountains are so compactly filled with God's beauty, no petty personal hope or experience has room to be. Drinking this champagne water is pure pleasure, so is breathing the living air, and every movement of limbs is pleasure, while the whole body seems to feel beauty when exposed to it as it feels the camp-fire or sunshine, entering not by the eyes alone, but equally through all one's flesh like radiant heat, making a passionate ecstatic pleasure-glow not explainable. One's body then seems homogeneous throughout, sound as a crystal.

Perched like a fly on this Yosemite dome, I gaze and sketch and bask, oftentimes settling down into dumb admiration without definite hope of ever learning much, yet with the longing, unresting effort that lies at the door of hope, humbly prostrate before the vast display of God's power, and eager to offer self-denial and renunciation with eternal toil to learn any lesson in the divine manuscript.

It is easier to feel than to realize, or in any way

explain, Yosemite grandeur. The magnitudes of the rocks and trees and streams are so delicately harmonized they are mostly hidden. Sheer precipices three thousand feet high are fringed with tall trees growing close like grass on the brow of a lowland hill, and extending along the feet of these precipices a ribbon of meadow a mile wide and seven or eight long, that seems like a strip a farmer might mow in less than a day. Waterfalls, five hundred to one or two thousand feet high, are so subordinated to the mighty cliffs over which they pour that they seem like wisps of smoke, gentle as floating clouds, though their voices fill the valley and make the rocks tremble. The mountains, too, along the eastern sky, and the domes in front of them, and the succession of smooth rounded waves between, swelling higher, higher, with dark woods in their hollows, serene in massive exuberant bulk and beauty, tend yet more to hide the grandeur of the Yosemite temple and make it appear as a subdued subordinate feature of the vast harmonious landscape. Thus every attempt to appreciate any one feature is beaten down by the overwhelming influence of all the others. And, as if this were not enough, lo! in the sky arises another mountain range with topography as rugged and substantial-looking as the one beneath it—snowy peaks and domes and shadowy Yosemite valleys—another version of the snowy Sierra, a new creation heralded by a thunder-storm. How fiercely, devoutly wild is Nature in the midst of her beauty-loving tenderness!—painting lilies, watering them, caressing them with gentle hand, going from flower to flower like a gardener while building rock mountains and cloud mountains full of lightning and rain. Gladly we run for shelter beneath an overhanging cliff and examine the reassuring ferns and mosses, gentle love tokens growing in cracks and chinks. Daisies, too, and ivesias, confiding wild children of light, too small to fear. To these one's heart goes home, and the voices of the storm become gentle. Now the sun breaks forth and fragrant steam arises. The birds are out singing on the edges of the groves. The west is flaming in gold and purple, ready for the ceremony of the sunset, and back I go to camp with my notes and pictures, the best of them printed in my mind as dreams. A fruitful day, without measured beginning or ending. A terrestrial eternity. A gift of good God.

Wrote to my mother and a few friends, mountain hints to each. They seem as near as if within voice-reach or touch. The deeper the solitude the less the sense of loneliness, and the nearer our friends. Now bread and tea, fir bed and good-night to Carlo, a look at the sky lilies, and death sleep until the dawn of another Sierra to-morrow.

July 21. Sketching on the Dome—no rain; clouds at noon about quarter filled the sky, casting shadows with fine effect on the white mountains at the heads of the streams, and a soothing cover over the gardens during the warm hours.

Saw a common house-fly and a grasshopper and a brown bear. The fly and grasshopper paid me a merry visit on the top of the Dome, and I paid a visit to the bear in the middle of a small garden meadow between the Dome and the camp where he was standing alert among the flowers as if willing to be seen to advantage. I had not gone more than half a mile from camp this morning, when Carlo, who was trotting on a few yards ahead of me, came to a sudden, cautious stand-still. Down went tail and ears, and forward went his knowing nose, while he seemed to be saying, "Ha, what's this? A bear, I guess." Then a cautious advance of a few steps, setting his feet down softly like a hunting cat, and questioning the air as to the scent he had caught until all doubt vanished. Then he came back to me, looked me in the face, and with his speaking eyes reported a bear near by; then led on softly, careful, like an experienced hunter, not to make the slightest noise; and frequently looking back as if whispering, "Yes, it's a bear; come and I'll show you." Presently we came to where the sunbeams were streaming through between the purple shafts of the firs, which showed that we were nearing an open spot, and here Carlo came behind me, evidently sure that the bear was very near. So I crept to a low ridge of moraine boulders on the edge of a narrow garden meadow, and in this meadow I felt pretty sure the bear must be. I was anxious to get a good look at the sturdy mountaineer without alarming him; so drawing myself up noise-lessly back of one of the largest of the trees I peered past its bulging buttresses, exposing only a part of my head, and there stood neighbor Bruin within a stone's throw, his hips covered by tall grass and flowers, and his front feet on the trunk of a fir that had fallen out into the meadow, which raised his head so high that he seemed to be standing erect. He had not yet seen me, but was looking and listening attentively, show-ing that in some way he was aware of our approach. I watched his gestures and tried to make the most of my opportunity to learn what I could about him, fearing he would catch sight of me and run away. For I had been told that this sort of bear, the cinnamon, always ran from his bad brother man, never showing fight unless wounded or in defense of young. He made a telling picture standing alert in the sunny forest garden. How well he played his part, harmonizing in bulk and color and shaggy hair with the trunks of the trees and lush vegetation, as natural a feature as any other in the landscape. After examining at leisure, noting the sharp muzzle thrust inquiringly forward, the long shaggy hair on his broad chest, the stiff, erect ears nearly buried in hair, and the slow, heavy way he moved his head, I thought I should like to see his gait in running, so I made a sudden rush at him, shouting and swinging my hat to frighten him, expecting to see him make haste to get away. But to my dismay he did not run or show any sign of running. On the contrary, he stood his ground ready to fight and defend himself, lowered his head, thrust it forward, and looked sharply and fiercely at me. Then I suddenly began to fear that upon me would fall the work of running; but I was afraid to run, and therefore, like the bear, held my ground. We stood staring at each other in solemn silence within a dozen yards or thereabouts, while I fervently hoped that the power of the human eye over wild beasts would prove as great as it is said to be. How long our awfully strenuous interview lasted, I don't know; but at length in the slow fullness of time he pulled his huge paws down off the log, and with magnificent deliberation turned and walked leisurely up the meadow, stopping frequently to look back over his shoulder to see whether I was pursuing him, then moving on again, evidently neither fearing me very much nor trusting me. He was probably about five hundred pounds in weight, a broad, rusty bundle of ungovernable wildness, a happy fellow whose lines have fallen in pleasant places. The flowery glade in which I saw him so well, framed like a picture, is one of the best of all I have yet discovered, a conservatory of Nature's precious plant people. Tall lilies were swinging their bells over that bear's back, with geraniums, larkspurs, columbines, and daisies brushing against his sides. A place for angels, one would say, instead of bears.

In the great cañons Bruin reigns supreme. Happy fellow, whom no famine can reach while one of his thousand kinds of food is spared him. His bread is sure at all seasons, ranged on the mountain shelves like stores in a pantry. From one to the other, up or down he climbs, tasting and enjoying each in turn in different climates, as if he had journeyed thousands of miles to other countries north or south to enjoy their varied productions. I should like to know my hairy brothers better—though after this particular Yosemite bear, my very neighbor, had sauntered out of sight this morning, I reluctantly went back to camp for the Don's rifle to shoot him, if necessary, in defense of the flock. Fortunately I couldn't find him, and after tracking him a mile or two towards Mount Hoffman I bade him Godspeed and gladly returned to my work on the Yosemite Dome.

The house-fly also seemed at home and buzzed about me as I sat sketching, and enjoying my bear interview now it was over. I wonder what draws house-flies so far up the mountains, heavy gross feeders as they are, sensitive to cold, and fond of domestic ease. How have they been distributed from continent to continent, across seas and deserts and mountain chains, usually so influential in determining boundaries of species both of plants and animals. Beetles and butterflies are sometimes restricted to small areas. Each mountain in a range, and even the different zones of a mountain, may have its own peculiar species. But the house-fly seems to be everywhere. I wonder if any island in mid-ocean is flyless. The bluebottle is abundant in these Yosemite woods, ever ready with his marvelous store of eggs to make all dead flesh fly. Bumblebees are here, and are well fed on boundless stores of nectar and pollen. The honey-bee, though abundant in the foothills, has not yet got so high. It is only a few years since the first swarm was brought to California.

A queer fellow and a jolly fellow is the grasshopper. Up the mountains he comes on excursions, how high I don't know, but at least as far and high as Yosemite tourists. I was much interested with the hearty enjoyment of the one that danced and sang for me on the Dome this afternoon. He seemed brimful of glad, hilarious energy, manifested by springing into the air to a height of twenty or thirty feet, then diving and springing up again and making a sharp musical rattle just as the lowest point in the descent was reached. Up and down a dozen times or so he danced and sang, then alighted to rest, then up and at it again. The curves he described in the air in diving and rattling resembled those made by cords hanging loosely and attached at the same height at the ends, the loops nearly covering each other. Braver, heartier, keener, care-free enjoyment of life I have never seen or heard in any creature, great or small. The life of this comic redlegs, the mountain's merriest child, seems to be made up of pure, condensed gayety. The Douglas squirrel is the only living creature that I can compare him with in exuberant, rollicking, irrepressible jollity. Wonderful that these

sublime mountains are so loudly cheered and brightened by a creature so queer. Nature in him seems to
be snapping her fingers in the face of all earthly dejec-
tion and melancholy with a boyish hip-hip-hurrah.
How the sound is made I do not understand. When
he was on the ground he made not the slightest noise,
nor when he was simply flying from place to place, but
only when diving in curves, the motion seeming to be
required for the sound; for the more vigorous the diving the more energetic the corresponding outbursts of
jolly rattling. I tried to observe him closely while he
was resting in the intervals of his performances; but
he would not allow a near approach, always getting
his jumping legs ready to spring for immediate flight,
and keeping his eyes on me. A fine sermon the little
fellow danced for me on the Dome, a likely place to
look for sermons in stones, but not for grasshopper
sermons. A large and imposing pulpit for so small a
preacher. No danger of weakness in the knees of the
world while Nature can spring such a rattle as this.
Even the bear did not express for me the mountain's
wild health and strength and happiness so tellingly as
did this comical little hopper. No cloud of care in his
day, no winter of discontent in sight. To him every day
is a holiday; and when at length his sun sets, I fancy
he will cuddle down on the forest floor and die like the
leaves and flowers, and like them leave no unsightly
remains calling for burial.

Sundown, and I must to camp. Good-night, friends
three,—brown bear, rugged boulder of energy in
groves and gardens fair as Eden; restless, fussy fly
with gauzy wings stirring the air around all the world;
and grasshopper, crisp, electric spark of joy enlivening
the massy sublimity of the mountains like the laugh of

a child. Thank you, thank you all three for your quickening company. Heaven guide every wing and leg.
Good-night friends three, good-night.

July 22. A fine specimen of the black-tailed deer
went bounding past camp this morning. A buck with
wide spread of antlers, showing admirable vigor and
grace. Wonderful the beauty, strength, and graceful movements of animals in wildernesses, cared for
by Nature only, when our experience with domestic
animals would lead us to fear that all the so-called
neglected wild beasts would degenerate. Yet the upshot
of Nature's method of breeding and teaching seems
to lead to excellence of every sort. Deer, like all wild
animals, are as clean as plants. The beauties of their
gestures and attitudes, alert or in repose, surprise yet
more than their bounding exuberant strength. Every
movement and posture is graceful, the very poetry of
manners and motion. Mother Nature is too often spoken of as in reality no mother at all. Yet how wisely,
sternly, tenderly she loves and looks after her children
in all sorts of weather and wildernesses. The more I
see of deer the more I admire them as mountaineers.
They make their way into the heart of the roughest solitudes with smooth reserve of strength, through dense
belts of brush and forest encumbered with fallen trees
and boulder piles, across cañons, roaring streams, and
snow-fields, ever showing forth beauty and courage.
Over nearly all the continent the deer find homes. In
the Florida savannas and hummocks, in the Canada
woods, in the far north, roaming over mossy tundras,
swimming lakes and rivers and arms of the sea from
island to island washed with waves, or climbing rocky
mountains, everywhere healthy and able, adding

beauty to every landscape,—a truly admirable creature and great credit to Nature.

Have been sketching a silver fir that stands on a granite ridge a few hundred yards to the eastward of camp—a fine tree with a particular snow-storm story to tell. It is about one hundred feet high, growing on bare rock, thrusting its roots into a weathered joint less than an inch wide, and bulging out to form a base to bear its weight. The storm came from the north while it was young and broke it down nearly to the ground, as is shown by the old, dead, weather-beaten top leaning out from the living trunk built up from a new shoot below the break. The annual rings of the trunk that have overgrown the dead sapling tell the year of the storm. Wonderful that a side branch forming a portion of one of the level collars that encircle the trunk of this species (*Abies magnifica*) should bend upward, grow erect, and take the place of the lost axis to form a new tree.

Many others, pines as well as firs, bear testimony to the crushing severity of this particular storm. Trees, some of them fifty to seventy-five feet high, were bent to the ground and buried like grass, whole groves vanishing as if the forest had been cleared away, leaving not a branch or needle visible until the spring thaw. Then the more elastic undamaged saplings rose again, aided by the wind, some reaching a nearly erect attitude, others remaining more or less bent, while those with broken backs endeavored to specialize a side branch below the break and make a leader of it to form a new axis of development. It is as if a man, whose back was broken or nearly so and who was compelled to go bent, should find a branch backbone sprouting straight up from below the break and should gradually develop new arms and shoulders and head, while the old damaged portion of his body died.

Grand white cloud mountains and domes created about noon as usual, ridges and ranges of endless variety, as if Nature dearly loved this sort of work, doing it again and again nearly every day with infinite industry, and producing beauty that never palls. A few zigzags of lightning, five minutes' shower, then a gradual wilting and clearing.

July 23. Another midday cloudland, displaying power and beauty that one never wearies in beholding, but hopelessly unsketchable and untellable. What can poor mortals say about clouds? While a description of their huge glowing domes and ridges, shadowy gulfs and cañons, and feather-edged ravines is being tried, they vanish, leaving no visible ruins. Nevertheless, these fleeting sky mountains are as substantial and significant as the more lasting upheavals of granite beneath them. Both alike are built up and die, and in God's calendar difference of duration is nothing. We can only dream about them in wondering, worshiping admiration, happier than we dare tell even to friends who see farthest in sympathy, glad to know that not a crystal or vapor particle of them, hard or soft, is lost; that they sink and vanish only to rise again and again in higher and higher beauty. As to our own work, duty, influence, etc., concerning which so much fussy pother is made, it will not fail of its due effect, though, like a lichen on a stone, we keep silent.

July 24. Clouds at noon occupying about half the sky gave half an hour of heavy rain to wash one of the cleanest landscapes in the world. How well it is washed! The sea is hardly less dusty than the ice-burnished pavements and ridges, domes and cañons, and summit peaks plashed with snow like waves with foam. How fresh the woods are and calm after the last films of clouds have been wiped from the sky! A few minutes ago every tree was excited, bowing to the roaring storm, waving, swirling, tossing their branches in glorious enthusiasm like worship. But though to the outer ear these trees are now silent, their songs never cease. Every hidden cell is throbbing with music and life, every fibre thrilling like harp strings, while incense is ever flowing from the balsam bells and leaves. No wonder the hills and groves were God's first temples, and the more they are cut down and hewn into cathedrals and churches, the farther off and dimmer seems the Lord himself. The same may be said of stone temples. Yonder, to the eastward of our camp grove, stands one of Nature's cathedrals, hewn from the living rock, almost conventional in form, about two thousand feet high, nobly adorned with spires and pinnacles, thrilling under floods of sunshine as if alive like a grove-temple, and well named "Cathedral Peak." Even Shepherd Billy turns at times to this wonderful mountain building, though apparently deaf to all stone sermons. Snow that refused to melt in fire would hardly be more wonderful than unchanging dullness in the rays of God's beauty. I have been trying to get him to walk to the brink of Yosemite for a view, offering to watch the sheep for a day, while he should enjoy what tourists come from all over the world to see. But though within a mile of the famous valley, he will not go to it even out of mere curiosity.

"What," says he, "is Yosemite but a cañon—a lot
of rocks—a hole in the ground—a place dangerous
about falling into—a d—d good place to keep away
from." "But think of the waterfalls, Billy—just think
of that big stream we crossed the other day, falling half a mile through the air—think of that, and
the sound it makes. You can hear it now like the
roar of the sea." Thus I pressed Yosemite upon him
like a missionary offering the gospel, but he would
have none of it. "I should be afraid to look over so
high a wall," he said. "It would make my head swim.
There is nothing worth seeing anywhere, only rocks,
and I see plenty of them here. Tourists that spend
their money to see rocks and falls are fools, that's
all. You can't humbug me. I've been in this country
too long for that." Such souls, I suppose, are asleep,
or smothered and befogged beneath mean pleasures
and cares.

July 25. Another cloudland. Some clouds have
an over-ripe decaying look, watery and bedraggled
and drawn out into wind-torn shreds and patches,
giving the sky a littered appearance; not so these
Sierra summer midday clouds. All are beautiful with smooth definite outlines and curves like
those of glacier-polished domes. They begin to grow
about eleven o'clock, and seem so wonderfully near
and clear from this high camp one is tempted to try
to climb them and trace the streams that pour like
cataracts from their shadowy fountains. The rain
to which they give birth is often very heavy, a sort
of waterfall as imposing as if pouring from rock
mountains. Never in all my travels have I found
anything more truly novel and interesting than

these midday mountains of the sky, their fine tones of color, majestic visible growth, and ever-changing scenery and general effects, though mostly as well let alone as far as description goes. I oftentimes think of Shelley's cloud poem, "I sift the snow on the mountains below."

MOUNT HOFFMAN AND LAKE TENAYA

July 26. Ramble to the summit of Mount Hoffman, eleven thousand feet high, the highest point in life's journey my feet have yet touched. And what glorious landscapes are about me, new plants, new animals, new crystals, and multitudes of new mountains far higher than Hoffman, towering in glorious array along the axis of the range, serene, majestic, snow-laden, sun-drenched, vast domes and ridges shining below them, forests, lakes, and meadows in the hollows, the pure blue bell-flower sky brooding them all,—a glory day of admission into a new realm of wonders as if Nature had wooingly whispered, "Come higher." What questions I asked, and how little I know of all the vast show, and how eagerly, tremulously hopeful of some day knowing more, learning the meaning of these divine symbols crowded together on this wondrous page.

Mount Hoffman is the highest part of a ridge or spur about fourteen miles from the axis of the main range, perhaps a remnant brought into relief and iso-lated by unequal denudation. The southern slopes shed their waters into Yosemite Valley by Tenaya and Dome Creeks, the northern in part into the Tuolumne River, but mostly into the Merced by Yosemite Creek. The rock is mostly granite, with some small piles and crests rising here and there in picturesque pillared and castellated remnants of red metamorphic slates.

Both the granite and slates are divided by joints, making them separable into blocks like the stones of artificial masonry, suggesting the Scripture "He hath builded the mountains." Great banks of snow and ice are piled in hollows on the cool precipitous north side forming the highest perennial sources of Yosemite Creek. The southern slopes are much more gradual and accessible. Narrow slot-like gorges extend across the summit at right angles, which look like lanes, formed evidently by the erosion of less resisting beds. They are usually called "devil's slides," though they lie far above the region usually haunted by the devil; for though we read that he once climbed an exceeding high mountain, he cannot be much of a mountaineer, for his tracks are seldom seen above the timber-line.

The broad gray summit is barren and desolate-looking in general views, wasted by ages of gnawing storms; but looking at the surface in detail, one finds it covered by thousands and millions of charming plants with leaves and flowers so small they form no mass of color visible at a distance of a few hundred yards. Beds of azure daisies smile confidingly in moist hollows, and along the banks of small rills, with several species of eriogonum, silky-leaved ivesia, pentstemon, orthocarpus, and patches of *Primula suffruticosa*, a beautiful shrubby species. Here also I found bryanthus, a charming heathwort covered with purple flowers and dark green foliage like heather, and three trees new to me—a hemlock and two pines. The hemlock (*Tsuga mertensiana*) is the most beautiful conifer I have ever seen; the branches and also the main axis droop in a singularly graceful way, and the dense foliage covers the delicate, sensitive, swaying branchlets all around. It is now in full bloom, and the flowers, together with thousands of last season's cones still clinging to the drooping sprays, display wonderful wealth of color, brown and purple and blue. Gladly I climbed the first tree I found to revel in the midst of it. How the touch of the flowers makes one's flesh tingle! The pistillate are dark, rich purple, and almost translucent, the staminate blue,—a vivid, pure tone of blue like the mountain sky,—the most uncommonly beautiful of all the Sierra tree flowers I have seen. How wonderful that, with all its delicate feminine grace and beauty of form and dress and behavior, this lovely tree up here, exposed to the wildest blasts, has already endured the storms of centuries of winters!

The two pines also are brave storm-enduring trees, the mountain pine (*Pinus monticola*) and the dwarf pine (*Pinus albicaulis*). The mountain pine is closely related to the sugar pine, though the cones are only about four to six inches long. The largest trees are from five to six feet in diameter at four feet above the ground, the bark rich brown. Only a few storm-beaten adventurers approach the summit of the mountain. The dwarf or white-bark pine is the species that forms the timber-line, where it is so completely dwarfed that one may walk over the top of a bed of it as over snow-pressed chaparral.

How boundless the day seems as we revel in these storm-beaten sky gardens amid so vast a congregation of onlooking mountains! Strange and admirable it is that the more savage and chilly and storm-chafed the mountains, the finer the glow on their faces and the finer the plants they bear. The myriads of flowers tingeing the mountain-top do not seem to have grown out of the dry, rough gravel of disintegration, but rather they appear as visitors, a cloud of witnesses to Nature's love in what we in our timid ignorance and unbelief call howling desert. The surface of the ground, so dull and forbidding at first sight, besides being rich in plants, shines and sparkles with crystals: mica, hornblende, feldspar, quartz, tourmaline. The radiance in some places is so great as to be fairly dazzling, keen lance rays of every color flashing, sparkling in glorious abundance, joining the plants in their fine, brave beauty-work—every crystal, every flower a window opening into heaven, a mirror reflecting the Creator.

From garden to garden, ridge to ridge, I drifted enchanted, now on my knees gazing into the face of a daisy, now climbing again and again among the purple and azure flowers of the hemlocks, now down into the treasuries of the snow, or gazing afar over domes and peaks, lakes and woods, and the billowy glaciated fields of the upper Tuolumne, and trying to sketch them. In the midst of such beauty, pierced with its rays, one's body is all one tingling palate. Who wouldn't be a mountaineer! Up here all the world's prizes seem nothing.

The largest of the many glacier lakes in sight, and the one with the finest shore scenery, is Tenaya, about a mile long, with an imposing mountain dipping its feet into it on the south side, Cathedral Peak a few miles above its head, many smooth swelling rock-waves and domes on the north, and in the distance southward a multitude of snowy peaks, the fountain-heads of rivers. Lake Hoffman lies shimmering beneath my feet, mountain pines around its shining rim. To the northward the picturesque basin of Yosemite Creek glitters with lakelets and pools; but the eye is soon drawn away from these bright mirror wells, however attractive, to

revel in the glorious congregation of peaks on the axis
of the range in their robes of snow and light.

Carlo caught an unfortunate woodchuck when
it was running from a grassy spot to its boulder-pile
home—one of the hardiest of the mountain animals.
I tried hard to save him, but in vain. After telling
Carlo that he must be careful not to kill anything, I
caught sight, for the first time, of the curious pika, or
little chief hare, that cuts large quantities of lupines
and other plants and lays them out to dry in the sun
for hay, which it stores in underground barns to last
through the long, snowy winter. Coming upon these
plants freshly cut and lying in handfuls here and there
on the rocks has a startling effect of busy life on the
lonely mountain-top. These little haymakers, endowed
with brain stuff something like our own,—God up here
looking after them,—what lessons they teach, how
they widen our sympathy!

An eagle soaring above a sheer cliff, where I suppose its nest is, makes another striking show of life,
and helps to bring to mind the other people of the
so-called solitude—deer in the forest caring for their
young; the strong, well-clad, well-fed bears; the lively
throng of squirrels; the blessed birds, great and small,
stirring and sweetening the groves; and the clouds of
happy insects filling the sky with joyous hum as part
and parcel of the down-pouring sunshine. All these
come to mind, as well as the plant people, and the
glad streams singing their way to the sea. But most
impressive of all is the vast glowing countenance of
the wilderness in awful, infinite repose.

Toward sunset, enjoyed a fine run to camp, down
the long south slopes, across ridges and ravines,
gardens and avalanche gaps, through the firs and

chaparral, enjoying wild excitement and excess of strength, and so ends a day that will never end.

July 27. Up and away to Lake Tenaya,—another big day, enough for a lifetime. The rocks, the air, everything speaking with audible voice or silent; joyful, wonderful, enchanting, banishing weariness and sense of time. No longing for anything now or hereafter as we go home into the mountain's heart. The level sunbeams are touching the fir-tops, every leaf shining with dew. Am holding an easterly course, the deep cañon of Tenaya Creek on the right hand, Mount Hoffman on the left, and the lake straight ahead about ten miles distant, the summit of Mount Hoffman about three thousand feet above me, Tenaya Creek four thousand feet below and separated from the shallow, irregular valley, along which most of the way lies, by smooth domes and wave-ridges. Many mossy emerald bogs, meadows, and gardens in rocky hollows to wade and saunter through—and what fine plants they give me, what joyful streams I have to cross, and how many views are displayed of the Hoffman and Cathedral Peak masonry, and what a wondrous breadth of shining granite pavement to walk over for the first time about the shores of the lake! On I sauntered in freedom complete; body without weight as far as I was aware; now wading through starry parnassia bogs, now through gardens shoulder deep in larkspur and lilies, grasses and rushes, shaking off showers of dew; crossing piles of crystalline moraine boulders, bright mirror pavements, and cool, cheery streams going to Yosemite; crossing bryanthus carpets and the scoured pathways of avalanches, and thickets of snow-pressed ceanothus; then down a broad, majestic stairway into the ice-sculptured lake-basin.

The snow on the high mountains is melting fast, and the streams are singing bankfull, swaying softly through the level meadows and bogs, quivering with sun-spangles, swirling in pot-holes, resting in deep pools, leaping, shouting in wild, exulting energy over rough boulder dams, joyful, beautiful in all their forms. No Sierra landscape that I have seen holds anything truly dead or dull, or any trace of what in manufactories is called rubbish or waste; everything is perfectly clean and pure and full of divine lessons. This quick, inevitable interest attaching to everything seems marvelous until the hand of God becomes visible; then it seems reasonable that what interests Him may well interest us. When we try to pick out anything by itself, we find it hitched to everything else in the universe. One fancies a heart like our own must be beating in every crystal and cell, and we feel like stopping to speak to the plants and animals as friendly fellow mountaineers. Nature as a poet, an enthusiastic workingman, becomes more and more visible the farther and higher we go; for the mountains are fountains—beginning places, however related to sources beyond mortal ken.

I found three kinds of meadows: (1) Those contained in basins not yet filled with earth enough to make a dry surface. They are planted with several species of carex, and have their margins diversified with robust flowering plants such as veratrum, larkspur, lupine, etc. (2) Those contained in the same sort of basins, once lakes like the first, but so situated in relation to the streams that flow through them and beds of transportable sand, gravel, etc., that they are now high and dry and well drained. This dry condition and corresponding difference in their vegetation may be caused by no superiority of position, or power of transporting filling material in the streams that belong to them, but simply by the basin being shallow and therefore sooner filled. They are planted with grasses, mostly fine, silky, and rather short-leaved, *Calamagrostis* and *Agrostis* being the principal genera. They form delightfully smooth, level sods in which one finds two or three species of gentian and as many of purple and yellow orthocarpus, violet, vaccinium, kalmia, bryanthus, and lonicera. (3) Meadows hanging on ridge and mountain slopes, not in basins at all, but made and held in place by masses of boulders and fallen trees, which, forming dams one above another in close succession on small, outspread, channelless streams, have collected soil enough for the growth of grasses, carices, and many flowering plants, and being kept well watered, without being subject to currents sufficiently strong to carry them away, a hanging or sloping meadow is the result. Their surfaces are seldom so smooth as the others, being roughened more or less by the projecting tops of the dam rocks or logs; but at a little distance this roughness is not noticed, and the effect is very striking—bright green, fluent, down-sweeping flowery ribbons on gray slopes. The broad shallow streams these meadows belong to are mostly derived from banks of snow and because the soil is well drained in some places, while in others the dam rocks are packed close and caulked with bits of wood and leaves, making boggy patches; the vegetation, of course, is correspondingly varied. I saw patches of willow, bryanthus, and a fine show of lilies on some of them, not forming a margin, but scattered about among the carex and grass. Most of these meadows are now in their prime. How wonderful must be the temper of the elastic leaves of grasses and sedges to make curves so perfect and fine. Tempered a little harder, they would stand erect, stiff and bristly, like strips of metal; a little softer, and every leaf would lie flat. And what fine painting and tinting there is on the glumes and pales, stamens and feathery pistils. Butterflies colored like the flowers waver above them in wonderful profusion, and many other beautiful winged people, numbered and known and loved only by the Lord, are waltzing together high over head, seemingly in pure play and hilarious enjoyment of their little sparks of life. How wonderful they are! How do they get a living, and endure the weather? How are their little bodies, with muscles, nerves, organs, kept warm and jolly in such admirable exuberant health? Regarded only as mechanical inventions, how wonderful they are! Compared with these, Godlike man's greatest machines are as nothing.

Most of the sandy gardens on moraines are in prime beauty like the meadows, though some on the north sides of rocks and beneath groves of sapling pines have not yet bloomed. On sunny sheets of crystal soil along the slopes of the Hoffman Mountains, I saw extensive patches of ivesia and purple gilia with scarce a green leaf, making fine clouds of color. Ribes bushes, vaccinium, and kalmia, now in flower, make beautiful rugs and borders along the banks of the streams. Shaggy beds of dwarf oak (*Quercus chrysolepis*, var. *vaccinifolia*) over which one may walk are common on rocky moraines, yet this is the same species as the large live oak seen near Brown's Flat. The most beautiful of the shrubs is the purple-flowered bryanthus, here making glorious carpets at an elevation of nine thousand feet.

The principal tree for the first mile or two from camp is the magnificent silver fir, which reaches perfection here both in size and form of individual trees, and in the mode of grouping in groves with open spaces between. So trim and tasteful are these silvery, spiry groves one would fancy they must have been placed in position by some master landscape gardener, their regularity seeming almost conventional. But Nature is the only gardener able to do work so fine. A few noble specimens two hundred feet high occupy central positions in the groups with younger trees around them; and outside of these another circle of yet smaller ones, the whole arranged like tastefully symmetrical bouquets, every tree fitting nicely the place assigned to it as if made especially for it; small roses and eriogonums are usually found blooming on the open spaces about the groves, forming charming pleasure grounds. Higher, the firs gradually become smaller and less perfect, many showing double summits, indicating storm stress. Still, where good moraine soil is found, even on the rim of the lake-basin, specimens one hundred and fifty feet in height and five feet in diameter occur nearly nine thousand feet above the sea. The saplings, I find, are mostly bent with the crushing weight of the winter snow, which at this elevation must be at least eight or ten feet deep, judging by marks on the trees; and this depth of compacted snow is heavy enough to bend and bury young trees twenty or thirty feet in height and hold them down for four or five months. Some are broken; the others spring up when the snow melts and at length attain a size that enables them to withstand the snow pressure. Yet even in trees five feet thick the traces of this early discipline are still plainly to be seen in their curved insteps, and frequently in old dried saplings protruding from the trunk, partially overgrown by the new axis developed from a branch below the break. Yet through all this stress the forest is maintained in marvelous beauty.

Beyond the silver firs I find the two-leaved pine (*Pinus contorta*, var. *Murrayana*) forms the bulk of the forest up to an elevation of ten thousand feet or more—the highest timber-belt of the Sierra. I saw a specimen nearly five feet in diameter growing on deep, well-watered soil at an elevation of about nine thousand feet. The form of this species varies very much with position, exposure, soil, etc. On stream-banks, where it is closely planted, it is very slender; some specimens seventy-five feet high do not exceed five inches in diameter at the ground, but the ordinary form, as far as I have seen, is well proportioned. The average diameter when full grown at this elevation is about twelve or fourteen inches, height forty or fifty feet, the straggling branches bent up at the end, the bark thin and bedraggled with amber-colored resin. The pistillate flowers form little crimson rosettes a fourth of an inch in diameter on the ends of the branchlets, mostly hidden in the leaf-tassels; the staminate are about three eighths of an inch in diameter, sulphur-yellow, in showy clusters, giving a remarkably rich effect—a brave, hardy mountaineer pine, growing cheerily on rough beds of avalanche boulders and joints of rock pavements, as well as in fertile hollows, standing up to the waist in snow every winter for centuries, facing a thousand storms and blooming every year in colors as bright as those worn by the sun-drenched trees of the tropics.

A still hardier mountaineer is the Sierra juniper (*Juniperus occidentalis*), growing mostly on domes and ridges and glacier pavements. A thickset, sturdy, picturesque highlander, seemingly content to live for more than a score of centuries on sunshine and snow; a truly wonderful fellow, dogged endurance expressed in every feature, lasting about as long as the granite he stands on. Some are nearly as broad as high. I saw one on the shore of the lake nearly ten feet in diameter, and many six to eight feet. The bark, cinnamon-colored, flakes off in long ribbon-like strips with a satiny luster. Surely the most enduring of all tree mountaineers, it never seems to die a natural death, or even to fall after it has been killed. If protected from accidents, it would perhaps be immortal. I saw some that had withstood an avalanche from snowy Mount Hoffman cheerily putting out new branches, as if repeating, like Grip, "Never say die." Some were simply standing on the pavement where no fissure more than half an inch wide offered a hold for its roots. The common height for these rock-dwellers is from ten to twenty feet; most of the old ones have broken tops, and are mere stumps, with a few tufted branches, forming picturesque brown pillars on bare pavements, with plenty of elbow-room and a clear view in every direction. On good moraine soil it reaches a height of from forty to sixty feet, with dense gray foliage. The rings of the trunk are very thin, eighty to an inch of diameter in some specimens I examined. Those ten feet in diameter must be very old—thousands of years. Wish I could live, like these junipers, on sunshine and snow, and stand beside them on the shore of Lake Tenaya for a thousand years. How much I should see, and how delightful it would be! Everything in the mountains would find me and come to me, and everything from the heavens like light.

The lake was named for one of the chiefs of the Yosemite tribe. Old Tenaya is said to have been a good Indian to his tribe. When a company of soldiers followed his band into Yosemite to punish them for cattle-stealing and other crimes, they fled to this lake by a trail that leads out of the upper end of the valley, early in the spring, while the snow was still deep; but being pursued, they lost heart and surrendered. A fine monument the old man has in this bright lake, and likely to last a long time, though lakes die as well as Indians, being gradually filled with detritus carried in by the feeding streams, and to some extent also by snow avalanches and rain and wind. A considerable portion of the Tenaya basin is already changed into a forested flat and meadow at the upper end, where the main tributary enters from Cathedral Peak. Two other tributaries come from the Hoffman Range. The outlet flows westward through Tenaya Cañon to join the Merced River in Yosemite. Scarce a handful of loose soil is to be seen on the north shore. All is bare, shining granite, suggesting the Indian name of the lake, Pywiack, meaning shining rock. The basin seems to have been slowly excavated by the ancient glaciers, a marvelous work requiring countless thousands of years. On the south side an imposing mountain rises from the water's edge to a height of three thousand feet or more, feathered with hemlock and pine; and huge shining domes on the east, over the tops of which the grinding, wasting, molding glacier must have swept as the wind does to-day.

July 28. No cloud mountains, only curly cirrus wisps scarce perceptible, and the want of thunder to strike the noon hour seems strange, as if the Sierra clock had stopped. Have been studying the *magnifica* fir—measured one near two hundred and forty feet high, the tallest I have yet seen. This species is the most symmetrical of all conifers, but though gigantic in size it seldom lives more than four or five hundred years. Most of the trees die from the attacks of a fungus at the age of two or three centuries. This dry-rot fungus perhaps enters the trunk by way of the stumps of limbs broken off by the snow that loads the broad palmate branches. The younger specimens are marvels of symmetry, straight and erect as a plumb-line, their branches in regular level whorls of five mostly, each branch as exact in its divisions as a fern frond, and thickly covered by the leaves, making a rich plush over all the tree, excepting only the trunk and a small portion of the main limbs. The leaves turn upward, especially on the branchlets, and are stiff and sharp, pointed on all the upper portion of the tree. They remain on the tree about eight or ten years, and as the growth is rapid it is not rare to find the leaves still in place on the upper part of the axis where it is three to four inches in diameter, wide apart of course, and their spiral arrangement beautifully displayed. The leaf-scars are conspicuous for twenty years or more, but there is a good deal of variation in different trees as to the thickness and sharpness of the leaves.

After the excursion to Mount Hoffman I had seen a complete cross-section of the Sierra forest, and I find that *Abies magnifica* is the most symmetrical tree of all the noble coniferous company. The cones are grand affairs, superb in form, size, and color, cylindrical, stand erect on the upper branches like casks, and are from five to eight inches in length by three or four in diameter, greenish gray, and covered with fine down which has a silvery luster in the sunshine, and their brilliance is augmented by beads of transparent balsam which seems to have been poured over each cone, bringing to mind the old ceremonies of anointing with oil. If possible, the inside of the cone is more beautiful than the outside; the scales, bracts, and seed wings are tinted with the loveliest rosy purple with a bright lustrous iridescence; the seeds, three fourths of an inch long, are dark brown. When the cones are ripe the scales and bracts fall off, setting the seeds free to fly to their predestined places, while the dead spike-like axes are left on the branches for many years to mark the positions of the vanished cones, excepting those cut off when green by the Douglas squirrel. How he gets his teeth under the broad bases of the sessile cones, I don't know. Climbing these trees on a sunny day to visit the growing cones and to gaze over the tops of the forest is one of my best enjoyments.

July 29. Bright, cool, exhilarating. Clouds about .05. Another glorious day of rambling, sketching, and universal enjoyment.

July 30. Clouds .20, but the regular shower did not reach us, though thunder was heard a few miles off striking the noon hour. Ants, flies, and mosquitoes seem to enjoy this fine climate. A few house-flies have discovered our camp. The Sierra mosquitoes are courageous and of good size, some of them measuring nearly an inch from tip of sting to tip of folded wings. Though less abundant than in most wildernesses, they occasionally make quite a hum and stir, and pay but little attention to time or place. They sting anywhere, any time of day, wherever they can find anything worth while, until they are themselves stung by frost. The large, jet-black ants are only ticklish and troublesome when one is lying down under the trees. Noticed a borer drilling a silver fir. Ovipositor about an inch and a half in length, polished and straight like a needle. When not in use, it is folded back in a sheath, which extends straight behind like the legs of a crane in flying. This drilling, I suppose, is to save nest building, and the after care of feeding the young. Who would guess that in the brain of a fly so much knowledge could find lodgment? How do they know that their eggs will hatch in such holes, or, after they hatch, that the soft, helpless grubs will find the right sort of nourishment in silver fir sap? This domestic arrangement calls to mind the curious family of gallflies. Each species seems to know what kind of plant will respond to the irritation or stimulus of the puncture it makes and the eggs it lays, in forming a growth that not only answers for a nest and home but also provides food for the young. Probably these gallflies make mistakes at times, like anybody else; but when they do, there is simply a failure of that particular brood, while enough to perpetuate the species do find the proper plants and nourishment. Many mistakes of this kind might be made without being discovered by us. Once a pair of wrens made the mistake of building a nest in the sleeve of a workman's coat, which was called for at sundown, much to the consternation and discomfiture of the birds. Still the marvel remains that any of the children of such small people as gnats and mosquitoes should escape their own and their parents' mistakes, as well as the vicis-situdes of the weather and hosts of enemies, and come forth in full vigor and perfection to enjoy the sunny world. When we think of the small creatures that are visible, we are led to think of many that are smaller still and lead us on and on into infinite mystery.

July 31. Another glorious day, the air as delicious to the lungs as nectar to the tongue; indeed the body seems one palate, and tingles equally throughout. Cloudiness about .05, but our ordinary shower has not yet reached us, though I hear thunder in the distance.

The cheery little chipmunk, so common about Brown's Flat, is common here also, and perhaps other species. In their light, airy habits they recall the familiar species of the Eastern States, which we admired in the oak openings of Wisconsin as they skimmed along the zigzag rail fences. These Sierra chipmunks are more arboreal and squirrel-like. I first noticed them on the lower edge of the conifer-ous belt, where the Sabine and yellow pines meet,—exceedingly interesting little fellows, full of odd, funny ways, and without being true squirrels, have most of their accomplishments without their aggres-sive quarrelsomeness. I never weary watching them as they frisk about in the bushes gathering seeds and berries, like song sparrows poising daintily on slen-der twigs, and making even less stir than most birds of the same size. Few of the Sierra animals inter-est me more; they are so able, gentle, confiding, and beautiful, they take one's heart, and get themselves adopted as darlings. Though weighing hardly more than field mice, they are laborious collectors of seeds, nuts, and cones, and are therefore well fed, but never in the least swollen with fat or lazily full. On the contrary, of their frisky, birdlike liveliness there is no end. They have a great variety of notes corresponding with their movements, some sweet and liquid, like water dripping with tinkling sounds into pools. They seem dearly to love teasing a dog, coming frequently almost within reach, then frisking away with lively chipping, like sparrows, beating time to their music with their tails, which at each chip describe half circles from side to side. Not even the Douglas squirrel is surer-footed or more fearless. I have seen them running about on sheer precipices of the Yosemite walls seemingly holding on with as little effort as flies, and as unconscious of danger, where, if the slightest slip were made, they would have fallen two or three thousand feet. How fine it would be could we mountaineers climb these tremendous cliffs with the same sure grip! The venture I made the other day for a view of the Yosemite Fall, and which tried my nerves so sorely, this little Tamias would have made for an ear of grass.

The woodchuck (*Arctomys monax*) of the bleak mountain-tops is a very different sort of mountaineer— the most bovine of rodents, a heavy eater, fat, aldermanic in bulk and fairly bloated, in his high pastures, like a cow in a clover field. One woodchuck would outweigh a hundred chipmunks, and yet he is by no means a dull animal. In the midst of what we regard as storm-beaten desolation he pipes and whistles right cheerily, and enjoys long life in his skyland homes. His burrow is made in disintegrated rocks or beneath large boulders. Coming out of his den in the cold hoarfrost mornings, he takes a sun-bath on some favorite flat-topped rock, then goes to breakfast in garden hollows, eats grass and flowers until comfortably swollen, then goes a-visiting to fight and play. How long a woodchuck lives in this bracing air I don't know, but some of them are rusty and gray like lichen-covered boulders.

August 1. A grand cloudland and five-minute shower, refreshing the blessed wilderness, already so fragrant and fresh, steeping the black meadow mold and dead leaves like tea.

The waycup, or flicker, so familiar to every boy in the old Middle West States, is one of the most common of the wood-peckers hereabouts, and makes one feel at home. I can see no difference in plumage or habits from the Eastern species, though the climate here is so different,—a fine, brave, confiding, beautiful bird. The robin, too, is here, with all his familiar notes and gestures, tripping daintily on open garden spots and high meadows. Over all America he seems to be at home, moving from the plains to the mountains and from north to south, back and forth, up and down, with the march of the seasons and food supply. How admirable the constitution and temper of this brave singer, keeping in cheery health over so vast and varied a range! Oftentimes, as I wander through these solemn woods, awe-stricken and silent, I hear the reassuring voice of this fellow wanderer ringing out, sweet and clear, "Fear not! fear not!"

The mountain quail (*Oreortyx ricta*) I often meet in my walks—a small brown partridge with a very long, slender, ornamental crest worn jauntily like a feather in a boy's cap, giving it a very marked appearance. This species is considerably larger than the valley quail, so common on the hot foothills. They seldom alight in trees, but love to wander in flocks of from five or six to twenty through the ceanothus and manzanita thickets and over open, dry meadows and rocks of the ridges where the forest is less dense or wanting, uttering a low clucking sound to enable them to keep together. When disturbed they rise with a strong birr of wing-beats, and scatter as if exploded to a distance of a quarter of a mile or so. After the danger is past they call one another together with a loud piping note—Nature's beautiful mountain chickens. I have not yet found their nests. The young of this season are already hatched and away—new broods of happy wanderers half as large as their parents. I wonder how they live through the long winters, when the ground is snow-covered ten feet deep. They must go down towards the lower edge of the forest, like the deer, though I have not heard of them there.

The blue, or dusky, grouse is also common here. They like the deepest and closest fir woods, and when disturbed, burst from the branches of the trees with a strong, loud whir of wing-beats, and vanish in a wavering, silent slide, without moving a feather—a stout, beautiful bird about the size of the prairie chicken of the old west, spending most of the time in the trees, excepting the breeding season, when it keeps to the ground. The young are now able to fly. When scattered by man or dog, they keep still until the danger is supposed to be passed, then the mother calls them together. The chicks can hear the call a distance of several hundred yards, though it is not loud. Should the young be unable to fly, the mother feigns desperate lameness or death to draw one away, throwing herself at one's feet within two or three yards, rolling over on her back, kicking and gasping, so as to deceive man or beast. They are said to stay all the year in the woods hereabouts, taking shelter in dense tufted branches of fir and yellow pine during snowstorms, and feeding on the young buds of these trees. Their legs are feathered down to their toes, and I have never heard of their suffering in any sort of weather. Able to live on pine and fir buds, they are forever independent in the matter of food, which troubles so many of us and controls our movements. Gladly, if I could, I would live forever on pine buds, however full of turpentine and pitch, for the sake of this grand independence. Just to think of our sufferings last month merely for grist-mill flour. Man seems to have more difficulty in gaining food than any other of the Lord's creatures. For many in towns it is a consuming, lifelong struggle; for others, the danger of coming to want is so great, the deadly habit of endless hoarding for the future is formed, which smothers all real life, and is continued long after every reasonable need has been over-supplied.

On Mount Hoffman I saw a curious dove-colored bird that seemed half woodpecker, half magpie, or crow. It screams something like a crow, but flies like a woodpecker, and has a long, straight bill, with which I saw it opening the cones of the mountain and white-barked pines. It seems to keep to the heights, though no doubt it comes down for shelter during winter, if not for food. So far as food is concerned, these bird-mountaineers, I guess, can glean nuts enough, even in winter, from the different kinds of conifers; for always there are a few that have been unable to fly out of the cones and remain for hungry winter gleaners.

A STRANGE EXPERIENCE

August 2. Clouds and showers, about the same as yesterday. Sketching all day on the North Dome until four or five o'clock in the afternoon, when, as I was busily employed thinking only of the glorious Yosemite landscape, trying to draw every tree and every line and feature of the rocks, I was suddenly, and without warning, possessed with the notion that my friend, Professor J. D. Butler, of the State University of Wisconsin, was below me in the valley, and I jumped up full of the idea of meeting him, with almost as much startling excitement as if he had suddenly touched me to make me look up. Leaving my work without the slightest deliberation, I ran down the western slope of the Dome and along the brink of the valley wall, looking for a way to the bottom, until I came to a side cañon, which, judging by its apparently continuous growth of trees and bushes, I thought might afford a practical way into the valley, and immediately began to make the descent, late as it was, as if drawn irresistibly. But after a little, common sense stopped me and explained that it would be long after dark ere I could possibly reach the hotel, that the visitors would be asleep, that nobody would know me, that I had no money in my pockets, and moreover was without a coat. I therefore compelled myself to stop, and finally succeeded in reasoning myself out of the notion of seeking my friend in the dark, whose presence I only felt in a strange, telepathic way. I succeeded in dragging myself back through the woods to camp, never for a moment wavering, however, in my determination to go down to him next morning. This I think is the most unexplainable notion that ever struck me. Had some one whispered in my ear while I sat on the Dome, where I had spent so many days, that Professor Butler was in the valley, I could not have been more surprised and startled. When I was leaving the university, he said, "Now, John, I want to hold you in sight and watch your career. Promise to write me at least once a year." I received a letter from him in July, at our first camp in the Hollow, written in May, in which he said that he might possibly visit California some time this summer, and therefore hoped to meet me. But inasmuch as he named no meeting-place, and gave no directions as to the course he would probably follow, and as I should be in the wilderness all summer, I had not the slightest hope of seeing him, and all thought of the matter had vanished from my mind until this afternoon, when he seemed to be wafted bodily almost against my face. Well, to-morrow I shall see; for, reasonable or unreasonable, I feel I must go.

August 3. Had a wonderful day. Found Professor Butler as the compass-needle finds the pole. So last evening's telepathy, transcendental revelation, or whatever else it may be called, was true; for, strange to say, he had just entered the valley by way of the Coulterville Trail and was coming up the valley past El Capitan when his presence struck me. Had he then looked toward the North Dome with a good glass when it first came in sight, he might have seen me jump up from my work and run toward him. This seems the one well-defined marvel of my life of the kind called supernatural; for, absorbed in glad Nature, spirit-rappings, second sight, ghost stories, etc., have never interested me since boyhood, seeming comparatively useless and infinitely less wonderful than Nature's open, harmonious, songful, sunny, everyday beauty.

This morning, when I thought of having to appear among tourists at a hotel, I was troubled because I had no suitable clothes, and at best am desperately bashful and shy. I was determined to go, however, to see my old friend after two years among strangers; got on a clean pair of overalls, a cashmere shirt, and a sort of jacket,—the best my camp wardrobe afforded,— tied my notebook on my belt, and strode away on my strange journey, followed by Carlo. I made my way though the gap discovered last evening, which proved to be Indian Cañon. There was no trail in it, and the rocks and brush were so rough that Carlo frequently called me back to help him down precipitous places. Emerging from the cañon shadows, I found a man making hay on one of the meadows, and asked him whether Professor Butler was in the valley. "I don't know," he replied; "but you can easily find out at the hotel. There are but few visitors in the valley just now. A small party came in yesterday afternoon, and I heard some one called Professor Butler, or Butterfield, or some name like that."

In front of the gloomy hotel I found a tourist party adjusting their fishing tackle. They all stared at me in silent wonderment, as if I had been seen dropping down through the trees from the clouds, mostly,

I suppose, on account of my strange garb. Inquiring for the office, I was told it was locked, and that the landlord was away, but I might find the landlady, Mrs. Hutchings, in the parlor. I entered in a sad state of embarrassment, and after I had waited in the big, empty room and knocked at several doors the landlady at length appeared, and in reply to my question said she rather thought Professor Butler *was* in the valley, but to make sure, she would bring the register from the office. Among the names of the last arrivals I soon discovered the Professor's familiar handwriting, at the sight of which bashfulness vanished; and having learned that his party had gone up the valley,—probably to the Vernal and Nevada Falls,—I pushed on in glad pursuit, my heart now sure of its prey. In less than an hour I reached the head of the Nevada Cañon at the Vernal Fall, and just outside of the spray discovered a distinguished-looking gentleman, who, like everybody else I have seen to-day, regarded me curiously as I approached. When I made bold to inquire if he knew where Professor Butler was, he seemed yet more curious to know what could possibly have happened that required a messenger for the Professor, and instead of answering my question he asked with military sharpness, "Who wants him?" "I want him," I replied with equal sharpness. "Why? Do *you* know him?" "Yes," I said. "Do *you* know him?" Astonished that any one in the mountains could possibly know Professor Butler and find him as soon as he had reached the valley, he came down to meet the strange mountaineer on equal terms, and courteously replied, "Yes, I know Professor Butler very well. I am General Alvord, and we were fellow students in Rutland, Vermont, long ago, when we were both young." "But where is he now?" I persisted, cutting short his story. "He has gone beyond the falls with a companion, to try to climb that big rock, the top of which you see from here." His guide now volunteered the information that it was the Liberty Cap Professor Butler and his companion had gone to climb, and that if I waited at the head of the fall I should be sure to find them on their way down. I therefore climbed the ladders alongside the Vernal Fall, and was pushing forward, determined to go to the top of Liberty Cap rock in my hurry, rather than wait, if I should not meet my friend sooner. So heart-hungry at times may one be to see a friend in the flesh, however happily full and care-free one's life may be. I had gone but a short distance, however, above the brow of the Vernal Fall when I caught sight of him in the brush and rocks, half erect, groping his way, his sleeves rolled up, vest open, hat in his hand, evidently very hot and tired. When he saw me coming he sat down on a boulder to wipe the perspiration from his brow and neck, and taking me for one of the valley guides, he inquired the way to the fall ladders. I pointed out the path marked with little piles of stones, on seeing which he called his companion, saying that the way was found; but he did not yet recognize me. Then I stood directly in front of him, looked him in the face, and held out my hand. He thought I was offering to assist him in rising. "Never mind," he said. Then I said, "Professor Butler, don't you know me?" "I think not," he replied; but catching my eye, sudden recognition followed, and astonishment that I should have found him just when he was lost in the brush and did not know that I was within hundreds of miles of him. "John Muir, John Muir, where have you come from?" Then I told him the story of my feeling his presence when he entered the valley last evening, when he was four or five miles distant, as I sat sketching on the North Dome. This, of course, only made him wonder the more. Below the foot of the Vernal Fall the guide was waiting with his saddle-horse, and I walked along the trail, chatting all the way back to the hotel, talking of school days, friends in Madison, of the students, how each had prospered, etc., ever and anon gazing at the stupendous rocks about us, now growing indistinct in the gloaming, and again quoting from the poets—a rare ramble.

It was late ere we reached the hotel, and General Alvord was waiting the Professor's arrival for dinner. When I was introduced he seemed yet more astonished than the Professor at my descent from cloudland and going straight to my friend without knowing in any ordinary way that he was even in California. They had come on direct from the East, had not yet visited any of their friends in the state, and considered themselves undiscoverable. As we sat at dinner, the General leaned back in his chair, and looking down the table, thus introduced me to the dozen guests or so, including the staring fisherman mentioned above: "This man, you know, came down out of these huge, trackless mountains, you know, to find his friend Professor Butler here, the very day he arrived; and how did he know he was here? He just felt him, he says. This is the queerest case of Scotch farsightedness I ever heard of," etc., etc. While my friend quoted Shakespeare: "More things in heaven and earth, Horatio, than are dreamt of in your philosophy," "As the sun, ere he has risen, sometimes paints his image in the firmament, e'en so the shadows of events precede the events, and in to-day already walks to-morrow."

Had a long conversation, after dinner, over Madison days. The Professor wants me to promise to go with him, sometime, on a camping trip in the Hawaiian Islands, while I tried to get him to go back with me to camp in the high Sierra. But he says, "Not now." He must not leave the General; and I was surprised to learn they are to leave the valley to-morrow or next day. I'm glad I'm not great enough to be missed in the busy world.

August 4. It seemed strange to sleep in a paltry hotel chamber after the spacious magnificence and luxury of the starry sky and silver fir grove. Bade farewell to my friend and the General. The old soldier was very kind, and an interesting talker. He told me long stories of the Florida Seminole war, in which he took part, and invited me to visit him in Omaha. Calling Carlo, I scrambled home through the Indian Cañon gate, rejoicing, pitying the poor Professor and General, bound by clocks, almanacs, orders, duties, etc., and compelled to dwell with lowland care and dust and din, where Nature is covered and her voice smothered, while the poor, insignificant wanderer enjoys the freedom and glory of God's wilderness.

Apart from the human interest of my visit to-day, I greatly enjoyed Yosemite, which I had visited only once before, having spent eight days last spring in rambling amid its rocks and waters. Wherever we go in the mountains, or indeed in any of God's wild fields, we find more than we seek. Descending four thousand feet in a few hours, we enter a new world— climate, plants, sounds, inhabitants, and scenery all new or changed. Near camp the goldcup oak forms sheets of chaparral, on top of which we may make our beds. Going down the Indian Cañon we observe this little bush changing by regular gradations to a large bush, to a small tree, and then larger, until on the rocky taluses near the bottom of the valley we find it developed into a broad, wide-spreading, gnarled, picturesque tree from four to eight feet in diameter, and forty or fifty feet high. Innumerable are the forms of water displayed. Every gliding reach, cascade, and fall has characters of its own. Had a good view of the Vernal and Nevada, two of the main falls of the valley, less than a mile apart, and offering striking differences in voice, form, color, etc. The Vernal, four hundred feet high and about seventy-five or eighty feet wide, drops smoothly over a round-lipped precipice and forms a superb apron of embroidery, green and white, slightly folded and fluted, maintaining this form nearly to the bottom, where it is suddenly veiled in quick-flying billows of spray and mist, in which the afternoon sunbeams play with ravishing beauty of rainbow colors. The Nevada is white from its first appearance as it leaps out into the freedom of the air. At the head it presents a twisted appearance, by an over-folding of the current from striking on the side of its channel just before the first free out-bounding leap is made. About two thirds of the way down, the hurrying throng of comet-shaped masses glance on an inclined part of the face of the precipice and are beaten into yet whiter foam, greatly expanded, and sent bounding outward, making an indescribably glorious show, especially when the afternoon sunshine is pouring into it. In this fall—one of the most wonderful in the world—the water does not seem to be under the dominion of ordinary laws, but rather as if it were a living creature, full of the strength of the mountains and their huge, wild joy.

From beneath heavy throbbing blasts of spray the broken river is seen emerging in ragged boulder-chafed strips. These are speedily gathered into a roaring torrent, showing that the young river is still gloriously alive. On it goes, shouting, roaring, exulting in its strength, passes through a gorge with sublime display of energy, then suddenly expands on a gently inclined pavement, down which it rushes in thin sheets and folds of lace-work into a quiet pool,—"Emerald Pool," as it is called,—a stopping-place, a period separating two grand sentences. Resting here long enough to part with its foam-bells and gray mixtures of air, it glides quietly to the verge of the Vernal precipice in a broad sheet and makes its new display in the Vernal Fall; then more rapids and rock tossings down the cañon, shaded by live oak, Douglas spruce, fir, maple, and dogwood. It receives the Illilouette tributary, and makes a long sweep out into the level, sun-filled valley to join the other streams which, like itself, have danced and sung their way down from snowy heights to form the main Merced—the river of Mercy. But of this there is no end, and life, when one thinks of it, is so short. Never mind, one day in the midst of these divine glories is well worth living and toiling and starving for.

Before parting with Professor Butler he gave me a book, and I gave him one of my pencil sketches for his little son Henry, who is a favorite of mine. He used to make many visits to my room when I was a student. Never shall I forget his patriotic speeches for the Union, mounted on a tall stool, when he was only six years old.

It seems strange that visitors to Yosemite should be so little influenced by its novel grandeur, as if their eyes were bandaged and their ears stopped. Most of those I saw yesterday were looking down as if wholly unconscious of anything going on about them, while the sublime rocks were trembling with the tones of the mighty chanting congregation of waters gathered from all the mountains round about, making music that might draw angels out of heaven. Yet respectable-looking, even wise-looking people were fixing bits of worms on bent pieces of wire to catch trout. Sport they called it. Should church-goers try to pass the time fishing in baptismal fonts while dull sermons were being preached, the so-called sport might not be so bad; but to play in the Yosemite temple, seeking pleasure in the pain of fishes struggling for their lives, while God himself is preaching his sublimest water and stone sermons!

Now I'm back at the camp-fire, and cannot help thinking about my recognition of my friend's presence in the valley while he was four or five miles away, and while I had no means of knowing that he was not thousands of miles away. It seems supernatural, but only because it is not understood. Anyhow, it seems silly to make so much of it, while the natural and common is more truly marvelous and mysterious than the so-called supernatural. Indeed most of the miracles we hear of are infinitely less wonderful than the commonest of natural phenomena, when fairly seen. Perhaps the invisible rays that struck me while I sat at work on the Dome are something like those which attract and repel people at first sight, concerning which so much nonsense has been written. The worst apparent effect of these mysterious odd things is blindness to all that is divinely common. Hawthorne, I fancy, could weave one of his weird romances out of this little telepathic episode, the one strange marvel of my life, probably replacing my good old Professor by an attractive woman.

August 5. We were awakened this morning before daybreak by the furious barking of Carlo and Jack and the sound of stampeding sheep. Billy fled from his punk bed to the fire, and refused to stir into the darkness to try to gather the scattered flock, or ascertain the nature of the disturbance. It was a bear attack, as we afterward learned, and I suppose little was gained by attempting to do anything before daylight. Nevertheless, being anxious to know what was up, Carlo and I groped our way through the woods, guided by the rustling sound made by fragments of the flock, not fearing the bear, for I knew that the runaways would go from their enemy as far as possible and Carlo's nose was also to be depended upon. About half a mile east of the corral we overtook twenty or thirty of the flock and succeeded in driving them back; then turning to the westward, we traced another band of fugitives and got them back to the flock. After daybreak I discovered the remains of a sheep carcass, still warm, showing that Bruin must have been enjoying his early mutton breakfast while I was seeking the runaways. He had eaten about half of it. Six dead sheep lay in the corral, evidently smothered by the crowding and piling up of the flock against the side of the corral wall when the bear entered. Making a wide circuit of the camp, Carlo and I discovered a third band of fugitives and drove them back to camp. We also discovered another dead sheep half eaten, showing there had been two of the shaggy freebooters at this early breakfast. They were easily traced. They had each caught a sheep, jumped over the corral fence with them, carrying them as a cat carries a mouse, laid them at the foot of fir trees a hundred yards or so back from the corral, and eaten their fill. After breakfast I set out to seek more of the lost, and found seventy-five at a considerable distance from camp. In the afternoon I succeeded, with Carlo's help, in getting them back to the flock. I don't know whether all are together again or not. I shall make a big fire this evening and keep watch.

When I asked Billy why he made his bed against the corral in rotten wood, when so many better places offered, he replied that he "wished to be as near the sheep as possible in case bears should attack them." Now that the bears have come, he has moved his bed to the far side of the camp, and seems afraid that he may be mistaken for a sheep.

This has been mostly a sheep day, and of course studies have been interrupted. Nevertheless, the walk through the gloom of the woods before the dawn was worth while, and I have learned something about these noble bears. Their tracks are very telling, and so are their breakfasts. Scarce a trace of clouds to-day, and of course our ordinary midday thunder is wanting.

August 6. Enjoyed the grand illumination of the camp grove, last night, from the fire we made to frighten the bears—compensation for loss of sleep and sheep. The noble pillars of verdure, vividly aglow, seemed to shoot into the sky like the flames that lighted them. Nevertheless, one of the bears paid us another visit, as if more attracted than repelled by the fire, climbed into the corral, killed a sheep and made off with it without being seen, while still another was lost by trampling and suffocation against the side of the corral. Now that our mutton has been tasted, I suppose it will be difficult to put a stop to the ravages of these freebooters.

The Don arrived to-day from the lowlands with provisions and a letter. On learning the losses he had sustained, he determined to move the flock at once to the Upper Tuolumne region, saying that the bears would be sure to visit the camp every night as long as we stayed, and that no fire or noise we might make would avail to frighten them. No clouds save a few thin, lustrous touches on the eastern horizon. Thunder heard in the distance.

THE MONO TRAIL

August 7. Early this morning bade good-bye to the bears and blessed silver fir camp, and moved slowly eastward along the Mono Trail. At sundown camped for the night on one of the many small flowery meadows so greatly enjoyed on my excursion to Lake Tenaya. The dusty, noisy flock seems outrageously foreign and out of place in these nature gardens, more so than bears among sheep. The harm they do goes to the heart, but glorious hope lifts above all the dust and din and bids me look forward to a good time coming, when money enough will be earned to enable me to go walking where I like in pure wildness, with what I can carry on my back, and when the bread-sack is empty, run down to the nearest point on the bread-line for more. Nor will these run-downs be blanks, for, whether up or down, every step and jump on these blessed mountains is full of fine lessons.

August 8. Camp at the west end of Lake Tenaya. Arriving early, I took a walk on the glacier-polished pavements along the north shore, and climbed the magnificent mountain rock at the east end of the lake, now shining in the late afternoon light. Almost every yard of its surface shows the scoring and polishing action of a great glacier that enveloped it and swept heavily over its summit, though it is about two thousand feet high above the lake and ten thousand above sea-level. This majestic, ancient ice-flood came from the eastward, as the scoring and crushing of the surface shows. Even below the waters of the lake the rock in some places is still grooved and polished; the lapping of the waves and their disintegrating action have not as yet obliterated even the superficial marks of glaciation. In climbing the steepest polished places I had to take off shoes and stockings. A fine region this for study of glacial action in mountain-making. I found many charming plants: arctic daisies, phlox, white spiræa, bryanthus, and rock-ferns,—pellæa, cheilanthes, allosorus,—fringing weathered seams all the way up to the summit; and sturdy junipers, grand old gray and brown monuments, stood bravely erect on fissured spots here and there, telling storm and avalanche stories of hundreds of winters. The view of the lake from the top is, I think, the best of all. There is another rock, more striking in form than this, standing isolated at the head of the lake, but it is not more than half as high. It is a knob or knot of burnished granite, perhaps about a thousand feet high, apparently as flawless and strong in structure as a wave-worn pebble, and probably owes its existence to the superior resistance it offered to the action of the overflowing ice-flood.

Made sketch of the lake, and sauntered back to camp, my iron-shod shoes clanking on the pavements disturbing the chipmunks and birds. After dark went out to the shore,—not a breath of air astir, the lake a perfect mirror reflecting the sky and mountains with their stars and trees and wonderful sculpture, all their grandeur refined and doubled,—a marvelously impressive picture, that seemed to belong more to heaven than earth.

August 9. I went ahead of the flock, and crossed over the divide between the Merced and Tuolumne Basins. The gap between the east end of the Hoffman spur and the mass of mountain rocks about Cathedral Peak, though roughened by ridges and waving folds, seems to be one of the channels of a broad ancient glacier that came from the mountains on the summit of the range. In crossing this divide the ice-river made an ascent of about five hundred feet from the Tuolumne meadows. This entire region must have been over-swept by ice.

From the top of the divide, and also from the big Tuolumne Meadows, the wonderful mountain called Cathedral Peak is in sight. From every point of view it shows marked individuality. It is a majestic temple of one stone, hewn from the living rock, and adorned with spires and pinnacles in regular cathedral style. The dwarf pines on the roof look like mosses. I hope some time to climb to it to say my prayers and hear the stone sermons.

The big Tuolumne Meadows are flowery lawns, lying along the south fork of the Tuolumne River at a height of about eighty-five hundred to nine thousand feet above the sea, partially separated by forests and bars of glaciated granite. Here the mountains seem to have been cleared away or set back, so that wide-open views may be had in every direction. The upper end of the series lies at the base of Mount Lyell, the lower below the east end of the Hoffman Range, so the length must be about ten or twelve miles. They vary in width from a quarter of a mile to perhaps three quarters, and a good many branch meadows put out along the banks of the tributary streams. This is the most spacious and delightful high pleasure-ground I have yet seen. The air is keen and bracing, yet warm during the day; and though lying high in the sky, the surrounding mountains are so much higher, one feels protected as if in a grand hall. Mounts Dana and Gibbs, massive red mountains, perhaps thirteen thousand feet high or more, bound the view on the east, the Cathedral and Unicorn Peaks, with many nameless peaks, on the south, the Hoffman Range on the west, and a number of peaks unnamed, as far as I know, on the north. One of these last is much like the Cathedral. The grass of the meadows is mostly fine and silky, with exceedingly slender leaves, making a close sod, above which the panicles of minute purple flowers seem to float in airy, misty lightness, while the sod is enriched with at least three species of gentian and as many or more of orthocarpus, potentilla, ivesia, solidago, pentstemon, with their gay colors,—purple, blue, yellow, and red,—all of which I may know better ere long. A central camp will probably be made in this region, from which I hope to make long excursions into the surrounding mountains.

On the return trip I met the flock about three miles east of Lake Tenaya. Here we camped for the night near a small lake lying on top of the divide in a clump of the two-leaved pine. We are now about nine thousand feet above the sea. Small lakes abound in all sorts of situations,—on ridges, along mountain sides, and in piles of moraine boulders, most of them mere pools. Only in those cañons of the larger streams at the foot of declivities, where the down thrust of the glaciers was heaviest, do we find lakes of considerable size and depth. How grateful a task it would be to trace them all and study them! How pure their waters are, clear as crystal in polished stone basins! None of them, so far as I have seen, have fishes, I suppose on account of falls making them inaccessible. Yet one would think their eggs might get into these lakes by some chance or other; on ducks' feet, for example, or in their mouths, or in their crops, as some plant seeds are distributed. Nature has so many ways of doing such things. How did the frogs, found in all the bogs and pools and lakes, however high, manage to get up these mountains? Surely not by jumping. Such excursions through miles of dry brush and boulders would be very hard on frogs. Perhaps their stringy gelatinous spawn is occasionally entangled or glued on the feet of water birds. Anyhow, they are here and in hearty health and voice. I like their cheery tronk and crink. They take the place of songbirds at a pinch.

August 10. Another of those charming exhilarating days that make the blood dance and excite nerve currents that render one unweariable and well-nigh immortal. Had another view of the broad ice-ploughed divide, and gazed again and again at the Sierra temple and the great red mountains east of the meadows.

We are camped near the Soda Springs on the north side of the river. A hard time we had getting the sheep across. They were driven into a horseshoe bend and fairly crowded off the bank. They seemed willing to suffer death rather than risk getting wet, though they swim well enough when they have to. Why sheep should be so unreasonably afraid of water, I don't know, but they do fear it as soon as they are born and perhaps before. I once saw a lamb only a few hours old approach a shallow stream about two feet wide and an inch deep, after it had walked only about a hundred yards on its life journey. All the flock to which it belonged had crossed this inch-deep stream, and as the mother and her lamb were the last to cross, I had a good opportunity to observe them. As soon as the flock was out of the way, the anxious mother crossed over and called the youngster. It walked cautiously to the brink, gazed at the water, bleated piteously, and refused to venture. The patient mother went back to it again and again to encourage it, but long without avail. Like the pilgrim on Jordan's stormy bank it feared to launch away. At length, gathering its trembling inexperienced legs for the mighty effort, throwing up its head as if it knew all about drowning, and was anxious to keep its nose above water, it made the tremendous leap, and landed in the middle of the inch-deep stream. It seemed astonished to find that, instead of sinking over head and ears, only its toes were wet, gazed at the shining water a few seconds, and then sprang to the shore safe and dry through the dreadful adventure. All kinds of wild sheep are mountain animals, and their descendants' dread of water is not easily accounted for.

August 11. Fine shining weather, with a ten minutes' noon thunderstorm and rain. Rambling all day getting acquainted with the region north of the river. Found a small lake and many charming glacier meadows embosomed in an extensive forest of the two-leaved pine. The forest is growing on broad, almost continuous deposits of moraine material, is remarkably even in its growth, and the trees are much closer together than in any of the fir or pine woods farther down the range. The evenness of the growth would seem to indicate that the trees are all of the same age or nearly so. This regularity has probably been in great part the result of fire. I saw several large patches and strips of dead bleached spars, the ground beneath them covered with a young even growth. Fire can run in these woods, not only because the thin bark of the trees is dripping with resin, but because the growth is close, and the comparatively rich soil produces good crops of tall broad-leaved grasses on which fire can travel, even when the weather is calm. Besides these fire-killed patches there are a good many fallen uprooted trees here and there, some with the bark and needles still on, as if they had lately been blown down in some thunderstorm blast. Saw a large black-tailed deer, a buck with antlers like the upturned roots of a fallen pine.

After a long ramble through the dense encumbered woods I emerged upon a smooth meadow full of sunshine like a lake of light, about a mile and a half long, a quarter to half a mile wide, and bounded by tall arrowy pines. The sod, like that of all the glacier meadows hereabouts, is made of silky agrostis and calamagrostis chiefly; their panicles of purple flowers and purple stems, exceedingly light and airy, seem to float above the green plush of leaves like a thin misty cloud, while the sod is brightened by several species of gentian, potentilla, ivesia, orthocarpus, and their corresponding bees and butterflies. All the glacier meadows are beautiful, but few are so perfect as this one. Compared with it the most carefully leveled, licked, snipped artificial lawns of pleasure-grounds are coarse things. I should like to live here always. It is so calm and withdrawn while open to the universe in full communion with everything good. To the north of this glorious meadow I discovered the camp of some Indian hunters. Their fire was still burning, but they had not yet returned from the chase.

From meadow to meadow, every one beautiful

beyond telling, and from lake to lake through groves and belts of arrowy trees, I held my way northward toward Mount Conness, finding telling beauty everywhere, while the encompassing mountains were calling "Come." Hope I may climb them all.

August 12. The sky-scenery has changed but little so far with the change in elevation. Clouds about .05. Glorious pearly cumuli tinted with purple of ineffable fineness of tone. Moved camp to the side of the glacier meadow mentioned above. To let sheep trample so divinely fine a place seems barbarous. Fortunately they prefer the succulent broad-leaved triticum and other woodland grasses to the silky species of the meadows, and therefore seldom bite them or set foot on them.

The shepherd and the Don cannot agree about methods of herding. Billy sets his dog Jack on the sheep far too often, so the Don thinks; and after some dispute to-day, in which the shepherd loudly claimed the right to dog the sheep as often as he pleased, he started for the plains. Now I suppose the care of the sheep will fall on me, though Mr. Delaney promises to do the herding himself for a while, then return to the lowlands and bring another shepherd, so as to leave me free to rove as I like.

Had another rich ramble. Pushed northward beyond the forests to the head of the general basin, where traces of glacial action are strikingly clear and interesting. The recesses among the peaks look like quarries, so raw and fresh are the moraine chips and boulders that strew the ground in Nature's glacial workshops.

Soon after my return to camp we received a visit from an Indian, probably one of the hunters whose camp I had discovered. He came from Mono, he said, with others of his tribe, to hunt deer. One that he had killed a short distance from here he was carrying on his back, its legs tied together in an ornamental bunch on his forehead. Throwing down his burden, he gazed stolidly for a few minutes in silent Indian fashion, then cut off eight or ten pounds of venison for us, and begged a "lill" (little) of everything he saw or could think of—flour, bread, sugar, tobacco, whiskey, needles, etc. We gave a fair price for the meat in flour and sugar and added a few needles. A strangely dirty and irregular life these dark-eyed, dark-haired, half-happy savages lead in this clean wilderness,—starvation and abundance, deathlike calm, indolence, and admirable, indefatigable action succeeding each other in stormy rhythm like winter and summer. Two things they have that civilized toilers might well envy them—pure air and pure water. These go far to cover and cure the grossness of their lives. Their food is mostly good berries, pine nuts, clover, lily bulbs, wild sheep, antelope, deer, grouse, sage hens, and the larvæ of ants, wasps, bees, and other insects.

August 13. Day all sunshine, dawn and evening purple, noon gold, no clouds, air motionless. Mr. Delaney arrived with two shepherds, one of them an Indian. On his way up from the plains he left some provisions at the Portuguese camp on Porcupine Creek near our old Yosemite camp, and I set out this morning with one of the pack animals to fetch them. Arrived at the Porcupine camp at noon, and might have returned to the Tuolumne late in the evening, but concluded to stay over night with the Portuguese shepherds at their pressing invitation. They had sad stories to tell of losses from the Yosemite bears, and were so discouraged they seemed on the point of leaving the mountains; for the bears came every night and helped themselves to one or several of the flock in spite of all their efforts to keep them off.

I spent the afternoon in a grand ramble along the Yosemite walls. From the highest of the rocks called the Three Brothers, I enjoyed a magnificent view comprehending all the upper half of the floor of the valley and nearly all the rocks of the walls on both sides and at the head, with snowy peaks in the background. Saw also the Vernal and Nevada Falls, a truly glorious picture,—rocky strength and permanence combined with beauty of plants frail and fine and evanescent; water descending in thunder, and the same water gliding through meadows and groves in gentlest beauty. This standpoint is about eight thousand feet above the sea, or four thousand feet above the floor of the valley, and every tree, though looking small and feathery, stands in admirable clearness, and the shadows they cast are as distinct in outline as if seen at a distance of a few yards. They appeared even more so. No words will ever describe the exquisite beauty and charm of this mountain park—Nature's landscape garden at once tenderly beautiful and sublime. No wonder it draws nature-lovers from all over the world.

Glacial action even on this lofty summit is plainly displayed. Not only has all the lovely valley now smiling in sunshine been filled to the brim with ice, but it has been deeply overflowed.

I visited our old Yosemite camp-ground on the head of Indian Creek, and found it fairly patted and smoothed down with bear-tracks. The bears had eaten all the sheep that were smothered in the corral, and some of the grand animals must have died, for Mr. Delaney, before leaving camp, put a large quantity of poison in the carcasses. All sheep-men carry strychnine to kill coyotes, bears, and panthers, though neither coyotes nor panthers are at all numerous in the upper mountains. The little dog-like wolves are far more numerous in the foothill region and on the plains, where they find a better supply of food,—saw only one panther-track above eight thousand feet.

On my return after sunset to the Portuguese camp I found the shepherds greatly excited over the behav-ior of the bears that have learned to like mutton. "They are getting worse and worse," they lamented. Not willing to wait decently until after dark for their suppers, they come and kill and eat their fill in broad daylight. The evening before my arrival, when the two shepherds were leisurely driving the flock toward camp half an hour before sunset, a hungry bear came out of the chaparral within a few yards of them and shuffled deliberately toward the flock. "Portuguese Joe," who always carried a gun loaded with buckshot, fired excitedly, threw down his gun, fled to the near-est suitable tree, and climbed to a safe height without waiting to see the effect of his shot. His companion also ran, but said that he saw the bear rise on its hind legs and throw out its arms as if feeling for somebody, and then go into the brush as if wounded.

At another of their camps in this neighborhood, a bear with two cubs attacked the flock before sun-set, just as they were approaching the corral. Joe promptly climbed a tree out of danger, while Antone, rebuking his companion for cowardice in abandoning his charge, said that he was not going to let bears

"eat up his sheeps" in daylight, and rushed towards
the bears, shouting and setting his dog on them. The
frightened cubs climbed a tree, but the mother ran
to meet the shepherd and seemed anxious to fight.
Antone stood astonished for a moment, eyeing the
oncoming bear, then turned and fled, closely pursued.
Unable to reach a suitable tree for climbing, he ran
to the camp and scrambled up to the roof of the little cabin; the bear followed, but did not climb to the
roof,—only stood glaring up at him for a few minutes,
threatening him and holding him in mortal terror,
then went to her cubs, called them down, went to the
flock, caught a sheep for supper, and vanished in the
brush. As soon as the bear left the cabin, the trembling Antone begged Joe to show him a good safe tree,
up which he climbed like a sailor climbing a mast, and
remained as long as he could hold on, the tree being
almost branchless. After these disastrous experiences
the two shepherds chopped and gathered large piles
of dry wood and made a ring of fire around the corral
every night, while one with a gun kept watch from
a comfortable stage built on a neighboring pine that
commanded a view of the corral. This evening the
show made by the circle of fire was very fine, bringing
out the surrounding trees in most impressive relief,
and making the thousands of sheep eyes glow like a
glorious bed of diamonds.

August 14. Up to the time I went to bed last night all
was quiet, though we expected the shaggy freebooters
every minute. They did not come till near midnight,
when a pair walked boldly to the corral between two of
the great fires, climbed in, killed two sheep and smothered ten, while the frightened watcher in the tree did

not fire a single shot, saying that he was afraid he might kill some of the sheep, for the bears got into the corral before he got a good clear view of them. I told the shepherds they should at once move the flock to another camp. "Oh, no use, no use," they lamented; "where we go, the bears go too. See my poor dead sheeps—soon all dead. No use try another camp. We go down to the plains." And as I afterwards learned, they were driven out of the mountains a month before the usual time. Were bears much more numerous and destructive, the sheep would be kept away altogether.

It seems strange that bears, so fond of all sorts of flesh, running the risks of guns and fires and poison, should never attack men except in defense of their young. How easily and safely a bear could pick us up as we lie asleep! Only wolves and tigers seem to have learned to hunt man for food, and perhaps sharks and crocodiles. Mosquitoes and other insects would, I suppose, devour a helpless man in some parts of the world, and so might lions, leopards, wolves, hyenas, and panthers at times if pressed by hunger,—but under ordinary circumstances, perhaps, only the tiger among land animals may be said to be a man-eater,— unless we add man himself.

Clouds as usual about .05. Another glorious Sierra day, warm, crisp, fragrant, and clear. Many of the flowering plants have gone to seed, but many others are unfolding their petals every day, and the firs and pines are more fragrant than ever. Their seeds are nearly ripe, and will soon be flying in the merriest flocks that ever spread a wing.

On the way back to our Tuolumne camp, I enjoyed the scenery if possible more than when it first came to view. Every feature already seems familiar as if I had lived here always. I never weary gazing at the wonderful Cathedral. It has more individual character than any other rock or mountain I ever saw, excepting perhaps the Yosemite South Dome. The forests, too, seem kindly familiar, and the lakes and meadows and glad singing streams. I should like to dwell with them forever. Here with bread and water I should be content. Even if not allowed to roam and climb, tethered to a stake or tree in some meadow or grove, even then I should be content forever. Bathed in such beauty, watching, the expressions ever varying on the faces of the mountains, watching the stars, which here have a glory that the lowlander never dreams of, watching the circling seasons, listening to the songs of the waters and winds and birds, would be endless pleasure. And what glorious cloudlands I should see, storms and calms,—a new heaven and a new earth every day, aye and new inhabitants. And how many visitors I should have. I feel sure I should not have one dull moment. And why should this appear extravagant? It is only common sense, a sign of health, genuine, natural, all-awake health. One would be at an endless Godful play, and what speeches and music and acting and scenery and lights!—sun, moon, stars, auroras. Creation just beginning, the morning stars "still singing together and all the sons of God shouting for joy."

BLOODY CAÑON AND MONO LAKE

August 21. Have just returned from a fine wild excursion across the range to Mono Lake, by way of the Mono or Bloody Cañon Pass. Mr. Delaney has been good to me all summer, lending a helping, sympathizing hand at every opportunity, as if my wild notions and rambles and studies were his own. He is one of those remarkable California men who have been overflowed and denuded and remodeled by the excitements of the gold fields, like the Sierra landscapes by grinding ice, bringing the harder bosses and ridges of character into relief,—a tall, lean, big-boned, big-hearted Irishman, educated for a priest in Maynooth College,—lots of good in him, shining out now and then in this mountain light. Recognizing my love of wild places, he told me one evening that I ought to go through Bloody Cañon, for he was sure I should find it wild enough. He had not been there himself, he said, but had heard many of his mining friends speak of it as the wildest of all the Sierra passes. Of course I was glad to go. It lies just to the east of our camp and swoops down from the summit of the range to the edge of the Mono Desert, making a descent of about four thousand feet in a distance of about four miles. It was known and traveled as a pass by wild animals and the Indians long before its discovery by white men in the gold year of 1858, as is shown by old trails which come together at the head of it. The name may have been suggested by the red color of the metamorphic slates in which the cañon abounds, or by the blood stains on the rocks from the unfortunate animals that were compelled to slide and shuffle over the sharp-angled boulders.

Early in the morning I tied my notebook and some bread to my belt, and strode away full of eager hope, feeling that I was going to have a glorious revel. The glacier meadows that lay along my way served to soothe my morning speed, for the sod was full of blue gentians and daisies, kalmia and dwarf vaccinium, calling for recognition as old friends, and I had to stop many times to examine the shining rocks over which the ancient glacier had passed with tremendous pressure, polishing them so well that they reflected the sunlight like glass in some places, while fine striæ, seen clearly through a lens, indicated the direction in which the ice had flowed. On some of the sloping polished pavements abrupt steps occur, showing that occasionally large masses of the rock had given way before the glacial pressure, as well as small particles; moraines, too, some scattered, others regular like long curving embankments and dams, occur here and there, giving the general surface of the region a young, new-made appearance. I watched the gradual dwarfing of the pines as I ascended, and the corresponding dwarfing of nearly all the rest of the vegetation. On the slopes of Mammoth Mountain, to the south of the pass, I saw many gaps in the woods reaching from the upper edge of the timber-line down to the level meadows, where avalanches of snow had descended, sweeping away every tree in their paths as well as the soil they were growing in, leaving the bedrock bare.

The trees are nearly all uprooted, but a few that had been extremely well anchored in clefts of the rock were broken off near the ground. It seems strange at first sight that trees that had been allowed to grow for a century or more undisturbed should in their old age be thus swished away at a stroke. Such avalanches can only occur under rare conditions of weather and snowfall. No doubt on some positions of the mountain slopes the inclination and smoothness of the surface is such that avalanches must occur every winter, or even after every heavy snowstorm, and of course no trees or even bushes can grow in their channels. I noticed a few clean-swept slopes of this kind. The uprooted trees that had grown in the pathway of what might be called "century avalanches" were piled in windrows, and tucked snugly against the wall-trees of the gaps, heads downward, excepting a few that were carried out into the open ground of the meadows, where the heads of the avalanches had stopped. Young pines, mostly the two-leaved and the white-barked, are already springing up in these cleared gaps. It would be interesting to ascertain the age of these saplings, for thus we should gain a fair approximation to the year that the great avalanches occurred. Perhaps most or all of them occurred the same winter. How glad I should be if free to pursue such studies!

Near the summit at the head of the pass I found a species of dwarf willow lying perfectly flat on the ground, making a nice, soft, silky gray carpet, not a single stem or branch more than three inches high; but the catkins, which are now nearly ripe, stand erect and make a close, nearly regular gray growth, being larger than all the rest of the plants. Some of these interesting dwarfs have only one catkin—willow bushes reduced to their lowest terms. I found patches of dwarf vaccinium also forming smooth carpets, closely pressed to the ground or against the sides of stones, and covered with round pink flowers in lavish abundance as if they had fallen from the sky like hail. A little higher, almost at the very head of the pass, I found the blue arctic daisy and purple-flowered bryanthus, the mountain's own darlings, gentle mountaineers face to face with the sky, kept safe and warm by a thousand miracles, seeming always the finer and purer the wilder and stormier their homes. The trees, tough and resiny, seem unable to go a step farther; but up and up, far above the tree-line, these tender plants climb, cheerily spreading their gray and pink carpets right up to the very edges of the snow-banks in deep hollows and shadows. Here, too, is the familiar robin, tripping on the flowery lawns, bravely singing the same cheery song I first heard when a boy in Wisconsin newly arrived from old Scotland. In this fine company sauntering enchanted, taking no heed of time, I at length entered the gate of the pass, and the huge rocks began to close around me in all their mysterious impressiveness. Just then I was startled by a lot of queer, hairy, muffled creatures coming shuffling, shambling, wallowing toward me as if they had no bones in their bodies. Had I discovered them while they were yet a good way off, I should have tried to avoid them. What a picture they made contrasted with the others I had just been admiring. When I came up to them, I found that they were only a band of Indians from Mono on their way to Yosemite for a load of acorns. They were wrapped in blankets made of the skins of sage-rabbits. The dirt on some of the faces seemed almost old enough and thick enough to have a geological significance; some were strangely blurred and divided into sections by seams and wrinkles that looked like cleavage joints, and had a worn abraded look as if they had lain exposed to the weather for ages. I tried to pass them without stopping, but they wouldn't let me; forming a dismal circle about me, I was closely besieged while they begged whiskey or tobacco, and it was hard to convince them that I hadn't any. How glad I was to get away from the gray, grim crowd and see them vanish down the trail! Yet it seems sad to feel such desperate repulsion from one's fellow beings, however degraded. To prefer the society of squirrels and woodchucks to that of our own species must surely be unnatural. So with a fresh breeze and a hill or mountain between us I must wish them Godspeed and try to pray and sing with Burns, "It's coming yet, for a' that, that man to man, the warld o'er, shall brothers be for a' that."

How the day passed I hardly know. By the map I have come only about ten or twelve miles, though the sun is already low in the west, showing how long I must have lingered, observing, sketching, taking notes among the glaciated rocks and moraines and Alpine flower-beds.

At sundown the somber crags and peaks were inspired with the ineffable beauty of the alpenglow, and a solemn, awful stillness hushed everything in the landscape. Then I crept into a hollow by the side of a small lake near the head of the cañon, smoothed a sheltered spot, and gathered a few pine tassels for a bed. After the short twilight began to fade I kindled a sunny fire, made a tin cupful of tea, and lay down to watch the stars. Soon the night-wind began to flow from the snowy peaks overhead, at first only a gentle breathing, then gaining strength, in less than an hour

rumbled in massive volume something like a boisterous stream in a boulder-choked channel, roaring and
moaning down the cañon as if the work it had to do
was tremendously important and fateful; and mingled
with these storm tones were those of the waterfalls on
the north side of the cañon, now sounding distinctly,
now smothered by the heavier cataracts of air, making
a glorious psalm of savage wildness. My fire squirmed
and struggled as if ill at ease, for though in a sheltered nook, detached masses of icy wind often fell like
icebergs on top of it, scattering sparks and coals, so
that I had to keep well back to avoid being burned.
But the big resiny roots and knots of the dwarf pine
could neither be beaten out nor blown away, and the
flames, now rushing up in long lances, now flattened
and twisted on the rocky ground, roared as if trying
to tell the storm stories of the trees they belonged to,
as the light given out was telling the story of the sunshine they had gathered in centuries of summers.

The stars shone clear in the strip of sky between
the huge dark cliffs; and as I lay recalling the lessons
of the day, suddenly the full moon looked down over
the cañon wall, her face apparently filled with eager
concern, which had a startling effect, as if she had
left her place in the sky and had come down to gaze
on me alone, like a person entering one's bedroom. It
was hard to realize that she was in her place in the
sky, and was looking abroad on half the globe, land
and sea, mountains, plains, lakes, rivers, oceans,
ships, cities with their myriads of inhabitants sleeping and waking, sick and well. No, she seemed to be
just on the rim of Bloody Cañon and looking only
at me. This was indeed getting near to Nature. I
remember watching the harvest moon rising above

the oak trees in Wisconsin apparently as big as a
cart-wheel and not farther than half a mile distant.
With these exceptions I might say I never before had
seen the moon, and this night she seemed so full of
life and so near, the effect was marvelously impressive and made me forget the Indians, the great black
rocks above me, and the wild uproar of the winds and
waters making their way down the huge jagged gorge.
Of course I slept but little and gladly welcomed the
dawn over the Mono Desert. By the time I had made
a cupful of tea the sunbeams were pouring through
the cañon, and I set forth, gazing eagerly at the tremendous walls of red slates savagely hacked and
scarred and apparently ready to fall in avalanches
great enough to choke the pass and fill up the chain
of lakelets. But soon its beauties came to view, and I
bounded lightly from rock to rock, admiring the polished bosses shining in the slant sunshine with glorious effect in the general roughness of moraines and
avalanche taluses, even toward the head of the cañon
near the highest fountains of the ice. Here, too, are
most of the lowly plant people seen yesterday on the
other side of the divide now opening their beautiful
eyes. None could fail to glory in Nature's tender care
for them in so wild a place. The little ouzel is flitting from rock to rock along the rapid swirling Cañon
Creek, diving for breakfast in icy pools, and merrily
singing as if the huge rugged avalanche-swept gorge
was the most delightful of all its mountain homes.
Besides a high fall on the north wall of the cañon,
apparently coming direct from the sky, there are
many narrow cascades, bright silvery ribbons zigzagging down the red cliffs, tracing the diagonal cleavage joints of the metamorphic slates, now contracted

and out of sight, now leaping from ledge to ledge in filmy sheets through which the sunbeams sift. And on the main Cañon Creek, to which all these are tributary, is a series of small falls, cascades, and rapids extending all the way down to the foot of the cañon, interrupted only by the lakes in which the tossed and beaten waters rest. One of the finest of the cascades is outspread on the face of a precipice, its waters separated into ribbon-like strips, and woven into a diamond-like pattern by tracing the cleavage joints of the rock, while tufts of bryanthus, grass, sedge, saxifrage form beautiful fringes. Who could imagine beauty so fine in so savage a place? Gardens are blooming in all sorts of nooks and hollows,—at the head alpine eriogonums, erigerons, saxifrages, gentians, cowania, bush primula; in the middle region larkspur, columbine, orthocarpus, castilleia, harebell, epilobium, violets, mints, yarrow; near the foot sunflowers, lilies, brier rose, iris, lonicera, clematis.

One of the smallest of the cascades, which I name the Bower Cascade, is in the lower region of the pass, where the vegetation is snowy and luxuriant. Wild rose and dogwood form dense masses overarching the stream, and out of this bower the creek, grown strong with many indashing tributaries, leaps forth into the light, and descends in a fluted curve thick-sown with crisp flashing spray. At the foot of the cañon there is a lake formed in part at least by the damming of the stream by a terminal moraine. The three other lakes in the cañon are in basins eroded from the solid rock, where the pressure of the glacier was greatest, and the most resisting portions of the basin rims are beautifully, tellingly polished. Below Moraine Lake at the foot of the cañon there are several old lake-basins lying between the large lateral moraines which extend out into the desert. These basins are now completely filled up by the material carried in by the streams, and changed to dry sandy flats covered mostly by grass and artemisia and sun-loving flowers. All these lower lake-basins were evidently formed by terminal moraine dams deposited where the receding glacier had lingered during short periods of less waste, or greater snowfall, or both.

Looking up the cañon from the warm sunny edge of the Mono plain my morning ramble seems a dream, so great is the change in the vegetation and climate. The lilies on the bank of Moraine Lake are higher than my head, and the sunshine is hot enough for palms. Yet the snow round the arctic gardens at the summit of the pass is plainly visible, only about four miles away, and between lie specimen zones of all the principal climates of the globe. In little more than an hour one may swoop down from winter to summer, from an Arctic to a torrid region, through as great changes of climate as one would encounter in traveling from Labrador to Florida.

The Indians I had met near the head of the cañon had camped at the foot of it the night before they made the ascent, and I found their fire still smoking on the side of a small tributary stream near Moraine Lake; and on the edge of what is called the Mono Desert, four or five miles from the lake, I came to a patch of elymus, or wild rye, growing in magnificent waving clumps six or eight feet high, bearing heads six to eight inches long. The crop was ripe, and Indian women were gathering the grain in baskets by bending down large handfuls, beating out the seed, and fanning it in the wind. The grains are about five eighths of an inch long, dark-colored and sweet. I fancy the bread made from it must be as good as wheat bread. A fine squirrel-ish employment this wild grain gathering seems, and the women were evidently enjoying it, laughing and chattering and looking almost natural, though most Indians I have seen are not a whit more natural in their lives than we civilized whites. Perhaps if I knew them better I should like them better. The worst thing about them is their uncleanliness. Nothing truly wild is unclean. Down on the shore of Mono Lake I saw a number of their flimsy huts on the banks of streams that dash swiftly into that dead sea,—mere brush tents where they lie and eat at their ease. Some of the men were feasting on buffalo berries, lying beneath the tall bushes now red with fruit. The berries are rather insipid, but they must needs be wholesome, since for days and weeks the Indians, it is said, eat nothing else. In the season they in like manner depend chiefly on the fat larvæ of a fly that breeds in the salt water of the lake, or on the big fat corrugated caterpil-lars of a species of silkworm that feeds on the leaves of the yellow pine. Occasionally a grand rabbit-drive is organized and hundreds are slain with clubs on the lake shore, chased and frightened into a dense crowd by dogs, boys, girls, men and women, and rings of sage brush fire, when of course they are quickly killed. The skins are made into blankets. In the autumn the more enterprising of the hunters bring in a good many deer, and rarely a wild sheep from the high peaks. Ante-lopes used to be abundant on the desert at the base of the interior mountain-ranges. Sage hens, grouse, and squirrels help to vary their wild diet of worms; pine nuts also from the small interesting *Pinus monophylla*, and good bread and good mush are made from acorns and wild rye. Strange to say, they seem to like the lake larvæ best of all. Long windrows are washed up on the shore, which they gather and dry like grain for winter use. It is said that wars, on account of encroachments on each other's worm-grounds, are of common occurrence among the various tribes and families. Each claims a certain marked portion of the shore. The pine nuts are delicious—large quantities are gathered every autumn. The tribes of the west flank of the range trade acorns for worms and pine nuts. The squaws carry immense loads on their backs across the rough passes and down the range, making journeys of about forty or fifty miles each way.

The desert around the lake is surprisingly flowery. In many places among the sage bushes I saw mentzelia, abronia, aster, bigelovia, and gilia, all of which seemed to enjoy the hot sunshine. The abronia, in particular, is a delicate, fragrant, and most charming plant.

Opposite the mouth of the cañon a range of volcanic cones extends southward from the lake, rising abruptly out of the desert like a chain of mountains. The largest of the cones are about twenty-five hundred feet high above the lake level, have well-formed craters, and all of them are evidently comparatively recent additions to the landscape. At a distance of a few miles they look like heaps of loose ashes that have never been blest by either rain or snow, but, for a' that and a' that, yellow pines are climbing their gray slopes, trying to clothe them and give beauty for ashes. A country of wonderful contrasts. Hot deserts bounded by snow-laden mountains,—cinders and ashes scattered on glacier-polished pavements,—frost and fire working together in the making of beauty. In the lake are several volcanic islands, which show that the waters were once mingled with fire.

Glad to get back to the green side of the mountains, though I have greatly enjoyed the gray east side and hope to see more of it. Reading these grand mountain manuscripts displayed through every vicissitude of heat and cold, calm and storm, upheaving volcanoes and down-grinding glaciers, we see that everything in Nature called destruction must be creation—a change from beauty to beauty.

Our glacier meadow camp north of the Soda Springs seems more beautiful every day. The grass covers all the ground though the leaves are thread-like in fineness, and in walking on the sod it seems like a plush carpet of marvelous richness and softness, and the purple panicles brushing against one's feet are not felt. This is a typical glacier meadow, occupying the basin of a vanished lake, very definitely bounded by walls of the arrowy two-leaved pines drawn up in a handsome orderly array like soldiers on parade. There are many other meadows of the same kind hereabouts imbedded in the woods. The main big meadows along the river are the same in general and extend with but little interruption for ten or twelve miles, but none I have seen are so finely finished and perfect as this one. It is richer in flowering plants than the prairies of Wisconsin and Illinois were when in all their wild glory. The showy flowers are mostly three species of gentian, a purple and yellow orthocarpus, a golden-rod or two, a small blue pentstemon almost like a gentian, potentilla, ivesia, pedicularis, white violet, kalmia, and bryanthus. There are no coarse weedy plants. Through this flowery lawn flows a stream silently gliding, swirling, slipping as if careful not to make the slightest noise. It is only about three feet wide in most places, widening here and there into pools six or eight feet in diameter with no apparent current, the banks bossily rounded by the down-curving mossy sod, grass panicles over-leaning like miniature pine trees, and rugs of bryanthus spreading here and there over sunken boulders. At the foot of the meadow the stream, rich with the juices of the plants it has refreshed, sings merrily down over shelving rock ledges on its way to the Tuolumne River. The sublime, massive Mount Dana and its companions, green, red, and white, loom impressively above the pines along the eastern horizon; a range or spur of gray rugged granite crags and mountains on the north; the curiously crested and battlemented Mount Hoffman on the west; and the Cathedral Range on the south with its grand Cathedral Peak, Cathedral Spires, Unicorn Peak, and several others, gray and pointed or massively rounded.

THE TUOLUMNE CAMP

August 22. Clouds none, cool west wind, slight hoarfrost on the meadows. Carlo is missing; have been seeking him all day. In the thick woods between camp and the river, among tall grass and fallen pines, I discovered a baby fawn. At first it seemed inclined to come to me; but when I tried to catch it, and got within a rod or two, it turned and walked softly away, choosing its steps like a cautious, stealthy, hunting cat. Then, as if suddenly called or alarmed, it began to buck and run like a grown deer, jumping high above the fallen trunks, and was soon out of sight. Possibly its mother may have called it, but I did not hear her. I don't think fawns ever leave the home thicket or follow their mothers until they are called or frightened. I am distressed about Carlo. There are several other camps and dogs not many miles from here, and I still hope to find him. He never left me before. Panthers are very rare here, and I don't think any of these cats would dare touch him. He knows bears too well to be caught by them, and as for Indians, they don't want him.

August 23. Cool, bright day, hinting Indian summer. Mr. Delaney has gone to the Smith Ranch, on the Tuolumne below Hetch-Hetchy Valley, thirty-five or forty miles from here, so I'll be alone for a week or more,—not really alone, for Carlo has come back.

He was at a camp a few miles to the northwestward. He looked sheepish and ashamed when I asked him where he had been and why he had gone away without leave. He is now trying to get me to caress him and show signs of forgiveness. A wondrous wise dog. A great load is off my mind. I could not have left the mountains without him. He seems very glad to get back to me.

Rose and crimson sunset, and soon after the stars appeared the moon rose in most impressive majesty over the top of Mount Dana. I sauntered up the meadow in the white light. The jet-black tree-shadows were so wonderfully distinct and substantial looking, I often stepped high in crossing them, taking them for black charred logs.

August 24. Another charming day, warm and calm soon after sunrise, clouds only about .01,— faint, silky cirrus wisps, scarcely visible. Slight frost, Indian summerish, the mountains growing softer in outline and dreamy looking, their rough angles melted off, apparently. Sky at evening with fine, dark, subdued purple, almost like the evening purple of the San Joaquin plains in settled weather. The moon is now gazing over the summit of Dana. Glorious exhilarating air. I wonder if in all the world there is another mountain range of equal height blessed with weather so fine, and so openly kind and hospitable and approachable.

August 25. Cool as usual in the morning, quickly changing to the ordinary serene generous warmth and brightness. Toward evening the west wind was cool and sent us to the camp-fire. Of all Nature's flowery carpeted mountain halls none can be finer than this glacier meadow. Bees and butterflies seem as abundant as ever. The birds are still here, showing no sign of leaving for winter quarters though the frost must bring them to mind. For my part I should like to stay here all winter or all my life or even all eternity.

August 26. Frost this morning; all the meadow grass and some of the pine needles sparkling with irised crystals,—flowers of light. Large picturesque clouds, craggy like rocks, are piled on Mount Dana, reddish in color like the mountain itself; the sky for a few degrees around the horizon is pale purple, into which the pines dip their spires with fine effect. Spent the day as usual looking about me, watching the changing lights, the ripening autumn colors of the grass, seeds, late-blooming gentians, asters, goldenrods; parting the meadow grass here and there and looking down into the underworld of mosses and liverworts; watching the busy ants and beetles and other small people at work and play like squirrels and bears in a forest; studying the formation of lakes and meadows, moraines, mountain sculpture; making small beginnings in these directions, charmed by the serene beauty of everything.

The day has been extra cloudy, though bright on the whole, for the clouds were brighter than common. Clouds about .15, which in Switzerland would be considered extra clear. Probably more free sunshine falls on this majestic range than on any other in the world I've ever seen or heard of. It has the brightest weather, brightest glacier-polished rocks, the greatest abundance of irised spray from its glorious waterfalls, the brightest forests of silver firs and silver pines, more star-shine, moonshine, and perhaps more crystal-shine than any other mountain chain, and its countless mirror lakes, having more light poured into them, glow and spangle most. And how glorious the shining after the short summer showers and after frosty nights when the morning sunbeams are pouring through the crystals on the grass and pine needles, and how ineffably spiritually fine is the morning-glow on the mountain-tops and the alpenglow of evening. Well may the Sierra be named, not the Snowy Range, but the Range of Light.

August 27. Clouds only .05,—mostly white and pink cumuli over the Hoffman spur towards evening,—frosty morning. Crystals grow in marvelous beauty and perfection of form these still nights, every one built as carefully as the grandest holiest temple, as if planned to endure forever.

Contemplating the lace-like fabric of streams outspread over the mountains, we are reminded that everything is flowing—going somewhere, animals and so-called lifeless rocks as well as water. Thus the snow flows fast or slow in grand beauty-making glaciers and avalanches; the air in majestic floods carrying minerals, plant leaves, seeds, spores, with streams of music and fragrance; water streams carrying rocks both in solution and in the form of mud particles, sand, pebbles, and boulders. Rocks flow from volcanoes like water from springs, and animals flock together and flow in currents modified by stepping, leaping, gliding, flying, swimming, etc. While the stars go streaming through space pulsed on and on forever like blood globules in Nature's warm heart.

August 28. The dawn a glorious song of color. Sky absolutely cloudless. A fine crop of hoarfrost. Warm after ten o'clock. The gentians don't mind the first frost though their petals seem so delicate; they close every night as if going to sleep, and awake fresh as ever in the morning sun-glory. The grass is a shade browner since last week, but there are no nipped wilted plants of any sort as far as I have seen. Butterflies and the grand host of smaller flies are benumbed every night, but they hover and dance in the sunbeams over the meadows before noon with no apparent lack of playful, joyful life. Soon they must all fall like petals in an orchard, dry and wrinkled, not a wing of all the mighty host left to tingle the air. Nevertheless new myriads will arise in the spring, rejoicing, exulting, as if laughing cold death to scorn.

August 29. Clouds about .05, slight frost. Bland serene Indian summer weather. Have been gazing all day at the mountains, watching the changing lights. More and more plainly are they clothed with light as a garment, white tinged with pale purple, palest during the midday hours, richest in the morning and evening. Everything seems consciously peaceful, thoughtful, faithfully waiting God's will.

August 30. This day just like yesterday. A few clouds motionless and apparently with no work to do beyond looking beautiful. Frost enough for crystal building,—glorious fields of ice-diamonds destined to last but a night. How lavish is Nature building, pulling down, creating, destroying, chasing every material particle from form to form, ever changing, ever beautiful.

Mr. Delaney arrived this morning. Felt not a trace of loneliness while he was gone. On the contrary, I never enjoyed grander company. The whole wilderness seems to be alive and familiar, full of humanity. The very stones seem talkative, sympathetic, brotherly. No wonder when we consider that we all have the same Father and Mother.

August 31. Clouds .05. Silky cirrus wisps and fringes so fine they almost escape notice. Frost enough for another crop of crystals on the meadows but none on the forests. The gentians, goldenrods, asters, etc., don't seem to feel it; neither petals nor leaves are touched though they seem so tender. Every day opens and closes like a flower, noiseless, effortless. Divine peace glows on all the majestic landscape like the silent enthusiastic joy that sometimes transfigures a noble human face.

September 1. Clouds .05—motionless, of no particular color—ornaments with no hint of rain or snow in them. Day all calm—an other grand throb of Nature's heart, ripening late flowers and seeds for next summer, full of life and the thoughts and plans of life to come, and full of ripe and ready death beautiful as life, telling divine wisdom and goodness and immortality. Have been up Mount Dana, making haste to see as much as I can now that the time of departure is drawing nigh. The views from the summit reach far and wide, eastward over the Mono Lake and Desert; mountains beyond mountains looking strangely barren and gray and bare like heaps of ashes dumped from the sky. The lake, eight or ten miles in diameter, shines like a burnished disk of silver, no trees about its gray, ashy, cindery shores. Looking westward, the glorious forests are seen sweeping over countless ridges and hills, girdling domes and subordinate mountains, fringing in long curving lines the dividing ridges, and filling every hollow where the glaciers have spread soil-beds however rocky or smooth. Looking northward and southward along the axis of the range, you see the glorious array of high mountains, crags and peaks and snow, the fountain-heads of rivers that are flowing west to the sea through the famous Golden Gate, and east to hot salt lakes and deserts to evaporate and hurry back into the sky. Innumerable lakes are shining like eyes beneath heavy rock brows, bare or tree fringed, or imbedded in black forests. Meadow openings in the woods seem as numerous as the lakes or perhaps more so. Far up the moraine-covered slopes and among crumbling rocks I found many delicate hardy plants, some of them still in flower. The best gains of this trip were the lessons of unity and interrelation of all the features of the landscape revealed in general views. The lakes and meadows are located just where the ancient glaciers bore heaviest at the foot of the steepest parts of their channels, and of course their longest diameters are approximately parallel with each other and with the belts of forests growing in long curving lines on the lateral and medial moraines, and in broad outspreading fields on the terminal beds deposited toward the end of the ice period when the glaciers were receding. The domes, ridges, and spurs also show the influence of glacial action in their forms, which approximately seem to be the forms of greatest strength with reference to the stress of oversweeping, past-sweeping, down-grinding ice-streams; survivals of the most resisting masses, or those most favorably situated. How interesting everything is! Every rock, mountain, stream, plant, lake, lawn, forest, garden, bird, beast, insect seems to call and invite us to come and learn something of its history and relationship. But shall the poor ignorant scholar be allowed to try the lessons they offer? It seems too great and good to be true. Soon I'll be going to the lowlands. The bread camp must soon be removed. If I had a few sacks of flour, an axe, and some matches, I would build a cabin of pine logs, pile up plenty of firewood about it and stay all winter to see the grand fertile snow-storms, watch the birds and animals that winter thus high, how they live, how the forests look snow-laden or buried, and how the avalanches look and sound on their way down the mountains. But now I'll have to go, for there is nothing to spare in the way of provisions. I'll surely be back, however, surely I'll be back. No other place has ever so overwhelmingly attracted me as this hospitable, Godful wilderness.

September 2. A grand, red, rosy, crimson day,—a perfect glory of a day. What it means I don't know. It is the first marked change from tranquil sunshine with purple mornings and evenings and still, white noons. There is nothing like a storm, however. The average cloudiness only about .08, and there is no sighing in the woods to betoken a big weather change. The sky was red in the morning and evening, the color not diffused like the ordinary purple glow, but loaded upon separate well-defined clouds that remained motionless, as if anchored around the jagged mountain-fenced horizon. A deep-red cap, bluffy around its sides, lingered a long time on Mount Dana and Mount Gibbs, drooping so low as to hide most of their bases, but leaving

Dana's round summit free, which seemed to float separate and alone over the big crimson cloud. Mammoth Mountain, to the south of Gibbs and Bloody Cañon, striped and spotted with snow-banks and clumps of dwarf pine, was also favored with a glorious crimson cap, in the making of which there was no trace of economy—a huge bossy pile colored with a perfect passion of crimson that seemed important enough to be sent off to burn among the stars in majestic independence. One is constantly reminded of the infinite lavishness and fertility of Nature—inexhaustible abundance amid what seems enormous waste. And yet when we look into any of her operations that lie within reach of our minds, we learn that no particle of her material is wasted or worn out. It is eternally flowing from use to use, beauty to yet higher beauty; and we soon cease to lament waste and death, and rather rejoice and exult in the imperishable, unspendable wealth of the universe, and faithfully watch and wait the reappearance of everything that melts and fades and dies about us, feeling sure that its next appearance will be better and more beautiful than the last.

I watched the growth of these red-lands of the sky as eagerly as if new mountain ranges were being built. Soon the group of snowy peaks in whose recesses lie the highest fountains of the Tuolumne, Merced, and North Fork of the San Joaquin were decorated with majestic colored clouds like those already described, but more complicated, to correspond with the grand fountain-heads of the rivers they overshadowed. The Sierra Cathedral, to the south of camp, was overshadowed like Sinai. Never before noticed so fine a union of rock and cloud in form and color and substance, drawing earth and sky together as one; and so human is it, every feature and tint of color goes to one's heart, and we shout, exulting in wild enthusiasm as if all the divine show were our own. More and more, in a place like this, we feel ourselves part of wild Nature, kin to everything. Spent most of the day high up on the north rim of the valley, commanding views of the clouds in all their red glory spreading their wonderful light over all the basin, while the rocks and trees and small Alpine plants at my feet seemed hushed and thoughtful, as if they also were conscious spectators of the glorious new cloud-world.

Here and there, as I plodded farther and higher, I came to small garden-patches and ferneries just where one would naturally decide that no plant-creature could possibly live. But, as in the region about the head of Mono Pass and the top of Dana, it was in the wildest, highest places that the most beautiful and tender and enthusiastic plant-people were found. Again and again, as I lingered over these charming plants, I said, How came you here? How do you live through the winter? Our roots, they explained, reach far down the joints of the summer-warmed rocks, and beneath our fine snow mantle killing frosts cannot reach us, while we sleep away the dark half of the year dreaming of spring.

Ever since I was allowed entrance into these mountains I have been looking for cassiope, said to be the most beautiful and best loved of the heathworts, but, strange to say, I have not yet found it. On my high mountain walks I keep muttering, "Cassiope, cassiope." This name, as Calvinists say, is driven in upon me, notwithstanding the glorious host of plants that come about me uncalled as soon as I show myself. Cassiope seems the highest name of all the small mountain-heath people, and as if conscious of her worth, keeps out of my way. I must find her soon, if at all this year.

September 4. All the vast sky dome is clear, filled only with mellow Indian summer light. The pine and hemlock and fir cones are nearly ripe and are falling fast from morning to night, cut off and gathered by the busy squirrels. Almost all the plants have matured their seeds, their summer work done; and the summer crop of birds and deer will soon be able to follow their parents to the foothills and plains at the approach of winter, when the snow begins to fly.

September 5. No clouds. Weather cool, calm, bright as if no great thing was yet ready to be done. Have been sketching the North Tuolumne Church. The sunset gloriously colored.

September 6. Still another perfectly cloudless day, purple evening and morning, all the middle hours one mass of pure serene sunshine. Soon after sunrise the air grew warm, and there was no wind. One naturally halted to see what Nature intended to do. There is a suggestion of real Indian summer in the hushed, brooding, faintly hazy weather. The yellow atmosphere, though thin, is still plainly of the same general character as that of eastern Indian summer. The peculiar mellowness is perhaps in part caused by myriads of ripe spores adrift in the sky.

Mr. Delaney now keeps up a solemn talk about the need of getting away from these high mountains, telling sad stories of flocks that perished in storms that broke suddenly into the midst of fine innocent weather like this we are now enjoying. "In no case," said he, "will I venture to stay so high and far back in the mountains as we now are later than the middle of this month, no matter how warm and sunny it may be." He would move the flock slowly at first, a few miles a day until the Yosemite Creek basin was reached and crossed, then while lingering in the heavy pine woods should the weather threaten he could hurry down to the foothills, where the snow never falls deep enough to smother a sheep. Of course I am anxious to see as much of the wilderness as possible in the few days left me, and I say again,—May the good time come when I can stay as long as I like with plenty of bread, far and free from trampling flocks, though I may well be thankful for this generous foodful inspiring summer. Anyhow we never know where we must go nor what guides we are to get,—men, storms, guardian angels, or sheep. Perhaps almost everybody in the least natural is guarded more than he is ever aware of. All the wilderness seems to be full of tricks and plans to drive and draw us up into God's Light.

Have been busy planning, and baking bread for at least one more good wild excursion among the high peaks, and surely none, however hopefully aiming at fortune or fame, ever felt so gloriously happily excited by the outlook.

September 7. Left camp at daybreak and made direct for Cathedral Peak, intending to strike eastward and southward from that point among the peaks and ridges at the heads of the Tuolumne, Merced, and San Joaquin Rivers. Down through the pine woods I made my way, across the Tuolumne River and meadows, and up the heavily timbered slope forming the south boundary of the upper Tuolumne basin, along the east side of Cathedral Peak, and up to its topmost spire, which I reached at noon, having loitered by the way to study the fine trees—two-leaved pine, mountain pine, albicaulis pine, silver fir, and the most charming, most graceful of all the evergreens, the mountain hemlock. High, cool, late-flowering meadows also detained me, and lakelets and avalanche tracks and huge quarries of moraine rocks above the forests.

All the way up from the Big Meadows to the base of the Cathedral the ground is covered with moraine material, the left lateral moraine of the great glacier that must have completely filled this upper Tuolumne basin. Higher there are several small terminal moraines of residual glaciers shoved forward at right angles against the grand simple lateral of the main Tuolumne Glacier. A fine place to study mountain sculpture and soil making. The view from the Cathedral Spires is very fine and telling in every direction. Innumerable peaks, ridges, domes, meadows, lakes, and woods; the forests extending in long curving lines and broad fields wherever the glaciers have left soil for them to grow on, while the sides of the highest mountains show a straggling dwarf growth clinging to rifts in the rocks apparently independent of soil. The dark heath-like growth on the Cathedral roof I found to be dwarf snow-pressed albicaulis pine, about three or four feet high, but very old looking. Many of them are bearing cones, and the noisy Clarke crow is eating the seeds, using his long bill like a woodpecker in digging them out of the cones. A good many flowers are still in bloom about the base of the peak, and even on the roof among the little pines, especially a woody yellow-flowered eriogonum and a handsome aster. The body of the Cathedral is nearly square, and the roof slopes are wonderfully regular and symmetrical, the ridge trending northeast and southwest. This direction has apparently been determined by structure joints in the granite. The gable on the northeast end is magnificent in size and simplicity, and at its base there is a big snow-bank protected by the shadow of the building. The front is adorned with many pinnacles and a tall spire of curious workmanship. Here too the joints in the rock are seen to have played an important part in determining their forms and size and general arrangement. The Cathedral is said to be about eleven thousand feet above the sea, but the height of the building itself above the level of the ridge it stands on is about fifteen hundred feet. A mile or so to the westward there is a handsome lake, and the glacier-polished granite about it is shining so brightly it is not easy in some places to trace the line between the rock and water, both shining alike. Of this lake with its silvery basin and bits of meadow and groves I have a fine view from the spires; also of Lake Tenaya, Cloud's Rest and the South Dome of Yosemite, Mount Starr King, Mount Hoffman, the Merced peaks, and the vast multitude of snowy fountain peaks extending far north and south along the axis of the range. No feature, however, of all the noble landscape as seen from here seems more wonderful than the Cathedral itself, a temple displaying Nature's best masonry and sermons in stones. How often I have gazed at it from the tops of hills and ridges, and through openings in the forests on my many short excursions, devoutly wondering, admiring, longing! This I may say is the first time I have been at church in California, led here at last, every door graciously opened for the poor lonely worshiper. In our best times everything turns into religion, all the world seems a church and the mountains altars. And lo, here at last in front of the Cathedral is blessed cassiope, ringing her thousands of sweet-toned bells, the sweetest church music I ever enjoyed. Listening, admiring, until late in the afternoon I compelled myself to hasten away eastward back of rough, sharp, spiry, splintery peaks, all of them granite like the Cathedral, sparkling with crystals—feldspar, quartz, hornblende, mica, tourmaline. Had a rather difficult walk and creep across an immense snow and ice cliff which gradually increased in steepness as I advanced until it was almost impassable. Slipped on a dangerous place, but managed to stop by digging my heels into the thawing surface just on the brink of a yawning ice gulf. Camped beside a little pool and a group of crinkled dwarf pines; and as I sit by the fire trying to write notes the shallow pool seems fathomless with the infinite starry heavens in it, while the onlooking rocks and trees, tiny shrubs and daisies and sedges, brought forward in the fire-glow, seem full of thought as if about to speak aloud and tell all their wild stories. A marvelously impressive meeting in which every one has something worth while to tell. And beyond the fire-beams out in the solemn darkness, how impressive is the music of a choir of rills singing their way down from the snow to the river! And when we call to mind that thousands of these rejoicing rills are assembled in each one of the main streams, we wonder the less that our Sierra rivers are songful all the way to the sea.

About sundown saw a flock of dun grayish sparrows going to roost in crevices of a crag above the big snow-field. Charming little mountaineers! Found a species of sedge in flower within eight or ten feet of a snow-bank. Judging by the looks of the ground, it can hardly have been out in the sunshine much longer than a week, and it is likely to be buried again in fresh snow in a month or so, thus making a winter about ten months long, while spring, summer, and autumn are crowded and hurried into two months. How delightful it is to be alone here! How wild everything is—wild as the sky and as pure! Never shall I forget this big, divine day—the Cathedral and its thousands of cassiope bells, and the landscapes around them, and this camp in the gray crags above the woods, with its stars and streams and snow.

September 8. Day of climbing, scrambling, sliding on the peaks around the highest source of the Tuolumne and Merced. Climbed three of the most commanding of the mountains, whose names I don't know; crossed streams and huge beds of ice and snow more than I could keep count of. Neither could I keep count of the lakes scattered on tablelands and in the cirques of the peaks, and in chains in the cañons, linked together by the streams—a tremendously wild gray wilderness of hacked, shattered crags, ridges, and peaks, a few clouds drifting over and through the midst of them as if looking for work. In general views all the immense round landscape seems raw and lifeless as a quarry, yet the most charming flowers were found rejoicing in countless nooks and garden-like patches everywhere. I must have done three or four days' climbing work in this one. Limbs perfectly tireless until near sundown, when I descended into the main upper Tuolumne valley at the foot of Mount Lyell, the camp still eight or ten miles distant. Going up through the pine woods past the Soda Springs Dome in the dark, where there is much fallen timber, and when all the excitement of seeing things was wanting, I was tired. Arrived at the main camp at nine o'clock, and soon was sleeping sound as death.

BACK TO THE LOWLANDS

September 9. Weariness rested away and I feel eager and ready for another excursion a month or two long in the same wonderful wilderness. Now, however, I must turn toward the lowlands, praying and hoping Heaven will shove me back again.

The most telling thing learned in these mountain excursions is the influence of cleavage joints on the features sculptured from the general mass of the range. Evidently the denudation has been enormous, while the inevitable outcome is subtle balanced beauty. Comprehended in general views, the features of the wildest landscape seem to be as harmoniously related as the features of a human face. Indeed, they look human and radiate spiritual beauty, divine thought, however covered and concealed by rock and snow.

Mr. Delaney has hardly had time to ask me how I enjoyed my trip, though he has facilitated and encouraged my plans all summer, and declares I'll be famous some day, a kind guess that seems strange and incredible to a wandering wilderness-lover with never a thought or dream of fame while humbly trying to trace and learn and enjoy Nature's lessons.

The camp stuff is now packed on the horses, and the flock is headed for the home ranch. Away we go, down through the pines, leaving the lovely lawn where we have camped so long. I wonder if I'll ever see it again. The sod is so tough and close it is scarcely at all injured by the sheep. Fortunately they are not fond of silky glacier meadow grass. The day is perfectly clear, not a cloud or the faintest hint of a cloud is visible, and there is no wind. I wonder if in all the world, at a height of nine thousand feet, weather so steadily, faithfully calm and bright and hospitable may anywhere else be found. We are going away fearing destructive storms, though it is difficult to conceive weather changes so great.

Though the water is now low in the river, the usual difficulty occurred in getting the flock across it. Every sheep seemed to be invincibly determined to die any sort of dry death rather than wet its feet. Carlo has learned the sheep business as perfectly as the best shepherd, and it is interesting to watch his intelligent efforts to push or frighten the silly creatures into the water. They had to be fairly crowded and shoved over the bank; and when at last one crossed because it could not push its way back, the whole flock suddenly plunged in headlong together, as if the river was the only desirable part of the world. Aside from mere money profit one would rather herd wolves than sheep. As soon as they clambered up the opposite bank, they began baaing and feeding as if nothing unusual had happened. We crossed the meadows and drove slowly up the south rim of the valley through the same woods I had passed on my way to Cathedral Peak, and camped for the night by the side of a small pond on top of the big lateral moraine.

September 10. In the morning at daybreak not one of the two thousand sheep was in sight. Examining the tracks, we discovered that they had been scattered, perhaps by a bear. In a few hours all were found and gathered into one flock again. Had fine view of a deer. How graceful and perfect in every way it seemed as compared with the silly, dusty, tousled sheep! From the high ground hereabouts had another grand view to the northward—a heaving, swelling sea of domes and round-backed ridges fringed with pines, and bounded by innumerable sharp-pointed peaks, gray and barren-looking, though so full of beautiful life. Another day of the calm, cloudless kind, purple in the morning and evening. The evening glow has been very marked for the last two or three weeks. Perhaps the "zodiacal light."

September 11. Cloudless. Slight frost. Calm. Fairly started downhill, and now are camped at the west end meadows of Lake Tenaya—a charming place. Lake smooth as glass, mirroring its miles of glacier-polished pavements and bold mountain walls. Find aster still in flower. Here is about the upper limit of the dwarf form of the goldcup oak,—eight thousand feet above sea-level,—reaching about two thousand feet higher than the California black oak (*Quercus Californica*). Lovely evening, the lake reflections after dark marvelously impressive.

September 12. Cloudless day, all pure sun-gold. Among the magnificent silver firs once more, within two miles of the brink of Yosemite, at the famous Portuguese bear camp. Chaparral of goldcup oak, manzanita, and ceanothus abundant hereabouts, wanting about the Tuolumne meadows, although the elevation is but little higher there. The two-leaved pine, though far more abundant about the Tuolumne meadow region, reaches its greatest size on stream-sides hereabouts and around meadows that are rather boggy. All the best dry ground is taken by the magnificent silver fir, which here reaches its greatest size and forms a well-defined belt. A glorious tree. Have fine bed of its boughs to-night.

September 13. Camp this evening at Yosemite Creek, close to the stream, on a little sand flat near our old camp-ground. The vegetation is already brown and yellow and dry; the creek almost dry also. The slender form of the two-leaved pine on its banks is, I think, the handsomest I have anywhere seen. It might easily pass at first sight for a distinct species, though surely only a variety (*Murrayana*), due to crowded and rapid growth on good soil. The yellow pine is as variable, or perhaps more so. The form here and a thousand feet higher, on crumbling rocks, is broad branching, with closely furrowed, reddish bark, large cones, and long leaves. It is one of the hardiest of pines, and has wonderful vitality. The tassels of long, stout needles shining silvery in the sun, when the wind is blowing them all in the same direction, is one of the most splendid spectacles these glorious Sierra forests have to show. This variety of *Pinus ponderosa* is regarded as a distinct species, *Pinus Jeffreyi*, by some botanists. The basin of this famous Yosemite stream is extremely rocky,—seems fairly to be paved with domes like a street with big cobblestones. I wonder if I shall ever be allowed to explore it. It draws me so strongly, I would make any sacrifice to try to read its lessons. I thank God for this glimpse of it. The charms of these mountains are beyond all common reason, unexplainable and mysterious as life itself.

September 14. Nearly all day in magnificent fir forest, the top branches laden with superb erect gray cones shining with beads of pure balsam. The squirrels are cutting them off at a great rate. Bump, bump, I hear them falling, soon to be gathered and stored for winter bread. Those that chance to be left by the industrious harvesters drop the scales and bracts when fully ripe, and it is fine to see the purple-winged seeds flying in swirling, merry-looking flocks seeking their fortunes. The bole and dead limbs of nearly every tree in the main forest-belt are ornamented by conspicuous tufts and strips of a yellow lichen.

Camped for the night at Cascade Creek, near the Mono Trail crossing. Manzanita berries now ripe. Cloudiness to-day about .10. The sunset very rich, flaming purple and crimson showing gloriously through the aisles of the woods.

September 15. The weather pure gold, cloudiness about .05, white cirrus flecks and pencilings around the horizon. Move two or three miles and camp at Tamarack Flat. Wandering in the woods here back of the pines which bound the meadows, I found very noble specimens of the magnificent silver fir, the tallest about two hundred and forty feet high and five feet in diameter four feet from the ground.

September 16. Crawled slowly four or five miles to-day through the glorious forest to Crane Flat, where we are camped for the night. The forests we so admired in summer seem still more beautiful and sublime in this mellow autumn light. Lovely starry night, the tall, spiring tree-tops relieved in jet black against the sky. I linger by the fire, loath to go to bed.

September 17. Left camp early. Ran over the Tuolumne divide and down a few miles to a grove of sequoias that I had heard of, directed by the Don. They occupy an area of perhaps less than a hundred acres. Some of the trees are noble, colossal old giants, surrounded by magnificent sugar pines and Douglas spruces. The perfect specimens not burned or broken are singularly regular and symmetrical, though not at all conventional, showing infinite variety in general unity and harmony; the noble shafts with rich purplish brown fluted bark, free of limbs for one hundred and fifty feet or so, ornamented here and there with leafy rosettes; main branches of the oldest trees very large, crooked and rugged, zigzagging stiffly outward seemingly lawless, yet unexpectedly stooping just at the right distance from the trunk and dissolving in dense bossy masses of branchlets, thus making a regular though greatly varied outline,—a cylinder of leafy, outbulging spray masses, terminating in a noble dome, that may be recognized while yet far off upheaved against the sky above the dark bed of pines and firs and spruces, the king of all conifers, not only in size but in sublime majesty of behavior and port. I found a black, charred stump about thirty feet in diameter and eighty or ninety feet high—a venerable, impressive old monument of a tree that in its prime may have been the monarch of the grove; seedlings and saplings growing up here and there, thrifty and hopeful, giving no hint of the dying out of the species. Not any unfavorable change of climate, but only fire, threatens the existence of these noblest of God's trees. Sorry I was not able to get a count of the old monument's annual rings.

Camp this evening at Hazel Green, on the broad back of the dividing ridge near our old camp-ground when we were on the way up the mountains in the spring. This ridge has the finest sugar-pine groves and finest manzanita and ceanothus thickets I have yet found on all this wonderful summer journey.

September 18. Made a long descent on the south side of the divide to Brown's Flat, the grand forests now left above us, though the sugar pine still flourishes fairly well, and with the yellow pine, libocedrus, and Douglas spruce, makes forests that would be considered most wonderful in any other part of the world.

The Indians here, with great concern, pointed to an old garden patch on the flat and told us to keep away from it. Perhaps some of their tribe are buried here.

September 19. Camped this evening at Smith's Mill, on the first broad mountain bench or plateau reached in ascending the range, where pines grow large enough for good lumber. Here wheat, apples, peaches, and grapes grow, and we were treated to wine and apples. The wine I didn't like, but Mr. Delaney and the Indian driver and the shepherd seemed to think the stuff divine. Compared to sparkling Sierra water fresh from the heavens, it seemed a dull, muddy, stupid drink. But the apples, best of fruits, how delicious they were—fit for gods or men.

On the way down from Brown's Flat we stopped at Bower Cave, and I spent an hour in it—one of the most novel and interesting of all Nature's underground mansions. Plenty of sunlight pours into it through the leaves of the four maple trees growing in its mouth, illuminating its clear, calm pool and marble chambers,—a charming place, ravishingly beautiful, but the accessible parts of the walls sadly disfigured with names of vandals.

September 20. The weather still golden and calm, but hot. We are now in the foot-hills, and all the conifers are left behind, except the gray Sabine pine. Camped at the Dutch Boy's Ranch, where there are extensive barley fields now showing nothing save dusty stubble.

September 21. A terribly hot, dusty, sunburned day, and as nothing was to be gained by loitering where the flock could find nothing to eat save thorny twigs and chaparral, we made a long drive, and before sundown reached the home ranch on the yellow San Joaquin plain.

September 22. The sheep were let out of the corral one by one, this morning, and counted, and strange to say, after all their adventurous wanderings in bewildering rocks and brush and streams, scattered by bears, poisoned by azalea, kalmia, alkali, all are accounted for. Of the two thousand and fifty that left the corral in the spring lean and weak, two thousand and twenty-five have returned fat and strong. The losses are: ten killed by bears, one by a rattlesnake, one that had to be killed after it had broken its leg on a boulder slope, and one that ran away in blind terror on being accidentally separated from the flock,— thirteen all told. Of the other twelve doomed never to return, three were sold to ranchmen and nine were made camp mutton.

Here ends my forever memorable first High Sierra excursion. I have crossed the Range of Light, surely the brightest and best of all the Lord has built; and rejoicing in its glory, I gladly, gratefully, hopefully pray I may see it again.

The End

Also Available

Continue your journey with adventure writers and literary naturalists, from Gibbs Smith:

Wild Animals I Have Known
By Ernest Thompson Seton
Hardcover, $16.99
ISBN: 978-1-4236-5488-9

Nature and Other Essays
By Ralph Waldo Emerson
Hardcover, $16.99
ISBN: 978-1-4236-5269-4

Canoeing in the Wilderness
By Henry David Thoreau
Hardcover, $14.99
ISBN: 978-1-4236-4914-4

Walden: Life in the Woods
By Henry David Thoreau
Hardcover, $16.99
ISBN: 978-1-4236-4679-2

Natural History Essays
By Henry David Thoreau
Hardcover, $16.99
ISBN: 978-1-4236-2228-4

Leaves of Grass
By Walt Whitman
Hardcover, $16.99
ISBN: 978-1-4236-4774-4

Call of the Wild
By Jack London
Hardcover, $14.99
ISBN: 978-1-4236-4677-8

Roughing It
By Mark Twain
Hardcover, $16.99
ISBN: 978-1-4236-4772-0

The Grand Canyon Expedition
By John Wesley Powell
Hardcover, $16.99
ISBN: 978-1-4236-5166-6

GIBBS SMITH
TO ENRICH AND INSPIRE HUMANKIND

JOHN MUIR

WILDERNESS ESSAYS

JOHN MUIR

WILDERNESS ESSAYS

GIBBS SMITH
TO ENRICH AND INSPIRE HUMANKIND

Revised Edition
26 25 24 23 22   27 26 25 24 23

Published by
Gibbs Smith
P.O. Box 667
Layton, Utah 84041

1.800.835.4993 orders
www.gibbs-smith.com

Cover art by Seth Lucas
Printed and bound in China

Gibbs Smith books are printed on either recycled, 100% post-consumer
waste, FSC-certified papers or on paper produced from sustainable PEFC-
certified forest/controlled wood source. Learn more at www.pefc.org.

The Library of Congress has cataloged the earlier edition as follows:

Muir, John. 1838–1914.
Wilderness essays.

(Literature of the American wilderness)
1. Natural history—United States—Addresses, essays, lectures.
I. Title. II. Series.
QH104.M85   917.9'042   80-10844

ISBN: 0-87905-072-1 (first edition)
ISBN: 978-1-4236-0712-0 (updated edition)

CONTENTS

In 1975, during spring quarter at the University of California, Davis, I taught a course for the Division of Environmental Studies called "Nature Writers in Nineteenth-Century America." The final works the students read were by John Muir: *The Mountains of California* and several of the essays included in this volume, "Twenty Hill Hollow," "Wild Wool," and "The Animals of Yosemite."

The next weekend the class and I travelled to Yosemite, which had provided much of the material for *The Mountains of California,* to look at—and try to see—the things that Muir had seen and described. We found a water ouzel's nest, with newly-hatched young, under a footbridge over the Merced River; we walked close to Yosemite Falls and found the place where Muir had once built a cabin; we saw Half Dome and climbers on El Capitan. That night we sat atop Sentinel Dome and listened to the music of the waterfalls as the stars came out; the next morning we had breakfast at Glacier Point and fed the birds and animals that gathered in friendly fashion around us. If we had been less inhibited, we might have exalted, as Muir once did upon returning from a trip to the High Sierras: "It is still the morning of creation, the morning stars are singing together and all

WILDERNESS ESSAYS

the Sons of God shouting for joy!"

Who was this man John Muir whose words, written scores of years before, still had the power to move readers to try to appreciate the wonders of the world as he saw them? My own interest in Muir was rather easily explained: I had grown up on a farm in Wisconsin not far from the region in which Muir, his parents and brothers and sisters, had cleared a homestead in the wilderness. Later, after moving to Alaska, I had travelled through the same areas to which Muir had thrilled on his early visits there and saw the huge ice masses still sculpting the landscape, the glacier mills still grinding the rocks into soil, the mountain fountains in ceaseless flow. The air was still soft and like a poultice; the land and waters still teemed with plant and animal life. Much had changed, but it was still a land John Muir would have recognized and in which he would have felt comfortable.

John Muir, born in Scotland in 1838, crossed the Atlantic in a sailing ship in 1849 with his father Daniel, his brother David, and his sister Sarah. After they had settled in Wisconsin, clearing the land and building a house, the rest of the family joined them: Mrs. Muir, two brothers and a sister.

For the next ten years, John Muir knew a life that would have been familiar to any pioneer on any of America's frontiers. Although he had attended school regularly in Scotland, there was time for only two months of formal education during

INTRODUCTION

the next decade. He was too busy with the breaking plow, chiselling a well through a thick limestone layer (and nearly losing his life when gas collected in the bottom of the excavation), and doing all the other chores normal to making a living under those circumstances. Daniel Muir believed that the good life, for his sons and daughters, consisted of long hours of hard work during the day and learning Bible verses at night. In Scotland, Muir had read whenever possible, as much as he could, and although his father believed that the Bible was the only book human beings could possibly require throughout their journey from earth to heaven, he did relent when he could be persuaded of the strong moral purpose of a work. Milton and Shakespeare were permitted, but Plutarch was forbidden until Muir suggested that the work might contain valuable dietary advice (this at a time when his father was attempting to enforce strict vegetarianism on the family).

And yet life on the frontier did have its rewards. In writing of "that glorious Wisconsin wilderness" in *The Story of My Boyhood and Youth*, Muir spoke of the "sudden plash into pure wildness—baptism in Nature's warm heart," and of the lessons in nature that he and his brothers and sisters learned. These experiences became the solid background for the life he would later choose to lead.

Muir left home in the autumn of 1860 without any clear purpose in mind except to display his inventions at the state fair in Madison. Early in

WILDERNESS ESSAYS

1861, just short of his twenty-third birthday, he entered the University of Wisconsin after a brief preparatory course to make up for his lack of formal schooling.

At the university, Muir signed up for courses with James Davie Butler, professor of classics, and Ezra Slocum Carr, professor of natural history, both of whom befriended Muir and were to influence him profoundly. In addition, he met Carr's wife, Jean, an intelligent and energetic woman with a strong interest in botany and plant collecting. During their years in Madison, the Carrs had met and become friends with America's most eminent transcendentalist, Ralph Waldo Emerson, on one of his lecture trips to that city. Mrs. Carr read Muir Emerson's poem, "Woodnotes," and introduced him to other works of Emerson and to the writings of Henry David Thoreau. She also introduced him to those of her friends in Madison who shared her interests in nature and the relationship of God and man to it.

Muir's years at the University were an exhilarating and liberating experience; they were also times of difficulty for him. Desperately poor—he received no help from his father—he worked at whatever jobs he could find to try to stay in school, even teaching one winter in a grammar school in a small community near Madison. Also, the Civil War had broken out; he was appalled by the senselessness of war and troubled by his visits to young men from his home neighborhood whom he visited at a camp

INTRODUCTION

near Madison. It must have occured to him that he might be called to serve. After deciding to enter medical school at the University of Michigan, he set out in June of 1863 on a plant-gathering summer's ramble through Indiana and Michigan, finally making his way to Canada.

The ramble lasted for four years. Muir stopped at least twice during this time to work in factories, putting his inventive talents to work to improve production. He might, in fact, have had a successful career in industry. But when a dropped file was propelled into his eye by a moving belt and he nearly lost his sight, Muir decided to devote his life to a study of the natural world.

During his travels, Muir collected plant specimens and kept up a correspondence with Mrs. Carr. In a letter to her, written while recovering from his eye injury, he recalled that he had read an account of the Yosemite Valley the year before, and the two of them discussed in subsequent letters the possibility that one day the Carrs and Muir would, in fact, see Yosemite Valley. In good health again, Muir returned to Wisconsin to say goodbye to his family and shortly thereafter began the journey that took him to California.

It was in September, 1867, that Muir left Indianapolis to begin his 1,000 mile walk to the Gulf of Mexico, a journey that he expected to continue on to the Amazon in South America. He carried in his pack small volumes of the poems of Robert Burns, Milton's *Paradise Lost*, the New Testament, and a journal on the inside cover of which he had written, "John Muir, Earth-Planet, Universe." Professor Butler had urged him years before to keep a journal; he was now ready to heed that advice.

The journal that Muir kept during his walk was his first conscious literary effort, his first attempt to express what he saw and what he felt about what he saw. The South, and the people who lived there, then in the troubled times of the Reconstruction, did not interest him nearly as much as the new plants he was seeing. He put down his skepticism about the importance of man in the universe: "Why should man value himself as more than a small part of the great creation?" True, the universe would be incomplete without man, but it would also be incomplete without even the smallest microscopic creature. Man had arrived rather late on planet earth and would one day take his place among creatures that had once existed and had since returned to dust.

By the time Muir reached Cuba, he had suffered two attacks of fever which left him too weak for strenuous travel. His money was running low; he took passage to California by way of Panama and a connecting ship to San Francisco. Upon arrival there, he started to walk eastward, toward the Sierras, which became for him the "Range of Light." To support himself, he took a job herding sheep—"hoofed locusts" he would call them later—and began his systematic study of the Yosemite

INTRODUCTION

region.

The official version of the origin of Yosemite Valley, promulgated by Dr. Josiah Whitney, California State Geologist, was that some cataclysm had caused the formation of the huge valley; Muir became convinced that glacial action had been responsible for carving it. Learning of Muir's theories, Whitney dismissed Muir as "a mere sheepherder"; but other scientists were more impressed: Joseph Le Conte, professor of geology at the University of California, and John Daniel Runkle, president of the Massachusetts Institute of Technology, who offered him a position teaching at his school. Muir's theories were beginning to gain acceptance.

In 1869, Professor Carr resigned his professorship at the University of Wisconsin and the Carrs moved west to Oakland. Muir's correspondence with Mrs. Carr had continued, but now the friends could exchange visits as well. In addition to sending Muir letters, Mrs. Carr also sent him visitors, the most famous of these being Ralph Waldo Emerson who arrived in the valley in May, 1871. It would be interesting to know what the two men talked about, but neither man ever wrote a detailed account of their conversations. The two became friends; Emerson wanted Muir to come back to the east coast to spread his knowledge about glacial action, but Muir felt that his work in the Yosemite was not yet complete. Muir sent Emerson cedar boughs with blossoms; Emerson sent Muir books. Late in life, Emerson added John Muir's name to his list of "My Men," men who had had the greatest effect on him.

From the beginning of his studies in Yosemite Valley, friends had urged Muir to publish accounts of his findings and theories. It was a period during which the nature essay was gaining in popularity: during the 1860s, collections of Thoreau's essays had come into print and John Burroughs was beginning to write his essays about familiar birds, animals and plants. Muir had sent several accounts of his experiences in Yosemite Valley to the New York *Tribune,* all of which had been published. Mrs. Carr was particularly anxious that Muir write not only articles, but possibly even a book, detailing his glacier theories and observations, though she did have some reservations about the lack of polish in his writing style. Finally, Muir came down from the mountains and began to organize his materials and to put them into articles. The *Overland Monthly* began printing them in April, 1872.

At this stage in his life, Muir certainly did not regard himself as a literary figure of any kind—the fact that he had to so regard himself in later years was painful to him. But he had always been fond of words and the way they could be used, and he had a gift for precise observation and the ability to express his thoughts in vivid imagery. Early in his life he had made the discovery "that the poetry of the Bible, Shakespeare, and Milton was a source of inspiring, exhilarating, uplifting pleasure." The

INTRODUCTION

nature essay was probably as congenial a genre as he could have found.

"Twenty Hill Hollow," which appeared in the *Overland Monthly* in July, 1872, describes a spot Muir had visited during his first summer in California. Muir's piece gives a careful description of the geology of the area, the plants, animals, birds, and weather to be found there, but it is the conclusion that startles. Muir writes that for a visitor, "plain, sky, and mountains ray beauty which you feel. You bathe in these spirit-beams.... Presently you lose consciousness of your own separate existence; you blend with the landscape, and become part and parcel of nature." This state of mystic communion with nature was very like the transparent eyeball that Emerson had described in his important essay, "Nature."

Early in his studies in the Yosemite, Muir formulated his most famous image, the metaphor of mountains as "fountains of men." The process began with one of the simplest of all of nature's manifestations, the snowflake (he called them "snowflowers"). The snowflakes fell, accumulating in huge layers over the land. When the climate warmed, these great snow masses, now compressed into ice as glaciers, began to melt and to move, becoming a powerful sculpting force that carved the mountains into ridges and canyons and becoming, too, a mighty mill that ground the rocks into soils. The water from the melting carried these soils down slope, depositing them in meadows and

WILDERNESS ESSAYS

on flatlands where plants and trees began to grow. Soon animals came to live in these areas, then men. And the process was continuous. Wherever there were glaciers, the world was in a constant state of creation. Snowflowers also provided man with another kind of beauty, however. When conditions were right, the wind picked up these snowflowers, whirled them through the air, and they streamed from the mountain tops in long snow banners, fluttering against a vivid, clear blue sky.

In "A Near View of the High Sierra," Muir presents one of his most artful pieces of writing. He begins with an almost painterly (he made many fine, quick sketches during his travels) description of the Sierras in autumn while returning to the Yosemite Valley. There he meets two painters who want to do some sketching so he guides them to a place where they will find the kinds of scenery they wish to draw. Then he leaves them to make an ascent of Mount Ritter. When he reaches the top he beholds a panorama they will never be able to see or to paint and the contrast between the two painters who are satisfied with the part and with Muir who sees the whole is particularly striking.

The Sierra was filled with many wonders for Muir, not the least of them the wild animals. He had always had a fondness for animals since his boyhood in Scotland and Wisconsin, and though he had to overcome aversions to alligators and rattlesnakes, he came to believe that all living things were brothers and sisters to man (though it is

INTRODUCTION

doubtful that he ever learned to like sheep). He loved the Douglas squirrel and liked to listen to— and retell—bear stories. In fact, Muir liked anything that was wild, and in "Wild Wool" he has no difficulty demonstrating to his satisfaction that wool from wild sheep is far superior to that of domesticated breeds. Anything and anyone living in a direct relationship with nature he could appreciate.

In 1874, Muir began writing a series of letters for the San Francisco *Bulletin,* describing his investigations in the Sierra. When, in 1878, he crossed the Sierras into Nevada and Utah, he sent back to the newspaper descriptions of the landscape and some rather biased accounts of his meetings with the Mormons. One of his most enjoyable experiences was a "Great Storm in Utah," an experience as vivid as the night he clung to a pine tree during a wind storm in the Sierras. All natural phenomena thrilled Muir: on one occasion he was so enthusiastic about an earthquake in the Yosemite that people thought he must be out of his mind!

By 1879, Muir had completed most of the studies he wished to make in Yosemite Valley. At a Sunday School convention there in June of that year, he met Sheldon Jackson, a Presbyterian missionary who had pioneered a mission effort in Alaska. Muir had been thinking about travelling northward; he determined to go to Alaska.

Alaska became the great adventure of Muir's life. There were glaciers everywhere, fronting on

WILDERNESS ESSAYS

rivers and bays of the ocean; the climate was mild and invigorating; the land was even more remote and untouched than that of the Yosemite. Although he had become engaged to be married just before leaving for Alaska, he could not tear himself away from this new land. In October, 1879, Muir and the resident missionary at Fort Wrangel, S. Hall Young, set out with four Indian paddlers—Toyatte, Kadachan, Stickeen John and Sitka Charley—to look for a bay filled with ice. When they reached their destination, Muir and Young became the first white men to explore what later came to be known as Glacier Bay; the largest ice mass in it was later named Muir Glacier.

After Muir's marriage in 1880, his travel and writing activities decreased for the next decade while he engaged in fruit ranching in Martinez, California, to provide for his wife and the two daughters born to them. His major literary effort was to edit *Picturesque California and the Regions West of the Rocky Mountains from Alaska to Mexico*, an over-size, two-volume set for which he got some of the West's most prominent authors and artists to contribute articles, drawings and paintings. Muir wrote seven of the essays, and in his description of the Columbia River basin included material which later appeared separately as "The Forests of Oregon." The piece gave him an opportunity to enthuse about his favorite tree, the sugar pine, together with an account of its discovery by David Douglas, a Scottish botanical

INTRODUCTION

explorer. The book also contains a brief account of Muir and Young's exploration of Glacier Bay, the first time an account of that voyage, written by Muir, had appeared in print.

After 1890, Muir relinquished management of his fruit ranch and turned to writing up some of the notes he had accumulated during his years of exploration, and to the cause of the preservation of America's forests and natural wonders. One of the founders of the Sierra Club in 1891, he became its first president, a post in which he served until his death. Muir's interest in conservation was no recent thing. In February of 1876, the Sacramento *Union* had published his letter, "How Shall We Preserve Our Forests?" His first-hand knowledge of the destructive activity of the sheep in the Sierras made him a passionate advocate of those who would save the beauties of nature from those who would despoil or destroy them.

During the 1890s, Muir's writing took on more and more a purpose he had declared in an earlier letter to Mrs. Carr: "I care to live only to entice people to look at Nature's loveliness." *The Mountains of California*, Muir's first, and considered by many readers his best, book appeared in 1894. The book contained many of the essays that had appeared earlier and that had established Muir's fame as a nature writer, particularly "The Water Ouzel," which is still widely anthologized. Muir was interested not only in describing the landscape but also in showing man's relationship to it. The feeling was explicit that any reader who would travel to the Sierras would be able to realize great benefits from the experience.

His travels in Alaska had so inspired Muir that he always said that he wanted to write a number of books about them, but he did not actually begin to write extensively about the area until after his fourth trip there in 1890 (he would make three more during his lifetime). "The Discovery of Glacier Bay" appeared in *Century Magazine* in June of 1895; by that time thousands of tourists had seen not only the Bay but also Muir Glacier. Tourist steamships had begun including Glacier Bay on their itineraries as early as 1883, and a number of Alaskan guide books had already extolled its beauties; even the Baedeker handbook for the United States recommended Muir Glacier as an outstanding tourist attraction. Muir's account, written sixteen years after that voyage of discovery, recalls vividly that dark and huge journey through the gloomy autumn weather, the hardships and the dangers. It is one of the great travel narratives in American literature.

"The Alaska Trip," made a timely appearance in *Century Magazine*, August, 1897, the very month the gold rush to the Klondike was at a peak of feverish intensity. In the article, Muir frankly extolled the beauties of Alaska and urged tourists to go to see them, claiming that not only will travellers be impressed with the beauty they find there, but also their health will be vastly improved by the

INTRODUCTION

bracing, invigorating air. Materials for this article were drawn from the newspaper letters Muir had sent back to the San Francisco *Bulletin* during his trips to Alaska in 1879 and 1880. Muir later claimed that it was he who had made Alaska a popular tourist attraction, and there was considerable merit in the claim.

In an effort to promote greater interest in the national parks and forests, Muir wrote a series of articles for the *Atlantic Monthly.* Yellowstone Park, which he had visited in 1885, was the subject of an article in April, 1898. It was an area that particularly intrigued Muir because of the activity of the bubbling pots of hot mud, the sulphurous cauldrons, and the jetting geysers. The account was later included in Muir's second book, *Our National Parks*, which came out in 1901.

By the early 1900s, Muir had a worldwide reputation as a writer and naturalist. President Theodore Roosevelt went camping with him in the Yosemite Valley; his help was constantly sought in battles involving conservation. After the death of his wife in 1905, Muir undertook some of the travels he'd always dreamed of: to the rain forests of the Amazon and to see the baobab tree in Africa. There was no time for all the things he wanted to do; he did not get to write all the books he planned.

Muir's most popular book, *Stickeen*, the story of crossing Taylor Glacier with S. Hall Young's mongrel dog, became an immediate popular success when it appeared in 1909. John Burroughs complained that when anyone asked Muir to tell the story they always got the whole theory of glacial activity thrown in! *My First Summer in the Sierra*, Muir's journal of his earliest explorations in the Sierra, appeared in 1911. *The Yosemite*, a tourist guidebook to that region, was published in 1912. He told of the years of his growing up in *The Story of My Boyhood and Youth* in 1913. The book that he had waited so long to write, *Travels in Alaska*, lay unfinished on his bedside table when Muir died on Christmas Eve, 1914. In a world, in a universe, which Muir regarded as being in a continuing state of creation, this seems, at least, appropriate.

Muir's reputation as a writer rests not only on the books and articles he published during his lifetime. *Travels in Alaska* was published posthumously and the latter portions of the book show that he had not worked the materials into final form. William Frederic Badè, Muir's literary executor, fashioned three more books from Muir's papers. *A Thousand Mile Walk to the Gulf*, Muir's first journal, on which he had done some editorial work, came out in 1917. *The Cruise of the Corwin*, made up of letters Muir had written to the San Francisco *Bulletin* while aboard the *Corwin* which searched for the *Jeanette*, a ship lost in the ice of the Arctic Ocean, appeared in 1917. *Steep Trails* was made up of articles from various sources, newspaper and magazine, describing Muir's travels in areas of the West other than California; it was published in 1918. In 1938, Linnie Marsh Wolfe edited the mate-

INTRODUCTION

rials in the notebooks and on the scraps of papers found after Muir's death, compiling *John of the Mountains: The Unpublished Journals of John Muir*. In addition, Muir's daughters arranged for the appearance of a significant work, *Letters to a Friend, Written to Mrs. Ezra S. Carr, 1866-1879*, in 1915, showing Muir's developing interest in nature and his commitment to a vocation of the study of it.

How shall we assess the importance of Muir as a nature writer? As in the case of Thoreau, Muir's personality frequently intrudes on our evaluation of him as a writer. Muir was a quintessential romantic frontier figure. Unarmed, carrying only a few crusts of bread, a tin cup, a small portion of tea, a notebook and a few scientific instruments, Muir walked into the vastness of the Sierras to search out truths. Single-minded, he did not hesitate to challenge the accepted authorities and their explanations regarding the wilderness he loved: he formulated his own theories and carefully searched out the evidence. America has always loved its rebels, even if it turns out later that they have not discovered the whole truth.

Part of Muir's attractiveness to modern readers is the fact that he was an activist. He not only explored the west and wrote about its beauties—he fought for their preservation. His successes dot the landscape in all the natural features that bear his name: forests, lakes, trails, glaciers. His writings still stimulate readers to try to retrace his footsteps through areas about which he wrote so compellingly.

Muir's prose is clean and direct, because his powers of observation were keen, and he drew his figures of speech, his similes and metaphors from the natural world. He is frequently "adjectivorous," as he admits, but at least part of his problem arises from the vastness of the landscape he is trying to describe. His transcendental brother, Thoreau, had found his correspondences between man and nature at Walden Pond, a physical area which would have filled only a small portion of Yosemite Valley which, in turn, is only a small corner of the Sierras, in turn only a fragment of the American West.

In commenting on Muir's achievement, Norman Foerster, in *Nature in American Literature,* wrote: "Whoever would know the Far West, from Alaska to Mexico, from the coast to the Rockies, must know John Muir.... [he] gave this region to the country— both to those who could not go to see and to those who, having eyes, saw not. That is his foremost achievement."

But Muir did much more than that: in the forests and national parks he helped to preserve, he gave the natural world back to the people of America. Had he never written a single word, that alone would be an impressive monument.

Frank E. Buske

THE DISCOVERY OF GLACIER BAY BY ITS DISCOVERER

My first visit to the now famous Glacier Bay of Alaska was made toward the end of October, 1879, when young ice was beginning to form in the branch inlets occupied by the glaciers, and the mountains were mantled with fresh snow all the way down from the highest peaks and ridges of the Fairweather Range nearly to the level of the sea.

I had spent most of the season exploring the cañon of the Stickeen River and its glaciers, and a small portion of the interior region beyond the Coast Mountains, on the divide of some of the southerly tributaries of the Yukon and Mackenzie rivers. When I got back to my headquarters at Fort Wrangel, about the beginning of October, it seemed too late for new undertakings in this icy northland. The days were growing short, and winter, with its heavy storms, was drawing nigh, when avalanches would be booming down the long white slopes of the peaks, and all the land would be buried. But, on the other hand, though this white wilderness was new to me, I was familiar with storms, and enjoyed them, knowing well that in right relations with them they are ever kindly. The main inland channels, extending in every direction along the coast, remain open all winter;

The Century Magazine (June, 1895)

and their shores being well forested, it would be easy to keep warm in camp, while in a large canoe abundance of provisions could be carried. I determined, therefore, to go ahead as far north as possible, with or without companions, to see and learn what I could, especially with reference to future work. When I made known my plans to Mr. Young, the Wrangel missionary, he offered to go with me, and with his assistance I procured a good canoe and a crew of Indians, gathered a large stock of provisions, blankets, etc., and on October 14 set forth, eager to welcome whatever wildness might offer, so long as food and firewood should last.

Our crew numbered four: Toyatte, a grand old Stickeen nobleman, who was elected captain, not only because he owned the canoe, but for his skill in woodcraft and seamanship; Kadechan, the son of a Chilcat chief; John, a Stickeen who acted as interpreter; and Sitka Charlie. Mr. Young is one of those fearless and adventurous evangelists who in seeking to save others save themselves, and it was the opportunities the trip might afford to meet the Indians of the different tribes along our route that induced him to join me.

After all our bundles were stowed aboard, and we were about to cast loose from the wharf, Kadechan's mother, a woman of great natural dignity and force of character, came down the steps alongside the canoe, oppressed with anxious fears for the safety of her son. Standing silent for a few moments, she held the missionary with her dark, bodeful eyes, and at length, with great solemnity of speech and gesture, accused him of using undue influence in gaining her son's consent to go on a dangerous voyage among tribes that were unfriendly to the Stickeens. Then, like an ancient sibyl, she foretold a long train of disasters from stormwinds and ice, and in awful majesty of mother-love finished by saying: "If my son comes not back, on you will be his blood, and you shall pay. I say it." Mr. Young tried in vain to calm her fears, promising Heaven's care as well as his own for her precious son, assuring her that he would faithfully share every danger that might assail him, and, if need be, willingly die in his defense. "We shall see whether or not you die," she said as she turned away.

Toyatte also encountered domestic difficulties in getting away. When he stepped into the canoe I noticed a cloud on his grand old face, as if his sad doom, now drawing near, was already beginning to overshadow him. When he took leave of his wife she wept bitterly, saying that the Chilcat chiefs would surely kill him in case he should escape the winter storms. But it was not on this trip that the old hero was to meet his fate, and when we were fairly free in the wilderness these gloomy forebodings vanished, and a gentle breeze pressed us joyfully onward over the shining waters.

We first pursued a westerly course through Sumner Strait, between Kupreanof and Prince of Wales islands; then, turning northward, we sailed

WILDERNESS ESSAYS

up the charming Kiku Strait, through the midst of innumerable picturesque islets, across Prince Frederick Sound, up Chatham Strait, and thence northwestward through Icy Strait and around Glacier Bay. Thence, returning through Icy Strait, we urged our way up the grand Lynn Canal to the Davidson Glacier and Chilcat, and returned to Wrangel along the coast of the mainland, visiting the icy Sum Dum Bay and the Le Conte Glacier on our route. Thus we made a journey more than eight hundred miles long; and though hardships were encountered, and a few dangers, the wild wonderland made compensation beyond our most extravagant hopes.

The first stages of our journey were mostly enjoyment. The weather was about half bright, and we glided along the green and yellow shores in comfort, the lovely islands passing in harmonious succession, like ideas in a fine poem. The rain did not hinder us, but when the wind was too wild we stayed in camp, the Indians usually improving such storm times in deer-hunting, while I examined the rocks and woods. Most of our camps were made in nooks that were charmingly embowered, and fringed with bushes and late flowers. After supper we sat long around the fire, listening to the stories of the Indians about the wild animals they were acquainted with, their hunting adventures, wars, traditions, religion, and customs. Every Indian party we met we interviewed, and every village we came to we visited.

DISCOVERY OF GLACIER BAY

Thus passed our days and nights until we reached the west coast of Admiralty Island, intending to make a straight course thence up Lynn Canal, when we learned from a party of traveling Hoonas that the Chilcats had been drinking and quarreling, that Kadechan's father had been shot, and that we could not go safely into their country before these whisky quarrels were settled. My Indians evidently believed this news, and dreaded the consequences; therefore I decided to turn to the westward through Icy Strait, and to go in search of the wonderful ice-mountains to which Sitka Charlie, the youngest of my crew, had frequently referred. Having noticed my interest in glaciers, he told me that when he was a boy he had gone with his father to hunt seals in a large bay full of ice, and that he thought he could find it if I cared to have him try. I was rejoiced to find all the crew now willing to go on this adventure, judging, perhaps, that ice-mountains under the present circumstances might prove less dangerous than Chilcats.

On the 24th, about noon, as we came near a small island in Icy Strait, Charlie said that we must procure some dry wood there, for in the ice-mountain country which we were now approaching not a single tree of any kind could be found. This seemed strange news to the rest of the crew, and I had to make haste to end an angry dispute that was rising by ordering as much wood to be taken aboard as we could carry. Then we set sail direct for the ice-country, holding a northwesterly course until long after dark, when we reached a small inlet that sets in near the mouth of Glacier Bay, on the west side. Here we made a cold camp on a desolate snow-covered beach in stormy sleet and darkness. At daybreak I looked eagerly in every direction to learn what kind of place we were in; but gloomy rainclouds covered the mountains, and I could see nothing that could give me a clue, while Vancouver's chart, hitherto a faithful guide, here failed us altogether. Nevertheless, we made haste to be off; and fortunately, just as we were leaving the shore, a faint smoke was seen across the inlet, toward which Charlie, who now seemed lost, gladly steered. Our sudden appearance so early that gray morning had evidently alarmed our neighbors, for as soon as we were within hailing distance an Indian with his face blackened fired a shot over our heads, and in a blunt, bellowing voice roared, "Who are you?" Our interpreter shouted, "Friends and the Fort Wrangel missionary." Then men, women, and children swarmed out of the hut, and awaited our approach on the beach. One of the hunters having brought his gun with him, Kadechan sternly rebuked him, asking with superb indignation whether he was not ashamed to bring a gun in his hand to meet a missionary. Friendly relations, however, were speedily established, and as a cold rain was falling, they invited us into their hut. It seemed small for two persons; nevertheless, twenty-one managed to find shelter in it about a smoky fire. Our hosts proved to be Hoona seal-hunters laying in their winter stores of meat and skins. The packed hut was passably well ventilated, but its oily, meaty smells were not the same to our noses as those of the briny, sprucy nooks we were accustomed to, and the circle of black eyes peering at us through a fog of reek and smoke made a novel picture. We were glad, however, to get within reach of information, and of course asked many questions concerning the ice-mountains and the strange bay, to most of which our inquisitive Hoona friends replied with counter-questions as to our object in coming to such a place, especially so late in the year. They had heard of Mr. Young and his work at Fort Wrangel, but could not understand what a missionary could be doing in such a place as this. Was he going to preach to seals and gulls, they asked, or to the ice-mountains? and could they take his word? Then John explained that only the friend of the missionary was seeking ice-mountains; that Mr. Young had already preached many good words in the villages we had visited on our way, in their own among the rest; that our hearts were good; and that every Indian was our friend. Then we gave them a little rice, sugar, tea, and tobacco, after which they began to gain confidence and to speak freely. They told us that the main bay was called by them Sit-a-da-kay, or Ice Bay; that there were many large ice-mountains in it, but no gold mines; and that the ice-mountain they knew best was at the head of the bay, where most seals were found.

WILDERNESS ESSAYS

Notwithstanding the rain, I was anxious that we should push and grope our way beneath the clouds as best we could, in case worse weather should come; but Charlie was ill at ease, and wanted one of the seal-hunters to go with us, for the place was much changed. I promised to pay well for a guide, and in order to lighten the canoe proposed to leave most of our heavy stores with our friends until our return. After a long consultation one of them consented to go. His wife got ready his blanket and a piece of cedar matting for his bed, and some provisions—mostly dried salmon, and seal sausage made of strips of lean meat plaited around a core of fat. She followed us to the beach, and just as we were pushing off said with a pretty smile: "It is my husband that you are taking away. See that you bring him back." We got under way about 10 A.M. The wind was in our favor, but a cold rain pelted us, and we could see but little of the dreary, treeless wilderness which we had now fairly entered. The bitter blast, however, gave us good speed; our bedraggled canoe rose and fell on the icy waves, solemnly bowing to them, and mimicking the gestures of a big ship. Our course was northwestward, up the southwest side of the bay, near the shore of what seemed to be the mainland, some smooth marble islands being on our right. About noon we discovered the first of the great glaciers—the one I afterward named for Geikie, the noted Scotch geologist. Its lofty blue cliffs, looming up through the draggled skirts of the clouds, gave a tremendous impression of savage power, while the roar of the new-born icebergs thickened and emphasized the general roar of the storm. An hour and a half beyond the Geikie Glacier we ran into a slight harbor where the shore is low, dragged the canoe beyond the reach of drifting icebergs, and, much against my desire to push ahead, encamped, the guide insisting that the big ice-mountain at the head of the bay could not be reached before dark, that the landing there was dangerous even in daylight, and that this was the only safe harbor on the way to it. While camp was being made I strolled along the shore to examine the rocks and the fossil timber that abound here. All the rocks are freshly glaciated even below the sea-level, nor have the waves as yet worn off the surface polish, much less the heavy scratches and grooves and lines of glacial contour.

The next day being Sunday, the minister wished to stay in camp; and so, on account of the weather, did the Indians. I therefore set out on an excursion, and spent the day alone on the mountain slopes above the camp, and to the north of it, to see what I might learn. Pushing on through rain and mud and sludgy snow, crossing many brown, boulder-choked torrents, wading, jumping, wallowing in snow to my shoulders, I had a desperately hard and dangerous time. After crouching cramped and benumbed in the canoe, poulticed in wet clothes and blankets night and day, my limbs had been long asleep. This day they were awake, and in the hour of trial proved that they had not lost the cunning learned on many a mountain peak of the high Sierra. I reached a height of 1500 feet, on the ridge that bounds the second of the great glaciers on the south. All the landscape was smothered in clouds, and I began to fear that I had climbed in vain, as far as wide views were concerned. But at length the clouds lifted a little, and beneath their gray fringes I saw the berg-filled expanse of the bay, and the feet of the mountains that stand about it, and the imposing fronts of five of the huge glaciers, the nearest being immediately beneath me. This was my first general view of Glacier Bay, a solitude of ice and snow and new-born rocks, dim, dreary, mysterious. I held the ground I had so dearly won for an hour or two, sheltering myself as best I could from the blast, while with benumbed fingers I sketched what I could see of the landscape, and wrote a few lines in my note-book. Then I breasted the snow again, crossed the muffled, shifting avalanche tali, forded the torrents in safety, and reached camp about dark, wet and weary, but rich in a notable experience.

While I was getting some coffee, Mr. Young told me that the Indians were discouraged, and had been talking about turning back, fearing that I would be lost, or that in some way the expedition would come to grief if I persisted in going farther. They had been asking him what possible motive I could have in climbing dangerous mountains when blinding storms were blowing; and when he replied that I was only seeking knowledge, Toyatte said, "Muir must be a witch to seek knowledge in such a place as this, and in such miserable weather." After supper, crouching about a dull fire of fossil wood, they became still more doleful, and talked in tones that accorded well with the growling torrents about us, and with the wind and rain among the rocks, telling sad old stories of crushed canoes and drowned Indians, and of hunters lost and frozen in snow-storms. Toyatte, dreading the treeless, forlorn appearance of the region, said that his heart was not strong, and that he feared his canoe, on the safety of which our lives depended, might be entering a skookum-house (jail) of ice, from which there might be no escape; while the Hoona guide said bluntly that if I was so fond of danger, and meant to go close up to the noses of the ice-mountains, he would not consent to go any farther: for we should all be lost, as many of his tribe had been, by the sudden rising of bergs from the bottom. They seemed to be losing heart with every howl of the storm, and fearing that they might fail me now that I was in the midst of so grand a congregation of glaciers, which possibly I might not see again, I made haste to reassure them, telling them that for ten years I had wandered along among mountains and storms, and that good luck always followed me; that with me, therefore, they need fear nothing; that the storm would soon cease, and the sun would shine; and that

WILDERNESS ESSAYS

Heaven cared for us, and guided us all the time, whether we knew it or not: but that only brave men had a right to look for Heaven's care, therefore all childish fear must be put away. This little speech did good. Kadechan, with some show of enthusiasm, said he liked to travel with good-luck people; and dignified old Toyatte declared that now his heart was strong again, and he would venture on with me as far as I liked, for my "wawa" was "delait" (my talk was very good). The old warrier even became a little sentimental, and said that if the canoe were crushed he would not greatly care, because on the way to the other world he would have pleasant companions.

Next morning it was still raining and snowing, but the wind was from the south, and swept us bravely forward, while the bergs were cleared from our course. In about an hour we reached the second of the big glaciers, which I afterward named for Hugh Miller. We rowed up its fiord, and landed to make a slight examination of its grand frontal wall. The berg-producing portion we found to be about a mile and a half wide. It presents an imposing array of jagged spires and pyramids, and flat-topped towers and battlements, of many shades of blue, from pale, shimmering, limpid tones in the crevasses and hollows, to the most startling, chilling, almost shrieking vitriol blue on the plain mural spaces from which bergs had just been discharged. Back from the front for a few miles the surface is rendered inaccessible by a series of wide, weathered crevasses, with the spaces between them rising like steps, as if the entire mass of this portion of the glacier had sunk in successive sections as it reached deep water, and the sea had found its way beneath it. Beyond this the glacier extends indefinitely in a gently rising prairie-like expanse, and branches among the slopes and cañons of the Fairweather Range.

From here a run of two hours brought us to the head of the bay, and to the mouth of the northwest fiord, at the head of which lie the Hoona sealing-grounds, and the great glacier now called the Pacific, and another called the Hoona. The fiord is about five miles long, and is two miles wide at the mouth. Here the Hoona guide had a store of dry wood, which we took aboard. Then, setting sail, we were driven wildly up the fiord, as if the storm-wind were saying: "Go, then, if you will, into my ice chamber; but you shall stay until I am ready to let you out." All this time sleety rain was falling on the bay, and snow on the mountains; but soon after we landed the sky began to open. The camp was made on a rocky bench near the front of the Pacific Glacier, and the canoe was carried beyond reach of the bergs and berg-waves. The bergs were now crowded in a dense pack against the ice-wall, as if the storm-wind had determined to make the glacier take back her crystal offspring and keep them at home.

While camp affairs were being attended to, I set out to climb a mountain for comprehensive views; and before I had reached a height of a thousand feet the rain ceased, and the clouds began to rise from the lower altitudes, slowly lifting their white skirts, and lingering in majestic, wing-shaped masses about the mountains that rise out of the broad, icy sea. These were the highest and whitest of all the white mountains, and the greatest of all the glaciers I had yet seen. Climbing higher for a still broader outlook, I made notes and sketched, improving the precious time while sunshine streamed through the luminous fringes of the clouds, and fell on the green waters of the fiord, the glittering bergs, the crystal bluffs of the two vast glaciers, the intensely white, far-spreading fields of ice, and the ineffably chaste and spiritual heights of the Fairweather Range, which were now hidden, now partly revealed, the whole making a picture of icy wildness unspeakably pure and sublime.

Looking southward, a broad ice-sheet was seen extending in a gently undulating plain from the Pacific Fiord in the foreground to the horizon, dotted and ridged here and there with mountains which were as white as the snow-covered ice in which they were half, or more than half, submerged. Several of the great glaciers flow from this one grand fountain. It is an instructive example of a general glacier covering the hills and dales of a country that is not yet ready to be brought to the light of day—not only covering, but creating, a landscape with all the features it is destined to have when, in the fullness of time, the fashioning ice-sheet shall be lifted by the sun, and the land shall become warm and fruitful. The view to the westward is bounded and almost filled by the glorious Fairweather Mountains, the highest of them springing aloft in sublime beauty to a height of nearly 16,000 feet, while from base to summit every peak and spire and dividing ridge of all the mighty host was of a spotless, solid white, as if painted. It would seem that snow could never be made to lie on the steepest slopes and precipices unless plastered on when wet, and then frozen. But this snow could not have been wet. It must have been fixed by being driven and set in small particles like the storm-dust of drifts, which, when in this condition, is fixed not only on sheer cliffs, but in massive overcurling cornices. Along the base of this majestic range sweeps the Pacific Glacier, fed by innumerable cascading tributaries, and discharging into the head of the fiord by two mouths, each nearly a mile wide. This is the largest of all the Glacier Bay glaciers that are at all river-like, the trunk of the larger Muir Glacier being more like a lake than a river. After the continuous rainy or snowy weather which we had had since leaving Wrangel, the clear weather was most welcome. Dancing down the mountain to camp, my mind glowing like the sun-beaten glaciers, I found the Indians seated around a good fire, entirely happy now that the farthest point of the journey had been reached. How keenly bright were the stars that night in the frosty sky, and how impressive was the thunder of the icebergs, rolling, swelling, reverberating through the solemn stillness! I was too happy to sleep.

About daylight next morning we crossed the fiord, and landed on the south side of the island that divides the front wall of the Pacific Glacier. The whiskered faces of seals dotted the water between the bergs, and I could not prevent John and Charlie and Kadechan from shooting at them. Fortunately, they were not skilled in this kind of hunting, and few, if any, were hurt. Leaving the Indians in charge of the canoe, I climbed the island, and gained a good general view of the glacier. At one favorable place I descended about fifty feet below the side of the glacier, where its denuding, fashioning action was clearly shown. Pushing back from here, I found the surface crevassed and sunken in steps, like the Hugh Miller Glacier, as if it were being undermined by the action of the tide-waters. For a distance of fifteen or twenty miles the river-like ice-flood is nearly level, and when it recedes the ocean water will follow it, and thus form a long extension of the fiord, with features essentially the same as those now extending into the continent farther south, where many great glaciers once poured into the sea, though scarce a vestige of them now exists. Thus the domain of the sea has been, and is being, extended in these ice-sculptured lands, and the scenery of the shores is enriched. The dividing island is about a thousand feet high, and is hard beset by the glacier, which still crushes heavily against and around it. A short time ago its summit was at least two thousand feet below the surface of the over-sweeping ice; now three hundred feet of the top is free, and under present climatic conditions it will soon be wholly free from the ice, and will take its place as a glacier-polished island in the middle of the fiord, like a thousand others in this magnificent archipelago. Emerging from its icy sepulcher, it gives a most telling illustration of the birth of a marked feature of a landscape. In this instance it is not the mountain, but the glacier, that is in labor, and the mountain itself is being brought forth.

The Hoona Glacier enters the fiord on the south side, a short distance below the Pacific, displaying a broad and far-reaching expanse, over which many of the lofty peaks of the Fairweather Range are seen; but the front wall, thrust into the fiord, is not nearly so interesting as that of the Pacific, and I did not observe any bergs discharged from it.

After we had seen the unveiling of the majestic peaks and glaciers that evening, and their baptism in the down-pouring sunbeams, it was inconceivable that nature could have anything finer to show us. Nevertheless, compared with what was coming the next morning, all that was as nothing. As far as we could see, the lovely dawn gave no promise of anything uncommon. Its most impressive features were the frosty clearness of the sky, and a deep, brooding calm, made all the more striking by the intermittent thunder of the bergs. The sunrise we did not see at all, for we were beneath the shadows of the fiord cliffs; but in the midst of our studies we were startled by the sudden appearance of a red light burning with a strange, unearthly splendor on the topmost peak of the Fairweather Mountains. Instead of vanishing as suddenly as it had appeared, it spread and spread until the whole range down to the level of the glaciers was filled with the celestial fire. In color it was at first a vivid crimson, with a thick, furred appearance, as fine as the alpenglow, yet indescribably rich and deep—not in the least like a garment or mere external flush or bloom through which one might expect to see the rocks or snow, but every mountain apparently glowing from the heart like molten metal fresh from a furnace. Beneath the frosty shadows of the fiord we stood hushed and awe-stricken, gazing at the holy vision; and had we seen the heavens open and God made manifest, our attention could not have been more tremendously strained. When the highest peak began to burn, it did not seem to be steeped in sunshine, however glorious, but rather as if it had been thrust into the body of the sun itself. Then the supernal fire slowly descending, with a sharp line of demarkation separating it from the cold, shaded region beneath, peak after peak, with their spires and ridges and cascading glaciers, caught the heavenly glow, until all the mighty host stood transfigured, hushed, and thoughtful, as if awaiting the coming of the Lord. The white, rayless light of the morning, seen when I was alone amid the silent peaks of the Sierra, had always seemed to me the most telling of the terrestrial manifestations of God. But here the mountains themselves were made divine, and declared his glory in terms still more impressive. How long we gazed I never knew. The glorious vision passed away in a gradual, fading change through a thousand tones of color to pale yellow and white, and then the work of the ice-world went on again in every-day beauty. The green waters of the fiord were filled with sun-spangles; with the upspringing breeze the fleet of icebergs set forth on their voyages; and on the innumerable mirrors and prisms of these bergs, and on those of the shattered crystal walls of the glaciers, common white light and rainbow light began to glow, while the mountains, changing to stone, put on their frosty jewelry, and loomed again in the thin azure in serene terrestrial majesty. We turned and sailed away, joining the outgoing bergs, while "Gloria in excelsis" still seemed to be sounding over all the white landscape, and our burning hearts were ready for any fate, feeling that whatever the future might have in store, the treasures we had gained would enrich our lives forever.

When we arrived at the mouth of the fiord, and rounded the massive granite headland that stands guard at the entrance on the north side, another large glacier, now named the Reid, was discovered at the head of one of the northern branches of the bay. Pushing ahead into this new fiord, we found that it was not only packed with bergs, but that the spaces between the bergs were crusted with new ice, compelling us to turn back while we were yet several miles from the discharging frontal wall. But though we were not then allowed to set foot on this magnificent glacier, we obtained a fine view of it, and I made the Indians cease rowing while I sketched its principal features. Thence, after steering northeastward a few miles, we discovered still another great glacier, now named the Carroll. But the fiord into which this glacier flows was, like the last, utterly inaccessible on account of ice, and we had to be content with a general view and a sketch of it, gained as we rowed slowly past at a distance of three or four miles. The mountains back of it and on each side of its inlet are sculptured in a singularly rich and striking style of architecture, in which subordinate peaks and gables appear in wonderful profusion, and an imposing conical mountain with a wide, smooth base stands out in the main current of the glacier, a mile or two back from the great ice-wall.

We now turned southward down the eastern shore of the bay, and in an hour or two discovered a large glacier of the second class, at the head of a comparatively short fiord that winter had not yet closed. Here we landed, and climbed across a mile or so of rough boulder-beds, and back upon the wildly broken receding snout of the glacier, which, though it descends to the level of the sea, no longer sends off bergs. Many large masses were detached from the wasting snout by irregular melting, and were buried beneath the mud, sand, gravel, and boulders of the terminal moraine. Thus protected, these fossil icebergs remain unmelted for many years, some of them for a century or more, as shown by the age of trees growing above them, though there are no trees here as yet. At length melting, a pit with sloping sides is formed by the falling of the overlying moraine material into the space at first occupied by the buried ice. In this way are formed the curious depressions in drift-covered regions called kettles, or sinks. On these decaying glaciers we may also find many interesting lessons on the formation of boulders and boulder-beds, which in all glaciated countries exert a marked influence on scenery, health, and fruitfulness.

Three or four miles farther down the bay we came to another fiord, up which we sailed in quest of more glaciers, discovering one in each of the two branches into which the fiord divides. Neither of these glaciers quite reaches tide-water. Notwithstanding their great size and the apparent fruitfulness of their fountains, they are in the first stage of decadence, the waste from melting and evaporation being greater now than the supply of new ice from the snow. We reached the one in the north branch after a comfortable scramble, and climbed over its huge, wrinkled brow, from the top of which we gained a good view of the trunk and some of the tributaries, and also of the sublime gray cliffs that tower on each hand above the ice.

Then we sailed up the south branch of the inlet, but failed to reach the glacier there, on account of a thin sheet of new ice. With the tent-poles we broke a lane for the canoe for a little distance; but it was slow, hard work, and we soon saw that we could not reach the glacier before dark. Nevertheless, we gained a fair view of it as it came sweeping down through its gigantic gateway of massive Yosemite rocks three and four thousand feet high. Here we lingered until sundown, gazing and sketching; then we turned back, and encamped on a bed of cobble-stones between the forks of the fiord.

Our fire was made of fossil wood gathered on the beach. This wood is found scattered or in wave-washed windrows all about the bay where the shores are low enough for it to rest. It also occurs in abundance in many of the ravines and gorges, and in roughly stratified beds of moraine material, some of which are more than a thousand feet in thickness. The bed-rocks on which these deposits rest are scored and polished by glacial action, like all the rocks hereabouts up to at least three thousand feet above the sea. The timber is mostly in the form of broken trunks of the Merten, Paton, and Menzies spruce, the largest sections being twenty to thirty feet long, and from one to three feet in diameter, some of them, with the bark on, sound and tough. It appears, therefore, that these shores were, a century or so ago, as generously forested as those of the adjacent bays and inlets are to-day; though, strange to say, not one tree is left standing, with the exception of a few on mountain-tops near the mouth of the bay and on the east side of the Muir Glacier. How this disforestment was effected I have not space to tell here. I will only say that all I have seen goes to show that the moraine soil on which the forests were growing was held in place on the steep mountain slopes by the grand trunk glacier that recently filled the entire bay as its channel, and that when it melted the soil and forests were sloughed off together.

As we sat by the camp-fire the brightness of the sky brought on a long talk with the Indians about the stars; and their eager, childlike attention was refreshing to see as compared with the decent, deathlike apathy of weary civilized people, in whom natural curiosity has been quenched in toil and care and poor, shallow comfort.

After sleeping a few hours, I stole quietly out of the camp, and climbed the mountain that stands guard between the two glaciers. The ground was frozen, making the climbing difficult in the steepest places; but the views over the icy bay, sparkling beneath the glorious effulgence of the sky, were enchanting. It seemed then a sad thing that any part of so precious a night had been lost in sleep. The starlight was so full that I distinctly saw not only the bay with its multitude of glittering bergs, but most of the lower portions of the glaciers, lying pale and spirit-like amid the huge silent mountains.

WILDERNESS ESSAYS

The nearest glacier in particular was so distinct that it seemed to be glowing with light that came from within itself. Not even in dark nights have I ever found any difficulty in seeing large glaciers; but on this mountain-top, amid so much ice, in the heart of so clear and frosty a night, everything was luminous, and I seemed to be poised in a vast hollow between two skies of equal brightness. How strong I felt after my exhilarating scramble, and how glad I was that my good angel had called me before the glorious night succeeding so glorious a morning had been spent!

I got back to camp in time for an early breakfast, and by daylight we had everything packed and were again under way. The fiord was frozen nearly to its mouth, and though the ice was so thin that it gave us but little trouble in breaking a way, yet it showed us that the season for exploration in these waters was well-nigh over. We were in danger of being imprisoned in a jam of icebergs, for the water-spaces between them freeze rapidly, binding the floes into one mass. Across such floes it would be almost impossible to drag a canoe, however industriously we might ply the ax, as our Hoona guide took great pains to warn us. I would have kept straight down the bay from here, but the guide had to be taken home, and the provisions we left at the bark hut had to be got on board. We therefore crossed over to our Sunday storm-camp, cautiously boring a way through the bergs. We found the shore lavishly adorned with a fresh arrival of assorted bergs that had been left stranded at high tide. They were arranged in a broad, curving row, looking intensely clear and pure on the gray sand, and, with the sunbeams pouring through them, suggested the jewel-paved streets of the New Jerusalem.

On our way down the coast, after examining the front of the beautiful Geikie Glacier, we obtained our first broad view of the Muir Glacier, the last of all the grand company to be seen, the stormy weather having hidden it when we first entered the bay. It was now perfectly clear, and the spacious, prairie-like glacier, with its many tributaries extending far back into the snowy recesses of the mountains, made a magnificent display of its wealth, and I was strongly tempted to go and explore it at all hazards. But winter had come, and the freezing of its fiord was an insurmountable obstacle. I had, therefore, to be content for the present with sketching and studying its main features at a distance. When we arrived at the Hoona hunting-camp, the men, women, and children came swarming out to welcome us. In the neighborhood of this camp I carefully noted the lines of demarkation between the forested and disforested regions. Several mountains here are only in part disforested, and the lines separating the bare and the forested portions are well defined. The soil, as well as the trees, had slid off the steep slopes, leaving the edges of the woods raw-looking and rugged.

WILDERNESS ESSAYS

At the mouth of the bay a series of moraine islands shows that the trunk glacier that occupied the bay halted here for some time, and deposited this island material as a terminal moraine; that more of the bay was not filled in shows that, after lingering here, it receded comparatively fast. All the level portions of trunks of glaciers occupying ocean fiords, instead of melting back gradually in times of general shrinking and recession, as inland glaciers with sloping channels do, melt almost uniformly over all the surface until they become thin enough to float. Then, of course, with each rise and fall of the tide the seawater, with a temperature usually considerably above the freezing-point, rushes in and out beneath them, causing rapid waste of the nether surface, while the upper is being wasted by the weather, until at length the fiord portions of these great glaciers become comparatively thin and weak, and are broken up, and vanish almost simultaneously from the mouths of their fiords to the heads of them.

Glacier Bay is undoubtedly young as yet. Vancouver's chart, made only a century ago, shows no trace of it, though found admirably faithful in general. It seems probable, therefore, that even then the entire bay was occupied by a glacier of which all those described above, great though they are, were only tributaries. Nearly as great a change has taken place in Sum Dum Bay since Vancouver's visit, the main trunk glacier there having receded from eighteen to twenty-five miles from the line marked on his chart.

The next season (1880), on September 1, I again entered Glacier Bay, and steered direct for the Muir Glacier. I was anxious to make my main camp as near the ice-wall as possible, to watch the discharge of the bergs. Toyatte, the grandest Indian I ever knew, had been killed soon after our return to Fort Wrangel; and my new captain, Tyeen, was inclined to keep at a safe distance from the "big ice-mountain," the threatening cliffs of which rose to a height of 300 feet above the water. After a good deal of urging he ventured within half a mile of them, on the east side of the fiord, where with Mr. Young I went ashore to seek a camp-ground on the moraine, leaving the Indians in the canoe. In a few minutes after we landed a huge berg sprung aloft with tremendous commotion, and the frightened Indians incontinently fled, plying their paddles in the tossing waves with admirable energy until they reached a safe shelter around the south end of the moraine, a mile down the inlet. I found a good place for a camp in a slight hollow where a few spruce stumps afforded abundance of firewood. But all efforts to get Tyeen out of his harbor failed. Nobody knew, he said, how far the ice-mountain could dash waves up the beach, and his canoe would be broken. Therefore I had my bedding and some provision carried to a high camp, and enjoyed the wildness alone.

Next morning at daybreak I pushed eagerly back over the snout and along the eastern margin of the glacier, to see as much as possible of the upper fountain region. About five miles back from the front I climbed a mountain 2500 feet high, from the flowery summit of which, the day being clear, the vast glacier and all of its principal branches were displayed in one magnificent view. Instead of a stream of ice winding down a mountain-walled valley, like the largest of the Swiss glaciers, the Muir is a broad, gently undulating prairie surrounded by innumerable icy mountains, from the far, shadowy depths of which flow the many tributary glaciers that form the great central trunk. There are seven large tributaries, from two to six miles wide where they enter the trunk, and from ten to twenty miles long, each of them fed by many secondary tributaries; so that the whole number of branches, great and small, pouring from the mountain fountains must number upward of two hundred, not counting the smallest. The area drained by this one grand glacier can hardly be less than 1000 square miles, and it probably contains as much ice as all the 1100 Swiss glaciers combined. The length of the glacier from the frontal wall back to the head of the farthest fountain is estimated at fifty miles, and the width of the main trunk just below the confluence of the large tributaries is about twenty-five miles. Though apparently as motionless as the mountains, it flows on forever, the speed varying in every part with the seasons, but mostly with the depth of the current, and the declivity, smoothness, and directness of the different portions of the basin. The flow of the central cascading portion near the front, as recently determined by Professor Reid, is at the rate of from two and a half to five inches an hour or from five to ten feet a day. A strip of the main trunk about a mile in width, extending along the eastern margin about fourteen miles to a large lake filled with bergs, has but little motion, and is so little broken by crevasses that one hundred horsemen might ride abreast over it without encountering much difficulty.

But far the greater portion of the vast expanse is torn and crumpled into a bewildering network of hummocky ridges and blades, separated by yawning gulfs and crevasses, so that the explorer, crossing the glacier from shore to shore, must always have a hard time. Here and there in the heart of the icy wilderness are spacious hollows containing beautiful lakes, fed by bands of quick-glancing streams that flow without friction in blue crystal channels, making most delightful melody, singing and ringing in silvery tones of peculiar sweetness, sun-filled crystals being the only flowers on their banks. Few, however, will be likely to enjoy them. Fortunately, to most travelers the thundering ice-wall, while comfortably accessible, is also by far the most interesting portion of the glacier.

The mountains about the great glacier were also seen from this standpoint in exceedingly grand and telling views, peaked and spired in end-

WILDERNESS ESSAYS

less variety of forms, and ranged and grouped in glorious array. Along the valleys of the main tributaries to the northwestward I saw far into their shadowy depths, one noble peak appearing beyond the other in its snowy robes in long, fading perspective. One of the most remarkable, fashioned like a superb crown with delicately fluted sides, stands in the middle of the second main tributary, counting from right to left. To the westward the majestic Fairweather Range lifted its peaks and glaciers into the blue sky in all its glory. Mount Fairweather, though not the highest, is by far the noblest of all the sky-dwelling company, the most majestic in port and architecture of all the mountains I have ever seen. It is a mountain of mountains. La Pérouse, at the south end of the range, is also a magnificent mountain, symmetrically peaked and sculptured, and wears its robes of snow and glaciers in noble style. Lituya, as seen from here, is an immense double tower, severely plain and massive. Crillon, though the loftiest of all (being nearly 16,000 feet high), presents no well-marked features. Its ponderous glaciers have ground it away into long, curling ridges until, from this point of view, it resembles a huge twisted shell. The lower summits about the Muir Glacier, like this one, the first that I climbed, are richly adorned and enlivened with beautiful flowers, though they make but a faint show in a general view. Lines and flashes of bright green appear on the lower slopes as one approaches them from the glacier, and a fainter green tinge may be noticed on the subordinate summits at a height of 2000 or 3000 feet. The lower are made mostly by alder bushes, and the topmost by a lavish profusion of flowering plants, chiefly cassiope, vaccinium, pyrola, erigeron, gentiana, campanula, anemone, larkspur, and columbine, with a few grasses and ferns. Of these cassiope is at once the commenest and the most beautiful and influential. In some places its delicate stems make mattresses on the mountain-tops two feet thick over several acres, while the bloom is so abundant that a single handful plucked at random will contain hundreds of its pale pink bells. The very thought of this, my first Alaskan glacier garden, is an exhilaration. Though it is 2500 feet high, the glacier flowed over its ground as a river flows over a boulder; and since it emerged from the icy sea as from a sepulcher it has been sorely beaten with storms; but from all those deadly, crushing, bitter experiences comes this delicate life and beauty, to teach us that what we in our faithless ignorance and fear call destruction is creation.

As I lingered here night was approaching, so I reluctantly scrambled down out of my blessed garden to the glacier, and returned to my lonely camp, and, getting some coffee and bread, again went up the moraine close to the end of the great ice-wall. The front of the glacier is about three miles wide, but the sheer middle, berg-producing portion that stretches across the inlet from side to side, like a huge green-and-blue barrier, is only about two miles wide, and its height above the water is from 250 to 300 feet. But soundings made by Captain Carroll show that 720 feet of the wall is below the surface, while a third unmeasured portion is buried beneath the moraine detritus that is constantly deposited at the foot of it. Therefore, were the water and rocky detritus cleared away, a sheer precipice of ice would be presented nearly two miles long and more than a thousand feet high. Seen from a distance, as you come up the fiord, it seems comparatively regular in form; but it is far otherwise: bold, jagged capes jut forward into the fiord, alternating with deep reëntering angles and sharp, craggy hollows with plain bastions, while the top is roughened with innumerable spires and pyramids and sharp, hacked blades leaning and toppling, or cutting straight into the sky.

The number of bergs given off varies somewhat with the weather and the tides, the average being about one every five or six minutes, counting only those large enough to thunder loudly, and make themselves heard at a distance of two or three miles. The very largest, however, may, under favorable conditions, be heard ten miles, or even farther. When a large mass sinks from the upper fissured portion of the wall, there is first a keen, piercing crash, then a deep, deliberate, prolonged, thundering roar, which slowly subsides into a low, muttering growl, followed by numerous smaller, grating, clashing sounds from the agitated bergs that dance in the waves about the newcomer as if in welcome; and these again are followed by the swash and roar of the waves that are raised and hurled against the moraines. But the largest and most beautiful of the bergs, instead of thus falling from the upper weathered portion of the wall, rise from the submerged portion with a still grander commotion, springing with tremendous voice and gestures nearly to the top of the wall, tons of water streaming like hair down their sides, plunging and rising again and again before they finally settle in perfect poise, free at last, after having formed part of a slow-crawling glacier for centuries. And as we contemplate their history, as we see them sailing past in their charming crystal beauty, how wonderful it seems that ice formed from pressed snow on the far-off mountains two or three hundred years ago should still be pure and lovely in color, after all its travel and toil in the rough mountain quarries in grinding and fashioning the face of the coming landscape! When the sunshine is sifting through the midst of this multitude of icebergs, and through the jets of radiant spray ever plashing from the blows of the falling and rising bergs, the effect is indescribably glorious. Glorious, too, are the nights along these crystal cliffs when the moon and stars are shining. Then the ice-thunder seems far louder than by day, and the projecting buttresses seem higher, as they stand forward in the pale light, relieved by the gloomy hollows, while the new bergs are dimly seen, crowned with faint lunar bows in the midst of the dashing spray. But it is in the darkest nights, when storms are blowing and the agitated waves are phosphorescent, that the most impressive displays are made. Then the long range of ice-bluffs, faintly illumined, is seen stretching through the gloom in weird, unearthly splendor, luminous foam dashing against it, and against every drifting berg; and amid all this wild, auroral splendor ever and anon some huge new-born berg dashes the living water into a yet brighter foam, and the streaming torrents pouring from its sides are worn as robes of light, while they roar in awful accord with the roaring winds, deep calling unto deep, glacier to glacier, from fiord to fiord.

THE ALASKA TRIP

To the lover of wildness Alaska offers a glorious field for either work or rest: landscape beauty in a thousand forms, things great and small, novel and familiar, as wild and pure as paradise. Wander where you may, wildness ever fresh and ever beautiful meets you in endless variety: ice-laden mountains, hundreds of miles of them peaked and pinnacled and crowded together like trees in groves, and so high and so divinely clad in clouds and air that they seem to belong more to heaven than to earth; inland plains grassy and flowery, dotted with groves and extending like seas all around to the rim of the sky; lakes and streams shining and singing, outspread in sheets of mazy embroidery in untraceable, measureless abundance, brightening every landscape, and keeping the ground fresh and fruitful forever; forests of evergreens growing close together like leaves of grass, girdling a thousand islands and mountains in glorious array; mountains that are monuments of the work of ice, mountains mounuments of volcanic fires; gardens filled with the fairest flowers, giving their fragrance to every wandering wind; and far to the north thousands of miles of ocean ice, now wrapped in fog, now glowing in sunshine through nightless days, and again shining in wintry

The Century Magazine (August, 1897)

WILDERNESS ESSAYS

splendor beneath the beams of the aurora—sea, land, and sky one mass of white radiance like a star. Storms, too, are here as wild and sublime in size and scenery as the landscapes beneath them, displaying the glorious pomp of clouds on the march over mountain and plain, the flight of the snow when all the sky is in bloom, trailing rainfloods, and the booming plunge of avalanches and icebergs and rivers in their rocky glens; while multitudes of wild animals and wild people, clad in feathers and furs, fighting, loving, getting a living, make all the wildness wilder. All this, and unspeakably more, lies in wait for those who love it, sufficient in kind and quantity for gods and men. And notwithstanding that this vast wilderness with its wealth is in great part inaccessible to the streams of careworn people called "tourists," who go forth on ships and railroads to seek rest with nature once a year, some of the most interesting scenery in the territory has lately been brought within easy reach even of such travelers as these, especially in southeastern Alaska, where are to be fond the finest of the forests, the highest mountains, and the largest glaciers.

During the summer season good steamships carrying passengers leave Tacoma on Puget Sound for Alaska about once a week. After touching at Seattle, Port Townsend, Victoria, and Nanaimo, they go through a wilderness of islands to Wrangel, where the first stop in Alaska is made. Thence a charming, wavering course is pursued still north-

THE ALASKA TRIP

ward through the grandest scenery to Tahkou, Juneau, Chilcat, Glacier Bay, and Sitka, affording fine glimpses of the innumerable evergreen islands, the icy mountain-ranges of the coast, the forests, glaciers, etc. The round trip of two thousand miles is made in about twelve days, and costs about a hundred dollars: and though on ocean waters, there is no seasickness, for all the way lies through a network of sheltered inland channels and sounds that are about as free from heaving waves as rivers are.

No other excursion that I know of can be made into any of the wild portions of America where so much fine and grand and novel scenery is brought to view at so cheap and easy a price. Anybody may make this trip and be blest by it—old or young, sick or well, soft, succulent people whose limbs have never ripened, as well as sinewy mountaineers; for the climate is kindly, and one has only to breathe the exhilarating air and gaze and listen while being carried smoothly onward over the glassy waters. Even the blind may be benefited by laving and bathing in the balmy, velvety atmosphere, and the unjust as well as the just; for I fancy that even sins must be washed away in such a climate, and at the feet of such altars as the Alaska mountains are.

Between Tacoma and Port Townsend you gain a general view of the famous Puget Sound, for you sail down the middle of it. It is an arm and many-fingered hand of the sea reaching a hundred miles

37

into the heart of one of the richest forest-regions on the globe. The scenery in fine weather is enchanting, the water as smooth and blue as a mountain lake, sweeping in beautiful curves around bays and capes and jutting promontories innumerable, and islands with soft, wavering outlines passing and overlapping one another, richly feathered with tall, spiry spruces, many of the trees 300 feet in height, their beauty doubled in reflections on the shiny waters. The Cascade Mountains bound the view on the right, the Olympic Range on the left, both ranges covered nearly to their summits with dense coniferous woods.

Doubling cape after cape, and passing uncounted islands that stud the shores, so many new and charming views are offered that one begins to feel there is no need of going farther. Sometimes clouds come down, blotting out all the land; then, lifting a little, perhaps a single island will be given back to the landscape, the tops of its trees dipping out of sight in trailing fringes of mist. Then the long ranks of spruce and cedar along the mainland are set free; and when at length the cloud-mantle vanishes, the colossal cone of Mount Rainier, 14,000 feet high, appears in spotless white, looking down over the dark woods like the very god of the landscape. A fine beginning is this for the Alaska trip! Crossing the Strait of Juan de Fuca from Port Townsend, in a few hours you are in Victoria and a foreign land. Victoria is a handsome little town, a section of old England set down

THE ALASKA TRIP

nearly unchanged in the western American wilderness. It is situated on the south end of Vancouver Island, which is 280 miles long, the largest and southernmost of the wonderful archipelago that stretches northward along the margin of the continent for nearly a thousand miles. The steamer usually stops a few hours here, and most of the tourists go up town to the stores of the famous Hudson Bay Company to purchase fur or some wild Indian trinket as a memento. At certain seasons of the year, when the hairy harvests from the North have been gathered, immense bales of skins may be seen in the unsavory warehouses, the clothing of bears, wolves, beavers, otters, fishers, martens, lynxes, panthers, wolverenes, reindeer, moose, elk, wild sheep, foxes, seals, muskrats, and many others of "our poor earth-born companions and fellow-mortals."

The wilderness presses close up to the town, and it is wonderfully rich and luxuriant. The forests almost rival those of Puget Sound; wild roses are three inches in diameter, and ferns ten feet high. And strange to say, all this exuberant vegetation is growing on moraine material that has been scarcely moved or modified in any way by postglacial agents. Rounded masses of hard, resisting rocks rise everywhere along the shore and in the woods, their scored and polished surfaces still unwasted, telling of a time, so lately gone, when the whole region lay in darkness beneath an all-embracing mantle of ice. Even in the streets of the town glaciated bosses are exposed, the telling inscriptions of which have not been effaced by the wear of either weather or travel. And in the orchards fruitful boughs shade the edges of glacial pavements, and drop apples and peaches on them. Nowhere, as far as I have seen, are the beneficent influences of glaciers made manifest in plainer terms or with more striking contrasts. No tale of enchantment is so marvelous, so exciting to the imagination, as the story of the works and ways of snowflowers marching forth from their encampments on the mountains to develop the beauty of land scenes and make them fruitful.

Leaving Victoria, instead of going to sea we go into a shady wilderness that looks as though it might be in the heart of the continent. Most of the channels through which we glide are narrow as compared with their length and with the height of the mountain walls of the islands which bound their shores. But however sheer the walls, they are almost everywhere densely forested from the water's edge to a height of two thousand feet; and almost every tree may be seen as they rise above one another like an audience on a gallery—the blue-green, sharply spired Menzies spruce; the warm, yellow-green Merten spruce, with finger-like tops all pointing in the same direction or gracefully drooping; and the airy, feathery, brownish Alaska cedar. Most of the way we seem to be tracing a majestic river with lake-like expansions, the tide-currents, the fresh driftwood brought down by avalanches, the inflowing torrents, and the luxuriant foliage of the shores making the likeness complete. The steamer is often so near the shore that we can see the purple cones on the top branches of the trees, and the ferns and bushes at their feet. Then, rounding some bossy cape, the eye perchance is called away into a far-reaching vista, headlands on each side in charming array, one dipping gracefully beyond the other and growing finer in the distance, while the channel, like a strip of silver, stretches between, stirred here and there by leaping salmon and flocks of gulls and ducks that float like lilies among the sun-spangles. While we may be gazing into the depths of this leafy ocean lane, the ship, turning suddenly to right or left, enters an open space, a sound decorated with small islands, sprinkled or clustered in forms and compositions such as nature alone can invent. The smallest of the islands are mere dots, but how beautiful they are! The trees growing on them seem like handfuls that have been culled from the neighboring woods, nicely sorted and arranged, and then set in the water to keep them fresh, the fringing trees leafing out like flowers against the rim of a vase.

The variety we find, both as to the contours and collocation of the islands, whether great or small, is chiefly due to differences in the composition and physical structure of the rocks out of which they are made, and the unequal amount of glaciation to which they have been subjected. All the islands of

WILDERNESS ESSAYS

the archipelago, as well as the headlands and promontories of the mainland, have a rounded, overrubbed, sandpapered appearance, a finish free from
angles, which is produced by the grinding of an
oversweeping, ponderous flood of ice.

FORT WRANGEL

Seven hundred miles of this scenery, and we
arrive at Fort Wrangel, on Wrangel Island, near
the mouth of the Stickeen River. It is a quiet,
rugged, dreamy place of no particular number of
inhabitants—a few hundreds of whites and Indians,
more or less, sleeping in a bog in the midst of the
purest and most delightful scenery on the continent. Baron Wrangel established a trading-post
here about a hundred years ago, and the fort, a
quadrangular stockade, was built by the United
States shortly after the purchase of the territory;
but in a few years it was abandoned and sold to
private parties. Indians, mostly of the Stickeen
tribe, occupy the two long, draggled ends of the
town along the shore; the whites, numbering about
fifty, the middle portion. Stumps and logs roughen
its two crooked streets, each of these picturesque
obstructions mossy and tufted with grass and
bushes on account of the dampness of the climate.

On the arrival of the steamer, most of the
passengers make haste to go ashore to see the
curious totem-poles in front of the massive timber
houses of the Indians, and to buy curiosities,
chiefly silver bracelets hammered from dollars

and half-dollars and tastefully engraved by Indian workmen; blankets better than those of civilization, woven from the wool of wild goats and sheep; carved spoons from the horns of these animals; Shaman rattles, miniature totem-poles, canoes, paddles, stone hatchets, pipes, baskets, etc. The traders in these curious wares are mostly women and children, who gather on the front platforms of the half-dozen stores, sitting in their blankets, seemingly careless whether they sell anything or not, every other face blackened hideously, a naked circle about the eyes and on the tip of the nose, where the smut has been weathered off. The larger girls and the young women are brilliantly arrayed in ribbons and calico, and shine among the blackened and blanketed old crones like scarlet tanagers in a flock of blackbirds. Besides curiosities, most of them have berries to sell, red, yellow and blue, fresh and dewy, and looking wondrous clean as compared with the people. These Indians are proud and intelligent, nevertheless, and maintain an air of self-respect which no amount of raggedness and squalor can wholly subdue.

Many canoes may be seen along the shore, all fashioned alike, with long, beak-like sterns and prows, the largest carrying twenty or thirty persons. What the mustang is to the Mexican vaquero the canoe is to the Indian of the Alaska coast. They skim over the glassy, sheltered waters far and near to fish and hunt and trade, or merely to visit their neighbors. Yonder goes a whole family, grand-

WILDERNESS ESSAYS

parents and all, the prow of their canoe blithely decorated with handfuls of the purple epilobium. They are going to gather berries, as the baskets show. Nowhere else in my travels, north or south, have I seen so many berries. The woods and meadows and open spaces along the shores are full of them—huckleberries of many species, salmon-berries, raspberries, blackberries, currants, and gooseberries, with fragrant strawberries and service-berries on the drier grounds, and cran-berries in the bogs, sufficient for every worm, bird, and human being in the territory, and thousands of tons to spare. The Indians at certain seasons, roving in merry bands, gather large quantities, beat them into paste, and then press the paste into square cakes and dry them for winter use, to be eaten as a kind of bread with their oily salmon. Berries alone, with the lavish bloom that belongs to them, are enough to show how fine and rich this Northern wilderness must be.

ALASKA WEATHER

The climate of all that portion of the coast that is bathed by the Japan current, extending from the southern boundary of the territory northward and westward to the island of Atoo, a distance of nearly twenty-five hundred miles, is remarkably bland, and free from extremes of heat and cold throughout the year. It is rainy, however; but the rain is of good quality, gentle in its fall, filling the fountains of the streams, and keeping the whole

THE ALASKA TRIP

land fresh and fruitful, while anything more delightful than the shining weather after the rain—the great, round sun-days of June, July, and August—can hardly be found elsewhere. An Alaska midsummer day is a day without night. In the extreme northern portion of the territory the sun does not set for weeks, and even as far south as Sitka and Fort Wrangel it sinks only a few degrees below the horizon, so that the rosy colors of the evening blend with those of the morning, leaving no gap of darkness between. Nevertheless, the full day opens slowly. At midnight, from the middle point between the gloaming and the dawn, a low arc of light is seen stealing along the horizon, with gradual increase of height and span and intensity of tone, accompanied usually by red clouds, which make a striking advertisement of the sun's progress long before he appears above the mountain-tops. For several hours after sunrise everything in the landscape seems dull and uncommunicative. The clouds fade, the islands and the mountains, with ruffs of mist about them, cast ill-defined shadows, and the whole firmament changes to pale pearl-gray with just a trace of purple in it. But toward noon there is a glorious awakening. The cool haziness of the air vanishes, and the richer sunbeams, pouring from on high, make all the bays and channels shine. Brightly now play the round-topped ripples about the edges of the islands, and over many a plume-shaped streak between them, where the water is stirred by some passing breeze.

WILDERNESS ESSAYS

On the mountains of the mainland, and in the high-walled fiords that fringe the coast, still finer is the work of the sunshine. The broad white bosoms of the glaciers glow like silver, and their crystal fronts, and the multitude of icebergs that linger about them, drifting, swirling, turning their myriad angles to the sun, are kindled into a perfect blaze of irised light. The warm air throbs and wavers, and makes itself felt as a life-giving, energizing ocean embracing all the earth. Filled with ozone, our pulses bound, and we are warmed and quickened into sympathy with everything, taken back into the heart of nature, whence we came. We feel the life and motion about us, and the universal beauty: the tides marching back and forth with weariless industry, laving the beautiful shores, and swaying the purple dulse of the broad meadows of the sea where the fishes are fed; the wild streams in rows white with waterfalls, ever in bloom and ever in song, spreading their branches over a thousand mountains; the vast forests feeding on the drenching sunbeams, every cell in a whirl of enjoyment; misty flocks of insects stirring all the air; the wild sheep and goats on the grassy ridges above the woods, bears in the berry-tangles, mink and beaver and otter far back on many a river and lake; Indians and adventurers pursuing their lonely ways; birds tending their young—everywhere, everywhere, beauty and life, and glad, rejoicing action.

Through the afternoon all the way down to the

west the air seems to thicken and become soft, without losing its fineness. The breeze dies away, and everything settles into a deep, conscious repose. Then comes the sunset with its purple and gold—not a narrow arch of color, but oftentimes filling more than half the sky. The horizontal clouds that usually bar the horizon are fired on the edges, and the spaces of clear sky between them are filled in with greenish yellow and amber; while the flocks of thin, overlapping cloudlets are mostly touched with crimson, like the outleaning sprays of a maple-grove in the beginning of Indian summer; and a little later a smooth, mellow purple flushes the sky to the zenith, and fills the air, fairly steeping and transfiguring the islands and mountains, and changing all the water to wine.

According to my own observations, in the year 1879 about one third of the summer weather at Wrangel was cloudy, one third rainy, and one third clear. Rain fell on eighteen days in June, eight in July, and twenty in September. But on some of these days only a light shower fell, scarce enough to count, and even the darkest and most bedraggled of them all had a dash of late or early color to cheer them, or some white illumination about the noon hours, while the lowest temperature was about 50°, and the highest 75°.

It is only in late autumn and winter that grand, roaring storms come down and solidly fill all the hours of day and night. Most of them are steady, all-day rains with high winds. Snow on the low-

WILDERNESS ESSAYS

lands is not uncommon, but it never falls to a great depth, or lies long, and the temperature is seldom more than a few degrees below the freezing-point. On the mountains, however, and back in the interior, the winter months are intensely cold— so cold that mercury may at times be used for bullets by the hunters, instead of lead.

EXCURSIONS ABOUT WRANGEL

By stopping over a few weeks at Fort Wrangel, and making excursions into the adjacent region, many near and telling views may be had of the noble forests, glaciers, streams, lakes, wild gardens, Indian villages, etc.; and as the Alaska steamers call here about once a week, you can go on northward and complete your round trip when you like.

THE FORESTS

Going into the woods almost anywhere, you have first to force a way through an outer tangle of *Rubus*, huckleberry, dogwood, and elder-bushes, and a strange woody plant, about six feet high, with limber, rope-like stems beset with thorns, and a head of broad, translucent leaves like the crown of a palm. This is the *Echino panax horrida*, or devil's-club. It is used by the Indians for thrashing witches, and, I fear, deserves both of its bad names. Back in the shady deeps of the forest the walking is comparatively free, and you will be charmed with the majestic beauty and grandeur of the trees, as well as with the solemn stillness and the beauty of the elastic carpet of golden mosses flecked and barred with the sunbeams that sift through the leafy ceiling.

The bulk of the forests of southeastern Alaska is made up of three species of conifers—the Menzies and Merten spruces, and the yellow cedar. These trees cover nearly every rod of the thousand islands, and the coast and the slopes of the mountains of the mainland to a height of about 2000 feet above the sea.

The Menzies spruce, or Sitka pine (*Picea Sitchensis*), is the commonest species. In the heaviest portions of the forest it grows to a height of 175 feet or more, with a diameter of from three to six feet, and in habit and general appearance resembles the Douglas spruce, so abundant about Puget Sound. The timber is tough, close-grained, white, and looks like pine. A specimen that I examined back of Fort Wrangel was a little over six feet in diameter inside the bark four feet above the ground, and at the time it was felled was about 500 years old. Another specimen, four feet in diameter, was 385 years old; and a third, a little less than five feet thick, had attained the good old age of 764 years without showing any trace of decay. I saw a raft of this spruce that had been brought to Wrangel from one of the neighboring islands, three of the logs of which were one hundred feet in length, and nearly two feet in diameter at the small ends. Perhaps half of all the trees in southeastern Alaska are of this species. Menzies, whose name is associated with this grand tree, was a Scotch botanist who accompanied Vancouver in his voyage of discovery to this coast a hundred years ago.

The beautiful hemlock-spruce (*Tsuga Mertensiana*) is more slender than its companion, but nearly as tall, and the young trees are more graceful and picturesque in habit. Large numbers of this species used to be cut down by the Indians for the astringent bark, which they pounded into meal for bread to be eaten with oily fish.

The third species of this notable group, *Chamoecyparis Nutkaensis*, called yellow cedar or Alaska cedar, attains a height of 150 feet and a diameter of from three to five feet. The branches are pinnate, drooping, and form beautiful light-green sprays like those of *Libocedrus*, but the foliage is finer and the plumes are more delicate. The wood of this noble tree is the best the country affords, and one of the most valuable of the entire Pacific coast. It is pale yellow, close-grained, tough, durable, and takes a fine polish. The Indians make their paddles and totem-poles of it, and weave matting and coarse cloth from the inner bark. It is also the favorite fire-wood. A yellow-cedar fire is worth going a long way to see. The flames rush up in a multitude of quivering, jagged-edged lances, displaying admirable enthusiasm, while the burning surfaces of the wood snap and crackle and explode and throw off showers of coals with such noise that conversation at such firesides is well-nigh impossible.

The durability of this timber is forcibly illustrated by fallen trunks that are perfectly sound after lying in the damp woods for centuries. Soon after these trees fall they are overgrown with moss, in which seeds lodge and germinate and grow up into vigorous saplings, which stand in a row on the backs of their dead ancestors. Of this company of young trees perhaps three or four will grow to full stature, sending down straddling roots on each side, and establishing themselves in the soil; and after they have reached an age of two or three hundred years, the downtrodden trunk on which they are standing, when cut into, is found as fresh in the heart as when it fell.

The species is found as far south as Oregon, and is sparsely distributed along the coast and through the islands as far north as Chilcat (latitude 59°). The most noteworthy of the other trees found in the southern portion of these forests, but forming only a small portion of the whole, is the giant arbor-vitae (*Thuja gigantea*). It is distributed all the way up the coast from California to about latitude 56°. It is from this tree that the Indians make their best canoes, some of them being large enough to carry fifty or sixty men. Of pine I have seen only one species (*Pinus contorta*), a few specimens of which, about fifty feet high, may be found on the margins of lakes and bogs. In the interior beyond the mountains it forms extensive forests. So also does *Picea alba*, a slender, spiry tree which attains a height of one hundred feet or more. I saw this species growing bravely on frozen ground on the banks of streams that flow into Kotzebue Sound, forming there the margin of the arctic forest.

In the cool cañons and fiords, and along the banks of the glaciers, a species of silver fir and the beautiful Paton spruce abound. The only hard-wood trees I have found in Alaska are birch, alder, maple, and wild apple, one species of each. They grow mostly about the margins of the main forests and back in the mountain cañons. The lively yellow-green of the birch gives pleasing variety to the colors of the conifers, especially on slopes of river-cañons with a southern exposure. In general views all the coast forests look dark in the middle ground and blue in the distance, while the foreground shows a rich series of gray and brown and yellow trees. In great part these colors are due to lichens which hang in long tresses from the limbs, and to mosses which grow in broad, nest-like beds on the horizontal palmate branches of the Menzies and Merten spruces. Upon these moss-bed gardens high in the air ferns and grasses grow luxuriantly, and even seedling trees five or six feet in height, presenting the curious spectacle of old, venerable trees holding hundreds of their children in their arms.

Seward expected Alaska to become the ship-yard of the world, and so perhaps it may. In the meantime, as good or better timber for every use still abounds in California, Oregon, Washington, and

THE ALASKA TRIP

British Columbia; and let us hope that under better management the waste and destruction that have hitherto prevailed in our forests will cease, and the time be long before our Northern reserves need to be touched. In the hands of nature these Alaska tribes of conifers are increasing from century to century as the glaciers are withdrawn. May they be saved until wanted for worthy use—so worthy that we may imagine the trees themselves willing to come down the mountains to their fate!

THE RIVERS

The most interesting of the excursions that may be made from Fort Wrangel is the one up the Stickeen River. Perhaps twenty or thirty of the Alaska streams may be called rivers, but not one of them all, from the mighty Yukon, 2000 miles long, to the shortest of the mountain torrents pouring white from the glaciers, has been fully explored. From St. Elias the coast mountains extend in a broad, lofty chain beyond the southern boundary of the territory, gashed by stupendous cañons, each of which carries a stream deep enough and broad enough to be called a river, though comparatively short, as the highest sources of most of them lie in the icy solitudes of the range within forty or fifty miles of the coast. A few, however, of this foaming brotherhood—the Chilcat, Chilcoot, Tahkou, Stickeen, and perhaps others—come from beyond the range, heading with the Mackenzie and Yukon.

WILDERNESS ESSAYS

The tributary cañons of the main-trunk cañons of all these streams are still occupied by glaciers which descend in glorious ranks, their massy, bulging snouts lying back a little distance in the shadows, or pushed grandly forward among the cottonwoods that line the banks of the rivers, or all the way across the main cañons, compelling the rivers to find a way beneath them through long, arching tunnels.

The Stickeen is perhaps better known than any other river in Alaska, because it is the way to the Cassiar gold-mines. It is about 350 miles long, and is navigable for small steamers 150 miles to Glenora. It first pursues a westerly course through grassy plains darkened here and there with patches of evergreens; then, curving southward, and receiving numerous tributaries from the north, it enters the Coast Range, and sweeps across it to the sea, through a yosemite that is more than a hundred miles long, one to three miles wide and from 5000 to 8000 feet deep, and marvelously beautiful from end to end. To the appreciative tourist sailing up the river, the cañon is a gallery of sublime pictures, an unbroken series of majestic mountains, glaciers, waterfalls, cascades, groves, gardens, grassy meadows, etc., in endless variety of form and composition; while back of the walls, and thousands of feet above them, innumerable peaks and spires and domes of ice and snow tower grandly into the sky.

Gliding along the swift-flowing river, the views

change with bewildering rapidity. Wonderful, too, are the changes dependent on the seasons and the weather. In winter avalanches from the snow-laden heights boom and reverberate from side to side like majestic waterfalls; storm-winds from the arctic highlands, sweeping the cañon like a flood, choke the air with ice-dust; while the rocks, glaciers, and groves are in spotless white. In spring you enjoy the chanting of countless waterfalls; the gentle breathing of warm winds; the opening of leaves and flowers; the humming of bees over beds of honeybloom; birds building their nests; clouds of fragrance drifting hither and thither from miles of wild roses, clover, and honeysuckle, and tangles of sweet chaparral; swaths of birch and willow on the lower slopes following the melting snow-banks; bossy cumuli swelling in white and purple piles above the highest peaks; gray rain-clouds wreathing the outstanding brows and battlements of the walls; then the breaking forth of the sun after the rain, the shining of the wet leaves and the river and the crystal architecture of the glaciers; the rising of fresh fragrance, the song of the happy birds, the looming of the white domes in the azure, and the serene color-grandeur of the morning and evening. In summer you find the groves and gardens in full dress; glaciers melting rapidly under warm sunshine and rain; waterfalls in all their glory; the river rejoicing in its strength; butterflies wavering and drifting about like ripe flower-bloom in springtime; young birds trying their wings;

bears enjoying salmon and berries; all the life of the cañon brimming full like the streams. In autumn comes rest, as if the year's work were done; sunshine, streaming over the cliffs in rich, hazy beams, calls forth the last of the gentians and goldenrods; the groves and tangles and meadows bloom again, every leaf changing to a petal, scarlet and yellow; the rocks also bloom, and the glaciers, in the mellow golden light. And so goes the song, change succeeding change in glorious harmony through all the seasons and years.

Leaving Wrangel, you go up the coast to Juneau. After passing through the picturesque Wrangel Narrows into Souchoi Channel and Prince Frederick Sound, a few icebergs come in sight, the first you have seen on the trip. They are derived from a large, showy glacier, the Leconte, which discharges into a wild fiord near the mouth of the Stickeen River, which the Indians call *Hutli*, or Thunder Bay, on account of the noise made by the discharge of the icebergs. This, so far as I know, is the southernmost of the glaciers that flow into the sea. Gliding northward, you have the mountains of the mainland on one hand, Kuprianof and countless smaller islands on the other. The views extend far into the wilderness, all of them as wild and clean as the sky; but your attention will chiefly be turned to the mountains, now for the first time appreciably near. As the steamer crawls along the coast, the cañons are opened to view and closed again in regular succession, like the leaves of a book, allowing the attentive observer to see far back into their icy depths. About halfway between Wrangel Narrows and Cape Fanshaw, you are opposite a noble group of glaciers which come sweeping down through the woods from their white fountains nearly to the level of the sea, swaying in graceful, river-like curves around the feet of lofty granite mountains and precipices like those of the Yosemite valley. It was at the largest of these, the Paterson glacier, that the ships of the Alaska Ice Company were loaded for San Francisco and the Sandwich Islands.

An hour or two farther north another fleet of icebergs come in sight, which have their sources in Sum Dum or Holkam Bay. This magnificent inlet, with its long, icy arms reaching deep into the mountains, is one of the most interesting of all the Alaska fiords; but the icebergs in it are too closely compacted to allow a passage for any of the excursion-steamers.

About five miles from the mouth the bay divides into two main arms, about eighteen and twenty miles long, in the farthest-hidden recesses of which there are four large glaciers which discharge bergs. Of the smaller glaciers of the second and third class that melt before reaching tidewater, a hundred or more may be seen along the walls from a canoe, and about as many snowy cataracts, which, with the plunging bergs from the main glaciers, keep all the fiord in a roar. The scenery in both of the long arms and their side branches is of the wildest description, especially in their upper reaches, where the granite walls rise in sheer, massive precipices, like those of the Yosemite valley, to a height of from 3000 to 5000 feet. About forty miles farther up the coast another fleet of icebergs come in sight, through the midst of which the steamer passes into the Tahkou Inlet. It is about eighteen miles into the heart of the Coast Mountains, draining many glaciers, great and small, all of which were once tributary branches of one grand glacier that formed and occupied the inlet as its channel. This inlet more plainly than any other that I have examined illustrates the mode of formation of the wonderful system of deep channels extending northward from Puget Sound; for it is a marked portion of that system, a branch of Stephen's Passage still in process of formation at the head; while its trends and sculpture are as distinctly glacial as those of the smaller fiords.

Sailing up the middle of it, you may count some forty-five glaciers. Three of these reach the level of the sea, descending from a group of lofty mountains at the head of the inlet, and making a grand show. Only one, however, the beautiful Tahkou glacier, discharges bergs. It comes sweeping forward in majestic curves, and discharges its bergs through a western branch of the inlet next the one occupied by the Tahkou River. Thus we see here a river of ice and a river of water flowing into the sea side by side, both of them abounding in cascades and rapids; yet how different in their rate of motion, and in the songs they sing, and in their influence on the landscape! A rare object-lesson this, worth coming round the world to see.

Once, while I sat sketching among the icebergs here, two Tahkou Indians, father and son, came gliding toward us in an exceedingly small cottonwood canoe. Coming alongside with a good-natured "Sahgaya," they inquired who we were, what we were doing, etc., while they in turn gave information concerning the river, their village, and two other large glaciers a few miles up the river-cañon. They were hunting hair-seals, and as they slipped softly away in pursuit of their prey, crouching in their tiny shell of a boat among the bergs, with barbed spear in place, they formed a picture of icy wildness as telling as any to be found amid the drifts and floes of Greenland.

After allowing the passengers a little time—half an hour or so—to admire the crystal wall of the great glacier and the huge bergs that plunge and rise from it, the steamer goes down the inlet to Juneau. This young town is the mining-center, and, so far as business is concerned, the chief place in the territory. Here, it is claimed, you may see the largest quartz-mill in the world, the two hundred and forty stamps of which keep up a "steady, industrious growl that may be heard a mile away."

Alaska, generally speaking, is a hard country for the prospector, because most of the ground is either permanently frozen or covered with glaciers, forests, or a thick blanket of moss. Nevertheless, thousands of hardy miners from the gulches and ledges of California and Arizona are rapidly over-running the territory in every direction, and making it tell its wealth. And though perhaps not one vein or placer in a hundred has yet been touched, enough has been discovered to warrant the opinion that this icy country holds at least a fair share of the gold of the world. After time has been given for a visit to the mines and a saunter through the streets of Juneau, the steamer passes between Douglass and Admiralty islands into Lynn Canal, the most beautiful and spacious of all the mountain-walled channels you have yet seen. The Auk and Eagle glaciers appear in one view on the right as you enter the canal, swaying their crystal floods through the woods with grand effect. But it is on the west side of the canal, near the head, that the most striking feature of the landscape is seen—the Davidson glacier. It first appears as an immense ridge of ice thrust forward into the channel; but when you have gained a position directly in front, it presents a broad current issuing from a noble gateway at the foot of the mountains, and spreading out to right and left in a beautiful fanshaped mass three or four miles in width, the front of which is separated from the water by the terminal moraine. This is one of the most notable of the large glaciers that are in the first stage of decadence, reaching nearly to tide-water, but failing to enter it and send off bergs. Excepting the Tahkou, all the great glaciers you have yet seen on

THE ALASKA TRIP

the trip belong to this class; but this one is perhaps the most beautiful of its kind, and you will not be likely to forget the picture it makes, however icy your after-travels may be. Shortly after passing the Davidson glacier the northernmost point of the trip is reached at the head of the canal, a little above latitude 59°. At the canning-establishments here you may learn something of the inhabitants of these beautiful waters. Whatever may be said of other resources of the territory,—furs, minerals, timber, etc.,—it is hardly possible to overestimate the importance of the fisheries. Besides whales in the far North, and the cod, herring, halibut, and other food fishes that swarm over immense areas along the shores and inlets, there are probably not fewer than a thousand salmon streams in Alaska that are crowded with fine salmon for months every year. Their numbers are beyond conception. Oftentimes there seem to be more fish than water in the rapid portions of the streams. On one occasion one of my men waded out into the middle of a crowded run, and amused himself by picking up the fish and throwing them over his head. In a single hour these Indians may capture enough to last a year. Surely in no part of the world may one's daily bread be more easily obtained. Sailing into these streams on dark nights, when the waters are phosphorescent and the salmon are running, is a very beautiful and exciting experience; the myriad fins of the on-rushing multitude crowding against one another churn all the water from bank to bank into silver fire, making a glorious glow in the darkness.

From Chilcat we now go down Lynn Canal, through Icy Strait, and into the famous Glacier Bay. All the voyage thus far after leaving Wrangel has been icy, and you have seen hundreds of glaciers great and small; but this bay, and the region about it and beyond it toward Mount St. Elias, are pre-eminently the iceland of Alaska, and of all the west coast of the continent.

GLACIERS OF THE PACIFIC COAST

Glancing for a moment at the results of a general exploration of the mountain-ranges of the Pacific coast, we find that there are between sixty and seventy small residual glaciers in the California Sierra. Northward through Oregon and Washington, glaciers, some of them of considerable extent, still exist on all the higher volcanic mountains of the Cascade Range,—the Three Sisters, Mounts Jefferson, Hood, St. Helen's, Adams, Rainier, Baker, and others,—though none of them approach the sea. Through British Columbia and southeastern Alaska the broad, sustained chain of coast mountains is generally glacier-bearing. The upper branches of nearly every one of its cañons are still occupied by glaciers, which gradually increase in size and descend lower until the lofty region between Glacier Bay and Mount St. Elias is reached, where a considerable number discharge into the sea. About Prince William's Sound and Cook's Inlet many grand glaciers are displayed; but

THE ALASKA TRIP

farther to the west, along the Alaska peninsula and the chain of the Aleutian Islands, though a large number of glaciers occur on the highest peaks, they are mostly small, and melt far above sea-level, while to the north of latitude 62° few, if any, remain in existence, the ground being comparatively low and the snowfall light.

ON THE MUIR GLACIER

The largest of the seven glaciers that discharge into Glacier Bay is the Muir; and being also the most accessible, it is the one to which tourists are taken and allowed to go ashore for a few hours, to climb about its crystal cliffs and watch the huge icebergs as with tremendous, thundering roar they plunge and rise from the majestic frontal sea-wall in which the glacier terminates. The front, or snout, of the glacier is about three miles wide, but the central berg-discharging portion, which stretches across from side to side of the inlet like a huge jagged white-and-blue barrier, is only about half as wide. The height of the ice-wall above the water is from 250 to 300 feet, but soundings made by Captain Carroll show that 720 feet of the wall is below the surface, while still a third unmeasured portion is buried beneath the moraine material that is being constantly deposited at the foot of it. Therefore, were the water and rocky detritus removed, there would be presented a sheer precipice of ice a mile and a half wide and more than a thousand feet in height. Seen from the inlet as you approach it, at a distance of a mile or two it seems massive and comparatively regular in form, but it is far from being smooth. Deep rifts and hollows alternate with broad, plain bastions, which are ever changing as the icebergs are discharged, while it is roughened along the top with innumerable spires and pyramids and sharp, hacked blades, leaning and toppling, or cutting straight into the sky.

THE BIRTH OF THE ICEBERGS

The number of bergs given off varies somewhat with the weather and the tides. For twelve consecutive hours I counted the number discharged that were large enough to make themselves heard like thunder at a distance of a mile or two, and found the average rate to be one in five or six minutes. The thunder of the largest may be heard, under favorable circumstances, ten miles or more. When a large mass sinks from the upper fissured portion of the wall, there is first a keen, piercing crash, then a deep, deliberate, long-drawn-out, thundering roar, which slowly subsides into a comparatively low, far-reaching, muttering growl; then come a crowd of grating, clashing sounds from the agitated bergs that dance in the waves about the newcomer as if in welcome; and these, again, are followed by the swash and roar of the berg-waves as they reach the shore and break among the boulders. But the largest and most beautiful of the bergs, instead of falling from the

THE ALASKA TRIP

exposed weathered portion of the wall, rise from the submerged portion with a still grander commotion, heaving aloft nearly to the top of the wall with awful roaring, tons of water streaming like hair down their sides, while they heave and plunge again and again before they settle in poise and sail away as blue crystal islands, free at last after being held fast as part of a slow-crawling glacier for centuries. And how wonderful it seems that ice formed from pressed snow on the mountains two or three hundred years ago should, after all its toil and travel in grinding down and fashioning the face of the landscape, still remain pure and fresh and lovely in color! When the sunshine is pouring and sifting in iris colors through the midst of all this wilderness of angular crystal ice, and through the grand, flame-shaped jets and sheets of radiant spray ever rising from the blows of the falling bergs, the effect is indescribably glorious.

GLACIAL NIGHTS

Glorious, too, are the nights along these crystal cliffs, when the moon and the stars are shining; the projecting buttresses and battlements, seemingly far higher than by day, standing forward in the moonlight, relieved by the shadows of the hollows; the new-born bergs keeping up a perpetual storm of thunder, and the lunar bows displaying faint iris colors in the up-dashing spray. But it is in the darkest nights, when storms are blowing and the waters of the inlet are phosphorescent, that the

65

most terribly impressive show is displayed. Then the long range of crystal bluffs, faintly illumined, is seen stretching away in the stormy gloom in awful, unearthly grandeur, luminous waves dashing beneath in a glowing, seething, wavering fringe of foam, while the new-born bergs, rejoicing in their freedom, plunging, heaving, grating one against another, seem like living creatures of some other world, dancing and roaring with the roaring storm and the glorious surges of auroral light.

CHARACTERISTICS OF THE MUIR GLACIER

If you go ashore as soon as the steamer drops anchor, you will have time to push back across the terminal moraine on the east side, and over a mile or so of the margin of the glacier, climb a yellow ridge that comes forward there and is easy of access, and gain a good, comprehensive, telling view of the greater portion of the glacier and its principal tributaries—that is, if you are so fortunate as to have clear weather. Instead of a river of ice winding down a narrow, mountain-walled valley, like the largest of the Swiss glaciers, you will see here a grand lake or sea of ice twenty-five or thirty miles wide, more than two hundred times as large as the celebrated Mer de Glace of the Alps, a broad, gently undulating prairie surrounded by a forest of mountains from the shadowy cañons and amphitheaters of which uncounted tributary glaciers flow into the grand central reservoir. There are seven main tributaries, from two to six miles wide where they enter the trunk, and from twenty to thirty miles long; each of these has many secondary tributaries, so that the whole number, great and small, pouring from the mountain fountains into the grand central trunk must number at least two hundred, not counting the smallest. The views up the main tributaries in bright weather are exceedingly rich and beautiful; though far off from your standpoint, the broad white floods of ice are clearly seen issuing in graceful lines from the depths of the mysterious solitudes. The area drained by this one grand glacier and its branches can hardly be less than a thousand square miles, and it probably contains more ice than all the eleven hundred glaciers of the Swiss Alps combined. The distance back from the front to the head of the farthest fountain is about fifty miles, and the width of the trunk below the confluence of the tributaries is about twenty-five miles. Though apparently as motionless as the mountains about its basin, the whole glacier flows on like a river, unhalting, unresting, through all the seasons from century to century, with a motion varying in every part with the depth of the current and the declivity, smoothness, and directness of different portions of the channel. The rate of motion in the central cascading portion of the current near the front, as determined by Professor Reid, is from two and a half to five inches an hour, or from five to ten feet a day.

WILDERNESS ESSAYS

Along the eastern margin of the main trunk the ice is so little broken that a hundred horsemen might ride abreast for miles without encountering much difficulty. But far the greater portion of the vast expanse is torn and crumpled into a bewildering network of ridges and blades, and rough, broken hummocks, separated by yawning gulfs and crevasses unspeakably beautiful and awful. Here and there the adventurous explorer, picking a way in long, patient zigzags through the shining wilderness, comes to spacious hollows, some of them miles in extent, where the ice, closely pressed and welded, presents beautiful blue lakes fed by bands of streams that sing and ring and gurgle, and make sheets of melody as sweet as ever were made by larks in springtime over their nests in the meadows.

Besides the Muir there are here six other noble glaciers which send off fleets of icebergs, and keep the whole bay in a roar. These are the Geikie, Hugh Miller, Pacific, Reid, Carroll, and Hoona glaciers. Of the second class of grand size descending to the level of the sea, but separated from it by mud floats and flood-washed terminal moraines, there are eight, and the smaller ones are innumerable.

With these views of the ice-world the duty-laden tourist is gladly content, knowing that nowhere else could he have sailed in a comfortable steamer into new-born landscapes and witnessed the birth of icebergs. Returning down the bay in a zigzag course, dodging the drifting bergs, you may

THE ALASKA TRIP

see the lofty summits of the Fairweather Range—
Mounts Fairweather, Lituya, Crillon, and La Pérouse. Then, leaving Icy Strait, you enter Chatham
Strait, and thence pass through the picturesque
Peril Strait to Sitka, the capital of the territory.
Here the steamer usually stops for a day, giving
time to see the interesting old Russian town and
its grand surroundings. After leaving Sitka the
steamer touches again at Wrangel for the mails.
Then, gliding through the green archipelago by
the same way that you came you speedily arrive
in civilization, rich in wildness forevermore.

TWENTY HILL HOLLOW

I WISH to say a word for the great central plain of California in general, and for Twenty Hill Hollow, in Merced County, in particular; because, in reading descriptions of California scenery, by the literary racers who annually make a trial of their speed here, one is led to fancy, that, outside the touristical see-saw of Yosemite, Geysers, and Big Trees, our State contains little else worthy of note, excepting, perhaps, certain wine-cellars and vineyards, and that our great plain is a sort of Sahara, whose narrowest and least dusty crossing they benevolently light-house. But to the few travelers who are in earnest – true lovers of the truth and beauty of wildness – we would say, Heed nothing you have heard; put no questions to "agent," or guide-book, or dearest friend; cast away your watches and almanacs, and go at once to our garden-

Overland Monthly (April, 1872)

This is the hub of the region where Mr. Muir spent the greater part of the summer of 1868 and the spring of 1869.

TWENTY HILL HOLLOW

wilds – the more planless and ignorant the better. Drift away confidingly into the broad gulf-streams of Nature, helmed only by Instinct. No harsh storm, no bear, no snake, will harm you. Those who submissively allow themselves to be packed and brined down in the sweats of a stage-coach, who are hurled into Yosemite by "favorite routes," are not aware that they are crossing a grander Yosemite than that to which they are going.

The whole State of California, from Siskiyou to San Diego, is one block of beauty, one matchless valley; and our great plain, with its mountain-walls, is the true California Yosemite – exactly corresponding in its physical character and proportions to that of the Merced. Moreover, as Yosemite the less is outlined in the lesser Yosemites of Indian Cañon, Glacier Cañon, Illilouette, and Pohono, so is Yosemite the great by the Yosemites of King's River, Fresno, Merced, and Tuolumne. The only important difference between the great central Yosemite – bottomed by the plain of the Sacramento and San Joaquin, and walled by the Sierras and mountains of the coast – and the Merced Yosemite – bottomed by a glacier meadow, and walled by glacier rocks – is, that the former is double – two Yosemites in one, each proceeding from a tangle of glacier *cañons*, meeting opposite Suisun Bay, and sending their united waters to the sea by the Golden Gate.

Were we to cross-cut the Sierra Nevada into blocks a dozen miles or so in thickness, each section would contain a Yosemite Valley and a river, together with a bright array of lakes and meadows, rocks and forests. The grandeur and inexhaustible beauty of each block would be so vast and over-satisfying that to choose among them would be like selecting slices of bread cut from the same loaf. One bread-slice might have burnt spots, answering to craters; another would be more browned; another, more crusted or raggedly cut; but all essentially the same. In no greater degree would the Sierra slices differ in general character. Nevertheless, we all would choose the Merced slice, because, being easier of access, it has been nibbled and tasted, and pronounced very good; and because of the concentrated form of its Yosemite, caused by certain conditions of baking, yeasting, and glacier-frosting of this portion of the great Sierra loaf. In like manner, we readily perceive that the great central plain is one batch of bread — one golden cake — and we are loath to leave these magnificent loaves for

TWENTY HILL HOLLOW

crumbs, however good.

After our smoky sky has been washed in the rains of winter, the whole complex row of Sierras appear from the plain as a simple wall slightly beveled, and colored in horizontal bands laid one above another, as if entirely composed of partially straightened rainbows. So, also, the plain seen from the mountains has the same simplicity of smooth surface, colored purple and yellow, like a patchwork of irised clouds. But when we descend to this smooth-furred sheet, we discover complexity in its physical conditions equal to that of the mountains, though less strongly marked. In particular, that portion of the plain lying between the Merced and the Tuolumne, within ten miles of the slaty foothills, is most elaborately carved into valleys, hollows, and smooth undulations, and among them is laid the Merced Yosemite of the plain – Twenty Hill Hollow.

This delightful Hollow is less than a mile in length, and of just sufficient width to form a well-proportioned oval. It is situated about midway between the two rivers, and five miles from the Sierra foothills. Its banks are formed of twenty hemispherical hills; hence its name. They surround and enclose it on all sides, leaving only one narrow opening

toward the southwest for the escape of its
waters. The bottom of the Hollow is about
two hundred feet below the level of the surrounding plain, and the tops of its hills are
slightly below the general level. Here is no
towering dome, no Tissiack, to mark its
place; and one may ramble close upon its rim
before he is made aware of its existence. Its
twenty hills are as wonderfully regular in
size and position as in form. They are like
big marbles half buried in the ground, each
poised and settled daintily into its place at
a regular distance from its fellows, making
a charming fairy-land of hills, with small,
grassy valleys between, each valley having a
tiny stream of its own, which leaps and sparkles
out into the open hollow, uniting to form
Hollow Creek.

Like all others in the immediate neighborhood, these twenty hills are composed of
stratified lavas mixed with mountain drift
in varying proportions. Some strata are almost
wholly made up of volcanic matter — lava and
cinders — thoroughly ground and mixed
by the waters that deposited them; others
are largely composed of slate and quartz
boulders of all degrees of coarseness, forming conglomerates. A few clear, open sections
occur, exposing an elaborate history of seas,

and glaciers, and volcanic floods — chapters
of cinders and ashes that picture dark days,
when these bright snowy mountains were
clouded in smoke, and rivered and laked with
living fire. A fearful age, say mortals, when
these bright Sierras flowed lava to the sea.
What horizons of flame! What atmospheres of
ashes and smoke!

The conglomerates and lavas of this region
are readily denuded by water. In the time
when their parent sea was removed to form
this golden plain, their regular surface,
in great part covered with shallow lakes,
showed little variation from motionless level
until torrents of rain and floods from the
mountains gradually sculptured the simple
page to the present diversity of bank and
brae, creating, in the section between the
Merced and the Tuolumne, Twenty Hill Hollow, Lily Hollow, and the lovely valley of
Cascade and Castle Creeks, with many others
nameless and unknown, seen only by hunters
and shepherds, sunk in the wide bosom of
the plain, like undiscovered gold. Twenty Hill
Hollow is a fine illustration of a valley created
by erosion of water. Here are no Washington columns, no angular El Capitans. The
hollow cañons, cut in soft lavas, are not so
deep as to require a single earthquake at

the hands of science, much less a baker's dozen of those convenient tools demanded for the making of mountain Yosemites, and our moderate arithmetical standards are not outraged by a single magnitude of this simple, comprehensible hollow.

The present rate of denudation of this portion of the plain seems to be about one tenth of an inch per year. This approximation is based upon observations made upon stream-banks and perennial plants. Rains and winds remove mountains without disturbing their plant or animal inhabitants. Hovering petrels, the fishes and floating plants of ocean, sink and rise in beautiful rhythm with its waves; and, in like manner, the birds and plants of the plain sink and rise with these waves of land, the only difference being that the fluctuations are more rapid in the one case than in the other.

In March and April the bottom of the Hollow and every one of its hills are smoothly covered and plushed with yellow and purple flowers, the yellow predominating. They are mostly social *Compositæ*, with a few claytonias, gilias, eschscholtzias, white and yellow violets, blue and yellow lilies, dodecatheons, and eriogonums set in a half-floating maze of purple grasses. There is but one vine in the Hollow — the *Megarrhiza* [*Echinocystis* T. & D.] or

"Big Root." The only bush within a mile of it, about four feet in height, forms so remarkable an object upon the universal smoothness that my dog barks furiously around it, at a cautious distance, as if it were a bear. Some of the hills have rock ribs that are brightly colored with red and yellow lichens, and in moist nooks there are luxuriant mosses — *Bartramia*, *Dicranum*, *Funaria*, and several *Hypnums*. In cool, sunless coves the mosses are companioned with ferns — a *Cystopteris* and the little gold-dusted rock fern, *Gymnogramma triangularis*.

The Hollow is not rich in birds. The meadowlark homes there, and the little burrowing owl, the killdeer, and a species of sparrow. Occasionally a few ducks pay a visit to its waters, and a few tall herons — the blue and the white — may at times be seen stalking along the creek; and the sparrow hawk and gray eagle [1] come to hunt. The lark, who does nearly all the singing for the Hollow, is not identical in species with the meadowlark of the East, though closely resembling it; richer flowers and skies have inspired him with a better song than was ever known to the Atlantic lark.

I have noted three distinct lark-songs here. The words of the first, which I committed to

[1] Mr. Muir doubtless meant the golden eagle (*Aquila chrysaëtos*).

memory at one of their special meetings, spelled as sung, are "Wee-ro spee-ro wee-o weer-ly wee-it." On the 20th of January, 1869, they sang "Queed-lix boodle," repeating it with great regularity, for hours together, to music sweet as the sky that gave it. On the 22d of the same month, they sang "Chee chool chee-dildy choodildy." An inspiration is this song of the blessed lark, and universally absorbable by human souls. It seems to be the only bird-song of these hills that has been created with any direct reference to us. Music is one of the attributes of matter, into whatever forms it may be organized. Drops and sprays of air are specialized, and made to plash and churn in the bosom of a lark, as infinitesimal portions of air plash and sing about the angles and hollows of sand-grains, as perfectly composed and predestined as the rejoicing anthems of worlds; but our senses are not fine enough to catch the tones. Fancy the waving, pulsing melody of the vast flower-congregations of the Hollow flowing from myriad voices of tuned petal and pistil, and heaps of sculptured pollen. Scarce one note is for us; nevertheless, God be thanked for this blessed instrument hid beneath the feathers of a lark.

The eagle does not dwell in the Hollow; he only floats there to hunt the long-eared hare.

TWENTY HILL HOLLOW

One day I saw a fine specimen alight upon a hillside. I was at first puzzled to know what power could fetch the sky-king down into the grass with the larks. Watching him attentively, I soon discovered the cause of his earthiness. He was hungry and stood watching a long-eared hare, which stood erect at the door of his burrow, staring his winged fellow mortal full in the face. They were about ten feet apart. Should the eagle attempt to snatch the hare, he would instantly disappear in the ground. Should long-ears, tired of inaction, venture to skim the hill to some neighboring burrow, the eagle would swoop above him and strike him dead with a blow of his pinions, bear him to some favorite rock table, satisfy his hunger, wipe off all marks of grossness, and go again to the sky.

Since antelopes have been driven away, the hare is the swiftest animal of the Hollow. When chased by a dog he will not seek a burrow, as when the eagle wings in sight, but skims wavily from hill to hill across connecting curves, swift and effortless as a bird-shadow. One that I measured was twelve inches in height at the shoulders. His body was eighteen inches, from nose-tip to tail. His great ears measured six and a half inches in length and two in width. His ears — which, notwithstanding their great size, he wears gracefully and becomingly — have procured for him the homely nickname, by which he is commonly known, of "Jackass rabbit." Hares are very abundant over all the plain and up in the sunny, lightly wooded foothills, but their range does not extend into the close pine forests.

Coyotes, or California wolves, are occasionally seen gliding about the Hollow; but they are not numerous, vast numbers having been slain by the traps and poisons of sheep-raisers. The coyote is about the size of a small shepherd-dog, beautiful and graceful in motion, with erect ears, and a bushy tail, like a fox. Inasmuch as he is fond of mutton, he is cordially detested by "sheep-men" and nearly all cultured people.

The ground-squirrel is the most common animal of the Hollow. In several hills there is a soft stratum in which they have tunneled their homes. It is interesting to observe these rodent towns in time of alarm. Their one circular street resounds with sharp, lancing outcries of "Seekit, seek, seek, seekit!" Near neighbors, peeping cautiously half out-of-doors, engage in low, purring chat. Others, bolt upright on the doorsill or on the rock above, shout excitedly, as if calling attention to the motions and aspects of the enemy. Like the wolf, this little animal is accursed, because of his relish for grain. What a pity that Nature should have made so many small mouths palated like our own!

All the seasons of the Hollow are warm and bright, and flowers bloom through the whole year. But the grand commencement of the annual genesis of plant and insect life is governed by the setting-in of the rains, in December or January. The air, hot and opaque, is then washed and cooled. Plant seeds, which for six months have lain on the ground dry as if garnered in a farmer's bin, at once unfold their treasured life. Flies hum their delicate tunes. Butterflies come from their coffins, like cotyledons from their husks. The network of dry water-courses, spread over valleys and hollows, suddenly gushes with bright waters, sparkling and pouring from pool to pool, like dusty mummies risen from the dead and set living and laughing with color and blood. The weather grows in beauty, like a flower. Its roots in the ground develop day-clusters a week or two in size, divided by and shaded in foliage of clouds; or round hours of ripe sunshine wave and spray in sky-shadows, like racemes of berries half hidden in leaves.

These months of so-called rainy season are not filled with rain. Nowhere else in North

America, perhaps in the world, are Januarys so balmed and glowed with vital sunlight. Referring to my notes of 1868 and 1869, I find that the first heavy general rain of the season fell on the 18th of December. January yielded to the Hollow, during the day, only twenty hours of rain, which was divided among six rainy days. February had only three days on which rain fell, amounting to eighteen and one half hours in all. March had five rainy days. April had three, yielding seven hours of rain. May also had three wet days, yielding nine hours of rain, and completed the so-called "rainy season" for that year, which is probably about an average one. It must be remembered that this rain record has nothing to do with what fell in the night.

The ordinary rainstorm of this region has little of that outward pomp and sublimity of structure so characteristic of the storms of the Mississippi Valley. Nevertheless, we have experienced rainstorms out on these treeless plains, in nights of solid darkness, as impressively sublime as the noblest storms of the mountains. The wind, which in settled weather blows from the northwest, veers to the southeast; the sky curdles gradually and evenly to a grainless, seamless, homogeneous cloud; and then comes the rain, pouring steadily and often driven aslant by strong winds. In 1869, more than three fourths of the winter rains came from the southeast. One magnificent storm from the northwest occurred on the 21st of March; an immense, round-browed cloud came sailing over the flowery hills in most imposing majesty, bestowing water as from a sea. The passionate rain-gush lasted only about one minute, but was nevertheless the most magnificent cataract of the sky mountains that I ever beheld. A portion of calm sky toward the Sierras was brushed with thin, white cloud-tissue, upon which the rain-torrent showed to a great height — a cloud waterfall, which, like those of Yosemite, was neither spray, rain, nor solid water. In the same year the cloudiness of January, omitting rainy days, averaged 0.32; February, 0.13; March, 0.20; April, 0.10; May, 0.08. The greater portion of this cloudiness was gathered into a few days, leaving the others blocks of solid, universal sunshine in every chink and pore.

At the end of January, four plants were in flower: a small white cress, growing in large patches; a low-set, umbelled plant, with yellow flowers; an eriogonum, with flowers in leafless spangles; and a small boragewort. Five or six mosses had adjusted their hoods, and were in the prime of life. In February, squirrels, hares, and flowers were in springtime joy. Bright plant-constellations shone everywhere about the Hollow. Ants were getting ready for work, rubbing and sunning their limbs upon the husk-piles around their doors; fat, pollen-dusted, "burly, dozing humble-bees" were rumbling among the flowers; and spiders were busy mending up old webs, or weaving new ones. Flowers were born every day, and came gushing from the ground like gayly dressed children from a church. The bright air became daily more songful with fly-wings, and sweeter with breath of plants.

In March, plant-life is more than doubled. The little pioneer cress, by this time, goes to seed, wearing daintily embroidered silicles. Several claytonias appear; also, a large white leptosiphon [?], and two nemophilas. A small plantago becomes tall enough to wave and show silky ripples of shade. Toward the end of this month or the beginning of April, plant-life is at its greatest height. Few have any just conception of its amazing richness. Count the flowers of any portion of these twenty hills, or of the bottom of the Hollow, among the streams: you will find that there are from one to ten thousand upon every square yard, counting the heads of *Compositæ* as single flowers. Yellow *Compositæ* form by far the greater portion of this goldy-way. Well may the sun feed them with his richest light, for these shining sunlets are his very children — rays of his ray, beams of his beam! One would fancy that these California days receive more gold from the ground than they give to it. The earth has indeed become a sky; and the two cloudless skies, raying toward each other flower-beams and sunbeams, are fused and congolded into one glowing heaven. By the end of April most of the Hollow plants have ripened their seeds and died; but, undecayed, still assist the landscape with color from persistent involucres and corolla-like heads of chaffy scales.

In May, only a few deep-set lilies and eriogonums are left alive. June, July, August, and September are the season of plant rest, followed, in October, by a most extraordinary outgush of plant-life, at the very driest time of the whole year. A small, unobtrusive plant, *Hemizonia virgata*, from six inches to three feet in height, with pale, glandular leaves, suddenly bursts into bloom, in patches miles in extent, like a resurrection of the gold of April. I have counted upward of three thousand heads upon one plant. Both leaves and pedicels are so small as to be nearly invisible among so vast a number of daisy golden-heads that seem to keep their places unsupported, like stars in the sky. The heads are about five eighths of an inch in diameter; rays and disk-flowers, yellow; stamens, purple. The rays have a rich, furred appearance, like the petals of garden pansies. The prevailing summer wind makes all the heads turn to the southeast. The waxy secretion of its leaves and involucres has suggested its grim name of "tarweed," by which it is generally known. In our estimation, it is the most delightful member of the whole Composite Family of the plain. It remains in flower until November, uniting with an eriogonum that continues the floral chain across December to the spring plants of January. Thus, although nearly all of the year's plant-life is crowded into February, March, and April, the flower circle around the Twenty Hill Hollow is never broken.

The Hollow may easily be visited by tourists *en route* for Yosemite, as it is distant only about six miles from Snelling's. It is at all seasons interesting to the naturalist; but it has little that would interest the majority of tourists earlier than January or later than April. If you wish to see how much of light, life, and joy can be got into a January, go to this blessed Hollow. If you wish to see a plant-resurrection, — myriads of bright flowers crowding from the ground, like souls to a judgment, — go to Twenty Hills in February. If you are traveling for health, play truant to doctors and friends, fill your pocket with biscuits, and hide in the hills of the Hollow, lave in its waters, tan in its golds, bask in its flower-shine, and your baptisms will make you a new creature indeed. Or, choked in the sediments of society, so tired of the world, here will your hard doubts disappear, your carnal incrustations melt off, and your soul breathe deep and free in God's shoreless atmosphere of beauty and love.

Never shall I forget my baptism in this font. It happened in January, a resurrection day for many a plant and for me. I suddenly found myself on one of its hills; the Hollow overflowed with light, as a fountain, and only small, sun-less nooks were kept for mosseries and ferneries. Hollow Creek spangled and mazed like a river. The ground steamed with fragrance. Light, of unspeakable richness, was brooding the flowers. Truly, said I, is California the Golden State — in metallic gold, in sun gold, and in plant gold. The sunshine for a whole summer seemed condensed into the chambers of that one glowing day. Every trace of dimness had been washed from the sky; the mountains were dusted and wiped clean with clouds — Pacheco Peak and Mount Diablo, and the waved blue wall between; the grand Sierra stood along the plain, colored in four horizontal bands: — the lowest, rose purple; the next higher, dark purple; the next, blue; and, above all, the white row of summits pointing to the heavens.

It may be asked, What have mountains fifty or a hundred miles away to do with Twenty Hill Hollow? To lovers of the wild, these mountains are not a hundred miles away. Their spiritual power and the goodness of the sky make them near, as a circle of friends. They rise as a portion of the hilled walls of the Hollow. You cannot feel yourself out of doors; plain, sky, and mountains ray beauty which you feel. You bathe in these spirit-beams, turning round and round, as if warming at a camp-fire. Presently you lose consciousness of your own separate existence: you blend with the landscape, and become part and parcel of nature.

THE SNOW

THE first snow that whitens the Sierra usually falls about the end of October or early in November, to a depth of a few inches, after months of the most charming Indian summer weather imaginable. But in a few days, this light covering mostly melts from the slopes exposed to the sun and causes but little apprehension on the part of mountaineers who may be lingering among the high peaks at this time. The first general winter storm that yields snow that is to form a lasting portion of the season's supply, seldom breaks on the mountains before the end of November. Then, warned by the sky, cautious mountaineers, together with the wild sheep, deer, and most of the birds and bears, make haste to the lowlands or foothills; and burrowing marmots, mountain beavers, wood-rats, and such people go into winter quarters, some of them not again to see the light of day until the general awakening and resurrection of the spring in June or July. The first heavy fall is usually from about two to four feet in depth. Then, with intervals of splendid sunshine, storm succeeds storm, heaping snow

The Mountains of California, 1894

on snow, until thirty to fifty feet has fallen. But on account of its settling and compacting, and the almost constant waste from melting and evaporation, the average depth actually found at any time seldom exceeds ten feet in the forest region, or fifteen feet along the slopes of the summit peaks.

Even during the coldest weather evaporation never wholly ceases, and the sunshine that abounds between the storms is sufficiently powerful to melt the surface more or less through all the winter months. Waste from melting also goes on to some extent on the bottom from heat stored up in the rocks, and given off slowly to the snow in contact with them, as is shown by the rising of the streams on all the higher regions after the first snowfall, and their steady, sustained flow all winter.

The greater portion of the snow deposited around the lofty summits of the range falls in small crisp flakes and broken crystals, or, when accompanied by strong winds and low temperature, the crystals, instead of being locked together in their fall to form tufted flakes, are beaten and broken into meal and fine dust. But down in the forest region the greater portion comes gently to the ground, light and feathery, some of the flakes in mild weather being nearly an inch in diameter, and it is evenly distributed and kept from drifting to any great extent by the shelter afforded by the large trees. Every tree during the progress of gentle storms is loaded with fairy bloom at the coldest and darkest time of year, bending the branches, and hushing every singing needle. But as soon as the storm is over, and the sun shines, the snow at once begins to shift and settle and fall from the branches in miniature avalanches, and the white forest soon becomes green again. The snow on the ground also settles and thaws every bright day, and freezes at night, until it becomes coarsely granulated, and loses every trace of its rayed crystalline structure, and then a man may walk firmly over its frozen surface as if on ice. The forest region up to an elevation of seven thousand feet is usually in great part free from snow in June, but at this time the higher regions are still heavy-laden, and are not touched by spring weather to any considerable extent before the middle or end of July.

One of the most striking effects of the snow on the mountains is the burial of the rivers and small lakes.

> " As the snaw fa's in the river
> A moment white, then lost forever," —

sang Burns, in illustrating the fleeting character of human pleasure. The first snowflakes that fall into the Sierra rivers vanish thus suddenly; but in great storms, when the temperature is low, the abundance of the snow at length chills the water nearly to the freezing-point, and then, of course, it ceases to melt and consume the snow so suddenly. The falling flakes and crystals form cloud-like masses of blue sludge, which are swept forward with the current and carried down to warmer climates many miles distant, while some are lodged against logs and rocks and projecting points of the banks, and last for days, piled high above the level of the water, and show white again, instead of being at once "lost forever," while the rivers themselves are at length lost for months during the snowy period. The snow is first built out from the banks in bossy, overcurling drifts, compacting and cementing until the streams are spanned. They then flow in the dark beneath a continuous covering across the snowy zone, which is about thirty miles wide. All the Sierra rivers and their tributaries in these high regions are thus lost every winter, as if another glacial period had come on. Not a drop of running water is to be seen excepting at a few points where large falls occur, though the rush and rumble of the heavier currents may still be heard. Toward spring, when the weather is warm during the day and frosty at night, repeated thawing and freezing and new layers of snow render the bridging-masses dense and firm, so that one may safely walk across the streams, or even lead a horse across them without danger of falling through. In June the thinnest parts of the winter ceiling, and those most exposed to sunshine, begin to give way, forming dark, rugged-edged, pit-like sinks, at the bottom of which the rushing water may be seen. At the end of June only here and there may the mountaineer find a secure snow-bridge. The most lasting of the winter bridges, thawing from below as well as from above, because of warm currents of air passing through the tunnels, are strikingly arched and sculptured; and by the occasional freezing of the oozing, dripping water of the ceiling they become brightly and picturesquely icy. In some of the reaches, where there is a free margin, we may walk through them. Small skylights appearing here and there, these tunnels are not very dark. The roaring river fills all the arching way with impressively loud reverberating music, which is sweetened at times by the ouzel, a bird that is not afraid to go wherever a stream may go, and to sing wherever a stream sings.

All the small alpine pools and lakelets are in like manner obliterated from the winter landscapes, either by being first frozen and then covered by snow, or by being filled in by avalanches. The first avalanche of the season shot into a lake basin may perhaps find the surface frozen. Then there is a grand crashing of breaking ice and dashing of waves mingled with the low, deep booming of the avalanche. Detached masses of the invading snow, mixed with fragments of ice, drift about in sludgy, island-like heaps, while the main body of it forms a talus with its base wholly or in part resting on the bottom of the basin, as controlled by its depth and the size of the avalanche. The next avalanche, of course, encroaches still farther, and so on with each in succession until the entire basin may be filled and its water sponged up or displaced. This huge mass of sludge, more or less mixed with sand, stones, and perhaps timber, is frozen to a considerable depth, and much sun-heat is required to thaw it. Some of these unfortunate lakelets are not clear of ice and snow until near the end of summer. Others are never quite free, opening only on the side opposite the entrance of the avalanches. Some show only a narrow crescent of water lying between the shore and sheer bluffs of icy compacted snow, masses of which breaking off float in front like icebergs in a miniature Arctic Ocean, while the avalanche heaps leaning back against the mountains look like small glaciers. The frontal cliffs are in some instances quite picturesque, and with the berg-dotted waters in front of them lighted with sunshine are exceedingly beautiful. It often happens that while one side of a lake basin is hopelessly snow-buried and frozen, the other, enjoying sunshine, is adorned with beautiful flower-gardens. Some of the smaller lakes are extinguished in an instant by a heavy avalanche either of rocks or snow. The rolling, sliding, ponderous mass entering on one side sweeps across the bottom and up the opposite side, displacing the water and even scraping the basin clean, and shoving the accumulated rocks and sediments up the farther bank and taking full possession. The dislodged water is in part absorbed, but most of it is sent around the front of the avalanche and down the channel of the outlet, roaring and hurrying as if frightened and glad to escape.

SNOW-BANNERS

The most magnificent storm phenomenon I ever saw, surpassing in showy grandeur the most imposing effects of clouds, floods, or avalanches, was the peaks of the High Sierra, back of Yosemite Valley, decorated with snow-banners. Many of the starry snow-flowers, out of

95

which these banners are made, fall before they are ripe, while most of those that do attain perfect development as six-rayed crystals glint and chafe against one another in their fall through the frosty air, and are broken into fragments. This dry fragmentary snow is still further prepared for the formation of banners by the action of the wind. For, instead of finding rest at once, like the snow which falls into the tranquil depths of the forests, it is rolled over and over, beaten against rock ridges, and swirled in pits and hollows, like boulders, pebbles, and sand in the pot-holes of a river, until finally the delicate angles of the crystals are worn off, and the whole mass is reduced to dust. And whenever storm-winds find this prepared snow-dust in a loose condition on exposed slopes, where there is a free upward sweep to leeward, it is tossed back into the sky, and borne onward from peak to peak in the form of banners or cloudy drifts, according to the velocity of the wind and the conformation of the slopes up or around which it is driven. While thus flying through the air, a small portion makes good its escape, and remains in the sky as vapor. But far the greater part, after being driven into the sky again and again, is at length locked fast in bossy drifts, or in the wombs of glaciers, some of it to remain silent and rigid for centuries before it is finally melted and sent singing down the mountain-sides to the sea.

Yet, notwithstanding the abundance of winter snow-dust in the mountains, and the frequency of high winds, and the length of time the dust remains loose and exposed to their action, the occurrence of well-formed banners is, for causes we shall hereafter note, comparatively rare. I have seen only one display of this kind that seemed in every way perfect. This was in the winter of 1873, when the snow-laden summits were swept by a wild "norther." I happened at the time to be wintering in Yosemite Valley, that sublime Sierra temple where every day one may see the grandest sights. Yet even here the wild gala day of the north wind seemed surpassingly glorious. I was awakened in the morning by the rocking of my cabin and the beating of pine burs on the roof. Detached torrents and avalanches from the main wind flood overhead were rushing wildly down the narrow side cañons, and over the precipitous walls, with loud resounding roar, rousing the pines to enthusiastic action, and making the whole valley vibrate as though it were an instrument being played.

But afar on the lofty exposed peaks of the range standing so high in the sky, the storm was expressing itself in still grander characters, which I was soon to see in all their glory. I had long been anxious to study some points in the structure of the ice cone that is formed every winter at the foot of the Upper Yosemite Fall, but the blinding spray by which it is invested had hitherto prevented me from making a sufficiently near approach. This morning the entire body of the fall was torn into gauzy shreds, and blown horizontally along the face of the cliff, leaving the cone dry; and while making my way to the top of an overlooking ledge to seize so favorable an opportunity to examine the interior of the cone, the peaks of the Merced group came in sight over the shoulder of the South Dome, each waving a resplendent banner against the blue sky, as regular in form, and as firm in texture, as if woven of fine silk. So rare and splendid a phenomenon, of course, overbore all other considerations, and I at once let the ice cone go, and began to force my way out of the valley to some dome or ridge sufficiently lofty to command a general view of the main summits, feeling assured that I should find them bannered still more gloriously; nor was I in the least disappointed. Indian Cañon, through which I climbed, was choked with snow that had been shot down in avalanches from the high cliffs on either side, rendering the ascent difficult; but inspired by the roaring storm, the tedious wallowing brought no fatigue, and in four hours I gained the top of a ridge above the valley, eight thousand feet high. And there in bold relief, like a clear painting, appeared a most imposing scene. Innumerable peaks, black and sharp, rose grandly into the dark blue sky, their bases set in solid white, their sides streaked and splashed with snow, like ocean rocks with foam; and from every summit, all free and unconfused, was streaming a beautiful silky silvery banner, from half a mile to a mile in length, slender at the point of attachment, then widening gradually as it extended from the peak until it was about one thousand or fifteen hundred feet in breadth, as near as I could estimate. The cluster of peaks called the "Crown of the Sierra," at the head of the Merced and Tuolumne Rivers, — Mounts Dana, Gibbs, Conness, Lyell, Maclure, Ritter, with their nameless compeers, — each had its own refulgent banner, waving with a clearly visible motion in the sunglow, and there was not a single cloud in the sky to mar their simple grandeur. Fancy yourself standing on this Yosemite ridge looking eastward. You notice a strange garish glitter in the air. The gale drives wildly overhead with a fierce, tempestuous roar, but its violence is not felt, for you are looking through a sheltered opening in the woods as through a window. There, in the immediate foreground of your picture, rises a majestic forest of silver fir blooming in eternal freshness, the foliage yellow-green, and the snow beneath the trees strewn with their beautiful plumes, plucked off by the wind. Beyond, and extending over all the middle ground, are somber swaths of pine, interrupted by huge swelling ridges and domes; and just beyond the dark forest you see the monarchs of the High Sierra waving their magnificent banners. They are twenty miles away, but you would not wish them nearer, for every feature is distinct, and the whole glorious show is seen in its right proportions. After this general view, mark how sharply the dark snowless ribs and buttresses and summits of the peaks are defined, excepting the portions veiled by the banners, and how delicately their sides are streaked with snow, where it has come to rest in narrow flutings and gorges. Mark, too, how grandly the banners wave as the wind is deflected against their sides, and how trimly each is attached to the very summit of its peak, like a streamer at a masthead; how smooth and silky they are in texture, and how finely their fading fringes are penciled on the azure sky. See how dense and opaque they are at the point of attachment, and how filmy and translucent toward the end, so that the peaks back of them are seen dimly, as though you were looking through ground glass. Yet again observe how some of the longest, belonging to the loftiest summits, stream perfectly free all the way across intervening notches and passes from peak to peak, while others overlap and partly hide each other. And consider how keenly every particle of this wondrous cloth of snow is flashing out jets of light. These are the main features of the beautiful and terrible picture as seen from the forest window; and it would still be surpassingly glorious were the fore- and middle-grounds obliterated altogether, leaving only the black peaks, the white banners, and the blue sky.

Glancing now in a general way at the formation of snow-banners, we find that the main causes of the wondrous beauty and perfection of those we have been contemplating were the favorable direction and great force of the wind, the abundance of snow-dust, and the peculiar conformation of the slopes of the peaks. It is essential not only that the wind should move with great velocity and steadiness to supply a sufficiently copious and continuous stream of snow-dust, but that it should come from the north. No perfect banner is ever hung on the Sierra peaks by a south wind. Had the gale that day blown from the south, leaving other conditions unchanged, only a dull, confused, foglike drift would have been produced; for the snow, instead of being spouted up over the tops of the peaks in concentrated currents to be drawn out as streamers, would have been shed off around the sides, and piled down into the glacier wombs. The cause of the concentrated action of the north wind is found in the peculiar form of the north sides of the peaks, where the amphitheaters of the residual glaciers are. In general the south sides are convex and irregular, while the north sides are concave in both their vertical and horizontal sections; the wind in ascending these curves converges toward the summits, carrying the snow in concentrating currents with it, shooting it almost straight up into the air above the peaks, from which it is then carried away in a horizontal direction.

This difference in form between the north and south sides of the peaks was almost wholly produced by the difference in the kind and quantity of the glaciation to which they have been subjected, the north sides having been hollowed by residual shadow glaciers of a form that never existed on the sun-beaten sides.

It appears, therefore, that shadows in great part determine not only the forms of lofty icy mountains, but also those of the snow-banners that the wild winds hang on them.

A NEAR VIEW OF THE HIGH SIERRA

EARLY one bright morning in the middle of Indian summer, while the glacier meadows were still crisp with frost crystals, I set out from the foot of Mount Lyell, on my way down to Yosemite Valley, to replenish my exhausted store of bread and tea. I had spent the past summer, as many preceding ones, exploring the glaciers that lie on the head waters of the San Joaquin, Tuolumne, Merced, and Owen's Rivers; measuring and studying their movements, trends, crevasses, moraines, etc., and the part they had played during the period of their greater extension in the creation and development of the landscapes of this alpine wonderland. The time for this kind of work was nearly over for the year, and I began to look forward with delight to the approaching winter with its wondrous storms, when I would be warmly snow-bound in my Yosemite cabin with plenty of bread and books; but a tinge of regret came on when I considered that possibly I might not see this favorite region again until the next summer, excepting distant views from the heights about the Yosemite walls.

The Mountains of California, 1894

WILDERNESS ESSAYS

To artists, few portions of the High Sierra are, strictly speaking, picturesque. The whole massive uplift of the range is one great picture, not clearly divisible into smaller ones; differing much in this respect from the older, and what may be called, riper mountains of the Coast Range. All the landscapes of the Sierra, as we have seen, were born again, remodeled from base to summit by the developing ice floods of the last glacial winter. But all these new landscapes were not brought forth simultaneously; some of the highest, where the ice lingered longest, are tens of centuries younger than those of the warmer regions below them. In general, the younger the mountain landscapes, — younger, I mean, with reference to the time of their emergence from the ice of the glacial period, — the less separable are they into artistic bits capable of being made into warm, sympathetic, lovable pictures with appreciable humanity in them.

Here, however, on the head waters of the Tuolumne, is a group of wild peaks on which the geologist may say that the sun has but just begun to shine, which is yet in a high degree picturesque, and in its main features so regular and evenly balanced as almost to appear conventional — one somber cluster of snow-laden peaks with gray, pine-fringed, granite bosses braided around its base, the whole surging free into the sky from the head of a magnificent valley, whose lofty walls are beveled away on both sides so as to embrace it all without admitting anything not strictly belonging to it. The foreground was now aflame with autumn colors, brown and purple and gold, ripe in the mellow sunshine; contrasting brightly with the deep, cobalt blue of the sky, and the black and gray, and pure, spiritual white of the rocks and glaciers. Down through the midst, the young Tuolumne was seen pouring from its crystal fountains, now resting in glassy pools as if changing back again into ice, now leaping in white cascades as if turning to snow; gliding right and left between granite bosses, then sweeping on through the smooth, meadowy levels of the valley, swaying pensively from side to side with calm, stately gestures past dipping willows and sedges, and around groves of arrowy pine; and throughout its whole eventful course, whether flowing fast or slow, singing loud or low, ever filling the landscape with spiritual animation, and manifesting the grandeur of its sources in every movement and tone.

Pursuing my lonely way down the valley, I turned again and again to gaze on the glorious picture, throwing up my arms to inclose it as in a frame. After long ages of growth in the darkness beneath the glaciers, through sunshine and storms, it seemed now to be ready and waiting for the elected artist, like yellow wheat for the reaper; and I could not help wishing that I might carry colors and brushes with me on my travels, and learn to paint. In the mean time I had to be content with photographs on my mind and sketches in my notebooks. At length, after I had rounded a precipitous headland that puts out from the west wall of the valley, every peak vanished from sight, and I pushed rapidly along the frozen meadows, over the divide between the waters of the Merced and Tuolumne, and down through the forests that clothe the slopes of Cloud's Rest, arriving in Yosemite in due time — which, with me, is *any* time. And, strange to say, among the first people I met here were two artists who, with letters of introduction, were awaiting my return. They inquired whether in the course of my explorations in the adjacent mountains I had ever come upon a landscape suitable for a large painting; whereupon I began a description of the one that had so lately excited my admiration. Then, as I went on further and further into details, their faces began to glow, and I offered to guide them to it, while they declared that they would gladly follow, far or near, whithersoever I could spare the time to lead them.

Since storms might come breaking down through the fine weather at any time, burying the colors in snow, and cutting off the artists' retreat, I advised getting ready at once.

I led them out of the valley by the Vernal and Nevada Falls, thence over the main dividing ridge to the Big Tuolumne Meadows, by the old Mono Trail, and thence along the Upper Tuolumne River to its head. This was my companions' first excursion into the High Sierra, and as I was almost always alone in my mountaineering, the way that the fresh beauty was reflected in their faces made for me a novel and interesting study. They naturally were affected most of all by the colors — the intense azure of the sky, the purplish grays of the granite, the red and browns of dry meadows, and the translucent purple and crimson of huckleberry bogs; the flaming yellow of aspen groves, the silvery flashing of the streams, and the bright green and blue of the glacier lakes. But the general expression of the scenery — rocky and savage — seemed sadly disappointing; and as they threaded the forest from ridge to ridge, eagerly scanning the landscapes as they were unfolded, they said: "All this is huge and sublime, but we see nothing as yet at all available for effective pictures. Art is long, and art is limited, you know; and here are foregrounds, middle-grounds, backgrounds, all alike; bare rock waves, woods, groves, diminutive flecks of meadow, and strips of glittering water." "Never mind," I replied, "only bide a wee, and I will show you something you will like."

At length, toward the end of the second day, the Sierra Crown began to come into view, and when we had fairly rounded the projecting headland before mentioned, the whole picture stood revealed in the flush of the alpenglow. Their enthusiasm was excited beyond bounds, and the more impulsive of the two, a young Scotchman, dashed ahead, shouting and gesticulating and tossing his arms in the air like a madman. Here, at last, was a typical alpine landscape.

After feasting a while on the view, I proceeded to make camp in a sheltered grove a little way back from the meadow, where pine boughs could be obtained for beds, and where there was plenty of dry wood for fires, while the artists ran here and there, along the river bends and up the sides of the cañon, choosing foregrounds for sketches. After dark, when our tea was made and a rousing fire had been built, we began to make our plans. They decided to remain several days, at the least, while I concluded to make an excursion in the mean time to the untouched summit of Ritter.

It was now about the middle of October, the springtime of snow-flowers. The first winter clouds had already bloomed, and the peaks were strewn with fresh crystals, without, however, affecting the climbing to any dangerous extent. And as the weather was still profoundly calm, and the distance to the foot of the mountain only a little more than a day, I felt that I was running no great risk of being storm-bound.

Mount Ritter is king of the mountains of the middle portion of the High Sierra, as Shasta of the north and Whitney of the south sections. Moreover, as far as I know, it had never been climbed. I had explored the adjacent wilderness summer after summer, but my studies thus far had never drawn me to the top of it. Its height above sea-level is about 13,300 feet, and it is fenced round by steeply inclined glaciers, and cañons of tremendous depth and ruggedness, which render it almost inaccessible. But difficulties of this kind only exhilarate the mountaineer.

Next morning, the artists went heartily to their work and I to mine. Former experiences had given good reason to know that passionate storms, invisible as yet, might be brooding in the calm sungold; therefore, before bidding farewell, I warned the artists not to be alarmed should I fail to appear before a week or ten days, and advised them, in case a snowstorm should set in, to keep up big fires and shelter themselves as best they could, and on no account to become frightened and attempt to seek their way back to Yosemite alone through the drifts.

My general plan was simply this: to scale the cañon wall, cross over to the eastern flank of the range, and then make my way southward to the northern spurs of Mount Ritter in compliance with the intervening topography; for to push on directly southward from camp through the innumerable peaks and pinnacles that adorn this portion of the axis of the range, however interesting, would take too much time, besides being extremely difficult and dangerous at this time of year.

All my first day was pure pleasure; simply mountaineering indulgence, crossing the dry pathways of the ancient glaciers, tracing happy streams, and learning the habits of the birds and marmots in the groves and rocks. Before I had gone a mile from camp, I came to the foot of a white cascade that beats its way down a rugged gorge in the cañon wall, from a height of about nine hundred feet, and pours its throbbing waters into the Tuolumne. I was acquainted with its fountains, which, fortunately, lay in my course. What a fine traveling companion it proved to be, what songs it sang, and how passionately it told the mountain's own joy! Gladly I climbed along its dashing border, absorbing its divine music, and bathing from time to time in waftings of irised spray. Climbing higher, higher, new beauty came streaming on the sight: painted meadows, late-blooming gardens, peaks of rare architecture, lakes here and there, shining like silver, and glimpses of the forested middle region and the yellow lowlands far in the west. Beyond the range I saw the so-called Mono Desert, lying dreamily silent in thick purple light — a desert of heavy sunglare beheld from a desert of ice-burnished granite. Here the waters divide, shouting in glorious enthusiasm, and falling eastward to vanish in the volcanic sands and dry sky of the Great Basin, or westward to the Great Valley of California, and thence through the Bay of San Francisco and the Golden Gate to the sea.

Passing a little way down over the summit until I had reached an elevation of about ten thousand feet, I pushed on southward toward a group of savage peaks that stand guard about Ritter on the north and west, groping my way, and dealing instinctively with every obstacle as it presented itself. Here a huge gorge would be found cutting across my path, along the dizzy edge of which I scrambled until some less precipitous point was discovered where I might safely venture to the bottom and then, selecting some feasible portion of the opposite wall, re-ascend with the same slow caution. Massive, flat-topped spurs alternate with the gorges, plunging abruptly from the shoulders of the snowy peaks, and planting their feet in the warm desert. These were everywhere marked and adorned with characteristic sculptures of the ancient glaciers that swept over this entire region like one vast ice wind, and the polished surfaces produced by the ponderous flood are still so perfectly preserved that in many places the sunlight reflected from them is about as trying to the eyes as sheets of snow.

God's glacial mills grind slowly, but they have been kept in motion long enough in California to grind sufficient soil for a glorious abundance of life, though most of the grist has been carried to the lowlands, leaving these high regions comparatively lean and bare; while the post-glacial agents of erosion have not yet furnished sufficient available food over the general surface for more than a few tufts of the hardiest plants, chiefly carices and eriogonæ. And it is interesting to learn in this connection that the sparseness and repressed character of the vegetation at this height is caused more by want of soil than by harshness of climate; for, here and there, in sheltered hollows (countersunk beneath the general surface) into which a few rods of well-ground moraine chips have been dumped, we find groves of spruce and pine thirty to forty feet high, trimmed around the edges with willow and huckleberry bushes, and oftentimes still further by an outer ring of tall grasses, bright with lupines, larkspurs, and showy columbines, suggesting a climate by no means repressingly severe. All the streams, too, and the pools at this elevation are furnished with little gardens wherever soil can be made to lie, which, though making scarce any show at a distance, constitute charming surprises to the appreciative observer. In these bits of leafiness a few birds find grateful homes. Having no acquaintance with man, they fear no ill, and flock curiously about the stranger, almost allowing themselves to be taken in the hand. In so wild and so beautiful a region was spent my first day, every sight and sound inspiring, leading one far out of himself, yet feeding and building up his individuality.

Now came the solemn, silent evening. Long, blue, spiky shadows crept out across the snowfields, while a rosy glow, at first scarce discernible, gradually deepened and suffused every mountain-top, flushing the glaciers and the harsh crags above them. This was the alpenglow, to me one of the most impressive of all the terrestrial manifestations of God. At the touch of this divine light, the mountains seemed to kindle to a rapt, religious consciousness, and stood hushed and waiting like devout worshipers. Just before the alpenglow began to fade, two crimson clouds came streaming across the summit like wings of flame, rendering the sublime scene yet more impressive; then came darkness and the stars.

Icy Ritter was still miles away, but I could proceed no farther that night. I found a good camp-ground on the rim of a glacier basin about eleven thousand feet above the sea. A small lake nestles in the bottom of it, from which I got water for my tea, and a storm-beaten thicket near by furnished abundance of resiny firewood. Somber peaks, hacked and shattered, circled halfway around the horizon, wearing a savage aspect in the gloaming, and a waterfall chanted solemnly across the lake on its way down from the foot of a glacier. The fall and the lake and the glacier were almost equally bare; while the scraggy pines anchored in the rock-fissures were so dwarfed and shorn by storm-winds that you might walk over their tops. In tone and aspect the scene was one of the most desolate I ever beheld. But the darkest scriptures of the mountains are illumined with bright passages of love that never fail to make themselves felt when one is alone.

I made my bed in a nook of the pine thicket, where the branches were pressed and crinkled overhead like a roof, and bent down around the sides. These are the best bedchambers the high mountains afford — snug as squirrel nests, well-ventilated, full of spicy odors, and with plenty of wind-played needles to sing one asleep. I little expected company, but, creeping in through a low side door, I found five or six birds nestling among the tassels. The night wind began to blow soon after dark; at first only a gentle breathing, but increasing toward midnight to a rough gale that fell upon my leafy roof in ragged surges like a cascade, bearing wild sounds from the crags overhead. The waterfall sang in chorus, filling the old ice fountain with its solemn roar, and seeming to increase in power as the night advanced — fit voice for such a landscape. I had to creep out many times to the fire during the night, for it was biting cold and I had no blankets. Gladly I welcomed the morning star.

The dawn in the dry, wavering air of the desert was glorious. Everything encouraged my undertaking and betokened success. There was no cloud in the sky, no storm tone in the wind. Breakfast of bread and tea was soon made. I fastened a hard, durable crust to my belt by way of provision, in case I should be compelled to pass a night on the mountain-top; then, securing the remainder of my little stock against wolves and wood rats, I set forth free and hopeful.

How glorious a greeting the sun gives the mountains! To behold this alone is worth the pains of any excursion a thousand times over. The highest peaks burned like islands in a sea of liquid shade. Then the lower peaks and spires caught the glow, and long lances of light, streaming through many a notch and pass, fell thick on the frozen meadows. The majestic form of Ritter was full in sight, and I pushed rapidly on over rounded rock bosses and pavements, my iron-shod shoes making a clanking sound, suddenly hushed now and then in rugs of bryanthus, and sedgy lake margins soft as moss. Here, too, in this so-called "land of desolation," I met cassiope, growing in fringes among the battered rocks. Her blossoms had faded long ago, but they were still clinging with happy memories to the evergreen sprays, and still so beautiful as to thrill every fiber of one's being. Winter and summer, you may hear her voice, the low, sweet melody of her purple bells.

A NEAR VIEW OF THE HIGH SIERRA

No evangel among all the mountain plants speaks Nature's love more plainly than cassiope. Where she dwells, the redemption of the coldest solitude is complete. The very rocks and glaciers seem to feel her presence, and become imbued with her own fountain sweetness. All things were warming and awakening. Frozen rills began to flow, the marmots came out of their nests in boulder piles and climbed sunny rocks to bask, and the dun-headed sparrows were flitting about seeking their breakfasts. The lakes seen from every ridge-top were brilliantly rippled and spangled, shimmering like the thickets of the low dwarf pines. The rocks, too, seemed responsive to the vital heat — rock crystals and snow crystals thrilling alike. I strode on exhilarated, as if never more to feel fatigue, limbs moving of themselves, every sense unfolding like the thawing flowers, to take part in the new day harmony.

All along my course thus far, excepting when down in the cañons, the landscapes were mostly open to me, and expansive, at least on one side. On the left were the purple plains of Mono, reposing dreamily and warm; on the right, the near peaks springing keenly into the thin sky with more and more impressive sublimity. But these larger views were at length lost. Rugged spurs, and moraines, and huge, projecting buttresses began to shut me in. Every feature became more rigidly alpine, without, however, producing any chilling effect; for going to the mountains is like going home. We always find that the strangest objects in these fountain wilds are in some degree familiar, and we look upon them with a vague sense of having seen them before.

On the southern shore of a frozen lake, I encountered an extensive field of hard, granular snow, up which I scampered in fine tone, intending to follow it to its head, and cross the rocky spur against which it leans, hoping thus to come direct upon the base of the main Ritter peak. The surface was pitted with oval hollows, made by stones and drifted pine needles that had melted themselves into the mass by the radiation of absorbed sun-heat. These afforded good footholds, but the surface curved more and more steeply at the head, and the pits became shallower and less abundant, until I found myself in danger of being shed off like avalanching snow. I persisted, however, creeping on all fours, and shuffling up the smoothest places on my back, as I had often done on burnished granite, until, after slipping several times, I was compelled to retrace my course to the bottom, and made my way around the west end of the lake, and thence up to the sum-

mit of the divide between the head waters of
Rush Creek and the northernmost tributaries
of the San Joaquin.

Arriving on the summit of this dividing crest,
one of the most exciting pieces of pure wilderness was disclosed that I ever discovered in
all my mountaineering. There, immediately
in front, loomed the majestic mass of Mount
Ritter, with a glacier swooping down its face
nearly to my feet, then curving westward and
pouring its frozen flood into a dark blue lake,
whose shores were bound with precipices of
crystalline snow; while a deep chasm drawn
between the divide and the glacier separated
the massive picture from everything else. I
could see only the one sublime mountain, the
one glacier, the one lake; the whole veiled with
one blue shadow — rock, ice, and water close
together, without a single leaf or sign of life.
After gazing spellbound, I began instinctively
to scrutinize every notch and gorge and weathered buttress of the mountain, with reference
to making the ascent. The entire front above
the glacier appeared as one tremendous precipice, slightly receding at the top, and bristling
with spires and pinnacles set above one another
in formidable array. Massive lichen-stained
battlements stood forward here and there,
hacked at the top with angular notches, and

separated by frosty gullies and recesses that have been veiled in shadow ever since their creation; while to right and left, as far as I could see, were huge, crumbling buttresses, offering no hope to the climber. The head of the glacier sends up a few finger-like branches through narrow *couloirs;* but these seemed too steep and short to be available, especially as I had no axe with which to cut steps, and the numerous narrow-throated gullies down which stones and snow are avalanched seemed hopelessly steep, besides being interrupted by vertical cliffs; while the whole front was rendered still more terribly forbidding by the chill shadow and the gloomy blackness of the rocks.

Descending the divide in a hesitating mood, I picked my way across the yawning chasm at the foot, and climbed out upon the glacier. There were no meadows now to cheer with their brave colors, nor could I hear the dun-headed sparrows, whose cheery notes so often relieve the silence of our highest mountains. The only sounds were the gurgling of small rills down in the veins and crevasses of the glacier, and now and then the rattling report of falling stones, with the echoes they shot out into the crisp air.

I could not distinctly hope to reach the summit from this side, yet I moved on across the glacier as if driven by fate. Contending with myself, the season is too far spent, I said, and even should I be successful, I might be storm-bound on the mountain; and in the cloud darkness, with the cliffs and crevasses covered with snow, how could I escape? No; I must wait till next summer. I would only approach the mountain now, and inspect it, creep about its flanks, learn what I could of its history, holding myself ready to flee on the approach of the first storm cloud. But we little know until tried how much of the uncontrollable there is in us, urging over glaciers and torrents, and up perilous heights, let the judgment forbid as it may.

I succeeded in gaining the foot of the cliff on the eastern extremity of the glacier, and there discovered the mouth of a narrow avalanche gully, through which I began to climb, intending to follow it as far as possible, and at least obtain some fine wild views for my pains. Its general course is oblique to the plane of the mountain-face, and the metamorphic slates of which the mountain is built are cut by cleavage planes in such a way that they weather off in angular blocks, giving rise to irregular steps that greatly facilitate climbing on the sheer places. I thus made my way into a wilderness of crumbling spires and battlements, built together in bewildering combinations, and glazed in many places with a thin coating of ice, which I had to hammer off with stones. The situation was becoming gradually more perilous; but, having passed several dangerous spots, I dared not think of descending; for, so steep was the entire ascent, one would inevitably fall to the glacier in case a single misstep were made. Knowing, therefore, the tried danger beneath, I became all the more anxious concerning the developments to be made above, and began to be conscious of a vague foreboding of what actually befell; not that I was given to fear, but rather because my instincts, usually so positive and true, seemed vitiated in some way, and were leading me astray. At length, after attaining an elevation of about 12,800 feet, I found myself at the foot of a sheer drop in the bed of the avalanche channel I was tracing, which seemed absolutely to bar further progress. It was only about forty-five or fifty feet high, and somewhat roughened by fissures and projections; but these seemed so slight and insecure, as footholds, that I tried hard to avoid the precipice altogether, by scaling the wall of the channel on either side. But, though less steep, the walls were smoother than the obstructing rock, and repeated efforts only showed that I must either go right ahead or turn back. The tried dangers beneath seemed even greater than that of the cliff in front; therefore, after scanning its face again and again, I began to scale it, picking my holds with intense caution. After gaining a point about halfway to the top, I was suddenly brought to a dead stop, with arms outspread, clinging close to the face of the rock, unable to move hand or foot either up or down. My doom appeared fixed. I *must* fall. There would be a moment of bewilderment, and then a lifeless rumble down the one general precipice to the glacier below.

When this final danger flashed upon me, I became nerve-shaken for the first time since setting foot on the mountains, and my mind seemed to fill with a stifling smoke. But this terrible eclipse lasted only a moment, when life blazed forth again with preternatural clearness. I seemed suddenly to become possessed of a new sense. The other self, bygone experiences, Instinct, or Guardian Angel, — call it what you will, — came forward and assumed control. Then my trembling muscles became firm again, every rift and flaw in the rock was seen as through a microscope, and my limbs moved with a positiveness and precision with which I seemed to have nothing at all to do. Had I been borne aloft upon wings, my deliverance could not have been more complete.

WILDERNESS ESSAYS

Above this memorable spot, the face of the mountain is still more savagely hacked and torn. It is a maze of yawning chasms and gullies, in the angles of which rise beetling crags and piles of detached boulders that seem to have been gotten ready to be launched below. But the strange influx of strength I had received seemed inexhaustible. I found a way without effort, and soon stood upon the topmost crag in the blessed light.

How truly glorious the landscape circled around this noble summit! — giant mountains, valleys innumerable, glaciers and meadows, rivers and lakes, with the wide blue sky bent tenderly over them all. But in my first hour of freedom from that terrible shadow, the sunlight in which I was laving seemed all in all.

Looking southward along the axis of the range, the eye is first caught by a row of exceedingly sharp and slender spires, which rise openly to a height of about a thousand feet, above a series of short, residual glaciers that lean back against their bases; their fantastic sculpture and the unrelieved sharpness with which they spring out of the ice rendering them peculiarly wild and striking. These are "The Minarets." Beyond them you behold a sublime wilderness of mountains, their snowy summits towering together in crowded abundance, peak beyond peak, swelling higher, higher, as they sweep on southward, until the culminating point of the range is reached on Mount Whitney, near the head of the Kern River, at an elevation of nearly 14,700 feet above the level of the sea.

Westward, the general flank of the range is seen flowing sublimely away from the sharp summits, in smooth undulations; a sea of huge gray granite waves dotted with lakes and meadows, and fluted with stupendous cañons that grow steadily deeper as they recede in the distance. Below this gray region lies the dark forest zone, broken here and there by upswelling ridges and domes; and yet beyond lies a yellow, hazy belt, marking the broad plain of the San Joaquin, bounded on its farther side by the blue mountains of the coast.

Turning now to the northward, there in the immediate foreground is the glorious Sierra Crown, with Cathedral Peak, a temple of marvelous architecture, a few degrees to the left of it; the gray, massive form of Mammoth Mountain to the right; while Mounts Ord, Gibbs, Dana, Conness, Tower Peak, Castle Peak, Silver Mountain, and a host of noble companions, as yet nameless, make a sublime show along the axis of the range.

Eastward, the whole region seems a land of

desolation covered with beautiful light. The torrid volcanic basin of Mono, with its one bare lake fourteen miles long; Owen's Valley and the broad lava tableland at its head, dotted with craters, and the massive Inyo Range, rivaling even the Sierra in height; these are spread, map-like, beneath you, with countless ranges beyond, passing and overlapping one another and fading on the glowing horizon.

At a distance of less than three thousand feet below the summit of Mount Ritter you may find tributaries of the San Joaquin and Owen's Rivers, bursting forth from the ice and snow of the glaciers that load its flanks; while a little to the north of here are found the highest affluents of the Tuolumne and Merced. Thus, the fountains of four of the principal rivers of California are within a radius of four or five miles.

Lakes are seen gleaming in all sorts of places, — round, or oval, or square, like very mirrors; others narrow and sinuous, drawn close around the peaks like silver zones, the highest reflecting only rocks, snow, and the sky. But neither these nor the glaciers, nor the bits of brown meadow and moorland that occur here and there, are large enough to make any marked impression upon the mighty wilderness of mountains. The eye, rejoicing in its freedom, roves about the vast expanse, yet returns again and again to the fountain peaks. Perhaps some one of the multitude excites special attention, some gigantic castle with turret and battlement, or some Gothic cathedral more abundantly spired than Milan's. But, generally, when looking for the first time from an all-embracing standpoint like this, the inexperienced observer is oppressed by the incomprehensible grandeur, variety, and abundance of the mountains rising shoulder to shoulder beyond the reach of vision; and it is only after they have been studied one by one, long and lovingly, that their far-reaching harmonies become manifest. Then, penetrate the wilderness where you may, the main telling features, to which all the surrounding topography is subordinate, are quickly perceived, and the most complicated clusters of peaks stand revealed harmoniously correlated and fashioned like works of art — eloquent monuments of the ancient ice rivers that brought them into relief from the general mass of the range. The cañons, too, some of them a mile deep, mazing wildly through the mighty host of mountains, however lawless and ungovernable at first sight they appear, are at length recognized as the necessary effects of causes which followed each other in harmonious sequence — Nature's poems carved on tables of stone — simplest and most emphatic of her glacial compositions.

Could we have been here to observe during the glacial period, we should have overlooked a wrinkled ocean of ice as continuous as that now covering the landscapes of Greenland; filling every valley and cañon with only the tops of the fountain peaks rising darkly above the rock-encumbered ice waves like islets in a stormy sea — those islets the only hints of the glorious landscapes now smiling in the sun. Standing here in the deep, brooding silence all the wilderness seems motionless, as if the work of creation were done. But in the midst of this outer steadfastness we know there is incessant motion and change. Ever and anon, avalanches are falling from yonder peaks. These cliff-bound glaciers, seemingly wedged and immovable, are flowing like water and grinding the rocks beneath them. The lakes are lapping their granite shores and wearing them away, and every one of these rills and young rivers is fretting the air into music, and carrying the mountains to the plains. Here are the roots of all the life of the valleys, and here more simply than elsewhere is the eternal flux of Nature manifested. Ice changing to water, lakes to meadows, and mountains to plains. And while we thus contemplate Nature's methods of landscape creation, and, reading the records she has carved on the rocks, reconstruct, however imperfectly, the landscapes of the past, we also learn that as these we now behold have succeeded those of the pre-glacial age, so they in turn are withering and vanishing to be succeeded by others yet unborn.

But in the midst of these fine lessons and landscapes, I had to remember that the sun was wheeling far to the west, while a new way down the mountain had to be discovered to some point on the timber line where I could have a fire; for I had not even burdened myself with a coat. I first scanned the western spurs, hoping some way might appear through which I might reach the northern glacier, and cross its snout, or pass around the lake into which it flows, and thus strike my morning track. This route was soon sufficiently unfolded to show that, if it were practicable at all, it would require so much time that reaching camp that night would be out of the question. I therefore scrambled back eastward, and descended the southern slopes obliquely at the same time. Here the crags seemed less formidable, and the head of a glacier that flows northeast came in sight, which I determined to follow as far as possible, hoping thus to make my way to the foot of the peak on the east side, and thence across the intervening cañons and ridges to camp.

The inclination of the glacier is quite moderate at the head, and, as the sun had softened the *névé*, I made safe and rapid progress, running and sliding, and keeping up a sharp outlook for crevasses. About half a mile from the head, there is an ice cascade, where the glacier pours over a sharp declivity and is shattered into massive blocks separated by deep, blue fissures. To thread my way through the slippery mazes of this crevassed portion seemed impossible, and I endeavored to avoid it by climbing off to the shoulder of the mountain. But the slopes rapidly steepened and at length fell away in sheer precipices, compelling a return to the ice. Fortunately, the day had been warm enough to loosen the ice crystals so as to admit of hollows being dug in the rotten portions of the blocks, thus enabling me to pick my way with far less difficulty than I had anticipated. Continuing down over the snout, and along the left lateral moraine, was only a confident saunter, showing that the ascent of the mountain by way of this glacier is easy, provided one is armed with an axe to cut steps here and there.

The lower end of the glacier was beautifully waved and barred by the outcropping edges of the bedded ice layers which represent the annual snowfalls, and to some extent the irregularities of structure caused by the weathering of the walls of crevasses, and by separate snowfalls which have been followed by rain, hail, thawing and freezing, etc. Small rills were gliding and swirling over the melting surface with a smooth, oily appearance, in channels of pure ice — their quick, compliant movements contrasting most impressively with the rigid, invisible flow of the glacier itself, on whose back they all were riding.

Night drew near before I reached the eastern base of the mountain, and my camp lay many a rugged mile to the north; but ultimate success was assured. It was now only a matter of endurance and ordinary mountain-craft. The sunset was, if possible, yet more beautiful than that of the day before. The Mono landscape seemed to be fairly saturated with warm, purple light. The peaks marshaled along the summit were in shadow, but through every notch and pass streamed vivid sunfire, soothing and irradiating their rough, black angles, while companies of small, luminous clouds hovered above them like very angels of light.

Darkness came on, but I found my way by the trends of the cañons and the peaks projected against the sky. All excitement died with the light, and then I was weary. But the joyful sound of the waterfall across the lake was heard at last, and soon the stars were seen reflected in the lake itself. Taking my bearings from these, I discovered the little pine thicket in which my nest was, and then I had a rest such as only a tired mountaineer may enjoy. After lying loose and lost for a while, I made a sunrise fire, went down to the lake, dashed water on my head, and dipped a cupful for tea. The revival brought about by bread and tea was as complete as the exhaustion from excessive enjoyment and toil. Then I crept beneath the pine tassels to bed. The wind was frosty and the fire burned low, but my sleep was none the less sound, and the evening constellations had swept far to the west before I awoke.

After thawing and resting in the morning sunshine, I sauntered home, — that is, back to the Tuolumne camp, — bearing away toward a cluster of peaks that hold the fountain snows of one of the north tributaries of Rush Creek. Here I discovered a group of beautiful glacier lakes, nestled together in a grand amphitheater. Toward evening, I crossed the divide separating the Mono waters from those of the Tuolumne, and entered the glacier basin that now holds the fountain snows of the stream that forms the upper Tuolumne cascades. This stream I traced down through its many dells and gorges, meadows and bogs, reaching the brink of the main Tuolumne at dusk.

A loud whoop for the artists was answered again and again. Their camp-fire came in sight, and half an hour afterward I was with them. They seemed unreasonably glad to see me. I had been absent only three days; nevertheless, though the weather was fine, they had already been weighing chances as to whether I would ever return, and trying to decide whether they should wait longer or begin to seek their way back to the lowlands. Now their curious troubles were over. They packed their precious sketches, and next morning we set out homeward bound, and in two days entered the Yosemite Valley from the north by way of Indian Cañon.

AMONG THE ANIMALS OF THE YOSEMITE

THE Sierra bear, brown or gray, the sequoia of the animals, tramps over all the park, though few travelers have the pleasure of seeing him. On he fares through the majestic forests and cañons, facing all sorts of weather, rejoicing in his strength, everywhere at home, harmonizing with the trees and rocks and shaggy chaparral. Happy fellow! his lines have fallen in pleasant places, — lily gardens in silver-fir forests, miles of bushes in endless variety and exuberance of bloom over hill-waves and valleys and along the banks of streams, cañons full of music and waterfalls, parks fair as Eden, — places in which one might expect to meet angels rather than bears.

In this happy land no famine comes nigh him. All the year round his bread is sure, for some of the thousand kinds that he likes are always in season and accessible, ranged on the shelves of the mountains like stores in a pantry. From one to another, from climate to climate, up and down he climbs, feasting on each in turn, — enjoying as great variety as if he traveled to far-off countries north and

Our National Parks, 1901

south. To him almost everything is food except granite. Every tree helps to feed him, every bush and herb, with fruits and flowers, leaves and bark; and all the animals he can catch, — badgers, gophers, ground squirrels, lizards, snakes, etc., and ants, bees, wasps, old and young, together with their eggs and larvæ and nests. Craunched and hashed, down all go to his marvelous stomach, and vanish as if cast into a fire. What digestion! A sheep or a wounded deer or a pig he eats warm, about as quickly as a boy eats a buttered muffin; or should the meat be a month old, it still is welcomed with tremendous relish. After so gross a meal as this, perhaps the next will be strawberries and clover, or raspberries with mushrooms and nuts, or puckery acorns and chokecherries. And as if fearing that anything eatable in all his dominions should escape being eaten, he breaks into cabins to look after sugar, dried apples, bacon, etc. Occasionally he eats the mountaineer's bed; but when he has had a full meal of more tempting dainties he usually leaves it undisturbed, though he has been known to drag it up through a hole in the roof, carry it to the foot of a tree, and lie down on it to enjoy a siesta. Eating everything, never is he himself eaten except by man, and only man is an enemy to be feared. "B'ar meat," said a hunter from whom I was seeking information, "b'ar meat is the best meat in the mountains; their skins make the best beds, and their grease the best butter. Biscuit shortened with b'ar grease goes as far as beans; a man will walk all day on a couple of them biscuit."

In my first interview with a Sierra bear we were frightened and embarrassed, both of us, but the bear's behavior was better than mine. When I discovered him, he was standing in a narrow strip of meadow, and I was concealed behind a tree on the side of it. After studying his appearance as he stood at rest, I rushed toward him to frighten him, that I might study his gait in running. But, contrary to all I had heard about the shyness of bears, he did not run at all; and when I stopped short within a few steps of him, as he held his ground in a fighting attitude, my mistake was monstrously plain. I was then put on my good behavior, and never afterward forgot the right manners of the wilderness.

This happened on my first Sierra excursion in the forest to the north of Yosemite Valley. I was eager to meet the animals, and many of them came to me as if willing to show themselves and make my acquaintance; but the bears kept out of my way.

An old mountaineer, in reply to my questions, told me that bears were very shy, all save grim old grizzlies, and that I might travel the mountains for years without seeing one, unless I gave my mind to them and practiced the stealthy ways of hunters. Nevertheless, it was only a few weeks after I had received this information that I met the one mentioned above, and obtained instruction at first-hand.

I was encamped in the woods about a mile back of the rim of Yosemite, beside a stream that falls into the valley by the way of Indian Cañon. Nearly every day for weeks I went to the top of the North Dome to sketch; for it commands a general view of the valley, and I was anxious to draw every tree and rock and waterfall. Carlo, a St. Bernard dog, was my companion, — a fine, intelligent fellow that belonged to a hunter who was compelled to remain all summer on the hot plains, and who loaned him to me for the season for the sake of having him in the mountains, where he would be so much better off. Carlo knew bears through long experience, and he it was who led me to my first interview, though he seemed as much surprised as the bear at my unhunter-like behavior. One morning in June, just as the sunbeams began to stream through the trees, I set out for a day's sketching on the dome; and before we had gone half a mile

from camp Carlo snuffed the air and looked
cautiously ahead, lowered his bushy tail,
drooped his ears, and began to step softly like
a cat, turning every few yards and looking me
in the face with a telling expression, saying
plainly enough, "There is a bear a little way
ahead." I walked carefully in the indicated
direction, until I approached a small flowery
meadow that I was familiar with, then crawled
to the foot of a tree on its margin, bearing in
mind what I had been told about the shyness
of bears. Looking out cautiously over the instep of the tree, I saw a big, burly cinnamon
bear about thirty yards off, half erect, his
paws resting on the trunk of a fir that had
fallen into the meadow, his hips almost buried
in grass and flowers. He was listening attentively and trying to catch the scent, showing
that in some way he was aware of our approach.
I watched his gestures, and tried to make the
most of my opportunity to learn what I could
about him, fearing he would not stay long. He
made a fine picture, standing alert in the
sunny garden walled in by the most beautiful
firs in the world.

After examining him at leisure, noting the
sharp muzzle thrust inquiringly forward, the
long shaggy hair on his broad chest, the stiff
ears nearly buried in hair, and the slow, heavy

way in which he moved his head, I foolishly
made a rush on him, throwing up my arms
and shouting to frighten him, to see him run.
He did not mind the demonstration much; only
pushed his head farther forward, and looked
at me sharply as if asking, "What now? If you
want to fight, I'm ready." Then I began to
fear that on me would fall the work of running.
But I was afraid to run, lest he should be
encouraged to pursue me; therefore I held my
ground, staring him in the face within a dozen
yards or so, putting on as bold a look as I
could, and hoping the influence of the human
eye would be as great as it is said to be. Under
these strained relations the interview seemed
to last a long time. Finally, the bear, seeing
how still I was, calmly withdrew his huge
paws from the log, gave me a piercing look, as
if warning me not to follow him, turned, and
walked slowly up the middle of the meadow
into the forest; stopping every few steps and
looking back to make sure that I was not trying to take him at a disadvantage in a rear
attack. I was glad to part with him, and
greatly enjoyed the vanishing view as he
waded through the lilies and columbines.

Thenceforth I always tried to give bears respectful notice of my approach, and they usually kept well out of my way. Though they

often came around my camp in the night, only once afterward, as far as I know, was I very near one of them in daylight. This time it was a grizzly I met; and as luck would have it, I was even nearer to him than I had been to the big cinnamon. Though not a large specimen, he seemed formidable enough at a distance of less than a dozen yards. His shaggy coat was well grizzled, his head almost white. When I first caught sight of him he was eating acorns under a Kellogg oak, at a distance of perhaps seventy-five yards, and I tried to slip past without disturbing him. But he had either heard my steps on the gravel or caught my scent, for he came straight toward me, stopping every rod or so to look and listen: and as I was afraid to be seen running, I crawled on my hands and knees a little way to one side and hid behind a libocedrus, hoping he would pass me unnoticed. He soon came up opposite me, and stood looking ahead, while I looked at him, peering past the bulging trunk of the tree. At last, turning his head, he caught sight of mine, stared sharply a minute or two, and then, with fine dignity, disappeared in a manzanita-covered earthquake talus.

Considering how heavy and broad-footed bears are, it is wonderful how little harm they do in the wilderness. Even in the well-watered gardens of the middle region, where the flowers grow tallest, and where during warm weather the bears wallow and roll, no evidence of destruction is visible. On the contrary, under nature's direction, the massive beasts act as gardeners. On the forest floor, carpeted with needles and brush, and on the tough sod of glacier meadows, bears make no mark; but around the sandy margin of lakes their magnificent tracks form grand lines of embroidery. Their well-worn trails extend along the main cañons on either side, and though dusty in some places make no scar on the landscape. They bite and break off the branches of some of the pines and oaks to get the nuts, but this pruning is so light that few mountaineers ever notice it; and though they interfere with the orderly lichen-veiled decay of fallen trees, tearing them to pieces to reach the colonies of ants that inhabit them, the scattered ruins are quickly pressed back into harmony by snow and rain and over-leaning vegetation.

The number of bears that make the Park their home may be guessed by the number that have been killed by the two best hunters, Duncan and old David Brown. Duncan began to be known as a bear-killer about the year 1865. He was then roaming the woods, hunting and prospecting on the south fork of the Merced. A friend told me that he killed his first bear near his cabin at Wawona; that after mustering courage to fire he fled, without waiting to learn the effect of his shot. Going back in a few hours he found poor Bruin dead, and gained courage to try again. Duncan confessed to me, when we made an excursion together in 1875, that he was at first mortally afraid of bears, but after killing a half dozen he began to keep count of his victims, and became ambitious to be known as a great bear-hunter. In nine years he had killed forty-nine, keeping count by notches cut on one of the timbers of his cabin on the shore of Crescent Lake, near the south boundary of the Park. He said the more he knew about bears, the more he respected them and the less he feared them. But at the same time he grew more and more cautious, and never fired until he had every advantage, no matter how long he had to wait and how far he had to go before he got the bear just right as to the direction of the wind, the distance, and the way of escape in case of accident; making allowance also for the character of the animal, old or young, cinnamon or grizzly. For old grizzlies, he said, he had no use whatever, and he was mighty careful to avoid their acquaintance. He wanted to kill an even hundred; then he was going to confine himself to safer game. There was not much money in bears, anyhow, and a round hundred was enough for glory.

I have not seen or heard of him lately, and do not know how his bloody count stands. On my excursions, I occasionally passed his cabin. It was full of meat and skins hung in bundles from the rafters, and the ground about it was strewn with bones and hair, — infinitely less tidy than a bear's den. He went as hunter and guide with a geological survey party for a year or two, and was very proud of the scientific knowledge he picked up. His admiring fellow mountaineers, he said, gave him credit for knowing not only the botanical names of all the trees and bushes, but also the "botanical names of the bears."

The most famous hunter of the region was David Brown, an old pioneer, who early in the gold period established his main camp in a little forest glade on the north fork of the Merced, which is still called "Brown's Flat." No finer solitude for a hunter and prospector could be found; the climate is delightful all the year, and the scenery of both earth and sky is a perpetual feast. Though he was not much of a "scenery fellow," his friends say that he knew a pretty place when he saw it as well as any one, and

143

liked mightily to get on the top of a commanding ridge to "look off."

When out of provisions, he would take down
his old-fashioned long-barreled rifle from its
deer-horn rest over the fireplace and set out in
search of game. Seldom did he have to go far
for venison, because the deer liked the wooded
slopes of Pilot Peak ridge, with its open spots
where they could rest and look about them, and
enjoy the breeze from the sea in warm weather,
free from troublesome flies, while they found
hiding-places and fine aromatic food in the
deer-brush chaparral. A small, wise dog was
his only companion, and well the little mountaineer understood the object of every hunt,
whether deer or bears, or only grouse hidden
in the fir-tops. In deer-hunting Sandy had
little to do, trotting behind his master as he
walked noiselessly through the fragrant woods,
careful not to step heavily on dry twigs, scanning open spots in the chaparral where the
deer feed in the early morning and toward sunset, peering over ridges and swells as new outlooks were reached, and along alder and willow
fringed flats and streams, until he found a
young buck, killed it, tied its legs together,
threw it on his shoulder, and so back to camp.
But when bears were hunted, Sandy played an
important part as leader, and several times

saved his master's life; and it was as a bear-hunter that David Brown became famous. His method, as I had it from a friend who had passed many an evening in his cabin listening to his long stories of adventure, was simply to take a few pounds of flour and his rifle, and go slowly and silently over hill and valley in the loneliest part of the wilderness, until little Sandy came upon the fresh track of a bear, then follow it to the death, paying no heed to time. Wherever the bear went he went, however rough the ground, led by Sandy, who looked back from time to time to see how his master was coming on, and regulated his face accordingly, never growing weary or allowing any other track to divert him. When high ground was reached a halt was made, to scan the openings in every direction, and perchance Bruin would be discovered sitting upright on his haunches, eating manzanita berries; pulling down the fruit-laden branches with his paws and pressing them together, so as to get substantial mouthfuls, however mixed with leaves and twigs. The time of year enabled the hunter to determine approximately where the game would be found: in spring and early summer, in lush grass and clover meadows and in berry tangles along the banks of streams, or on pea-vine and lupine clad slopes; in late summer and autumn, beneath the pines, eating the cones cut off by the squirrels, and in oak groves at the bottom of cañons, munching acorns, manzanita berries, and cherries; and after snow had fallen, in alluvial bottoms, feeding on ants and yellow-jacket wasps. These food places were always cautiously approached, so as to avoid the chance of sudden encounters.

"Whenever," said the hunter, "I saw a bear before he saw me, I had no trouble in killing him. I just took lots of time to learn what he was up to and how long he would be likely to stay, and to study the direction of the wind and the lay of the land. Then I worked round to leeward of him, no matter how far I had to go; crawled and dodged to within a hundred yards, near the foot of a tree that I could climb, but which was too small for a bear to climb. There I looked well to the priming of my rifle, took off my boots so as to climb quickly if necessary, and, with my rifle in rest and Sandy behind me, waited until my bear stood right, when I made a sure, or at least a good shot back of the fore leg. In case he showed fight, I got up the tree I had in mind, before he could reach me. But bears are slow and awkward with their eyes, and being to windward they could not scent me, and often I got in a second shot before they saw the smoke. Usually,

146

however, they tried to get away when they were hurt, and I let them go a good safe while before I ventured into the brush after them. Then Sandy was pretty sure to find them dead; if not, he barked bold as a lion to draw attention, or rushed in and nipped them behind, enabling me to get to a safe distance and watch a chance for a finishing shot.

"Oh yes, bear-hunting is a mighty interesting business, and safe enough if followed just right, though, like every other business, especially the wild kind, it has its accidents, and Sandy and I have had close calls at times. Bears are nobody's fools, and they know enough to let men alone as a general thing, unless they are wounded, or cornered, or have cubs. In my opinion, a hungry old mother would catch and eat a man, if she could; which is only fair play, anyhow, for we eat them. But nobody, as far as I know, has been eaten up in these rich mountains. Why they never tackle a fellow when he is lying asleep I never could understand. They could gobble us mighty handy, but I suppose it's nature to respect a sleeping man."

Sheep-owners and their shepherds have killed a great many bears, mostly by poison and traps of various sorts. Bears are fond of mutton, and levy heavy toll on every flock driven into the mountains. They usually come to the corral at night, climb in, kill a sheep with a stroke of the paw, carry it off a little distance, eat about half of it, and return the next night for the other half; and so on all summer, or until they are themselves killed. It is not, however, by direct killing, but by suffocation through crowding against the corral wall in fright, that the greatest losses are incurred. From ten to fifteen sheep are found dead, smothered in the corral, after every attack; or the walls are broken, and the flock is scattered far and wide. A flock may escape the attention of these marauders for a week or two in the spring; but after their first taste of the fine mountain-fed meat the visits are persistently kept up, in spite of all precautions. Once I spent a night with two Portuguese shepherds, who were greatly troubled with bears, from two to four or five visiting them almost every night. Their camp was near the middle of the Park, and the wicked bears, they said, were getting worse and worse. Not waiting now until dark, they came out of the brush in broad daylight, and boldly carried off as many sheep as they liked. One evening, before sundown, a bear, followed by two cubs, came for an early supper, as the flock was being slowly driven toward the camp. Joe, the elder of the shepherds, warned by many exciting experiences, promptly climbed a tall tamarack pine, and left the freebooters to help themselves; while Antone, calling him a coward, and declaring that he was not going to let bears eat up his sheep before his face, set the dogs on them, and rushed toward them with a great noise and a stick. The frightened cubs ran up a tree, and the mother ran to meet the shepherd and dogs. Antone stood astonished for a moment, eyeing the oncoming bear; then fled faster than Joe had, closely pursued. He scrambled to the roof of their little cabin, the only refuge quickly available; and fortunately, the bear, anxious about her young, did not climb after him, — only held him in mortal terror a few minutes, glaring and threatening, then hastened back to her cubs, called them down, went to the frightened, huddled flock, killed a sheep, and feasted in peace. Antone piteously entreated cautious Joe to show him a good safe tree, up which he climbed like a sailor climbing a mast, and held on as long as he could with legs crossed, the slim pine recommended by Joe being nearly branchless. "So you, too, are a bear coward as well as Joe," I said, after hearing the story. "Oh, I tell you," he replied, with grand solemnity, "bear face close by look awful; she just as soon eat me

as not. She do so as eef all my sheeps b'long
every one to her own self. I run to bear no
more. I take tree every time."

After this the shepherds corraled the flock
about an hour before sundown, chopped large
quantities of dry wood and made a circle of
fires around the corral every night, and one
with a gun kept watch on a stage built in a
pine by the side of the cabin, while the other
slept. But after the first night or two this fire
fence did no good, for the robbers seemed to
regard the light as an advantage, after becoming used to it.

On the night I spent at their camp the show
made by the wall of fire when it was blazing
in its prime was magnificent, — the illumined
trees round about relieved against solid darkness, and the two thousand sheep lying down
in one gray mass, sprinkled with gloriously
brilliant gems, the effect of the firelight in
their eyes. It was nearly midnight when a
pair of the freebooters arrived. They walked
boldly through a gap in the fire circle, killed
two sheep, carried them out, and vanished in
the dark woods, leaving ten dead in a pile,
trampled down and smothered against the corral fence; while the scared watcher in the tree
did not fire a single shot, saying he was afraid
he would hit some of the sheep, as the bears

got among them before he could get a good sight.

In the morning I asked the shepherds why they did not move the flock to a new pasture. "Oh, no use!" cried Antone. "Look my dead sheeps. We move three four time before, all the same bear come by the track. No use. To-morrow we go home below. Look my dead sheeps. Soon all dead."

Thus were they driven out of the mountains more than a month before the usual time. After Uncle Sam's soldiers, bears are the most effective forest police, but some of the shepherds are very successful in killing them. Altogether, by hunters, mountaineers, Indians, and sheepmen, probably five or six hundred have been killed within the bounds of the Park, during the last thirty years. But they are not in danger of extinction. Now that the Park is guarded by soldiers, not only has the vegetation in great part come back to the desolate ground, but all the wild animals are increasing in numbers. No guns are allowed in the Park except under certain restrictions, and after a permit has been obtained from the officer in charge. This has stopped the barbarous slaughter of bears, and especially of deer, by shepherds, hunters, and hunting tourists, who, it would seem, can find no pleasure without blood.

WILDERNESS ESSAYS

The Sierra deer — the blacktail — spend the winters in the brushy and exceedingly rough region just below the main timber-belt, and are less accessible to hunters there than when they are passing through the comparatively open forests to and from their summer pastures near the summits of the range. They go up the mountains early in the spring as the snow melts, not waiting for it all to disappear; reaching the high Sierra about the first of June, and the coolest recesses at the base of the peaks a month or so later. I have tracked them for miles over compacted snow from three to ten feet deep.

Deer are capital mountaineers, making their way into the heart of the roughest mountains; seeking not only pasturage, but a cool climate, and safe hidden places in which to bring forth their young. They are not supreme as rock-climbing animals; they take second rank, yielding the first to the mountain sheep, which dwell above them on the highest crags and peaks. Still, the two meet frequently; for the deer climbs all the peaks save the lofty summits above the glaciers, crossing piles of angular boulders, roaring swollen streams, and sheer-walled cañons by fords and passes that would try the nerves of the hardiest mountaineers, — climbing with graceful ease and reserve of strength that cannot fail to arouse admiration.

THE ANIMALS OF THE YOSEMITE

Everywhere some species of deer seems to be at home, — on rough or smooth ground, lowlands or highlands, in swamps and barrens and the densest woods, in varying climates, hot or cold, over all the continent; maintaining glorious health, never making an awkward step. Standing, lying down, walking, feeding, running even for life, it is always invincibly graceful, and adds beauty and animation to every landscape, — a charming animal, and a great credit to nature.

I never see one of the common blacktail deer, the only species in the Park, without fresh admiration; and since I never carry a gun I see them well: lying beneath a juniper or dwarf pine, among the brown needles on the brink of some cliff or the end of a ridge commanding a wide outlook; feeding in sunny openings among chaparral, daintily selecting aromatic leaves and twigs; leading their fawns out of my way, or making them lie down and hide; bounding past through the forest, or curiously advancing and retreating again and again.

One morning when I was eating breakfast in a little garden spot on the Kaweah, hedged around with chaparral, I noticed a deer's head thrust through the bushes, the big beautiful eyes gazing at me. I kept still, and the deer ventured forward a step, then snorted and withdrew. In a few minutes she returned, and came into the open garden, stepping with infinite grace, followed by two others. After showing themselves for a moment, they bounded over the hedge with sharp, timid snorts and vanished. But curiosity brought them back with still another, and all four came into my garden, and, satisfied that I meant them no ill, began to feed, actually eating breakfast with me, like tame, gentle sheep around a shepherd, — rare company, and the most graceful in movements and attitudes. I eagerly watched them while they fed on ceanothus and wild cherry, daintily culling single leaves here and there from the side of the hedge, turning now and then to snip a few leaves of mint from the midst of the garden flowers. Grass they did not eat at all. No wonder the contents of the deer's stomach are eaten by the Indians.

While exploring the upper cañon of the north fork of the San Joaquin, one evening, the sky threatening rain, I searched for a dry bed, and made choice of a big juniper that had been pushed down by a snow avalanche, but was resting stubbornly on its knees high enough to let me lie under its broad trunk. Just below my shelter there was another juniper on the very brink of a precipice, and, examining it, I found a deer-bed beneath it, completely protected and concealed by drooping branches, a fine refuge and lookout as well as resting-place. About an hour before dark I heard the clear, sharp snorting of a deer, and looking down on the brushy, rocky cañon bottom, discovered an anxious doe that no doubt had her fawns concealed near by. She bounded over the chaparral and up the farther slope of the wall, often stopping to look back and listen, — a fine picture of vivid, eager alertness. I sat perfectly still, and as my shirt was colored like the juniper bark I was not easily seen. After a little she came cautiously toward me, sniffing the air and grazing, and her movements, as she descended the cañon side over boulder piles and brush and fallen timber, were admirably strong and beautiful; she never strained or made apparent efforts, although jumping high here and there. As she drew nigh she sniffed anxiously, trying the air in different directions until she caught my scent; then bounded off, and vanished behind a small grove of firs. Soon she came back with the same caution and insatiable curiosity, — coming and going five or six times. While I sat admiring her, a Douglas squirrel, evidently excited by her noisy alarms, climbed a boulder beneath me, and witnessed her performances as attentively as I did, while a frisky chipmunk, too restless or hungry for such shows, busied himself about his supper in a thicket of shadbushes, the fruit of which was then ripe, glancing about on the slender twigs lightly as a sparrow.

Toward the end of the Indian summer, when the young are strong, the deer begin to gather in little bands of from six to fifteen or twenty, and on the approach of the first snowstorm they set out on their march down the mountains to their winter quarters; lingering usually on warm hillsides and spurs eight or ten miles below the summits, as if loath to leave. About the end of November, a heavy, far-reaching storm drives them down in haste along the dividing ridges between the rivers, led by old experienced bucks whose knowledge of the topography is wonderful.

It is when the deer are coming down that the Indians set out on their grand fall hunt. Too lazy to go into the recesses of the mountains away from trails, they wait for the deer to come out, and then waylay them. This plan also has the advantage of finding them in bands. Great preparations are made. Old guns are mended, bullets moulded, and the hunters wash themselves and fast to some extent, to insure good luck, as they say. Men and women, old and young, set forth together. Central camps are made on the well-known highways of the deer, which are soon red with blood. Each hunter comes in laden, old crones as well as maidens smiling on the luckiest. All grow fat and merry. Boys, each armed with an antlered head, play at buck-fighting, and plague the industrious women, who are busily preparing the meat for transportation, by stealing up behind them and throwing fresh hides over them. But the Indians are passing away here as everywhere, and their red camps on the mountains are fewer every year.

There are panthers, foxes, badgers, porcupines, and coyotes in the Park, but not in large numbers. I have seen coyotes well back in the range at the head of the Tuolumne Meadows as early as June 1st, before the snow was gone, feeding on marmots; but they are far more numerous on the inhabited lowlands around ranches, where they enjoy life on chickens, turkeys, quail eggs, ground squirrels, hares, etc., and all kinds of fruit. Few wild sheep, I fear, are left hereabouts; for, though safe on the high peaks, they are driven down the eastern slope of the mountains when the deer are driven down the western, to ridges and outlying spurs where the snow does not fall to a great depth, and there they are within reach of the cattlemen's rifles.

The two squirrels of the Park, the Douglas and the California gray, keep all the woods lively. The former is far more abundant and more widely distributed, being found all the way up from the foothills to the dwarf pines on the Summit peaks. He is the most influential of the Sierra animals, though small, and the brightest of all the squirrels I know, — a squirrel of squirrels, quick mountain vigor and valor condensed, purely wild, and as free from disease as a sunbeam. One cannot think of such an animal ever being weary or sick. He claims all the woods, and is inclined to drive away even men as intruders. How he scolds, and what faces he makes! If not so comically small he would be a dreadful fellow. The gray, *Sciurus fossor*, is the handsomest, I think, of all the large American squirrels. He is something like the Eastern gray, but is brighter and clearer in color, and more lithe and slender. He dwells in the oak and pine woods up to a height of about five thousand feet above the sea, is rather common in Yosemite Valley, Hetch-Hetchy, Kings River Cañon, and indeed in all the main cañons and Yosemites, but does not like the high fir-covered ridges. Compared with the Douglas, the gray is more than twice as large; nevertheless, he manages to make his way through the trees with less stir than his small, peppery neighbor, and is much less influential in every way. In the spring, before the pine-nuts and hazel-nuts are ripe, he examines last year's cones for the few seeds that may be left in them between the half-open scales, and gleans fallen nuts and seeds on the ground among the leaves, after making sure that no enemy is nigh. His fine tail floats, now behind, now above him, level or gracefully curled, light and radiant as dry thistledown. His body seems hardly more substantial than his tail. The Douglas is a firm, emphatic bolt of life, fiery, pungent, full of brag and show and fight, and his movements have none of the elegant deliberation of the gray. They are so quick and keen they almost sting the onlooker, and the acrobatic harlequin gyrating show he makes of himself turns one giddy to see. The gray is shy and oftentimes stealthy, as if half expecting to find an enemy in every tree and bush and behind every log; he seems to wish to be let alone, and manifests no desire to be seen, or admired, or feared. He is hunted by the Indians, and this of itself is cause enough for caution. The Douglas is less attractive for game, and probably increasing in numbers in spite of every enemy. He goes his ways bold as a lion, up and down and across, round and round, the happiest, merriest of all the hairy tribe, and at the same time tremendously earnest and solemn, sunshine incarnate, making every tree tingle with his electric toes. If you prick him, you cannot think he will bleed. He seems above the chance and change that beset common mortals, though in busily gathering burs and nuts he shows that he has to work for a living, like the rest of us. I never found a dead Douglas. He gets into the world and out of it without being noticed; only in prime is he seen, like some little plants that are visible only when in bloom.

The little striped *Tamias quadrivittatus* is one of the most amiable and delightful of all the mountain tree-climbers. A brighter, cheerier chipmunk does not exist. He is smarter, more arboreal and squirrel-like, than the familiar Eastern species, and is distributed as widely on the Sierra as the Douglas. Every forest, however dense or open, every hilltop and cañon, however brushy or bare, is cheered and enlivened by this happy little animal. You are likely to notice him first on the lower edge of the coniferous belt, where the Sabine and yellow pines meet; and thence upward, go where you may, you will find him every day, even in winter, unless the weather is stormy.

THE ANIMALS OF THE YOSEMITE

He is an exceedingly interesting little fellow, full of odd, quaint ways, confiding, thinking no evil; and without being a squirrel — a true shadow-tail — he lives the life of a squirrel, and has almost all squirrelish accomplishments without aggressive quarrelsomeness.

I never weary of watching him as he frisks about the bushes, gathering seeds and berries; poising on slender twigs of wild cherry, shad, chinquapin, buckthorn, bramble; skimming along prostrate trunks or over the grassy, needle-strewn forest floor; darting from boulder to boulder on glacial pavements and the tops of the great domes. When the seeds of the conifers are ripe, he climbs the trees and cuts off the cones for a winter store, working diligently, though not with the tremendous lightning energy of the Douglas, who frequently drives him out of the best trees. Then he lies in wait, and picks up a share of the burs cut off by his domineering cousin, and stores them beneath logs and in hollows. Few of the Sierra animals are so well liked as this little airy, fluffy half squirrel, half spermophile. So gentle, confiding, and busily cheery and happy, he takes one's heart and keeps his place among the best-loved of the mountain darlings. A diligent collector of seeds, nuts, and berries, of course he is well fed, though

161

never in the least dumpy with fat. On the contrary, he looks like a mere fluff of fur, weighing but little more than a field mouse, and of his frisky, birdlike liveliness without haste there is no end. Douglas can bark with his mouth closed, but little quad always opens his when he talks or sings. He has a considerable variety of notes which correspond with his movements, some of them sweet and liquid, like water dripping into a pool with tinkling sound. His eyes are black and animated, shining like dew. He seems dearly to like teasing a dog, venturing within a few feet of it, then frisking away with a lively chipping and low squirrelish churring; beating time to his music, such as it is, with his tail, which at each chip and churr describes a half circle. Not even Douglas is surer footed or takes greater risks. I have seen him running about on sheer Yosemite cliffs, holding on with as little effort as a fly and as little thought of danger, in places where, if he had made the least slip, he would have fallen thousands of feet. How fine it would be could mountaineers move about on precipices with the same sure grip!

Before the pine-nuts are ripe, grass seeds and those of the many species of ceanothus, with strawberries, raspberries, and the soft red thimbleberries of *Rubus nutkanus*, form the

162

bulk of his food, and a neater eater is not to be found in the mountains. Bees powdered with pollen, poking their blunt noses into the bells of flowers, are comparatively clumsy and boorish. Frisking along some fallen pine or fir, when the grass seeds are ripe, he looks about him, considering which of the tufts he sees is likely to have the best, runs out to it, selects what he thinks is sure to be a good head, cuts it off, carries it to the top of the log, sits upright and nibbles out the grain without getting awns in his mouth, turning the head round, holding it and fingering it as if playing on a flute; then skips for another and another, bringing them to the same dining-log.

The woodchuck (*Arctomys monax*) dwells on high bleak ridges and boulder piles; and a very different sort of mountaineer is he, — bulky, fat, aldermanic, and fairly bloated at times by hearty indulgence in the lush pastures of his airy home. And yet he is by no means a dull animal. In the midst of what we regard as storm-beaten desolation, high in the frosty air, beside the glaciers he pipes and whistles right cheerily and lives to a good old age. If you are as early a riser as he is, you may oftentimes see him come blinking out of his burrow to meet the first beams of the morning and take a sunbath on some favorite flat-topped boulder. Afterward, well warmed, he goes to breakfast in one of his garden hollows, eats heartily like a cow in clover until comfortably swollen, then goes a-visiting, and plays and loves and fights.

In the spring of 1875, when I was exploring the peaks and glaciers about the head of the middle fork of the San Joaquin, I had crossed the range from the head of Owen River, and one morning, passing around a frozen lake where the snow was perhaps ten feet deep, I was surprised to find the fresh track of a woodchuck plainly marked, the sun having softened the surface. What could the animal be thinking of, coming out so early while all the ground was snow-buried? The steady trend of his track showed he had a definite aim, and fortunately it was toward a mountain thirteen thousand feet high that I meant to climb. So I followed to see if I could find out what he was up to. From the base of the mountain the track pointed straight up, and I knew by the melting snow that I was not far behind him. I lost the track on a crumbling ridge, partly projecting through the snow, but soon discovered it again. Well toward the summit of the mountain, in an open spot on the south side, nearly inclosed by disintegrating pinnacles among which the sun heat reverberated, making an isolated patch of warm climate, I found a nice garden, full of rock cress, phlox, silene, draba, etc., and a few grasses; and in this garden I overtook the wanderer, enjoying a fine fresh meal, perhaps the first of the season. How did he know the way to this one garden spot, so high and far off, and what told him that it was in bloom while yet the snow was ten feet deep over his den? For this it would seem he would need more botanical, topographical, and climatological knowledge than most mountaineers are possessed of.

The shy, curious mountain beaver, *Haplodon*, lives on the heights, not far from the woodchuck. He digs canals and controls the flow of small streams under the sod. And it is startling when one is camped on the edge of a sloping meadow near the homes of these industrious mountaineers, to be awakened in the still night by the sound of water rushing and gurgling under one's head in a newly formed canal. Pouched gophers also have a way of awakening nervous campers that is quite as exciting as the haplodon's plan; that is, by a series of firm upward pushes when they are driving tunnels and shoving up the dirt. One naturally cries out, "Who's there?" and then discovering the cause, "All right. Go on. Good-night," and goes to sleep again.

WILDERNESS ESSAYS

The haymaking pika, bob-tailed spermophile, and wood-rat are also among the most interesting of the Sierra animals. The last, *Neotoma*, is scarcely at all like the common rat, is nearly twice as large, has a delicate, soft, brownish fur, white on the belly, large ears thin and translucent, eyes full and liquid and mild in expression, most blunt and squirrelish, slender claws sharp as needles, and as his limbs are strong he can climb about as well as a squirrel; while no rat or squirrel has so innocent a look, is so easily approached, or in general expresses so much confidence in one's good intentions. He seems too fine for the thorny thickets he inhabits, and his big, rough hut is as unlike himself as possible. No other animal in these mountains makes nests so large and striking in appearance as his. They are built of all kinds of sticks (broken branches, and old rotten moss-grown chunks and green twigs, smooth or thorny, cut from the nearest bushes), mixed with miscellaneous rubbish and curious odds and ends, — bits of cloddy earth, stones, bones, bits of deer-horn, etc.: the whole simply piled in conical masses on the ground in chaparral thickets. Some of these cabins are five or six feet high, and occasionally a dozen or more are grouped together; less, perhaps, for society's sake than for advantages of food and shelter.

THE ANIMALS OF THE YOSEMITE

Coming through deep, stiff chaparral in the heart of the wilderness, heated and weary in forcing a way, the solitary explorer, happening into one of these curious neotoma villages, is startled at the strange sight, and may imagine he is in an Indian village, and feel anxious as to the reception he will get in a place so wild. At first, perhaps, not a single inhabitant will be seen, or at most only two or three seated on the tops of their huts as at the doors, observing the stranger with the mildest of mild eyes. The nest in the center of the cabin is made of grass and films of bark chewed to tow, and lined with feathers and the down of various seeds. The thick, rough walls seem to be built for defense against enemies — fox, coyote, etc. — as well as for shelter, and the delicate creatures in their big, rude homes, suggest tender flowers, like those of *Salvia carduacea*, defended by thorny involucres.

Sometimes the home is built in the forks of an oak, twenty or thirty feet from the ground, and even in garrets. Among housekeepers who have these bushmen as neighbors or guests they are regarded as thieves, because they carry away and pile together everything transportable (knives, forks, tin cups, spoons, spectacles, combs, nails, kindling-wood, etc., as well as eatables of all sorts), to strengthen their fortifications or to shine among rivals. Once, far back in the high Sierra, they stole my snow-goggles, the lid of my teapot, and my aneroid barometer; and one stormy night, when encamped under a prostrate cedar, I was awakened by a gritting sound on the granite, and by the light of my fire I discovered a handsome neotoma beside me, dragging away my ice-hatchet, pulling with might and main by a buckskin string on the handle. I threw bits of bark at him and made a noise to frighten him, but he stood scolding and chattering back at me, his fine eyes shining with an air of injured innocence.

A great variety of lizards enliven the warm portions of the Park. Some of them are more than a foot in length, others but little larger than grasshoppers. A few are snaky and repulsive at first sight, but most of the species are handsome and attractive, and bear acquaintance well; we like them better the farther we see into their charming lives. Small fellow mortals, gentle and guileless, they are easily tamed, and have beautiful eyes, expressing the clearest innocence, so that, in spite of prejudices brought from cool, lizardless countries, one must soon learn to like them. Even the horned toad of the plains and foothills, called horrid, is mild and gentle, with charming eyes, and so are the snakelike species found in the underbrush of the lower forests. These glide in curves with all the ease and grace of snakes, while their small, undeveloped limbs drag for the most part as useless appendages. One specimen that I measured was fourteen inches long, and as far as I saw it made no use whatever of its diminutive limbs.

Most of them glint and dart on the sunny rocks and across open spaces from bush to bush, swift as dragonflies and hummingbirds, and about as brilliantly colored. They never make a long-sustained run, whatever their object, but dart direct as arrows for a distance of ten or twenty feet, then suddenly stop, and as suddenly start again. These stops are necessary as rests, for they are short-winded, and when pursued steadily are soon run out of breath, pant pitifully, and may easily be caught where no retreat in bush or rock is quickly available.

If you stay with them a week or two and behave well, these gentle saurians, descendants of an ancient race of giants, will soon know and trust you, come to your feet, play, and watch your every motion with cunning curiosity. You will surely learn to like them, not only the bright ones, gorgeous as the rainbow, but the little ones, gray as lichened granite, and scarcely bigger than grasshoppers; and they will teach you that scales may cover as fine a nature as hair or feathers or anything tailored.

There are many snakes in the cañons and lower forests, but they are mostly handsome and harmless. Of all the tourists and travelers who have visited Yosemite and the adjacent mountains, not one has been bitten by a snake of any sort, while thousands have been charmed by them. Some of them vie with the lizards in beauty of color and dress patterns. Only the rattlesnake is venomous, and he carefully keeps his venom to himself as far as man is concerned, unless his life is threatened.

Before I learned to respect rattlesnakes I killed two, the first on the San Joaquin plain. He was coiled comfortably around a tuft of bunch-grass, and I discovered him when he was between my feet as I was stepping over him. He held his head down and did not attempt to strike, although in danger of being trampled. At that time, thirty years ago, I imagined that rattlesnakes should be killed wherever found. I had no weapon of any sort, and on the smooth plain there was not a stick or a stone within miles; so I crushed him by jumping on him, as the deer are said to do. Looking me in the face he saw I meant mischief, and quickly cast himself into a coil, ready to strike in defense. I knew he could not strike when traveling, therefore I threw handfuls of dirt and grass sods at him, to tease him out of coil. He held his ground a few minutes, threatening and striking, and then started off to get rid of me. I ran forward and jumped on him; but he drew back his head so quickly my heel missed, and he also missed his stroke at me. Persecuted, tormented, again and again he tried to get away, bravely striking out to protect himself; but at last my heel came squarely down, sorely wounding him, and a few more brutal stampings crushed him. I felt degraded by the killing business, farther from heaven, and I made up my mind to try to be at least as fair and charitable as the snakes themselves, and to kill no more save in self-defense.

The second killing might also, I think, have been avoided, and I have always felt somewhat sore and guilty about it. I had built a little cabin in Yosemite, and for convenience in getting water, and for the sake of music and society, I led a small stream from Yosemite Creek into it. Running along the side of the wall it was not in the way, and it had just fall enough to ripple and sing in low, sweet tones, making delightful company, especially at night when I was lying awake. Then a few frogs

came in and made merry with the stream, —
and one snake, I suppose to catch the frogs.

Returning from my long walks, I usually
brought home a large handful of plants, partly
for study, partly for ornament, and set them in
a corner of the cabin, with their stems in the
stream to keep them fresh. One day, when I
picked up a handful that had begun to fade, I
uncovered a large coiled rattler that had been
hiding behind the flowers. Thus suddenly
brought to light face to face with the rightful
owner of the place, the poor reptile was desperately embarrassed, evidently realizing that he
had no right in the cabin. It was not only fear
that he showed, but a good deal of downright
bashfulness and embarrassment, like that of a
more than half honest person caught under suspicious circumstances behind a door. Instead
of striking or threatening to strike, though
coiled and ready, he slowly drew his head
down as far as he could, with awkward, confused kinks in his neck and a shamefaced expression, as if wishing the ground would open
and hide him. I have looked into the eyes of so
many wild animals that I feel sure I did not
mistake the feelings of this unfortunate snake.
I did not want to kill him, but I had many visitors, some of them children, and I oftentimes
came in late at night; so I judged he must die.

THE ANIMALS OF THE YOSEMITE

Since then I have seen perhaps a hundred or more in these mountains, but I have never intentionally disturbed them, nor have they disturbed me to any great extent, even by accident, though in danger of being stepped on. Once, while I was on my knees kindling a fire, one glided under the arch made by my arm. He was only going away from the ground I had selected for a camp, and there was not the slightest danger, because I kept still and allowed him to go in peace. The only time I felt myself in serious danger was when I was coming out of the Tuolumne Cañon by a steep side cañon toward the head of Yosemite Creek. On an earthquake talus, a boulder in my way presented a front so high that I could just reach the upper edge of it while standing on the next below it. Drawing myself up, as soon as my head was above the flat top of it I caught sight of a coiled rattler. My hands had alarmed him, and he was ready for me; but even with this provocation, and when my head came in sight within a foot of him, he did not strike. The last time I sauntered through the big cañon I saw about two a day. One was not coiled, but neatly folded in a narrow space between two cobblestones on the side of the river, his head below the level of them, ready to shoot up like a jack-in-the-box for frogs

173

or birds. My foot spanned the space above within an inch or two of his head, but he only held it lower. In making my way through a particularly tedious tangle of buckthorn, I parted the branches on the side of an open spot and threw my bundle of bread into it; and when, with my arms free, I was pushing through after it, I saw a small rattlesnake dragging his tail from beneath my bundle. When he caught sight of me he eyed me angrily, and with an air of righteous indignation seemed to be asking why I had thrown that stuff on him. He was so small that I was inclined to slight him, but he struck out so angrily that I drew back, and approached the opening from the other side. But he had been listening, and when I looked through the brush I found him confronting me, still with a come-in-if-you-dare expression. In vain I tried to explain that I only wanted my bread; he stoutly held the ground in front of it; so I went back a dozen rods and kept still for half an hour, and when I returned he had gone.

One evening, near sundown, in a very rough, boulder-choked portion of the cañon, I searched long for a level spot for a bed, and at last was glad to find a patch of flood-sand on the river-bank, and a lot of driftwood close by for a camp-fire. But when I threw down my bundle,

THE ANIMALS OF THE YOSEMITE

I found two snakes in possession of the ground. I might have passed the night even in this snake den without danger, for I never knew a single instance of their coming into camp in the night; but fearing that, in so small a space, some late comers, not aware of my presence, might get stepped on when I was replenishing the fire, to avoid possible crowding I encamped on one of the earthquake boulders.

There are two species of *Crotalus* in the Park, and when I was exploring the basin of Yosemite Creek I thought I had discovered a new one. I saw a snake with curious divided appendages on its head. Going nearer, I found that the strange headgear was only the feet of a frog. Cutting a switch, I struck the snake lightly until he disgorged the poor frog, or rather allowed it to back out. On its return to the light from one of the very darkest of death valleys, it blinked a moment with a sort of dazed look, then plunged into a stream, apparently happy and well.

Frogs abound in all the bogs, marshes, pools, and lakes, however cold and high and isolated. How did they manage to get up these high mountains? Surely not by jumping. Long and dry excursions through weary miles of boulders and brush would be trying to frogs. Most likely their stringy spawn is carried on the feet of ducks, cranes, and other water-birds. Anyhow, they are most thoroughly distributed, and flourish famously. What a cheery, hearty set they are, and how bravely their krink and tronk concerts enliven the rocky wilderness!

None of the high-lying mountain lakes or branches of the rivers above sheer falls had fish of any sort until stocked by the agency of man. In the high Sierra, the only river in which trout exist naturally is the middle fork of Kings River. There are no sheer falls on this stream; some of the rapids, however, are so swift and rough, even at the lowest stage of water, that it is surprising any fish can climb them. I found trout in abundance in this fork up to seventy-five hundred feet. They also run quite high on the Kern. On the Merced they get no higher than Yosemite Valley, four thousand feet, all the forks of the river being barred there by sheer falls, and on the main Tuolumne they are stopped by a fall below Hetch-Hetchy, still lower than Yosemite. Though these upper waters are inaccessible to the fish, one would suppose their eggs might have been planted there by some means. Nature has so many ways of doing such things. In this case she waited for the agency of man, and now many of these hitherto fishless lakes and streams are full of fine trout, stocked by

176

individual enterprise, Walton clubs, etc., in great part under the auspices of the United States Fish Commission. A few trout carried into Hetch-Hetchy in a common water-bucket have multiplied wonderfully fast. Lake Tenaya, at an elevation of over eight thousand feet, was stocked eight years ago by Mr. Murphy, who carried a few trout from Yosemite. Many of the small streams of the eastern slope have also been stocked with trout transported over the passes in tin cans on the backs of mules. Soon, it would seem, all the streams of the range will be enriched by these lively fish, and will become the means of drawing thousands of visitors into the mountains. Catching trout with a bit of bent wire is a rather trivial business, but fortunately people fish better than they know. In most cases it is the man who is caught. Trout-fishing regarded as bait for catching men, for the saving of both body and soul, is important, and deserves all the expense and care bestowed on it.

THE YELLOWSTONE NATIONAL PARK

Of the four national parks of the West, the Yellowstone is far the largest. It is a big, wholesome wilderness on the broad summit of the Rocky Mountains, favored with abundance of rain and snow, — a place of fountains where the greatest of the American rivers take their rise. The central portion is a densely forested and comparatively level volcanic plateau with an average elevation of about eight thousand feet above the sea, surrounded by an imposing host of mountains belonging to the subordinate Gallatin, Wind River, Teton, Absaroka, and snowy ranges. Unnumbered lakes shine in it, united by a famous band of streams that rush up out of hot lava beds, or fall from the frosty peaks in channels rocky and bare, mossy and bosky, to the main rivers, singing cheerily on through every difficulty, cunningly dividing and finding their way east and west to the two far-off seas.

Glacier meadows and beaver meadows are outspread with charming effect along the banks of the streams, parklike expanses in the woods, and innumerable small gardens in

Our National Parks, 1901

rocky recesses of the mountains, some of them containing more petals than leaves, while the whole wilderness is enlivened with happy animals.

Beside the treasures common to most mountain regions that are wild and blessed with a kind climate, the park is full of exciting wonders. The wildest geysers in the world, in bright, triumphant bands, are dancing and singing in it amid thousands of boiling springs, beautiful and awful, their basins arrayed in gorgeous colors like gigantic flowers; and hot paint-pots, mud springs, mud volcanoes, mush and broth caldrons whose contents are of every color and consistency, plash and heave and roar in bewildering abundance. In the adjacent mountains, beneath the living trees the edges of petrified forests are exposed to view, like specimens on the shelves of a museum, standing on ledges tier above tier where they grew, solemnly silent in rigid crystalline beauty after swaying in the winds thousands of centuries ago, opening marvelous views back into the years and climates and life of the past. Here, too, are hills of sparkling crystals, hills of sulphur, hills of glass, hills of cinders and ashes, mountains of every style of architecture, icy or forested, mountains covered with honey-bloom sweet as Hymettus, mountains boiled soft like potatoes and colored like a sunset sky. A' that and a' that, and twice as muckle 's a' that, Nature has on show in the Yellowstone Park. Therefore it is called Wonderland, and thousands of tourists and travelers stream into it every summer, and wander about in it enchanted.

Fortunately, almost as soon as it was discovered it was dedicated and set apart for the benefit of the people, a piece of legislation that shines benignly amid the common dust-and-ashes history of the public domain, for which the world must thank Professor Hayden above all others; for he led the first scientific exploring party into it, described it, and with admirable enthusiasm urged Congress to preserve it. As delineated in the year 1872, the park contained about 3344 square miles. On March 30, 1891, it was to all intents and purposes enlarged by the Yellowstone National Park Timber Reserve, and in December, 1897, by the Teton Forest Reserve; thus nearly doubling its original area, and extending the southern boundary far enough to take in the sublime Teton range and the famous pasture lands of the big Rocky Mountain game animals. The withdrawal of this large tract from the public domain did no harm to any one; for its height, six thousand to over thirteen thousand feet above the sea, and its thick mantle of volcanic rocks, prevent its ever being available for agriculture or mining, while on the other hand its geographical position, reviving climate, and wonderful scenery combine to make it a grand health, pleasure, and study resort, — a gathering-place for travelers from all the world.

The national parks are not only withdrawn from sale and entry like the forest reservations, but are efficiently managed and guarded by small troops of United States cavalry, directed by the Secretary of the Interior. Under this care the forests are flourishing, protected from both axe and fire; and so, of course, are the shaggy beds of underbrush and the herbaceous vegetation. The so-called curiosities, also, are preserved, and the furred and feathered tribes, many of which, in danger of extinction a short time ago, are now increasing in numbers, — a refreshing thing to see amid the blind, ruthless destruction that is going on in the adjacent regions. In pleasing contrast to the noisy, ever-changing management, or mismanagement, of blundering, plundering, money-making vote-sellers who receive their places from boss politicians as purchased goods, the soldiers do their duty so quietly that the traveler is scarce aware of their presence.

WILDERNESS ESSAYS

This is the coolest and highest of the parks. Frosts occur every month of the year. Nevertheless, the tenderest tourist finds it warm enough in summer. The air is electric and full of ozone, healing, reviving, exhilarating, kept pure by frost and fire, while the scenery is wild enough to awaken the dead. It is a glorious place to grow in and rest in; camping on the shores of the lakes, in the warm openings of the woods golden with sunflowers, on the banks of the streams, by the snowy waterfalls, beside the exciting wonders or away from them in the scallops of the mountain walls sheltered from every wind, on smooth silky lawns enameled with gentians, up in the fountain hollows of the ancient glaciers between the peaks, where cool pools and brooks and gardens of precious plants charmingly embowered are never wanting, and good rough rocks with every variety of cliff and scaur are invitingly near for outlooks and exercise.

From these lovely dens you may make excursions whenever you like into the middle of the park, where the geysers and hot springs are reeking and spouting in their beautiful basins, displaying an exuberance of color and strange motion and energy admirably calculated to surprise and frighten, charm and shake up the least sensitive out of apathy into newness of life.

YELLOWSTONE NATIONAL PARK

However orderly your excursions or aimless, again and again amid the calmest, stillest scenery you will be brought to a standstill hushed and awe-stricken before phenomena wholly new to you. Boiling springs and huge deep pools of purest green and azure water, thousands of them, are plashing and heaving in these high, cool mountains as if a fierce furnace fire were burning beneath each one of them; and a hundred geysers, white torrents of boiling water and steam, like inverted waterfalls, are ever and anon rushing up out of the hot, black underworld. Some of these ponderous geyser columns are as large as sequoias, — five to sixty feet in diameter, one hundred and fifty to three hundred feet high, — and are sustained at this great height with tremendous energy for a few minutes, or perhaps nearly an hour, standing rigid and erect, hissing, throbbing, booming, as if thunderstorms were raging beneath their roots, their sides roughened or fluted like the furrowed boles of trees, their tops dissolving in feathery branches, while the irised spray, like misty bloom is at times blown aside, revealing the massive shafts shining against a background of pine-covered hills. Some of them lean more or less, as if storm-bent, and instead of being round are flat or fan-shaped, issuing from irregular slits in silex pavements with radiate structure, the sunbeams sifting through them in ravishing splendor. Some are broad and round-headed like oaks; others are low and bunchy, branching near the ground like bushes; and a few are hollow in the centre like big daisies or water-lilies. No frost cools them, snow never covers them nor lodges in their branches; winter and summer they welcome alike; all of them, of whatever form or size, faithfully rising and sinking in fairy rhythmic dance night and day, in all sorts of weather, at varying periods of minutes, hours, or weeks, growing up rapidly, uncontrollable as fate, tossing their pearly branches in the wind, bursting into bloom and vanishing like the frailest flowers, — plants of which Nature raises hundreds or thousands of crops a year with no apparent exhaustion of the fiery soil.

The so-called geyser basins, in which this rare sort of vegetation is growing, are mostly open valleys on the central plateau that were eroded by glaciers after the greater volcanic fires had ceased to burn. Looking down over the forests as you approach them from the surrounding heights, you see a multitude of white columns, broad, reeking masses, and irregular jets and puffs of misty vapor ascending from the bottom of the valley, or entangled like smoke among the neighboring trees, suggesting the factories of some busy town or the camp-fires of an army. These mark the position of each mush-pot, paint-pot, hot spring, and geyser, or gusher, as the Icelandic words mean. And when you saunter into the midst of them over the bright sinter pavements, and see how pure and white and pearly gray they are in the shade of the mountains, and how radiant in the sunshine, you are fairly enchanted. So numerous they are and varied, Nature seems to have gathered them from all the world as specimens of her rarest fountains, to show in one place what she can do. Over four thousand hot springs have been counted in the park, and a hundred geysers; how many more there are nobody knows.

These valleys at the heads of the great rivers may be regarded as laboratories and kitchens, in which, amid a thousand retorts and pots, we may see Nature at work as chemist or cook, cunningly compounding an infinite variety of mineral messes; cooking whole mountains; boiling and steaming flinty rocks to smooth paste and mush, — yellow, brown, red, pink, lavender, gray, and creamy white, — making the most beautiful mud in the world; and distilling the most ethereal essences. Many of these pots and caldrons have been boiling thousands of years. Pots of sulphurous mush, stringy and lumpy, and pots of broth as black as ink, are tossed and stirred with constant care, and thin transparent essences, too pure and fine to be called water, are kept simmering gently in beautiful sinter cups and bowls that grow ever more beautiful the longer they are used. In some of the spring basins, the waters, though still warm, are perfectly calm, and shine blandly in a sod of overleaning grass and flowers, as if they were thoroughly cooked at last, and set aside to settle and cool. Others are wildly boiling over as if running to waste, thousands of tons of the precious liquids being thrown into the air to fall in scalding floods on the clean coral floor of the establishment, keeping onlookers at a distance. Instead of holding limpid pale green or azure water, other pots and craters are filled with scalding mud, which is tossed up from three or four feet to thirty feet, in sticky, rank-smelling masses, with gasping, belching, thudding sounds, plastering the branches of neighboring trees; every flask, retort, hot spring, and geyser has something special in it, no two being the same in temperature, color, or composition.

In these natural laboratories one needs stout faith to feel at ease. The ground sounds hollow underfoot, and the awful subterranean thunder shakes one's mind as the ground is shaken, especially at night in the pale moonlight, or when the sky is overcast with storm-clouds. In the solemn gloom, the geysers, dimly visible, look like monstrous dancing ghosts, and their wild songs and the earthquake thunder replying to the storms overhead seem doubly terrible, as if divine government were at an end. But the trembling hills keep their places. The sky clears, the rosy dawn is reassuring, and up comes the sun like a god, pouring his faithful beams across the mountains and forest, lighting each peak and tree and ghastly geyser alike, and shining into the eyes of the reeking springs, clothing them with rainbow light, and dissolving the seeming chaos of darkness into varied forms of harmony. The ordinary work of the world goes on. Gladly we see the flies dancing in the sunbeams, birds feeding their young, squirrels gathering nuts, and hear the blessed ouzel singing confidingly in the shallows of the river, — most faithful evangel, calming every fear, reducing everything to love.

The variously tinted sinter and travertine formations, outspread like pavements over large areas of the geyser valleys, lining the spring basins and throats of the craters, and forming beautiful coral-like rims and curbs about them, always excite admiring attention; so also does the play of the waters from which they are deposited. The various minerals in them are rich in colors, and these are greatly heightened by a smooth, silky growth of brilliantly colored confervæ which lines many of the pools and channels and terraces. No bed of flower-bloom is more exquisite than these myriads of minute plants, visible only in mass, growing in the hot waters. Most of the spring borders are low and daintily scalloped, crenelated, and beaded with sinter pearls. Some of the geyser craters are massive and picturesque, like ruined castles or old burned-out sequoia stumps, and are adorned on a grand scale with outbulging, cauliflower-like formations. From these as centers the silex pavements slope gently away in thin, crusty, overlapping layers, slightly inter-rupted in some places by low terraces. Or, as in the case of the Mammoth Hot Springs, at the north end of the park, where the building waters issue from the side of a steep hill, the deposits form a succession of higher and broader terraces of white travertine tinged with purple, like the famous Pink Terrace at Rotomahana, New Zealand, draped in front with clustering stalactites, each terrace having a pool of indescribably beautiful water upon it in a basin with a raised rim that glistens with confervæ, — the whole, when viewed at a distance of a mile or two, looking like a broad, massive cascade pouring over shelving rocks in snowy purpled foam.

The stones of this divine masonry, invisible particles of lime or silex, mined in quarries no eye has seen, go to their appointed places in gentle, tinkling, transparent currents or through the dashing turmoil of floods, as surely guided as the sap of plants streaming into bole and branch, leaf and flower. And thus from century to century this beauty-work has gone on and is going on.

Passing through many a mile of pine and spruce woods, toward the center of the park you come to the famous Yellowstone Lake. It is about twenty miles long and fifteen wide, and lies at a height of nearly eight thousand feet above the level of the sea, amid dense black forests and snowy mountains. Around its winding, wavering shores, closely forested and picturesquely varied with promontories and bays, the distance is more than one hundred miles. It is not very deep, only from two hundred to three hundred feet, and contains less water than the celebrated Lake Tahoe of the California Sierra, which is nearly the same size, lies at a height of sixty-four hundred feet, and is over sixteen hundred feet deep. But no other lake in North America of equal area lies so high as the Yellowstone, or gives birth to so noble a river. The terraces around its shores show that at the close of the glacial period its surface was about one hundred and sixty feet higher than it is now, and its area nearly twice as great.

It is full of trout, and a vast multitude of birds — swans, pelicans, geese, ducks, cranes, herons, curlews, plovers, snipe — feed in it and upon its shores; and many forest animals come out of the woods, and wade a little way in shallow, sandy places to drink and look about them, and cool themselves in the free flowing breezes.

In calm weather it is a magnificent mirror for the woods and mountains and sky, now pattered with hail and rain, now roughened with sudden storms that send waves to fringe the shores and wash its border of gravel and sand. The Absaroka Mountains and the Wind River Plateau on the east and south pour their gathered waters into it, and the river issues from the north side in a broad, smooth, stately current, silently gliding with such serene majesty that one fancies it knows the vast journey of four thousand miles that lies before it, and the work it has to do. For the first twenty miles its course is in a level, sunny valley lightly fringed with trees, through which it flows in silvery reaches stirred into spangles here and there by ducks and leaping trout, making no sound save a low whispering among the pebbles and the dipping willows and sedges of its banks. Then suddenly, as if preparing for hard work, it rushes eagerly, impetuously forward rejoicing in its strength, breaks into foam-bloom, and goes thundering down into the Grand Cañon in two magnificent falls, one hundred and three hundred feet high.

The cañon is so tremendously wild and impressive that even these great falls cannot hold your attention. It is about twenty miles long and a thousand feet deep, — a weird, unearthly-looking gorge of jagged, fantastic architecture, and most brilliantly colored. Here the Washburn range, forming the northern rim of the Yellowstone basin, made up mostly of beds of rhyolite decomposed by the action of thermal waters, has been cut through and laid open to view by the river; and a famous section it has made. It is not the depth or the shape of the cañon, nor the waterfall, nor the green and gray river chanting its brave song as it goes foaming on its way, that most impresses the observer, but the colors of the decomposed volcanic rocks. With few exceptions, the traveler in strange lands finds that, however much the scenery and vegetation in different countries may change, Mother Earth is ever familiar and the same. But here the very ground is changed, as if belonging to some other world. The walls of the cañon from top to bottom burn in a perfect glory of color, confounding and dazzling when the sun is shining, — white, yellow, green, blue, vermilion, and various other shades of red indefinitely blending. All the earth hereabouts seems to be paint. Millions of tons of it lie in sight, exposed to wind and weather as if of no account, yet marvelously fresh and bright, fast colors not to be washed out or bleached out by either sunshine or storms. The effect is so novel and awful, we imagine that even a river might be afraid to enter such a place. But the rich and gentle beauty of the vegetation is reassuring. The lovely *Linnæa borealis* hangs her twin bells over the brink of the cliffs, forests and gardens extend their treasures in smiling confidence on either side, nuts and berries ripen well whatever may be going on below; blind fears vanish, and the grand gorge seems a kindly, beautiful part of the general harmony, full of peace and joy and good will.

The park is easy of access. Locomotives

drag you to its northern boundary at Cinnabar, and horses and guides do the rest. From Cinnabar you will be whirled in coaches along the foaming Gardiner River to Mammoth Hot Springs; thence through woods and meadows, gulches and ravines along branches of the Upper Gallatin, Madison, and Firehole rivers to the main geyser basins; thence over the Continental Divide and back again, up and down through dense pine, spruce, and fir woods to the magnificent Yellowstone Lake, along its northern shore to the outlet, down the river to the falls and Grand Cañon, and thence back through the woods to Mammoth Hot Springs and Cinnabar; stopping here and there at the so-called points of interest among the geysers, springs, paint-pots, mud volcanoes, etc., where you will be allowed a few minutes or hours to saunter over the sinter pavements, watch the play of a few of the geysers, and peer into some of the most beautiful and terrible of the craters and pools. These wonders you will enjoy, and also the views of the mountains, especially the Gallatin and Absaroka ranges, the long, willowy glacier and beaver meadows, the beds of violets, gentians, phloxes, asters, phacelias, goldenrods, eriogonums, and many other flowers, some species giving color to whole meadows and hillsides. And you will enjoy your short views of the great lake and river and cañon. No scalping Indians will you see. The Black-feet and Bannocks that once roamed here are gone; so are the old beaver-catchers, the Coulters and Bridgers, with all their attractive buckskin and romance. There are several bands of buffaloes in the park, but you will not thus cheaply in tourist fashion see them nor many of the other large animals hidden in the wilderness. The song-birds, too, keep mostly out of sight of the rushing tourist, though off the roads thrushes, warblers, orioles, grosbeaks, etc., keep the air sweet and merry. Perhaps in passing rapids and falls you may catch glimpses of the water-ouzel, but in the whirling noise you will not hear his song. For-tunately, no road noise frightens the Douglas squirrel, and his merry play and gossip will amuse you all through the woods. Here and there a deer may be seen crossing the road, or a bear. Most likely, however, the only bears you will see are the half tame ones that go to the hotels every night for dinner-table scraps, — yeast-powder biscuit, Chicago canned stuff, mixed pickles, and beefsteaks that have proved too tough for the tourists.

Among the gains of a coach trip are the ac-quaintances made and the fresh views into human nature; for the wilderness is a shrewd touchstone, even thus lightly approached, and brings many a curious trait to view. Setting out, the driver cracks his whip, and the four horses go off at half gallop, half trot, in trained, showy style, until out of sight of the hotel. The coach is crowded, old and young side by side, blooming and fading, full of hope and fun and care. Some look at the scenery or the horses, and all ask questions, an odd mixed lot of them: "Where is the umbrella? What is the name of that blue flower over there? Are you sure the little bag is aboard? Is that hollow yonder a crater? How is your throat this morning? How high did you say the geysers spout? How does the elevation affect your head? Is that a geyser reeking over there in the rocks, or only a hot spring?" A long ascent is made, the solemn mountains come to view, small cares are quenched, and all become natural and silent, save perhaps some unfortunate expounder who has been reading guidebook geology, and rumbles forth foggy subsidences and upheavals until he is in danger of being heaved overboard. The driver will give you the names of the peaks and meadows and streams as you come to them, call attention to the glass road, tell how hard it was to build, — how the obsidian cliffs naturally pushed the surveyor's lines to the right, and the industrious beavers, by flooding the valley in front of the cliff, pushed them to the left.

Geysers, however, are the main objects, and as soon as they come in sight other wonders are forgotten. All gather around the crater of the one that is expected to play first. During the eruptions of the smaller geysers, such as the Beehive and Old Faithful, though a little frightened at first, all welcome the glorious show with enthusiasm, and shout, "Oh, how wonderful, beautiful, splendid, majestic!" Some venture near enough to stroke the column with a stick, as if it were a stone pillar or a tree, so firm and substantial and permanent it seems. While tourists wait around a large geyser, such as the Castle or the Giant, there is a chatter of small talk in anything but solemn mood; and during the intervals between the preliminary splashes and upheavals some adventurer occasionally looks down the throat of the crater, admiring the silex formations and wondering whether Hades is as beautiful. But when, with awful uproar as if avalanches were falling and storms thundering in the depths, the tremendous outburst begins, all run away to a safe distance, and look on, awe-stricken and silent, in devout, worshiping wonder.

The largest and one of the most wonderfully

beautiful of the springs is the Prismatic, which the guide will be sure to show you. With a circumference of three hundred yards, it is more like a lake than a spring. The water is pure deep blue in the center, fading to green on the edges, and its basin and the slightly terraced pavement about it are astonishingly bright and varied in color. This one of the multitude of Yellowstone fountains is of itself object enough for a trip across the continent. No wonder that so many fine myths have originated in springs; that so many fountains were held sacred in the youth of the world, and had miraculous virtues ascribed to them. Even in these cold, doubting, questioning, scientific times many of the Yellowstone fountains seem able to work miracles. Near the Prismatic Spring is the great Excelsior Geyser, which is said to throw a column of boiling water sixty to seventy feet in diameter to a height of from fifty to three hundred feet, at irregular periods. This is the greatest of all the geysers yet discovered anywhere. The Firehole River, which sweeps past it, is, at ordinary stages, a stream about one hundred yards wide and three feet deep; but when the geyser is in eruption, so great is the quantity of water discharged that the volume of the river is doubled, and it is rendered too hot and rapid to be forded.

WILDERNESS ESSAYS

Geysers are found in many other volcanic regions, — in Iceland, New Zealand, Japan, the Himalayas, the Eastern Archipelago, South America, the Azores, and elsewhere; but only in Iceland, New Zealand, and this Rocky Mountain park do they display their grandest forms, and of these three famous regions the Yellowstone is easily first, both in the number and in the size of its geysers. The greatest height of the column of the Great Geyser of Iceland actually measured was two hundred and twelve feet, and of the Strokhr one hundred and sixty-two feet.

In New Zealand, the Te Pueia at Lake Taupo, the Waikite at Rotorna, and two others are said to lift their waters occasionally to a height of one hundred feet, while the celebrated Te Tarata at Rotomahana sometimes lifts a boiling column twenty feet in diameter to a height of sixty feet. But all these are far surpassed by the Excelsior. Few tourists, however, will see the Excelsior in action, or a thousand other interesting features of the park that lie beyond the wagon-roads and the hotels. The regular trips — from three to five days — are too short. Nothing can be done well at a speed of forty miles a day. The multitude of mixed, novel impressions rapidly piled on one another make only a dreamy, bewildering, swirling blur, most of which is unrememberable. Far more time should be taken. Walk away quietly in any direction and taste the freedom of the mountaineer. Camp out among the grass and gentians of glacier meadows, in craggy garden nooks full of Nature's darlings. Climb the mountains and get their good tidings. Nature's peace will flow into you as sunshine flows into trees. The winds will blow their own freshness into you, and the storms their energy, while cares will drop off like autumn leaves. As age comes on, one source of enjoyment after another is closed, but Nature's sources never fail. Like a generous host, she offers here brimming cups in endless variety, served in a grand hall, the sky its ceiling, the mountains its walls, decorated with glorious paintings and enlivened with bands of music ever playing. The petty discomforts that beset the awkward guest, the unskilled camper, are quickly forgotten, while all that is precious remains. Fears vanish as soon as one is fairly free in the wilderness.

Most of the dangers that haunt the unseasoned citizen are imaginary; the real ones are perhaps too few rather than too many for his good. The bears that always seem to spring up thick as trees, in fighting, devouring attitudes before the frightened tourist whenever a camping trip is proposed, are gentle now, finding they are no longer likely to be shot; and rattlesnakes, the other big irrational dread of over-civilized people, are scarce here, for most of the park lies above the snake-line. Poor creatures, loved only by their Maker, they are timid and bashful, as mountaineers know; and though perhaps not possessed of much of that charity that suffers long and is kind, seldom, either by mistake or by mishaps, do harm to any one. Certainly they cause not the hundredth part of the pain and death that follow the footsteps of the admired Rocky Mountain trapper. Nevertheless, again and again, in season and out of season, the question comes up, "What are rattlesnakes good for?" As if nothing that does not obviously make for the benefit of man had any right to exist; as if our ways were God's ways. Long ago, an Indian to whom a French traveler put this old question replied that their tails were good for toothache, and their heads for fever. Anyhow, they are all, head and tail, good for themselves, and we need not begrudge them their share of life.

Fear nothing. No town park you have been accustomed to saunter in is so free from danger as the Yellowstone. It is a hard place to leave.

YELLOWSTONE NATIONAL PARK

Even its names in your guidebook are attractive, and should draw you far from wagon-roads, — all save the early ones, derived from the infernal regions: Hell Roaring River, Hell Broth Springs, The Devil's Caldron, etc. Indeed, the whole region was at first called Coulter's Hell, from the fiery brimstone stories told by trapper Coulter, who left the Lewis and Clark expedition and wandered through the park, in the year 1807, with a band of Bannock Indians. The later names, many of which we owe to Mr. Arnold Hague of the U.S. Geological Survey, are so telling and exhilarating that they set our pulses dancing and make us begin to enjoy the pleasures of excursions ere they are commenced. Three River Peak, Two Ocean Pass, Continental Divide, are capital geographical descriptions, suggesting thousands of miles of rejoicing streams and all that belongs to them. Big Horn Pass, Bison Peak, Big Game Ridge, bring brave mountain animals to mind. Birch Hills, Garnet Hills, Amethyst Mountain, Storm Peak, Electric Peak, Roaring Mountain, are bright, bracing names. Wapiti, Beaver, Tern, and Swan lakes conjure up fine pictures, and so also do Osprey and Ouzel falls. Antelope Creek, Otter, Mink, and Grayling creeks, Geode, Jasper, Opal, Carnelian, and

Chalcedony creeks, are lively and sparkling names that help the streams to shine; and Azalea, Stellaria, Arnica, Aster, and Phlox creeks, what pictures these bring up! Violet, Morning Mist, Hygeia, Beryl, Vermilion, and Indigo springs, and many beside, give us visions of fountains more beautifully arrayed than Solomon in all his purple and golden glory. All these and a host of others call you to camp. You may be a little cold some nights on mountain tops above the timber-line, but you will see the stars, and by and by you can sleep enough in your town bed, or at least in your grave. Keep awake while you may in mountain mansions so rare.

If you are not very strong, try to climb Electric Peak when a big bossy, well-charged thunder-cloud is on it, to breathe the ozone set free, and get yourself kindly shaken and shocked. You are sure to be lost in wonder and praise, and every hair of your head will stand up and hum and sing like an enthusiastic congregation.

After this reviving experience, you should take a look into a few of the tertiary volumes of the grand geological library of the park, and see how God writes history. No technical knowledge is required; only a calm day and a calm mind. Perhaps nowhere else in the

YELLOWSTONE NATIONAL PARK

Rocky Mountains have the volcanic forces been so busy. More than ten thousand square miles hereabouts have been covered to a depth of at least five thousand feet with material spouted from chasms and craters during the tertiary period, forming broad sheets of basalt, andesite, rhyolite, etc., and marvelous masses of ashes, sand, cinders, and stones now consolidated into conglomerates, charged with the remains of plants and animals that lived in the calm, genial periods that separated the volcanic outbursts.

Perhaps the most interesting and telling of these rocks, to the hasty tourist, are those that make up the mass of Amethyst Mountain. On its north side it presents a section two thousand feet high of roughly stratified beds of sand, ashes, and conglomerates coarse and fine, forming the untrimmed edges of a wonderful set of volumes lying on their sides, — books a million years old, well bound, miles in size, with full-page illustrations. On the ledges of this one section we see trunks and stumps of fifteen or twenty ancient forests ranged one above another, standing where they grew, or prostrate and broken like the pillars of ruined temples in desert sands, — a forest fifteen or twenty stories high, the roots of each spread above the tops of the next beneath it, telling wonderful tales of the bygone centuries, with their winters and summers, growth and death, fire, ice, and flood.

There were giants in those days. The largest of the standing opal and agate stumps and prostrate sections of the trunks are from two or three to fifty feet in height or length, and from five to ten feet in diameter; artd so perfect is the petrifaction that the annual rings and ducts are clearer and more easily counted than those of living trees, centuries of burial having brightened the records instead of blurring them. They show that the winters of the tertiary period gave as decided a check to vegetable growth as do those of the present time. Some trees favorably located grew rapidly, increasing twenty inches in diameter in as many years, while others of the same species, on poorer soil or overshadowed, increased only two or three inches in the same time.

Among the roots and stumps on the old forest floors we find the remains of ferns and bushes, and the seeds and leaves of trees like those now growing on the southern Alleghanies, — such as magnolia, sassafras, laurel, linden, persimmon, ash, alder, dogwood. Studying the lowest of these forests, the soil it grew on and the deposits it is buried in, we see that it was rich in species, and flourished in a genial, sunny climate. When its stately trees were in their glory, volcanic fires broke forth from chasms and craters, like larger geysers, spouting ashes, cinders, stones, and mud, which fell on the doomed forest like hail and snow; sifting, hurtling through the leaves and branches, choking the streams, covering the ground, crushing bushes and ferns, rapidly deepening, packing around the trees and breaking them, rising higher until the topmost boughs of the giants were buried, leaving not a leaf or twig in sight, so complete was the desolation. At last the volcanic storm began to abate, the fiery soil settled; mud floods and boulder floods passed over it, enriching it, cooling it; rains fell and mellow sunshine, and it became fertile and ready for another crop. Birds, and the winds, and roaming animals brought seeds from more fortunate woods, and a new forest grew up on the top of the buried one. Centuries of genial growing seasons passed. The seedling trees became giants, and with strong outreaching branches spread a leafy canopy over the gray land.

The sleeping subterranean fires again awake and shake the mountains, and every leaf trembles. The old craters, with perhaps new ones, are opened, and immense quantities of ashes, pumice, and cinders are again thrown into the sky. The sun, shorn of his beams, glows like a dull red ball, until hidden in sulphurous clouds. Volcanic snow, hail, and floods fall on the new forest, burying it alive, like the one beneath its roots. Then come another noisy band of mud floods and boulder floods, mixing, settling, enriching the new ground, more seeds, quickening sunshine and showers; and a third noble magnolia forest is carefully raised on the top of the second. And so on. Forest was planted above forest and destroyed, as if Nature were ever repenting, undoing the work she had so industriously done, and burying it.

Of course this destruction was creation, progress in the march of beauty through death. How quickly these old monuments excite and hold the imagination! We see the old stone stumps budding and blossoming and waving in the wind as magnificent trees, standing shoulder to shoulder, branches interlacing in grand varied round-headed forests; see the sunshine of morning and evening gilding their mossy trunks, and at high noon spangling on the thick glossy leaves of the magnolia, filtering through translucent canopies of linden and ash, and falling in mellow patches on the ferny floor; see the shining after rain, breathe the exhaling fragrance, and hear the winds and birds and the murmur of brooks and insects.

YELLOWSTONE NATIONAL PARK

We watch them from season to season; see the swelling buds when the sap begins to flow in the spring, the opening leaves and blossoms, the ripening of summer fruits, the colors of autumn, and the maze of leafless branches and sprays in winter; and we see the sudden oncome of the storms that overwhelmed them.

One calm morning at sunrise I saw the oaks and pines in Yosemite Valley shaken by an earthquake, their tops swishing back and forth, and every branch and needle shuddering as if in distress like the frightened screaming birds. One many imagine the trembling, rocking, tumultuous waving of those ancient Yellowstone woods, and the terror of their inhabitants when the first foreboding shocks were felt, the sky grew dark, and rock-laden floods began to roar. But though they were close pressed and buried, cut off from sun and wind, all their happy leaf-fluttering and waving done, other currents coursed through them, fondling and thrilling every fibre, and beautiful wood was replaced by beautiful stone. Now their rocky sepulchres are partly open, and show forth the natural beauty of death.

After the forest times and fire times had passed away, and the volcanic furnaces were banked and held in abeyance, another great change occurred. The glacial winter came on. The sky was again darkened, not with dust and ashes, but with snow which fell in glorious abundance, piling deeper, deeper, slipping from the overladen heights in booming avalanches, compacting into glaciers, that flowed over all the landscape, wiping off forests, grinding, sculpturing, fashioning the comparatively featureless lava beds into the beautiful rhythm of hill and dale and ranges of mountains we behold to-day; forming basins for lakes, channels for streams, new soils for forests, gardens, and meadows. While this ice-work was going on, the slumbering volcanic fires were boiling the subterranean waters, and with curious chemistry decomposing the rocks, making beauty in the darkness; these forces, seemingly antagonistic, working harmoniously together. How wild their meetings on the surface were we may imagine. When the glacier period began, geysers and hot springs were playing in grander volume, it may be, than those of to-day. The glaciers flowed over them while they spouted and thundered, carrying away their fine sinter and travertine structures, and shortening their mysterious channels.

The soils made in the down-grinding required to bring the present features of the

landscape into relief are possibly no better
than were some of the old volcanic soils that
were carried away, and which, as we have
seen, nourished magnificent forests, but the
glacial landscapes are incomparably more
beautiful than the old volcanic ones were.
The glacial winter has passed away, like the
ancient summers and fire periods, though in
the chronology of the geologist all these times
are recent. Only small residual glaciers on the
cool northern slopes of the highest mountains
are left of the vast all-embracing ice-mantle,
as solfataras and geysers are all that are left
of the ancient volcanoes.

Now the post-glacial agents are at work on
the grand old palimpsest of the park region,
inscribing new characters; but still in its main
telling features it remains distinctly glacial.
The moraine soils are being leveled, sorted,
refined, re-formed, and covered with vegetation; the polished pavements and scoring and
other superficial glacial inscriptions on the
crumbling lavas are being rapidly obliterated;
gorges are being cut in the decomposed rhyolites and loose conglomerates, and turrets and
pinnacles seem to be springing up like growing
trees; while the geysers are depositing miles
of sinter and travertine. Nevertheless, the ice-
work is scarce blurred as yet. These later ef-

fects are only spots and wrinkles on the grand glacial countenance of the park.

Perhaps you have already said that you have seen enough for a lifetime. But before you go away you should spend at least one day and a night on a mountain top, for a last general, calming, settling view. Mount Washburn is a good one for the purpose, because it stands in the middle of the park, is unencumbered with other peaks, and is so easy of access that the climb to its summit is only a saunter. First your eye goes roving around the mountain rim amid the hundreds of peaks: some with plain flowing skirts, others abruptly precipitous and defended by sheer battlemented escarpments; flat-topped or round; heaving like sea-waves or spired and turreted like Gothic cathedrals; streaked with snow in the ravines, and darkened with files of adventurous trees climbing the ridges. The nearer peaks are perchance clad in sapphire blue, others far off in creamy white. In the broad glare of noon they seem to shrink and crouch to less than half their real stature, and grow dull and uncommunicative, — mere dead, draggled heaps of waste ashes and stone, giving no hint of the multitude of animals enjoying life in their fastnesses, or of the bright bloom-bordered streams and lakes. But when storms blow they awake and arise, wearing robes of cloud and mist in majestic speaking attitudes like gods. In the color glory of morning and evening they become still more impressive; steeped in the divine light of the alpenglow their earthiness disappears, and, blending with the heavens, they seem neither high nor low.

Over all the central plateau, which from here seems level, and over the foothills and lower slopes of the mountains, the forest extends like a black uniform bed of weeds, interrupted only by lakes and meadows and small burned spots called parks, — all of them, except the Yellowstone Lake, being mere dots and spangles in general views, made conspicuous by their color and brightness. About eighty-five per cent of the entire area of the park is covered with trees, mostly the indomitable lodge-pole pine (*Pinus contorta*, var. *Murrayana*), with a few patches and sprinklings of Douglas spruce, Engelmann spruce, silver fir (*Abies lasiocarpa*), *Pinus flexilis*, and a few alders, aspens, and birches. The Douglas spruce is found only on the lowest portions, the silver fir on the highest, and the Engelmann spruce on the dampest places, best defended from fire. Some fine specimens of the flexilis pine are growing on the margins of openings, — wide-branching, sturdy trees, as broad as high, with trunks five feet in diameter, leafy and shady, laden with purple cones and rose-colored flowers. The Engelmann spruce and sub-alpine silver fir are beautiful and notable trees, — tall, spiry, hardy, frost and snow defying, and widely distributed over the West, wherever there is a mountain to climb or a cold moraine slope to cover. But neither of these is a good firefighter. With rather thin bark, and scattering their seeds every year as soon as they are ripe, they are quickly driven out of fire-swept regions. When the glaciers were melting, these hardy mountaineering trees were probably among the first to arrive on the new moraine soil beds; but as the plateau became drier and fires began to run, they were driven up the mountains, and into the wet spots and islands where we now find them, leaving nearly all the park to the lodge-pole pine, which though as thin-skinned as they and as easily killed by fire, takes pains to store up its seeds in firmly closed cones, and holds them from three to nine years, so that, let the fire come when it may, it is ready to die and ready to live again in a new generation. For when the killing fires have devoured the leaves and thin resinous bark, many of the cones, only scorched, open as soon as the smoke clears away; the hoarded store of seeds is sown broadcast on the cleared ground, and a new growth immediately springs up triumphant out of the ashes. Therefore, this tree not only holds its ground, but extends its conquests farther after every fire. Thus the evenness and closeness of its growth are accounted for. In one part of the forest that I examined, the growth was about as close as a cane-brake. The trees were from four to eight inches in diameter, one hundred feet high, and one hundred and seventy-five years old. The lower limbs die young and drop off for want of light. Life with these close-planted trees is a race for light, more light, and so they push straight for the sky. Mowing off ten feet from the top of the forest would make it look like a crowded mass of telegraph-poles; for only the sunny tops are leafy. A sapling ten years old, growing in the sunshine, has as many leaves as a crowded tree one or two hundred years old. As fires are multiplied and the mountains become drier, this wonderful lodge-pole pine bids fair to obtain possession of nearly all the forest ground in the West.

How still the woods seem from here, yet how lively a stir the hidden animals are making; digging, gnawing, biting, eyes shining, at work and play, getting food, rearing young, roving through the underbrush, climbing the rocks, wading solitary marshes, tracing the banks of the lakes and streams! Insect swarms are dancing in the sunbeams, burrowing in the ground, diving, swimming, — a cloud of witnesses telling Nature's joy. The plants are as busy as the animals, every cell in a swirl of enjoyment, humming like a hive, singing the old new song of creation. A few columns and puffs of steam are seen rising above the treetops, some near, but most of them far off, indicating geysers and hot springs, gentle-looking and noiseless as downy clouds, softly hinting the reaction going on between the surface and the hot interior. From here you see them better than when you are standing beside them, frightened and confused, regarding them as lawless cataclysms. The shocks and outbursts of earthquakes, volcanoes, geysers, storms, the pounding of waves, the uprush of sap in plants, each and all tell the orderly love-beats of Nature's heart.

Turning to the eastward, you have the Grand Cañon and reaches of the river in full view; and yonder to the southward lies the great lake, the largest and most important of all the high fountains of the Missouri-Mississippi, and the last to be discovered.

In the year 1541, when De Soto, with a romantic band of adventurers, was seeking gold and glory and the fountain of youth, he found the Mississippi a few hundred miles above its mouth, and made his grave beneath its floods. La Salle, in 1682, after discovering the Ohio, one of the largest and most beautiful branches of the Mississippi, traced the latter to the sea from the mouth of the Illinois, through adventures and privations not easily realized now. About the same time Joliet and Father Marquette reached the "Father of Waters" by way of the Wisconsin, but more than a century passed ere its highest sources in these mountains were seen. The advancing stream of civilization has ever followed its guidance toward the west, but none of the thousand tribes of Indians living on its banks could tell the explorer whence it came. From those romantic De Soto and La Salle days to these times of locomotives and tourists, how much has the great river seen and done! Great as it now is, and still growing longer through the ground of its delta and the basins of receding glaciers at its head, it was immensely broader toward the close of the glacial period, when the ice-mantle of the mountains was melting: then with its three hundred thousand miles of branches outspread over the plains and valleys of the continent, laden with fertile mud, it made the biggest and most generous bed of soil in the world.

WILDERNESS ESSAYS

Think of this mighty stream springing in the first place in vapor from the sea, flying on the wind, alighting on the mountains in hail and snow and rain, lingering in many a fountain feeding the trees and grass; then gathering its scattered waters, gliding from its noble lake, and going back home to the sea, singing all the way! On it sweeps, through the gates of the mountains, across the vast prairies and plains, through many a wild, gloomy forest, cane-brake, and sunny savanna; from glaciers and snowbanks and pine woods to warm groves of magnolia and palm; geysers dancing at its head keeping time with the sea-waves at its mouth; roaring and gray in rapids, booming in broad, bossy falls, murmuring, gleaming in long, silvery reaches, swaying now hither, now thither, whirling, bending in huge doubling, eddying folds, serene, majestic, ungovernable, overflowing all its metes and bounds, frightening the dwellers upon its banks; building, wasting, uprooting, planting; engulfing old islands and making new ones, taking away fields and towns as if in sport, carrying canoes and ships of commerce in the midst of its spoils and drift, fertilizing the continent as one vast farm. Then, its work done, it gladly vanishes in its ocean home, welcomed by the waiting waves.

YELLOWSTONE NATIONAL PARK

Thus naturally, standing here in the midst of its fountains, we trace the fortunes of the great river. And how much more comes to mind as we overlook this wonderful wilderness! Fountains of the Columbia and Colorado lie before us, interlaced with those of the Yellowstone and Missouri, and fine it would be to go with them to the Pacific; but the sun is already in the west, and soon our day will be done.

Yonder is Amethyst Mountain, and other mountains hardly less rich in old forests, which now seem to spring up again in their glory; and you see the storms that buried them — the ashes and torrents laden with boulders and mud, the centuries of sunshine, and the dark, lurid nights. You see again the vast floods of lava, red-hot and white-hot, pouring out from gigantic geysers, usurping the basins of lakes and streams, absorbing or driving away their hissing, screaming waters, flowing around hills and ridges, submerging every subordinate feature. Then you see the snow and glaciers taking possession of the land, making new landscapes. How admirable it is that, after passing through so many vicissitudes of frost and fire and flood, the physiognomy and even the complexion of the landscape should still be so divinely fine!

Thus reviewing the eventful past, we see Nature working with enthusiasm like a man, blowing her volcanic forges like a blacksmith blowing his smithy fires, shoving glaciers over the landscapes like a carpenter shoving his planes, clearing, ploughing, harrowing, irrigating, planting, and sowing broadcast like a farmer and gardener, doing rough work and fine work, planting sequoias and pines, rosebushes and daisies; working in gems, filling every crack and hollow with them; distilling fine essences; painting plants and shells, clouds, mountains, all the earth and heavens, like an artist, — ever working toward beauty higher and higher. Where may the mind find more stimulating, quickening pasturage? A thousand Yellowstone wonders are calling, "Look up and down and round about you!" And a multitude of still, small voices may be heard directing you to look through all this transient, shifting show of things called "substantial" into the truly substantial spiritual world whose forms flesh and wood, rock and water, air and sunshine, only veil and conceal, and to learn that here is heaven and the dwelling-place of the angels.

The sun is setting; long, violet shadows are growing out over the woods from the mountains along the western rim of the park; the

Absaroka range is baptized in the divine light of the alpenglow, and its rocks and trees are transfigured. Next to the light of the dawn on high mountain tops, the alpenglow is the most impressive of all the terrestrial manifestations of God.

Now comes the gloaming. The alpenglow is fading into earthy, murky gloom, but do not let your town habits draw you away to the hotel. Stay on this good fire-mountain and spend the night among the stars. Watch their glorious bloom until the dawn, and get one more baptism of light. Then, with fresh heart, go down to your work, and whatever your fate, under whatever ignorance or knowledge you may afterward chance to suffer, you will remember these fine, wild views, and look back with joy to your wanderings in the blessed old Yellowstone Wonderland.

UTAH has just been blessed with one of the grandest storms I have ever beheld this side of the Sierra. The mountains are laden with fresh snow; wild streams are swelling and booming adown the cañons, and out in the valley of the Jordan a thousand rain-pools are gleaming in the sun.

With reference to the development of fertile storms bearing snow and rain, the greater portion of the calendar springtime of Utah has been winter. In all the upper cañons of the mountains the snow is now from five to ten feet deep or more, and most of it has fallen since March. Almost every other day during the last three weeks small local storms have been falling on the Wahsatch and Oquirrh Mountains, while the Jordan Valley remained dry and sun-filled. But on the afternoon of Thursday, the 17th ultimo, wind, rain, and snow filled the whole basin, driving wildly over valley and plain from range to range, bestowing their benefactions in most cordial and

[1] Letter dated "Salt Lake City, Utah, May 19, 1877." *San Francisco Bulletin*, (May, 1877)

A GREAT STORM IN UTAH

harmonious storm-measures. The oldest Saints
say they have never witnessed a more violent
storm of this kind since the first settlement of
Zion, and while the gale from the northwest,
with which the storm began, was rocking their
adobe walls, uprooting trees and darkening the
streets with billows of dust and sand, some of
them seemed inclined to guess that the terrible
phenomenon was one of the signs of the times
of which their preachers are so constantly reminding them, the beginning of the outpouring
of the treasured wrath of the Lord upon the
Gentiles for the killing of Joseph Smith. To
me it seemed a cordial outpouring of Nature's
love; but it is easy to differ with salt Latter-
Days in everything — storms, wives, politics,
and religion.

About an hour before the storm reached the
city I was so fortunate as to be out with a
friend on the banks of the Jordan enjoying the
scenery. Clouds, with peculiarly restless and
self-conscious gestures, were marshaling themselves along the mountain-tops, and sending
out long, overlapping wings across the valley;
and even where no cloud was visible, an obscuring film absorbed the sunlight, giving rise
to a cold, bluish darkness. Nevertheless, distant objects along the boundaries of the landscape were revealed with wonderful distinct-

ness in this weird, subdued, cloud-sifted light. The mountains, in particular, with the forests on their flanks, their mazy lacelike cañons, the wombs of the ancient glaciers, and their marvelous profusion of ornate sculpture, were most impressively manifest. One would fancy that a man might be clearly seen walking on the snow at a distance of twenty or thirty miles.

While we were reveling in this rare, ungarish grandeur, turning from range to range, studying the darkening sky and listening to the still small voices of the flowers at our feet, some of the denser clouds came down, crowning and wreathing the highest peaks and dropping long gray fringes whose smooth linear structure showed that snow was beginning to fall. Of these partial storms there were soon ten or twelve, arranged in two rows, while the main Jordan Valley between them lay as yet in profound calm. At 4.30 P.M. a dark brownish cloud appeared close down on the plain towards the lake, extending from the northern extremity of the Oquirrh Range in a northeasterly direction as far as the eye could reach. Its peculiar color and structure excited our attention without enabling us to decide certainly as to its character, but we were not left long in doubt, for in a few minutes it came sweeping over the valley in wild uproar, a torrent of wind thick with sand and dust, advancing with a most majestic front, rolling and overcombing like a gigantic sea-wave. Scarcely was it in plain sight ere it was upon us, racing across the Jordan, over the city, and up the slopes of the Wahsatch, eclipsing all the landscapes in its course — the bending trees, the dust streamers, and the wild onrush of everything movable giving it an appreciable visibility that rendered it grand and inspiring.

This gale portion of the storm lasted over an hour, then down came the blessed rain and the snow all through the night and the next day, the snow and rain alternating and blending in the valley. It is long since I have seen snow coming into a city. The crystal flakes falling in the foul streets was a pitiful sight.

Notwithstanding the vaunted refining influences of towns, purity of all kinds — pure hearts, pure streams, pure snow — must here be exposed to terrible trials. City Creek, coming from its high glacial fountains, enters the streets of this Mormon Zion pure as an angel, but how does it leave it? Even roses and lilies in gardens most loved are tainted with a thousand impurities as soon as they unfold. I heard Brigham Young in the Tabernacle the other day warning his people that if they did not mend their manners angels would not come into their houses, though perchance they might be sauntering by with little else to do than chat with them. Possibly there may be Salt Lake families sufficiently pure for angel society, but I was not pleased with the reception they gave the small snow angels that God sent among them the other night. Only the children hailed them with delight. The old Latter-Days seemed to shun them. I should like to see how Mr. Young, the Lake Prophet, would meet such messengers.

But to return to the storm. Toward the evening of the 18th it began to wither. The snowy skirts of the Wahsatch Mountains appeared beneath the lifting fringes of the clouds, and the sun shone out through colored windows, producing one of the most glorious after-storm effects I ever witnessed. Looking across the Jordan, the gray sagey slopes from the base of the Oquirrh Mountains were covered with a thick, plushy cloth of gold, soft and ethereal as a cloud, not merely tinted and gilded like a rock with autumn sunshine, but deeply muffled beyond recognition. Surely nothing in heaven, nor any mansion of the Lord in all his worlds, could be more gloriously carpeted. Other portions of the plain were flushed with red and purple, and all the mountains and the clouds above them were painted in corresponding loveliness. Earth and sky, round and round the entire landscape, was one ravishing revelation of color, infinitely varied and interblended.

I have seen many a glorious sunset beneath lifting storm-clouds on the mountains, but nothing comparable with this. I felt as if newarrived in some other far-off world. The mountains, the plains, the sky, all seemed new. Other experiences seemed but to have prepared me for this, as souls are prepared for heaven. To describe the colors on a single mountain would, if it were possible at all, require many a volume — purples, and yellows, and delicious pearly grays divinely toned and interblended, and so richly put on one seemed to be looking down through the ground as through a sky. The disbanding clouds lingered lovingly about the mountains, filling the cañons like tinted wool, rising and drooping around the topmost peaks, fondling their rugged bases, or, sailing alongside, trailed their lustrous fringes through the pines as if taking a last view of their accomplished work. Then came darkness, and the glorious day was done.

This afternoon the Utah mountains and valleys seem to belong to our own very world again. They are covered with common sunshine. Down here on the banks of the Jordan,

larks and redwings are swinging on the rushes;
the balmy air is instinct with immortal life;
the wild flowers, the grass, and the farmers'
grain are fresh as if, like the snow, they had
come out of heaven, and the last of the angel
clouds are fleeing from the mountains.

WILD WOOL

MORAL improvers have calls to preach. I have a friend who has a call to plough, and woe to the daisy sod or azalea thicket that falls under the savage redemption of his keen steel shares. Not content with the so-called subjugation of every terrestrial bog, rock, and moorland, he would fain discover some method of reclamation applicable to the ocean and the sky, that in due calendar time they might be brought to bud and blossom as the rose. Our efforts are of no avail when we seek to turn his attention to wild roses, or to the fact that both ocean and sky are already about as rosy as possible — the one with stars, the other with dulse, and foam, and wild light. The practical developments of his culture are orchards and clover-fields wearing a smiling, benevolent aspect, truly excellent in their way, though a near view discloses something barbarous in them all. Wildness charms not my friend, charm it never so wisely: and whatsoever may be the character of his heaven, his earth seems

Overland Monthly (April, 1875)

only a chaos of agricultural possibilities calling for grubbing-hoes and manures.

Sometimes I venture to approach him with a plea for wildness, when he good-naturedly shakes a big mellow apple in my face, reiterating his favorite aphorism, "Culture is an orchard apple; Nature is a crab." Not all culture, however, is equally destructive and inappreciative. Azure skies and crystal waters find loving recognition, and few there be who would welcome the axe among mountain pines, or would care to apply any correction to the tones and costumes of mountain waterfalls. Nevertheless, the barbarous notion is almost universally entertained by civilized man, that there is in all the manufactures of Nature something essentially coarse which can and must be eradicated by human culture. I was, therefore, delighted in finding that the wild wool growing upon mountain sheep in the neighborhood of Mount Shasta was much finer than the average grades of cultivated wool. This *fine* discovery was made some three months ago,[1] while hunting among the Shasta sheep between Shasta and Lower Klamath Lake. Three fleeces were obtained — one that belonged to a large ram about four years old, another to a ewe about the same age, and another to a

[1] This essay was written early in 1875. [Editor.]

yearling lamb. After parting their beautiful wool on the side and many places along the back, shoulders, and hips, and examining it closely with my lens, I shouted: "Well done for wildness! Wild wool is finer than tame!"

My companions stooped down and examined the fleeces for themselves, pulling out tufts and ringlets, spinning them between their fingers, and measuring the length of the staple, each in turn paying tribute to wildness. It *was* finer, and no mistake; finer than Spanish Merino. Wild wool *is* finer than tame.

"Here," said I, "is an argument for fine wildness that needs no explanation. Not that such arguments are by any means rare, for all wildness is finer than tameness, but because fine wool is appreciable by everybody alike — from the most speculative president of national wool-growers' associations all the way down to the gude-wife spinning by her ingleside."

Nature is a good mother, and sees well to the clothing of her many bairns — birds with smoothly imbricated feathers, beetles with shining jackets, and bears with shaggy furs. In the tropical south, where the sun warms like a fire, they are allowed to go thinly clad; but in the snowy northland she takes care to clothe warmly. The squirrel has socks and mittens, and a tail broad enough for a blanket; the grouse is densely feathered down to the ends of his toes; and the wild sheep, besides his undergarment of fine wool, has a thick overcoat of hair that sheds off both the snow and the rain. Other provisions and adaptations in the dresses of animals, relating less to climate than to the more mechanical circumstances of life, are made with the same consummate skill that characterizes all the love-work of Nature. Land, water, and air, jagged rocks, muddy ground, sand-beds, forests, underbrush, grassy plains, etc., are considered in all their possible combinations while the clothing of her beautiful wildlings is preparing. No matter what the circumstances of their lives may be, she never allows them to go dirty or ragged. The mole, living always in the dark and in the dirt, is yet as clean as the otter or the wave-washed seal; and our wild sheep, wading in snow, roaming through bushes, and leaping among jagged storm-beaten cliffs, wears a dress so exquisitely adapted to its mountain life that it is always found as unruffled and stainless as a bird.

On leaving the Shasta hunting-grounds I selected a few specimen tufts, and brought them away with a view to making more leisurely examinations; but, owing to the imperfectness of the instruments at my command, the results thus far obtained must be regarded only as rough approximations.

As already stated, the clothing of our wild sheep is composed of fine wool and coarse hair. The hairs are from about two to four inches long, mostly of a dull bluish-gray color, though varying somewhat with the seasons. In general characteristics they are closely related to the hairs of the deer and antelope, being light, spongy, and elastic, with a highly polished surface, and though somewhat ridged and spiraled, like wool, they do not manifest the slightest tendency to felt or become taggy. A hair two and a half inches long, which is perhaps near the average length, will stretch about one fourth of an inch before breaking. The diameter decreases rapidly both at the top and bottom, but is maintained throughout the greater portion of the length with a fair degree of regularity. The slender tapering point in which the hairs terminate is nearly black: but, owing to its fineness as compared with the main trunk, the quantity of blackness is not sufficient to affect greatly the general color. The number of hairs growing upon a square inch is about ten thousand; the number of wool fibers is about twenty-five thousand, or two and a half times that of the hairs. The wool fibers are white and glossy, and beautifully spired into ringlets. The average length of the staple is about an inch and a half. A fiber of this length, when growing undisturbed down among the hairs, measures about an inch; hence the degree of curliness may easily be inferred. I regret exceedingly that my instruments do not enable me to measure the diameter of the fibers, in order that their degrees of fineness might be definitely compared with each other and with the finest of the domestic breeds; but that the three wild fleeces under consideration are considerably finer than the average grades of Merino shipped from San Francisco is, I think, unquestionable.

When the fleece is parted and looked into with a good lens, the skin appears of a beautiful pale-yellow color, and the delicate wool fibers are seen growing up among the strong hairs, like grass among stalks of corn, every individual fiber being protected about as specially and effectively as if inclosed in a separate husk. Wild wool is too fine to stand by itself, the fibers being about as frail and invisible as the floating threads of spiders, while the hairs against which they lean stand erect like hazel wands; but, notwithstanding their great dissimilarity in size and appearance, the wool and hair are forms of the same thing, modified in just that way and to just that degree that renders them most perfectly subservient to the well-being of the sheep. Furthermore, it will be observed that these wild modifications are entirely distinct from those which are brought chancingly into existence through the accidents and caprices of culture; the former being inventions of God for the attainment of definite ends. Like the modifications of limbs — the fin for swimming, the wing for flying, the foot for walking — so the fine wool for warmth, the hair for additional warmth and to protect the wool, and both together for a fabric to wear well in mountain roughness and wash well in mountain storms.

The effects of human culture upon wild wool are analogous to those produced upon wild roses. In the one case there is an abnormal development of petals at the expense of the stamens, in the other an abnormal development of wool at the expense of the hair. Garden roses frequently exhibit stamens in which the transmutation to petals may be observed in various stages of accomplishment, and analogously the fleeces of tame sheep occasionally contain a few wild hairs that are undergoing transmutation to wool. Even wild wool presents here and there a fiber that appears to be in a state of change. In the course of my examinations of the wild fleeces mentioned above, three fibers were found that were wool at one end and hair at the other. This, however, does not necessarily imply imperfection, or any process of change similar to that caused by human culture. Water-lilies contain parts variously developed into stamens at one end, petals at the other, as the constant and normal condition. These half wool, half hair fibers may therefore subserve some fixed requirement essential to the perfection of the whole, or they may simply be the fine boundary-lines where an exact balance between the wool and the hair is attained.

I have been offering samples of mountain wool to my friends, demanding in return that the fineness of wildness be fairly recognized and confessed, but the returns are deplorably tame. The first question asked is, "Now truly, wild sheep, wild sheep, have you any wool?" while they peer curiously down among the hairs through lenses and spectacles. "Yes, wild sheep, you *have* wool; but Mary's lamb had more. In the name of use, how many wild sheep, think you, would be required to furnish wool sufficient for a pair of socks?" I endeavor to point out the irrelevancy of the latter question, arguing that wild wool was not made for man but for sheep, and that, however deficient as clothing for other animals, it is just the thing for the brave mountain-dweller that wears it. Plain, however, as all this appears, the quantity question rises again and again in all its commonplace tameness. For in my experience it seems well-nigh impossible to obtain a hearing on behalf of Nature from any other standpoint than that of human use. Domestic flocks yield more flannel per sheep than the wild, therefore it is claimed that culture has improved upon wildness; and so it has as far as flannel is concerned, but all to the contrary as far as a sheep's dress is concerned. If every wild sheep inhabiting the Sierra were to put on tame wool, probably only a few would survive the dangers of a single season. With their fine limbs muffled and buried beneath a tangle of hairless wool, they would become short-winded, and fall an easy prey to the strong mountain wolves. In descending precipices they would be thrown out of balance and killed, by their taggy wool catching upon sharp points of rocks. Disease would also be brought on by the dirt which always finds a lodgment in tame wool, and by the draggled and water-soaked condition into which it falls during stormy weather.

No dogma taught by the present civilization

seems to form so insuperable an obstacle in the way of a right understanding of the relations which culture sustains to wildness as that which regards the world as made especially for the uses of man. Every animal, plant, and crystal controverts it in the plainest terms. Yet it is taught from century to century as something ever new and precious, and in the resulting darkness the enormous conceit is allowed to go unchallenged.

I have never yet happened upon a trace of evidence that seemed to show that any one animal was ever made for another as much as it was made for itself. Not that Nature manifests any such thing as selfish isolation. In the making of every animal the presence of every other animal has been recognized. Indeed, every atom in creation may be said to be acquainted with and married to every other, but with universal union there is a division sufficient in degree for the purposes of the most intense individuality; no matter, therefore, what may be the note which any creature forms in the song of existence, it is made first for itself, then more and more remotely for all the world and worlds.

Were it not for the exercise of individualizing cares on the part of Nature, the universe would be felted together like a fleece of tame wool.

WILD WOOL

But we are governed more than we know, and most when we are wildest. Plants, animals, and stars are all kept in place, bridled along appointed ways, *with* one another, and *through the midst* of one another — killing and being killed, eating and being eaten, in harmonious proportions and quantities. And it is right that we should thus reciprocally make use of one another, rob, cook, and consume, to the utmost of our healthy abilities and desires. Stars attract one another as they are able, and harmony results. Wild lambs eat as many wild flowers as they can find or desire, and men and wolves eat the lambs to just the same extent.

This consumption of one another in its various modifications is a kind of culture varying with the degree of directness with which it is carried out, but we should be careful not to ascribe to such culture any improving qualities upon those on whom it is brought to bear. The water-ouzel plucks moss from the river-bank to build its nest, but it does not improve the moss by plucking it. We pluck feathers from birds, and less directly wool from wild sheep, for the manufacture of clothing and cradle-nests, without improving the wool for the sheep, or the feathers for the bird that wore them. When a hawk pounces upon a linnet and proceeds to pull out its feathers, preparatory to making a meal, the hawk may be said to be cultivating the linnet, and he certainly does effect an improvement as far as hawk-food is concerned; but what of the songster? He ceases to be a linnet as soon as he is snatched from the woodland choir; and when, hawklike, we snatch the wild sheep from its native rock, and, instead of eating and wearing it at once, carry it home, and breed the hair out of its wool and the bones out of its body, it ceases to be a sheep.

These breeding and plucking processes are similarly improving as regards the secondary uses aimed at; and, although the one requires but a few minutes for its accomplishment, the other many years or centuries, they are essentially alike. We eat wild oysters alive with great directness, waiting for no cultivation, and leaving scarce a second of distance between the shell and the lip; but we take wild sheep home and subject them to the many extended processes of husbandry, and finish by boiling them in a pot — a process which completes all sheep improvements as far as man is concerned. It will be seen, therefore, that wild wool and tame wool — wild sheep and tame sheep — are terms not properly comparable, nor are they in any correct sense to be considered as bearing any antagonism toward each other; they are different things, planned and accomplished for wholly different purposes.

Illustrative examples bearing upon this interesting subject may be multiplied indefinitely, for they abound everywhere in the plant and animal kingdoms wherever culture has reached. Recurring for a moment to apples. The beauty and completeness of a wild apple tree living its own life in the woods is heartily acknowledged by all those who have been so happy as to form its acquaintance. The fine wild piquancy of its fruit is unrivaled, but in the great question of quantity as human food wild apples are found wanting. Man, therefore, takes the tree from the woods, manures and prunes and grafts, plans and guesses, adds a little of this and that, selects and rejects, until apples of every conceivable size and softness are produced, like nut-galls in response to the irritating punctures of insects. Orchard apples are to me the most eloquent words that culture has ever spoken, but they reflect no imperfection upon Nature's spicy crab. Every cultivated apple is a crab, not improved, *but cooked*, variously softened and swelled out in the process, mellowed, sweetened, spiced, and rendered pulpy and foodful, but as utterly unfit for the uses of nature as a meadowlark killed and plucked and roasted. Give to Nature every cultured apple — codling, pippin, russet — and every sheep so laboriously compounded — muffled Southdowns, hairy Cotswolds, wrinkled Merinos — and she would throw the one to her caterpillars, the other to her wolves.

It is now some thirty-six hundred years since Jacob kissed his mother and set out across the plains of Padan-aram to begin his experiments upon the flocks of his uncle, Laban; and, notwithstanding the high degree of excellence he attained as a wool-grower, and the innumerable painstaking efforts subsequently made by individuals and associations in all kinds of pastures and climates, we still seem to be as far from definite and satisfactory results as we ever were. In one breed the wool is apt to wither and crinkle like hay on a sun-beaten hillside. In another, it is lodged and matted together like the lush tangled grass of a manured meadow. In one the staple is deficient in length, in another in fineness; while in all there is a constant tendency toward disease, rendering various washings and dippings indispensable to prevent its falling out. The problem of the quality and quantity of the carcass seems to be as doubtful and as far removed from a satisfactory solution as that of the wool.

WILD WOOL

Desirable breeds blundered upon by long series of groping experiments are often found to be unstable and subject to disease — bots, foot-rot, blind-staggers, etc. — causing infinite trouble, both among breeders and manufacturers. Would it not be well, therefore, for some one to go back as far as possible and take a fresh start?

The source or sources whence the various breeds were derived is not positively known, but there can be hardly any doubt of their being descendants of the four or five wild species so generally distributed throughout the mountainous portions of the globe, the marked differences between the wild and domestic species being readily accounted for by the known variability of the animal, and by the long series of painstaking selection to which all its characteristics have been subjected. No other animal seems to yield so submissively to the manipulations of culture. Jacob controlled the color of his flocks merely by causing them to stare at objects of the desired hue; and possibly Merinos may have caught their wrinkles from the perplexed brows of their breeders. The California species (*Ovis montana*)[1] is a

[1] The wild sheep of California are now classified as *Ovis nelsoni*. Whether those of the Shasta region belonged to the latter species, or to the bighorn species of Oregon, Idaho, and Washington, is still an unsettled question. [Editor.]

noble animal, weighing when full-grown some three hundred and fifty pounds, and is well worthy the attention of wool-growers as a point from which to make a new departure. That it will breed with the domestic sheep I have not the slightest doubt, and I cordially recommend the experiment to the various wool-growers' associations as one of great national importance. From my knowledge of the homes and habits of our wild sheep I feel confident that several hundred could be obtained for breeding purposes from the Sierra alone, and I am ready to undertake their capture. A little pure wildness is the one great present want, both of men and sheep.

THE FORESTS OF OREGON AND THEIR INHABITANTS

LIKE the forests of Washington, already described, those of Oregon are in great part made up of the Douglas spruce,[1] or Oregon pine (*Abies Douglasii*). A large number of mills are at work upon this species, especially along the Columbia, but these as yet have made but little impression upon its dense masses, the mills here being small as compared with those of the Puget Sound region. The white cedar, or Port Orford cedar (*Cupressus Lawsoniana*, or *Chamæcyparis Lawsoniana*), is one of the most beautiful of the evergreens, and produces excellent lumber, considerable quantities of which are shipped to the San Francisco market. It is found mostly about Coos Bay, along the Coquille River, and on the northern slopes of the Siskiyou Mountains, and extends down the coast into California. The silver firs, the spruces, and the colossal arbor-vitæ, or white cedar [2] (*Thuja gigantea*), described in the chapter on Washington, are

[1] *Pseudotsuga taxifolia*. Brit. [Editor.]
[2] *Thuja plicata* Don. [Editor.]

also found here in great beauty and perfection, the largest of these (*Picea grandis*, Loud.; *Abies grandis*, Lindl.) being confined mostly to the coast region, where it attains a height of three hundred feet, and a diameter of ten or twelve feet. Five or six species of pines are found in the State, the most important of which, both as to lumber and as to the part they play in the general wealth and beauty of the forests, are the yellow and sugar pines (*Pinus ponderosa* and *P. Lambertiana*). The yellow pine is most abundant on the eastern slopes of the Cascades, forming there the main bulk of the forest in many places. It is also common along the borders of the open spaces in Willamette Valley. In the southern portion of the State the sugar pine, which is the king of all the pines and the glory of the Sierra forests, occurs in considerable abundance in the basins of the Umpqua and Rogue Rivers, and it was in the Umpqua Hills that this noble tree was first discovered by the enthusiastic botanical explorer David Douglas, in the year 1826.

This is the Douglas for whom the noble Douglas spruce is named, and many a fair blooming plant also, which will serve to keep his memory fresh and sweet as long as beautiful trees and flowers are loved. The Indians of the lower Columbia River watched him with lively curiosity as he wandered about in the woods day after day, gazing intently on the ground or at the great trees, collecting specimens of everything he saw, but, unlike all the eager fur-gathering strangers they had hitherto seen, caring nothing about trade. And when at length they came to know him better, and saw that from year to year the growing things of the woods and prairies, meadows and plains, were his only object of pursuit, they called him the "Man of Grass," a title of which he was proud.

He was a Scotchman and first came to this coast in the spring of 1825 under the auspices of the London Horticultural Society, landing at the mouth of the Columbia after a long, dismal voyage of eight months and fourteen days. During this first season he chose Fort Vancouver, belonging to the Hudson's Bay Company, as his headquarters, and from there made excursions into the glorious wilderness in every direction, discovering many new species among the trees as well as among the rich underbrush and smaller herbaceous vegetation. It was while making a trip to Mount Hood this year that he discovered the two largest and most beautiful firs in the world (*Picea amabilis* and *P. nobilis* — now called *Abies*), and from the seeds which he then collected and sent home tall trees are now growing in Scotland.

In one of his trips that summer, in the lower Willamette Valley, he saw in an Indian's tobacco-pouch some of the seeds and scales of a new species of pine, which he learned were gathered from a large tree that grew far to the southward. Most of the following season was spent on the upper waters of the Columbia, and it was not until September that he returned to Fort Vancouver, about the time of the setting-in of the winter rains. Nevertheless, bearing in mind the great pine he had heard of, and the seeds of which he had seen, he made haste to set out on an excursion to the headwaters of the Willamette in search of it; and how he fared on this excursion and what dangers and hardships he endured is best told in his own journal, part of which I quote as follows: —

October 26th, 1826. Weather dull. Cold and cloudy. When my friends in England are made acquainted with my travels I fear they will think that I have told them nothing but my miseries. . . . I quitted my camp early in the morning to survey the neighboring country, leaving my guide to take charge of the horses until my return in the evening. About an hour's walk from the camp I met an Indian, who on perceiving me instantly strung his

bow, placed on his left arm a sleeve of raccoon skin
and stood on the defensive. Being quite sure that
conduct was prompted by fear and not by hostile
intentions, the poor fellow having probably never
seen such a being as myself before, I laid my gun
at my feet on the ground and waved my hand for
him to come to me, which he did slowly and with
great caution. I then made him place his bow and
quiver of arrows beside my gun, and striking a
light gave him a smoke out of my own pipe and
a present of a few beads. With my pencil I made
a rough sketch of the cone and pine tree which I
wanted to obtain and drew his attention to it, when
he instantly pointed with his hand to the hills
fifteen or twenty miles distant towards the south;
and when I expressed my intention of going thither,
cheerfully set about accompanying me. At midday
I reached my long-wished-for pines and lost no
time in examining them and endeavoring to collect
specimens and seeds. New and strange things seldom fail to make strong impressions and are therefore frequently overrated; so that, lest I should
never see my friends in England to inform them
verbally of this most beautiful and immensely
grand tree, I shall here state the dimensions of the
largest I could find among several that had been
blown down by the wind. At three feet from the
ground its circumference is fifty-seven feet, nine
inches; at one hundred and thirty-four feet, seventeen feet five inches; the extreme length two hundred and forty-five feet. . . . As it was impossible
either to climb the tree or hew it down, I endeavored
to knock off the cones by firing at them with ball,
when the report of my gun brought eight Indians,

all of them painted with red earth, armed with bows, arrows, bone-tipped spears, and flint knives. They appeared anything but friendly. I explained to them what I wanted and they seemed satisfied and sat down to smoke; but presently I saw one of them string his bow and another sharpen his flint knife with a pair of wooden pincers and suspend it on the wrist of his right hand. Further testimony of their intentions was unnecessary. To save myself by flight was impossible, so without hesitation I stepped back about five paces, cocked my gun, drew one of the pistols out of my belt, and holding it in my left hand, the gun in my right, showed myself determined to fight for my life. As much as possible I endeavored to preserve my coolness, and thus we stood looking at one another without making any movement or uttering a word for perhaps ten minutes, when one at last, who seemed to be the leader, gave a sign that they wished for some tobacco; this I signified they should have if they fetched a quantity of cones. They went off immediately in search of them, and no sooner were they all out of sight than I picked up my three cones and some twigs of the trees and made the quickest possible retreat, hurrying back to my camp, which I reached before dusk. The Indian who last undertook to be my guide to the trees I sent off before gaining my encampment, lest he should betray me. How irksome is the darkness of night to one under such circumstances. I cannot speak a word to my guide, nor have I a book to divert my thoughts, which are continually occupied with the dread lest the hostile Indians should trace me hither and make an attack. I now write lying on the grass with my

THE FORESTS OF OREGON

gun cocked beside me, and penning these lines by the light of my *Columbian candle*, namely, an ignited piece of rosin-wood.

Douglas named this magnificent species *Pinus Lambertiana*, in honor of his friend Dr. Lambert, of London. This is the noblest pine thus far discovered in the forests of the world, surpassing all others not only in size but in beauty and majesty. Oregon may well be proud that its discovery was made within her borders, and that, though it is far more abundant in California, she has the largest known specimens. In the Sierra the finest sugar pine forests lie at an elevation of about five thousand feet. In Oregon they occupy much lower ground, some of the trees being found but little above tide-water.

No lover of trees will ever forget his first meeting with the sugar pine. In most coniferous trees there is a sameness of form and expression which at length becomes wearisome to most people who travel far in the woods. But the sugar pines are as free from conventional forms as any of the oaks. No two are so much alike as to hide their individuality from any observer. Every tree is appreciated as a study in itself and proclaims in no uncertain terms the surpassing grandeur of the species. The branches, mostly near the summit, are sometimes nearly forty feet long, feathered richly all around with short, leafy branchlets, and tasselled with cones a foot and a half long. And when these superb arms are outspread, radiating in every direction, an immense crown-like mass is formed which, poised on the noble shaft and filled with sunshine, is one of the grandest forest objects conceivable. But though so wild and unconventional when full-grown, the sugar pine is a remarkably regular tree in youth, a strict follower of coniferous fashions, slim, erect, tapering, symmetrical, every branch in place. At the age of fifty or sixty years this shy, fashionable form begins to give way. Special branches are thrust out away from the general outlines of the trees and bent down with cones. Henceforth it becomes more and more original and independent in style, pushes boldly aloft into the winds and sunshine, growing ever more stately and beautiful, a joy and inspiration to every beholder.

Unfortunately, the sugar pine makes excellent lumber. It is too good to live, and is already passing rapidly away before the woodman's axe. Surely out of all of the abounding forest-wealth of Oregon a few specimens might be spared to the world, not as dead lumber, but as living trees. A park of moderate

THE FORESTS OF OREGON

extent might be set apart and protected for public use forever, containing at least a few hundreds of each of these noble pines, spruces, and firs. Happy will be the men who, having the power and the love and benevolent forecast to do this, will do it. They will not be forgotten. The trees and their lovers will sing their praises, and generations yet unborn will rise up and call them blessed.

Dotting the prairies and fringing the edges of the great evergreen forests we find a considerable number of hardwood trees, such as the oak, maple, ash, alder, laurel, madrone, flowering dogwood, wild cherry, and wild apple. The white oak (*Quercus Garryana*) is the most important of the Oregon oaks as a timber tree, but not nearly so beautiful as Kellogg's oak (*Q. Kelloggii*). The former is found mostly along the Columbia River, particularly about the Dalles, and a considerable quantity of useful lumber is made from it and sold, sometimes for eastern white oak, to wagon-makers. Kellogg's oak is a magnificent tree and does much for the picturesque beauty of the Umpqua and Rogue River Valleys where it abounds. It is also found in all the Yosemite valleys of the Sierra, and its acorns form an important part of the food of the Digger Indians. In the Siskiyou Mountains there is a live oak (*Q. chrysolepis*), wide-spreading and very picturesque in form, but not very common. It extends southward along the western flank of the Sierra and is there more abundant and much larger than in Oregon, oftentimes five to eight feet in diameter.

The maples are the same as those in Washington, already described, but I have not seen any maple groves here equal in extent or in the size of the trees to those on the Snoqualmie River.

The Oregon ash is now rare along the stream-banks of western Oregon, and it grows to a good size and furnishes lumber that is for some purposes equal to the white ash of the Western States.

Nuttall's flowering dogwood makes a brave display with its wealth of showy involucres in the spring along cool streams. Specimens of the flowers may be found measuring eight inches in diameter.

The wild cherry (*Prunus emarginata*, var. *mollis*) is a small, handsome tree seldom more than a foot in diameter at the base. It makes valuable lumber and its black, astringent fruit furnishes a rich resource as food for the birds. A smaller form is common in the Sierra, the fruit of which is eagerly eaten by the Indians and hunters in time of need.

THE FORESTS OF OREGON

The wild apple (*Pyrus rivularis*) is a fine, hearty, handsome little tree that grows well in rich, cool soil along streams and on the edges of beaver-meadows from California through Oregon and Washington to southeastern Alaska. In Oregon it forms dense, tangled thickets, some of them almost impenetrable. The largest trunks are nearly a foot in diameter. When in bloom it makes a fine show with its abundant clusters of flowers, which are white and fragrant. The fruit is very small and savagely acid. It is wholesome, however, and is eaten by birds, bears, Indians, and many other adventurers, great and small.

Passing from beneath the shadows of the woods where the trees grow close and high, we step into charming wild gardens full of lilies, orchids, heathworts, roses, etc., with colors so gay and forming such sumptuous masses of bloom, they make the gardens of civilization, however lovingly cared for, seem pathetic and silly. Around the great fire-mountains, above the forests and beneath the snow, there is a flowery zone of marvelous beauty planted with anemones, erythroniums, daisies, bryanthus, kalmia, vaccinium, cassiope, saxifrages, etc., forming one continuous garden fifty or sixty miles in circumference, and so deep and luxuriant and closely woven it seems as if Nature, glad to find an opening, were economizing space and trying to see how many of her bright-eyed darlings she can get together in one mountain wreath.

Along the slopes of the Cascades, where the woods are less dense, especially about the headwaters of the Willamette, there are miles of rhododendron, making glorious outbursts of purple bloom, and down on the prairies in rich, damp hollows the blue-flowered camassia grows in such profusion that at a little distance its dense masses appear as beautiful blue lakes imbedded in the green, flowery plains; while all about the streams and the lakes and the beaver-meadows and the margins of the deep woods there is a magnificent tangle of gaultheria and huckleberry bushes with their myriads of pink bells, reinforced with hazel, cornel, rubus of many species, wild plum, cherry, and crab apple; besides thousands of charming bloomers to be found in all sorts of places throughout the wilderness whose mere names are refreshing, such as linnæa, menziesia, pyrola, chimaphila, brodiæa, smilacina, fritillaria, calochortus, trillium, clintonia, veratrum, cypripedium, goodyera, spiranthes, habenaria, and the rare and lovely "Hider of the North," *Calypso borealis*, to find which is alone a sufficient object for a journey into the wilderness. And besides these there is a charming underworld of ferns and mosses flourishing gloriously beneath all the woods.

Everybody loves wild woods and flowers more or less. Seeds of all these Oregon evergreens and of many of the flowering shrubs and plants have been sent to almost every country under the sun, and they are now growing in carefully tended parks and gardens. And now that the ways of approach are open one would expect to find these woods and gardens full of admiring visitors reveling in their beauty like bees in a clover-field. Yet few care to visit them. A portion of the bark of one of the California trees, the mere dead skin, excited the wondering attention of thousands when it was set up in the Crystal Palace in London, as did also a few peeled spars, the shafts of mere saplings from Oregon or Washington. Could one of these great silver firs or sugar pines three hundred feet high have been transplanted entire to that exhibition, how enthusiastic would have been the praises accorded to it!

Nevertheless, the countless hosts waving at home beneath their own sky, beside their own noble rivers and mountains, and standing on a flower-enameled carpet of mosses thousands of square miles in extent, attract but little attention. Most travelers content themselves with what they may chance to see from car windows, hotel verandas, or the deck of a steamer on the lower Columbia — clinging to the battered highways like drowning sailors to a life-raft. When an excursion into the woods is proposed, all sorts of exaggerated or imaginary dangers are conjured up, filling the kindly, soothing wilderness with colds, fevers, Indians, bears, snakes, bugs, impassable rivers, and jungles of brush, to which is always added quick and sure starvation.

As to starvation, the woods are full of food, and a supply of bread may easily be carried for habit's sake, and replenished now and then at outlying farms and camps. The Indians are seldom found in the woods, being confined mainly to the banks of the rivers, where the greater part of their food is obtained. Moreover, the most of them have been either buried since the settlement of the country or civilized into comparative innocence, industry, or harmless laziness. There are bears in the woods, but not in such numbers nor of such unspeakable ferocity as town-dwellers imagine, nor do bears spend their lives in going about the country like the devil, seeking whom they may devour. Oregon bears, like most others, have no liking for man either as meat or as society; and while some may be curious at times to see what manner of creature he is, most of them have learned to shun people as deadly enemies. They have been poisoned, trapped, and shot at until they have become shy, and it is no longer easy to make their acquaintance. Indeed, since the settlement of the country, notwithstanding far the greater portion is yet wild, it is difficult to find any of the larger animals that once were numerous and comparatively familiar, such as the bear, wolf, panther, lynx, deer, elk, and antelope.

As early as 1843, while the settlers numbered only a few thousands, and before any sort of government had been organized, they came together and held what they called "a wolf meeting," at which a committee was appointed to devise means for the destruction of wild animals destructive to tame ones, which committee in due time begged to report as follows: —

It being admitted by all that bears, wolves, panthers, etc., are destructive to the useful animals owned by the settlers of this colony, your committee would submit the following resolutions as the sense of this meeting, by which the community may be governed in carrying on a defensive and destructive war on all such animals: —

WILDERNESS ESSAYS

Resolved, 1st. — That we deem it expedient for the community to take immediate measures for the destruction of all wolves, panthers and bears, and such other animals as are known to be destructive to cattle, horses, sheep and hogs.

2d. — That a bounty of fifty cents be paid for the destruction of a small wolf, $3.00 for a large wolf, $1.50 for a lynx, $2.00 for a bear and $5.00 for a panther.

This center of destruction was in the Willamette Valley. But for many years prior to the beginning of the operations of the "Wolf Organization" the Hudson's Bay Company had established forts and trading-stations over all the country, wherever fur-gathering Indians could be found, and vast numbers of these animals were killed. Their destruction has since gone on at an accelerated rate from year to year as the settlements have been extended, so that in some cases it is difficult to obtain specimens enough for the use of naturalists. But even before any of these settlements were made, and before the coming of the Hudson's Bay Company, there was very little danger to be met in passing through this wilderness as far as animals were concerned, and but little of any kind as compared with the dangers encountered in crowded houses and streets.

When Lewis and Clark made their famous

THE FORESTS OF OREGON

trip across the continent in 1804–05, when all the Rocky Mountain region was wild, as well as the Pacific Slope, they did not lose a single man by wild animals, nor, though frequently attacked, especially by the grizzlies of the Rocky Mountains, were any of them wounded seriously. Captain Clark was bitten on the hand by a wolf as he lay asleep; that was one bite among more than a hundred men while traveling through eight to nine thousand miles of savage wilderness. They could hardly have been so fortunate had they stayed at home. They wintered on the edge of the Clatsop plains, on the south side of the Columbia River near its mouth. In the woods on that side they found game abundant, especially elk, and with the aid of the friendly Indians who furnished salmon and "wapatoo" (the tubers of *Sagittaria variabilis*), they were in no danger of starving.

But on the return trip in the spring they reached the base of the Rocky Mountains when the range was yet too heavily snow-laden to be crossed with horses. Therefore they had to wait some weeks. This was at the head of one of the northern branches of Snake River, and, their scanty stock of provisions being nearly exhausted, the whole party was compelled to live mostly on bears and dogs; deer, antelope, and elk, usually abundant, were now scarce because the region had been closely hunted over by the Indians before their arrival.

Lewis and Clark had killed a number of bears and saved the skins of the more interesting specimens, and the variations they found in size, color of the hair, etc., made great difficulty in classification. Wishing to get the opinion of the Chopumish Indians, near one of whose villages they were encamped, concerning the various species, the explorers unpacked their bundles and spread out for examination all the skins they had taken. The Indian hunters immediately classed the white, the deep and the pale grizzly red, the grizzly dark-brown — in short, all those with the extremities of the hair of a white or frosty color without regard to the color of the ground or foil — under the name of *hoh-host*. The Indians assured them that these were all of the same species as the white bear, that they associated together, had longer nails than the others, and never climbed trees. On the other hand, the black skins, those that were black with white hairs intermixed or with a white breast, the uniform bay, the brown, and the light reddish-brown, were classed under the name *yack-ah*, and were said to resemble each other in being smaller and having shorter nails, in climbing trees, and being so little vicious that they could be pursued with safety.

Lewis and Clark came to the conclusion that all those with white-tipped hair found by them in the basin of the Columbia belonged to the same species as the grizzlies of the upper Missouri; and that the black and reddish-brown, etc., of the Rocky Mountains belong to a second species equally distinct from the grizzly and the black bear of the Pacific Coast and the East, which never vary in color.

As much as possible should be made by the ordinary traveler of these descriptions, for he will be likely to see very little of any species for himself; not that bears no longer exist here, but because, being shy, they keep out of the way. In order to see them and learn their habits one must go softly and alone, lingering long in the fringing woods on the banks of the salmon streams, and in the small openings in the midst of thickets where berries are most abundant.

As for rattlesnakes, the other grand dread of town-dwellers when they leave beaten roads, there are two, or perhaps three, species of them in Oregon. But they are nowhere to be found in great numbers. In western Oregon they are hardly known at all. In all my walks in the

Oregon forest I have never met a single specimen, though a few have been seen at long intervals.

When the country was first settled by the whites, fifty years ago, the elk roamed through the woods and over the plains to the east of the Cascades in immense numbers; now they are rarely seen except by experienced hunters who know their haunts in the deepest and most inaccessible solitudes to which they have been driven. So majestic an animal forms a tempting mark for the sportsman's rifle. Countless thousands have been killed for mere amusement and they already seem to be nearing extinction as rapidly as the buffalo. The antelope also is vanishing from the Columbia plains before the farmers and cattle-men. Whether the moose still lingers in Oregon or Washington I am unable to say.

On the highest mountains of the Cascade Range the wild goat roams in comparative security, few of his enemies caring to go so far in pursuit and to hunt on ground so high and so dangerous. He is a brave, sturdy, shaggy mountaineer of an animal, enjoying the freedom and security of crumbling ridges and overhanging cliffs above the glaciers, oftentimes beyond the reach of the most daring hunter. They seem to be as much at home on the ice and snow-fields as on the crags, making their way in flocks from ridge to ridge on the great volcanic mountains by crossing the glaciers that lie between them, traveling in single file guided by an old experienced leader, like a party of climbers on the Alps. On these ice-journeys they pick their way through networks of crevasses and over bridges of snow with admirable skill, and the mountaineer may seldom do better in such places than to follow their trail, if he can. In the rich alpine gardens and meadows they find abundance of food, venturing sometimes well down in the prairie openings on the edge of the timber-line, but holding themselves ever alert and watchful, ready to flee to their highland castles at the faintest alarm. When their summer pastures are buried beneath the winter snows, they make haste to the lower ridges, seeking the wind-beaten crags and slopes where the snow cannot lie at any great depth, feeding at times on the leaves and twigs of bushes when grass is beyond reach.

The wild sheep is another admirable alpine rover, but comparatively rare in the Oregon mountains, choosing rather the drier ridges to the southward on the Cascades and to the eastward among the spurs of the Rocky Mountain chain.

WILDERNESS ESSAYS

Deer give beautiful animation to the forests, harmonizing finely in their color and movements with the gray and brown shafts of the trees and the swaying of the branches as they stand in groups at rest, or move gracefully and noiselessly over the mossy ground about the edges of beaver-meadows and flowery glades, daintily culling the leaves and tips of the mints and aromatic bushes on which they feed. There are three species, the black-tailed, white-tailed, and mule deer; the last being restricted in its range to the open woods and plains to the eastward of the Cascades. They are nowhere very numerous now, killing for food, for hides, or for mere wanton sport, having well-nigh exterminated them in the more accessible regions, while elsewhere they are too often at the mercy of the wolves.

Gliding about in their shady forest homes, keeping well out of sight, there is a multitude of sleek fur-clad animals living and enjoying their clean, beautiful lives. How beautiful and interesting they are is about as difficult for busy mortals to find out as if their homes were beyond sight in the sky.